Eugene A. Marinelli, D.O.

Westminster Aids to the Study of the Scriptures

THE WESTMINSTER HISTORICAL ATLAS TO THE BIBLE

Revised Edition

WESTMINSTER AIDS

TO THE STUDY OF THE SCRIPTURES

THE WESTMINSTER DICTIONARY OF THE BIBLE

Edited by John D. Davis

Fifth edition revised and rewritten by Henry S. Gehman

THE WESTMINSTER HISTORICAL ATLAS TO THE BIBLE

Edited by G. Ernest Wright and Floyd V. Filson

THE WESTMINSTER STUDY EDITION OF THE HOLY BIBLE

THE WESTMINSTER

HISTORICAL ATLAS TO THE BIBLE

REVISED EDITION

Edited by

GEORGE ERNEST WRIGHT

Professor of Old Testament History and Theology,
McCormick Theological Seminary

AND

FLOYD VIVIAN FILSON

Professor of New Testament Literature and History
McCormick Theological Seminary

WITH AN INTRODUCTORY ARTICLE BY

WILLIAM FOXWELL ALBRIGHT

Professor of Semitic Languages, Johns Hopkins University

The Westminster Press

PHILADELPHIA

LIBRARY OF CONGRESS CATALOG CARD
NUMBER 56-9123

PRINTED IN THE UNITED STATES OF AMERICA

PREFACE

THE study of geography cannot give the ultimate explanation of human life. Nevertheless, life has a geographical basis which the study of history cannot neglect. For example, the peculiar conditions within Palestine and its setting in the Near East provided a background for a people who lived in the world, yet were never quite united with the world. They enjoyed enough detachment to preserve and develop their gifts, but in their constant contact with the stream of significant events they faced the deepest and most vital problems of life.

Careful study of the historical geography of Biblical lands is imperative for two reasons. First, these regions have exercised an immense influence upon our Western World. Indeed, the foundations of modern civilization are to be found in the heritage which the ancient civilizations of the Mediterranean area have left to us. This is true not only in such details as the alphabet, pen and ink, metallurgy, astronomy, medicine, and mathematics, but more basically in the heritage of the Judaeo-Christian religion, Greek philosophy, and Roman law. Hence he who would understand the major factors which have shaped our faith, thought, and life cannot neglect the historical geography of Biblical lands.

Second, the study of geography is necessary for understanding the Bible. The Scripture is not a treatise on philosophy or theology, nor does it present a manual of abstract ethics. It is primarily a historical literature, which tells how God confronted men at particular times and places. Geography, history, and religion are so inextricably bound together in it that the religious message cannot be truly understood without attention to the setting and conditions of the revelation. In this respect the Bible is unique among the world's scriptures; it is the only one for whose comprehension the study of historical geography is basic.

I. GEOGRAPHICAL INFLUENCE ON BIBLICAL HISTORY

The focal center of Biblical history is the small land of Palestine, and the geographical influence upon the Judaeo-Christian movement may be suggested by a brief discussion of four facts about this country's situation:

A. The basic cultural ties of Palestine were with Syria and the rest of the Fertile Crescent. From this region, which lay along the great Arabian Desert, came the dominant factors in the cultural life of Palestine. No permanent or thorough shaping of Palestinian life ever came from the west. Moreover, it was separated from Egypt by the barren coastal desert and the wilderness of Sinai. This does not mean that there were no contacts between Egypt and Palestine. The influence of Egypt on her northern neighbor was constant; in nearly every excavation of ancient Palestinian ruins, objects imported from Egypt have been found. Yet that influence was always superficial; it did not affect the basic elements of the native culture.

The conceptual life and material civilization of Palestine were oriented mainly toward the Fertile Crescent on the north and northeast. When we examine the Israelite beliefs about life after death, about the essentially anthropomorphic rather than theriomorphic nature of God, about man as created for the service of the Divine, and about the divine requirements concerning both the ritualistic and the moral law, it becomes clear that the closest kinship of these beliefs is with the conceptual life of the Fertile Crescent. In Egypt, on the other hand, as indeed also in Greece, the fundamental doctrines about human and divine life were very different. Similarly, the arts and crafts, architecture, agriculture, metallurgy, and ceramics of Palestine were dependent upon Syria. It was in the latter country that new inventions, new styles, and new fashions originated. From Syria they gradually filtered down into Palestine, where, however, they never possessed the same brilliance. In material culture Palestine was the borrower and imitator, rarely the originator.

This culturally dependent region of Palestine was never a center of wealth. It was comparatively poor in natural resources, and as a result was not fought for with quite the same intensity as were the richer portions of the ancient Near East. None of the world's large cities were located within its borders. A sophisticated urban culture, of a type common in such centers as Tyre, Byblos, Ugarit, and Babylon, did not exist in Palestine except as a weak reflection or imitation of the cultured and wealthy north. Here, therefore, was the providentially provided setting, in which the prophetic minds of Israel could understand that the real purpose and blessing of God for his people were not to be found in riches, political power, and cultural distinction. The prophets reacted against contemporary culture because of its pagan character and the easygoing, compromising tolerance which it promoted.

B. Proximity to the Arabian Desert was a second noteworthy feature of the geographical situation of Palestine. Between that land and the Desert to the east there was no barrier. Hence here, as in the other countries of the Fertile Crescent, there was the eternal struggle between the nomadic and the settled peoples.

> The struggle between the Desert and the Sown seems to be a perpetual one. The moment that the central political authority weakens or is destroyed, that moment the Bedouins sweep in . . . . Like the waters of the ocean, the Bedouins may be held in check, but the moment the barriers are weakened, in they sweep with a destructive force that cannot be stemmed. . . . They can always retreat into the desert whither few can follow, and they are always prepared to break into the fertile lands at the first appearance of weakness there.*

Before Israel invaded Palestine, the comparative poverty and culturally dependent nature of the country meant that there was no real political strength and no deeply seated urban culture which could successfully resist nomadic invasion and influence. The incoming Israelite hosts constituted a nomadic group with the typical patriarchal organization of Arabia, and in later times they continued to look back upon this organization as the ideal one. In addition, later Israel preserved the relatively high moral purity and austerity of the patriarchal, nomadic religion, so that when the people settled down to agriculture and became increasingly urbanized, the family God of the Fathers did not become another nature or weather deity. The close relation of God and people, as symbolized in the covenant, was Israel's nomadic heritage, and the most important factor in saving her from idolatry. These basic elements of patriarchal religious life were idealized in later Israel and always remained as a purifying agent, not only among such extremists as the Nazirites and Rechabites, but among the great prophets as well.

This does not mean, however, that we can explain away Israel's unique conception of God simply by reference to the Arabian Desert or nomadic life. Before the days of Mohammed, Arabs were polytheists. Geography may explain the conditions of divine revelation, but cannot provide a substitute for it. What can safely be said, however, is that the patriarchal influence upon Israel remained dominant throughout her struggle with Canaanite polytheism. The ideal background of her religion lay in the desert, not in the scenes of urban civilization, and to that background the prophets constantly appealed.

C. A third important geographical fact about Palestine was its situation on two of the most vital trade routes of the ancient world: one between Egypt and Asia, and the other running west from Arabia to reach the coastal plain and there branch off to Egypt or Syria. By reason of this involvement in the economic life of the world, Palestine inevitably was drawn into world affairs. The period of Biblical history was the first great epoch of empire-building. It witnessed the impressive rise and rule of such mighty empires as Egypt, Assyria, Babylonia, Persia, Macedonia, and Rome. Each in succession reached out to seize and dominate the trade routes which passed through Palestine. This little country was thus inescapably forced within the bounds of each succeeding kingdom. It is not surprising, therefore, that the prophets deal with the international situa-

*Glueck, Nelson, *The Other Side of the Jordan* (New Haven, 1940), pp. 6 f.

tion and see the far reach of the power of God. Nor is it strange that along the many lines of trade and travel Jews moved out from their homeland until in the early days of the Christian movement, settlements of Jews were found in every important city of the known world.

D. The geographical features of Palestine and the character of its borders offered its inhabitants the possibility of a definitely limited but nevertheless real detachment. It would be easy to exaggerate that detachment; indeed, this has often been done. Palestine was too much involved in the currents of the ancient world to live in "splendid isolation" at any period of its history, and the study of its life always requires attention to the surrounding world. In spite of this immensely significant fact, however, Palestine was set apart from every neighboring region. On the south and east were uninviting wilderness and desert. The almost unbroken shore line of the Mediterranean Sea severely limited maritime contacts with lands to the west. On the north the massive heights of the Lebanons and Hermon rendered complete identification with the life of Syria impossible.

Thus on every side the borders of Palestine marked it as destined to have its own peculiar history. This provision for detachment was further effected by the lack of geographical unity within the country itself. Galilee was separated from Samaria; the hills were distinct from the plains; Transjordan was divided from western Palestine by the deep cleft of the Jordan Valley. Thus when the Canaanites were in control, no unified state ever came into being. Instead, there were numerous city-states. Even the deities became localized and pluralized, so that we hear of Baals and Ashtoreths, although in the official religion Baal and Ashtoreth were a single god and goddess. The basic geography of the country, therefore, created divisive forces which naturally tended to separate people into groups.

When Israel entered the country, she possessed a common religious and historical tradition, but throughout her existence she had to struggle against the geographical factors which divided north from south and east from west. Yet the partial isolation of the country as a whole provided sufficient detachment to enable Israel to develop a unique spiritual heritage. In Judaism this detachment was magnified into a national and religious exclusiveness. So basic did this element become that it continued to shape the lives of Jews even when they moved out into Gentile lands, and the Jews as a strong religious and cultural group continued to exist even when deprived of homeland and political independence. Under the stimulus of Hellenistic influence and Roman rule, however, the setting was created in the first century for a fuller revelation of the world scope of God's purpose. The days when detachment could be creative and fruitful were past; it was the time for Israel to give her gifts to the world.

II. THE PLAN OF THE ATLAS

In this volume the Editors and Publisher have sought to supply a series of maps which will set forth clearly and vividly the geographical setting of the Biblical story. The explanatory chapters which accompany the maps attempt to provide the essential facts needed to comprehend the historical and geographical framework of Scripture. Carefully selected photographs supplement the maps and text.

A new Biblical atlas is urgently needed. In recent decades extensive exploration has added greatly to our geographical knowledge of the Biblical lands. The last generation has seen an epoch-making advance in the methods and achievements of archaeological work. A new degree of mastery of the languages of the ancient Near East, a hitherto unattained correlation of the discoveries in the Mediterranean and Near East, and the development of adequate methods of excavation have all combined to make this advance possible.

The volume begins with an introductory article on the methods that have been employed in the rediscovery of the Biblical world. Professor W. F. Albright, the acknowledged authority in this field, has been kind enough to supply it. Following this article is a table of dates for convenient reference; it places the persons and events of the Biblical story in the full setting of the ancient world.

In the main body of the book each map plate is accompanied by an explanatory discussion. Chapter I deals with the general geography of Palestine. Chapters II-VII are primarily historical, and cover the period beginning with the world of the Patriarchs and ending with Judah in Nehemiah's time. At this point the historical maps are interrupted to give enlarged section maps of Palestine and their accompanying geographical discussion in Chapters VIII-X. Chapter XI, with its four section maps, continues the historical discussion, dealing with the great empires between the ninth and second centuries B.C. Chapters XII-XVI carry the story to the fourth century A.D., discussions of Palestine alternating with discussions of the Mediterranean world into which Christianity spread. Chapter XVII traces the history of Jerusalem, and Chapter XVIII surveys the archaeological excavations in Palestine during the past century.

It is hoped that the Index of Sites at the close of the volume will prove to be one of the most useful features of the work. It is not limited to the sites that appear on the maps, but is enlarged to provide a geographical index to the Bible (the spelling used is generally that of the A.V.). It gives directions for finding any site shown on the maps, and in the case of other places gives the approximate location, if it can be determined. With the expert aid of Professor Albright, an attempt has also been made to present the accurate spelling of the modern Arabic names of the places with which the ancient Palestinian sites are identified.

The Editors have divided responsibilities as much as possible. In general, Professor Wright's work extended through the Old Testament period. Professor Filson was responsible for the later period, beginning with the time of Alexander the Great. Plates I-VII, XI: A-C, XVII:A, and XVIII, together with Chapters II-VII, X, XVIII, and portions of Chapters XI and XVII have been done by Professor Wright. Professor Filson edited Plates XI:D, XII-XVI, and XVII: B-D, and prepared Chapters VIII, XII-XVI, and parts of Chapters XI and XVII. They collaborated on Plates VIII-X and Chapters I and IX.

The Editors are greatly indebted to their advisory committee, consisting of Professors W. F. Albright, of Johns Hopkins University; Millar Burrows, of Yale University; and O R. Sellers, of McCormick Theological Seminary. These scholars gave generously of their time and interest in examining the material in the volume and making many suggestions. To Professor Albright in particular we owe a great debt for his sympathetic counsel and advice at every stage of the work. Professors George Cameron and I. J. Gelb and Dr. A. A. Hays also gave scholarly aid in connection with the preparation of Plates II, III, XI, and XVI. The Index of Arabic Names has been prepared by Mr. Herbert B. Huffmon.

Constant aid came from Rev. L. J. Trinterud and Mr. John Ribble, of The Westminster Press, and from Mr. W. R. Bowes and the technical staff of the R. R. Donnelley and Sons Company in Chicago during the preparation of the first edition, while Mr. Ribble, Mr. Harry F. Hynd and Mr. Kenneth L. Rapalee of the Donnelley Company have given similar service for the second edition. The interest of these men went far beyond the usual function of publisher and printer, and the results of their expert and patient counsel appear on every page. To them is due also the revolutionary method of map-making, developed especially for use in this atlas.

Dr. Georges Barrois, of Princeton Theological Seminary, drew the relief map of Palestine which was used on Plates I, IV, VI, VIII-X, XII, XIV, and XVIII. He began work on the relief map of the Mediterranean world, but pressure of other duties prevented him from completing it. Mr. Hal Arbo, of Chicago, completed this map, which is used on Plates II, III, XI, XIII, XV, XVI; he also prepared the special maps used on Plates V, VII, and XVII. Mrs. Jean Arbo prepared the maps for the engravers by lettering sites, drawing in roads and boundaries, et cetera, on the basis of original copy supplied by the Editors. To these artists we express our sincere appreciation for their painstaking and highly competent work.

G. ERNEST WRIGHT.
FLOYD V. FILSON.

McCormick Theological Seminary
January 12, 1956

TABLE OF CONTENTS

	PAGE
Preface	5
Table of Illustrations	8
Acknowledgments	8
The Rediscovery of the Biblical World, *by William Foxwell Albright*	9
Chronological Outline of Ancient History	15
The Geography of Palestine	17
Plate I: Relief Map of Palestine	21
Plate II: The World of the Patriarchs (c. 2000–1700 B.C.) Inset Map: The Hebrew Table of Nations	22
The World of the Patriarchs (c. 2000–1700 B.C.)	23
The Great Empires During the Sojourn in Egypt	27
Plate III: The Great Empires During the Sojourn in Egypt (c. Fifteenth Century B.C.)	31
Plate IV: The Land of Canaan Before the Israelite Conquest	32
The Land of Canaan Before the Israelite Conquest	33
The Exodus from Egypt	37
Plate V: The Exodus from Egypt (Thirteenth Century B.C.)	41
Plate VI: Tribal Claims During the Period of the Judges	42
Palestine During the Period of the Judges (c. 1200–1020 B.C.)	43
The Political History of Israel and Judah	47
Plate VII: A: The Empire of David and Solomon (c. 1000–930 B.C.) B: The Kingdoms of Israel and Judah in Elijah's Time (c. 860 B.C.) C: The Kingdom of Judah in Isaiah's Time (c. 700 B.C.) D: The Province of Judah in Nehemiah's Time (c. 440 B.C.)	51
Plate VIII: Northern Palestine in Biblical Times	52
Northern Palestine in Biblical Times	57
Central Palestine in Biblical Times	61
Plate IX: Central Palestine in Biblical Times	65
Plate X: Southern Palestine in Biblical Times	66
Southern Palestine in Biblical Times	67
The Great Empires of Israelite Times	71
Maccabean and Herodian Palestine	77
Plate XI: A: The Assyrian Empire in Isaiah's Time (c. 700 B.C.) B: The Rival Empires in Jeremiah's Time (c. 585 B.C.) C: The Persian Empire at Its Greatest Extent (c. 500 B.C.) D: The Hellenistic Empires (c. 275 B.C.)	79
Plate XII: A: Palestine in the Maccabean Period (168–63 B.C.) B: Palestine under Herod the Great (40–4 B.C.) C: Palestine under Herod Agrippa I (41–44 A.D.) D: Palestine in the Time of Herod Agrippa II and the Roman Procurators (54–66 A.D.)	80
The Roman Empire at the Birth of Jesus	85
Plate XIII: The Roman World at the Birth of Jesus	89
Plate XIV: Palestine During the Ministry of Jesus	90
Palestine During the Ministry of Jesus	91
The Journeys of Paul	95
Plate XV: The Journeys of Paul	99
Plate XVI: A: The Church Before Paul's Missionary Journeys (c. 45 A.D.) B: The Church at the Close of Paul's Ministry (c. 65 A.D.) C: The Church in the Time of Irenaeus (c. 185 A.D.) D: The Church in the Time of Constantine (c. 325 A.D.)	100
The Expansion of Christianity	101
The History of Jerusalem	105
Plate XVII: A: Jerusalem in Israelite Times B: Jerusalem in the Time of Christ C: The Walls of Jerusalem in Christian Times D: Jerusalem Today	109
Plate XVIII: Excavated Sites in Modern Palestine	110
Excavations in Modern Palestine	111
Index to the Text	118
Index to the Maps, Including a Topographical Concordance to the Bible	121
Index of Arabic Names Identified with Biblical Places in Syria and Palestine	129

TABLE OF ILLUSTRATIONS

FIGURE	PAGE
1. The Behistun "Rock"	9
2. The Sphinx and Pyramids	11
3. The Ruins of Persepolis	12
4. A Cedar of Lebanon	13
5. Esdraelon or the Valley of Jezreel	17
6. The Plain of Shechem	18
7. The Jordan River	19
8. The Northern Tip of the Dead Sea	20
9. Asiatics Entering Egypt	23
10. Canaanite Captives in Egypt	24
11. A Restoration of Babylon and the Tower of Babel	25
12. The Code of Hammurabi	26
13. The Ruins of *Karnak*, Ancient Thebes	27
14. A Hyksos Enclosure	28
15. The Euphrates River	28
16. Foreign Captives in Egypt	29
17. A Nuzi Tablet	30
18. A Canaanite City Besieged by Egyptians	33
19. Amenophis IV (Akhnaton)	34
20. Queen Nofretete	34
21. The Canaanite God Baal	35
22. Asiatics Making Bricks in Egypt	37
23. The Traditional Mount Sinai	38
24. *Wâdī Qudeirât*	39
25. The King's Highway	40
26. The Pass of Megiddo	43
27. The Plain of Lebonah in Ephraim	44
28. A Megiddo Ivory, Showing Canaanite King	45
29. A Megiddo Ivory, Showing Canaanite Girl	46
30. *Tell Zakarîyeh*, Biblical Azekah	47
31. A Reconstruction of Solomon's Temple	48
32. The Altar of Burnt Offering	49
33. The Mesha Stone	50
34. The Hill of Samaria	53
35. The Omri-Ahab Wall at Samaria	54
36. Sennacherib's Lachish Relief	55
37. A Reconstruction of Lachish	56
38. One Source of the River Jordan, near Caesarea Philippi	57
39. Mount Tabor	58
40. Tiberias and the Sea of Galilee	59
41. The Synagogue at Capernaum	60
42. The Dead Sea	61
43. The Coastal Plain near Ramleh	62
44. The Shepherd's Field near Bethlehem	63
45. Jerash, Site of Ancient Gerasa	64
46. Jeshimon or the Wilderness of Judah	67
47. A Dam at *Kurnub*	68
48. An Ancient Edomite Mine	68
49. A Moabite Fortress	69
50. The Mountain-Fortress Sela in Edom	69
51. A Nabataean-Roman Site	70
52. One of the Cilician Gates	71
53. The Black Obelisk of Shalmaneser III	72
54. Reliefs on the Cliff of the Dog River	73
55. Sargon II	74
56. Ruins of the Ishtar Gate, Babylon	75
57. A Reconstruction of the Ishtar Gate, Babylon	76
58. The *Sīq* and *el-Khazneh* at Petra	77
59. Beth-zur (Bethsura)	78
60. *Khirbet Qumrân*	81
61. Table and Bench from *Qumrân*	82
62. One of "Solomon's Pools"	83
63. Lake Huleh and Mount Hermon	84
64. The Appian Way	85
65. The Roman Emperor Augustus	86
66. The Roman Forum and Arch of Titus	87
67. The Corinth Canal	88
68. The Sea of Galilee	91
69. The Jerusalem-Jericho Road	92
70. The Garden of Gethsemane and Mount of Olives	93
71. The Wailing Wall in Jerusalem	94
72. The Theodotus Synagogue Inscription	95
73. "Straight Street," Damascus	96
74. The Areopagus, Athens	97
75. Ruins of the Theater at Ephesus	98
76. Pompeii and Mount Vesuvius	101
77. The Coliseum and Arch of Constantine at Rome	102
78. Air View of Dura-Europos	103
79. The Church of the Holy Sepulcher, Jerusalem	104
80. The Citadel and City Wall, Jerusalem	105
81. The Dome of the Rock, Jerusalem	107
82. Sketch of the Relief of Jerusalem	108
83. The Mound of Beth-shan	111
84. The American School of Oriental Research, Jerusalem	112
85. The Mound of Megiddo	113
86. The Mound of Jericho	114
87. The Fortifications of *Tell en-Naṣbeh*	115
88. Prehistoric Caves in the *Wâdī el-Mughârah*	116

ACKNOWLEDGMENTS *We gratefully give credit to the following sources for the illustrations used in this volume:*

Oriental Institute, University of Chicago, Figures 1 (Aerial Survey of the Oriental Institute), 3, 5, 10, 11 (Painting by M. Bardin after Unger), 12 (Cast in Oriental Institute), 16, 17, 18, 20 (Cast in Oriental Institute), 28, 29, 33 (Cast in Oriental Institute), 53 (Cast in Oriental Institute), 57 (Painting by M. Bardin after Unger), 85.
Ewing Galloway, ©, Figures 2, 4, 6, 8, 13, 15, 38, 39, 42, 43, 44, 46, 62, 65, 66, 67, 68, 69, 73, 75, 76, 79, 80.
Philip Gendreau, ©, Figures 7, 40, 56, 64, 70, 71.
Lepsius, *Denkmaeler*, Part 2, Pl. 133, and Part 3, Pl. 40, Figures, 9, 22.
Petrie, Sir W. M. F., *Hyksos and Israelite Cities* (Bernard Quaritch Press), Pl. IVa, Figure 14.
Boreux, *La Sculpture égyptienne au Musée du Louvre*, Pl. XXVIII, Figure 19.
Syria, Vol. 17, Pl. XXI, Photograph by C. F. A. Schaeffer, for the French expedition to Ugarit, Figure 21.
Wilson and Palmer, *Ordnance Survey of the Peninsula of Sinai*, Photographs, Vol. I, Numbers 48–50, Figure 23.
John Trever, Figures 30, 34, 35, 81, 84.
A. H. Layard, *The Monuments of Nineveh*, Pls. 21–22, Figure 36.
R. Dussaud, P. Deschamps and H. Seyrig, *La Syrie antique et médiévale illustrée* (Paris, Geuthner, 1928, Pl. 28), Figure 54.
Museo di Antichità, Turin, Figure 55.
Jericho Excavation Fund, Miss Kathleen Kenyon, Figure 86.
L'Abbé J. Starcky, Figure 60.
Palestine Archaeological Museum, Figure 61.
Dura Expedition, Yale University, Figure 78.
American Schools of Oriental Research, Figures 24, 25, 31, 32, 47, 48, 49, 51; Figures 25 and 51 being by courtesy of the Air Officer Commanding, Royal Air Force, Middle East; Figures 31 and 32 being the Solomonic Temple and Altar as drawn by C. F. Stevens from specifications by W. F. Albright and G. E. Wright.
H. G. May, Figures 26, 27, 63.
Wellcome-Marston Archaeological Research Expedition to the Near East, Figure 37.
G. Ernest Wright, Figures 50, 58, 77.
O. R. Sellers, Figure 59 (from the Beth-zur Excavation; courtesy, Royal Air Force Official, Crown Copyright Reserved).
Oxford University Press, Figure 72 (from Sukenik, *Ancient Synagogues in Palestine and Greece*, British Academy, Pl. XVI:A).
W. A. McDonald, Figure 74.
University Museum, Philadelphia, Figure 83.
Palestine Institute, Pacific School of Religion, Figure 87.
Vartan D. Melconian, Figures 41, 45, 88.

THE REDISCOVERY OF THE BIBLICAL WORLD

WILLIAM FOXWELL ALBRIGHT

I. INTRODUCTORY CONSIDERATIONS

THERE are few fields where the progress of discovery makes constant revision of handbooks and other aids to study more necessary than in Biblical research. This is not easy, even for scholars, to realize, since one instinctively feels that old books are more useful as guides to the study of old subjects than new books. On the other hand, there is danger in seeking new discoveries and novel points of view at the expense of more solid earlier work. This is particularly true in fields like Biblical archaeology and geography, where mastery of tools and of methods of investigation is so arduous that there is always a temptation to neglect sound method, substituting clever combinations and brilliant guesses for slower and more systematic work.

Since it is only in our generation that the progress of research has made real synthesis possible, all standard books appearing earlier are in imperative need of revision, often of complete rewriting. Moreover, many of the latest books and articles have been written by men who are not really competent. The reader who is not a specialist is naturally helpless in selecting a reliable authority to follow. The mere fact that an author occupies a distinguished academic position or has made some remarkable discoveries in the field or museum does not prove his scholarly competence. Hence the value of such an organization as the American Schools of Oriental Research, which is not tied to any one university or organization but gathers the best skills and selects only the most reliable scholars to present the results of excavation, exploration, and interpretation to the educated public.

In evaluating the information contained in standard Biblical handbooks, it is well to compare the dates of their publication with the dates of the most significant archaeological discoveries. To begin with standard English works of conservative character, Clarke's great *Commentary*, which is still used by many, appeared in 1810–1826; Kitto's famous *Cyclopaedia* came out in 1843–1845. If we consider fundamental German works, Eichhorn's *Introduction* (with which the history of the so-called higher criticism really begins) was published in 1783, while the first scientific Hebrew dictionary and grammar were brought out by Gesenius in 1810–1813. The most important developments in literary criticism of the Old Testament came in 1805 with De Wette's contention that Deuteronomy was composed in the reign of Josiah, in 1853 with Hupfeld's successful revival of Ilgen's view that there were three documents instead of two in Genesis, and in 1876 with Wellhausen's consolidation of the Graf-Kuenen view that the Priestly Code was the latest of the four documents of the Pentateuch.

Turning to compare the most important dates in the history of modern Biblical archaeology, we note that the Egyptian hieroglyphics were not deciphered until the years 1822–1841 and that Assyrian cuneiform was not decoded until 1845–1851. Systematic excavations were not begun in Assyria until 1843 and in Egypt until 1850; the first scientific excavations from our present point of view were undertaken by Flinders Petrie in Egypt (since 1883) and Palestine (1890). But it was not until 1887 that the Amarna Tablets (see p. 35) were found, while the Elephantine Papyri did not become available to scholars until 1911. The great Hittite archives of Boghazköy were unearthed in 1907, but it was not until the middle twenties that enough material became available to make synthesis possible. The long-lost Canaanite religious literature has been excavated only since 1929, while successful interpretation of its remains cannot be said to have begun until 1932. Scarcely any original Sumerian literature from the third millennium was available for scholarly research until S. N. Kramer began to publish in 1938. It was not until 1939 that the present writer felt that the time had come to begin the preparation of real syntheses of ancient Near-Eastern history and civilization. During the preceding decade our knowledge of archaeological chronology had increased so rapidly that it was then possible for the first time to date events and cultural phenomena in different lands correctly in relation to one another.

This tremendous improvement in knowledge and method applies not only to the broad field of ancient civilization but at the same time to such special aspects as geography and topography, with which this book is primarily concerned. Even in the field of map making there has been great advance since Robinson began his epochal researches in 1837. At that time few points in the entire Near East had been precisely located in latitude and longitude, while details were left to be roughly sketched in by cartographers who utilized naval observations and explorers' records of distance and direction.

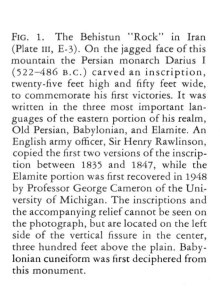

FIG. 1. The Behistun "Rock" in Iran (Plate III, E-3). On the jagged face of this mountain the Persian monarch Darius I (522–486 B.C.) carved an inscription, twenty-five feet high and fifty feet wide, to commemorate his first victories. It was written in the three most important languages of the eastern portion of his realm, Old Persian, Babylonian, and Elamite. An English army officer, Sir Henry Rawlinson, copied the first two versions of the inscription between 1835 and 1847, while the Elamite portion was first recovered in 1948 by Professor George Cameron of the University of Michigan. The inscriptions and the accompanying relief cannot be seen on the photograph, but are located on the left side of the vertical fissure in the center, three hundred feet above the plain. Babylonian cuneiform was first deciphered from this monument.

The Holy Land was the first country of southwestern Asia to be systematically surveyed, yet the Survey of Western Palestine was not undertaken until 1865 and was not finished until 1877. Schumacher's much sketchier survey of northern Transjordan, begun in 1885, was not finished until 1914. The region of Moab and Edom has never been properly mapped. In recent years a cadastral survey has been completed, though its distribution is as yet restricted. Moreover, a century ago nothing was known about geological formation, and little about soils and water supply, rainfall and temperature, etc. Above all, however, from our present standpoint, we have learned how to use archaeological data to locate, date, and often identify ancient sites. How this is done will be concisely explained below.

II. HOW WE EXCAVATE IN THE NEAR EAST

It is often supposed that the archaeologist digs merely for the purpose of unearthing monuments and finding museum objects in the buildings or tombs which he excavates. It is true that much excavation of the nineteenth century was undertaken for these ends; the outstanding example of it is Mariette's work in Egypt from 1850 to 1880. Fortunately, however, not nearly so much harm could be done in Egypt as in Mesopotamia by such rough-and-ready methods, since there was almost no stratification in the temples and tombs of the Nile Valley which Mariette cleared of their silt and sand. From the very beginning of the work of Botta and Layard in Assyria, about a century ago, much more care was devoted to the recording of the finds as they were made, to the planning of excavated buildings, and to the prompt publication of the principal objects discovered. Yet scientific archaeology cannot be said to have commenced until 1890, when Flinders Petrie dug for six weeks at *Tell el-Ḥesī* in southern Judah (Plate XVIII, B-5). At that time he was able to demonstrate once for all that most important ancient sites of southwestern Asia consist of more or less regular, superimposed layers of debris, and that it is possible to date them by the artifacts (objects made by man) which each layer contains. The most valuable artifacts for dating are pieces of pottery, whole or broken. These broken pieces are found in enormous numbers on these ancient sites. Pottery was fragile and seldom was usable for any great while. Moreover, pottery styles changed rapidly. In his brief season in Palestine, preceded and followed by many years of excavation in Egypt, Petrie showed that archaeological chronology could be based on a careful study of the relation of objects to one another in the light of the deposits in which they occur, as well as on equally systematic study of the evolution of pottery forms or styles (sequence dating). The study of the physical relationship of artifacts in the light of the strata in which they are found is called "stratigraphy," and the study of the relation between the forms of objects is called "typology." All scientific modern archaeology is based on the application of these two basic principles, to which we shall return presently.

The best recent archaeological method is associated with the name of George Andrew Reisner, a native of Indianapolis, who became the foremost excavator of modern times. Reisner combined the methods employed by the leading German excavators, who stressed the architectural and engineering side of archaeology, with the stratigraphy and typology of the Petrie school, employing both with the aid of American filing cabinets and recording systems. Fortunately, Reisner was always supplied with adequate funds to provide for assistants and apparatus, so he was able to set an example of comprehensive and accurate recording of his work in the field.

Today archaeological treasure hunts are no longer permitted in the Near East. In all the countries of this region, whether independent nations or colonies, there are organized departments of antiquities, headed by Government appointees who are generally scholars of distinction. The directors of antiquities are assisted by staffs of trained archaeologists, who care for the archaeological museum or museums, inspect ancient monuments and see that they are protected against injury, watch over the trade in antiquities and prevent illicit digging and smuggling as far as practicable, and control the excavations carried on by native and foreign institutions. Both Jordan and Israel possess highly trained officials in their departments of antiquities who work within the framework of detailed ordinances controlling all archaeological matters. For example, whenever ancient remains are discovered in the building of a modern house or street, the work must cease until a member of the antiquities department has gathered all essential information as to the nature of the deposit. If a foreign institution desires to excavate a site, permission must be secured from the department, which exercises care in the oversight of such proposals, makes a division of the objects found, and sees to it that all objects of special significance are kept within the country for study and display.

The excavator of today is expected to undertake his work with an adequate staff of assistants, who are provided with all necessary equipment, such as surveying instruments, photographic apparatus, drawing tools, picks, hoes, baskets, and sieves. In large sites light railways and cranes may be required. The work of the native diggers, who are generally untrained, must be supervised directly by the members of the excavating staff or by trained native foremen, whose own supervisory activity is carefully controlled by the director of the expedition. The site and its environs are surveyed first, if possible, and a survey grid, composed as a rule of squares twenty meters on a side, is prepared. All excavated remains are recorded on this grid as exactly as possible, in order to avoid errors. All artifacts found during the excavation are labeled with the number of the room or other locus where they were found. If desirable, the exact spot, as well as the precise level above the floor, is noted. Many photographs are taken to show the exact appearance of the ruins as they are cleared, and especially to record the relation of objects to one another as well as to the adjacent walls. The levels of the excavated ruins are also duly recorded, attention being concentrated mainly on tops of walls in each locus, floor levels, and foundation levels. When this task is finished and the excavator has taken careful notes on details, such as peculiarities of construction and indications of repair or reoccupation, the entire stratum may be removed down to its foundations and the next stratum below may be cleared in the same way. Sometimes, of course, there was so much reuse of older walls and so much partial reconstruction that it is not practicable to remove any walls until the excavator has cleared a sufficient number of superimposed foundations to make a systematic analysis of their relation to one another possible.

All significant objects of human manufacture found should be recorded summarily, with brief descriptions and identifying drawings or photographs, on cards or in a record book, the objects themselves being correspondingly labeled. When possible, objects are restored and cleaned, though final cleaning and restoration are generally left to be done in the museums where they are later deposited. It is particularly important, moreover, that pottery be cleaned and put together on the spot, since it is all of chronological interest and since most broken pottery is discarded after the close of an excavation. Accurate outline drawings and clear photographs are prepared on the spot as far as possible, so that errors and losses may be averted. Chemical treatment of objects and detailed technical study of them must nearly always be left until later, since few expeditions possess the necessary facilities or technologically trained staff.

In interpreting his finds as sources of historical information the archaeologist must be particularly careful not to allow his judgment to be biased by preconceived ideas. In other words, he must remember that archaeology is primarily an inductive science, and that the careful use of factual data precedes all deductive reasoning. Hence the importance of distinguishing throughout between stratigraphy and typology, which we have defined above. First of all, he must be sure of the limits and relations of his strata and must determine whether any unique piece from a given stratum really belongs there or is an intrusion from above or below. Strata are not always level, and later pieces were sometimes washed down from a higher level on a site, or earlier pieces were dropped on the surface after being brought up from an ancient pit, excavated for a cistern or silo. The trained excavator has little trouble with such intrusions, but care

FIG. 2. The Sphinx and Pyramids at *Gîzeh*, Egypt (Plate V, C-3). The great age of pyramid-building in Egypt was during the Old Kingdom between the twenty-seventh and the twenty-second centuries B.C. The pyramids are the most spectacular and tremendous tombs ever built by man. The Sphinx, while possessing the body of a lion, is actually the portrait head of Pharaoh Khafre, the builder of the pyramid behind it. The great Pyramid of Khufu stands just to the right of the photograph.

is obviously required in making deductions from the appearance of a singular object in a given stratum. Unwritten objects, such as pottery, must first be dated relatively to other comparable objects which recur in higher or lower deposits. Then one can give them a date in absolute chronology (B.C. or A.D.) by noting what kind of datable objects (inscriptions, scarabs, coins, etc.) are found with them or in known relation to them. For such evidence we may have to turn to another site, where identical objects may occur together with intrinsically datable remains. Typology is of the greatest importance in fixing chronology, since it enables the scholar to group archaeological objects into classes and species, to identify given types wherever they may recur—sometimes hundreds of miles apart—and to trace the evolution of a given form. When the successive steps of evolution of form are once known, it is possible, for instance, to assign approximate dates to objects which are a little later in type than objects found in a given datable stratum and a little earlier in type than corresponding objects found in the next stratum above. By the combination of inductive reasoning from stratigraphy and deduction from typological indications the archaeologist gradually builds up a coherent chronological system. After such a system has been built up it may be rectified and adjusted by reference to formal historic chronology (see below, section IV).

Once the excavator has accurately described and interpreted his data, they can be used for a great many historical purposes. Particularly significant, of course, are written objects and documents, since they enable the scholar to reconstruct the life of religion, politics, and commerce. But other remains have great and steadily increasing significance. Through them we learn about the arts and crafts of antiquity, how men built and where they lived, how they made pottery, practiced metallurgy, what crops and animals they possessed. Through them we also learn to follow the history of human settlement. Once the archaeologist has determined the pottery chronology of a given region by excavating a number of sites, he can proceed to date all other occupied sites of antiquity by the potsherds with which they are strewn. The outstanding illustration of the successful application of this principle is Nelson Glueck's archaeological survey of Transjordan, in which he has examined and described more than 1,500 ancient sites, dating them by their sherds.

III. HOW WRITTEN DOCUMENTS ARE INTERPRETED

As stated above, written documents form by far the most important single body of material discovered by archaeologists. Hence it is extremely important to gain a clear idea of their character and of our ability to interpret them. Just as in all archaeological work, the question of method takes first place. It must be remembered that every single script employed in the ancient Near East has had to be deciphered in modern times. Curiously enough, for every ancient script to be deciphered two new ones seem to be discovered. We have deciphered Assyro-Babylonian cuneiform and various other independent cuneiform scripts, three principal varieties of Egyptian hieroglyphics, and many other alphabetic and syllabic scripts, but an even greater number remain to be interpreted, and new ones turn up every few years.

As a characteristic example of the nature of our task, we may point to the cuneiform alphabet of Ugarit. First discovered in 1929, many hundreds of tablets in this script have been excavated by C. F. A. Schaeffer at *Râs Shamrah* (Ugarit) on the Syrian coast opposite Cyprus (Plate II, E-2). The first fragmentary tablets were published by Virolleaud in 1930 and almost immediately deciphered by Bauer and Dhorme, both of whom were distinguished as Semitic philologians and as cipher experts. First Bauer correctly identified over half the letters, then Dhorme added five more, after which Bauer made various corrections in his own system, raising the total number of letters identified by himself to nineteen. Subsequently, on the basis of a vastly increased body of texts, Virolleaud and others added six more characters, making thirty in all. However, decipherment was here again only the beginning, and it is characteristic of the difference in the type of skills required that neither Bauer nor Dhorme, in spite of their outstanding ability as Semitists, contributed much to the task of interpretation as such. The next step required schooled imagination, held constantly under control by a rigid sense of grammatical form. Many scholars now entered the field; outstanding among them was H. L. Ginsberg, whose keen grammatical instinct had been cultivated by a thorough training in Semitic philology. Thanks to Gordon's *Ugaritic Grammar*, which first appeared in 1940, we have a solid grammatical basis for further work. Students of Ugaritic are

FIG. 3. The ruins of Persepolis, the magnificent capital of the Persian Empire begun by Darius I (522–486 B.C.) and completed by his successors. The low building in the center is the royal treasury, which has been reconstructed as the expedition headquarters of modern excavators. Columns of the royal palaces can be seen as they were left standing by Alexander the Great, who wantonly set fire to the beautiful capital.

now concentrating on the explanation of passages in the texts hitherto published, with special attention to the meaning of words.

We must distinguish sharply between the earlier and the more recent periods of philological research in our field, since the translations of documents written in different languages depend for accuracy on the progress of grammatical and lexical knowledge. Thus it is unsafe to rely on any translations of Egyptian historical texts which appeared before Breasted's *Ancient Records* (1906), since Breasted was the first historian to take full advantage of the tremendous progress in the knowledge of Egyptian achieved by Erman and Sethe after 1880. It is equally unsafe to depend on any translations of Egyptian religious texts made before about 1925, since that year marked the publication of the first volume of the great Berlin dictionary of Egyptian, while the year 1927 saw the appearance of Gardiner's monumental *Egyptian Grammar*. The first reliable English translations of Egyptian religious texts appeared in Blackman's *Literature of the Ancient Egyptians* (1927) and Breasted's *Dawn of Conscience* (1933). Turning to Mesopotamia we find ourselves in a worse situation, since no English translations of cuneiform texts adequately represent the great progress in scientific philology marked by the brilliant work of Landsberger and his pupils since about 1923. Luckenbill's *Ancient Records of Assyria and Babylonia* (1926–1927) was far below the standard set twenty years earlier by Breasted in the corresponding Egyptian field. A selection of historical, legal, and religious texts has recently been translated by eminent scholars in the excellent volume edited by J. B. Pritchard, *Ancient Near Eastern Texts Relating to the Old Testament* (1950). This book, together with its companion, *The Ancient Near East in Pictures* (1954), is virtually indispensable for the student who does not handle at first hand the material surveyed. Assyriologists have been handicapped by the lack of a good Assyrian dictionary, but the Oriental Institute of the University of Chicago began publishing its great *Assyrian Dictionary* in 1956 to fill the need. The field of Sumerian was helped greatly with the publication of Poebel's grammar in 1923. Fortunately Poebel's gifted student, S. N. Kramer, is in charge of the publication of the Sumerian literature from the temple library at Nippur (Plate II, F-3). In 1938 he began to edit and translate Sumerian epics from the third millennium. Since this is the oldest body of narrative literature in the world, and since it influenced much of the religious literature of the Semites of later times, its importance can scarcely be overestimated.

Our understanding of cuneiform Hittite is now abreast of our knowledge of Sumerian, in spite of the fact that cuneiform Hittite was not deciphered until 1915 and that workers are few. On the other hand, decipherment of hieroglyphic Hittite has been making slow progress, but thanks to the discovery of bilinguals there is hope for greater success. We are still unable to translate a single inscription in hieroglyphic Hittite satisfactorily, though most of the phonetic characters and many ideograms can be read and a good deal is understood about the grammar. At present Helmuth Bossert, of the University of Istanbul, is the leader in this elusive field. The study of Horite (Hurrian), though begun more than fifty years ago after the publication of the first cuneiform tablets in that language, is still hampered by the small number of texts, which come from half a dozen different excavations, in Egypt, Syria, Mesopotamia, and Asia Minor. E. A. Speiser's excellent *Introduction to Hurrian* (1941) represents the high-water mark in this field.

IV. HOW ANCIENT DATES ARE FIXED

Since chronology is the backbone of history and since it is impossible to comprehend the relationship of events and movements unless we know their dates, it is extremely important for the thoughtful student of the past to get a clear idea how dates are fixed. Since 1938, Mesopotamian chronology has gradually become stabilized until it is probably correct to within half a century as far back as the twenty-fifth century B.C. Egyptian dates for the Old Kingdom have had to be rather drastically reduced to agree with the lower Mesopotamian chronology, and the archaeological chronology of Syria and Palestine has been adjusted to harmonize with the concurrent evidence from both sides. For the first time since the beginning of excavations we are, accordingly, in a position to validate our chronology of the ancient Near East. On what basis can we make this affirmation?

Assyrian chronology is now fixed back toward the middle of the second millennium B.C., thanks to the publication by Arno Poebel, in 1942–1943, of the so-called Khorsabad List of Assyrian kings, which begins in the late third millennium and ends in the eighth century B.C. Moreover, the latter part of this list overlaps other lists of annual magistrates, or eponyms, which are preserved intact from the early ninth century to the middle of the seventh. Part of the period is also covered by a terse chronicle, giving each eponym with the outstanding events of his year. Under one year a solar eclipse is recorded, thus enabling the astronomer to compute the precise date —763 B.C. In this way it is possible to fix the precise date of all the dated events recorded in the Babylonian Chronicle, covering the years from 745 to 667 B.C.—and the accessions of the kings of Babylon agree throughout to the year with the data of the Ptolemaic canon, compiled from Babylonian sources by the famous Greek astronomer of the second century A.D.! Further, thanks to many thousands of dated business documents, we are able to control practically all intercalary months employed in the Neo-Babylonian and Persian periods to adjust the calendar. With the aid of exact astronomical data, it thus becomes possible to give the Julian equivalents of nearly all dates in Mesopotamian records of the first millennium B.C. This means that we have invaluable pegs on which to hang our Biblical chronology from the ninth to the fifth century B.C.

Thanks to the agreement of the Khorsabad List (checked and controlled by numerous other Assyrian sources) with the astronomically fixed chronology of the New Kingdom in Egypt, we can be sure of our approximate dates back to the reign of Asshur-uballit (c.1354–1319), who came to the throne not long before the death of Amenophis IV (c. 1370–1353). Dead reckoning on the basis of the Khorsabad List brings us to about the middle of the eighteenth century for Shamshi-Adad I, the older Assyrian contemporary of the great Hammurabi of Babylon. The contemporaneity of these outstanding figures in ancient history was not discovered until 1937, with the sensational find of the Mari tablets, which flooded the age in question with historical illumination (see p. 24). Since lists of the annual events by which years were then dated in Babylonia have been recovered—confirmed by many thousand dated business documents of the age—we possess a record of the chronology of Babylonia from the beginning of the Third Dynasty of Ur to the end of the First Dynasty of Babylon, a period of over five centuries, so we can now fix the chronological position of every year in this series with reference to the Khorsabad List within thirty years or so. Moreover, in 1912 the German scholar F. X. Kugler discovered that a cuneiform table of movements of the planet Venus had originally been drawn up under King Ammiṣaduqa of Babylon, as proved by a date formula from that king's reign. This table makes it possible for the astronomer to calculate possible alternative dates for the reign of Ammiṣaduqa, and it becomes easy to show that only one of them fits the data provided by the Khorsabad List and the Mari documents. Employing this astronomically calculated date, the reign of Hammurabi falls between 1728 and 1686 B.C. and the beginning of the Third Dynasty of Ur between 2070 and 2050 B.C.

Turning from Mesopotamia to Egypt, we find one great advantage in the existence of the Sothic cycle, a period equivalent to 1,460 Julian years. When the Egyptian calendar was formally regularized, perhaps about 2780 B.C., it opened each year with the first day on which the star Sirius was visible on the eastern horizon before sunrise, which then coincided roughly with the appearance of the annual Nile inundation in Lower Egypt. But since there were only 365 days in the Egyptian civil (vague) year, each year the calendar fell behind about a quarter of a day. In the course of 1,461 vague years the date of any astronomically fixed event in the calendar returned to its original place in this calendar, so 1,461 vague years = 1,460 Julian years of 365¼ days each. Since the Egyptians celebrated the festival of the heliacal rising of Sirius every year, to the accompaniment of elaborate ritual and mythology, they could not help becoming aware of this discrepancy and its cyclic character. Fortunately for us, we have a definite, though not entirely clear, statement about the end of a Sothic cycle in the second century A.D. in Censorinus, and a probable allusion to the commencement of the same cycle in the monuments of Sethos I, toward the end of the fourteenth century B.C. These fixed dates, combined with new moons and other data, enable us to give fairly exact dates for the kings of the Twelfth Dynasty, between 1991 and 1778 B.C., for Amenophis I of the Eighteenth Dynasty, c. 1546 B.C., and for Tuthmosis III, c. 1490 B.C. (These dates follow the correlation of Borchardt, corrected in part by Edgerton, and may have to be moved up or down a few years.) For years many scholars fought the "low chronology" of Borchardt, Meyer, and Breasted, until overwhelmed by the weight of new evidence. I know of no competent ancient historian today who places the beginning of the Middle Kingdom before 2000 B.C. Thanks to the corroboratory evidence of Mesopotamian chronology, there can be no doubt about the substantial correctness of Borchardt's date.

All our chronology of the lands of the Aegean, including Crete, as well as of Palestine and Phoenicia during the Bronze Age, depends upon direct or cultural synchronisms between these regions and Egypt. The archaeological chronology of the entire Bronze Age in Palestine is based on Egyptian. The results are so reasonable throughout and are now so beautifully confirmed by Mesopotamian evidence (through Syria) that they cannot be changed more than a century or two in the future. Since our Palestinian dates depend largely on pottery, they are generally somewhat fluid, but even so they remain fixed within narrow limits. Before 3000 we must use conjecture, aided by computations based on geochronology and radioactive carbon.

V. HOW ANCIENT SITES ARE IDENTIFIED

Few scholarly matters have been as cavalierly handled as the identification of ancient sites. Owing to the intense interest of pilgrims and travelers in the Holy Land, well-meaning clergy and helpful guides have made many hasty identifications, generally on the flimsiest pretexts. Moreover, few of the modern scholars who have identified Biblical sites have possessed the necessary scholarly training. Most of what has been written on the subject of Palestinian topography since the seventeenth century is now virtually worthless. However, here and there are some outstanding names of men who made valuable contributions to our knowledge of the topography of the Holy Land. In 1714, Adrian Reland published a careful and comprehensive account of Palestine and its ancient towns, compiled from all available ancient literary sources—the Bible, Graeco-Roman literature, and the Talmud. In 1837, Edward Robinson undertook his epoch-making trip to Palestine, in the course of which he vastly

FIG. 4. A cedar of Lebanon. The cedar forests of the Lebanon range are now greatly diminished in size, but they were once extensive and the most important source of excellent furniture and building wood in the ancient East. Egyptian, Mesopotamian, Canaanite, and Israelite monarchs drew heavily from these forests for their luxurious palaces.

improved existing maps and located hundreds of modern sites, besides identifying for the first time scores of Biblical towns whose location was completely unknown. Dozens of Western scholars followed his footsteps during the following half century, but few of their identifications have stood the test of sound method. In 1865–1877 Conder, Kitchener, and others carried out the great Survey of Western Palestine (see above), followed by an abortive American expedition and later by a successful one-man German undertaking. In 1894, George Adam Smith published his *Historical Geography of the Holy Land*, which became astonishingly popular and passed through many editions. From the scholarly point of view it was abreast of the times when it first appeared, but it has become more and more antiquated with the progress of investigation. The next important step forward came in 1902, when the German Evangelical Institute for the Archaeology of the Holy Land was founded under the direction of Gustav Dalman. He and his pupils introduced much greater precision in their treatment of the material, observing the physical facts as accurately as possible, reproducing modern Arabic names correctly, and dealing with the literary and documentary sources as exhaustively and critically as possible. The German school added some good identifications and discarded many bad ones, as may be seen most conveniently from the *Atlas* of Hermann Guthe (latest edition: 1926). Dalman was succeeded in 1922 by Albrecht Alt, who has improved Dalman's method by utilizing inscriptions and results of archaeological excavations and surface explorations. Since 1922 the American Schools of Oriental Research has taken the lead in surface exploration, dating sites by the potsherds with which they are strewn. The high-water mark of its investigations is marked by the explorations of Nelson Glueck, who began a systematic examination of all ancient sites in Transjordan in 1932, completing it at the beginning of the Second World War. No such thorough archaeological survey has ever been made in any other comparable area in the Near East. For the first time we can analyze the fluctuations of population in Transjordan, from period to period, and delimit the boundaries of Edom, Moab, and Ammon on purely archaeological grounds.

The topographical student of today can begin with an admirable French work, Father Abel's *Géographie de la Palestine* (two volumes, 1933 and 1938). But he will soon find that this is only a convenient starting point for further research, especially on the basis of the rapidly accumulating archaeological and inscriptional material. The serious investigator must consider the following aspects of his problem: (1) criticism of the written sources in which ancient place names occur; (2) approximate location of sites from documentary indications; (3) toponymy, or the analysis of place names and their linguistic transmission; (4) archaeological indications; (5) the evidence of tradition.

The first requirement boils down to a very simple yet often neglected principle: all ancient literary works must be edited with the greatest possible exactness, after a methodical comparison of all preserved manuscripts (whose variant readings must be recorded); all inscriptions must be accessible in photographs or in good copies by scholars of recognized competence and precision. In the case of important places, such scientific editing of passages where they are mentioned frequently gives a clearer idea of their relation to other places in the neighborhood. In the case of less important places, it is well to know the most reliable form of their names before proceeding to locate them. Textual criticism becomes a matter of primary value in dealing with long lists of names such as we have in Joshua, where the Greek translation of the third or second century B.C. often corrects the Hebrew Bible, though it is sometimes not possible to restore the original Greek reading with any degree of confidence. The topographer is thus heavily dependent on the laborious work of textual critics of the Greek Bible. As one out of many possible illustrations we select Josh. 19:45, in a list of towns of Dan. The Hebrew text reads, "And Jehud, and Bene-berak," whereas the oldest Greek manuscript, from the fourth century A.D., offers, "And (I)azor and Banaibakat." The Taylor Prism of Sennacherib, in its account of the campaign of 701 B.C. against Hezekiah, offers, "Azuru and Banai-barqa." Today we find the two Arab villages of *Yazûr* and *Ibn-ibrâq*, with ancient names, only a mile and a half apart, thus proving the correctness of the Iazor of the oldest Greek text against the Jehud of the much younger Hebrew text of the Masoretic Bible (see Plate IX, C-4, where the traditional name Jehud is placed at modern *Yazûr*).

Our second approach depends more upon knowledge of the country, ancient and modern, as well as upon common sense, than upon any other considerations. The topographer must analyze accounts of journeys and campaigns, comparing routes and lists of different periods with one another; he must be able to select the most suitable location for an ancient town on the basis of terrain, communications, water supply, etc. If he can find different references to a place, he can often locate it approximately by the simple method of drawing lines or circles and noting where they intersect. The greatest danger here is that the scholar will content himself with the application of this method and perhaps the third one, without taking other approaches into consideration.

The third approach to topographic problems begins by comparing ancient place names with modern. Since this method is the most obvious of all, it has been sorely abused by amateur topographers, as well as by many scholars who should know better. Thus Palmer proposed the identification of Zephath (Hormah in the south) with modern *Isbeiṭā* (*Subaita*), though all Semitic vowels and consonants are different (Plate XVIII, B-7). It is quite true that both vowels and consonants shift in the course of history (thus Hebrew *g* becomes Arabic *j*), but these shifts are subject to regular phonetic laws, which can never be stated arbitrarily but must always be worked out inductively by first collecting all certain examples of correspondences between ancient and modern names. It is also true that popular etymology often modifies an ancient name slightly: e.g., ancient Shefar'am in Galilee is now called *Shefa'amr*, which means, "Healing of 'Amr." Note, however, that even here all the consonants and vowels are kept; the only change is in transposing two consonants. There is little excuse save ignorance for the frequent disregard of sound linguistic method by topographers, especially by archaeologists without any philological training, since Kampffmeyer published an admirable—now slightly antiquated—monograph on the subject as far back as 1892.

The fourth approach consists in utilizing the results of surface exploration and excavation for identifying sites. Thus, for instance, Palmer's identification of Zephath was disproved by the results of the Colt expedition ten years ago. No pottery or other remains from the Israelite period were discovered either at *Isbeiṭa* (*Subaita*) itself or in the vicinity, thus confirming the objections to the identification previously made by philologians and territorial geographers, who considered the site as much too far south of the mountains of Judah and the arable lands of the tribe of Simeon. An increasing number of identifications have been made on an archaeological basis and subsequently confirmed from other sources: e.g., *Tell ed-Duweir* as the site of Lachish (Plate XVIII, B-5). The archaeological method may be used together with territorial geography: if a town can be limited to a certain district, an exhaustive examination of all possible sites in the area in question often yields the correct identification without any further ado. In this way Garstang discovered the site of Hazor in Galilee (Plate XVIII, D-2).

Our final approach is that of tradition, which can be very valuable but must be employed with great caution. Modern "traditions" are often worthless: e.g., Masterman identified ancient Tarichaea on the Sea of Galilee with modern *Khirbet Kerak* (Plate XVIII, D-3) because the Jewish colonists of Chinnereth—established in the nineteenth century—told him that their ancestors had pickled fish there. Naturally the facts are that the colonists had learned about this once popular but quite erroneous identification from travelers or teachers!

CHRONOLOGICAL OUTLINE OF ANCIENT HISTORY

(*c.* = *circa* = *about*)

I. THE ANCIENT WORLD BEFORE THE PATRIARCHS

A. The Stone Age, beginning at least 100,000 years ago.

1. The Paleolithic or Old Stone Age, ending with the retreat of the last glacier c. 10,000–8000 B.C. Neanderthal man, the first distinguishable race, spread over Europe and W. Asia c. 75,000 years ago. In Palestine, Mt. Carmel man, a mixture with modern man (*homo sapiens*). In Europe, Cro-Magnon man and the remarkable cave paintings of France and Spain, between c. 50,000 and 15,000 years ago.
2. The Mesolithic or Middle Stone Age, c. 8000–5500 B.C. A transitional stage between the old food-gathering and the new food-producing economy. In Palestine, Natufian man, the first to domesticate animals and engage in agriculture.
3. The Neolithic or Late Stone Age, in the Near East c. 5500–4000 B.C. The first villages founded and pottery invented.

B. The Chalcolithic Age, c. 4000–3300 B.C. Copper introduced; the first great buildings erected; and writing begun (in Babylonia c. 3500 B.C.).

C. The Early Bronze Age, or first historical period, c. 3300–2000 B.C.—the age when the first great states emerged.

EGYPT:

1. The Early Dynastic Period (Dynasties I–II), c. 3000–2700.
2. The Old Kingdom or Pyramid Age (Dynasties III–VI), c. 2700–2200. Close commercial relations by sea and land with Syria and Palestine, involving also, perhaps, political control of these countries by Egypt.
3. The First Intermediate Period, c. 2200–2000—a dark age caused by Asiatic, perhaps Amorite, invaders.

BABYLONIA:

1. The Early Dynastic or Sumerian Age, c. 2800–2400.
2. The First Semitic or Accad Dynasty, c. 2400–2200, of which the chief ruler was Sargon I. The world's first great empire was founded, and expeditions were sent as far away as Syria and the Taurus (Silver) Mountains.
3. The Guti (highlander) rule, and Sumerian resurgence in the Third Dynasty of Ur, c. 2200–2000 B.C.

II. THE ANCIENT WORLD BETWEEN THE AGES OF ABRAHAM AND DAVID, c. 2000–1000 B.C.

A. The Middle Bronze Age, c. 2000–1500 B.C.

EGYPT:

1. The Middle Kingdom (Dynasty XII), c. 1991–1778. Palestine and Syria under Egyptian control.
2. The Second Intermediate Age, c. 1778–1550. Dynasties XIII–XIV, c. 1778–1710. The Hyksos Period, composed of Dynasties XV–XVII, c. 1710–1550, during which Asiatic rulers (probably mostly Canaanite) seized control of Egypt and established a great empire including Palestine-Syria. War of liberation led by Kamose and Ahmose, c. 1600–1550.
3. Beginning of the New Kingdom under Amenophis (Amenhotep) I, c. 1546.

MESOPOTAMIA:

The Amorite invasion and establishment of Amorite dynasties from the Mediterranean to Babylonia, c. 2000–1700. The Mari age, known from the archives found at the city of Mari, 18th century. The First Dynasty of Babylon (Amorite), c. 1830–1530 (according to the new "low" chronology), with Hammurabi reigning during the latter part of the 18th and perhaps early 17th century. Irruption of non-Semitic Indo-Iranian and Hurrian (Horite) peoples from the highlands into northern Mesopotamia, 18th and 17th centuries. Destruction of Babylon by the Hittites of Asia Minor, c. 1530.

PALESTINE:

Controlled politically from Egypt during most of the period. The wandering of the Patriarchs in the hill country and Negeb, c. 2000–1700. Descent into Egypt of the family of Jacob, c. 1700. Country exceedingly prosperous under Hyksos, c. 1710–1550. Conquered by native Egyptians under Ahmose and his successors, c. 1560 ff. Some portion of the House of Joseph (Ephraim and Manasseh) may have returned to Palestine from Egypt when the Hyksos were expelled.

B. The Late Bronze Age, c. 1500–1200 B.C.

EGYPT: This was the period of the New Kingdom, when Egyptian rulers expanded their empire to its greatest extent in all directions.

1. Dynasty XVIII, c. 1570–1310. According to recent revisions in chronology, the chief Pharaohs ruled as follows: Thutmose (Thothmes) III, c. 1490–1435, under whom some of the most brilliant campaigns in Egyptian military history were launched. After the capture of Megiddo,c. 1468, he had little Canaanite opposition, and controlled all territory between Egypt and the Euphrates, where his border touched that of Mitanni. Amenophis (Amenhotep) III, c. 1406–1370, and Amenophis IV (Akhnaton), c. 1370–1353, were the Pharaohs to whom the letters from Canaanite, Hittite, Mitannian, Assyrian, and Babylonian kings found at *Tell el-Amarna* (Akhetaton) were written. Akhnaton instituted a monotheistic religious revolution in Egypt; as a result of his concentration on that project, the Egyptian hold on Asia was greatly weakened.
2. Dynasty XIX, c. 1310–1200, during which energetic efforts were made to re-establish the empire in Asia, into which the Hittites had extended their control. The chief Pharaohs were: Sethos (Seti) I, c. 1308–1290; Rameses II, c. 1290–1224, who fought the drawn battle with the Hittites at Kadesh in Syria, c. 1286, and concluded the formal treaty with them which established the Syrian boundary, c. 1270; Merenptah, c. 1224–1216, who claims to have defeated Israel in Palestine, c. 1220. Moses and the Exodus of Israel, probably sometime after 1290 B.C.

MESOPOTAMIA:

Babylonia weak under Kassite (non-Semitic) rulership, c. 1500–1150. The Hurrian (Horite) or Mitannian state in northern Mesopotamia, c. 1500–1370. During the major part of that period almost continuous, but indecisive, warfare between Egypt and Mitanni. The state was conquered by the Hittites, c. 1370; but was kept as a buffer between Asia Minor and Assyria; finally taken over by Assyria, c. 1250.

ASIA MINOR:

The Hittite Empire, c. 1600–1200. A Hittite army raided Babylon, c. 1550; conquered northern Syria in the first half of the 14th century. Battle of Kadesh, c. 1286, and treaty with the Egyptians, c. 1270.

PALESTINE:

A province of Egypt, nominally at least, throughout the period. The Amarna Age, illuminated by the letters from Canaanite kings to the Egyptian court, c. 1400–1350. The main phase of the Israelite Conquest, c. 1250–1200, including the known destruction of Bethel, Lachish, Eglon, Debir and Hazor.

THE GREEK WORLD:

The golden age of Crete and the Minoan civilization achieved its peak in the 15th century. The downfall of Crete, c. 1400. The Mycenaean civilization in Greece and establishment of active trade with Asia, 14th–13th centuries.

C. The Beginning of the Iron Age, c. 1200–1000 B.C.

EGYPT:

Dynasty XX, c. 1180–1065. Invasion of the Sea Peoples (among whom were the Philistines) thrown back by Rameses III, c. 1175. After c. 1150 the power of the Pharaohs declined and the priests became the real rulers, and the Asiatic empire was lost.

MESOPOTAMIA:

No strong rulers, except the Assyrian Tiglath-pileser I, who c. 1100 held northern Syria for a time.

PALESTINE:

The Period of the Judges, c. 1200–1020. The Aramean invasion of Bashan (and eastern Syria), 12th–11th centuries. The Philistines, thrown back from Egypt, settled along the southern coastal plain, early 12th century. The great battle with the Canaanites in the Valley of Jezreel and the Song of Deborah, c. 1100. The struggle with the Philistines, 11th century, with the fall of Shiloh and the death of Eli, c. 1050. Saul and the beginning of the Israelite monarchy, c. 1020–1000.

III. THE PERIOD OF THE HEBREW KINGS, c. 1000–587 B.C.

A. Palestine: The dates of the Israelite and Judean kings are not fixed with absolute certainty. The following is an approximate chronology prepared by W. F. Albright (from *Bulletin of the American Schools of Oriental Research*, No. 100, Dec., 1945, pp. 16–22).

(1) The United Monarchy: David, c. 1000–994 (as king of Judah), c. 994–961 (over all Israel); Solomon, c. 961–922. The division of the kingdom, c. 922.

(2) The Divided Monarchy, c. 922–587 (the cross lines mark changes in dynasties).

ISRAEL				JUDAH		
RULER	REIGN	PROPHET	EVENTS	PROPHET	RULER	REIGN
JEROBOAM I	c. 922–901		*Shishak's invasion, c. 918*		REHOBOAM	c. 922–915
Nadab	c. 901–900				Abijam	c. 915–913
Baasha	c. 900–877				ASA	c. 913–873
Elah	c. 877–876				JEHOSHAPHAT	c. 873–849
Zimri	c. 876				Jehoram	
OMRI	c. 876–869				(or Joram)	c. 849–842
AHAB	c. 869–850	*ELIJAH*	*Battle of Karkar; coalition vs. Assyria, 853*		Ahaziah	c. 842
Ahaziah	c. 850–849				Athaliah	c. 842–837
Jehoram	c. 849–842				Joash	
JEHU	c. 842–815	*ELISHA*			(or Jehoash)	c. 837–800
Jehoahaz	c. 815–801				Amaziah	c. 800–783
Joash	c. 801–786				UZZIAH	
JEROBOAM II	c. 786–746	*AMOS*			(or Azariah)	c. 783–742
Zechariah	c. 746–745				Jotham	
Shallum	c. 745		*Syro-Ephraimitic war, c. 734*		(regent and king)	c. 750–735
Menahem	c. 745–738	*HOSEA*	*Tiglath-pileser III's invasion, 733–732*	*ISAIAH*	AHAZ	c. 735–715
Pekahiah	c. 738–737		*Siege of Samaria by Assyrians, 724-Feb., 721*	*MICAH*	HEZEKIAH	c. 715–687
Pekah	c. 737–732		*Sennacherib invasion, 701*		MANASSEH	c. 687–642
Hoshea	c. 732–724		*Deuteronomic Reform, 622*		Amon	c. 642–640
Fall of Samaria	722–721		*Josiah killed by Pharaoh Necho, 609*		JOSIAH	c. 640–609
			Nebuchadnezzar's first invasion, 598–597		Jehoiahaz	609
			Nebuchadnezzar's second invasion, 589–587	*JEREMIAH*	Jehoiakim	609–598
					Jehoiachin	598–597
				EZEKIEL	Zedekiah	597–587
					Fall of Jerusalem	587

B. Mesopotamia:

The Assyrian Empire, c. 1000–612. Conquest of northern Syria, early ninth century. Beginning of the push southward under Shalmaneser III (859–824) checked by the drawn battle with the Syrian coalition (in which Ahab of Israel participated) at Karkar, 853. A new attempt to seize southern Syria and Palestine succeeded under Tiglath-pileser III (745–727), who in 733–732 conquered the Plain of Sharon, Galilee, Gilead, and Damascus, turning them into subject provinces and leaving the small kingdoms of Palestine as client states. As the result of rebellion, Israel was reduced by Shalmaneser V (727–722) and Sargon II (722–705), and 27,290 leading citizens were carried into exile, 721. Sennacherib (705–681) invaded Judah in 701. Esarhaddon (681–669) succeeded in the conquest of Egypt, but he and Asshurbanapal (669–633) were engaged chiefly in defensive warfare against threatening powers on all sides. Fall of Asshur to the Medes, 614, and of Nineveh to the Medes and Babylonians, 612.
The Babylonian Empire, c. 612–539. Defeat of the Assyrians and Egyptians under Pharaoh Necho at Haran, 609. Nebuchadnezzar (605–562), after his defeat of Pharaoh Necho at Carchemish in 605, took over Syria-Palestine, leaving small principalities like Judah as client states.

C. Egypt:

The Libyan Dynasties (XXII–XXIV), of which the first Pharaoh was Shishak, c. 935–709. Shishak's raid on Palestine, c. 918. The Ethiopian Dynasty (XXV), c. 709–663. Assyrian conquest of Egypt, c. 663.
The Saite Dynasty (XXVI), c. 663–525. Pharaoh Necho (609–593) and Hophra (588–569). The former attempted to recover the Egyptian Asiatic empire, defeating Josiah in 609, but being defeated by the Babylonians at Haran in 609 and decisively at Carchemish in 605.

IV. THE EXILIC AND POST-EXILIC PERIODS, 587–333 B.C.

A. Palestine:

Leading Judean citizens exiled from the country in 598 and 587, among them Ezekiel. The Edict of Cyrus, permitting the return from Exile, c. 538. Temple rebuilt by Zerubbabel, 520–515.—Rival dates for Ezra: 458, c. 432, c. 428, and 398. Nehemiah's return, 445. Malachi, c. 500–450.

B. The Persian Empire:

Cyrus united Persia and Media, 549; conquered Lydia, 546; conquered Babylon (which was ruled by Nabonidus and the crown prince Belshazzar), 539. Cambyses (530–522) conquered Egypt, 525. Darius I (522–486); campaign against Greece and defeat at Marathon, 490. Xerxes I or Ahasuerus (486–465); campaign against Greece and defeat at Thermopylae and Salamis, 480. Subsequent rulers: Artaxerxes I (465–424); Xerxes II (424–423); Darius II (423–404); Artaxerxes II (404–358); Artaxerxes III (358–338); Arses (338–336); and Darius III (336–331).

C. Greece:

The defeat of the Persians at Marathon, 490; at Thermopylae and Salamis, 480. The golden age of Pericles, 460–429. Herodotus (c. 484–425). Socrates (c. 470–399). Plato (c. 428–348). Aristotle (384–322).

V. THE HELLENISTIC PERIOD, 333–63 B.C.*

A. Macedonian Empire: Period of rapid expansion.

Philip (359–336) extended power over Greece; battle of Chaeronea (338) marked end of power of Greek city-states.
Alexander the Great (336–323) conquered Persia and extended rule to western India; decisive battles: River Granicus (334), Issus (333), Gaugamela (331). He reached India (327); died in Babylon (323).

B. Hellenistic Empires Which Emerged From Alexander's Empire:

Alexander's Generals Compete for Power. At first Perdiccas was in control in Asia, Antipater and Craterus in Europe. By 301 Cassander held Macedon, Lysimachus Thrace and Asia Minor, Seleucus Mesopotamia and Syria, and Ptolemy Africa. Conditions remained unsettled. By 277 three leading empires had emerged; they remained until absorbed by Rome.

The Three Great Hellenistic Empires:

1. Macedonia: Antigonus Gonatas (277–239). The line of kings ends with Perseus (179–168); in 168 Macedonia became dependent upon Rome, and in 146 was made a Roman province.
2. Egypt: Ptolemy had been satrap since 323; he founded the dynasty which bears his name. Ptolemy I (323–283); Ptolemy II (285–246); Ptolemy III (246–221); Ptolemy IV (221–203); Ptolemy V (203–181/0). Thereafter the line of Ptolemies continued, under Roman dominance, until 30 B.C., when Egypt became a Roman province.
3. Syria: Seleucus gained control of southern Asia Minor, Syria, and the eastern portions of Alexander's empire, and founded the Seleucid dynasty: Seleucus I (312–280); Antiochus I (280–262/1); Antiochus II (261–247); Seleucus II (247–226); Seleucus III (226–223); Antiochus III, the Great (223–187); Seleucus IV (187–175); Antiochus IV, Epiphanes (175–163), Antiochus V (163–162); Demetrius I (162–150); Alexander Balas (150–145); Demetrius II (145–139/8); Antiochus VI (145–142/1); Antiochus VII (139/8–129). The weak, unsettled Syrian kingdom continued until 64 B.C., when Pompey took over Syria and made it a Roman province.

Smaller Kingdoms Which Emerged from Alexander's Empire:

1. Pergamum: Continued under the Attalids until Attalus III (139/8–133), who willed his kingdom to Rome.
2. Bithynia: Established by Ziboetes (327–c. 279) and Nicomedes I (c. 279–c. 250); continued until Nicomedes III (94–75/4), who willed his kingdom to Rome.

C. Other Kingdoms of Asia Minor:

1. Pontus: Under the Mithridatids beginning with Mithridates I (337/6–302/1); mastered by Rome in middle of first century B.C.
2. Galatia: On the Halys River in Asia Minor; settled by the Gauls, c. 278; passed to Rome on the death of Amyntas (37–25).

*The dates from this point follow the *Cambridge Ancient History*.

D. Parthian Empire:

Threw off the rule of the Seleucids (tradition says this happened under Arsaces); the Parthian era began c. 247 B.C. The Empire grew until it reached from the Euphrates to the borders of India. In 53 the Parthians defeated Crassus and threatened Syria and Asia Minor; in 40 they succeeded in entering Jerusalem; but in 39/38 the Romans repulsed the threat. Their kingdom continued, but with declining power, until A.D. 224.

E. The Greek Cities:

Resisted Macedonian rule; made alliances with Rome. But Rome gradually took Greece over; the destruction of Corinth (146 B.C.) ended resistance. Greece organized as the Roman province of Achaia, 27 B.C.

F. Palestine:

Continued under Egypt until 198 B.C., when Syria gained control. In 167 the Maccabean revolt against Syria occurred. The Maccabean leaders were: Judas Maccabaeus (166/5–160); Jonathan (160–142); Simon (142–134); John Hyrcanus (134–104); Aristobulus I (104–103); Alexander Jannaeus (103–76); Alexandra (76–67); Aristobulus II (66–63). In 63 Pompey established Roman control over Palestine.

VI. THE ROMAN PERIOD, 63 B.C. to A.D. 325

A. Earlier History of Rome:

Etruscan control from about 750 B.C. Establishment of Roman Republic about 500. Rome dissolved the Latin League in 338, and controlled central Italy. Subjugation of Italy to Po Valley complete about 266. Period of Punic Wars, 264–146; destruction of Carthage, 146. Achaian League crushed, Corinth destroyed, 146. Wars against peoples in Spain, Numidia, Helvetia, etc., spread Roman rule in western Mediterranean world. Wars against Mithridates VI of Pontus (121/0–63) and against pirates in eastern Mediterranean extended Roman rule in east. In 64–63 Pompey organized as provinces Pontus, Cilicia, and Syria; he took over Palestine (63).

B. Period of Conspiracies and Civil Wars:

Catiline's conspiracy; opposed by Cicero; Catiline slain (62). First Triumvirate: Pompey, Caesar, Crassus (60). Caesar's Gallic Wars (58–51). Civil war between Caesar and Pompey (49–46). Assassination of Julius Caesar (44). Second Triumvirate: Antony, Octavian, Lepidus (43); defeats republican forces under Brutus and Cassius at Philippi (42). Battle of Actium (31); Octavian, later called Augustus, sole ruler.

C. The Roman Emperors:

The Five Julian Emperors: Augustus (31 B.C. to A.D. 14); division of provinces into senatorial and imperial; golden age of Latin literature, e.g., Virgil; birth of Jesus. Tiberius (14–37); ministry of John the Baptist and Jesus. Caligula (37–41). Claudius (41–54); Paul leads missionary expansion of Church. Nero (54–68); Rome burned; Christians persecuted there (64). Rival Contenders for Power: Galba, Otho, Vitellius, Vespasian (68–69).
The Three Flavian Emperors: Vespasian (69–79); Jewish revolt (66–70); destruction of Jerusalem (70). Titus (79–81). Domitian (81–96); persecution of Christians in latter part of reign.
Emperors in Period of Maximum Expansion: Nerva (96–98). Trajan (98–117); provinces Dacia, Armenia, Mesopotamia, Assyria, and Arabia added to empire; letters of Ignatius, Bishop of Antioch, c. A.D. 115. Hadrian (117–138); revolt of Jews (132–135); Jerusalem rebuilt as Aelia Capitolina. Antoninus Pius (138–161); Marcion in Rome, c. 138–140; Polycarp and Justin Martyr important Christian leaders. Marcus Aurelius, Stoic philosopher-king (161–180).
Emperors in Century of Disorder: Commodus (180–192); leadership of Irenaeus in Church. Septimius Severus (193–211). Caracalla (211–217); grant of universal citizenship. Severus Alexander (222–235); new Persian empire, 226. Decius (249–251); general persecution of Christians. Death of Christian scholar Origen, c. 254. Aurelian (270–275).
Emperors with Absolute Power: Diocletian (284–305); reorganization of imperial administration; removal of imperial residence to the east; general persecution of Christians. Contest for power after Diocletian's death. Constantine the Great, sole ruler (323–337). First ecumenical council, Nicaea (325).

D. Palestine Under the Romans:

Rule of the Herods: Hyrcanus appointed ethnarch and high priest under Roman control (63 B.C.). Antipater, the Idumaean, virtual ruler of Palestine under Roman grant (c. 55–43). His sons, Herod and Phasael, tetrarchs (41). Antigonus, son of Aristobulus, high priest and king by aid of Parthians (40–37). Herod the Great, king of Judaea by grant of Roman Senate (40–4 B.C.). Upon his death, kingdom divided: Archelaus, tetrarch of Judaea, Samaria, and Idumaea (4 B.C. to A.D. 6); Herod Antipas, tetrarch of Galilee and Peraea (4 B.C. to A.D. 39), until banished for suspected plotting against Rome; Philip, tetrarch of Gaulonitis, Trachonitis, Batanaea, Auranitis, and Panias (4 B.C. to A.D. 34).
Roman procurators ruled (A.D. 6–41) after Augustus deposed Archelaus. Of these procurators, Pontius Pilate was in office 26–36.
Herod Agrippa I was made king by Caligula in 37 over the former tetrarchies of Philip and Lysanias (Abilene); in 39 or 40 he was given the tetrarchy of Herod Antipas; in 41, the rest of Palestine. He died in 44.
Roman procurators again ruled Palestine, 44–66: Cuspius Fadus (44–?); Tiberius Alexander (?–48); Cumanus (48–52); Felix (52–60; or, 52–c. 55?); Festus (60–62); Albinus (62–64); Gessius Florus (64–66).
Herod Agrippa II, made king of Chalcis (A.D. 50), exchanged this realm for the former tetrarchy of Philip about 53. Nero later added to this kingdom some cities of Galilee and Peraea. His long reign lasted until c. 93.
Jewish revolt against Rome (66–70). Destruction of Jerusalem and the Temple by Titus (70). Judaea again under Roman procurators.
Renewed revolt, led by Bar-Cochba (132–135). Jerusalem rebuilt, after revolt was crushed; renamed Aelia Capitolina; only Gentiles allowed in it.

E. Nabataean Kingdom:

By the beginning of the Hellenistic era the Nabataeans were in possession of the territory of the ancient Edomites. From their capital at Petra they extended their control in all directions. Their independence was limited by the Romans from 63 B.C. on, but their land did not become a Roman province until A.D. 106. Aretas IV was their king from 9 B.C. to A.D. 40.

FIG. 5. Esdraelon or the Valley of Jezreel. This plain separates Galilee from Samaria. In the background are the Galilean hills, in which, just left of center, some houses of Nazareth can be seen. At the top right is Mount Tabor (see Fig. 35). In the left foreground the pass of Megiddo (Fig. 26) opens out into the plain. At the left, above the pass, the flat-topped mound of Megiddo, comprising some thirteen acres, juts out into the plain. Megiddo was the fortress city which guarded the pass.

THE GEOGRAPHY OF PALESTINE

PLATE I

PALESTINE has wielded an influence in world history quite out of proportion to its size and natural resources. Its prominent role in determining the cultural and particularly the religious life of the modern world is the more surprising in view of its remarkably small dimensions. West of the River Jordan (Plate I, D 2-5), its total area is only 6,000 square miles. If the portion east of the Jordan is included, there are but 10,000 square miles in the entire region. Thus in its full extent Palestine is barely larger than the State of Vermont, and exceeds the size of Wales by only twenty-five per cent.

With patriotic pride the Israelites spoke of their country as extending "from Dan even to Beer-sheba" (I Kings 4:25). Yet from Dan (I, D-2), at the southwest foot of snow-capped Mount Hermon, to Beer-sheba (I, B-6), where the Hill Country ends and the southern desert region begins, it is slightly less than 150 miles. The distances from east to west are even smaller. From Accho (I, C-3) to the Sea of Galilee (I, D-3) it is only 28 miles. Even in the south, where the shore line curves gradually toward the southwest, it is but 54 miles from Gaza (I, A-6) to the Dead Sea (I, C-D 5-6).

Within such meager limits occur surprising contrasts of terrain and climate. Along the coastal plain a mild climate prevails; the average annual temperature is about 67° F. at Joppa. Only thirty-four miles from the Mediterranean Sea, at an altitude of nearly 2,600 feet, Jerusalem (I, C-5) enjoys a delightful temperate climate with an average annual temperature of 63°. To the east of the "holy city," however, there is such a sharp drop in altitude that fifteen miles away, at Jericho (I, C-5), one stands 3,400 feet below the level of Jerusalem, and nearly 800 feet below the level of the Mediterranean Sea. In this region a warm, virtually tropical climate prevails. Indeed, the heat of the summer months is so intense as to enervate the natives who live there. Farther east, however, where the plateau of Transjordan (I, D-E 3-7) stretches away at an altitude some 4,000 feet above Jericho, snow falls in winter and the rather temperate climate approximates that of Jerusalem.

The same striking contrasts of altitude and climate may be traced from north to south. From the heights of Mount Hermon (I, D-2), 9,100 feet above sea level, where the temperature has an alpine range and snow lies on the mountaintop the year round, the land slopes down in a rapid descent until the Jordan Valley, just after leaving Lake Huleh (I, D-2), reaches sea level. Continuing to the south, the valley offers a mild climate about the Sea of Galilee (I, D-3), 696 feet below sea level, and when it finally reaches the Dead Sea, 1,290 feet below sea level and the lowest body of water on the surface of the earth, the summer climate is intensely hot. From this deep gorge the Arabah ascends until at a point southwest of Petra (I, C-8) it is 650 feet above sea level, whence it rapidly drops to the Gulf of Aqabah.

Climatic conditions, however, depend not only upon altitude but also upon other factors. Of great importance are the winds, which usually blow from the west. In the winter, coming from the west or southwest, they bring the clouds which drop their moisture as they reach the cool Hill Country, and thus cause the rainy season, which extends from October to April. During the summer season, the northwest breezes bring a welcome coolness but almost no rainfall.

In addition to the prevailing breezes from the west, winds from other directions blow occasionally. Particularly in the early fall, cool winds come down from the north. More important, however, is the occasional sirocco or hot "east wind," which blows in from the eastern desert. Because of its excessive dryness, heat, and violence, it

FIG. 6. The Plain of Shechem in the heart of Samaria. In the center, surrounded by a modern wall, is the ancient Well of Jacob. In the left background is the modern village *'Askar*, often wrongly identified as ancient Sychar (John 4:5). This view looks northeast from the eastern slopes of Mount Gerizim. Behind *'Askar*, the slope of Mount Ebal begins its rise to the left. Between these two mountain slopes is the mouth of the important pass for roads leading west and north. The mound of ancient Shechem, which once guarded the pass, is just left of the area here shown. The road running up past 'Askar leads to Beth-shan (Scythopolis) in the upper Jordan Valley. The road to Jerusalem runs to the right at the very foot of Mount Gerizim.

is the country's chief climatic curse (cf. Job 1:19; Jer. 18:17; Ezek. 17:10; 27:26).

For a more detailed study of its physical features, resources, and climate, Palestine may be divided into four main sections: (1) the *Coastal Plain;* (2) the central *Hill Country*, including its spur, Mount Carmel (I, B-C 3), which juts out northwest into the sea; (3) the deep cleft of the *Jordan Valley;* and (4) the *Plateau of Transjordan.*

I. THE COASTAL PLAIN

The almost unbroken coast line of Palestine distinctly discouraged commerce on the Mediterranean Sea. In this respect Palestine was in a quite different situation from her northern neighbor Phoenicia. The latter possessed harbor facilities in such places as Tyre (I, C-2) and Sidon (I, C-1). Moreover, the rough terrain of Phoenicia comes down practically to the sea, and deprives its people of adequate opportunities for agriculture. Inevitably, therefore, the Phoenicians became a seafaring people.

With their interest in the sea, the Phoenicians often reached southward and took possession of Accho (I, C-3). This port, called Ptolemais in New Testament times (Acts 21:7), though poorly sheltered from sea winds, was the most attractive harbor location afforded by the coast of Palestine proper. By including Mount Carmel in her borders Phoenicia could completely control the Bay of Accho and the port.

However, even when the Israelites controlled Accho and its bay, they had there no adequate harbor. It was not until recent years, when British engineers built a breakwater running out from the northeast side of the Carmel spur, that this bay provided a really safe anchorage. South of Mount Carmel the coast line was even more discouraging to sea trade. Dor (IV, B-3) was used as a port in Biblical times, but it had no stormproof harbor. Joppa (I, B-4) likewise could boast no real harbor; a line of irregular rocks a short distance from shore appeared to offer a little protection, and with this meager encouragement Joppa has rendered mediocre service through the centuries as a fair-weather port.

Perhaps the most striking proof of the fact that Palestine did not face the sea is the location of Gaza (I, A-6). It was the greatest trading center of ancient Palestine, yet it lay some three miles inland, and no attempt to provide it with a port proved permanently successful. It was land trade from south, east, and north that made Gaza rich.

Yet, although Palestine could never develop a maritime people, it did possess, except where Mount Carmel made its northwest thrust into the sea, a fertile coastal plain. This plain may be divided into three sections. To the north of Mount Carmel was the *Plain of Accho* or Acre (I, C-3), located on the small bay north of Carmel. In Biblical times this small but fertile area was dotted with many important towns, only a few of which are shown on Plate VIII.

Between Mount Carmel and Joppa lay the *Plain of Sharon* (I, B-4). This was a well-watered region which in spots, partly because of the drainage barrier of low hills along the coast, was even marshy. In ancient times it probably possessed extensive forests, and the combination of marshy tendencies and forests kept it from being thickly settled. Its maximum width was a little over twelve miles.

By far the most important section of the coastal plain in Biblical times was *Philistia* or the *Philistine Plain* (I, A-B 5-6). Here once lived those ancient enemies of Israel, the Philistines, who subsequently gave their name to the whole country, for the word "Palestine" is derived from "Philistia." In this well-watered and generally level plain there were few trees, and almost everywhere the rich brown soil invited agricultural development (see Fig. 43). Recently the success achieved in extensive citrus groves has demonstrated anew the fruitfulness of this plain. The one threat to the productivity of the area was the drifting sand, which tended to encroach upon the region near the coast.

Attractive as the Coastal Plain has proved for modern agriculture in Palestine, it is noteworthy that this section was never a center of Israelite settlement or power in Old Testament times; nor in the New Testament period was it dominated by the Jewish people and culture. The chief center of Israelite population and interest was not the Coastal Plain but the Hill Country.

II. THE HILL COUNTRY

The rough and rocky Hill Country forms part of an almost continuous range of hills which runs south through southern Syria and extends almost unbroken down the length of Palestine until it drops to a lower level in the desert country south of Judah. This range is composed of a soft, porous, and eroded limestone which outcrops and crumbles continuously throughout the country's extent.

Within the limits of Palestine, the three divisions of the Hill Country are Galilee, Samaria, and Judah. *Galilee* (I, C 2-3), in its northern portion, is quite rugged, and at one point, near Merom (VIII, E-5), attains an altitude of nearly 4,000 feet above sea level. The southern half, however, is less hilly, and enjoys a somewhat milder climate. Much of its rolling land can be tilled; level plains a few miles north of Nazareth (I, C-3) and just northwest of the Sea of Galilee invite intensive cultivation. The entire series of hills in Galilee, sloping down from north to south, constitute in reality extensive foothills of Mount Lebanon (I, D-1).

At the southern end of Galilee the range of the Hill Country is cut by the great *Valley of Jezreel* or Esdraelon (I, C-3). From very ancient times important cities were built in this valley; of these Megiddo (VIII, D-7) was of particular significance, because it guarded and controlled the pass which permitted the easiest movement of caravans and troops from the Plain of Sharon to the Valley of Jezreel (Figs. 5 and 26). Mount Carmel, to the northwest, pushed its foot to within two hundred yards of the Mediterranean Sea and if its slopes were manned by a hostile army, the use of the shore road around the point was impossible. To save time and distance and to secure safety of passage, it proved desirable to keep control of the pass which led directly from the southern Coastal Plain to the Valley of Jezreel. Megiddo was thus a location of strategic military importance. Control of the Valley of Jezreel was likewise crucial in military maneuvers in Northern Palestine. Hence it came about that again and again this region became a decisive battleground, until, according to the probable interpretation of Rev. 16:16, it gave its name to the scene of the expected final battle of God's hosts with the powers of evil. "Har-Magedon" seems to be the Mount or Hill of Megiddo.

This fertile and inviting valley, which prosperous colonies of Zionists in recent years have turned into a garden, is drained to the west by the River Kishon (*Nahr Muqaṭṭa'*), a small brook which may overflow and prove impassable in the rainy season. It flows out to the Mediterranean Sea through the Plain of Accho. To the east two valleys lead down to the Jordan. Their ancient names are unknown. One of them passes between Mount Tabor (I, C-3 and Fig. 39) and the Hill of Moreh (VIII, E-7); the other runs between the Hill of Moreh and Mount Gilboa (I, C 3-4). Thus, except in the heavy rainy season, Esdraelon offered easy, unimpeded passage from the coast to the Jordan Valley.

The hills of *Samaria* form the geographical center of the country. They rise abruptly at the north in Mount Gilboa and the southern extension of Mount Carmel, and reach their highest point at Baal-hazor (I, C-5). The two most conspicuous peaks, however, are Mount Ebal and Mount Gerizim (I, C-4), which stand in the heart of the district of Samaria. They were always heights of great military importance, because between them ran the main pass on the north and south road, and at the eastern mouth of this pass was a crossroads from which highways ran in all directions (Fig. 6). Religious significance was soon attached to these twin peaks, and in later days the Samaritan religious group had its center on Mount Gerizim.

The third main division of the Hill Country is *Judah*. In this district the hills are not quite so lofty as in Samaria. Approaching Jerusalem (I, C-5) the hills descend to some 2,600 feet above sea level, and then rise as they go south until the highest point (3,346′) is reached just north of Hebron (I, C-6). On the western, more gentle slope of this central watershed, clouds coming in from the Mediterranean bring considerable rainfall and thus sustain plant life on a reasonably adequate level. To the east of the watershed, however, is found the bleak "Wilderness of Judah" or wasteland, deprived of adequate moisture, deeply cut by the valleys leading to the Dead Sea, and dropping down so sharply as to offer little opportunity for agricultural development (see Fig. 46).

The natural result of this contrast was that population and history centered much more upon the fertile western slope of the Judaean Hill Country. Here geographical considerations compelled the people of the upper Hill Country to take deep interest in the *Shephelah* (I, B-5) or Lowlands. The latter region was a distinct district, formed by the broken foothills of the Judaean plateau, but partially severed from it by longitudinal valleys. The Shephelah was important to Judah, not only because of the grain of its valleys and the vineyards and olive groves of its hills, but even more for defensive reasons. In Israelite times such strongly fortified towns as Lachish, Debir, Libnah, Azekah, and Beth-shemesh were situated in it.

To the south the hills gradually descend to the *Negeb* or Southland, which centers in the area between Beer-sheba (I, B-6) and Kadesh-barnea (I, A-7). In this broken, semiarid country people can exist only with the most careful conservation of the water supply. At various times in its history careful water conservation, irrigation systems, and dams have made possible the support of a considerable population. Life proved precarious in this region, however, and the general dryness of the Negeb is shown by the fact that in recent years a number of ancient papyri, which survive only in very dry climates, have been found there (see pp. 67 f.).

FIG. 7. The Jordan River shortly before it enters the Dead Sea. In the background may be seen the wilderness of the Jordan Valley and the steep slopes of the Hill Country on the west.

FIG. 8. The northern tip of the Dead Sea where the Jordan flows into it.

III. THE JORDAN VALLEY

The Jordan Valley is part of a great rift or geological fault. This rift extends down through Syria, where it divides Mount Lebanon from the Anti-Lebanon range known in the Bible as Hermon and Amana; it continues through Palestine as the Jordan Valley; farther south it forms the Arabah (I, C 7-8) and the Red Sea, and thence extends to Africa.

The sources of the River Jordan are located on the western side of Mount Hermon (I, D-2 and Fig. 38). In its upper course the river runs above the level of the sea, but after the stream arrives at Lake Huleh (I, D-2), or Lake Semechonitis, as the first-century Jewish historian Josephus calls it, it soon falls to sea level. Thence it tumbles rapidly to the Sea of Galilee, a beautiful fresh-water lake some 696 feet below sea level, which in the days of Jesus supported a considerable fishing industry.

The one area on the lake shore which invited extensive cultivation was the fertile Plain of Gennesaret, located at the northwest shore and aided by mild climate in yielding a year-round supply of fruits, grains, and vegetables. Elsewhere around the lake the surrounding hills come down to the shore on almost all sides (Fig. 40). Down from these hills rush the winds which cause the sudden storms mentioned in the Gospels (e.g., Mark 4:37). On the east side of the lake the slope rises sharply to the high plateau beyond. Since communication with the plateau region is therefore not easy, the Sea of Galilee has been linked almost entirely with life on its western side.

Other names for the Sea of Galilee are the Sea of Chinnereth, a name used in Old Testament times; the Lake of Gennesaret, a New Testament designation derived from the fertile plain on its northwest; and the Sea of Tiberias, a name derived from the city which Herod Antipas built on the western shore c. A.D. 20.

Leaving the Sea of Galilee as a clear and quiet stream, the Jordan winds down its serpentine course toward the Dead Sea (Fig. 7). By the time it has reached the traditional site of the baptism of Jesus by John the Baptist, it has become a muddy carrier of the soil picked up on its journey. When it empties into the Dead Sea it has reached a level some 1,290 feet below the Mediterranean.

The Jordan rift was naturally something of a barrier to communication between east and west Palestine. Yet the ancient Israelites and the later Arabs found many places where the river could be forded except in time of high water, and government and trade have often proved able to bind the two sides of the valley together. In the early Christian period the Romans first bridged the Jordan, at a point not far below Lake Huleh; a bridge centuries old still stands at that spot. There are also modern bridges just south of the Sea of Galilee and at a point east of Jericho.

The Valley of the Jordan, both to the north and south of the Sea of Galilee, was intensively cultivated throughout ancient times. Tributary streams were utilized in the construction of networks of irrigation channels. Such settlement and cultivation, like the occupation of the Valley of Jezreel and the Coastal Plain, occurred before the coming of the Israelites. Precisely in these fertile plain areas the early centers of civilized life developed, and the invading Israelites found the inhabitants already in control of the level land. Hence the newcomers first seized the comparatively undeveloped Hill Country, and only gradually obtained control of the plains. The grazing of flocks and herds, the cultivation of olive, fig, and vine, and the less-crowded life of the hills seemed better to suit the nomadic Israelites; and they found it easier to defend the Hill Country with their more individualistic ways of war than to cope with the professional military forces and equipment which they met in the plains.

The Dead Sea (Figs. 8 and 42), like the Great Salt Lake in Utah, has no outlet. Hence about 25 per cent of the water consists of salt deposits, from which it has recently proved profitable to extract potash and other chemicals. In ancient times the sea did not extend so far south as it does today. The peninsula which extends out into the sea west of Kir-hareseth in Moab (I, D-6) is called the "Tongue." South of this "Tongue" is the area which the Israelites called the Vale of Siddim (Gen. 14:3). Here were situated Sodom, Gomorrah, Admah, Zeboiim, and Zoar (X, H-3). About 2000 B.C. or shortly thereafter (in the time of Abraham) a great catastrophe occurred, presumably an earthquake. Following this event the Vale of Siddim was filled with water, the extent of which has been increasing ever since (see pp. 69 f.).

In Old Testament times the Dead Sea was called "Salt Sea" or "Sea of the Arabah." Josephus speaks of it as "Lake Asphaltitis." However, the Dead Sea had little importance in the history of Bible times. Its oppressive heat in summer, its unnatural saltiness, and the forbidding heights on east and west combined to make it a rather desolate place.

IV. THE PLATEAU OF TRANSJORDAN

The Plateau of Transjordan is divided into five sections by four main streams: the *Yarmûk*, the Jabbok (*Nahr Zerqā*), the Arnon (*Wâdī Môjib*), and the Zered (*Wâdī Ḥesā*). North of the *Yarmûk* was the Biblical *Bashan* (I, D-E 2-3), roughly identical with later Ḥaurân. Signs of prehistoric volcanic activity are frequent in this region; extinct craters, large patches of lava, and a layer of black basalt over the common limestone of Palestine still witness to early eruptions. Trees are rare but the soil is rich. While a somewhat limited rainfall prevents the fullest agricultural development, the region is noted for extensive grain production.

Stretching both north and south of the Jabbok (I, D-4) was *Gilead*. Since it was well watered, possessing a larger number of streams and springs than Bashan, it was capable of sustaining a larger population. This fact, coupled with its greater nearness to the western Hill Country, caused it to play a more prominent role than Bashan in the history of Israel. The most important stream in Gilead was the Jabbok, which took its rise near Rabbath-ammon (I, D-5) and flowed east and north in a semicircle before descending to the Jordan Valley. In the upper reaches of the Jabbok watershed centered the kingdom of *Ammon* (I, D-E 4-5). To the north of the Jabbok are well-wooded regions, but farther south trees become fewer and are not found on the plateau south of Mount Nebo (I, D-5). The area east of Gilead and Ammon is a rather dry region of gently sloping low hills, beyond which is the great desert.

South of the deep valley of the Arnon (I, D-6) lay the original area of the kingdom of *Moab*. To its high and level plateau Israel rarely laid claim. Farther south was *Edom* (I, C-D 7-8), which centered in strategically located and picturesque Petra (I, C-8). Apparently doomed to unimportance by the semidesert climate in this region, Edom was strong for two reasons. It controlled the trade from the desert to Gaza, Egypt, and Phoenicia. Furthermore, it possessed what Palestine proper lacked—quantities of copper and iron ore (cf. Deut. 8:9 and Fig. 48). This ore is found along the border of the Arabah, where the valleys have cut into old sandstone underlying the heavy deposits of limestone, which are never far below the surface in Palestine.

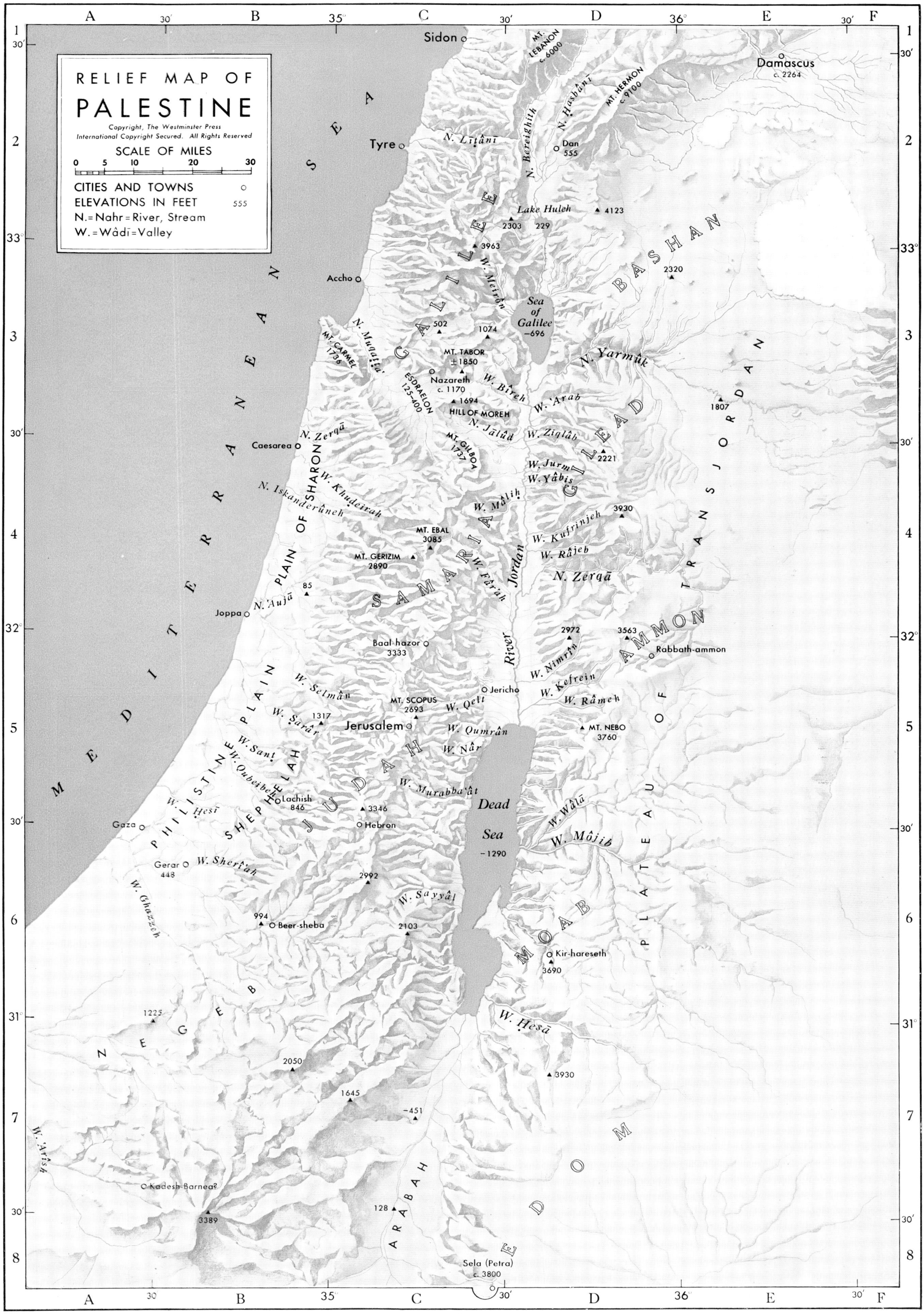
RELIEF MAP OF
PALESTINE
Copyright, The Westminster Press
International Copyright Secured. All Rights Reserved
SCALE OF MILES
0 5 10 20 30
CITIES AND TOWNS
ELEVATIONS IN FEET 555
N.=Nahr=River, Stream
W.=Wâdī=Valley
MEDITERRANEAN SEA
Sidon
Tyre
Accho
Caesarea
Joppa
Gaza
Gerar 448
Damascus c. 2264
MT. LEBANON c. 6000
MT. HERMON c. 9100
N. Hasbânī
N. Bareighith
N. Lîtânî
Dan 555
Lake Huleh 229
2303
4123
3963
BASHAN
2320
W. Meirôn
Sea of Galilee -696
GALILEE
502
1074
MT. CARMEL 1736
N. Muqaṭṭaʻ
MT. TABOR ±1850
Nazareth c. 1170
ESDRAELON 125-400
1694
HILL OF MOREH
N. Jâlûd
W. Bîreh
N. Yarmûk
W. ʻArab
W. Ziqlâb
MT. GILBOA 1737
GILEAD
2221
1807
TRANSJORDAN
N. Zerqā
PLAIN OF SHARON
W. Khudeirah
N. Iskanderûneh
W. Jurm
W. Yâbis
W. Mâlih
3930
W. Kufrinjeh
W. Râjeb
MT. EBAL 3085
MT. GERIZIM 2890
SAMARIA
W. Fârʻah
Jordan
N. Zerqā
85
N. ʻAujā
AMMON
2972
3563
Rabbath-ammon
Baal-hazor 3333
River
W. Nimrîn
W. Kefrein
W. Râmeh
Jericho
W. Selmân
W. Sarâr
1317
MT. SCOPUS 2693
W. Qelt
Jerusalem
W. Qumrân
MT. NEBO 3760
W. Sant
W. Qubeibeh
W. Nâr
PHILISTINE PLAIN
SHEPHELAH
JUDAH
W. Murabbaʻât
Lachish 846
W. Hesī
3346
Hebron
Dead Sea -1290
W. Wâlā
W. Môjib
PLATEAU OF
W. Sherîʻah
2992
W. Ghazzeh
W. Sayyâl
994
Beer-sheba
2103
MOAB
Kir-hareseth
3690
NEGEB
1225
W. Hesā
2050
3930
1645
-451
EDOM
W. ʻArîsh
Kadesh-Barnea?
ARABAH
128
3389
Sela (Petra) c. 3800
A B C D E F
1 2 3 4 5 6 7 8
30′ 35° 36° 33° 32° 31°

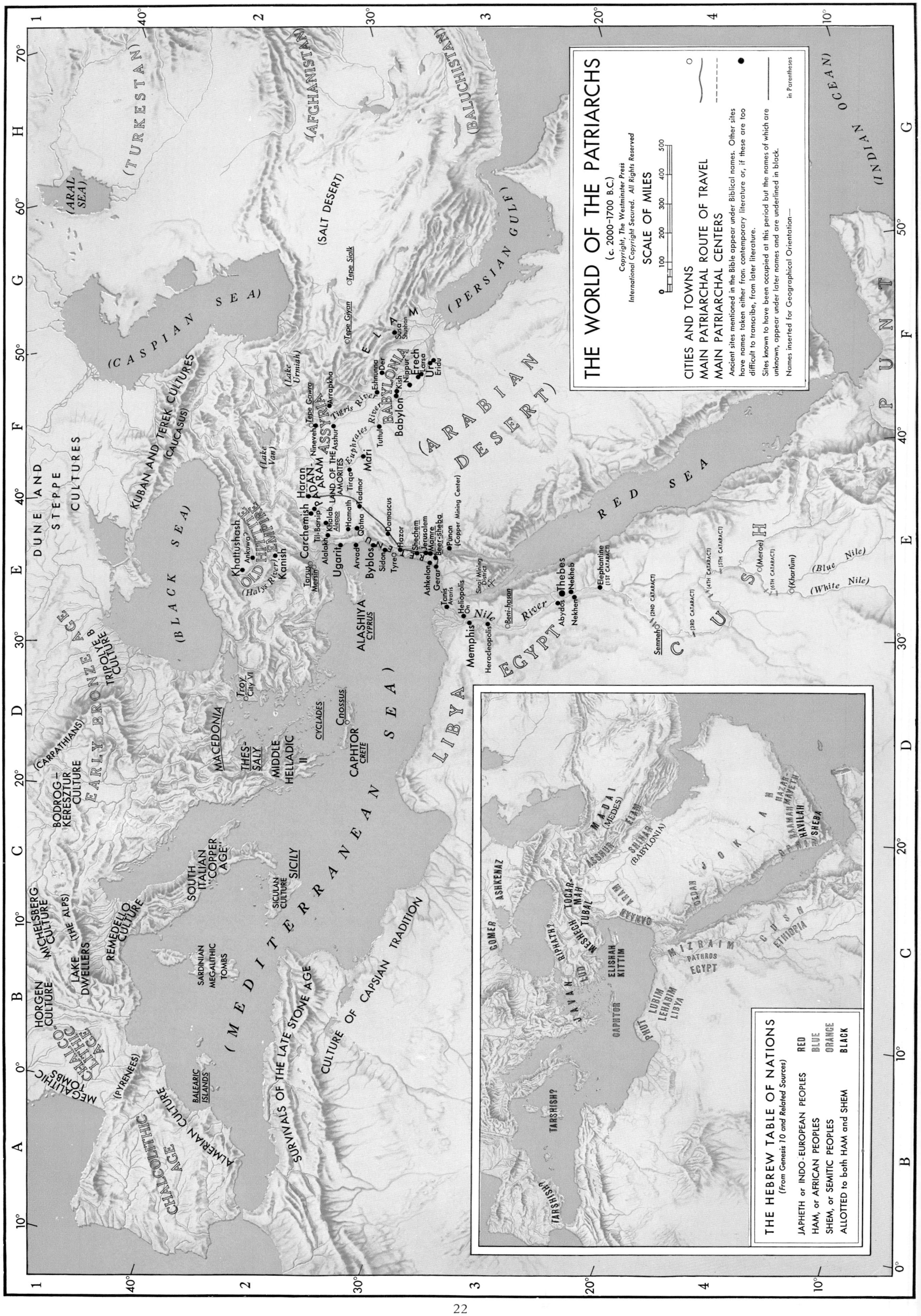
THE WORLD OF THE PATRIARCHS
(c. 2000–1700 B.C.)
Copyright, The Westminster Press
International Copyright Secured. All Rights Reserved
SCALE OF MILES
0 100 200 300 400 500
CITIES AND TOWNS
MAIN PATRIARCHAL ROUTE OF TRAVEL
MAIN PATRIARCHAL CENTERS
Ancient sites mentioned in the Bible appear under Biblical names. Other sites have names taken either from contemporary literature or, if these are too difficult to transcribe, from later literature.
Sites known to have been occupied at this period but the names of which are unknown, appear under later names and are underlined in black.
Names inserted for Geographical Orientation—in Parentheses
(TURKESTAN)
(ARAL SEA)
(AFGHANISTAN)
(BALUCHISTAN)
(SALT DESERT)
(CASPIAN SEA)
(PERSIAN GULF)
(ARABIAN DESERT)
(INDIAN OCEAN)
PUNT
RED SEA
ELAM
Susa Shushan
Tepe Sialk
Tepe Giyan
Tepe Gawra
Nineveh
ASSYRIA
Asshur
Arrapkha
(Lake Urmiah)
(Lake Van)
Tigris River
Euphrates River
BABYLONIA
Eshnunna
Der
Kish
Nippur
Babylon
Erech
Larsa
Ur
Eridu
Tuttul
Mari
Haran
PADAN-ARAM
LAND OF THE AMORITES
Carchemish
Til-Barsip
Khalab
Aleppo
Alalakh
Tirqa
Tadmor
Hamath
Qatna
Ugarit
Arvad
Byblos
Sidon
Tyre
Damascus
Hazor
Shechem
Jerusalem
Mamre
Beer-sheba
Ashkelon
Gerar
Punon (Copper Mining Center)
Sinai Mining District
Tanis Avaris
Heliopolis On
Memphis
Heracleopolis
Nile River
Beni-hasan
EGYPT
Abydos
Thebes
Nekhen
Nekheb
Elephantine (1ST CATARACT)
(2ND CATARACT)
(3RD CATARACT)
(4TH CATARACT)
(5TH CATARACT)
(6TH CATARACT)
Semneh
CUSH
(Meroe)
(Khartum)
(Blue Nile)
(White Nile)
LIBYA
ALASHIYA CYPRUS
Tarsus
Mersin
Khattushash
Ankuwa?
Kanish
OLD HITTITE EMPIRE
(Halys River)
(BLACK SEA)
DUNE AND STEPPE CULTURES
KUBAN AND TEREK CULTURES
(CAUCASUS)
TRIPOLYE CULTURE
EARLY BRONZE AGE B
(CARPATHIANS)
BODROG-KERESZTUR CULTURE
Troy City VI
MACEDONIA
THESSALY
MIDDLE HELLADIC II
CYCLADES
Cnossus
CAPHTOR CRETE
(MEDITERRANEAN SEA)
SOUTH ITALIAN "COPPER AGE"
SICULAN CULTURE
SICILY
MICHELSBERG CULTURE
(THE ALPS)
LAKE DWELLERS
REMEDELLO CULTURE
HORGEN CULTURE
SARDINIAN MEGALITHIC TOMBS
CHALCOLITHIC AGE
MEGALITHIC TOMBS
(PYRENEES)
BALEARIC ISLANDS
ALMERIAN CULTURE
SURVIVALS OF THE LATE STONE AGE
CULTURE OF CAPSIAN TRADITION
THE HEBREW TABLE OF NATIONS
(From Genesis 10 and Related Sources)
JAPHETH or INDO-EUROPEAN PEOPLES RED
HAM, or AFRICAN PEOPLES BLUE
SHEM, or SEMITIC PEOPLES ORANGE
ALLOTTED to both HAM and SHEM BLACK
GOMER
ASHKENAZ
RIPHATH?
TOGARMAH
MESHECH
TUBAL
MADAI (MEDES)
ASSHUR
ELAM
SHINAR (BABYLONIA)
ARAM
CANAAN
JAVAN
LUD
ELISHAH
KITTIM
CAPHTOR
TARSHISH?
PHUT
LUBIM
LEHABIM
LIBYA
MIZRAIM
PATHROS
EGYPT
CUSH
ETHIOPIA
DEDAN
JOKTAN
HAZARMAVETH
RAAMAH
HAVILAH
SHEBA
OPHIR

THE WORLD OF THE PATRIARCHS

(c. 2000-1700 B.C.)

PLATE II

IF ONE were to draw a line from Egypt up through Palestine and Syria, then down the Euphrates to the Persian Gulf, he would have marked out an area in the shape of a semicircle which has been called "the Fertile Crescent." This was the center of civilization from the Stone Age to the golden age of Greece in the fifth century B.C. In the time of Abraham (c. 2000–1700 B.C.) world history centered in this region. The farther we move from it in any direction, the more primitive were the people. The two great foci of political and cultural energy were Egypt and Mesopotamia. There the first great states were established during the early third millennium because the Nile, Euphrates, and Tigris rivers made irrigation and a stable economy possible. Acting as a bridge between them was the narrow coastal strip of Syria-Palestine, across which moved caravans and armies, involving its peoples in the economic, political, and intellectual life of the two states. East and south of this bridge lay the arid Arabian Peninsula, joined to Asia on the north by the Fertile Crescent and to Africa on the west by Sinai. The peninsula of Arabia was the home of the Semites, or the children of Shem (Plate II, Inset), a proud, nomadic people who throughout history have treasured their patriarchal society and their pastoral traditions. Arabia is not a desert of shifting sand like the Sahara west of Egypt; it is a tableland, with sufficient rainfall in the interior and in the south for the needs of a considerable population. The Israelites, Canaanites (native inhabitants of Palestine-Syria), Babylonians, and Assyrians were all Semitic peoples, who in successive waves had moved from the Arabian Desert into the fertile lands.

North and east of the Fertile Crescent lay the highland regions of the children of Japheth (II, Inset, and Gen., ch. 10). These were the Aryan or Indo-European peoples. The history of the lands of the Bible, both before and during the period of Israel in Palestine, is largely the story of the successive invasions from Arabia on the one hand, and from the highland zone on the other, together with the conflicts of these invaders with each other and the kingdoms and civilizations which they developed.

A study of Plate II will reveal quite clearly the state of our knowledge about the world of Abraham's day. The cities and towns which are known to have existed are concentrated in the Fertile Crescent and in Egypt. Comparatively little is known about the peoples of the highlands surrounding the Fertile Crescent, of Europe to the northwest, or of Africa to the southwest. Between 1900 and 1600 B.C. an early Hittite state was formed in central Asia Minor, but we know very little about it. The records of an Assyrian trading colony at Kanish (II, E-2) have been recovered, revealing that before 1800 B.C. a highly developed trade was in existence between Assyria and Asia Minor, its chief object being the exploitation of the silver mines of the Taurus Mountains (III, B-2).

FIG. 9. This picture, painted on the wall of the tomb of an Egyptian noble at *Beni-ḥasan* (II, E-3), is the best representation from antiquity of Asiatics, probably Amorites, of the time of Abraham. It shows the family of a chieftain named Absha entering Egypt about 1900 B.C. Note the elaborately woven, many-colored woolen clothes (compare Joseph's "coat of many colors"), the shoes and sandals, the skin water bottles, the bows, javelins, heavy throw sticks (upper left), ax and eight-stringed lyre (lower left). Asses were used for transportation, since so far as is known the camel was not yet domesticated. In the upper right corner are two Egyptian scribes who are introducing the family to an official who is not here shown. They wear the white linen skirts so common in Egypt. At the top is a good example of Egyptian hieroglyphs. At the right the scribe shows a letter written in ink on papyrus, which was the Egyptian method of communication. On the bottom line of the letter the number in the family is given as thirty-seven.

The European areas on Plate II are marked with a number of archaeological terms which are not derived from contemporary records. In the time of Abraham, Europe had not yet emerged from the comparatively dark prehistoric age into the historical period when the people began to write about themselves and to achieve a high degree of social organization and intellectual advancement. Consequently, all that we know about the country has been discovered by archaeologists, who have given to various cultural units names which serve as convenient designations to aid in the discussion.

Greece and the island of Crete were far in advance of the rest of Europe at this time and in the following centuries were to emerge into the historical period. The Balkans were still in the "Early Bronze Age": that is, in a period when metal tools and weapons were coming into use, though the people had been living in villages and engaging in agriculture for some time. Farther west the manner of life was more primitive. In western Spain and southern France the cultures were still in the Chalcolithic Age: that is, in the transitional period when metal was first being introduced, though agriculture, pottery, and domesticated animals were known. Western France and Sardinia were still characterized by megalithic tombs; these were tombs constructed of stones so large that later peoples believed that their predecessors in the land had been giants. In Palestine also such structures had been built, but by a pastoral people in the late Stone Age, some three to four thousand years earlier. In England during this age some part at least of the famous Stonehenge was in existence, but on the whole the great age of megalithic dolmens (tombs), menhirs (upright stone shafts), and cromlechs (stone circles) was coming to an end.*

THE AGE OF THE PATRIARCHS

During the period following 2000 B.C. the whole Fertile Crescent was flooded with Semitic invaders from the Arabian Desert (Figs. 9, 10), who in Mesopotamia were called "Westerners," a name which appears as "Amorites" in the Old Testament. By 1750 B.C. the main cities from Syria to Babylon were ruled by Amorite dynasties. The chief source of our knowledge is the city of Mari (II, F-2), the capital of the most important state of the area. This kingdom extended some three hundred miles from the frontier of Babylon to the border of Syria. Its king was a man named Zimri-Lim, whose remarkable archives have been recovered, consisting of over 20,000 clay documents. Some 5,000 of them were letters written to him by kings, officials, and commoners from various parts of Syria and Mesopotamia. These documents and others like them have caused a revolution in our knowledge of the age, including a reduction in the date of the great Babylonian king, Hammurabi, by some three hundred years.

*For more detailed information about prehistoric Europe, see V. G. Childe, *The Dawn of European Civilization* (4th ed., 1948); *Prehistoric Migrations in Europe* (1950); and J. G. D. Clark, *Prehistoric Europe: The Economic Basis* (1952).

FIG. 10. Canaanite captives in Egypt being led before the Pharaoh. This relief, which portrays the general appearance of Israelites as well as Canaanites, is a good representation of the typical Semite of the day. Note the noble, aristocratic features, particularly the finely cut noses, and the long hair and beards. It is commonly thought that Israelites had "hooked noses," but this was originally a Hittite or Armenoid feature. (From the Temple of Rameses III at *Medînet Habu* in Egypt.)

Zimri-Lim's palace was one of the show places of the day. It contained nearly three hundred rooms, and comprised more than fifteen acres. The detailed records and reports which were kept indicate that it was both the commercial and political center of a most efficient state. Other discoveries show the widespread interest in divination and "fortune telling." While in Egypt there was a firm and sure faith in a beautiful hereafter, the Mesopotamian people paid less attention to the matter. In fact, they appear to have varied between faith and doubt. One of their great epics was concerned with the adventures of a hero named Gilgamesh, who was overtaken by a morbid fear of death and began a long search for immortality, but never quite found it. Consequently, the Mesopotamian (and the Canaanite and Israelite as well) was primarily interested in living this life as successfully as possible. To do so he developed elaborate techniques for piercing the veil of the future, and Babylonian diviners became so famous that they were soon scattered throughout the Fertile Crescent. Balaam, hired by the king of Moab to curse Israel, is a good example (Num., chs. 22 to 24). (Cf. the stern prohibition of these practices in Deut. 18:9–14.)

Mari was conquered about 1700 B.C. by the greatest king of the age, the illustrious Hammurabi of Babylonia. Under his rule the small village of Babylon became an even more impressive city than Mari, and the commercial center of a rich empire which extended from Nineveh (II, F-2) and the Upper Euphrates to Ur (II, F-3). The most famous building of Babylon was the temple-tower named *Etemenanki*, one of the wonders of the ancient world (Fig. 11). Babylon, being the polyglot city that it was, and possessing the great temple-tower second in size only to the great Pyramid of Egypt, was the perfect setting for the Israelite story of the confusion of tongues. It was indeed a city with a tower whose top reached the heavens (Gen. 11:4).

One of Hammurabi's notable achievements was his code of laws, a collection and adaptation of old Sumerian laws and customs (Fig. 12). This code has long interested students of the Bible, for many of its provisions are similar to those found in secular Israelite law. The latter, however, is no copy of the former. The Code of Hammurabi is merely typical of the common law of the day, and from this law Israel later adapted much that she needed.

Palestine had entered its first great cultural age during the Early Bronze Age, beginning c. 3300 B.C., though east of the Jordan the people had remained nomadic. Between c. 2400 and 2100 B.C., however, this early civilization was destroyed, and the nomads in Transjordan began to settle in villages. After 1900 B.C. there was a new culture in Palestine, while Transjordan was again nomadic—evidence of the shifting relations between the Desert and the Sown.

During the age of the Patriarchs the coastal areas of Syria-Palestine appear to have been largely under Egypt's control. Monuments belonging to important Egyptians have been found at Gezer and Megiddo in Palestine (IV, B-5 and C-3) and at Byblos and Ugarit in Syria (II, E-3 and E-2). Recently discovered Egyptian texts on which are listed numerous Asiatic enemies mention a number of towns, among them Jerusalem, Shechem, and Hazor (II, E-3)—the earliest reference to these important places outside the Bible. Each town is ruled by one or more chieftains, and the implication of the documents is that the social organization was patriarchal and quite different from the city-state system in vogue after the seventeenth century (see pp. 33 ff.).

A most interesting Egyptian story, the Tale of Sinuhe (c. 1900 B.C.), describes contemporary life among the Amorites in eastern Syria. Sinuhe was a high Egyptian official who had to flee from his country for political reasons. He found refuge with an Amorite chieftain in the country of the "East" (*Kedem*), presumably the same general territory as "the land of the children of the east" to which Jacob went, according to Gen. 29:1. The comparative wealth of the seminomadic life which Sinuhe lived in this region is vividly described. It is the same type of life as that of the Patriarchs described in Genesis, who lived from flocks and herds while occasionally engaging in simple agriculture. Further illustration of patriarchal life is to be found in a beautiful Egyptian painting which pictures a family of Asiatics, presumably Amorites, entering Egypt about 1900 B.C. (Fig. 9). The families of Abraham and Jacob undoubtedly looked and dressed very much like these people when they journeyed to Egypt during periods of famine (Gen., chs. 12; 42 ff.).

Egypt at the time of Abraham was ruled by the Pharaohs of the illustrious Twelfth Dynasty (c. 1991–1778 B.C.). Besides exercising political control over Palestine and Syria they organized an extensive sea trade with Syria, Cyprus, Crete, and Punt (II, F-4). The southern boundary of the country was pushed southward to the second cataract of the Nile, where a border fortress was erected at *Semneh* (II, E-4). Expeditions were sent to Sinai to exploit the copper and turquoise deposits existing there (II, E-3), and also to Nubia (Cush, II, E-4), where gold had been discovered. Later Egyptians looked back upon this period as a golden age. Not only was a high degree of prosperity attained; it was an age of great literature as well, the style of which formed the model for succeeding periods.

FIG. 11. A restoration of Babylon and the Tower of Babel. The tower, properly known as *Etemenanki*, "the House of the Foundation Platform of Heaven and Earth," was begun in the third millennium B.C. but not completed until Nebuchadnezzar's reign. The tower is an example of the common Mesopotamian *ziqqurat*, a high, stepped platform surmounted by a temple, in this instance one dedicated to Marduk who was believed to be the chief god of the land. The structure was about three hundred feet square at the base and approximately the same in height. Portions of the enormous city walls built by Nebuchadnezzar c. 600 B.C. are also shown. In the foreground is the Euphrates River, which flowed along the western edge of the city.

THE HEBREW PATRIARCHS

Thus far no contemporary record of Abraham has been found outside the Bible. Yet the background of the narratives about him and his descendants has been considerably illumined. Genesis 11:31 informs us that his family migrated from Ur of the Chaldees (II, F-3) to Haran (II, F-2). Ur was a great Sumerian city before the days of Abraham, and it continued to be an important place for centuries. Yet the reference here is obscure both textually and historically. In any event there is no reliable information which indicates any influence of that city on patriarchal life.

With the case of Haran, however, the situation is different. When Abraham and his family reached Canaan, they continued to keep in close touch with their relatives there, and apparently looked upon that area as their homeland (Gen., chs. 24; 29 ff.). Haran was the chief town of the region called Paddan-aram (Field of Aram) by later Israel. An earlier name appears to have been Aram of the Two Rivers (Gen. 24:10, R.V. marg.). This was one of the centers of the new Amorite settlement, and it is tempting to connect the journeys of the family of Abraham either directly or indirectly with the Amorite movement. Several lines of evidence lead to the conclusion that this can be done.

For one thing, certain of the names of the ancestors and family of Abraham were also names of towns in the area of Haran: that is, Peleg, Serug, Nahor, and Terah (Gen. 11:16 ff.). The name of the city Haran sounds very much like that of one of Abraham's brothers, though the initial letter in the original language is slightly different. The identification of one name with an ancient town might be mere coincidence, but in this case there are at least four in the precise area from which Abraham came. These names were probably patriarchal clan names which either were given by the clans to towns they founded or were taken from the towns which they seized during the disturbances around 2000 B.C.

Further, the names Abram (in the form *Abamram*) and Jacob (in the form *Jacob-el*) are known as personal names among the Amorites. In the Mari archives there is also frequent mention of a tribe of Benjamin which was causing some trouble in the area, though it is to be identified only in name with the later Israelite tribe. Even more interesting is the light thrown on patriarchal customs by the archives of a later city of northern Mesopotamia named Nuzi (III, D-2). The customs reflected in these documents explain a number of patriarchal laws and practices which have been obscure, and they demonstrate that patriarchal life as described in Genesis is that of the second millennium, and not that of the first millennium, when Israelites were retelling the stories and putting them into writing. Thus, the relations between Jacob and Laban, the hitherto obscure "teraphim" (Gen. 31:19 ff.), Esau's sale of his birthright, patriarchal deathbed blessings, etc., are now seen in clearer perspective (see further p. 30).

It is also a significant fact that the Hebrew traditions about the Creation and the Flood (Gen., chs. 1 to 11) contain many resemblances to similar accounts of Mesopotamian people, while they resemble nothing in either Egyptian or Canaanite literature. In the case of the Creation and of the Garden of Eden the resemblances are superficial. Though the views regarding the structure of the world were essentially similar (the firmament or heavens as a bowl covering the earth, with waters both above and below, etc.), the refinement produced by the purity of the Israelite faith sets a great gulf between the Old Testament accounts and the crassly pagan traditions of Babylon. The same is true regarding the Flood account, but in this case the parallels with Babylonian documents (which in turn are based upon Sumerian sources of the third millennium) are so close that a relation must exist between them. The Babylonian ark, however, grounded on the Zagros Mountains to the east and north of Babylon (III, E-3), while according to the Old Testament it rested on the mountains of Ararat (III, D-1, Armenia; Gen. 8:4)—another indication of the influence of northern Mesopotamia on Israel.

It must be asked, therefore, why it was that the country which was the farthest from Israel should have had the greatest influence upon her thinking about the early days of man's life on earth. Today almost the only possible explanation is that the essential outlines of the accounts of the Creation, the Garden of Eden, the Flood, Nimrod (Gen. 10:8 ff.), and the Tower of Babel (Gen., ch. 11) were brought from the homeland in Haran by the Patriarchs themselves. It was once thought that the Canaanites acted as the intermediaries between Israel and Mesopotamia, but since the recovery of the Ugaritic literature (pp. 30, 36) this view has become increasingly difficult to hold. The story regarding the Tower of Babel must have arisen at a time when Babylon and its great temple-tower were flourishing and well-known: that is, between the eighteenth and sixteenth centuries B.C., before the city was destroyed by the Hittites (see p. 29). The story of the tower, then, gives the approximate age, while the story of the Flood indicates that we are dealing, not with a Babylonian, but with a North Mesopotamian edition.

These and other facts enable us for the first time to answer with confidence the questions as to who the Patriarchs were and whence they came.

Various sources of information also illuminate the life of the Patriarchs in Canaan. The main centers around which they lived (Mamre, Beer-sheba, Bethel, Shechem, Dothan) were all located in the central hill country of Palestine. This region was rather sparsely populated at the time, and therefore particularly suited for pastoral life.

FIG. 12. The Code of Hammurabi. This is a replica of the diorite shaft nearly eight feet in height on which Hammurabi had inscribed his code of laws. This code, one of the oldest which has survived, was compiled by the great king from the ancient laws of his predecessors. At the top of the shaft he is represented as receiving these laws from the enthroned sun-god. At a later time an Elamite conqueror took the shaft as a trophy for his capital at Susa (II, G-3), where it was found during the winter of 1901–1902. At the base of the shaft part of the original text has been erased, probably to make room for another inscription which was never executed.

Dothan, Shechem, and Bethel were all in existence, according to archaeological information. In Num. 13:22 we are informed that Hebron was founded "seven years before Zoan in Egypt." This means that Hebron was established about 1700 B.C., or just before, because the reference here to Zoan (Avaris) refers to its establishment as the Hyksos capital of Egypt (V, C-3, and p. 28). Consequently, Hebron as a city was not in existence in Abraham's day. This accounts for his association with Mamre and the mention of Hebron in an explanatory note to indicate where Mamre was (Gen. 13:18; 23:19). We now have interesting information regarding "the cities of the Plain" and the destruction of Sodom and Gomorrah (Gen. 13:10 ff.; 19:23 ff.). Genesis informs us that the Jordan Valley was thriving and well populated in the days of Abraham, but that subsequently a part of the area that contained Sodom and Gomorrah was destroyed. We know that these cities were situated in the Vale of Siddim (Gen. 14:3), and that this was the area at the southern end of the Dead Sea, now covered with water (X, H-3). Evidence from both archaeological and historical sources outside the Bible supports the tradition of a terrific catastrophe in this area about the time of Abraham (see further, p. 69 f.).

Unfortunately, we lack precise knowledge of the nature of Abraham's religion, but a number of features have been clarified. Particularly important is the apparent fact that the name of the patriarchal family God was "*El Shaddai*" (Ex. 6:2, 3; Gen. 17:1; etc.). This has been translated "God Almighty"; in reality *Shaddai* is a Mesopotamian word meaning "The Mountain One"—further evidence of the connection of the Patriarchs with northern Mesopotamia. This was the name of the "God of the Fathers," whom the successive patriarchal generations deliberately chose as their Deity. The relationship between the family and its chosen God was very close, so that he was addressed as "father," "brother," "kinsman," and was considered an actual member of the group. When treaties or covenants were made, he was the third party who sealed the agreement and saw that it was kept (cf. the Mizpah benediction in Gen. 31:49). These factors played a prominent part in the later religion of Israel, in which the same close relationship between God and people continued to exist and was symbolized in the special covenant relationship freely contracted by God and Israel at Mount Sinai (Ex., ch. 24). Thus the patriarchal religion played a most important part in the later religion of Israel and was a central factor in distinguishing it from the degrading, polytheistic nature worship of Canaan.

The above is but a partial list of the results of recent investigation. Archaeology and historical study in recent years have done a great deal to illumine the background of the patriarchal stories—and this is one of the important accomplishments of this generation's Old Testament students. Of course, the stories were occasionally modernized by the addition of such references as those to the "Philistines," a people who were not in Palestine until after 1200 B.C. (VI, B-5; see pp. 45 f.). In addition, the narratives were written by later Israelite teachers whose interest was to interpret their meaning in terms of God's choice and promise to the Fathers, a fact in which the real significance of this literature resides. Yet the recovery of the life and times of the Patriarchs is a most important achievement, one which has revolutionized our understanding of the book of Genesis and to some extent our whole approach to the historical books of the Old Testament.

THE HEBREW TABLE OF NATIONS

(PLATE II, INSET)

The Inset of Plate II shows the countries and peoples of the world as they were known to the Israelites and listed in Gen., ch. 10. The inhabitants of the world were believed by Israel to have descended from the three sons of Noah: Shem was the father of the Semites; Ham, the father of the African peoples; and Japheth, the father of the Aryan or Indo-European peoples. The list does not include the inhabitants of northern Europe nor of the Far East, because Hebrew life had no contact with them. The area included in the Table of Nations extends from Asia Minor (Turkey) to Abyssinia (Cush or Ethiopia), and from Elam, east of Babylon, to Greece and the distant Tarshish. From the peoples and places mentioned we know immediately that the list in its present form comes from the period between 1000 and 800 B.C. Thus Tarshish, for example, was the name for "smelter" and was used for certain colonies of the Phoenicians in the Mediterranean. One such "tarshish" was on Sardinia and another perhaps in Spain, and we are not sure in this case just which one was meant.

The list is arranged on the whole from a racial point of view, though certain exceptions are to be noted. For example, we know from their language that the Canaanites were a Semitic people, though here they are listed as descendants of Ham (Africa). The reason may be that when Israel entered Canaan, the latter had long been under the control of Egypt (see pp. 34, 35). Thus its inclusion as a Hamitic people is for political and geographical, rather than for racial, reasons. Similarly, Elam is listed as a son of Shem; but we know from the language there spoken that the majority of its people were non-Semitic. Its inclusion under Shem was, therefore, not a matter of race but of historical geography. Apart from such exceptions, however, this division of the peoples of the ancient world into three main groups is very convenient and is still used to some extent by historians and ethnographers.

FIG. 13. The ruins of *Karnak*, a portion of the chief city of ancient Egypt named Thebes (called No or No-amon in the Old Testament). Here the successive Pharaohs spent lavishly of their wealth in the building of magnificent temples and palaces. This picture shows the remains of the chief sanctuary of the city, the imperial temple of the god Amun. The main structure is in the left center. Surrounding the sacred precinct is a massive brick wall, and in the center is the bed of the sacred lake. The view is toward the east, with the Nile River back of the camera. On the west side of the Nile were other temples and the Valley of the Tombs of the Kings, where the tomb of Tutankhamun was found in 1922, untouched by either ancient or modern tomb robbers.

THE GREAT EMPIRES DURING THE SOJOURN IN EGYPT

PLATE III

THE four centuries which Israel spent in Egypt are a "dark age" in her history. From this entire period little or no information about the Israelites has come down to us. Some record of the beginnings of this era has been preserved in the story of Joseph and the account of Jacob's descent into Egypt. The intervening years are passed over in silence and the narrative of Israel's history does not take up again until it reaches the time of Moses and of the Exodus of Israel from Egypt. If, however, little is known directly of Israel in these centuries, much can be learned by indirection from a study of the great empires which flourished in the Near East during her sojourn in Egypt, especially the empires of the Late Bronze Age (c. 1500–1200 B.C.). These empires, while not the first to appear in history, were the earliest of the great rival empires to contend for conquest and dominion in the Fertile Crescent. The story of this international rivalry and strife is the principal motif in the history of this era. Israel's Sojourn and Exodus were, no doubt, a part of the migrations and upheavals of the age.

For a thorough understanding of this period it is necessary, however, to consider briefly the two centuries just preceding the rise of these empires. Between the Age of the Patriarchs (Plate II) and the era of the rival empires came two tumultuous centuries. The stability which had been achieved in Egypt by the Egyptian Middle Kingdom (i.e., contemporary with the Age of the Patriarchs) and later in Babylon by the First Dynasty under Hammurabi (p. 24) was interrupted during the seventeenth and sixteenth centuries by foreign invasions. Non-Semitic highlanders poured down into the Mesopotamian plains and brought an end to Semitic rule there, while Semitic rulers from Canaan established themselves in Egypt.

THE HYKSOS PERIOD IN SYRIA-PALESTINE AND EGYPT

Although information about these events in Mesopotamia is very scant, sufficient data are at hand from Syria-Palestine and Egypt to enable us to piece together something of the history of all these countries during this era. About 1720 B.C. Egypt was invaded and conquered by an Asiatic people whom the Egyptians called *Hyksos*, "Rulers of Foreign Lands." The later Egyptian historian Manetho wrote about them as follows:

> "There was a king of ours whose name was Timaios, in whose reign it came to pass, I know not why, that God was displeased with us, and there came unexpectedly men of ignoble birth out of the eastern parts, who had

FIG. 14. Reproduction of the great Hyksos enclosure at *Tell el-Yehûdîyeh* in Egypt (v, C-3). The Hyksos introduced a new weapon of war, the horse and chariot. Beaten earth embankments of this sort were built by them about 1700 B.C. throughout Syria, Palestine, and the Egyptian Delta as enclosures for the horses.

boldness enough to make an expedition into our country, and easily subdued it by force without a battle. And when they had got our rulers under their power, they afterwards savagely burnt down our cities and demolished the temples of the gods, and used all the inhabitants in a most hostile manner, for they slew some and led the children and wives of others into slavery. At length they made one of themselves king, whose name was Salatis, and he lived at Memphis and made both upper and lower Egypt pay tribute, and left garrisons in places that were most suitable for them . . . and as he found in the Saite nome [county] a city very fit for his purpose (which lay east of the arm of the Nile near Bubastis, and with regard to a certain theological notion was called Avaris), he rebuilt it and made it very strong by the walls he built around it and by a numerous garrison of 240,000 men, whom he put into it to keep it. There Salatis went every summer, partly to gather his corn and pay his soldiers their wages, and partly to train his armed men and so to awe foreigners."

These invaders, whom the Egyptians so despised and hated, built a powerful empire, including Palestine and Syria. Objects belonging to one of their greatest kings have been found in lands as far separated as Crete and Mesopotamia. Recent evidence indicates that most, if not all, of the Hyksos were of western Semitic, i.e., Canaanite, stock. Syria-Palestine, the home of these peoples, enjoyed a period of great prosperity during the period when they were in power. The population increased during one and one half centuries of peace; and great advances can be observed in the arts and crafts. The Hyksos were evidently able to carry out their conquest of Egypt by the introduction of a new weapon of war, the horse and chariot. Great earthwork enclosures were built for chariotry at numerous places in Syria-Palestine and in the Egyptian Delta (Fig. 14). At Shechem and Jericho in Palestine tremendous fortifications were erected, and the country was organized into a feudal city-state system (see pp. 33 ff.). Though Canaan was prosperous, the age was a dark one for Egypt and no extensive writings from it have been recovered.

The Hyksos period is of particular interest to the student of the Old Testament because several lines of evidence suggest that it was during this time, probably not far from 1700 B.C., that Joseph came to power in Egypt. In the Genesis story it is evident that the court of the Pharaoh was not far from Goshen (Gen. 46:28 ff.). This would mean that the Egyptian capital at that time was in the Delta area. This is precisely where it was during the Hyksos period (see Avaris, III, B-4), whereas both before and after the Hyksos the Egyptian Pharaohs used as their capital the city of Thebes in Upper Egypt (Fig. 13 and II, E-3). If, therefore, the family of Jacob entered Egypt either before or after the Hyksos age, we should be at a loss to explain the obvious implication of Genesis concerning the location of the capital, unless, of course, we assume that in this respect the book is mistaken. Further, Ex. 12:40 states that "the time that the children of Israel dwelt in Egypt was four hundred and thirty years." Since it is almost certain that the Exodus from Egypt under Moses took place sometime after 1300 B.C. (see pp. 37 ff.), we are brought back to about 1700 B.C. for the date of Joseph. This and other evidence suggests that the Sojourn of Israel began at a time when Canaanite foreigners were ruling Egypt. Thus the rise to power of a foreigner like Joseph would easily be explained.

It has long been known that the local color of the story of Joseph is so good that the narratives must have been recounted by those who knew Egypt well. The titles "chief of the butlers" and "chief of the bakers" (Gen. 40:2) are those of palace officials mentioned in Egyptian writings. Dreams were regarded by Egyptians as extremely important. The birthday of Pharaoh was an occasion for feasting, and possibly for the release of prisoners (cf. Gen. 40:20). We know also that magicians were plentiful in Egypt (cf. ch. 41:8), that Asiatic shepherds were indeed "an abomination unto the Egyptians" (chs. 46:34; 43:32), that seven-year famines had occurred in Egypt, that Joseph's life span of 110 years (ch. 50:22) was the traditional length of a happy and prosperous life in Egyptian writings, and that the embalming or mummification of Jacob and Joseph (ch. 50:2, 26) was the customary Egyptian manner of preparing the bodies of important people for burial.

Potiphar made Joseph "overseer over his house" (Gen. 39:4), a title which is a direct translation of an office in the houses of great Egyptian nobles. Pharaoh gave him an office with similar title in the administration of the realm (ch. 41:40), corresponding exactly to the office of prime minister or vizier of Egypt, who was the chief official in the country, second in power to no one but the Pharaoh The Pharaoh's gifts to Joseph upon the latter's induction into office would be quite in keeping with Egyptian custom: "And Pharaoh took off his signet ring from his hand, and put it upon Joseph's hand, and arrayed him in vestures of fine linen, and put a gold chain about his neck; and he made him to ride in the second chariot which he had; and they cried before him, Bow the knee" (ch. 41:42, 43). In Egypt there was also an office of "superintendent of the granaries." This was especially important since the stability of the country lay in its grain. Because of the approaching famine Joseph may have carried on the functions of this office in addition to his duties as prime minister.

As indicated, the Biblical story of the seven years of famine (Gen., ch. 41) is not unusual. Various Egyptian writings speak of famines in the land, and at least two officials, giving laudatory summaries of their good deeds on the walls of their tombs, tell of distributing food to the hungry "in each year of want." One inscription which was written about 100 B.C. tells how Pharaoh Zoser (c. 2700 B.C., one thousand years before Joseph) appealed to one of his gods because of a severe seven-year famine in which the people suffered terrible hardships, robbery became prevalent, and though storehouses had been built their contents were gone.

Joseph's father and brethren were settled in Egypt in the land of *Goshen* (Gen. 46:26 ff.). While this name does not occur outside the Bible, its locality is known to have comprised the area around the

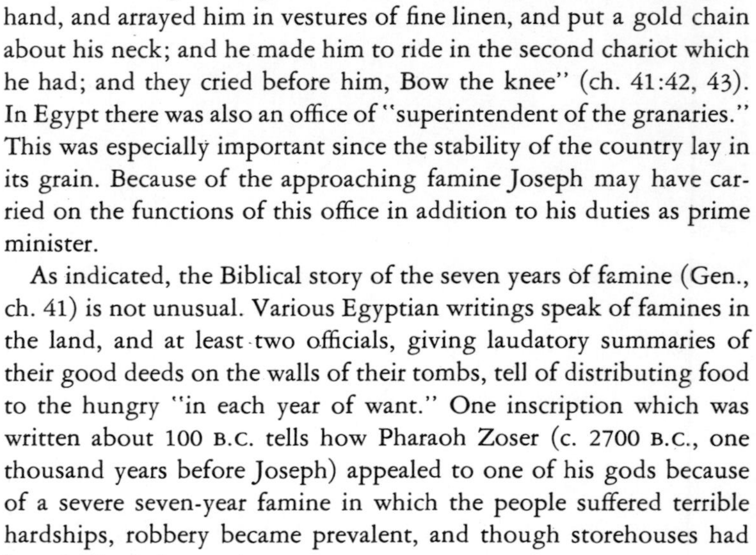

FIG. 15. The Euphrates, the largest river of southwestern Asia and a commercial highway from times immemorial. It rises in the mountains of Armenia and flows south into Syria, where instead of emptying into the Mediterranean Sea it moves southeastward, falling one thousand feet in its seven-hundred-mile journey to the Persian Gulf. In ancient times a network of canals led from it, fertilizing Babylonia and making possible the erection there of a strong state. The modern boat here shown is built of reeds and coated with bitumen, precisely as were the river boats of ancient Babylonia.

Wâdī Tumilât in the eastern part of the Nile Delta (III, B-4; V, C-D 3). This *Wâdī* (the Arabic name for a river bed which is usually dry except in the rainy season) is a narrow valley between thirty and forty miles long connecting the Nile with Lake Timsâḥ (V, D-3). In both ancient and modern times the area around this valley, especially to the north of it, has been one of the richest sections of Egypt, truly "the best of the land," as it is described in Gen. 47:11.

Two Egyptian writings indicate that it was the customary thing for frontier officials to allow people from Palestine and Sinai to enter this section of Egypt during hard times. One, dating about 1350 B.C., is written from frontier officials to the Pharaoh, telling him that such a group "who knew not how they should live, have come begging a home in the domain of Pharaoh . . ., after the manner of your [the Pharaoh's] fathers' fathers since the beginning . . . ." The family of Jacob was seventy in number (Gen. 46:26, 27). Fig. 9 shows a portion of the Asiatic family of Absha, as it entered Egypt about 1900 B.C. This family was thirty-seven in number; and during the course of the following centuries many such families must have been admitted to the country. It is small wonder, therefore, that no record of Jacob has been preserved in Egyptian writings.

THE ANCIENT WORLD DURING THE FIFTEENTH CENTURY B.C.

Shortly after 1600 B.C. native rulers at Thebes in Upper Egypt (II, E-3) became sufficiently strong to begin the war of liberation against the hated Hyksos. By c. 1550 B.C. the foreigners had been driven from the Delta and a great siege of three years' duration at Sharuhen in southern Canaan (IV, A-6) had been brought to a successful conclusion. The Hyksos' power was now completely broken. During the succeeding decades the Egyptians took over the Hyksos empire in Palestine and Syria. This brought them into direct conflict with the newly formed powers in the north, to which we must now turn.

The highlands of Armenia, Media, and Elam to the northeast and east of the Fertile Crescent were not consolidated into one great power before the sixth century B.C. (Plates XI: B and C). The inhabitants of these upland regions were, however, a constant menace to the civilized world since periodically they poured out of the mountains into the plains.

Babylonian tradition preserves the record of a brief surge to power of the Kingdom of Elam (III, E-3) about 1600 B.C., when a king of that country sacked and burned the cities of lower Babylonia. The First Dynasty of Babylonia, which had attained such illustrious heights under the great administrator Hammurabi (p. 24), was finally brought to an end by highlanders known as the Kassites, causing a dark age in Babylonia similar to the Hyksos period in Egypt. They maintained their control over the country for a period of almost four centuries (c. 1500–1150 B.C.). Under their rule the country remained weak and no effectual effort was made to establish an empire.

Between 1750 and 1600 B.C. non-Semitic Indo-Iranian and Hurrian peoples invaded northern Mesopotamia from the eastern highlands. By 1500 B.C. these invaders had established a powerful kingdom called Mitanni which controlled the whole area between the Mediterranean Sea and the highlands of Media. Their capital was at Washshukanni (III, D-2) on a tributary of the River Habor (*Khabûr*). The royal family and the nobles were the Indo-Iranians (i.e., Aryans). They worshiped Indian gods such as Mithra, Indra, and Varuna. The national sport of these aristocrats was horse racing. Judging from one of their treatises on horse-training which has been preserved in Hittite, far more care was given to the horse than to the average peasant of the time. The Hurrians who came in with the ruling Aryan peoples were of a different, though also non-Semitic, stock. Their language is only just beginning to yield to the efforts of the scholars who are attempting to translate it. In the Old Testament these people are called Horites (see pp. 35 f.). During the fifteenth and fourteenth centuries they spread so widely over the Canaanite lands of Syria-Palestine that one of the Egyptian names for Canaan was

FIG. 16. Foreign captives led before the Egyptian Pharaoh at Thebes. Types of people are clearly shown. On the left is a Libyan from the desert east of lower Egypt. Next to him is a Semite, perhaps from Syria or Palestine (cf. Fig. 10). The third has the typical profile of a Hittite from Asia Minor. The fourth, wearing a feathered headdress, is one of the sea peoples from the Aegean world, among whom were the Philistines. The last is another Semite. (From the temple of Rameses III at *Medînet Habu* in Egypt.)

Khûru, a word derived from the same source as "Hurrian" and "Horite" (see Plate IV).

To the north in central Asia Minor (Turkey) was the Hittite kingdom, centering in the region watered by the Halys River. Its capital was Khattushash (III, B-1), about ninety miles east of the modern Turkish capital, Ankara. By 1600 B.C. strong rulers had consolidated the area into a powerful state. Soon they began to push into northern Syria and Mesopotamia, and even succeeded in devastating Babylon (III, E-3) about 1550 B.C. Pressure from all sides, especially from Mitanni and Egypt, soon called a halt to this advance so that the Hittites do not play an important role until after 1400 B.C.

Plate III shows the extent of the various empires as they existed during the fifteenth century when Egypt had achieved its golden age. The neighbor of Egypt to the northeast was Mitanni, against which she waged continuous but indecisive war. Mitanni itself in this period lay mainly east of the Euphrates, but its territory reached to Lake Van on the north and included Assyria on the east. The Hittites remained quiet in Asia Minor. Babylon was weak under Kassite rulership, while the power and extent of Elam at this time is unknown. The borders as here drawn must not be considered as exact. Not only did they fluctuate constantly, but at no time in this age is our knowledge sufficient to fix them precisely.

THE FATE OF THE EMPIRES

After 1400 B.C. the balance of power achieved in the fifteenth century was broken by two factors: the rise of the Hittite kingdom into a position as the dominant power in the northern part of Western Asia, and the weakening of Egyptian foreign policy under the religious revolutionary, Amenophis IV or Akhnaton (c. 1370-1353 B.C.; Fig. 19). While the Hittites were passive, Egypt and Mitanni had been free to engage in almost continual warfare. When the Hittites began to exert pressure from the north, Mitanni hastened to make peace with Egypt, and the successive kings sent princesses to the Egyptian royal harem to secure the alliance. By about 1370, however, the Hittites had conquered Mitanni, reducing it to the status of a tributary state which acted as a buffer between Asia Minor and Assyria. The Hittites then pushed into Egyptian territory in Syria, and from this time to about 1200 B.C. the border between Egypt and Khatti (the Hittite Empire) lay in the area of Qatna, Kadesh, and Irqata (III, C-3). For the greater part of the fourteenth century the two empires were so occupied with internal affairs that they had little time for disputes with one another. The kings of the Nineteenth Egyptian Dynasty, Sethos I (1308-1290) and Rameses II (1290-1224), however, were vitally concerned with the recovery of the lost portions of their empire, and led their armies through Palestine to Syria. This

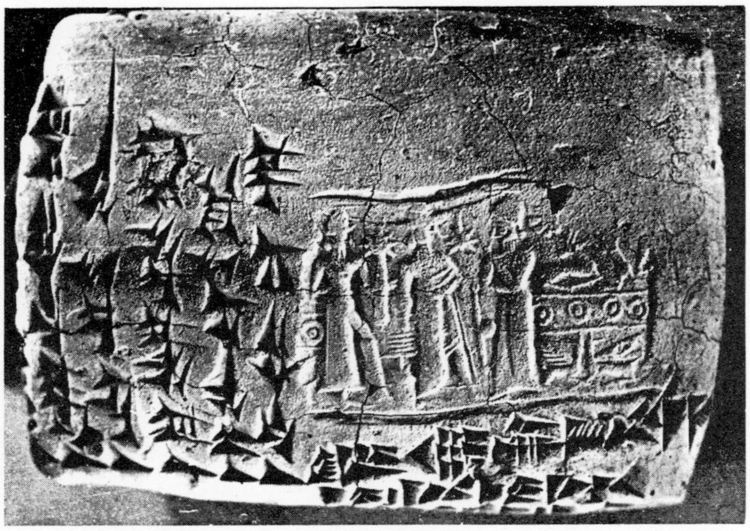

FIG. 17. One of the Nuzi tablets. This is an example of the cuneiform (wedge-shaped) method of writing developed in Mesopotamia. A reed or stylus was used to make the signs while the clay was wet. The figures were impressed by a small cylindrical seal, used instead of a signature by the one who had the document prepared. For the Egyptian method of writing with pen and ink on papyrus, see Fig. 9. The latter was the method adopted by Phoenicians and Israelites, passed on to the Greeks and thence to us.

campaign culminated in the great battle at Kadesh (III, C-3) about 1286 B.C., with results that appeared on the whole unfavorable to Egypt, though the Hittites were never able to take advantage of their success. In 1270 B.C., a formal peace, or nonaggression pact, was made, copies of which have been found in Egyptian at Thebes and in Babylonian at Khattushash (III, B-1).

Thus ended the major wars of the fourteenth and thirteenth centuries B.C. Regional conflicts, however, continued. Assyria, relieved of the yoke of Mitanni, began to spread rapidly and by 1250 B.C. had subjugated that country. For the next six hundred years, except for periods of decline in the twelfth and tenth centuries, the Assyrians were the dominant political force in Western Asia (Plate XI: A). The golden ages of Egypt and Khatti were now over. Invading hordes about 1200 B.C. brought an end to the Hittite Empire. After 1150 B.C. the Egyptian Government was controlled by an inept priesthood which made no attempt to interfere in the affairs of Western Asia.

In the Greek world before 1400 B.C. the political and cultural center was the island of Crete (called "Caphtor" in the Old Testament; III, A-2). Here for hundreds of years had flourished the "Minoan" civilization with its capital at Cnossus (or Knossos), where the magnificent palace of the legendary King Minos has been excavated (II, D-2). About 1400 B.C. Crete was overrun by mainlanders from Greece. During the two centuries which followed they controlled the sea trade with Palestine-Syria and Egypt, flooding those countries with products exported in beautiful vases (Mycenaean ware) and establishing colonies in various places, particularly on Alashiya (Cyprus). Because of internal disorders or invasions in Greece this trade appears to have been stopped by about 1225 B.C. and was not revived until the period of Phoenician (Canaanite) commercial expansion into the Mediterranean beginning about the time of Solomon in the tenth century B.C. (see pp. 33, 46).

The period about 1200 B.C. marks the end of an epoch in the history of the ancient world. In the Aegean the golden ages of "Minoan" and "Mycenaean" civilization had come to an end. In Asia Minor the Hittite power had been destroyed. To the south the Mitannian state had been taken over by Assyria. Most of Palestine was in the control of the Israelites (Plate VI and pp. 43 ff.), while Egypt was suffering from an internal weakness from which she was never fully to recover.

WRITTEN DOCUMENTS OF THE PERIOD OF THE SOJOURN

The art of writing had been highly developed and widely cultivated by the time of the Sojourn. Numerous important collections of political, religious, and legal documents have been recovered from this age in a great variety of scripts and languages, some of which cannot yet be translated. For the Biblical student the most important are the libraries of *Tell el-Amarna* (V, B-6), Ugarit (III, C-2), and Nuzi (III, D-2). The Accadian cuneiform method of writing was that most commonly used. The scribe wrote on clay tablets with a stylus which made wedge-shaped (that is, "cuneiform") characters (see Fig. 17). The *Tell el-Amarna* documents were letters written in this manner by the local kings of Palestine and Syria to the Pharaoh of Egypt about political matters, and they form a most valuable source of information about the Land of Canaan before the Israelite Conquest (see further pp. 34, 35).

The Ugarit texts, dating about 1400 B.C., are largely religious in character and were found in the ruins of a scribal school adjoining a temple. Using a new cuneiform alphabet, the scribes invented a new way of writing the Canaanite language. The dialect employed is closely akin to the Hebrew of the Old Testament, the differences between the two being in part dialectical and in part a matter of respective age. Most significant is the fact that these documents contain a portion of the long-lost Canaanite religious literature and mythology, frequent allusions to which occur in the Old Testament (see further p. 36). Moreover, the texts contain many words and phrases borrowed by Israel, some of which are now explained for the first time. In addition, they provide a store of information about Canaanite poetry, certain forms of which were learned by the Israelites and used in their own psalmody (e.g., in Judg., ch. 5; II Sam. 1:19 ff.; Ps. 29; 68, etc.).

The Nuzi texts are largely concerned with social and business transactions in the small Assyrian city when it was under the control of Mitanni during the fifteenth century B.C. The most significant fact about them is that they throw a flood of light upon social customs of the northern Mesopotamian area in the second millennium B.C., and for the first time illustrate and explain many customs in the stories of Genesis. Such practices as the deathbed blessing or will of the Patriarch (Gen., ch. 27), and the giving of concubines for the purpose of raising family heirs (Gen., chs. 16 and 30), are here seen to be customs of the day. Another custom was for childless people to adopt a son to take care of them as long as they lived and to provide them with proper burial when they died. In return for this service the adopted son was designated as heir of the family's property. This explains the peculiar relation between Eliezer, a man from Damascus, and Abraham. Though a servant he was to be Abraham's heir if no son were born (Gen. 15:1 ff.). The relations between Jacob and Laban are also explained (Gen., chs. 29 to 31). At a time when Laban had no sons Jacob was adopted as son and heir. After a period of service, he was permitted by custom to marry Leah and Rachel, though he could not marry the daughter of any other family (Gen. 31:50). Complications appear to have arisen when sons were born to Laban (first mentioned in Gen. 31:1). The Nuzi law provided that if a son were born after the adoption had taken place, that son and the adopted son were to share the inheritance, but only the son was privileged to take the household idols or "gods," possession of which implied leadership of the family. In Gen. 31:19, 34, 35 the idols of the family are called "teraphim" (compare vs. 30-32). Apparently Rachel stole them from the house to insure the future position of her husband, though the act was in violation of the law of adoption. These and other Nuzi parallels to Genesis show that the description of Patriarchal society is not distorted, but actually reflects the age which the stories purport to describe (see further p. 25).

Many other important documents of the age have been recovered, among them the Assyrian and Hittite legal codes. These together with the code of Hammurabi (Fig. 12) illustrate the secular law of the ancient Near East, portions of which are to be found adapted to Israelite usage in Ex., chs. 21 to 23. The alphabet (in which the Old Testament was written and which was borrowed by the Greeks and transferred through the Romans to us) was being developed and used in Palestine-Syria during the period of the Sojourn, and a number of inscriptions which employ it have been discovered. In addition, a large number of incidental discoveries fill out our picture of Old Testament lands and peoples of which comparatively little was known until recent years.

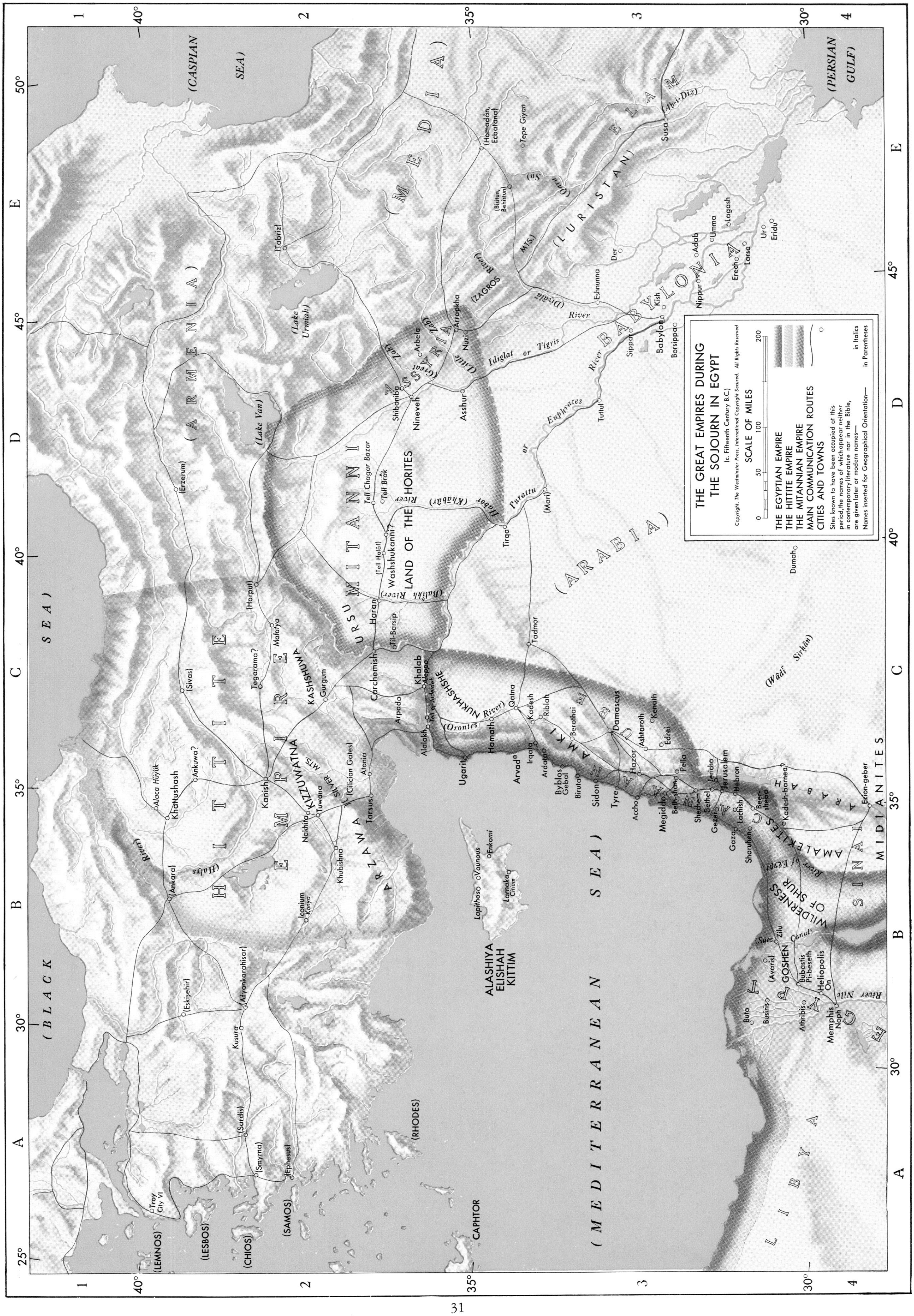
THE GREAT EMPIRES DURING
THE SOJOURN IN EGYPT
(c. Fifteenth Century B.C.)
Copyright, The Westminster Press, International Copyright Secured. All Rights Reserved
SCALE OF MILES
0 50 100 200
THE EGYPTIAN EMPIRE
THE HITTITE EMPIRE
THE MITANNIAN EMPIRE
MAIN COMMUNICATION ROUTES
CITIES AND TOWNS
Sites known to have been occupied at this period the names of which appear neither in contemporary literature nor in the Bible, are given later or modern names— in Italics
Names inserted for Geographical Orientation— in Parentheses
(BLACK SEA)
(CASPIAN SEA)
(PERSIAN GULF)
(MEDITERRANEAN SEA)
HITTITE EMPIRE
URSU MITANNI
LAND OF THE HORITES
ASSYRIA
(MEDIA)
(ARMENIA)
ELAM
(LURISTAN)
BABYLONIA
(ARABIA)
EGYPT
(LIBYA)
SINAI
MIDIANITES
AMALEKITES
WILDERNESS OF SHUR
GOSHEN
KIZZUWATNA
KASHSHUWA
ARZAWA
NUKHASHSHE
AMKI
CANAAN
EDOM
ARABAH
ALASHIYA
ELISHAH
KITTIM
CAPHTOR
(RHODES)
(LEMNOS)
(LESBOS)
(CHIOS)
(SAMOS)
Troy City VI
(Smyrna)
(Ephesus)
(Sardis)
Kusura
(Eskişehir)
(Afyonkarahisar)
Iconium Konya
(Ankara)
(Halys) River
Khattushash
Alaca Hüyük
Ankuwa?
Kanish
Nakhita
Tuwana
Khubishna
Tarsus
Atania
(Cilician Gates)
TAURUS MTS.
(Sivas)
Tegarama?
Malatya
(Harput)
(Erzerum)
(Lake Van)
(Lake Urmiah)
(Tabriz)
Gurgum
Carchemish
Til-Barsip
Haran
Washshukanni?
(Tell Halaf)
(Tell Brak)
Tell Chagar Bazar
(Balikh River)
(Khabur) River
Habor
Tirqa
(Mari)
Puratta or Euphrates River
Shibaniba
Nineveh
Asshur
Arbela
Arrapkha
Nuzi
(Great Zab)
(Little Zab)
Idiglat or Tigris River
(ZAGROS MTS.)
(Diyala) River
Eshnunna
Der
(Bisitun, Behistun)
(Hamadan, Ecbatana)
Tepe Giyan
(Qara Su)
Susa
(Ab-i-Diz)
Sippar
Kish
Babylon
Borsippa
Nippur
Adab
Umma
Lagash
Erech
Larsa
Ur
Eridu
Tutul
Dumah
(Wadi Sirhan)
Tadmor
Arpad
Khalab Aleppo
Tell Atchana
Alalakh
(Orontes River)
Ugarit
Hamath
Qatna
Kadesh
Riblah
Arvad
Irqata
Ardata
Byblos Gebal
Biruta
Sidon
Tyre
Barathai
Damascus
Ashtaroth
Edrei
Kenath
Hazor
Accho
Megiddo
Beth-shan
Pella
Shechem
Bethel
Jericho
Jerusalem
Hebron
Gezer
Lachish
Gaza
Sharuhen
Beer-sheba
Kadesh-barnea
Ezion-geber
Enkomi
Vounous
Lapithos
Larnaka Citium
River of Egypt
(Suez Canal)
Zilu
(Avaris)
Bubastis Pi-beseth
Heliopolis On
Athribis
Busiris
Buto
Memphis Noph
Nile River
A B C D E
1 2 3 4
25° 30° 35° 40° 45° 50°

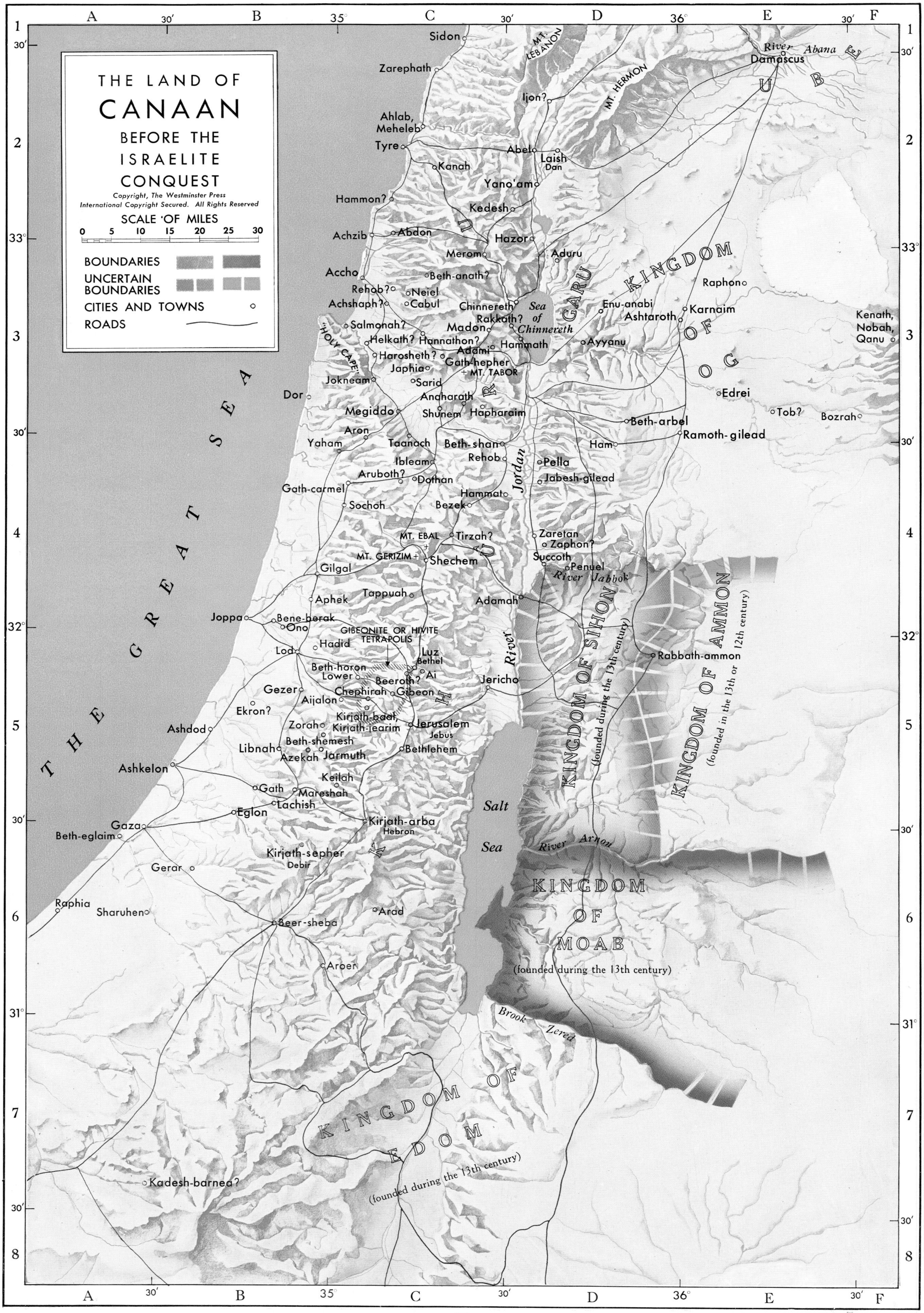
THE LAND OF
CANAAN
BEFORE THE
ISRAELITE
CONQUEST
Copyright, The Westminster Press
International Copyright Secured. All Rights Reserved
SCALE OF MILES
0 5 10 15 20 25 30
BOUNDARIES
UNCERTAIN BOUNDARIES
CITIES AND TOWNS
ROADS
THE GREAT SEA
Sidon
Zarephath
MT. LEBANON
MT. HERMON
River Abana
Damascus
Ijon?
Ahlab, Meheleb
Tyre
Abel
Laish
Dan
Kanah
Yano'am
Hammon?
Kedesh
Achzib
Abdon
Hazor
Merom
Aduru
Accho
Beth-anath?
Rehob?
Neiel
Achshaph?
Cabul
Chinnereth
Sea of Chinnereth
Rakkath?
Madon
Hammath
Enu-anabi
Ashtaroth
Karnaim
Raphon
Ayyanu
Salmonah?
HOLY CAPE
Helkath?
Hannathon?
Adami
Harosheth?
Gath-hepher
MT. TABOR
Japhia
Sarid
Jokneam
Dor
Anaharath
Megiddo
Shunem
Hapharaim
Edrei
Tob?
Bozrah
Kenath, Nobah, Qanu
Beth-arbel
Ramoth-gilead
Aron
Yaham
Taanach
Beth-shan
Ham
Rehob
Pella
Ibleam
Aruboth?
Dothan
Jabesh-gilead
Jordan
Gath-carmel
Hammath
Sochoh
Bezek
MT. EBAL
Tirzah?
Zaretan
Zaphon?
MT. GERIZIM
Shechem
Succoth
Penuel
River Jabbok
Gilgal
Aphek
Tappuah
Adamah
Joppa
Bene-berak
Ono
GIBEONITE OR HIVITE TETRAPOLIS
Hadid
Lod
Luz
Bethel
Beth-horon Lower
Ai
Beeroth?
Rabbath-ammon
Gezer
Chephirah
Gibeon
Jericho
River
Aijalon
Ekron?
Kirjath-baal, Kirjath-jearim
Jerusalem
Jebus
Ashdod
Zorah
Beth-shemesh
Bethlehem
Libnah
Azekah
Jarmuth
Ashkelon
Keilah
Gath
Mareshah
Lachish
Salt Sea
Eglon
Gaza
Kirjath-arba
Hebron
Beth-eglaim
Kirjath-sepher
Debir
River Arnon
Gerar
Raphia
Sharuhen
Arad
Beer-sheba
Aroer
KINGDOM OF OG
GARU
KINGDOM OF SIHON
(founded during the 13th century)
KINGDOM OF AMMON
(founded in the 13th or 12th century)
KINGDOM OF MOAB
(founded during the 13th century)
Brook Zered
KINGDOM OF EDOM
(founded during the 13th century)
Kadesh-barnea?

FIG. 18. The Canaanite city of Tunip in Syria being stormed by the Egyptian army. The Egyptian artist shows the Canaanite defenders at the moment of surrender. Around the fortress is a dry moat; but the attackers, protected by the formidable Egyptian bowmen, have succeeded in placing ladders against the battlements and in gaining access to the first parapet, where an Egyptian soldier is blowing a trumpet as a signal that the battle is over. At the top the defenders have laid down their arms and raised their hands beseeching mercy. Note that the Canaanites are distinguished from the Egyptians by their long hair and beards. Such Egyptian battle reliefs indicate the appearance of Canaanite fortresses and the manner in which they were attacked. (From the temple of Rameses III at *Medînet Habu* in Egypt.)

THE LAND OF CANAAN BEFORE THE ISRAELITE CONQUEST

PLATE IV

CANAAN" was the name by which the original inhabitants of Syria-Palestine designated their territory. In Gen. 10: 15–19 the name "Canaanite" is defined as including the pre-Israelite inhabitants from Gaza on the south to Arvad and Hamath on the north (Plate III, B-C 3). The accuracy of this definition is vouched for by the Canaanites themselves, who used this name for their land as early as the fourteenth century B.C. It originated from one of the most celebrated industries of ancient times—the Canaanite manufacture of purple dye; for in all probability its original meaning was "Land of the Purple." Good dyes for clothing were difficult to obtain, but Canaanites in Syria discovered the murex shellfish, which was native to the eastern Mediterranean coast, and from it obtained a deep crimson color which became the most famous and coveted textile dye of the ancient world. Since it was very expensive, only the wealthy could purchase it, and robes of this color became a mark of high rank—whence the familiar phrases "born to the purple" and "promoted to the purple." When the Greeks became acquainted with the Canaanites, they called them "Phoenicians" and their land "Phoenicia" from the Greek word meaning "purple." Historically, geographically, and culturally, then, the terms "Canaanite" and "Phoenician" mean precisely the same thing.

THE IMPORTANCE OF THE CANAANITES

From an early time the Canaanites played a very important role in the history of civilization. By 3000 B.C. important cities like Jerusalem (C-5), Ai (C-5), Jericho (C-5), Gezer (B-5), Megiddo (C-3), Beth-shan (C-4), Beth-yerah (XVIII, D-3), Byblos (III, C-3), and Hamath (III, C-3) were already in existence. During the subsequent two thousand years the inhabitants of these and other cities formed the bridge between the great centers of civilization on the Euphrates and the Nile, across which moved not only the currents of war and politics but also ideas, techniques, literature, art, music, religion, and science. Thus when Greece after the ninth century B.C. began its steady climb to the great age of Socrates and Plato, she found among the Canaanites ready teachers in many rudiments of civilized living. From them she borrowed the alphabet and passed it on to us; and today practically all literate people on the globe (except for the Japanese and Chinese) use some modified form of the Canaanite or Phoenician alphabet. Even our word "Bible" is to be traced back to Canaan, for the Greeks learned so much about writing and writing materials from the Canaanites that their word for "book" (*biblion*, whence "Bible") was derived from the name of the Syrian city, Byblos (III, C-3).

By 1200 B.C. a disaster had overtaken the Canaanites. The Israelites had deprived them of most of Palestine, and shortly thereafter Syrians (Aramaeans) took the hinterland of Syria east of Mt. Lebanon. Now confined to the coast of northern Palestine and southern Syria they took to the sea and became one of the greatest sea-trading people of history, founding commercial colonies on the shores and islands of the Mediterranean as far west as Spain. One of the best descriptions of this activity is to be found in Ezek., ch. 27, in which the extensive trade by sea and also by land is described.

It was inevitable that such an energetic people should exert considerable influence upon Israel. Excavations in Israelite towns show that the Hebrews imitated Canaanite dishes, jugs, cooking pots, weapons, jewelry, and the like. From the Canaanites Israel borrowed the alphabet with which the Old Testament is written. A large part of the Old Testament is in poetry and some of the poetry is in particular styles now known to have been borrowed from the Canaanites. The Canaanites excelled in and were famous for their music, and we now know that Israel borrowed or imitated their instruments and learned from them musical arts which were used in Temple worship. Solomon had a business agreement with Hiram of Tyre and hired from him the services of trained Canaanite artists and architects to direct his great building program, of which the Temple in Jerusalem is the best-known example (I Kings, ch. 5–7). Jezebel, before marrying Ahab of Israel, was a princess of Sidon (I Kings 16:31); and we hear of Israelite housewives selling homemade linen clothes to the Canaanites (Prov. 31:24, R.V. marg.), of Canaanite businessmen in a quarter in Jerusalem (Zeph. 1:11), of the barter of wheat, oil, honey, and balm for Canaanite luxuries (Ezek. 27:17). Even the religious life of Israel was affected by the pagan religion of Canaan, and many of the common people fell into idolatry by this means (Judg., ch. 2; I Kings 19:18; etc.). Canaanite civilization had many bad features, but it also possessed much that was good to which Israel was indebted.

LOCATION OF CANAANITE CITIES

One of the ways in which geography influenced the history of the Canaanites is to be seen in the fact that politically they never were a united people. The country of Palestine and Syria is so cut by mountains, rivers, and valleys that local differences had a tendency to be emphasized, and a strong Canaanite state or empire was never formed. Instead, before the conquest of Palestine by Israel, the country was split up among numerous city-states. Each of the larger cities tried to control as much of the territory around it as possible. Each was ruled by a king, and each king was independent of the others. In The Book of Joshua a number of these city-states and their kings are mentioned (see especially chs. 10 to 12). Five of them banded together against Joshua, but were defeated in the Valley of Aijalon (IX, D-E 5). They were Jerusalem (C-5), Hebron (of which the old name was Kirjath-arba, Josh. 15:13, C-5), Jarmuth (B-5), Lachish (B-5), and Eglon (B-5). Other important city-states were Kirjath-sepher or Debir (B-6), Libnah (B-5), Gezer (B-5), Luz or Bethel (C-5), Jericho (C-5), Shechem (C-4), Dor (B-3), Megiddo (C-3), Beth-shan (C-4), Pella (D-4), Hazor (D 2), Kedesh (D-2), Yano'am (D-2), Tyre (C-2), Sidon (C-1), and Damascus (E-1).

The distribution of these Canaanite royal cities should be noted. Few of them are located in the central hill country. Apart from Kirjath-arba (Hebron), Jerusalem, Luz (Bethel), and Shechem, the most important are located in the Judaean Lowlands or Shephelah (I, B-C 5–6 and p. 19), along the coast, or in the valleys of Jezreel (Plate I, C-3) and the Jordan. In other words, the centers of Canaanite civilization were largely in the plains and not in the hill country. In fact, before the conquest of Canaan by Israel the latter was sparsely populated. In all probability this hill country was thickly wooded with areas where grazing was possible for cattle, sheep, and goats. The Patriarchs wandered up and down the central ridge with their flocks and herds; and the men of the Joseph tribes (Ephraim and Manasseh) were told by Joshua to make room for themselves by clearing the forest (Josh. 17:15).

It was precisely in this region and in the thinly populated Transjordan that the Hebrews secured their first foothold in Canaanite territory. Unequipped as the Israelite invaders were for siege operations, we are not surprised that at first they were unable to capture such fortified cities as Dor, Megiddo, Beth-shan, and Gezer (Judg. 1:27 ff.). Fighting on foot with no weapons but bows, slings, stones, staves, and a few swords and spears, they would have been weak in pitched battles in the open plains where formidable chariots could maneuver. Thus, we are told, Judah "could not drive out the inhabitants of the valley, because they had chariots of iron" (Judg. 1:19). It is interesting to hear Syrian (Aramean) enemies of Israel at a later period discuss this weakness and strength of Israelite tactics. The God of the Israelites, they said, "is a god of the hills; therefore they are stronger than we: but let us fight against them in the plain, and surely we shall be stronger than they" (I Kings 20:23).

POLITICS IN CANAAN BEFORE THE CONQUEST

From about 1550 to 1200 B.C. Palestine was a province of the Egyptian empire (Plate III), except for occasional brief rebellions. Gaza (A-6) and Joppa (B-4) were two of the main provincial administrative centers. Other cities were governed by the local kings whose work and interests were unmolested by the Egyptian administration as long as they paid their taxes or tribute and provided their share of laborers for Egyptian royal projects. The country was thus governed by a double administration. On the one hand there were the local rulers, called "governors" in correspondence with the Egyptian state department; and on the other there were Egyptian commissioners, called "inspectors." The native rulers were allowed to have armed forces, consisting of chariots, owned and operated by the aristocracy, and footmen drawn from the peasant classes of the society. With these forces the Canaanite kings could war with one another as they wished, provided that such conflicts did not reach proportions of sufficient size to endanger the steady flow of royal taxes to Egypt. The Egyptian commissioners levied and raised the taxes and directed the compulsory labor groups in work on roads, in the Valley of Jezreel (I, C-3) where wheat was grown for the Royal Court, in the forest preserves of Mt. Lebanon, and elsewhere. Troops were at their disposal, composed

FIG. 19. The Pharaoh Amenophis IV or Akhnaton (c. 1370–1353 B.C.), a remarkable personage, who was intensely interested in religion. He was the first clear monotheist of history, worshiping the Aton, the personification of the sun disk. In his palace at Akhetaton (*Tell el-Amarna*) were found a large group of letters which form our most important source of information about politics in Canaan during the period preceding the Israelite Conquest. The Egyptian Pharaohs were believed by their people to be gods; and the greatness of the artist of this statue is to be seen in his portrayal in stone of the quiet, serene nobility which is above and beyond the turmoil of this world.

FIG. 20. A reproduction of the bust of Queen Nofretete, wife of Akhnaton. This remarkable portrait was found in the studio of the royal sculptor at *Tell el-Amarna*, and is one of the best known and most beautiful objects of art found in Egypt. Such works as this and Fig. 19 illustrate the high cultural level and refinement of the Egyptians, and help us to understand the sense of superiority which they bore toward all foreigners, particularly the Asiatics. Cf. Gen. 46:34, "For every shepherd is an abomination unto the Egyptians."

of slaves and mercenaries from Cush (Nubia; II, E-4), the Mediterranean islands (especially Crete), and local Bedouin or nomads, supported by a few Egyptians soldiers. As a result of repeated revolts, Egyptian fortresses were built in various parts of the country, one of which has been excavated at Beth-shan (C-4). It was first erected about 1450 B.C., and was rebuilt several times before the decline of Egyptian power. Unhappily for the country, the Egyptian bureaucracy was notoriously corrupt and the Egyptian troops frequently failed to receive their wages or proper maintenance, with the result that they often plundered the local villages and contributed to the general instability of the age.

Under strong Egyptian Pharaohs this double system of administration probably operated in a satisfactory manner; but under weak rulers, corruption of officials, local rivalry and warfare between the Canaanite kings, and predatory operations of Egyptian troops increased to such an extent that the political situation was little short of chaos. Our most important source of information about Canaan during this age is a portion of the archives of the Egyptian foreign office found in the palace of the Pharaoh Amenophis IV, also named Akhnaton (c. 1370-1353, Fig. 19), at the modern *Tell el-Amarna* in Egypt (V, B-6). This king was far more interested in religious matters (he was the first clear monotheist whom we know in history) than he was in the military and administrative affairs of the empire, and the letters from the Canaanite kings which were found in his archives bear witness to the disorder and confusion existing in Canaan. Numerous kings were actively engaged in extending their domains at the expense of their neighbors. Each accuses others of disloyalty and rebellion; yet those accused write to profess their utter devotion to the crown and denounce their enemies as slanderers. The letters so abound with accusations and counteraccusations that it is difficult to discover when the truth is being told. Indeed, one gets the impression that all parties involved are indulging in an intricate game of political and military maneuvering, each with the express purpose of "feathering his own nest," though moving adroitly so that the Egyptian court may not consider him disloyal.

One of the most reviled of the Canaanite kings of the Palestine area was Lab'aya, who controlled a large section of the hill country from his center at Shechem (C-4). He and his sons for a considerable period of time terrorized their neighbors in every direction. Yet in letters to the Pharaoh he humbly protested his innocence of "sin" and rebellion. His father and his grandfather before him were loyal servants of the king, and so is he! He says further that he had to fight to protect himself against his enemies, and, quoting an old proverb, he adds: "If ants are smitten, they do not receive [the smiting passively], but they bite the hand of the man who smites them!" (Cf. Prov. 6:6; 30:25.) The king of Megiddo (C-3), however, was apparently ordered to capture Lab'aya and send him to Egypt. This he did and turned him over to the king of Accho (C-3), so that the latter could send him to Egypt by sea. Instead, the king of Accho finally freed him after being bribed to do so. Lab'aya was unable to reach home, however, before being murdered by his enemies.

In southern Palestine the main city-states of this period were Gezer (B-5), Lachish (B-5), Jerusalem (C-5), and Hebron-Keilah (C-5); and these four states apparently met at a point near Beth-shemesh or Jarmuth (B-5). Over a hundred years later, when Israelites were engaged in the conquest of this area, the number had increased to nine (Josh., ch. 10); and in addition Jericho, Luz (Bethel), and the four Hivite cities (Gibeon, Beeroth, Chephirah, and Kirjath-baal; C-5) were under separate rulers. Thus between about 1375 and 1250 B.C. an increase in the number of these city-states brought on a decrease in their power; and this undoubtedly aided Israel in her conquest.

Among the troublemakers of the early fourteenth century were a people who are called *'Apiru*. Many of them appear to have been mercenary or slave troops in the employ of the Canaanite kings. Several scholars in the past have assumed that they were new invaders, who in some way are to be identified with either the Patriarchal or Mosaic invasions of Israel. It is now doubtful, however, that the Amarna letters can be used to indicate new invasions. The *'Apiru* were a people already in the land. In all probability their name refers, not to a special race, but to any group in a given country which did not adhere to the customs of the existing legal community. They were thus the "lawless" ones, who were usually foreigners.

The words *Khabiru* and *Hebrew* seem to come from the same root and are somehow related. It is interesting to note that the great majority of the references to the word *Hebrew* in the Old Testament belong to the period of the Patriarchs and of the Sojourn in Egypt. The term is usually used when an Egyptian speaks of an Israelite, or when an Israelite identifies himself to an Egyptian (cf. Gen. 39:17; 40:15). It is thus probable that the word *Hebrew* referred originally to a much larger group than Israel alone. The latter were "Hebrews," but many other seminomadic peoples were designated originally by the same name. The term was confined to Israelites at a very much later time. On the other hand, it is quite possible that some of the *Khabiru* mentioned in the Amarna tablets, especially those associated with Lab'aya in the Shechem area, may have been related to the Israelites in Egypt, and later may have become members of the Israelite nation (see p. 39).

FIG. 21. A bronze figure representing the Canaanite god Baal, found at Ugarit in northern Syria. Idols such as these were the "graven and molten images" of the Old Testament. Most of them were cast in copper or bronze, and then "graven." Frequently their helmets and short skirts were made of gold leaf (cf. Hab. 2:19; Isa. 40:19; Jer. 10:14).

THE PEOPLE OF CANAAN

After 1600 B.C. the population of Canaan became increasingly mixed. When Israel entered the country under Joshua, numerous groups were encountered which are mentioned in the Old Testament. Joshua 9:1, for example, mentions the Hittite, the Amorite, the Canaanite, the Perizzite, the Hivite, and the Jebusite. As we have noted, the Canaanites were the original inhabitants of the country. The Jebusites were possibly Canaanites who lived in the City of Jebus, another name for Jerusalem (Josh. 18:28; Judg. 19:10). The Hittites were from Asia Minor where a great state was in existence at this time (Plate III, and pp. 29 f.). The Amorites were survivors of a great invasion of peoples from the Arabian Desert about 2000 B.C. (Plate II and pp. 24 f.). The Hivites were probably the same as the Horites; a large group of the latter appear to have been settled in Edom or Seir (Gen. 36:20; Deut. 2:12). Their homeland was in northern Mesopotamia, in the country of Mitanni which was a powerful state during the fifteenth and fourteenth centuries before it was conquered by the Hittites about 1370 and before its final subjugation by the Assyrians a century later (Plate III and pp. 29 f.). In the days of Joshua the Hivites were in possession of four federated cities northwest of Jerusalem: Gibeon, Beeroth, Chephirah, and Kirjath-baal (C-5; Josh. 9:17). They avoided annihilation by obtaining a treaty or covenant with Joshua through trickery (Josh., ch. 9). The Perizzites were a people about whom we know nothing. The Girgashites (Josh. 3:10; 24:11) are equally obscure.

On Plate IV are to be seen the five kingdoms which Israel found east of the Jordan and the Dead Sea (Num. 20:14 ff.; Deut., chs. 2; 3). To the north was the Kingdom of Og, a giant of a man whose bedstead was on exhibition in Rabbath-ammon (D-5) for a long time after his death (Deut. 3:11). The origin of this state is not known; but the very existence of such kingdoms as these in Transjordan at a time when the city-state system was in vogue in western Palestine suggests that a new type of life and a new people have invaded this area. In the Amarna period, correspondence from the city of Pella (D-4) indicates that about 1375 B.C. the northern area of Transjordan, where the Kingdom of Og was later established, was still organized in city-states. One of Og's capitals, Ashtaroth (E-3; Deut. 1:4; Josh. 12:4), was at that time ruled by a man named Ayyab (an early spelling of the name "Job"). It is thus evident that the kingdom ruled by Og was established sometime after this period. An intensive archaeological survey of Transjordan carried out during the years 1932–1943 has revealed that the cities in the region to the south of the River Jabbok (D-4) in the territory controlled by the Amorite state of King Sihon, and by the kingdoms of Ammon, Moab, and Edom, were not founded before the thirteenth or twelfth centuries. Edom and Moab thus had barely been established when the Israelites from Egypt appeared in their area (see pp. 39 f.). The latter avoided conflict with them; but in the territory controlled by Sihon and Og, the tribes of Reuben, Gad, and half-Manasseh established themselves (Plate VI). The origin of the Ammonites, Moabites, and Edomites is unknown except that they were related to Israel: Edom through Esau (Gen., ch. 36) and Ammon and Moab through Lot (Gen. 19:30–38).

The establishment of these kingdoms in Transjordan and the gradual weakening of the power of the old city-states in central and southern Palestine might lead us to suppose that the energy and power of Canaanite civilization was dwindling by the thirteenth century, when Israel appeared on the scene from Egypt. Excavations in such cities as Kirjath-sepher (B-6), Lachish (B-5), Beth-shemesh (B-5), Gezer (B-5), Bethel (C-5), Jericho (C-5), Megiddo (C-3), and Beth-shan (C-4) indicate that this was precisely the case. From the sixteenth to the end of the thirteenth century a gradual deterioration in the arts and crafts can be observed. Reasons for this decline are not difficult to discover. Certainly the oppressive Egyptian taxation and corrupt administration made life difficult for the Canaanites. In addition, the system of government which fostered the city-state system, permitting and perhaps even encouraging continual warfare and bickering between the cities, would drain the energy and vitality from any people. The social organization of Canaanite society was likewise unhealthy. It was a feudal system with a king and an aristocracy of partly foreign "chariot-warriors" at the top, while at the bottom was a lower class of serfs and slaves. An independent and energetic middle class was nonexistent. This situation of affairs is illustrated by excavations in Canaanite cities. The chief building in the typical city is the palace of the local king, while around it is a maze of rooms and huts which once housed the lower class. Enclosing the city were great fortification walls, with protecting towers and well-guarded gates. These fortifications are so strong and often so elaborate that they could have been built only by a strongly centralized government which had at its disposal a large supply of inexpensive labor. The towns of the Canaanite kinglets were thus akin to great castles. They reflect the unsettled conditions of a country torn by constant internal warfare, which made the erection of such structures a necessity.

THE RELIGION OF CANAAN

Still another factor which may have hindered the development of Canaanite civilization was the extremely low level of its religion. While it is difficult to tell just what influence Canaanite religion had on community life, its barbarous character should at least be pointed out. As in other countries, many gods were believed to exist. The father of the gods was named El. He was "the father of man" as well as of gods, "the father of years," and "creator of creatures." One of his epithets was "bull," with which he was likened to a bull in a herd of cows and calves. He was believed to have a wife named Asherah (as her name is spelled in the Old Testament; e.g., I Kings 18:19), who was supposed to have borne him a sizable family, composed of some seventy gods and goddesses. Chief among the offspring, as son or grandson, was Hadad, whom the people called familiarly Baal ("Lord"). Baal was the personification of those forces in nature which produce rain and vegetation. He was the lord of heaven and earth, whose kingdom was "eternal, to all generations." In northern Syria his wife was believed to be Anath, though in Palestine later another goddess named Ashtoreth (Greek, Astarte) was his wife. In any event both goddesses were the personifications of love and fertility. Anath was also a goddess who loved war. One of her bloody adventures is described in a Canaanite poem. Deciding on a massacre, she smote and slew from seacoast (west) to sunrise. Filling her temple with men, she barred the doors and hurled at them chairs, tables, and footstools. Soon she waded in blood up to her knees—nay, up to her neck. "Her liver swelled with laughter; her heart was full of joy." She then washed her hands in gore and proceeded to other occupations! Other gods were Mot (Death), Baal's enemy; Resheph, the god of pestilence and lord of the underworld; Shulman or Shalim, the god who brings health; Koshar (or Kothar), the god of arts and crafts including music; et cetera.

The various stories told about these gods and goddesses (i.e., the mythology) were actually means of explaining how the natural forces of the world operate. Chief among them was the saga about Baal (Rain and Vegetation) being murdered each spring by Mot (Death) and coming to life again in the fall. Thus the cycle of climate in Canaan (dry, rainless summers and rainy winters) was explained. The amazing thing about the gods, as they were conceived in Canaan, is that they had no moral character whatsoever. In fact, their conduct was on a much lower level than that of society as a whole, if we can judge from ancient codes of law. Certainly the brutality of the mythology is far worse than anywhere else in the Near East at that time. Worship of these gods carried with it some of the most demoralizing practices then in existence. Among them were child sacrifice, a practice long since discarded in Egypt and Babylonia, sacred prostitution, and snake-worship on a scale unknown among other peoples. It is difficult to see how a religion of such debasing character could have had any stabilizing or vitalizing effect whatsoever upon the civilization. Indeed, one would expect just the opposite to have been the case.

We have thus seen that when Israel under Joshua entered Palestine during the thirteenth century B.C., Canaanite civilization was weak and decaying. It was small loss to the world when in parts of the Palestinian hill country it was virtually annihilated. The purity and righteous holiness of the God of Israel were now to be demonstrated against this background of pagan and immoral religion. The intransigence and hostility of the religious leaders of Israel toward the people and religion of Canaan is thus to be seen in its true perspective. There could be no compromise between Jehovah and Baal.

FIG. 22. Asiatic captives making bricks in an Egyptian brickyard, as the Israelites were forced to do during their oppression. At the top left water is drawn from a pool and in the center the clay is mixed. At the top right a molder shapes the clay in a rectangular mold while an overseer sits watching. Near the pool another man lays the completed bricks out to dry in the sun.

THE EXODUS FROM EGYPT

PLATE V

AT THE beginning of Israel's history as a nation there occurred the stirring events of the oppression in Egypt, the Exodus, the organization of the people into a covenant nation at Mount Sinai, and the conquest of Canaan. Years of study, exploration, and excavation have been spent in the attempt to solve the historical and geographical problems which these events present. As a result of the work of the last twenty years in particular, it is possible to reconstruct the history and geography involved with more certainty and clarity than ever before.

THE OPPRESSION

The book of Exodus opens near the end of the four-hundred-year sojourn of Israel in Egypt. At that time "there arose a new king over Egypt, who knew not Joseph," and who, no doubt because he desired cheap labor for his elaborate construction plans, forced the Hebrews to work as slaves on two "store-cities," Pithom and Raamses (Ex. 1:11). From a number of references outside the Bible we know that on the borders of every settled country in the Near East were groups of nomads who often worked in various capacities for the wealthy, as servants and slaves, scribes, soldiers, laborers, et cetera. Such a group were the Hebrews in Goshen (Plate V, C-D 3), and the unscrupulous Pharaoh found them an easy prey for exploitation.

After many years of debate, it now appears that the two cities which the Hebrews built under Egyptian coercion and direction have been located. Pithom (V, C-3) is probably to be identified with an ancient site in the valley which connects the Nile and Lake Timsâh. (When first excavated in 1905-1906, it was thought that this site was Raamses, but the latter must now be located elsewhere.) The ruins were found to have been those of an old town which had been beautified and furnished with a temple by the great builder, Rameses II (1290–1224 B.C.). No earlier royal construction was found, so the Israelites probably worked there in his day.

More definite is the evidence from the city of Raamses (or Rameses, Ex. 12:37). This was obviously the same as the great capital of Egypt in the Delta during the Nineteenth Dynasty (c. 1310–1200), named the "House of Rameses." The location of this site is now best fixed at Tanis (V, C-3), the city chosen also by the Hyksos as their capital (see p. 28). While the attempt has recently been made to fix it at modern *Qanṭîr* a few miles away (V, C-3), the weight of the evidence still favors Tanis. After the expulsion of the Hyksos and the destruction of Avaris about 1550 B.C., the Pharaohs again made Thebes (II, E-3) in Upper Egypt their capital. Judging from both the excavations and the ancient inscriptions they did no royal building in the Delta. In the story of Moses, however, the court of the Pharaoh is not far from the land of Goshen, where the Hebrews lived. This immediately brings us to the Nineteenth Dynasty when the capital was moved to the Delta, in order that the Royal Court might be in better position to reconquer and control the lost Asiatic Empire. The new city, evidently built in part at least with Hebrew slave labor, was celebrated for its beauty. Court poets sang that "none resembles it in its likeness to Thebes"; and the richness of the country around, known as "the land of Rameses," was a subject of frequent comment (cf. Gen. 47:11, where Israelite writers use the familiar name for the area in which Goshen was located, though it was not called by this name in Joseph's day).

This information, therefore, is important in fixing the approximate time when Moses lived. As will be shown later, Israel was in Palestine by the third quarter of the thirteenth century (1250-1225 B.C.), and if this be so, then the Pharaoh of the Oppression "who knew not Joseph" must have been Seti (or Sethos) I (1308–1290 B.C.), the king who began the work on the city of Rameses, according to a monument found at the site. The Pharaoh of the Exodus would then have been Rameses II (1290–1224 B.C.), a great builder who tried desperately to recover the lost glory of Egypt. After the nonaggression pact with the Hittites in 1270 B.C. (see p. 30), he became less active in Asiatic affairs and more and more concerned with the attempt to immortalize his name in Egypt by the vastness of his architectural enterprises.

We are not to think that the number of the Hebrews involved in the Exodus was so large that it caused a tremendous economic blow to Egypt. Even accounting for the provision of manna (a honeylike substance given off by an insect while it sucks the sap of tamarisk trees in Sinai), between two and six thousand people would appear to

FIG. 23. The traditional Mount Sinai where Moses received the Law and before which Israel encamped. The mountain in the center is *Râs eṣ-Ṣafṣâf*, the beginning of the range of which *Jebel Mûsā* is the chief peak. The precise spot where Moses received the Law, whether on *Râs eṣ-Ṣafṣâf* itself or on *Jebel Mûsā* is unknown. The small plain of *er-Râḥa* in the foreground is probably to be identified with the "desert of Sinai" in Ex. 19:2 and Num. 33:16.

be a reasonable figure. Numbers, chs. 1 and 26, contains census lists which state that the male population of the Hebrews in the wilderness was over 600,000, a figure which would mean a total of at least two or three million when women and children are included. Most Biblical scholars have assumed that these figures are completely unhistorical, but a saner view which has recently been gaining acceptance holds that they are the misplaced census records of the time of David. II Samuel, ch. 24, describes the one census of united Israel of which we know, and the lists in Numbers represent the population of Israel which we would expect at that time according to calculations from archaeological investigation. Numbers, chs. 1 and 26, might thus represent two different editions of the Davidic lists from which the title pages had been lost and which were later thought to come from the time of Moses. This explanation would avoid treating the figures as forgeries and at the same time would permit us to fix the approximate number involved in the Exodus from other sources of information which require a much more modest figure.

THE ROUTE OF THE EXODUS

After permission was finally secured for the Children of Israel and the "mixed multitude" that joined them (Ex. 12:38) to leave Egypt, the initial stages of the journey are described as follows:

> And the children of Israel journeyed from Rameses to Succoth [Ex. 12:37]. . . . And it came to pass, when Pharaoh had let the people go, that God led them not by the way of the land of the Philistines, although that was near. (For God said, Lest the people repent when they see war, and return to Egypt.) But God led the people around by the wilderness of the Reed Sea [not Red Sea; ch. 13:17, 18]. . . . And they set out from Succoth, and encamped in Etham on the edge of the wilderness [v. 20]. . . . And the Lord spake to Moses, saying, Speak to the children of Israel, that they turn back and encamp before Pihahiroth, between Migdol and the sea, before Baal-zephon. Before it ye shall encamp by the sea [ch. 14:1, 2].

At that point the Pharaoh sent a detachment of chariots after them, but they were delivered by the miraculous crossing of the sea when a strong wind backed up the waters.

Does this itinerary make geographical sense? Before the second quarter of this century it did not because of wrong or uncertain identifications. Now, however, the picture is clearer (see Plate v). Leaving Rameses-Tanis the Israelites or their leaders headed directly for the center of the area of Goshen at Succoth (modern *Tell el-Maskhûṭah*, formerly mistakenly identified with Pithom). Perhaps the reason was to gather together all Hebrews who wished to go and to leave Egypt by way of the *Wâdī Ṭumilât* in the area of Lake Timsâḥ. In any event, the decision was against going to Palestine by way of the well-traveled commercial and military route, here named "the way of the land of the Philistines." The long line of Egyptian fortifications along this route is known to us from an inscription of Pharaoh Seti I at Karnak. Instead the plan was to take a circuitous route "by the wilderness of the Reed Sea." This Reed or Marsh Sea can no longer be identified with the Red Sea. For one thing, the latter has no reeds in it; for another, the Reed Sea is mentioned in thirteenth-century Egyptian sources as a body of water near Rameses. Since the Suez Canal was constructed, the topography of this area seems to have changed somewhat, and at least one lake, Lake Balaḥ, has disappeared. The Reed Sea which the Israelites crossed was in this area, perhaps at a southern extension of the present Lake Menzaleh.

In Biblical times the Pharaohs guarded their eastern frontier with a string of fortresses, none of which can be located with any certainty with the exception of Zilu (Thel), guarding the border on the main highway to Canaan (v, D-3). The narrative of the crossing of the Sea suggests that the problem of Israel was precisely that of getting by these fortresses. After arriving at Succoth and then moving to the edge of the wilderness at the unknown site of Etham, Israel turned back northeastward and encamped "before Pihahiroth, between Migdol and the Sea, before Baal-zephon." Pihahiroth and Migdol are mentioned in Egyptian inscriptions but are not yet identified with certainty. During World War II a Phoenician letter was published which mentions the god "Baal-zephon and all the gods of Tahpanhes." The latter was located at modern *Tell Defneh* (Greek Daphne), and the letter proves that a temple of Baal-zephon existed there. The name in the Exodus story is probably a reference to the town that contained this temple (v, D-3).

There has been considerable debate as to where the Hebrews went after entering the wilderness, since Mount Sinai or Horeb (it was called by both names) has not been located with certainty. The Sinai peninsula is triangular in shape, 260 miles long and 150 miles wide at the north. Along the Mediterranean there is a sandy belt some 15 miles deep. To the south is a gravel and limestone plateau stretching some 150 miles. Below that is the apex of the peninsula with its mass of granite mountains, the highest of which rise some 8,000 feet above sea level. Among these mountains were the ancient copper and turquoise mines to which the Egyptians sent regular expeditions. Here also is the traditional site of Mount Sinai where Moses received the Law and bound the people together in a joint covenant with the Lord. The tradition that this is the Mount Sinai of Israel is at least fifteen hundred years old, and it is difficult to see how the tradition could have arisen if it did not have some historical basis. In addition, it is possible to point to several stations along the route to this area which correspond to those mentioned in the Bible, but it is not possible to do this for any other route through the peninsula. Further, if the tradition is correct, we should be able to understand the presence of the Midianites at Sinai, among whom was Moses' father-in-law, Jethro or Reuel (Ex. 2:16 ff.; 18:1 ff.). One Midianite clan was called the "Kenites," meaning "metal smiths" (cf. Num. 10:29 and Judg. 4:11). We may assume, therefore, that one of the occupations of the Midianites was copper mining and smelting, and their interest in the mines of Sinai would be obvious.

The attempt has been made to locate Mount Sinai in Arabia east of the Gulf of Aqabah, the homeland of Midian. Some extinct volcanoes exist there, and the "thunders and lightnings, and a thick cloud upon the mount" in Ex. 19:16 are interpreted as evidence of an active volcano. In this case the Hebrews would have journeyed across Sinai to Ezion-geber along the present Mohammedan pilgrim route to Mecca (v, D-F 4); but the stages of the journey as described in Exodus hardly fit this route.

On Plate v the stations of the Israelite journey which can be identified with the most probability along the traditional route have been designated. Among the first springs on the ancient road to the Sinai mines is *'Ain Ḥawârah*. This, therefore, is probably Marah, the first station of the Israelite journey which was reached after three waterless days in the wilderness (v, D-4; Ex. 15:22 ff.). The next oasis to the south is in the *Wâdī Gharandel*, which corresponds to the Biblical Elim where twelve springs and seventy palm trees are said to have existed (v, D-4; Ex. 16:1; Num. 33:9). The next stages of the journey took them along the Red Sea, and thence inland to the Wilderness of Sin and to Dophkah (Num. 33:10-12). The exact route at this point depends upon the location of Dophkah. From its etymological meaning in Hebrew we should judge that this name was probably connected with smelting operations. If so, then the best identification of the site is with the Egyptian mining center of *Serâbîṭ el-Khâdim* (v, E-5). The Wilderness of Sin would then be the plain along the edge of the Sinai plateau called *Debbet er-Ramleh*. From this point a series of valleys lead directly to *Jebel Mûsā* past Rephidim (*Wâdī Refâyid;* v, E-5). While various mountains in the neighborhood have been identified with the Biblical Mount Sinai, the most probable location is the range designated at v, F-5 (see Fig. 23), of which the chief peak is called *Jebel Mûsā*, "Mountain of Moses."

After spending a year at Mount Sinai, Israel left it and journeyed through the Wilderness of Paran (v, F-4; Num. 10:11, 12). None of the stations along the way which are listed in Num. 33:16-35 can be identified with any degree of certainty except Hazeroth (v, F-5) and Ezion-geber (v, G-4). From the latter the itinerary led to Kadesh-barnea in the Wilderness of Zin (v, F-3). Judging from the implications of the narrative as it now stands, the purpose of the Hebrews was to storm Canaan from the south. The pessimistic report of the spies (Num., ch. 13) and the defeat at Hormah (Num. 14:39 ff.) so weakened their morale, however, that they were forced to live in the area of Kadesh-barnea (for description see pp. 67 ff.) until the older generation had been replaced by a new one.

THE CONQUEST OF CANAAN

After considerable time had passed, Moses led the new generation of Israelites from Kadesh-barnea with the purpose of going through Transjordan to storm Canaan from the east instead of from the south (Num. 20:22 ff.). The exact route which was taken is somewhat obscure, partly because the location of Mount Hor is uncertain. Apparently they circled northward in order to descend into the Arabah (v, F-G 3-4). According to Deut. 2:1 ff. they continued south in the Arabah to Ezion-geber (v, G-4) in order to traverse the King's Highway (v, G 2-4, and Fig. 25), while Num., ch. 33, implies a northern route past Punon (v, G-3). In any event, the king of Edom refused permission for them to traverse his country, and no attempt was made to force the matter (Num. 20: 14 ff.). According to Num., ch. 33, Moses led the people northward in the Arabah past the mining center of Punon (see p. 69) and the spring at Oboth (v, G-3), crossing eastward at the northern border of Edom along the Brook Zered (v, G-3). Ije-abarim on the border of Moab (Num. 33:44) cannot be located with certainty at present, but there is no doubt that the itinerary as shown on Plate v is at least approximately correct.

Likewise unwilling to join battle with Moab, the people circled its territory to the east, and crossing the River Arnon they found themselves at the border of the Amorite Kingdom of Sihon (v, G 1-2 and IV, D 4-5; Num. 21:10 ff.). The latter was defeated in the battle of Jahaz (IX, I-6), the first great triumph of Israelite arms (Num. 21:21 ff.). Then followed the defeat of the giant king Og, whose kingdom north of the Jabbok had capitals at Edrei and Ashtaroth (IV, E-3; Num. 21:33 ff.) Thus ended the first phase of the conquest, with Israel in possession of the territory of Transjordan between Bashan and the River Arnon, the regions called Gilead and "the Plain" (Deut. 3:10).

The conquest of Western Palestine as led by Joshua is described as being effected in three stages: (1) Gaining a foothold in the central hill country through the capture of Jericho and Ai (v, G-2; Josh., chs. 2 to 8); (2) the Gibeonite alliance (see p. 36) and the battle of Gibeon, followed by the defeat of the Canaanite coalition and the campaign against the territory later occupied by Judah (Josh., chs. 9 to 10); and (3) a campaign in Galilee which gained territory, but unlike that in Judah destroyed no fortified cities except Hazor (IV, D-2; Josh., ch. 11).

This story of a unified assault on the whole land with spectacular success has long troubled scholars because the first chapter of The Book of Judges seems to present a different picture with the individual tribes bearing the responsibility for the subjugation of their respective territories. Scholars have been inclined to assume in the past that Judg., ch. 1, preserves primary data from the time of the conquest and that the land was subdued, not by a single unified campaign under Joshua, but by a series of struggles on the part of the individual tribes. Today, however, we find it necessary to take account of two different groups of archaeological data. One group suggests a major and violent disturbance during the thirteenth century which brought to an end several important Canaanite cities. The other group of data is from the period of the Judges during the twelfth and eleventh centuries. It indicates that this was one of the most disturbed times in the country's history. Every town thus far excavated was destroyed from one to four times during these centuries.

When we put the historical and archaeological data together, we seem forced to a conclusion somewhat as follows: There was a campaign of great violence and success during the thirteenth century. Its purpose was to destroy the existing Canaanite city-state system, weakening local power to such an extent that new settlement, at least in the hill country, became possible. The centuries that followed, however, record a continuous struggle with the inhabitants who still offered resistance, though major centers of power had been reduced, a struggle complicated by the Philistine and other invasions and by the remaining unconquered city-states, notably those of Megiddo and Jerusalem.

One of the curious features of the Joshua story is its silence with regard to a conquest of central Palestine, where the Joseph tribes, Ephraim and Manasseh, settled (see Plate VI). The capital of this region at that time was Shechem (IV, C-4), situated between Mount Ebal and Mount Gerizim, and known from excavations to have been an exceedingly strong city. While nothing is said about its capture, it was nevertheless deeply fixed in Israelite tradition; its area was the scene of the gathering of all the tribes for covenant ceremonies during the period of the conquest and at its end. Furthermore it was an early center of the northern Israelite tribes (see Deut., ch. 27;

FIG. 24. The small *Wâdī Qudeirât* in which was possibly located the site of Hazar-addar (Plate v, F-3 and p. 64). This valley is watered by the largest spring in the area of Kadesh-barnea. The neighboring spring, *'Ain Qedeis*, where Kadesh-barnea is located on Plate v is very small, and the Israelites during their long stay in this area probably made use of *'Ain Qudeirât* as well.

FIG. 25. A section of the King's Highway (Num. 20:17; 21:22) as it runs north along a valley to cross the Brook Zered in the background (Plate V, G 2-4). This was the old road through Transjordan used by the four invading kings in Gen., ch. 14. It is here so clearly marked because it was paved by the Romans and is still used. Today it is being constructed anew by the Government of Transjordan. Note the ruins of an ancient watchtower beside it.

Josh. 8: 30-35; and Josh., ch. 24). Most scholars are inclined to believe that in control of Shechem were Hebrews whom Joshua did not have to conquer, who had never been in Egypt or possibly had come out at an earlier time, but who nevertheless in Joshua's time entered into the Israelite covenant and accepted its traditions. For years afterwards at Shechem regular covenant ceremonies were celebrated.

The best-known story connected with the conquest is the stirring account of the fall of Jericho (V, G-2; Josh., ch. 6). After the excavations of John Garstang at the site between 1930 and 1936, it was believed that Jericho fell after a violent destruction sometime during the fourteenth century. Beginning in 1952, however, a new expedition began work on the site (see p. 114). A redating of the major architectural remains has occurred, with the resulting conclusion that very little remains on the site from the period between 1500 and 1200 B.C. The nature of the town or fort that existed there during the fourteenth and thirteenth centuries, is something we know little about, nor can we say much about the date of its capture by Joshua.

Any invaders of the hill country from the Jericho area would first be forced to seize a foothold in the region of Bethel and Ai, rather than around Jerusalem, because the valleys leading from the Jordan give easy access to the former, but not to the latter (cf. IX, G 5-6). Consequently, when Josh., chs. 7; 8, describes the capture of Ai, it is describing the first great victory over the Canaanites in the hill country. From excavations it is known that the city involved was not Ai, but rather the nearby Bethel (see p. 116), the ruins of which bear eloquent testimony to a violent destruction during the thirteenth century.

In the tenth chapter of Joshua the itinerary of the conquest of the southern hill country is described. After the defeat of the five Canaanite kings in the Valley of Aijalon (IX, D-E 5), Joshua turned south into the Shephelah or Lowlands (I, B 5-6), carefully avoiding the strong fortress of Gezer, which did not come into Israelite hands until the time of Solomon (V, F-2; IX, D-5; I Kings 9:16). He first captured Makkedah (Josh. 10:28), a city near Beth-shemesh and Azekah (IX, D-6) but one which cannot be located with certainty. Next, he took Libnah at the head of the Valley of Elah (where David was later to fight Goliath; V, F-2; IX, D-6). A small excavation was made at this site in 1898–1899, and while it was found to have been occupied during this period, the precise date of its fall to Israel was not determined. The next Canaanite royal city to the south of Libnah was Lachish (V, F-2; IX, D-7). From excavations this exceedingly strong fortress is known to have been violently destroyed about 1220 B.C., and the conflagration is certainly to be attributed to Israel (Josh. 10:31 ff.). Joshua then proceeded to Eglon, seven miles southwest of Lachish (V, F-2; IX, C-7). The evidence gained from excavations indicates that this city was also destroyed about the same age, though the date of its conflagration cannot be as precisely determined as that of Lachish.

Now in control of the most important fortresses guarding the passes to the later Judean capital at Hebron, Israel turned upon Hebron itself, presumably following the pass by Mareshah (see the road drawn on Plates IV and VI, B-C 5-6). When Hebron was captured, it was a simple matter to take the remaining frontier fortress of Debir (V, F-2; IX, D-8; Josh. 10:38, 39), the Canaanite name of which was Kirjath-sepher. Excavations at this site show that it too was violently destroyed at approximately the same period as Lachish.

One feature of Joshua's Judean campaign is the evidence of sound military strategy which it exhibits. In conquering Palestine, Israel did not waste her strength on the strongest military fortresses at Jerusalem and Gezer (see pp. 44, 112). The strategy employed was the same as that used by the Assyrians and Babylonians later on. That was to conquer first the string of fortresses in the Shephelah which guarded the approaches to the Judean hill country. After that was accomplished, the capture of the hill country was a comparatively simple operation.

We have no information about the Galilean campaign other than evidence from recent excavation at Hazor (IV, D-2) which suggests that this city too was destroyed during the thirteenth century. We may summarize our evidence for the date of Joshua's conquest, therefore, as follows: (1) As noted on p. 35, the city-state system of early fourteenth-century Canaan was not the same as it was in the time of Joshua. The Canaan described in The Book of Joshua is later than the *Tell el-Amarna* period of the early fourteenth century. (2) Explorations in Transjordan have shown that the kingdoms of Edom, Moab, and Ammon were not founded before the thirteenth century. Edom and Moab may have been established in their homelands as early as 1250 B.C. Ammon, however, may not have entered the scene until sometime later (c. 1200), inasmuch as she plays no role in the conquest narratives. (3) The Egyptian cities of Pithom and Rameses which Israel built for Pharaoh must have been constructed after c. 1308 B.C. (see above). (4) The destruction of Bethel, Lachish, Eglon, Debir, and Hazor during the thirteenth century can surely be attributed with some confidence to Joshua. Indeed, the evidence from Lachish and Debir brings us down to the latter part of the century for the completion of the Judean campaign. That Israel was in Palestine at that time is proved by an Egyptian monument of Pharaoh Merenptah (c. 1224-1216 B.C.), who claims to have defeated "the people of Israel" in Palestine during the fifth year of his reign. This event is not mentioned in the Old Testament; it certainly was of minor significance and without lasting effect, for the Egyptian control of Canaan was then very weak. The reference does show, however, that Israel was already established in her later home by 1220 B.C.

By way of conclusion it should be stated, however, that these historical questions must not obscure the central facts: namely, that at least some Israelites suffered slavery in Egypt, that they were freed in a wonderful deliverance, that they were led victoriously into the Promised Land after years of murmuring and faintheartedness, and that in these remarkable events the Israelites saw the hand of their God, a gracious God who had taken pity on their afflictions, and saved them for his providential purpose.

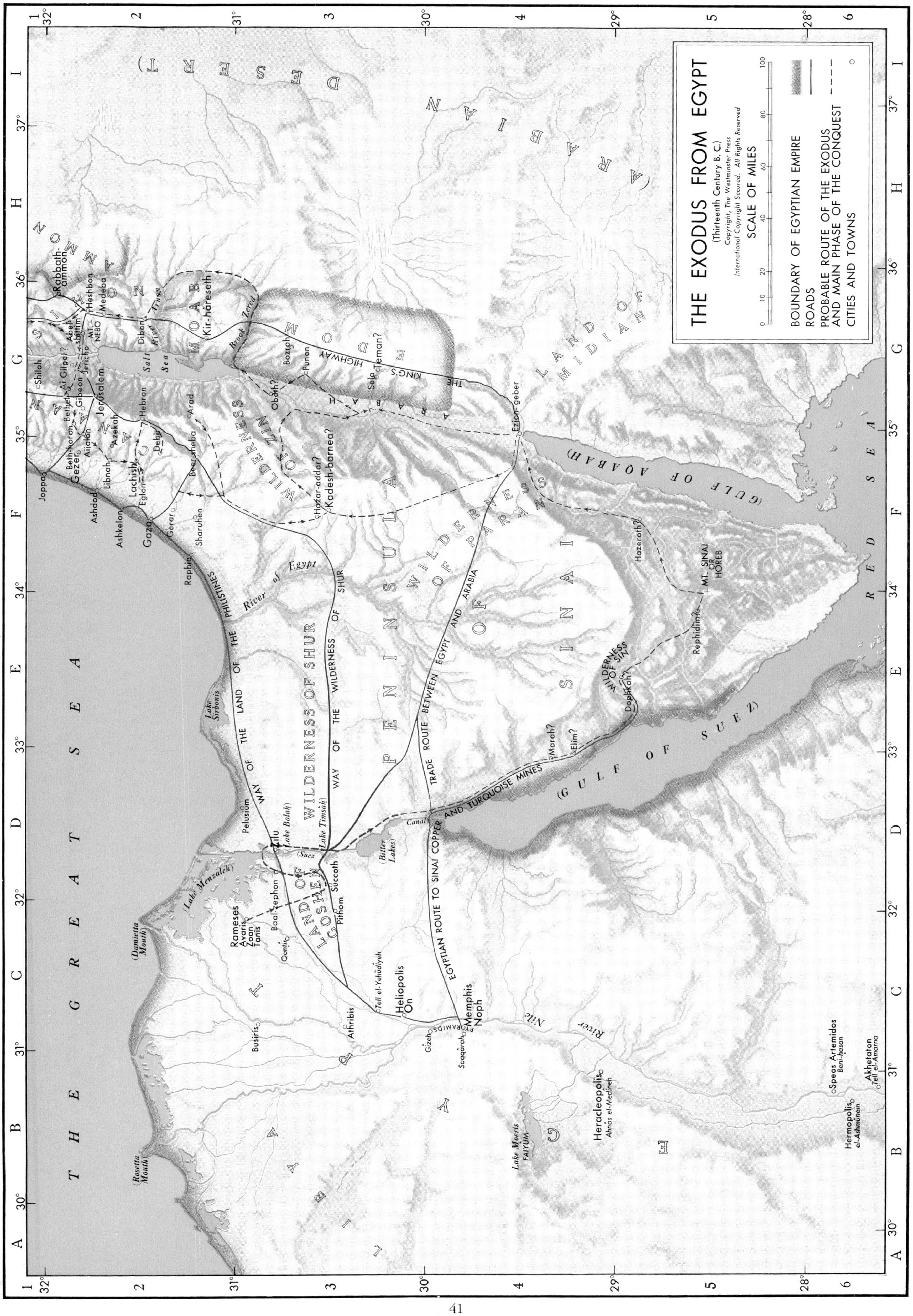
THE EXODUS FROM EGYPT
(Thirteenth Century B. C.)
Copyright, The Westminster Press
International Copyright Secured. All Rights Reserved
SCALE OF MILES
0 10 20 40 60 80 100
BOUNDARY OF EGYPTIAN EMPIRE
ROADS
PROBABLE ROUTE OF THE EXODUS AND MAIN PHASE OF THE CONQUEST
CITIES AND TOWNS
THE GREAT SEA
LIBYA
EGYPT
PENINSULA OF SINAI
ARABIAN DESERT
LAND OF MIDIAN
EDOM
MOAB
AMMON
WILDERNESS OF SHUR
WILDERNESS OF ZIN
WILDERNESS OF PARAN
WILDERNESS OF SIN
LAND OF GOSHEN
WAY OF THE LAND OF THE PHILISTINES
WAY OF THE WILDERNESS OF SHUR
TRADE ROUTE BETWEEN EGYPT AND ARABIA
EGYPTIAN ROUTE TO SINAI COPPER AND TURQUOISE MINES
THE KING'S HIGHWAY
ARABAH
GULF OF SUEZ
GULF OF AQABAH
RED SEA
River Nile
River of Egypt
Brook Zered
River Arnon
Salt Sea
Lake Menzaleh
Lake Sirbonis
Lake Balah
Lake Timsah
Bitter Lakes
Canal
Suez
Lake Moeris
FAIYUM
Damietta Mouth
Rosetta Mouth
Rameses
Avaris
Zoan
Tanis
Qantir
Baal-zephon
Zilu
Pelusium
Succoth
Pithom
Tell el-Yehudiyeh
Heliopolis
On
Memphis
Noph
PYRAMIDS
Saqqarah
Gizeh
Athribis
Busiris
Heracleopolis
Ahnas el-Medineh
Speos Artemidos
Beni-hasan
Hermopolis
el-Ashmunein
Akhetaton
Tell el-Amarna
Marah?
Elim?
Dophkah?
Rephidim?
MT. SINAI OR HOREB
Hazeroth?
Ezion-geber
Kadesh-barnea?
Hazar-addar?
Oboth?
Punon
Bozrah
Sela
Teman?
Kir-hareseth
Dibon
Medeba
MT. NEBO
Heshbon
Rabbath-ammon
Abel-shittim
Jericho
Ai
Gilgal?
Gibeon
Bethel
Shiloh
Jerusalem
Beth-horon
Aijalon
Azekah
Gezer
Libnah
Lachish
Eglon
Debir
Hebron
Arad
Beer-sheba
Sharuhen
Gerar
Gaza
Ashkelon
Ashdod
Joppa
Raphia
CANAAN
SIHON

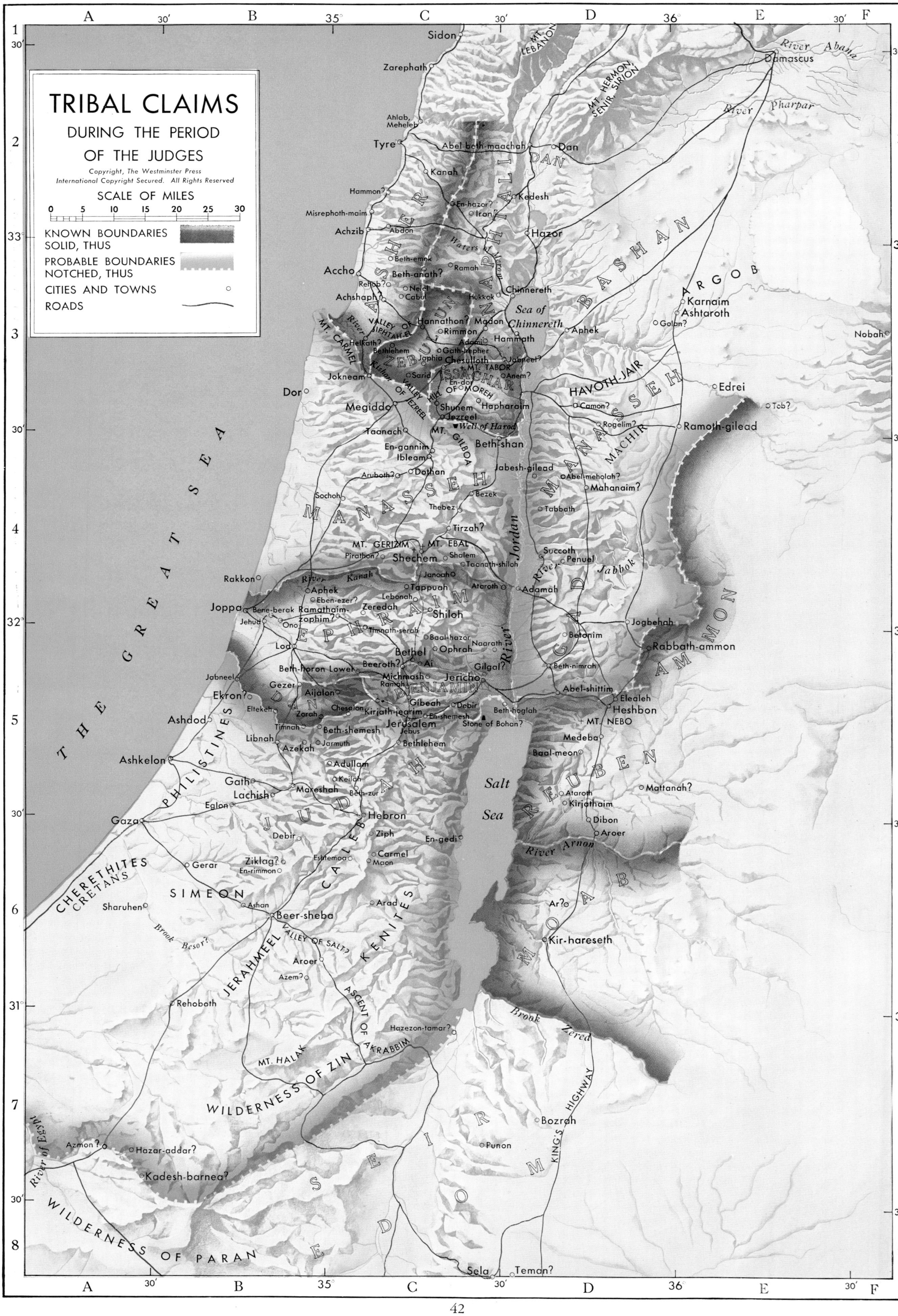
TRIBAL CLAIMS
DURING THE PERIOD
OF THE JUDGES
Copyright, The Westminster Press
International Copyright Secured. All Rights Reserved
SCALE OF MILES
0 5 10 15 20 25 30
KNOWN BOUNDARIES SOLID, THUS
PROBABLE BOUNDARIES NOTCHED, THUS
CITIES AND TOWNS
ROADS
THE GREAT SEA
ASHER
NAPHTALI
ZEBULUN
ISSACHAR
MANASSEH
EPHRAIM
BENJAMIN
DAN
JUDAH
SIMEON
PHILISTINES
CHERETHITES
CRETANS
JERAHMEEL
KENITES
CALEB
GAD
REUBEN
AMMON
MOAB
EDOM
SEIR
BASHAN
ARGOB
HAVOTH-JAIR
MACHIR
Sidon
Zarephath
Tyre
Dan
Kedesh
Hazor
Accho
Megiddo
Beth-shan
Shechem
Shiloh
Joppa
Bethel
Jericho
Jerusalem
Hebron
Gaza
Ashkelon
Ashdod
Beer-sheba
Kadesh-barnea?
Damascus
Ramoth-gilead
Rabbath-ammon
Heshbon
Dibon
Aroer
Kir-hareseth
Bozrah
Sela
Teman?
Salt Sea
Sea of Chinnereth
River Jordan
River Arnon
Brook Zered
Jabbok
WILDERNESS OF ZIN
WILDERNESS OF PARAN
KING'S HIGHWAY
MT. CARMEL
MT. TABOR
MT. GILBOA
MT. GERIZIM
MT. EBAL
MT. NEBO
MT. HERMON, SENIR, SIRION
MT. LEBANON

PALESTINE DURING THE PERIOD OF THE JUDGES

(c. 1200–1020 B.C.)

Plate VI

THE settlement of the Israelite tribes in their newly won territory is described in Josh., chs. 13 to 19. Israelite society was patriarchal in structure; that is, it was composed of families, each headed by a patriarchal head or father. A number of related families made up a clan, and a varying number of clans made up a tribe. During and at the conclusion of the conquest, the country was parceled out among the eleven tribes, while the tribe of Levi, which was to attend to religious matters, was distributed among the others by the allotment to it of specific towns (Josh., ch. 21). In each tribal area the land was further subdivided among the clans and families. The process by which the distribution east of the Jordan was effected is described as a drawing by lot. Reuben, Gad, and one half of Manasseh (of which the chief clan was Machir) were given the territory of Sihon and Og (Num., ch. 32; Josh., ch. 13). West of the Jordan the house of Joseph, composed of Ephraim and Manasseh, was settled first (Josh., chs. 16; 17), after which the rest of the country was divided at an assembly in Shiloh (Plate VI, C-4). The land thus allotted became the ancestral property of each family, and laws were made to protect the inheritance. The well-known story of Ahab and Naboth's vineyard makes it plain that not even the later kings of Israel had the right to confiscate family property. Naboth was quite within his legal rights when he exclaimed to King Ahab: "The Lord forbid it me, that I should give the inheritance of my fathers unto thee" (I Kings 21:3).

In recent years a great advance has been made in the accuracy with which the tribal boundaries can be traced. This is due primarily to the work of archaeologists in locating the places where the ancient towns once stood (see pp. 13, 14). On Plate VI the districts claimed by the tribes are shown as they can now be located.

THE SETTLEMENT OF TRANSJORDAN

South, east, and northeast of the Dead Sea were the kingdoms of Edom, Moab, and Ammon, which Israel made no attempt to conquer at this time. The plateau of Edom proper lay directly south of the Brook Zered (VI, D-7; see X, H-J 5-7), although the Arabah (X, G-H 5-6) and some of the wilderness west of it were probably also under Edomite control. Moab at this time was confined between the Brook Zered and the River Arnon, while Ammon lay east of the River Jabbok as the latter turned in a wide loop southward to the capital at Rabbath-ammon (VI, D-5). The tribes of Reuben and Gad were situated in the territory formerly ruled by King Sihon (cf. Plates IV and VI, D 4-5). The northern boundary of Reuben was the *Wâdī Hesbân*, a valley leading to the Jordan from Heshbon (VI, D-5). To the south Reuben bordered on Moab at the River Arnon. Gad extended from the *Wâdī Hesbân* to a point north of the River Jabbok near Mahanaim (VI, D-4), but we cannot establish the boundary precisely. These two tribes were located in a precarious position, since Moab and Ammon were always a threat to their independence. During the eleventh century Moab took over Reuben's territory, and that tribe disappeared from history (see Plate VII:C). Similarly, Gad was pressed by the Ammonites, who as early as the eleventh century were in position to threaten the Israelite territory as far west as Jabesh-gilead (VI, D-4; I Sam., ch. 11).

To the north the half tribe of Manasseh occupied the kingdom of Og (cf. IV and VI, D-E 3-4) with its strong cities of Ramoth-gilead, Edrei, Ashtaroth, and Karnaim (VI, E-3). The northern boundary is not shown on Plate VI because it cannot be precisely located, but Argob (VI, E-3), Nobah (VI, F-3), and Salcah (VII:A, D-4) were included (Num. 32:42; Deut. 3:14; Josh. 13:11 ff.). During the ninth and eighth centuries this region became a battleground between Israel and the Aramean kingdom of Damascus, while the Ammonites pressed against it on the southeast (see Plate VII:B). King Ahab was mortally wounded in battle at Ramoth-gilead (I Kings 22:29 ff.; VI, E-3).

THE SETTLEMENT OF WESTERN PALESTINE

For the tribal settlement of the country west of the Jordan more information is available, and the core of the documentary lists in Josh., chs. 15 to 19, is very old. Thus among the towns of Simeon, Sharuhen (VI, A-6) is listed (Josh. 19:6). We know from the excavations at the site that it was destroyed during the ninth century and not reoccupied for four centuries. Consequently, a list of villages containing this town must date before 800 B.C. Similarly, we are told that the tribe of Ephraim did not drive out "the Canaanites that dwelt in

FIG. 26. The pass of Megiddo, on the main highway from the Plain of Sharon across Mount Carmel to the Valley of Jezreel (Esdraelon). This highway is the main road between Syria and Egypt. Along it armies and caravans have moved for millennia. This view, looking toward the southwest, is taken at the point where a side road branches off at the left to Taanach (VI, C-3).

FIG. 27. The small plain of Lebonah (modern *Lubban*) in the hill country of Ephraim near Shiloh (VI, C-4). The road shown is the highway from Jerusalem through the hill country to Nablus by ancient Shechem. In the background at the foot of the hill is the modern village on the approximate site of ancient Lebonah (Judg. 21:19).

Gezer [VI, B-5]: but the Canaanites dwell in the midst of Ephraim unto this day, and are become servants to do taskwork" (Josh. 16:10). This verse must certainly have been written in the time of David or Solomon in the tenth century. Not only did Gezer first come under Israelite control at that time (I Kings 9:16), but it was only then that Israel was strong enough to place the Canaanites in labor battalions as slaves (I Kings 9:21). Gezer was destroyed and abandoned at the end of the tenth century and the verse must date, therefore, before that period. We may be confident that the boundary lists in their present form rest on still older sources, and that the tribal claims as represented on Plate VI are in general reliable.

At first glance Plate VI would indicate that during the period of the Judges (c. 1200-1020 B.C.) the Israelites were in control of the whole country. Yet a careful reading of Joshua and Judg., ch. 1, indicates that this was not the case. While the tribal lists divided up the land and Israel laid claim to all of it, there were portions which could not be subdued. As mentioned above, Gezer was not conquered until the time of Solomon, and Jerusalem was first taken by David (Judg. 1:21; II Sam. 5:6 ff.). Judges 1:19 states that Judah occupied the hill country, but "he could not drive out the inhabitants of the valley, because they had chariots of iron." This refers primarily to the coastal plain from Gaza to Ekron and extending inland as far as Gath (VI, A-B 5-6). Similarly, the tribe of Manasseh failed to subdue a string of Canaanite fortresses along its northern boundary, and these separated it from the tribes in Galilee (Judg. 1:27). Chief among them were Beth-shan, Ibleam, Taanach, Megiddo, and Dor (VI, B-C 3-4). From the excavations it appears likely that Megiddo, a strong city guarding the main pass from the Plain of Sharon (Plate I, and VI, B-C 3-4) to the north (see Figs. 5 and 26) fell to Israel at least temporarily between c. 1140 and 1100 B.C. After the destruction at this time, the town was deserted for at least half a century. During the period of desertion the battle between the forces of Barak and Sisera as described in the Song of Deborah (Judg., ch. 5) probably took place. The location of the battle was "in Taanach by the waters of Megiddo" (v. 19). These waters are those of the River Kishon (VI, C-3), the sources of which were at Megiddo. Since, however, the town which is mentioned to give the general location was not Megiddo but Taanach some distance away, we may infer that the former was not in existence at that time. Beth-shan (see Fig. 83) continued in Canaanite and Philistine hands and was not destroyed until the time of David, judging from the evidence found in the ruins (cf. also I Sam. 31:10; the temple there mentioned has been excavated).

It is evident, therefore, that the Israelites during the period of the Judges were not in possession of the whole country but chiefly of the central ridge, while Canaanites continued to live around them—a situation that was little altered until the great conquests of David.

THE "JUDGES" OF ISRAEL

There was a striking difference between the political organization of Israel and that of the surrounding peoples during this period. The latter were highly organized. Edom, Moab, and Ammon to the east and southeast were monarchies, controlling numerous cities and with capitals at Sela (see Fig. 50) or Teman (VI, C-D 8), Kir-hareseth (VI, D-6), and Rabbath-ammon (VI, D-5) respectively. The Canaanites continued their old city-state organization (see pp. 34 ff.), each major city possessing its own ruler (for example, Jerusalem, Gezer, Megiddo, Beth-shan, Dor, Sidon, etc.). There was no great power to interfere in the local struggles; effective Egyptian control was at an end (see pp. 29, 30), and the Assyrian Empire had not yet extended its power this far. Assyria, about 1100 B.C., conquered northern Syria, but the success was ephemeral and scarcely affected Palestine.

In contrast to her strongly organized neighbors, Israel was only a loose federation of tribes. These were held together, not by a central political figure who exercised dictatorial control, but solely by a common tradition and a religious bond or "covenant." The visible symbol of the bond was the "Ark of the Covenant," which during most of the period of the Judges rested in the central sanctuary at Shiloh (VI, C-4). With no central government we should expect the tribes to be in constant danger of attack from raiders and "oppressors" on every hand, unless the Israelite sense of religious unity were kept so strong that danger to one tribe would immediately cause all tribes to come to its defense. But according to The Book of Judges the people in settling down to an agricultural life succumbed in large measure to the seductive nature worship which was the religion of Canaan (see p. 36). Whenever they did this, we are told, God sent "oppressors" to afflict them (Judg., ch. 2). In other words, the more paganism they adopted, the weaker the covenant bond between them became, and the more each tribe tended to live by and for itself, isolated from the other tribes. This disunity made subjugation and oppression by outsiders relatively easy.

Several of these oppressors are mentioned: Moabites (Judg. 3:12 ff.), Canaanites (Judg., chs. 4; 5), Midianites from Arabia (Judg., chs. 6; 7; V, G 4-5), Ammonites (Judg., ch. 11), and Philistines (Judg. 3:31; chs. 13 ff.; I Sam., chs. 4 ff.). As previously indicated, the Moabites and Ammonites were peoples of Transjordan whom Israel had not conquered. During this period they took advantage of the separatist tendencies of the tribes and tried to gain control over Transjordan. Apart from the Philistine oppression (see below) the most dangerous threats to Israel were from the Canaanites and Midianites. A formidable Canaanite army was assembled in the Valley of Jezreel (I, C-3) under the leadership of one Sisera from the village of Harosheth (IV, C-3). A call to arms was issued to the tribes of Israel by the prophetess Deborah. Six of the tribes responded and an army was assembled at Mount Tabor (VI, C-3) under the leadership of Barak from Kedesh-naphtali (VI, D-2; Judg. 4:6 ff.). The subsequent defeat of the Canaanites in a battle near Megiddo (VI, C-3) was celebrated by the remarkable poem, composed by an eyewitness, which is preserved in Judg., ch. 5. The Midianite oppression was also exceedingly serious, since it was an invasion from the Arabian Desert of Bedouins who for the first time were using domesticated camels on a large scale. This use of the camel made the Midianites dangerous; they could travel long distances with comparative rapidity without concern for water supply. The story of their defeat by Gideon in the valley leading from Jezreel to the Jordan, between Mount Gilboa and the Hill of Moreh (VI, C-3), is well known.

Complete disaster for Israel in these crises was avoided by spontaneous leaders who were called "judges." These figures have been called "charismatic" leaders, because they were believed to possess some special gift of God's grace. They were set apart from others by special abilities, such as military prowess, wisdom, honesty, and natural capacities for leadership. In disputes between individuals and families, it was only natural that the cases be taken before such leaders for decision. In this way the name "judges" was given them, though for the most part in the stories about them they appear as military leaders. The charismatic nature of the leadership during this period is a remarkable feature of Israel, and distinguishes its history sharply from that of the surrounding peoples.

ARCHAEOLOGY AND THE PERIOD OF THE JUDGES

During the period of the Judges considerable difference can be observed between the material civilization and wealth of Israelite towns and those of the neighbors who were not driven out. Canaanite cities which have been excavated, such as Beth-shan (VI, C-4), Megiddo (VI, C-3), and Salmonah (the probable name of modern *Tell Abū Hawâm*, IV, C-3), show a considerable degree of wealth. Houses were well built, and their contents indicate that an active trade with Syria and Cyprus was carried on. Occasionally objects of art from Egypt are found. At Beth-shan, after Egyptian control came to an end, the temples of the Canaanite deities Dagon and Ashtaroth were built (I Sam. 31:10; I Chron. 10:10); and in their precincts were placed numerous coveted objects, including three Egyptian stelae (monumental stones) set up by the Pharaohs Seti I and Rameses II some two hundred years before.

At Megiddo during the early twelfth century was an elaborate palace of the local king, in all probability as large as the palace which Solomon later built for himself in Jerusalem. In its basement was the treasure room which had been looted of its finest objects when the city was destroyed by some enemy about 1150 B.C. Left on the floor in a confused mass were a large number of gold, ivory, and alabaster objects, which while unimportant to the looters are of great value to us, since they so vividly illustrate the wealth and culture of the Canaanite king (Figs. 28, 29).

In contrast to the wealth of these Canaanite towns the Israelites were extremely poor. Between 1200 and 1000 B.C. the hill country, for the first time, became dotted with towns, indicating an increase in the population and witnessing to the Israelite settlement. Several of these towns have been excavated (see Plate XVIII), and their ruins testify to a civilization very different from that of the Canaanites. Everywhere there is evidence of poverty. House walls are crude and ill-planned. Art is exceedingly primitive. Before about 1050 B.C. there is no evidence of trade with foreign peoples other than with the immediate neighbors. City fortifications, when constructed, were poorly built and scarcely capable of withstanding serious attack. All this was to change during the period of David and Solomon after 1000 B.C., when strong government and military success brought an economic revolution to Israel.

THE PHILISTINES

Shortly after 1200 B.C. there appeared in the southern coastal plain a people called "Philistines" (VI, B-5), from whom the name "Palestine" was later derived. The Philistines were one group of a large number of sea peoples from the Greek islands and particularly from Crete (Caphtor; see Amos 9:7). This we know, not only from references in the Bible and in Egyptian records, but from the characteristic pottery which they made in Palestine. The shapes of the vessels were quite unlike the traditional forms of Canaan, but were patterned after styles well known in the Greek world whence the people came.

While attempting to invade Egypt the sea peoples suffered a severe defeat at the hands of Pharaoh Rameses III (c. 1175 B.C.), and some at least fell back on Palestine (see Fig. 16). One group settled at Dor in the Plain of Sharon (VI, B-3), though we hear about them, not from the Old Testament, but from the Egyptian story of a certain Wenamon, an Egyptian emissary who stopped there on his way to

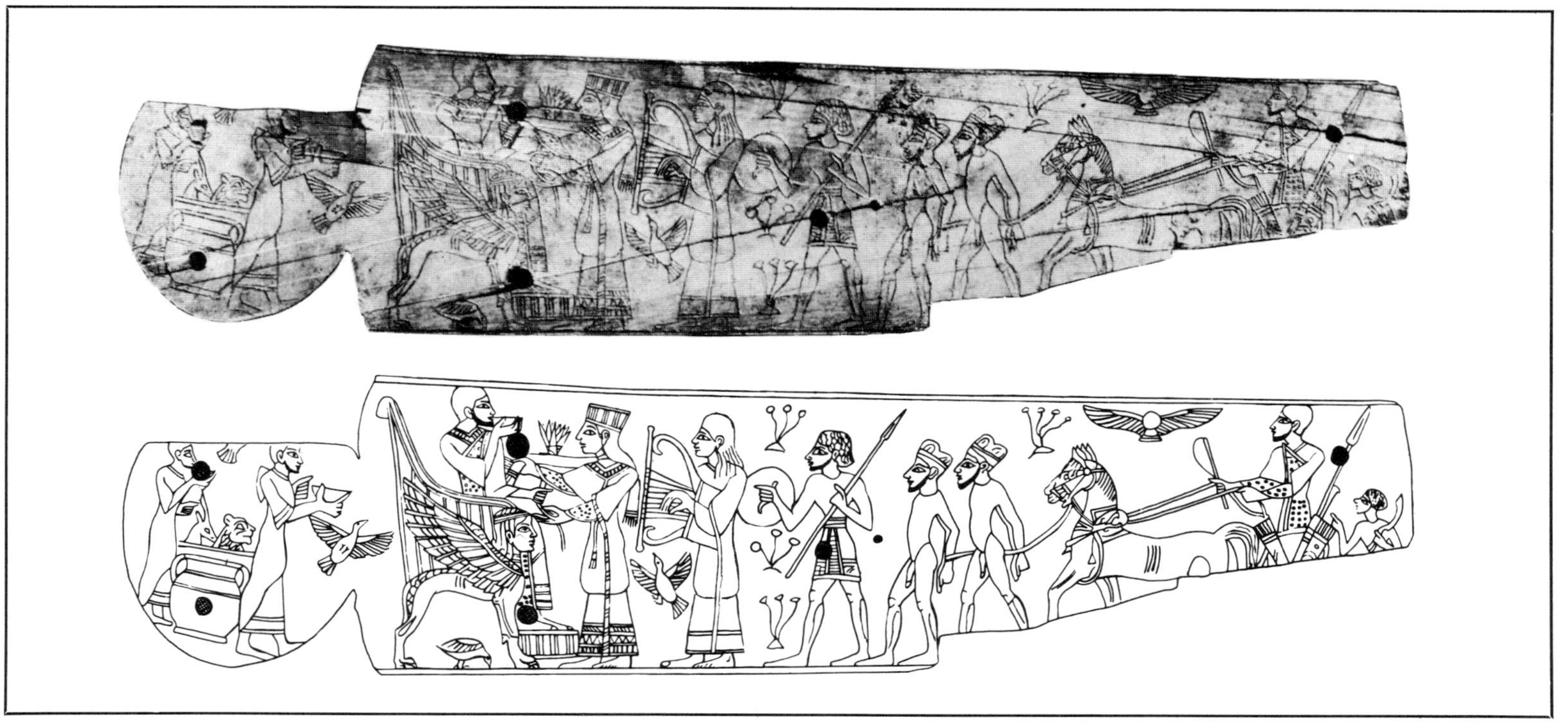

FIG. 28. One of the ivories from the collection of the king of Megiddo, dating c. 1200 B.C. A Canaanite ruler is shown sitting on his throne, drinking from a small bowl. Before him are an official and a musician plucking the strings of a lyre. The latter reminds us of David playing the lyre (not the "harp") before the moody Saul (I Sam. 16:23). The king's throne is supported by winged lions with human heads. These are the imaginary, composite beings which the Israelites called "cherubim" (which were not the small winged children that appear as "cherubs" in modern art). In Solomon's Temple there were two large figures of this type in the Holy of Holies, on which the Lord was believed to be enthroned, though invisibly, precisely as Canaanite kings such as this were enthroned (see p. 49; cf. I Sam. 4:4).

Syria for cedar. South of Gerar was another group called the "Cherethites" (VI, A-6), but we know nothing about them apart from three references in the Old Testament (I Sam. 30:14; Ezek. 25:16; Zeph. 2:5).

By far the most important of the sea peoples in Palestine was the Philistine group, which was organized around five cities: Gaza (VI, A-5), Ashkelon, Ashdod, Ekron, and Gath (VI, B-5). Each city, with the area it controlled, was ruled by a "lord," who, though independent, co-operated with the others in important matters. Thus in political and military affairs the people were able to act as a united group. As a result they proved to be the most serious threat to the independence of Israel during the period of the Judges. Most disastrous was the battle at Eben-ezer and Aphek (VI, B-4) about 1050 B.C., when the Israelite Ark was captured and taken to Ashdod (I Sam., ch. 4). After the trouble it caused in the Temple of Dagon, it was sent to Ekron, and from there up the Valley of Sorek past Beth-shemesh to Kirjath-jearim (VI, C-5; see also IX, C-E 5-6). The primary interest of the writer of this story was to tell about the Ark, and we are left to infer what happened to Israel politically. From archaeological investigation we know that Israel's central sanctuary, Shiloh (VI, C-4), where the Ark had been kept, was violently destroyed at this time, making the reference of Jeremiah to its destruction quite clear (Jer. 7:12 ff.; 26:6 ff.). Later we hear of Philistine garrisons in the hill country itself (I Sam. 13:3), and also in possession of such a far-away city as Beth-shan (VI, C-4), on the wall of which was hung the body of Saul after his defeat at Mount Gilboa (VI, C-4; I Sam., ch. 31). This means that between c. 1050 and 1020 B.C. the Philistines were able to dominate Israel politically, and it is small wonder that the people of Israel came to Samuel demanding a king who would organize them and drive off the oppressor.

One direct consequence of the Philistine pressure was the fact that the small tribe of Dan was forced to leave the territory originally assigned to it (Josh. 19:47; Judg., ch. 18). This tribe had been allotted an area from Beth-shemesh, Zorah, and Aijalon (VI, B-5), to Ekron (VI, B-5), Jehud, Bene-berak, and Rakkon (VI, B-4; Josh. 19:40 ff.). Philistine power drove the Danites from the plains, whereupon they traveled to the foot of Mount Hermon and settled there, after taking a Canaanite city called Laish and renaming it for themselves (VI, D-2; Judg. 18:27-29).

The period of the Judges marks the beginning of the Iron Age; that is, the time when iron came into common use. The metal used for tools and weapons since 4000 B.C. had been copper, though since the Hyksos period (pp. 27 f.) it had been common practice to introduce tin into the copper to produce a harder product, bronze. Before 1200 B.C. iron appears to have been a magic product in Western Asia, valued almost as much as gold and silver. This was not because of the scarcity of the ore, but because the secrets of the rather complicated smelting process seem to have been jealously guarded by the Hittites.

Throughout the period of the Judges the Israelites, who were poor in material possessions, were thwarted time and again because of their lack of this important metal for agricultural implements, nails, and weapons. They were unable to drive out the Canaanites from the plains because these people owned iron chariots (Josh. 17:16; Judg. 1:19; 4: 2, 3).

From excavations in Philistine territory it has been learned that the Philistines possessed iron weapons and jewelry, while the Israelites appear to have had none. It is very probable, therefore, that the metal was introduced into common use in Palestine by the Philistines who had learned about it in the north. They held a "corner" on the iron market, however, and closely guarded the trade secrets of its production. This we infer from the excavations and also from the interesting passage in I Sam. 13:19-22.

Once the Philistine power was broken by the first kings of Israel, Saul and David, the secret of the iron-smelting process became public property, and the metal came into use in Israel. This promptly resulted in an economic revolution and higher standard of living for the common man. The war with the Philistines was one of survival for Israel. Small wonder that it was celebrated in song and story, since it furnished the occasion for great exploits, notably those of Samson (Judg., chs. 13 to 16) and of David against Goliath (I Sam., ch. 17).

ISRAEL'S NORTHERN NEIGHBORS

During the period of the Judges the people of Israel were not troubled by oppressors from Syria. Yet to the north and northeast Phoenician and Aramean states were in process of formation which were to influence greatly the course of events in Palestine.

The coast line of Syria apparently suffered severely in the twelfth century from the depredations of the invading sea peoples. The great city of Ugarit (III, C-2), and probably Tyre (VI, C-2) also, was destroyed and abandoned at this time. Yet by the time of David and Solomon in the tenth century the Canaanites in the Tyre-Sidon (VI, C 1-2) area had been united into a strong state with its capital at Tyre. This Phoenician state came into being during the period of the Judges and was apparently quite unique among the world's kingdoms. Instead of concentrating its energies on expanding its territory by force of arms, it spread its influence, its raw materials, and its artisans throughout the Mediterranean by trade and treaties. We are unable to trace its boundaries at any one period or to determine how much territory it comprised. The tribe of Asher, following the conquest, laid claim to the whole coast from Mount Carmel well into Syria (VI, C 2-3), but it is improbable that Israelites ever really controlled this area (see Judg. 1: 31, 32). By the time of Solomon the tribe had virtually ceased to exist, having become a dependency of Phoenicia (VII:A, B-C 2-3).

East of the Syrian mountains to the north and south of Damascus new invaders from Arabia were settling down during the period of the Judges. These were the Aramaeans (a name which is translated "Syrians" in the A.V. and R.V.). Towns were founded by them throughout this area as far south as the Yarmuk (I, D-3), so that by the end of the tenth century the whole of Bashan and eastern Syria was under Aramean control (VII: A-B). By 1000 B.C. the Aramean kingdom of Zobah had extended its frontiers to the Euphrates and was conquering Assyrian territory there, but this was stopped by the Davidic conquest of Zobah (p. 48). During the ninth and eighth centuries the Aramaeans were a formidable enemy of Israel. Even after their subjugation by the Assyrians in 733-732 they continued to be great traders who by commercial means became as influential in Western Asia as Phoenicia was in the Mediterranean.

FIG. 29. A Canaanite maiden, as restored from a Megiddo ivory. Note the long hair and flowing robe which were characteristic of the Canaanite fashions of the day.

FIG. 30. *Tell ez-Zakarîyeh*, Biblical Azekah, in the Vale of Elah. It was not far from here that the traditional battle between David and Goliath took place (I Sam., ch. 17). The ancient city on this strong point guarded the inner reaches of the valley, while Libnah protected the entrance to the east in the Philistine Plain (Plate IX, D-E 6; cf. II Kings 19:8; II Chron. 11:9; Jer. 34:7).

THE POLITICAL HISTORY OF ISRAEL AND JUDAH

PLATE VII

THE period between the beginning of the tenth and the middle of the eight century was one of the most prosperous times in Palestinian history before the days of the Romans. The population increased and appears to have flourished. Indeed, for the archaeologist the age between 1000 and 600 B.C. shows a remarkable uniformity of material culture with none of the radical shifts and starts that accompany frequent invasion of new peoples and the destruction of old values. Nevertheless, following the golden age of empire during the tenth century under the leadership of David, the territory controlled by the Israelite people was gradually diminished in extent until by 585 B.C. all land had been taken from them and by the fifth century, after a small restoration, they constituted but a tiny province in the Fifth Satrapy of the vast Persian empire. Excavations in Israelite and Judean towns reveal the progressive weakening and impoverishment of the people after the Assyrians appear on the scene during the third quarter of the eight century.

Plates VII and XII, supplemented by Plates XI, XIII, and XIV, picture the political fortunes of the Israelite-Jewish people from the time of David to the period of Paul. Plate VII shows the state of affairs in Palestine during the tenth, ninth, seventh, and fifth centuries B.C.

THE EMPIRE OF DAVID AND SOLOMON

By the third quarter of the eleventh century the whole of Western Palestine south of the Esdraelon or Valley of Jezreel (VI, C-3) was virtually a Philistine dependency. The freedom permitted by the tribal confederacy, with its dependence upon the local rule of elders and the prowess of a spontaneous or charismatic leader to unite the people and save them from invaders—all this had proved insufficient to cope with the Philistine menace. By popular demand the last of the Judges, an Ephraimite named Samuel who was a priest and the sponsor of the budding prophetic movement, became the unwilling initiator of a new form of government, a monarchy. It was adopted as a necessity in conscious imitation of other peoples (I Sam. 8:5). Opposition to it centered around the assertion that the God of Israel was the true King of his people while the human king was at best no more than God's concession to human sin. The result was that in Israel kingship never was quite able to achieve or sustain the unqualified absolutism that it possessed among surrounding peoples. In the case of Samuel and Saul the problem was partially solved by considering the king the "anointed" (messiah) of the Lord (I Sam., ch. 10), who was to rule his people under the dictates of God's will as it was revealed to him by God's spokesmen. Thus when Saul was anointed as the first king, Samuel was the spokesman who was to make God's will known to him. An innate instability on the part of Saul and an inflexibility on the part of Samuel, however, soon brought a rupture in their relations. This fact, coupled with Saul's largely irrational jealousy of David, weakened his efficiency as king. Yet his reign was Israel's political salvation. The Philistines were expelled from the hill country following the battle of Michmash (IX, F-5), and the Ammonites were thrown back from Jabesh-gilead (IX, H-2; I Sam., chs. 11 and 14 ff.). Saul's fortress at Gibeah (IX, F-6) has been excavated. It was located just three miles north of Jerusalem on a hill that commanded an excellent view of the surrounding country. A double wall surrounded the building, the outer fortification being about seven feet in width. The corners were protected by stout towers, and, though the exact size is unknown, it was at least 169 feet long by 114 feet wide, the most elaborate defensive work that Israel had erected up to this time.

At the death of Saul (c. 1000 B.C.) David was made king and began an illustrious reign, forty years in duration (ending c. 961 B.C.). During that period the centralization of power in the throne was vastly increased and strongly supported by a large standing army of sworn loyalty to the king.

FIG. 31. A reconstruction of the Temple of Solomon, based upon a combination of archaeological and Biblical information. It was built according to Phoenician designs and was notable, not for its size, but for its beauty and artistic workmanship. Its main walls were so thick (c. 10 feet) that we must think of it as belonging to a certain old tradition in temple architecture in which the sacred building was erected both as a house of God and as a fortress. The crenelated parapet or battlement has been documented archaeologically. We know that it was used for defensive purposes on city walls and forts, and we also know that all buildings were required to have some kind of parapet around their flat roofs (Deut. 22:8). Drawing by C. F. Stevens, based on specifications of W. F. Albright and G. E. Wright.

David's first acts exhibited a high degree of political sagacity. Jerusalem, which had never been conquered by Israel, was captured and made the political center of the state (II Sam. 5:6 ff.). Owing to its strategic position between the northern and southern groups, its choice prevented charges of favoritism from arising against David. The Ark of the Covenant was then brought to Jerusalem and placed under the royal protection, so that the court became not only the center of political unity but the symbol of religious unity as well (II Sam., ch. 6).

A brief summary of the remarkable conquests of David is found in II Sam., chs. 8; 10; 12:26 ff. First, he confined the Philistines to a small area on the coast (VII:A, B-5) and dominated them economically. The kingdoms of Edom, Moab, and Ammon across the Jordan were next subjugated and their inhabitants made to work on royal projects. The road to the Red Sea and the trade routes between Arabia and Syria were now in David's control. His greatest military triumph, however, was his conquest of Aram ("Syria"; VII:A-B, D-E 2-3). The Aramaeans in this region (see p. 46) had come to the assistance of the Ammonites during David's siege of their capital at Rabbah (VII:A, D-5), but they had been defeated. Now he seized Damascus and also subdued Zobah (VII:A, D 2-3), the leading Aramean kingdom. Assyrian records indicate that the state of Zobah had become sufficiently powerful to begin the conquest of Assyrian territory along the upper Euphrates. It is part of the irony of history that David's subjugation of this kingdom may have saved Assyria and made it possible for her to rise rapidly to power and during the subsequent centuries to conquer the whole of the Fertile Crescent.

Just where David finally fixed the northern boundary of his empire is not recorded in II Samuel. It is known only that his empire bordered on the state of Hamath (ch. 8:9 ff.; VII:A, D-1). Numbers 34:7 ff. and Ezek., ch. 48, however, describe the ideal northern border of Israel as extending from Hazar-enan and Zedad to "the entrance of Hamath" (in the area of Riblah and Kadesh; VII:A, D-2). From that point it would have descended the valley along the eastern side of the Lebanons. This description probably reflects the actual northern extent of the Davidic empire. Otherwise we should be at a loss to explain how the tradition could have arisen that this was Israel's true boundary.

After Edom had been subjugated, David had nothing to fear from the south, because Egypt at that time was unable to interfere in Asia. Treaties were made with the states of Hamath and Tyre to the north, so that the borders of the empire were now firmly established and remained so through most of the days of Solomon. As to the internal fiscal policies of David's administration very little is known except a small amount of information from archaeological discovery. We know that there was a great deal of material prosperity, that population increased, and that the introduction of iron into common use, after the breaking of the Philistine control over it (see p. 46), brought a technological revolution which was certainly felt in the agricultural and building trades. Two city walls of the Davidic era were erected at Beth-shemesh (VI, B-5) and Debir (VI, B-6). They are precisely the same in type and size and must have been under common supervision. In their day they represented a new type of fortification in Palestine. Instead of using sheer mass for strength, two parallel walls were connected with cross walls. The latter created small inner rooms or casemates, which were then frequently filled with rubble.

At Beth-shemesh also and at Lachish (VI, B-5) sizable palaces were built, probably by David. Associated with each was a thick-walled, long-roomed structure which was evidently a granary for taxes collected in kind. These structures can be interpreted only as governmental headquarters of district officials. They suggest that David had divided the country of Judah into districts for purposes of local administration and taxation.

Solomon (c. 961-922 B.C.) did not add to the Davidic conquests, but instead devoted his reign to the cultural and economic development of his empire. Political ties with the smaller countries and with Egypt were strengthened by the addition to his harem of numerous princesses, chief among whom was the daughter of the Egyptian Pharaoh. He set out on a vast building program, remains of which have been recovered in various parts of the country, notably at Megiddo (VI, C-3), Gezer (VI, B-5), and Eglon (VI, B-5; I Kings 9:15 ff.). Megiddo (see Fig. 5) seems to have been taken over for governmental purposes entirely. A city wall averaging twelve feet in width was erected, together with a magnificent covered gateway composed of four sets of piers and four entryways. The latter is the first gateway found that answers to the description of the east gate in the enclosure to the Solomonic Temple in Jerusalem, as described in Ezek. 40: 5-16. The construction of the gate and of portions of the wall marks the first use in Palestine of carefully drafted masonry, with stones fitted and bonded together on the wall faces, often with such precision that not even a thin knife blade can be inserted between them. Within the walled enclosure the most astonishing features were an excellent palace for the local provincial governor, set in a walled courtyard of its own, and four large stables for horses. The total capacity of the stables was approximately five hundred horses. Megiddo is thus our best illustration of Solomonic building activity. The royal government had taken over the city for its purposes, converting it into a military reservation and housing there a portion of the newly introduced chariotry.

In Jerusalem, Solomon's architectural efforts were expended on an expansion of the city to the north in order to provide room for the construction of new administrative buildings, a royal palace, and a temple (see Plate XVII:A). The last-mentioned is described in such detail in I Kings, chs. 6; 7, and Ezek., chs. 40-43, that with the aid of a wealth of archaeological data it is possible to reconstruct it in a general way, even though no remains of it have ever been found in Jerusalem (see p. 105).

In a world that had attained a high level of artistry in architecture and the plastic arts, it should be remembered that Israel was not noted for her achievements in either area. In literature by the end of the tenth century she had already produced works that far surpassed anything in her world. The plastic arts, however, were so largely used in the service of pagan gods that Israel had little to do with them. Similarly up to that time she had had nothing to do with temple architecture nor had she any interest in the subject. Consequently, when Solomon desired to make his new Jerusalem a reflection of the finest work in his environment, he had to go outside Palestine for assistance. As the Bible tells us in the story of the relations between Solomon and Hiram of Tyre, the Temple was a product of Phoenician craftsmanship and artistic genius.

Figure 31 is an attempt on the part of archaeologists working with an artist to visualize what the Temple was like. It was a comparatively small building standing on a platform in a walled-in courtyard. Within it were three rooms: (1) a vestibule before the great doors of (2) the nave or main room, and (3) the Holy of Holies. The interior width of the building was twenty cubits, and the length of the three rooms mentioned was ten, forty, and twenty cubits. The long or sacred cubit was evidently used as the unit of measurement; this was slightly less than twenty-one inches. The over-all interior length, including the width of the dividing walls, would thus have been c. 135 feet, and the interior width c. 35 feet. Side chambers in three stories were attached to the sides of the Temple for storage purposes. The structure was probably built entirely of the type of hewn and carefully bonded stone which we have previously noted in Solomonic construction at Megiddo, but the interior was lined with cedar and was highly decorated with Phoenician motifs of the type illustrated on the doors in Fig. 31. The main sidewalls are said by Ezek. 41:5 to have been six cubits or c. ten feet thick. This suggests that the structure is to be associated with earlier *migdal* or fortress-temples, examples of which have been excavated at Megiddo and Shechem. Indeed, the Herodian Temple of New Testament times was also considered a fortress.

In the rear room (Holy of Holies) were two olivewood cherubim (cf. Fig. 28), standing c. seventeen feet high and overlaid with gold leaf, under whose outstretched wings the Ark was placed. In the vacant place above them God was believed to be invisibly enthroned. In the exterior court were the large altar of burnt offering, the lavers, and the bronze "sea." The latter was a tremendous bronze bowl, c. seventeen feet in diameter, c. eight feet high, and holding c. 10,000 gallons of water. It was cast in the clay beds of the Jordan Valley at Adamah (VII:A, C-4). The "sea" and the bronze pillars placed in front of the Temple (I Kings 7:15 ff.) were so large that we marvel at the genius of the artisan Hiram who cast them. Figure 32 is an attempt to reconstruct the great altar of burnt offering on the basis of Ezek. 43: 13-17. It was constructed in stages like a Babylonian ziggurat or temple tower (cf. Fig. 11). Its dimensions were c. seventeen and one-half feet high by c. twenty-one feet square at the top.

To obtain both material and artists for the work Solomon had a trading agreement with the Phoenician, Hiram of Tyre (I Kings, ch. 5). At the end of twenty years Solomon had accumulated a serious deficit and had to cede to Hiram twenty Galilean cities in the vicinity of Cabul (I Kings 9:10 ff.; VII:A, C-4). To finance this elaborate building program and to support his great court Solomon en-

FIG. 32. The altar of burnt offering in the Jerusalem Temple, as described in Ezek. 43:13-17. It was like a Babylonian ziggurat or temple-tower, and was built in stages with stairs leading to the top on the east. The height of the whole was c. 17½ feet, and the hearth or topmost stage was about 21 feet square. Drawing by C. F. Stevens, based on specifications of W. F. Albright and G. E. Wright.

tered into numerous business ventures. With Hiram's aid he built a fleet of ships for the Red Sea trade (I Kings 10:22), with port at Ezion-geber (VII:A, B-7). This site has been excavated, and has revealed a totally new phase of Solomon's activity. Here the king had built a huge smelter, the largest ever found in the ancient Near East, in which to smelt the ores obtained from the Arabah mines (see p. 69). Another phase of his commercial activity is revealed by I Kings 10:28, 29, which though long regarded as untranslatable, can now be rendered as follows: "And Solomon's horses were exported from Egypt and Cilicia [XI:B, B-2]: the merchants of the king procured them from Cilicia at the current price; and a chariot was exported from Egypt at the rate of 600 shekels of silver and a horse from Cilicia at the rate of 150; and thus they delivered them by their agency to all the kings of the Hittites and the kings of Aram."

In fiscal administration Solomon's reign is notable for his division of northern Israel into provinces for taxation purposes (see I Kings 4:7 ff.), an act which meant the end of the tribe as an administrative unit. In a general way the provinces followed the old tribal districts (cf. VII:A and VI), though certain exceptions are to be noticed. The Plain of Sharon in the area of Dor was made a separate district; Zebulun had disappeared and in its place was a district of which a chief city was Megiddo; Reuben and Gad were joined as one province, while Manasseh across the Jordan was divided into two. The areas as outlined on Plate VII:A are given numbers which represent the order in which the districts are listed in I Kings 4:7 ff. How the territory of Judah was administered is not stated, and some scholars have concluded that Judah enjoyed a favored status. It is far more likely, however, that Solomon did not need to reorganize Judah into provinces for the reason that David had already done so (see above).

The fame of Solomon spread far beyond the borders of his realm. Yet by the end of his reign the country was rocked by disaffection, caused by the heavy taxes, the forced labor on royal projects, and the

FIG. 33. A replica of the stele or monumental stone of Mesha, king of Moab. It was set up by him in Dibon (IX, I-8) to commemorate his victory over Israel shortly after the middle of the ninth century, a victory which for the first time in a century and a half made his country independent.

traditional jealousy between north and south. A new dynasty, the Twenty-second, had come to power in Egypt, headed by the Libyan Shishak. As a result, the political tie between the two countries was broken, and Egypt now became a haven for political refugees who were able to plot in safety against the Israelite monarch.

THE EARLY DIVIDED MONARCHY

The kingdom of Solomon split apart and remained permanently separated after his death c. 922 B.C. Jeroboam, one of the political refugees in Egypt, returned to lead Israel away from the Dynasty of David, while Rehoboam, Solomon's son, retained the throne in Judah. The large empire of David was no more. The Aramean state centering in Damascus had attained its freedom and was shortly to seize virtually all of Bashan, east of the Sea of Galilee. The Kingdom of Ammon across the Jordan had either gained independence or very soon would do so. Even Moab and Edom were evidently lost for a time, though they were soon reconquered. Jeroboam refortified Shechem and at first made it his capital (VII:A, C-4; I Kings 12:25); a portion of his repair of older fortifications at the site has been discovered. Subsequently, however, the capital was shifted to Tirzah (IX, F-3; cf. I Kings 14:17; 15:33). Recent excavation at the mound of *Tell el-Far'ah*, northeast of Shechem, appears to confirm its identification with Tirzah; it was a great city throughout the Bronze Age and was destroyed during the ninth century (cf. I Kings 16:15-18).

Meanwhile Rehoboam in Judah busied himself in fortifying a number of cities in his shrunken realm, especially in the Lowland or Shephelah of Judah (II Chron. 11:5-12). All these cities can now be identified; two of them, Lachish and Azekah (IX, D 6-7), have been excavated and Rehoboam's fortifications have been found. Azekah was provided with a large walled stockade at the highest point on the mound, while Lachish was given a double wall around the summit and a protected gateway (cf. Fig. 37).

During Rehoboam's fifth year Shishak of Egypt raided the country and destroyed numerous cities (I Kings 14:25). This Pharaoh was attempting to re-establish the Egyptian empire of former times, but his early death defeated his dream. On the walls of the great temple of Karnak in Upper Egypt, Shishak portrayed the event for all to see. From the names there listed we gather that the campaign was not directed against Judah alone but against northern Palestine and Edom as well. Excavations have given further indication of the severity of the campaign. A number of towns were evidently destroyed at the time; among them were Megiddo, Debir, *Tell Jemmeh* (Jorda?), Solomon's refinery at Ezion-geber, and probably Beth-shemesh and Lachish. Shishak even erected a stele or monument to the event at Megiddo; a fragment of it has been discovered. At Sharuhen in the South (X, B-2) a huge brick wall, twenty-three feet wide, was constructed around the city at this time, and it is thought that Shishak built it in order to use the city as a base for his operations.

In the years that followed, the strength of the two Hebrew kingdoms was weakened by frequent conflict between them. The tribal district of Benjamin was included in Judah while that once occupied by Dan seems to have been divided (cf. VI, B-C 5). The tension that existed along this border for a half century after Solomon's death is illustrated by the exceedingly strong fortifications at *Tell en-Naṣbeh* (XVIII, C-5). They were erected about this time, and their great size (Fig. 87) illustrates the bitterness with which the civil war was fought. If *Tell en-Nasbeh* is ancient Mizpah, then the story related in I Kings 15:16-22 receives archaeological confirmation. King Baasha of Israel had begun to fortify the town of Ramah, some distance south of his border. He was forced to desist when Asa of Judah secured the aid of Ben-hadad of Damascus, who attacked Galilee. Asa then took "the stones of Ramah and its timber, with which Baasha had been building, and King Asa built with them Gibeah of Benjamin [so the Greek translation] and Mizpah." Excavations at Gibeah show that Saul's ruined fortress was rebuilt not far from 900 B.C. We thus can say that Asa in order to protect Judah from Israel fortified the two main sites on the highroad from Bethel to Jerusalem, thus providing a defense in depth (cf. IX, F-6).

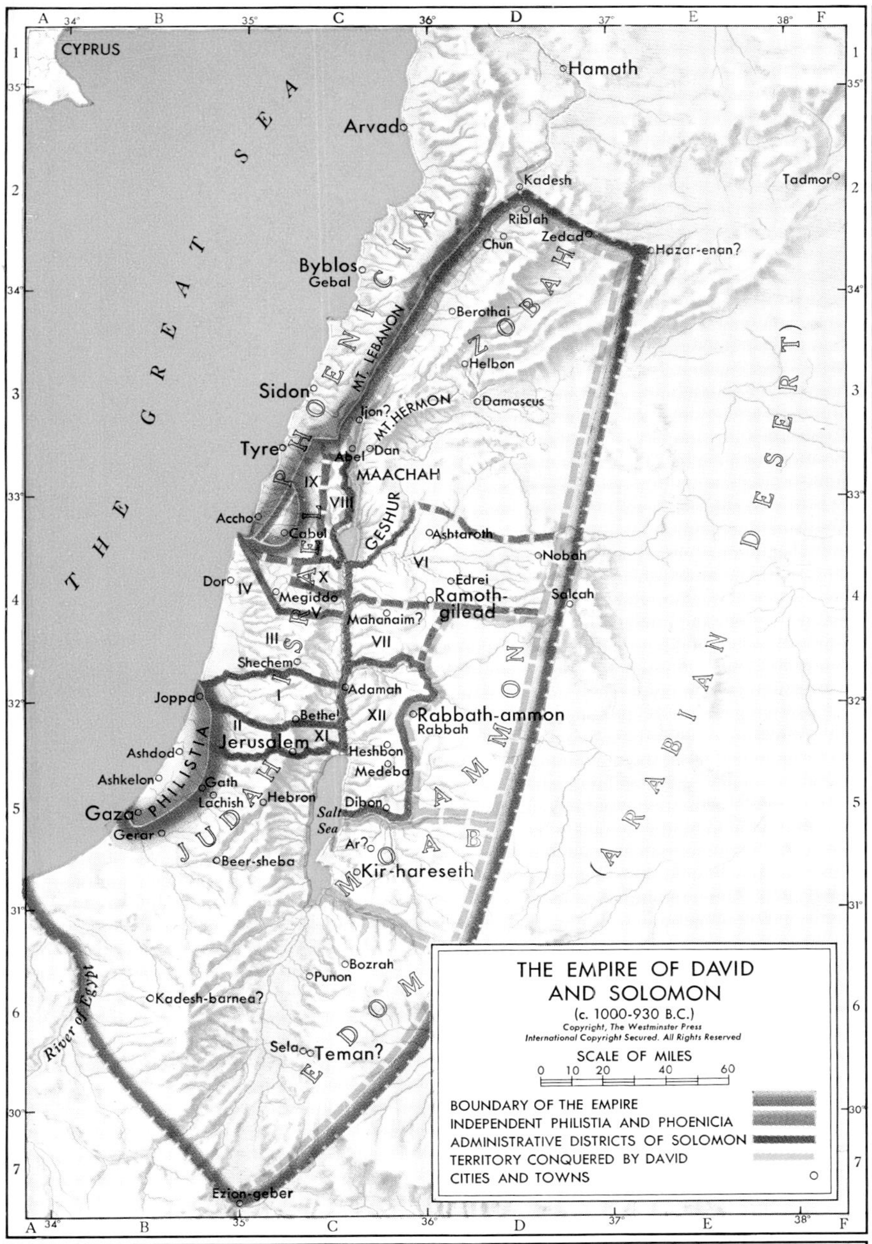
THE EMPIRE OF DAVID AND SOLOMON
(c. 1000-930 B.C.)
Copyright, The Westminster Press
International Copyright Secured. All Rights Reserved
SCALE OF MILES
0 10 20 40 60
BOUNDARY OF THE EMPIRE
INDEPENDENT PHILISTIA AND PHOENICIA
ADMINISTRATIVE DISTRICTS OF SOLOMON
TERRITORY CONQUERED BY DAVID
CITIES AND TOWNS
CYPRUS
THE GREAT SEA
Hamath
Arvad
Kadesh
Riblah
Chun
Zedad
Hazar-enan?
Tadmor
Byblos
Gebal
PHOENICIA
MT. LEBANON
ZOBAH
Berothai
Helbon
Sidon
MT. HERMON
Damascus
Ijon?
Tyre
Abel
Dan
MAACHAH
GESHUR
Accho
Cabul
Ashtaroth
Nobah
Dor
Megiddo
Edrei
Ramoth-gilead
Salcah
Mahanaim?
Shechem
Joppa
Adamah
Bethel
Rabbath-ammon
Rabbah
Ashdod
Jerusalem
Heshbon
Medeba
Ashkelon
Gath
PHILISTIA
Lachish
Hebron
Gaza
Gerar
JUDAH
ISRAEL
Dibon
Salt Sea
Ar?
Kir-hareseth
Beer-sheba
MOAB
AMMON
(ARABIAN DESERT)
Bozrah
Punon
Kadesh-barnea?
EDOM
River of Egypt
Sela
Teman?
Ezion-geber
I
II
III
IV
V
VI
VII
VIII
IX
X
XI
XII

B

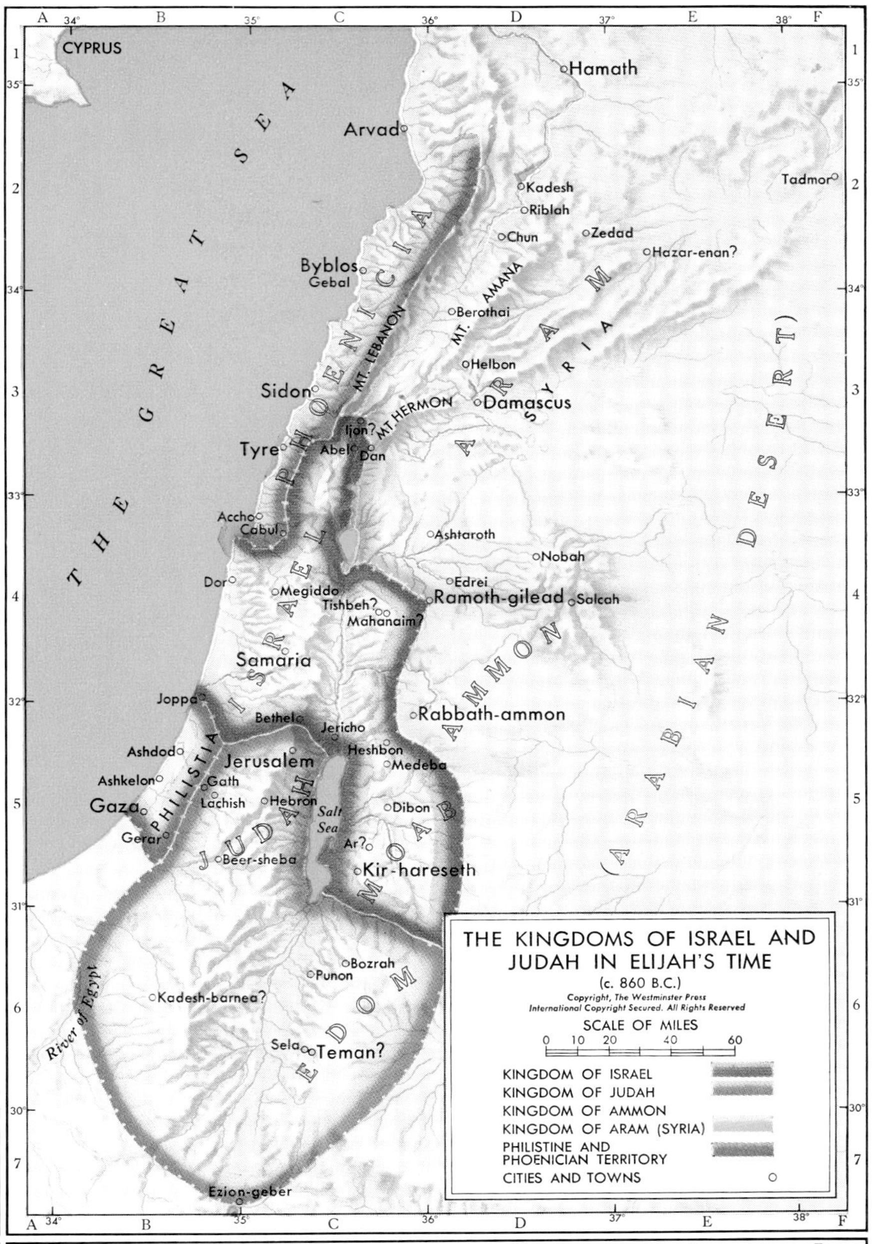
THE KINGDOMS OF ISRAEL AND JUDAH IN ELIJAH'S TIME
(c. 860 B.C.)
Copyright, The Westminster Press
International Copyright Secured. All Rights Reserved
SCALE OF MILES
0 10 20 40 60
KINGDOM OF ISRAEL
KINGDOM OF JUDAH
KINGDOM OF AMMON
KINGDOM OF ARAM (SYRIA)
PHILISTINE AND PHOENICIAN TERRITORY
CITIES AND TOWNS
CYPRUS
THE GREAT SEA
Hamath
Arvad
Kadesh
Riblah
Chun
Zedad
Hazar-enan?
Tadmor
Byblos
Gebal
MT. AMANA
ARAM
SYRIA
Berothai
PHOENICIA
MT. LEBANON
Helbon
Sidon
MT. HERMON
Damascus
Ijon?
Tyre
Abel
Dan
Accho
Cabul
Ashtaroth
Nobah
Dor
Megiddo
Tishbeh?
Mahanaim?
Edrei
Ramoth-gilead
Salcah
Samaria
ISRAEL
AMMON
Joppa
Bethel
Jericho
Rabbath-ammon
Ashdod
Heshbon
Jerusalem
Medeba
Ashkelon
Gath
PHILISTIA
Gaza
Lachish
Hebron
Dibon
Gerar
Salt Sea
Ar?
JUDAH
MOAB
Beer-sheba
Kir-hareseth
(ARABIAN DESERT)
Bozrah
Punon
Kadesh-barnea?
EDOM
River of Egypt
Sela
Teman?
Ezion-geber

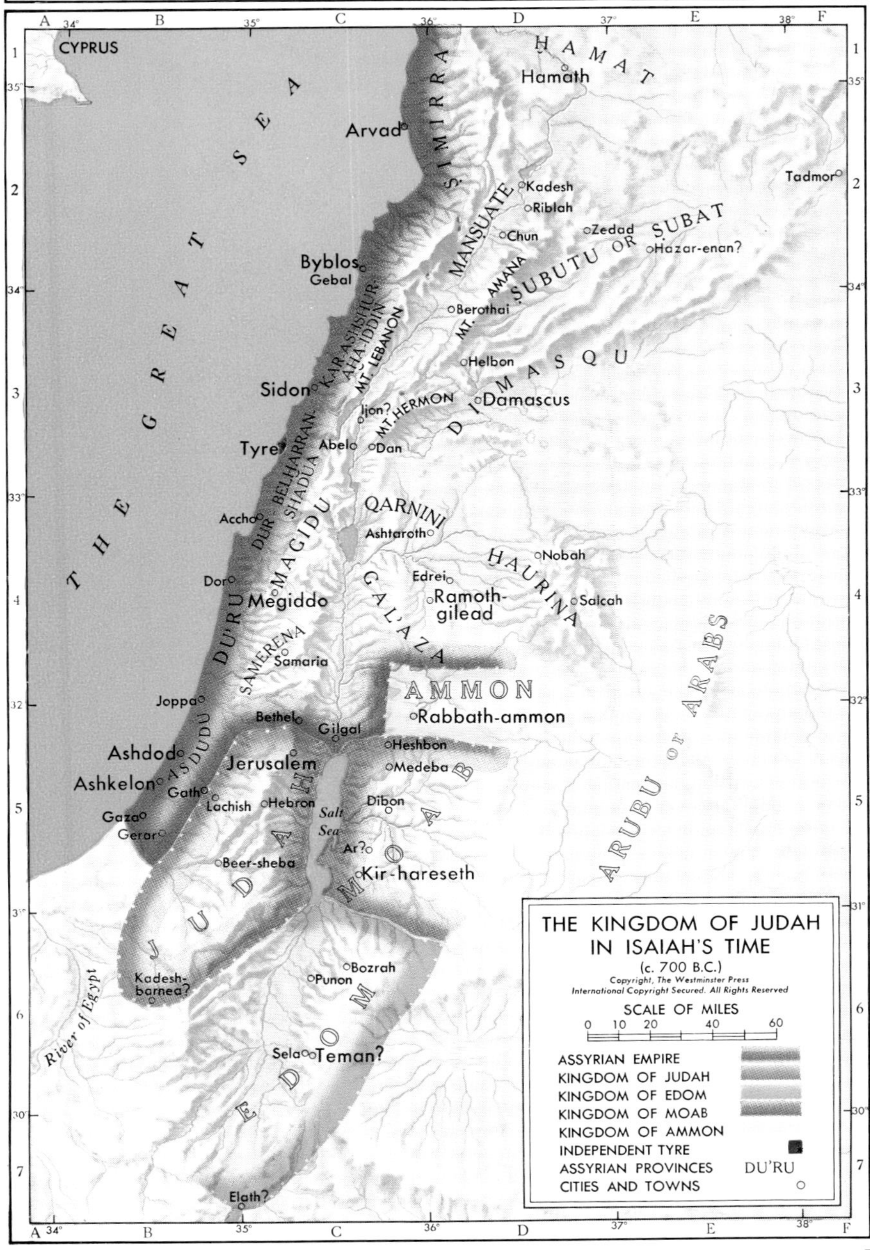
THE KINGDOM OF JUDAH IN ISAIAH'S TIME
(c. 700 B.C.)
Copyright, The Westminster Press
International Copyright Secured. All Rights Reserved
SCALE OF MILES
0 10 20 40 60
ASSYRIAN EMPIRE
KINGDOM OF JUDAH
KINGDOM OF EDOM
KINGDOM OF MOAB
KINGDOM OF AMMON
INDEPENDENT TYRE
ASSYRIAN PROVINCES DU'RU
CITIES AND TOWNS
CYPRUS
THE GREAT SEA
HAMAT
Hamath
Arvad
SIMIRRA
MANSUATE
Kadesh
Riblah
Chun
Zedad
SUBUTU OR SUBAT
Hazar-enan?
Tadmor
Byblos
Gebal
MT. AMANA
Berothai
KAR-ASSHUR-AHA-IDDIN
MT. LEBANON
Helbon
DIMASQU
Sidon
MT. HERMON
Damascus
Ijon?
Tyre
Abel
Dan
DUR-BELHARRAN-SHADUA
QARNINI
Accho
MAGIDU
Ashtaroth
HAURINA
Nobah
Dor
Edrei
GAL'AZA
Megiddo
Ramoth-gilead
Salcah
DURU
SAMERENA
Samaria
AMMON
ARUBU OR ARABS
Joppa
Bethel
Gilgal
Rabbath-ammon
Ashdod
ASDUDU
Heshbon
Jerusalem
Medeba
Ashkelon
Gath
Gaza
Lachish
Hebron
Dibon
Gerar
Salt Sea
Ar?
MOAB
Beer-sheba
Kir-hareseth
JUDAH
Kadesh-barnea?
Bozrah
Punon
River of Egypt
EDOM
Sela
Teman?
Elath?

D

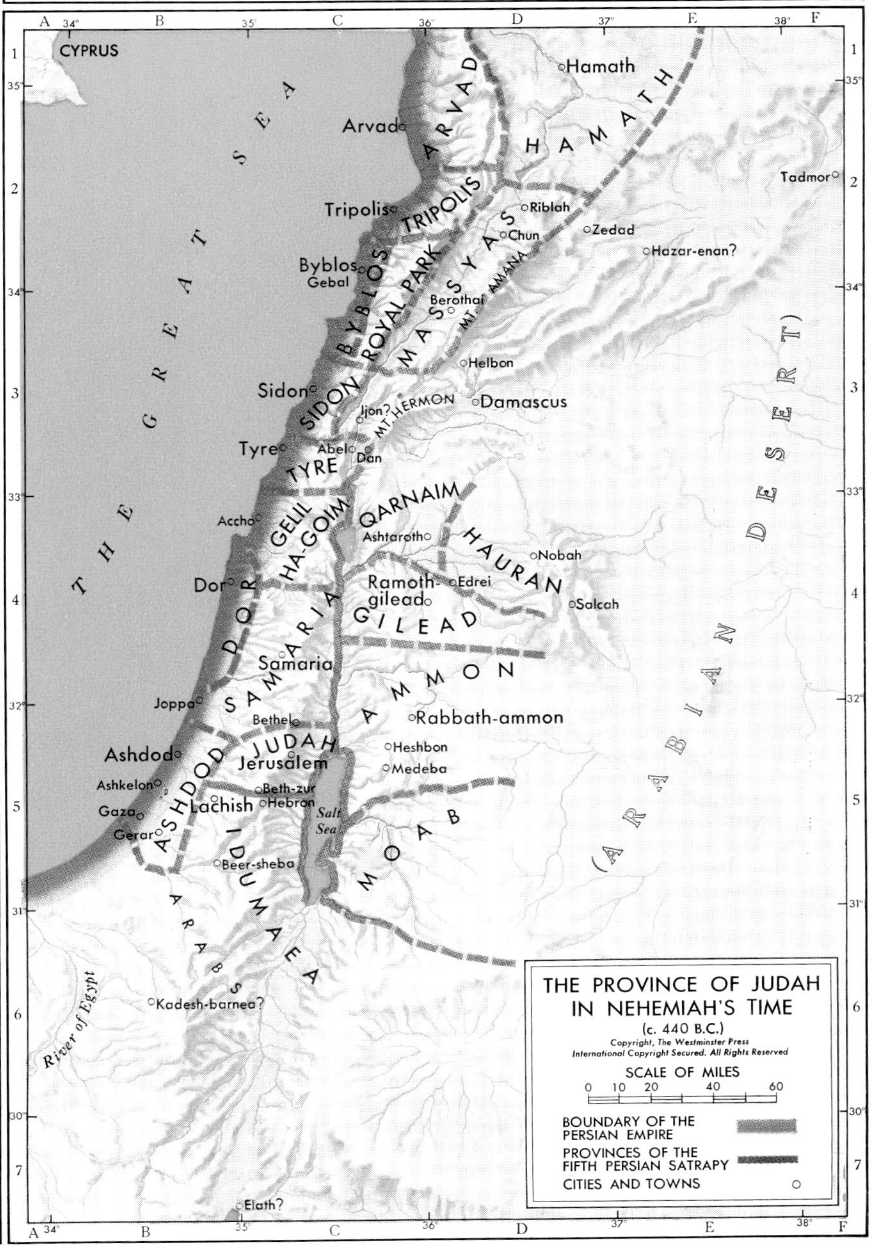
THE PROVINCE OF JUDAH IN NEHEMIAH'S TIME
(c. 440 B.C.)
Copyright, The Westminster Press
International Copyright Secured. All Rights Reserved
SCALE OF MILES
0 10 20 40 60
BOUNDARY OF THE PERSIAN EMPIRE
PROVINCES OF THE FIFTH PERSIAN SATRAPY
CITIES AND TOWNS
CYPRUS
THE GREAT SEA
Hamath
ARVAD
Arvad
HAMATH
Tripolis
TRIPOLIS
Riblah
Chun
Zedad
Hazar-enan?
Tadmor
Byblos
Gebal
BYBLOS
ROYAL PARK
MASSYAS
MT. AMANA
Berothai
Helbon
Sidon
SIDON
MT. HERMON
Damascus
Ijon?
Tyre
Abel
Dan
TYRE
QARNAIM
Accho
GELIL HA-GOIM
Ashtaroth
HAURAN
Nobah
Dor
DOR
Ramoth-gilead
Edrei
Salcah
GILEAD
SAMARIA
Samaria
AMMON
Joppa
Bethel
Rabbath-ammon
Ashdod
JUDAH
Jerusalem
Heshbon
Medeba
Ashkelon
ASHDOD
Beth-zur
Gaza
Lachish
Hebron
Gerar
Salt Sea
MOAB
IDUMAEA
Beer-sheba
ARABS
(ARABIAN DESERT)
Kadesh-barnea?
River of Egypt
Elath?

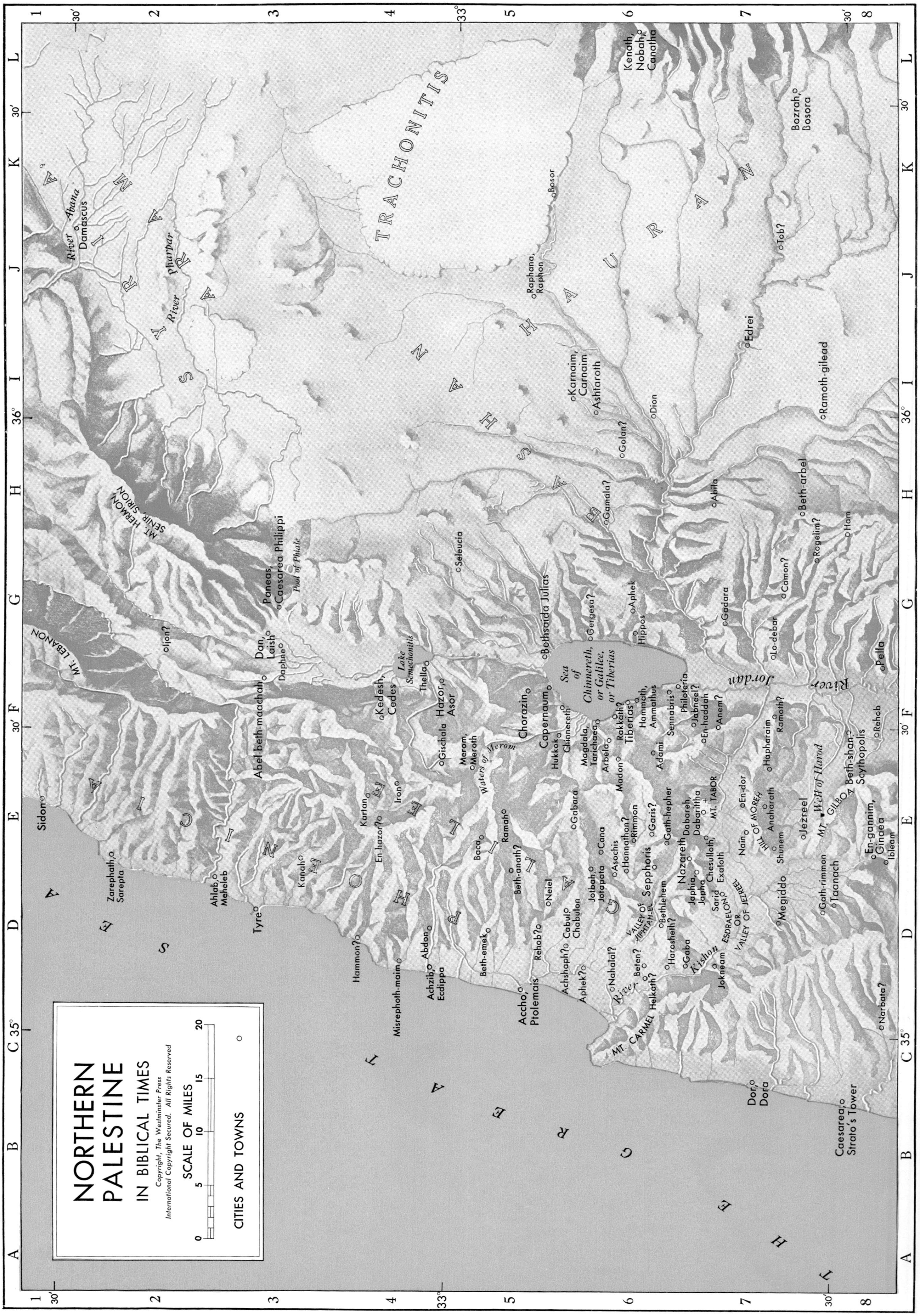
NORTHERN PALESTINE
IN BIBLICAL TIMES
Copyright, The Westminster Press
International Copyright Secured. All Rights Reserved
SCALE OF MILES
0
5
10
15
20
CITIES AND TOWNS
THE GREAT SEA
PHOENICIA
GALILEE
BASHAN
HAURAN
TRACHONITIS
SYRIA
MT. LEBANON
MT. HERMON, SENIR, SIRION
Sidon
Zarephath, Sarepta
Ahlab, Mehaleb
Tyre
Abel-beth-maachah
Ijon?
Dan, Laish
Daphne
Paneas, Caesarea Philippi
Pool of Phiale
Lake Semechonitis
Kedesh, Cedes
Thella
Hazor, Asor
Gischala
Merom, Meroth
Waters of Merom
Kanah
Kartan
En-hazor?
Iron
Hammon?
Misrephoth-maim
Achzib, Ecdippa
Abdon
Beth-emek
Baca
Ramah
Beth-anath?
Neiel
Rehob?
Cabul, Chabulon
Accho, Ptolemais
Achshaph?
Aphek?
Nahalal?
Helkath?
Beten?
River Kishon
MT. CARMEL
Harosheth?
Gaba
Jokneam
Bethlehem
Valley of Jiphtah-el
Jotbah, Jotapara
Asochis
Hannathon?
Sepphoris
Rimmon
Cana
Gabara
Garis?
Gath-hepher
Nazareth
Japhia, Japha
Sarid
Chesulloth, Exaloth
Daberath, Dabarittha
MT. TABOR
Esdraelon or Valley of Jezreel
Megiddo
Gath-rimmon
Taanach
Ibleam
En-gannim, Ginaea
Shunem
Nain
Hill of Moreh
En-dor
Anaharath
Jezreel
Well of Harod
MT. GILBOA
Beth-shan, Scythopolis
Hapharaim
Ramoth?
Rehob
Narbata?
Dor, Dora
Caesarea, Strato's Tower
Chorazin
Capernaum
Chinnereth
Hukkok
Magdala, Tarichaea
Arbela
Madon
Rakkath?
Tiberias
Hammath, Ammathus
Adami
Sennabris
Philoteria
Jabneel?
En-haddah
Anem?
Sea of Chinnereth, or Galilee, or Tiberias
Bethsaida Julias
Gergesa?
Hippos
Aphek
Gadara
Lo-debar
Camon?
Pella
River Jordan
Seleucia
Gamala?
Golan?
Abila
Ragelim?
Beth-arbel
Ham
Dion
Karnaim, Carnaim
Ashtaroth
Raphana, Raphon
Bosor
Edrei
Ramoth-gilead
Tob?
Bozrah, Bosora
Kenath, Nobah, Canatha
Damascus
River Abana
River Pharpar
A B C D E F G H I J K L
1 2 3 4 5 6 7 8
35° 30' 36° 30' 33° 30'

About 876 B.C. the throne of Israel was seized by an army officer named Omri (I Kings 16:15 ff.), who became one of the most illustrious rulers of Israel, in spite of the fact that he reigned only twelve years, half of which time he struggled with civil war in his land. He was so well known that for more than a century the official name for Samaria in the Assyrian records was "House of Omri," while Israel could be called "the land of Omri," even though his dynasty was swept from the throne in the bloody Elijah-Elisha-Jehu revolution c. 842 B.C. One of his first acts was to purchase the hill of Samaria, some seven miles northwest of Shechem, and there to begin the erection of a beautiful new capital (Fig. 34; IX, F-3). By this act he created a city which, like Jerusalem, the "City of David," was the personal possession of the king and one which could be wholly utilized for governmental purposes. Excavations have uncovered some of the constructions begun by Omri and completed by his son, Ahab. On the mound's summit a wall was built to surround the palace and its courtyard. This was in turn enclosed by two more walls, the first on a terrace and the other around the base of the hill. The masonry is like the finest used in the Solomonic building at Megiddo; its superb workmanship has probably never been surpassed in Palestine. The summit wall was only about five feet wide, but the stones were cut and bonded so carefully and the foundation, usually in trenches in the natural rock, so well prepared, that it would have been very difficult to break through. The city gate was at the east, approached through a monumental court, the walls of which had pilasters with capitals of the Ionic type, that is, carved in curved volutes in a style that the Greeks were later to develop into their Ionic column. In the ruins of the city there were also found a large number of carved ivory pieces that had been used as inlays for boxes and fine furniture. From I Kings 22:39 we learn that Ahab had built what is called an "ivory house," and a century later Amos spoke about Israelites who lay on beds of ivory (Amos 6:4; cf. ch. 3:15).

Following the policy of David and Solomon, close commercial relations were established between Israel and Phoenicia, and they were strengthened by the political marriage of Ahab, Omri's son, with Jezebel, the daughter of the king of Tyre. She was an extremely forceful person, who attempted to impose her own religion and the totalitarian methods of Tyre upon Israel. The reaction to her was led by the prophets Elijah and Elisha, who did not rest until every vestige of the dynasty of Omri had been swept away and a new dynasty formed under an army leader named Jehu (II Kings, chs. 9; 10).

Plate VII:B shows the state of affairs at this time. Aram or Syria, having secured its independence during the days of Solomon, was now united as a formidable kingdom with its capital at Damascus (VII, D-3). By the time of Ahab this kingdom was Israel's most potent enemy, and a succession of battles was fought as far south as Ramoth-gilead, an Israelite city which was now on the frontier (VII:B, D-4) and at which Ahab lost his life when "a certain man drew a bow at a venture" (I Kings 22:34). By 853 B.C., however, Assyria was strong enough to have gained control over northern Syria and to begin its first push southward against Aram and Israel. These two countries composed their differences and joined with Hamath (VII, D-1) long enough to meet the Assyrian emperor, Shalmaneser III, in battle at Qarqar on the River Orontes, north of Damascus. For some reason, the Bible does not mention this battle; but Shalmaneser tells us that his opposition was Hadadezer of Damascus with 1,200 chariots, 1,200 cavalrymen and 20,000 infantry; Irhuleni of Hamath with 700 chariots, 700 cavalrymen, and 10,000 infantry; and "Ahab, the Israelite," with 2,000 chariots and 10,000 infantry.*

The horse and chariot as a weapon of war had been introduced by the Hyksos during the eighteenth century B.C. (see p. 28), but Israel first made use of this weapon during the reigns of David and Solomon (II Sam. 8:4; I Kings 10:26). Ahab now had more of them than his northern neighbors, though as yet he made no use of cavalry

FIG. 34. The hill where once stood Samaria, Palestine's most famous city after Jerusalem. The site was purchased by Omri c. 875 B.C. and made the capital of the Northern Kingdom. He and his son, Ahab, built a wall (Fig. 35) around the summit and two more around the slopes. The city gate was to the right of the picture and was approached on the other side (north) of the hill. In Roman times a new roadway to the gate was built and lined with columns on this (the south) side, about one fourth of the way from the top within what is now a line of trees.

which had only recently been introduced in the warfare of the area and of which Hamath and Damascus had a considerable number. Shalmaneser claimed a marvelous victory at Qarqar, but it could not have been as successful as he implies because he withdrew from Syria without following up any advantage he may have secured, thus leaving Aram and Israel free to resume their private war with one another. Israel was aided in this conflict by Jehoshaphat, king of Judah, for the Dynasty of Omri had ended the rivalry between the two Palestinian kingdoms by a treaty (cf. I Kings, ch. 22).

By c. 842 B.C. both Moab and Edom had successfully rebelled against Israel and Judah respectively (II Kings 3:4 ff.; 8:20 ff.) and become independent. Mesha, the king of Moab, commemorated his triumph by erecting a stele in his capital city, Dibon (VII:B, C-5; see Fig. 33). On this monument Mesha tells us that Omri, king of Israel, had humbled Moab for many years because the Moabite god "Chemosh was angry at his land. And his son (grandson) followed him and said, 'I will humble Moab.' In my time he spoke (thus), but I have triumphed over him and over his house, while Israel hath perished forever!"

The violent revolution that shook Israel c. 842 B.C. placed another army general, Jehu, on the throne (II Kings, ch. 9). The Jehu revolt broke the alliances that the Omri dynasty had made with Phoenicia and with Judah, and Israel did not again join with Damascus in an attempt to repel Shalmaneser III of Assyria. The result was that the latter had no difficulty in forcing the separated powers to pay him tribute in 841 B.C. The Assyrian king thought sufficiently highly of this event that he portrays Jehu kissing the ground before him, and followed by a line of Israelites bearing tribute to him. This portrayal was on his well-known "Black Obelisk"; it is the first picture of Israelites that we have from the ancient world (see Fig. 53).

ISRAEL AND JUDAH DURING THE EIGHTH CENTURY B.C.

During the latter part of the ninth and the first half of the eighth century Assyria gave little further trouble to the peoples of Palestine. Their great enemy was Hazael, king of Damascus, whom the Assyrians called a "son of nobody" (that is, a commoner; cf. II Kings 8:7-15). Until the devastation of Damascus by Assyria in 805 B.C., Hazael was able to deal blow upon blow to both Israel and Judah, until by 815 B.C. Israel was scarcely able to defend herself further and Judah had paid tribute to him (II Kings 12:17 to 13:23).

After Hazael's demise, there came to Israel the long reigns of Joash and Jeroboam II, which together extended from c. 801 to 746 B.C. During that time, Israel reached the height of her power and prosperity. Either earlier in the reign of Jehu or during the first two decades of the eighth century the capital city of Samaria was refortified and the Omri-Ahab palace was repaired or rebuilt (Periods II

*For translations of the original text of this and other inscriptions to which allusion is made in this chapter, see J. B. Pritchard, ed., *Ancient Near Eastern Texts Relating to the Old Testament*, Princeton, 1950.

FIG. 35. Some remains of the Omri-Ahab wall built around the summit of the hill of Samaria. While the wall was only about five feet wide, the stones were so carefully dressed and laid that it would have been difficult to break down. The embossing on the surface of the stones indicates that this portion was probably meant to be underground; above the ground the stones were generally cut smooth. Note the header-stretcher method by which the stones were laid: that is, two stones laid crosswise so that only their ends (headers) show, and then a stone laid lengthwise. In the adjoining courses above and below, the headers appear in the middle of the stretchers of the intervening layer so that the bonding is perfect and no weakness is apparent.

and III of the archaeologists). Around the more vulnerable parts of the summit of the mound a casemate wall was erected, that is, there were two parallel walls joined by cross walls, an outer one nearly six feet thick, an inner one about three and one half feet thick. On the north, the total width of the two walls and the intervening space which was filled up with rubble was nearly thirty-one feet. The stones of the walls and the foundations prepared for them were so well laid and made that it is probably to be considered as the finest city fortification in Palestinian history before the Herodian work in Jerusalem. It was kept in repair, used for centuries and not replaced until c. 150 B.C.

The most astonishing feat of arms during this age was Jeroboam's defeat of Aram, his capture of Damascus and the restoration of the northern Davidic border in Syria (II Kings 14:25; cf. Plate VII:A). Two prophets were closely related to this victory, but they were of a very different type. One, Jonah, son of Amittai, gave the divine sanction to Jeroboam's enterprise (II Kings 14:25), thus earning a reputation as a popular, nationalistic prophet which made it possible for a later writer in the book that bears his name to use him as an example of all that a prophet should not be. For Amos, however, the victory of Jeroboam had a different meaning, and he took the occasion as a time to issue the warning in God's name that the pride of victory was mere prelude to the national ruin that was soon to come (see Amos 6:13, 14, R. S. V.).

Amos, together with the prophets Hosea and Isaiah, shared a belief in impending crisis and doom—a belief which events fully justified. In 745 B.C. a new Assyrian king came to the throne in Nineveh after a revolt; he was Tiglath-pileser III (c.745–727 B.C.). Soon he was in Syria with a great army and was beginning the subjugation of the Syro-Palestinian coastland. Northern Syria was shortly conquered and formed into an Assyrian province, ruled from Arpad (III, C-2; cf. II Kings 19:13). Jeroboam II, Israel's last strong king, had died c. 746 B.C., and now, as the political pressure on the country increased, the inner strength evaporated in frequent civil war and revolt, with king succeeding king, until the country was in virtual chaos. In Syria, Tiglath-pileser was confronted with a coalition headed by one Azriau of Yauda. These two words are the Assyrian spelling for Azariah (Uzziah) and Judah. It has seemed so improbable that Judeans would have been fighting in Syria that scholars have sought another Judah in the north. Yet it would be an extraordinary coincidence if there were another strong state named Judah with another king named Azariah, who by his name indicated that he was a worshiper of another god named Yahweh. Recently several scholars have returned to the view generally held in the last century that there was only one Judah in western Asia at this time, and that was in southern Palestine. Under Uzziah (c. 783-742) it had one of the most stable governments in its area and in him it possessed one of the outstanding personalities of his time. It need not be presumed that he personally led the coalition against Tiglath-pileser in battle. Nevertheless, he was the focus of the western opposition to Assyria in the years 744-742 B.C. Then he died (a leper) and his name suddenly disappeared from the Assyrian records.

The coalition evidently was successful in preventing Assyrian penetration as far south as Palestine. This success and that against Shalmaneser III a century before would explain why new coalitions were subsequently formed in spite of repeated failure and why such bitter anger was exhibited against Judah when in 734 B.C. she refused again to join her neighbors (see below). In any event, the first tribute paid to Tiglath-pileser from Israel was that given by Menahem in 738 B.C. when he used that means of buying Assyrian support in order to preserve his seat on a shaky throne (II Kings 15:19). The crucial years, however, were those between 735 and 732 B.C. To ward off a coming attack Rezin, king of Damascus, and Pekah, king of Israel, formed a new coalition against Assyria, and tried to get Judah to enter it. Yet this time King Ahaz, Uzziah's grandson, refused to join, was attacked by the other two, defeated, and finally saved only by the actual approach of the Assyrian army (II Kings 16:5ff.; II Chron., ch. 28; Isa., ch. 7). In 733-732 B.C. Tiglath-pileser conquered the Palestinian coast line, Galilee, Gilead, and Damascus. He says: "Officers of mine I installed as governors upon them." That is, as a result of this campaign, the conquered territory was turned into Assyrian provinces and was no longer allowed to govern itself. Israel was left as a small territory in the hill country west of the Jordan, while Galilee and Gilead were separated from it and administered by Assyrian officials. This was in accord with a new policy begun by Tiglath-pileser and supported by the mass deportation of large numbers of people from one area and resettling them elsewhere. All the remaining small states of the Palestinian region now became tributary to Assyria, paying regular tribute though left to regulate their own internal affairs. These were Ammon, Moab, Edom, Philistia, and Judah. Indeed the Bible presents an eloquent portrayal of the disillusionment of King Ahaz: after paying his homage to Tiglath-pileser in Damascus, he gave up what little of his ancestral faith he had left, closed the Temple, and became a polytheist (II Chron. 28:20ff.).

A few years later, however, as a result of refusal to pay tribute, Shalmaneser V, the successor of Tiglath-pileser III, laid siege to Samaria. He died before the city was captured, but Sargon II (722-705 B.C.) completed the task in the first months of 721 B.C. According to his own statement, he carried 27,290 Israelites (presumably all the political leaders, the elders, the artisans, and the well-to-do) into exile, settling them in the region of "Gozan, and in the cities of the Medes" (II Kings 17:6; XI:A, C-2 and D-2). In their place new settlers were brought from Babylonia, Elam, and Syria by Sargon and his successors. Thus, what the prophets had foretold came to pass; the Kingdom of Israel was ended. The central interest of the Biblical story now shifts to Judah.

Plate VII:C shows the state of affairs in Palestine about 700 B.C., several years after the fall of Israel. Judah had barely escaped the fate of Israel in 701 B.C. when Sennacherib had attacked the country (II Kings, chs. 18; 19; Isa., chs. 36; 37). Hezekiah, against the advice of Isaiah, had entered into a defensive alliance with the Philistine cities, after having secured the promise of Egyptian help. Among his preparations for the battle was the digging of the Siloam Tunnel in Jerusalem to insure the water supply in case of siege (see p. 106, and Plate XVII:A). Isaiah denounced these acts in strong terms (chs. 22; 30:1-4; 31:1-3); yet the revolt was carried out. Sennacherib crushed it severely, destroying, he says, forty-six Judean cities, chief among which was Lachish (VII:C, B-5; Figs. 36-37). Jerusalem was saved by payment of a heavy tribute (II Kings 18:13ff.). Both archaeological evidence and Sennacherib's own account of the event suggest that the Assyrian king did not want to destroy the country.

He simply broke down all fortified centers of resistance; except Jerusalem, in order to force the country again to acknowledge his rule and resume tribute. He says that he drove out of the walled cities of Judah 200,150 people. This does not mean that he took that number captive; the figure was probably a rough computation of the size of the population of Judah outside Jerusalem. As such it is very valuable because it suggests a total Judean population of approximately a quarter million. The Kingdom of Judah was left in a weakened condition, controlling only its hill country, the lowlands (Shephelah), and part of the barren wilderness to the south of Beer-sheba (in the Negeb), where its boundary with Edom cannot now be clearly defined (VII:C).

THE LAST DAYS OF JUDAH (c. 700-587 B.C.)

For the better part of the seventh century Judah continued as a vassal of Assyria, paying regular tribute. In lists of western client kings the Assyrian emperors Esarhaddon (681-669 B.C.) and Asshurbanapal (669-c.633 B.C.) both mention Manasseh, king of Judah, and in each case he is second in the list, following the king of Tyre, which would suggest that he was by no means unimportant. A serious revolt against Assyria, led by Babylon, occurred between 652 and 648 B.C., and this is probably the occasion for the revolt of Manasseh as described in II Chron. 33:11. In any event, except for this one event or because of it Manasseh appears to have been a very pliant figure for the Assyrians, even introducing Assyrian religious cults into the Temple in Jerusalem and ruthlessly suppressing all opposition. In 640 B.C. his son, Amon, was murdered, probably by extremists who wished to throw off the Assyrian yoke. The moderates prevailed, however, and placed another son, Josiah, on the throne, even though he was only an eight-year-old boy.

During the next few years the decline of Assyrian power was rapid and Judah was able to take progressive advantage of the situation. In 632 B.C. after the death of Asshurbanapal, Josiah repudiated the Assyrian religious cults and the syncretistic policies of his father (II Chron. 34:3). In 628 B.C., evidently after the death of Asshurbanapal's successor, a religious reform was initiated not only in Judah but also in Israel as far as Galilee (II Chron. 34: 3-7). The political significance of this religious act was that Josiah took control of the Assyrian provinces of Samaria and Megiddo (see Plate VII: C), thus reasserting the ancient Davidic claim to a united Israel. It was also at this juncture that Jeremiah received his call as a prophet and during the years that followed warned about the northern peril. In 622 B.C. Josiah carried out a great religious reform (II Kings, chs. 22;23) under the influence of an old law book (Deuteronomy or some portion of it) found during repair work in the Temple. Sacrifice at shrines and high places about the country was prohibited by royal decree; worship was now centralized in Jerusalem where pagan excesses could be kept under control. This reform probably marked the final break with Assyria, and it came at a time when Babylon had just secured its independence and was preparing to invade Assyria itself.

After the fall of Nineveh in 612 B.C., the Assyrian army fell back to Haran (III, C-2). Pharaoh Necho of Egypt then decided to intervene, assist the Assyrians (II Kings 23:29, R. S. V.) and keep them a buffer between himself and Babylon. This policy would enable him to recover Palestine and most of Syria as an Egyptian dependency. Josiah seems quickly to have analyzed the situation and to have seen that the only hope for him, the lesser of the evils, was to do what he could to prevent Necho from reaching Haran in time to save the Assyrians from the Babylonians. In 609 B.C. Josiah placed his army in the path of Necho at the pass of Megiddo. His plan succeeded; Necho was unable to help the Assyrians, but Josiah was killed in the attempt to stop him. For the next four years (609-605 B.C.) Necho controlled Palestine; but, after the battle of Carchemish in 605 B.C. in which Necho was defeated by Nebuchadnezzar, the country was taken over by the Babylonians.

The dominant prophetic figure of this period was Jeremiah, who warned the Judeans against the disaster that would surely come if their current policies were not altered. His famous Temple sermon was given at a festival during the year following Josiah's death when the Egyptians were in control (Jer., chs. 7;26; 608 B.C.). He emerged from hiding to deliver a scourging attack on Jehoiakim and to call Nebuchadnezzar the Lord's "servant" after the battle of Carchemish (chs. 36; 25; 605 B.C.). A recently published portion of the Babylonian Chronicle, an official document which lists the chief events in the Babylonian empire (see further p. 74), reports that at Carchemish Nebuchadnezzar so annihilated the Egyptian army "that not a single man escaped." Nevertheless, the document continues, the Egyptians managed to defeat Nebuchadnezzar in 601 B.C. It is probable that this event encouraged Jehoiakim to revolt. He died before Nebuchadnezzar retaliated. The Chronicle gives the official Babylonian report of what happened. It says that in Nebuchadnezzar's seventh year he marched his army into the land of Khatti (Syria-Palestine) and besieged Jerusalem. He captured the city on the second day of the twelfth month (mid-March, 597 B.C.) and took the king (the youthful Jehoiachin) prisoner (cf. II Kings 24:1-17; Jer. 22:24-30).

In 594-593 the atmosphere among both Judeans and the exiles had again become electric. In the international situation popular prophets and political leaders had combined to convince many of the people that freedom was at hand. Revolt was planned in which Edom, Moab, Ammon, Tyre, and Sidon joined. Jeremiah did everything in his power to prevent it, sending messages to the foreign ambassadors, addressing the Judean king, Zedekiah, and writing to the exiles, asking them to settle down and even to pray for the welfare of their captors (chs. 27 to 29). Zedekiah was summoned to Babylon (Jer. 51:59), the tension quieted, and in 592 official Babylonian documents list Jehoiachin as "king of Judah" and as receiving regular court rations, indicating that they are holding him as a hostage and allowing him the title "king." Yet within four years revolt had again flared, and in 588-587 Nebuchadnezzar utterly laid waste every important town of Judah, destroying Jerusalem and the Temple in August, 587 (II Kings, ch. 25; Jer.,

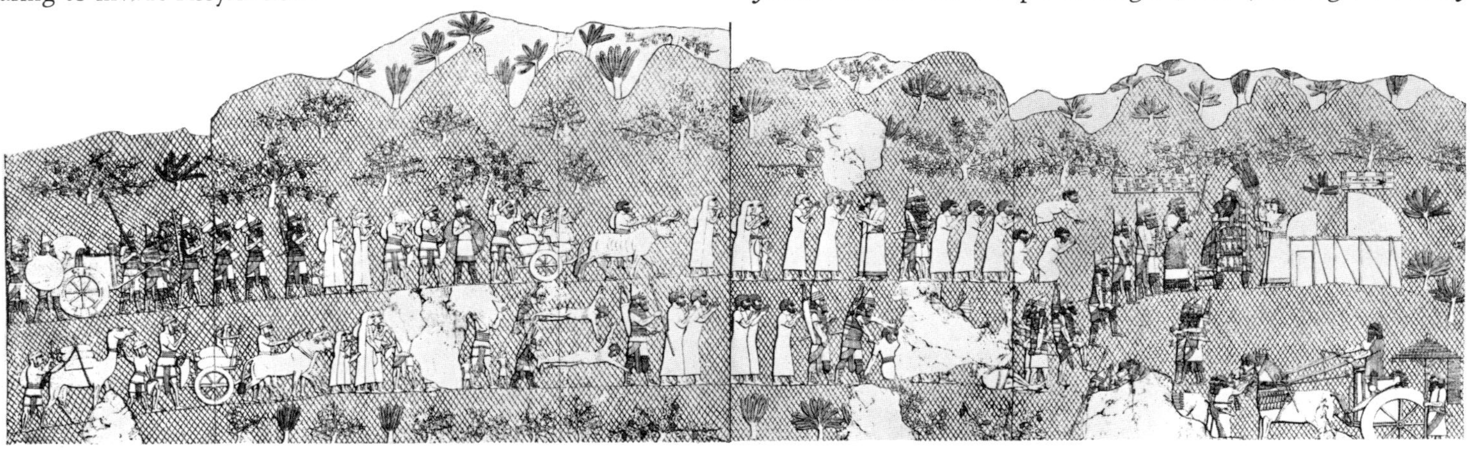

FIG. 36. A relief from the Assyrian palace of Sennacherib at Nineveh, which depicts his capture of Lachish in Judah in 701 B.C. The king is shown enthroned in full splendor, his tent and chariot waiting behind him. His officials are presenting the captives: Judean elders of the city in their long white tunics bow before him while behind them is a long line of Judean men, women, and children, accompanied by Assyrian soldiers, carts, and valuables, evidently prepared for the long journey into exile.

FIG. 37. A reconstruction of the Judean fortress-city of Lachish (VII: A-D, B-5). Note the double fortification walls, the strongly protected city gate, and the palace of the local Judean governor in the midst of the city—all probably erected by the command of Rehoboam (II Chron. 11:9). A group of letters written by the officer in charge of a near-by outpost to the commandant of Lachish was found in the ruins of the gate. They date from c. 589 or 588 B.C., before Nebuchadnezzar's subjection of Judah in 588-587 B.C.

ch. 39). The devastation was so complete that town after town was never reinhabited, and it was centuries before the country recovered. In the ruins of the final devastation of the city gate of Lachish excavators have found a group of letters written by the commander of a neighboring outpost to his superior in the city. They reveal the same state of tension and excitement in the country that is reflected in The Book of Jeremiah.

Thousands of Judeans were now scattered in the Babylonian Empire, among them Ezekiel. The poor who were left in Judah were prey to the hostile neighbors. Edom in particular was never forgotten because of the cruelty of her raids upon Judah, and because her people rapidly took over complete control of the southern part of the country (cf. Ps. 137:7; Ezek., ch. 35; Obadiah).

POST-EXILIC JUDAH

Within two decades after the death of Nebuchadnezzar in 562 B.C. the Babylonian empire was crumpling. Shortly after the Persian conquest in 539 B.C. (cf. p. 74) permission was given for the exiles to return to Judah, and over a period of years a considerable company did so (Ezra, chs. 1ff.). The first group to return was led by one Sheshbazzar, who immediately laid the foundation for a new temple on the site of the one that had been destroyed (Ezra 5:16). He was unable to complete it, however, because of the interference of the hostile neighbors and of "the people of the land" (Judeans who had not been in exile). When Darius I came to the throne in 522 B.C. he appointed Zerubbabel, the grandson of King Jehoiachin (Jechoniah; Matt. 1:12), as governor of the province. Zerubbabel returned from Babylon with a considerable company of priests and Levites (Neh. 12:1), and with the help of the high priest Joshua and with the encouragement of the prophets Haggai and Zechariah he completed the Temple between 520 and 515 B.C. The obstacles in the meantime had partially been cleared away by a decree of Darius (Ezra, chs. 5; 6). The prophecies of Haggai and Zechariah were delivered at a time of unrest in the reign of Darius (520-519 B.C.), and they believed the Persian empire would soon fall. They even implied that Zerubbabel was the Lord's Anointed (Messiah) to reign over a new Israel. When these things did not come to pass, disillusionment seems to have fallen over the Judeans and prophets of that type did not receive a wide hearing from this time forth. The Persians appear to have deprived the Davidic family of all political power after this time. Governors were appointed, but more power seems to have been turned over to the Judean high priest.

Plate VII:D shows the approximate size of Judah during this age. It was a tiny province in the Fifth Persian Satrapy, extending from Bethel to Beth-zur. Its population during the fifth century was probably at the maximum not more than about 50,000 (cf. Ezra 2:64; Neh. 7:66). After the fall of Jerusalem in 587 B.C., it seems probable that the province of Samaria to the north had gradually assumed more and more influence over the Jerusalem area. The Persian creation of the new province of Judah was met, therefore, with every type of local opposition that the interested parties could muster. The Temple was finally completed only after direct orders had been received from the Persian chancellery for all opposition to cease. In 445 B.C., however, Nehemiah returned with an additional group of exiles. He had been appointed governor of the province with permission to rebuild the walls of Jerusalem (Neh., chs. 1ff.). He immediately encountered the strongest kind of opposition from Sanballat, governor of the province of Samaria, from Tobiah, governor of Ammon across the Jordan, and from Geshem "the Arab." It was not in their interest that Jerusalem be strengthened. Nehemiah in a moving narrative describes how their plots were frustrated (Neh. 2:19-20; chs. 4; 6).

Both Sanballat and Tobiah were formally worshipers of the God of Israel. The sons of the former are mentioned in the archives of the Jewish community, found at Elephantine in Upper Egypt. The family of Tobiah can also be traced from archaeological sources; their tomb and palace, the latter dating from about 200 B.C., still exist at 'Araq el-Emir in Transjordan. Recent archaeological information identifies the formerly enigmatic "Geshem the Arab." His territory had replaced the Edomites on the southern boundary of Judah. At the time of Jerusalem's fall to the Babylonians the Edomites had taken over southern Judah, and this was followed by prophetic judgments of doom on that country by Jeremiah, Ezekiel, Obadiah, and Second Isaiah (Isa., ch. 34). By the time of Nehemiah, however, the Edomites are no more. Their territory has been taken over by Arabs, and Geshem appears now on two inscriptions as king of a confederation of Arabian tribes which had its center at Kedar (XI, A-C, B-3). While the Kingdom of Kedar was under nominal Persian control in the time of Nehemiah, it had absorbed Edom and extended its power over a wide territory in North Arabia, Sinai and even into the eastern reaches of Egypt. Three silver vessels, bearing inscriptions, have recently been acquired by the Brooklyn Museum. They were originally gifts to an Arabian goddess worshiped at a shrine in ancient Succoth (V, D-3), and one of them says that it was given by "Cain (Qaynu), son of Geshem (Gashmu), king of Kedar." There is no doubt that this Cain is the son of the adversary of Nehemiah and that he was able to exercise a control over the eastern Delta of Egypt where his people had built a shrine.

Beginning in the time of Nehemiah and continuing into the fourth century, the province of Judah was given the status of a semiautonomous priestly commonwealth, with the right to levy its own taxes and issue its own coinage. A number of jar handles have been found that have been stamped with the word *Yehud* (the official Aramaic spelling of "Judah") or with "Jerusalem." The first coins in Palestine of Jewish mintage appear also at this time, bearing the province name, *Yehud*. Before the fifth century sums of money (gold or silver) were weighed in scales. The Persian government, however, got the idea of coined money from the Greeks and introduced it into the empire. The earliest coins in Judah were modeled after the Greek daric (cf. Ezra 8:27; Neh. 7:70-72).

During this age another group of exiles returned to Jerusalem under the leadership of Ezra. He bore with him a commission from the Persian monarch which authorized him to reform Jewish religious life "according to the law of your God, which is in your hand" (Ezra 7:11-26). Precisely what this document was we are not informed. Evidently, it was a work which Jewish scholars had completed in Babylon. It is not impossible that Ezra brought with him the final priestly edition of the first four books of the Old Testament. In any event, Ezra's mission meant that Jewish life from this time on was to be governed by a written law. For the first time the variety of old legal traditions was collected into one written form and used as constitutional law. In this sense Ezra can be said to be the father of Judaism. The date of his work in Judah is a matter of much debate. There appears to be an increasing body of scholarly opinion that would date his return to Jerusalem after that of Nehemiah, sometime toward the end of the reign of Artaxerxes I (465-424 B.C.) or in 398 B.C. which would be the seventh year of the reign of Artaxerxes II (cf. Ezra 7:7).

NORTHERN PALESTINE IN BIBLICAL TIMES

Plate VIII

THE center of interest in Northern Palestine is Galilee and Esdraelon (Plate viii, D-F 4-7). Here, as a survey of the map reveals, the cities and towns were thickest. Here, too, the history of Northern Palestine found its focus. Galilee particularly witnessed religious developments of the greatest significance for both Judaism and Christianity.

THE UNINVITING SEA

In order to understand the history which took place in the Galilean region, it is necessary to make a brief study of the physical features of the surrounding areas and observe how they affected Galilee. Turning first to the west, we note that the seacoast of Palestine proper lacks the broken shore lines and safe harbors which would encourage maritime ventures. South of Mount Carmel (viii, C-6) the coast offers no harbor; when Herod the Great (40-4 B.C.) rebuilt Strato's Tower and renamed it Caesarea (viii, B-8), he provided an adequate harbor only by building sea walls out from the shore, a feat which required unusual engineering skill. This Herodian city, however, which later became the residence of the Roman procurator who governed Judaea in the days of Jesus, had its connection with central Palestine rather than with the region north of Carmel.

Mount Carmel itself, an impressive wooded height projecting northwest into the Mediterranean, never attained great political or military significance. Though famed as the home of an ancient sanctuary of Baal (I Kings 18:19 ff.), it was separated from the main body of Palestine by passes running through the hills on its southeast flank (cf. Fig. 26), and was thus too isolated to be a center of power. Nor did its promontory protect a harbor. Just north of Carmel was a bay which offered partial shelter to shipping. Here Accho, later called Ptolemais (viii, C-5), was used as a port (Acts 21:7), but it had no adequately protected harbor. There were numerous towns just east of the bay, but they did not face the sea. Their main connection was with the area north and east.

PHOENICIA FACES SEAWARD

Further north, in the district of Phoenicia proper (viii, D-E 1-4), the situation was entirely different. The closely crowding hills and the lack of an extensive coastal plain made it impossible to support life by agriculture and grazing. Settlers in this section were forced to turn to the sea. Moreover, although there were roads which led from Galilee to the Phoenician ports, they were not the major routes for caravan trade from the east. Therefore no adequate economic basis existed for intimate relations between Phoenicia and Galilee. Accordingly, this stretch of seacoast which developed a seafaring people had no great influence upon the country immediately to the east. The course of history in Galilee and Transjordan was not determined by nearness to the sea.

In full harmony with the physical features of the region, Phoenicia was never part of Israel. Even the golden age of Israelite expansion under David and Solomon saw no attempt to conquer or control this region. Nor did the interest of the city-states of Phoenicia lead them to make any serious attempt to master the country to the east, although they usually controlled the coast as far south as Mount Carmel, and at one time took over certain border villages of Galilee (I Kings 9:11). Phoenicia faced west; her life was centered in sea trade; her expansion was achieved by founding numerous colonies as outposts for her life and commerce (see pp. 33, 34). Most noted of these was Carthage (xiii, B-2).

The chief cities of Phoenicia were Sidon (viii, E-1) and Tyre (viii, D-3). The former was more prominent in the second millennium B.C., but the latter, situated in Old Testament times on an island just off the coast, had outstripped her northern neighbor by the time of the Hebrew monarchy. Tyre was a city of unusual strength. Shalmaneser V, Sennacherib, Esarhaddon, Asshurbanapal, and Nebuchadnezzar failed in attempts to capture it. Alexander the Great had to spend seven months before he succeeded in taking it by building a great causeway from the mainland to the island.

By reason of manifold contacts and wide expansion, Phoenicia became the middleman of the ancient world for the distribution of cultural possessions. She is given credit for having carried the alphabet from Asia to Greek lands. She was also famous for her articles of merchandise and extensive trade, so well described in Ezek., ch. 27. Her purple dyes, made from the murex shells found along her shores (see p. 33), were widely known and eagerly sought. Her art, architecture, and types of artifacts always were the dominant influence on the material culture of Palestine. David, Solomon, and Omri made use of her building skill in the construction of cities, palaces, and the Temple (see pp. 48 ff.). Phoenician seamen helped to build and man Solomon's fleet for the purpose of capturing the Arabian and African trade (I Kings 10:22). Solomon's smelter (*tarshîsh*) at Ezion-geber (see pp. 50, 69) was probably built from Phoenician models.

In view of these relations between Israel and Phoenicia it is not surprising to read that in a time of famine the Prophet Elijah found refuge in Zarephath (viii, E-2; cf. I Kings 17:9). But such facts must not be used to argue that Phoenicia and Israel were united in life and interests, even in the Old Testament period. In New Testament times, it is significant that the Elijah incident mentioned above is treated as quite exceptional (Luke 4:26), and the journey of Jesus into "the parts of Tyre and Sidon" (Matt. 15:21) is regarded as a definite withdrawal from the bounds of Israel. Phoenicia was a separate country, and in New Testament times, when the Romans had taken over the entire region of Palestine and Syria, they grouped Phoenicia and the Carmel region with Syria rather than with Palestine.

THE NORTHERN MOUNTAIN BARRIER

The rugged slopes of Mount Lebanon (viii, F-G 1) and Mount Hermon (viii, H-2), with the broken surface of the intervening valleys, made travel too difficult and dangerous to encourage regular intercourse between Galilee and the country north of the Lebanons. For this reason Israel rarely attempted to expand in that direction.

Fig. 38. Source of the River Jordan near Caesarea Philippi (viii, G-3). The water rushes from the southwestern foot of Mount Hermon. This, however, is only one of four sources of the Jordan. Another is just north of Abel-beth-maachah (viii, F-3); a third on the west slope of Mount Hermon; the fourth in the valley at Dan (viii, G-3). The sources at Dan and Caesarea Philippi are the largest.

FIG. 39. Mount Tabor, c. 1,850 feet above sea level. Here met the borders of the tribes of Issachar, Zebulun, and Naphtali. It controlled one of the eastern exits from Esdraelon. From this strategic height Barak started his charge against Sisera (Judg., ch. 4). One Christian tradition locates the scene of Christ's transfiguration on Tabor.

The traditional northern limit was Dan (VIII, G-3; cf. I Sam. 3:20), not far from the sources of the Jordan (see Fig. 38). Only under her strongest rulers did she seek to extend her borders farther north, into the region east of Mount Lebanon; such efforts were crowned with but temporary success.

THE FERTILE REGION OF DAMASCUS

East of Mount Hermon lies a much more inviting area. The rivers Abana and Pharpar (VIII, H-L 1-2), rising on the mountain slopes, flow off to the east. On their way they irrigate a fertile and attractive region, until they break up into many smaller streams and lose themselves in trying to water the thirsty soil. Here was found what might be called an immense oasis. It invited settlers, and offered a center of interest and trade to nomads of the desert.

In this favored spot arose the ancient city of Damascus (VIII, J-1). Her situation guaranteed a permanent life of trade and influence. Nevertheless, her environment set firm limits to her power. To the north and west mountains prevented any direct expansion. On the east the desert offered no great opportunity for development. She might exercise considerable influence upon the rather sparsely settled plateau to the southwest, but Palestine was too far away to be within effective reach of her power.

Thus the region of Damascus, which is what the Old Testament means when it refers to Syria or Aram, had a history somewhat separate from that of Palestine. Strong kings such as Hazael (II Kings 10:32 f.; 12:17 f.) extended their influence across the plateau country into the life of Israel, and there were almost constant trade contacts between the two regions. The famous "Way of the Sea" was one of the trade routes which connected Damascus with Palestine. This ancient caravan route ran southwest to cross the Jordan below Lake Huleh or Semechonitis (VIII, F-G 4), touched the Sea of Galilee on the northwest, passed through Galilee to Esdraelon, and thence either proceeded to the sea or branched off southward to reach points in Palestine or Egypt. Evidence of commercial contact along such roads is given by the Samarian quarter in Damascus and the Damascene quarter in the city of Samaria, in the ninth century B.C. (I Kings 20:34). But direct and effective political control of Palestine was more difficult, and Damascus never achieved this. She usually played the role of a rival power, or of a small kingdom that sought alliance with neighboring rulers against threatened aggression.

At the end of the fourth century B.C. Damascus lost much of her political importance when Antioch on the Orontes River (XI:D, B-2) was founded as the capital of Syria. Even then, however, her importance continued as a center of trade and an outpost on the desert frontier. In New Testament times Damascus had a link southward with the Hellenistic cities of the Decapolis (Plate XIV), which included Scythopolis west of the Jordan (VIII, F-8) as well as Canatha (VIII, L-6), Raphana (VIII, J-5), Dion (VIII, I-6), Hippos (VIII, G-6), Abila (VIII, H-7), Gadara (VIII, G-7), and Pella (VIII, F-8). It is somewhat surprising that a city so far north as Damascus should be a member of this league of Hellenistic cities in Transjordan; her inclusion is a witness to her importance as a trade center and as a bulwark against eastern forces which might threaten this region.

THE ḤAURÂN PLATEAU

South of the Pharpar River lay a broad, high plateau, 2,000 feet above sea level. It was called Bashan in Old Testament times, and Ḥaurân in later centuries (VIII, H-K 4-7). Signs of volcanic action are numerous in this section. The huge mass of hardened lava labeled Trachonitis (VIII, J-L 4-5), and the smaller mass of lava some ten miles northwest, are striking evidence of extensive volcanic activity in prehistoric times. Along the east rim of the Jordan Valley and on the eastern side of the plateau are many extinct volcanoes.

Furthermore, the prevailing limestone of Palestine is here covered with a layer of black basalt, which extends into parts of Galilee. The modern traveler is reminded of these formations when he sees the black basalt ruins of an ancient synagogue at Chorazin (VIII, F-5). The volcanic character of the plateau extends south to the Yarmuk River (I, D-3). In this region the soil is a rich red, and nothing but the limitations of its water supply keep it from being more populous and prosperous. Only to the south of the Yarmuk, however, does water become more plentiful and provide the basis for a considerable population.

The plateau east of the Sea of Galilee was generally affected by the fortunes of Damascus, yet was rarely an integral part of the political and social life of that state. On the other hand, it was little settled by Israelites and seldom mastered by Israelite rulers. Nevertheless, it was too close to the Jordan and Galilee, and too much in contact with the more Israelite section of Gilead south of the Yarmuk, to be entirely independent of the course of events in Palestine. The tribe of Manasseh settled both north and south of the Yarmuk (Deut. 3:13), although the extent of its occupation in Bashan is a question. Solomon taxed this region (I Kings 4:13). In the ninth century B.C., however, the rulers of Syria wrested it from Israelite control.

The later Maccabees gained control of part of the area (Plate XII:A), and later Herod the Great included all of it in his kingdom. His son Philip ruled it as a separate tetrarchy (Luke 3:1). Philip built his capital at Bethsaida Julias (VIII, F-5), which is probably to be located on the shore of the Sea of Galilee rather than two miles north at *et-Tell.* This location of his capital shows that his tetrarchy was related to Galilee in life and trade; but his territory was not really Jewish. He built also the pagan city of Caesarea Philippi at Paneas (VIII, G-3; cf. Mark 8:27), and the population of this area was predominantly Gentile. It should be noticed that it was only to non-Jewish rulers such as Herod the Great, Philip, Herod Agrippa I (A.D. 37-44; cf. Acts 12:1), and Herod Agrippa II (A.D. 53-c.100; cf. Acts 25:13) that the Romans entrusted the rule of this essentially non-Jewish region (Plates XII:B-D; XIV).

Because Transjordan was constantly threatened from the desert, the Romans were interested in strengthening it. When Rome first took over Palestine, the Nabataeans were constantly pressing on the east and south; Bosora, i.e., Bozrah (VIII, L-7), and *Jebel Ḥaurân*, the mountainous region southeast of Canatha (VIII, L-6), were in Nabataean hands. This desert people also extended its influence further north, and either pressed close to Damascus or occasionally gained temporary control of it. The kingdom of Parthia (XIII, F-G 2-3) also endangered the eastern border of Palestine and Syria. The Romans therefore took steps to make Ḥaurân a secure outpost against such threats, and the Hellenistic cities founded and fostered there were largely intended to fulfill this end. From the time of Trajan (A.D. 98-117) there was a remarkable development of city life and architecture in this region. Christianity made progress, and Bosora became the chief center of Christian life for the area. The Mohammedan conquest in the seventh century, however, marked the end of Christian strength here as elsewhere in the Levant.

GALILEE FACES SOUTH

Thus the regions to the west, north, and east of Galilee do not offer the basis for a large population, nor do their physical features lead naturally to intimate contacts with Galilee. Only to the south does the geographical situation favor more vital ties.

One factor in promoting southern associations is the Jordan Valley (VIII, F 3-8). Its fertile valley and the inviting shores of the Sea of Galilee (VIII, F-G 5-6) tended to turn the attention of inhabitants of the hill country away from the west. On the east side of the Jordan Valley, the steep rise of nearly 2,700 feet from the Sea of Galilee to the Ḥaurân plateau presents a forbidding barrier, and has the effect of binding the Sea of Galilee, including its eastern shore, exclusively to the district of Galilee. Once drawn into living connection with the Jordan Valley, however, and given a focal point in the Sea of Galilee, the people of the hills were naturally connected with the country farther south.

Another factor leading Galilee to face south was the fertile, well-watered plain, Esdraelon. Northern or Upper Galilee, rugged and mountainous, is but the southward extension of the Lebanon range. In Southern or Lower Galilee the foothills drop to more even slopes and offer more level areas, which invite settlement and cultivation. Outstanding in this section is the small but fertile Plain of Gennesaret (XIV, C-D 3), where there is farming throughout the year, and the larger Plain of Asochis (VIII, E-6), on the edge of which were Hannathon and, later, Cana (VIII, E-6). These plains, however, could satisfy only local needs. Esdraelon was wide, well-watered, fertile, and thus inevitably a magnet to draw the interest of Galilee.

Yet the heights of Mount Carmel, and the line of hills which continued southeast and east to Mount Gilboa (VIII, E-8), formed a barrier between Galilee and central Palestine. As a result, Samaria (Plate IX) had a history rather distinct from that of the northern hills. Nevertheless, the pass running southwest from Megiddo (VIII, D-7; see Fig. 26), the road southward from En-gannim (VIII, E-8) into the Samarian hills, together with the route down the Jordan Valley, offered lines of trade and travel, and gave Galilee, in spite of partial isolation, a vital link with central Palestine.

Geography to a considerable extent determines history, and physical features in and around Galilee tell what its life had to be. It would be a meeting place of roads from all directions, and would have some relations with countries on all sides. It could have no secure independence and no completely isolated life. But it could never have intimate unity with the regions to the west, north, and east. It must center about the Sea of Galilee and find its chief contacts in the south. Yet even there it was doomed to have a somewhat loose association.

PRE-ISRAELITE GALILEE AND ESDRAELON

The Biblical student thus comes back to Galilee and Esdraelon as his main center of interest in this region. Galilee has had a long history. As shown by the discussion on p. 117, archaeologists have found there and in valleys south of Carmel some of the most important remains yet discovered of prehistoric man.

At a much later date, but prior to the coming of the Israelites, the

FIG. 40. Tiberias and the Sea of Galilee looking southeast. In the foreground is a Mohammedan mosque; note the tower from which the call to prayer is given. Palm trees indicate mild climate. Observe how the hills enclose the lake on both sides.

FIG. 41. Partially restored ancient synagogue at Capernaum. View from the southeast corner. Steps lead up to entrances on the south. The colonnade of pillars once supported a balcony for women, which ran around the west, north, and east sides; entrance to the balcony was by an outside stairway on the north. It was built about the third century A.D.

Canaanites were strongly established in this region. The chief city was Hazor (VIII, F-4), in Upper Galilee, and still farther north were Kedesh (VIII, F-4) and Yano'am (IV, D-2). The Canaanites were also found on all sides of Esdraelon. Among their cities were Madon in Lower Galilee (VIII, F-6), Achshaph (VIII, D-5) not far southeast of Accho, Dor (VIII, C-7) on the coast south of Carmel, Megiddo (VIII, D-7) and Taanach (VIII, D-8) on the southern rim of Esdraelon, and Beth-shan, Rehob, and Pella (VIII, F-8) near the Jordan. The latter group of three cities is mentioned in the Amarna tablets (see p. 30); of them, Beth-shan was by far the most important. From the fifteenth to the middle of the twelfth century B.C. it was a strong Egyptian outpost. It was also a center of Canaanite religious life, as its successive temples bear witness.

THE BIBLICAL PERIOD

The league of Canaanite city-states offered strong opposition to the incoming Israelites. Except for the occupation of the Hill of Moreh (VIII, E-7) by Issachar, the Esdraelon region was not brought under Israelite control until David captured the strongholds there (see p. 44). Prior to this, however, the Galilean hill country had been conquered, and from Mount Tabor, the meeting place of the tribes of Issachar, Zebulun, and Naphtali (VIII, E-7; Fig. 35; cf. Plate VI), Israelite forces made a victorious sally against Sisera, a Canaanite ruler (Judg., ch. 4). Solomon made the plain his fifth Israelite administrative district, with its capital at Megiddo (see p. 50 and Plate VII:A).

From the time of Solomon to that of Jesus the role of Galilee was relatively unimportant. The region was included in the Northern Kingdom, Israel, and in the wars and invasions of subsequent centuries it evidently suffered considerably, since it was situated on the northern border of the kingdom and was always difficult to defend. Its participation in the life of Israel reached the lowest ebb in the early days of the Maccabean revolt, when Simon marched north, rescued all the Jews who wished to remain loyal to the Law, and took them to Judaea (c. 163 B.C.; see p. 78). Not long after this, however, the return of faithful Jews to Galilee must have begun, for by the end of the second century B.C. the Maccabeans were in control of Galilee, a situation which assumes a considerable Jewish group there. Certainly in the first century A.D., while the population was mixed, as it had been through the centuries, the region was predominantly Jewish, dotted with synagogues, and often the scene of fanatical outbursts of zeal for the ancestral faith.

Nevertheless, Gentile population, cities, and influence were present. The two chief centers of such Gentile influence were Sepphoris and Tiberias. Sepphoris (VIII, E-6) was the capital of the tetrarchy of Herod Antipas in the early years of his rule. Some years later he built Tiberias (VIII, F-6; Fig. 36) and made it his capital. South of Tiberias were the hot springs at Ammathus (VIII, F-6), supposed to possess curative properties, and therefore visited then as now by people from distant places. Tarichaea, often sought at the southwest corner of the Sea of Galilee, was probably another name for Magdala (VIII, F-6); it was a center of fishing, fish-packing, and shipbuilding. A hippodrome indicated Gentile influence.

Such facts help us to see why there existed in Jerusalem and southern Palestine a certain contempt for the somewhat suspect Judaism of Galilee. The northern district had been so long a place of mixed population, and so often cut off from normal relations with the "holy city," that the Jewish leaders in the capital regarded it with condescension. When Jesus came from Galilee, and from the obscure village of Nazareth (VIII, E-7), a place not mentioned in any Jewish source of the Biblical period, and presumed not merely to teach in Jerusalem but even to interfere with Temple arrangements (Mark 11:15), it is little wonder that the recognized leaders rose up in resentment. Galilee was inferior; an unauthorized teacher from Galilee could expect no official favor (cf. John 1:46; 7:52).

In such a region, prevailingly Jewish, rather deprecated in Jerusalem, and mixed in population, language, and cultural factors, Jesus grew up. Here he carried on the main part of his ministry. His work centered at Capernaum (VIII, F-5), and he seems to have labored chiefly around the north end of the Sea of Galilee. However, references to Cana (VIII, E-6) and Nain (VIII, E-7), and reports of journeys among the villages to preach and heal (cf. Mark 1:39), show that he must have traveled over most of Galilee (see further p. 94).

POST-BIBLICAL JUDAISM

It is amazing that after the death of Jesus Galilee figures so little in the story of early Christianity. The region is mentioned but once in The Acts, and then in a general way (ch. 9:31). But the obscurity into which Galilee fell in Christian history, until pilgrims began visiting the country to see the Gospel sites, is in sharp contrast with the new importance which this section assumed for Judaism after the fall of Jerusalem (A.D. 70). The continuing Jewish faith found a new center in Galilee. Such cities as Sepphoris and Tiberias became centers of Jewish learning; here the rabbinic tradition was preserved and elaborated.

The vigor and extent of Galilean Judaism in the next few centuries are clear from the many ruins of synagogues discovered and excavated in this region (see p. 117). A decisive majority of the Palestinian synagogues known to belong to this period are located in northern Palestine. Among the most interesting of such synagogues for Christian students, though built definitely later than the days of Jesus, is the one at Capernaum (see Fig. 41). A striking structure is the black basalt synagogue at Chorazin (VIII, F-5). Here, as in the synagogue at Hammath (VIII, F-6), south of Tiberias, an example has been found of the "Seat of Moses" (cf. Matt. 23:2), the seat of honor reserved for the most distinguished elder or visitor, who thus sat facing the congregation. There was noteworthy variety of ornamentation in the synagogues of this period; characteristic features are the seven-branched candlesticks and elaborate floor mosaics. The free use, not only of human figures, but even of the signs of the Zodiac, shows that Judaism then permitted a freedom in ornamentation which in earlier and later days was not tolerated.

Another striking evidence of the prominent place of Galilee in the Judaism of this period has been found at *Sheikh Abreiq* (XVIII, C-3). In addition to synagogue ruins at this site, extensive catacombs have been discovered.

Such significant discoveries throw much light on post-Biblical Judaism. It is still highly desirable, however, for excavators to seek further evidence of first-century Judaism, in order to illuminate that period of Jewish life and reveal the setting of the ministry of Jesus.

CENTRAL PALESTINE IN BIBLICAL TIMES

Plate IX

Fig. 42. View of the Dead Sea, taken from the northwestern edge, not far from the area of *Qumrân* where the Dead Sea Scrolls were found. The surface of the sea is 1,290 feet below sea level. In its deepest portions the water is at least 1,300 feet deep, which means that at this point the Jordan rift or fault attains a depth of some 2,600 feet.

Biblical history, apart from the ministry of Jesus in Galilee, has its focus in central Palestine. This area begins on the north at the border of Esdraelon or Valley of Jezreel (Plate viii, D-7), and extends southward below Hebron (ix, E-8) to the beginning of the Negeb (see pp. 67 ff.). It is about eighty miles long and has between the Mediterranean and the Jordan an average width of fifty miles. Its total area is thus approximately 4,000 square miles.

The district was thickly populated. Judging from the exceptionally large number of inhabited places in so small an area, one might conclude that ancient Palestine was largely urban rather than agricultural. The country, however, was and still is largely agricultural and pastoral. The basic foods were wheat, barley, vegetables, grapes, figs, and olives; in modern times the coastal plain has also proved ideal for citrus fruits. The grain ripens during the early spring rains and is harvested in May and June. From April to November there is little rain. Certain varieties of vegetables, however, thrive during the summer months; they are sustained by the early morning dew, which appears regularly, except in occasional hot spells caused by the country's chief climatic curse, the hot wind (sirocco) from the Arabian Desert.

In ancient times, however, farmers found it necessary, as they still do, to live in towns for protection. They did not build their houses in the midst of their fields. Instead, they lived in towns and journeyed daily to their work. Each main city of Old Testament times was located on an easily fortified hill, near a spring or springs. It was surrounded by strong walls and protected by gates, so that it could withstand siege (cf. Fig. 37). Around it were numerous unfortified villages. The farmers lived in them, but when war came they sought safety within the city's fortifications. During the times when a strong government, such as Rome, preserved peace, the number of unwalled villages increased greatly, as did the population. In troubled times, however, both villages and population diminished greatly in number.

In spite of such fluctuations, the general trend showed an increase of population through Old and New Testament times and down to the Byzantine period (fourth to sixth centuries A.D.). In the reign of David, the first time stability of government had been achieved, the population of Palestine was probably less than one million. The most densely inhabited areas were the southern coastal plain (Philistia) and the hill country north and south of Jerusalem (ix, F-6). During the Roman rule, when the country reached the greatest degree of agricultural and commercial development which it attained in ancient times, it probably contained between one million and a half and two million people. The population is about the same or a little more today, but this is due to a recent increase, brought about very largely by the creation of the new state of Israel.

The map indicates where population was most dense. The district between Jerusalem and Bethel (ix, F-5), once occupied by the tribe of Benjamin (cf. Plate vi), contained the largest number of villages. Here were Gibeah (ix, F-6), which Saul made his capital; Anathoth (ix, F-6), the home of Jeremiah; Michmash (ix, F-5), famous as the scene of a battle with the Philistines (I Sam., chs. 13; 14); and Gibeon (ix, F-5), where Solomon in prayer chose wisdom instead of riches (I Kings 3:4 ff.).

JUDAEAN AND SAMARITAN RIVALRY

In this territory of Benjamin lay the border between Samaria and Judah. One of the peculiar facts about the history of ancient Palestine was the rivalry which existed between Judah (ix, D-G 5-8) and Samaria (ix, E-G 2-5). It is not explained by geography. Judah and Samaria form a continuous geographical and economic unit; there is no natural boundary between them. This is shown by the fact that the border, which in an earlier day lay just south of Bethel (ix, F-5), was placed in New Testament times north of Borcaeus (ix, F-4). Yet, in spite of the geographical unity of these districts, the people of the two areas were more or less hostile to one another from the early days of Israelite settlement through the New Testament period.

The cause of this tension goes back to the time of the conquest, when different groups took possession of these two continuous sections of Palestine. Though temporarily united by Saul against a common danger, the two were led by their rivalry to fall apart after his death; Judah anointed David as king, while Israel accepted Ishbaal.

When David became king of Israel on the death of Ishbaal, he was faced with the problem of where to locate his capital. Gibeah, Saul's home, was too small. Hebron, important in Judah, was too far south; its choice would have provoked renewed jealousy in Israel. On the other hand, any Israelite town would have alienated Judah. David chose the Canaanite (Jebusite) city of Jerusalem, which lay on the border between the two areas but belonged to neither. It was claimed by Benjamin, whose border ascended past the Valley of Achor (ix, G-6) from the Jordan and circled Jerusalem by the Hinnom Valley (Josh. 18:15 ff.; Plates vi and xvii:a); but this tribe had never subjugated the city. David did, and the city owned by him (the "City of David") proved the ideal choice for the capital (see p. 48).

On the death of Solomon, the two districts again separated, into rival kingdoms, which periodically waged war with each other (see pp. 50, 53). The border between them lay north of the old tribal area of Benjamin. During the first half of the ninth century it lay as far north as Baal-hazor (ix, F-5; II Chron. 13:19; 15:8; 17:2; and Josh. 19:22-24, which probably reflects this time). Early in the days of Jeroboam I and from the eighth century on it lay farther south near Bethel (see Plate vii:b; I Kings 12:28 f.; Amos 7:10-13).

When Israel fell in 721 B.C., some twenty-seven thousand of the intellectual and well-to-do classes were deported, and eastern foreigners were settled in their place. Israel became a province of Assyria, Babylonia, and Persia in turn (see pp. 54 ff.). The presence of foreigners intensified the traditional hostility, and when Judah was reconstituted as a religious state under Ezra and Nehemiah, the northern neighbors, now called Samaritans after their chief city, Samaria (IX, F-3), were excluded from the Temple at Jerusalem.

Thus began the Jewish-Samaritan schism which existed in the time of Jesus (cf. John 4:9). It led to the building of a rival Temple on Mount Gerizim (IX, F-3). During the second century B.C. it found expression in the hostility of the Samaritans to the Jews during the Maccabean struggle for religious and political independence. When, about 128 B.C., John Hyrcanus ravaged Samaria and extended Maccabean control northward from Judaea, he destroyed the Samaritan sanctuary, and it was never rebuilt. This, however, did not stop the use of Mount Gerizim for Samaritan worship. Indeed, such use continued through New Testament times (John 4:20), and even today the small Samaritan sect, centered in *Nâblus*, still celebrates the Passover on the top of Gerizim.

This persistent division of central Palestine cannot be explained by geographical and economic factors. It was rooted in historical and cultural rivalries and jealousies.

PHILISTIA AND JUDAH

In the area south of Jerusalem four vertical zones can be distinguished. Along the coast is the fertile, rolling plain where the Philistines once lived. Their chief cities were Gaza (IX, A-8), Ashkelon (IX, B-7), Ashdod (IX, C-6), Ekron (IX, C-6), and Gath (IX, C-7). This plain was rarely under Israelite or Jewish control. The Philistines early made a determined effort to subdue the whole of Palestine. They were checked only when Saul and David united Israel to resist the danger (see p. 45 f.). During the reigns of David and Solomon, Israel dominated Philistia economically, but did not subjugate it (see Plate VII:A). Uzziah is said to have conquered the plain during the first half of the eighth century B.C. (II Chron. 26:6); the conquest, however, had no lasting effect.

Control of Philistia was important for political reasons; it was the outpost of Palestine and Syria facing Egypt on the south. Economic reasons also were involved; Philistia not only dominated the best land route between Egypt and the north countries, but also in Gaza possessed the natural western terminus for trade from the eastern desert. Hence with the weakening of the Kingdom of Judah, it was inevitable that the region should become a scene of conflict. After the fall of Jerusalem in 587 B.C., the Persians held control until the coming of Alexander the Great in 332 B.C. At this time Gaza felt strong enough to resist, and held out for two months. Its fall meant that Hellenistic influence gained the ascendancy in the Philistine plain. After a century under Egypt, Philistia came under the control of Syria. A few decades later the Maccabees brought the district into their kingdom, but they did not succeed in making it Jewish. Ascalon became an independent city and a seat of Hellenistic culture. Gaza, a strong trade center, at times was free from Palestinian control and under the protection of the Roman governor of Syria. Other cities, such as Azotus and Jamnia, were given as sources of revenue and prestige to favorites of the Herods or the Romans.

FIG. 43. Coastal plain near Ramleh, looking toward Lydda. In the foreground appear olive trees, scattered through the fields.

After the destruction of Jerusalem in A.D. 70, Jamnia (IX, C-5) became a center of rabbinic studies, but in general Galilee proved more important in the rabbinic movement than either Philistia or Judaea (see p. 60). In the first five centuries A.D. Philistia was the scene of vigorous Christian activity, one phase of which, a strong monastic movement, spread eastward into the hill country and flourished about Eleutheropolis (XVIII, B-5).

Between the plain and the Judaean upland is a series of foothills, partially separated from the highland by longitudinal valleys. This is called the Shephelah ("Lowland"; see p. 19 and I, B-5). A series of valleys run across it westward to the plain. The northernmost is the Valley of Aijalon, protected by the two Beth-horons (IX, D-E 5). Next below it is the Valley of Sorek, along which the modern railroad runs from Tell Aviv to Jerusalem (IX, D-6). Ekron and Gezer (IX, D-5) protected its outer reaches in the plain, and Beth-shemesh (IX, D-6) was the chief town within it. This valley was the scene of Samson's exploits; he lived at Zorah, and Delilah at Timnah (IX, D-6; cf. Judg., chs. 13 to 16). Along this valley the Ark passed when sent back to Israel by the Philistines (I Sam. 6:12 ff.). Next on the south is the Valley of Elah, protected by the fortresses of Libnah and Azekah (IX, D-6) and famous as the place where David slew Goliath (I Sam. 17:19 ff.). Below it is the Valley of Zephathah (IX, C-D 7), in which occurred the battle between Asa and the Ethiopians (II Chron. 14:10). Further south are the valleys, unnamed in the Bible, protected by Gath (IX, C-7) and Lachish (IX, D-7), Eglon (IX, C-7) and Debir (IX, D-8).

The Shephelah was a very fertile region. It was filled with towns, only a few of which are shown on the map. It was greatly desired by Judah as a protective frontier, for unless the Shephelah was in the control of Judah the hill country was left exposed. Indeed, the usual strategy of invaders was first to conquer the Shephelah and then attack the heart of Judah.

The third vertical zone in the southern part of Plate IX is the rugged hill country between the Shephelah and the Judaean watershed. The latter extends southward from Jerusalem to Carmel (IX, E-8). It is clearly marked on the map, not merely by the relief, but also by the absence of towns some two miles east of this line. In this third zone was the cultivatable district of Judah. In its northern part, as in the Shephelah, the grape industry was especially prosperous (cf. Num. 13:23). In the south, around Debir and Carmel, the raising of sheep, weaving, and dyeing were more common.

East of the Judaean watershed was the forbidding and barren wasteland called Jeshimon or the Wilderness of Judah (IX, F-G 6-8; see pp. 19, 69 and Fig. 46). On its western and northern edges were Tekoa (IX, F-7), whence Amos came, and Herodium (IX, F-7) and Hyrcania (IX, G-6), two of the many fortresses with which Herod the Great gave strength to his rule of Palestine. Below Hyrcania just above the Dead Sea there is a barren and forbidding plateau, called today the *Buqei'ah* (IX, G-6) and in Old Testament times the "Valley of Achor" ("trouble"). Archaeological investigation in 1955 has shown that the main period in which this "valley" was used was between the ninth and sixth centuries B.C. At that time a series of towns or forts was erected, together with the first datable examples of Judean water conservation by means of dams. This region would appear to have belonged to a special Judean province mentioned in the document quoted in Josh., ch. 15 (vs. 61-62). Among the occupied villages there mentioned is the City of (the) Salt (Sea). This is now identified with *Khirbet Qumrân* (XVIII, C-5), which in New Testament times was the community center of the main group of the Jewish sect known as the Essenes (see further pp. 82 f.).

SAMARIA

In contrast to the four vertical zones south of Jerusalem, the region to the north possesses but two: the hills and the plain. The hill country of Samaria is more open to outside influence and more richly endowed than is that of Judah. To the west, north, and east, broad valleys give easy access to the Plain of Sharon (IX, D 1-3), Esdraelon, and the Jordan Valley (IX, G-H 1-6). Between the Plain of Sharon and Samaria there is no protecting Shephelah. Along the Jordan the wilderness is not so forbidding as it is west of the Dead Sea.

Perhaps because outside influences here had easy access to the hills, Israelites in the Old Testament period succumbed more easily than did Judah to the paganism of northern neighbors. However, since Samaria was a richer agricultural country, the resulting economic superiority and greater population meant that for a time a stronger state than Judah could be erected there.

It is no surprise, therefore, to note that before the fall of the Northern Kingdom to Assyria in 721 B.C., the center of interest in the Biblical narrative lay in the north. Elijah and Elisha, concerning whose lives and times nineteen of the forty-seven chapters of the books of the Kings were written, labored here. Queen Jezebel, who rivals Judas for the doubtful distinction of being the most notorious figure of the Bible, lived in Samaria as the wife of King Ahab. A century later, Amos and Hosea prophesied in the area. After the fall of the Israelite kingdom, however, this region was never again so significant in the Biblical story. It has little importance for the New Testament narrative. Perhaps the Aenon of John the Baptist's ministry (John 3:23) was near the Salim in eastern Samaria (IX, F-3), though another possible site is near the Salim south of Scythopolis (IX, H-2). John, ch. 4, mentions a brief contact of Jesus with Samaritans at Jacob's Well near "Sychar," which probably is not at modern *'Askar* but may refer to Sychem (Shechem; IX, F-3).

Whereas in the south there was a conflict of interest between Philistia and Judah, in the north no comparable situation occurred, because there was never an intensive settlement in the Plain of Sharon (IX, D 1-3). The latter was probably rather swampy and thickly wooded, and hence largely undeveloped. In the first century B.C., however, Herod the Great, vassal king under Rome, chose the site of Strato's Tower (IX, D-1), renamed it Caesarea in honor of the emperor, and spent twelve years rebuilding it on a grand scale. He thus made the city the chief port and virtual capital of Palestine.

During the Old Testament period, however, the political center of gravity for Samaria was always at or near Mount Ebal and Mount Gerizim. At this point all roads through the hill country met (see Fig. 6, and Plates IV, VI, XVIII). Between the mountains was the earliest chief city of the area, Shechem (IX, F-3). It was a strong Canaanite city, which played an active role in the political affairs of Canaan before the time of Israel (see p. 35). Later an unsuccessful attempt was made here to establish the first Israelite monarchy, with Abimelech, son of Gideon, as king (Judg., ch. 9; see also Gen., ch. 34, which reflects early tribal conflicts in the area).

After the division of the kingdom of Solomon, the first Israelite capital was at Tirzah (IX, F-3; see I Kings 15:21, 33; 16:6, 23; S. of Sol. 6:4). Shechem was not in a well-protected spot for a capital, and Tirzah, situated in a valley leading east and northeast, was not a suitable site for wider contacts. When, therefore, King Omri, about 880 B.C., wished to orient his capital toward the west and north, he chose the site of Samaria (IX, F-3), and built there a magnificent capital, which subsequent builders made so strong that it took the Assyrians the better part of three years to capture it (see p. 73).

After this disaster, the city of Samaria was never again so important politically. Its situation, on an isolated hill with a good water supply, invited military use, and in the troubled centuries that followed it was repeatedly fortified and destroyed. When Herod the Great received Samaria from the Roman emperor Augustus, he spared no expense to make it an outstanding city of his kingdom. Ruins of the large Temple of Augustus on the hilltop, including a great altar and a fragment of a colossal statue apparently representing the emperor, still reflect clearly Herod's friendship for Rome and his adoption of Hellenistic influences in architecture and religion. There was a thriving Christian community here in later centuries; striking evidence of this is the Church of John the Baptist which has been excavated.

FIG. 44. Shepherds' field near Bethlehem. Traditional site of the appearance of angels to the shepherds on the night of Jesus' birth. Many sturdy olive trees are seen in the center of the picture. Note how stones are taken from the fields and used to build fences and terraces.

THE JORDAN VALLEY

The western side of the Jordan Valley was for the most part never intensively occupied. A noteworthy exception was in the north, around Beth-shan (IX, G-1). In the Roman period a considerable use of irrigation in the region of Phasaelis and Archelais (IX, G 4-5) resulted in a fruitful section which was given usually to some favorite of the ruling power (see p. 92). At this same time Jericho (IX, G-5) underwent expansion. The city spread to the south and east of the old site, and Herod the Great constructed here a palace, baths, theater, and citadels. The area was then noted for its palm groves, balsam trees, and garden products.

The eastern side of the valley, however, was and still is a more prosperous area. North of the Jabbok (IX, H-3) are numerous perennial streams, along which lay such towns as Succoth, Zaphon, and Zaretan (IX, H-3), Jabesh-gilead and Pella (IX, H-2). Between the Jabbok and Beth-nimrah (IX, H-5) is an area without streams, though it has been cultivated to some extent by irrigation. Between Beth-nimrah and the Dead Sea were several villages. Here Israel encamped before crossing the Jordan to conquer Canaan; the region was then called "the plains of Moab" (Num. 22:1). Considerable development of this area occurred in the New Testament period; a number of towns were then moved further down the little valleys in which they were situated, and relocated on more level ground. This trend reflects a time of rather stable conditions in the area.

TRANSJORDAN

Ascent up the valleys to the east soon leads one to the hilly plateau of Transjordan. The tribe of Reuben received as its inheritance the territory between Heshbon (IX, I-6) and the River Arnon (IX, H-I 8), but during the period of the Judges this tribe disappears from history because of pressure from the Kingdom of Moab. To the north was Gilead, occupied by Gad and one half of the tribe of Manasseh (see Plate VI). Subsequently Israel contended for Gilead with both the Aramaeans (Damascus) and the Ammonites.

Ammon proper was a semiarid region between Gilead and the desert. Its border was the River Jabbok as it turned in a large semicircle southward (Deut. 3:16). Rabbah or Rabbath-ammon, the chief city of the kingdom (IX, J-5), was a naturally strong place, possessed by Israel only for a short time after its capture by David (II Sam. 12:26 ff.). In the succeeding period Ammon pressed westward, enlarging its territory in proportion to Israel's weakness.

During the period of the divided monarchy both Judah and Israel made attempts to hold the borders of the Davidic empire (see Plate VII: A-B). It was Israel, however, which laid claim to the whole Jordan Valley and Transjordan, including Moab, as far south as the Brook Zered (X, H-I 3-4; VII:B). The reason was that the valleys from the district of Samaria led easily across the Jordan, while the one route from Jerusalem to the Jordan was winding, steep, and difficult (Fig. 69). Hence, of the districts of Transjordan once conquered by David, Judah laid claim to Edom alone.

Yet the intervening Jordan Valley made it impossible for Transjordan ever to become integrally united with Samaria. The later history of the eastern plateau was rather more strongly affected by the proximity of the desert. It may have been with the thought of protecting the region from possible attack by desert peoples that Greek cities were founded and encouraged in this region from the time of Alexander the Great. At some time not later than the first century B.C., ten of these, including Scythopolis (IX, G-1), Pella (IX, H-2), Gerasa (IX, J-3), and Philadelphia (IX, J-5), banded together to form the Decapolis (XIV, D-F 1-5), a league of Hellenistic cities. The later Maccabees were able for a time to control almost the entire area, including the eastern side of the Dead Sea. But the Nabataeans, centered in Petra, were extending their control north as well as west, and in the days of the Herods, Machaerus (IX, H-7) was the southernmost fortress under Herodian control. The problem of how to deal with the Nabataeans and their threat to the Roman outposts was not solved effectively until the early second century A.D., when Rome was able to organize the Nabatean territory into the Roman province of Arabia (A.D. 106).

While the region of Transjordan was never the center of Israelite life, it figured continually in the Biblical history. The tribes of Israel came from the east to cross the Jordan and invade Palestine. Balaam viewed the hosts of Israel from Mount Pisgah (IX, I-6; Num. 23:14), and the death of Moses is reported to have occurred there or on Mount Nebo (IX, I-6; cf. Deut. 32:49; 34:1). Two and a half tribes settled in Transjordan, and through the centuries Israel fought with only intermittent success to hold these eastern regions. During the second half of the eighth century the whole territory was permanently lost to the Hebrews, as may be seen from Plate VII:C. In the New Testament period, Peraea (XIV, D 4-5), a name which means the land "across" the Jordan, was combined with Galilee and placed under the rule of Herod Antipas. John the Baptist evidently preached and baptized on the east side of the Jordan; his work at Bethany beyond Jordan is mentioned (XIV, D-5; cf. John 1:28), and he was taken prisoner by Antipas, who had no jurisdiction on the west bank. John was imprisoned and executed at Machaerus, according to Josephus. Jesus, to judge by popular Galilean custom, probably traveled through Peraea on some of his trips to Jerusalem. When the early Christian group left Jerusalem at the outbreak of the Jewish rebellion against Rome (A.D. 66-70), they went to Pella. Christianity had a great expansion in Transjordan in the early centuries. Prominent in this period were Gerasa, where the ruins of many splendid churches have been excavated and studied, and Medeba (IX, I-6), where a marvelous mosaic map of Palestine, laid in the sixth century A.D., has been found in the floor of a church. Yet this rapid expansion of the Church was shortly to be checked throughout Asia and Africa by the conquests of Islam in the seventh century. Groups of Christians still remain, but they are comparatively few in number.

FIG. 45. Jerash, site of the ancient Gerasa. In the foreground a semicircle of columns still marks the location of the ancient forum. Running north from the forum was the main north-south street, with columns on either side. Some columns are still in place. Trees mark the course of the stream which runs through the site. Beyond the picture to the right the modern village begins, built mainly with stones taken from the ruins. At the extreme left are the columns of what was once the temple of Artemis, a pagan goddess.

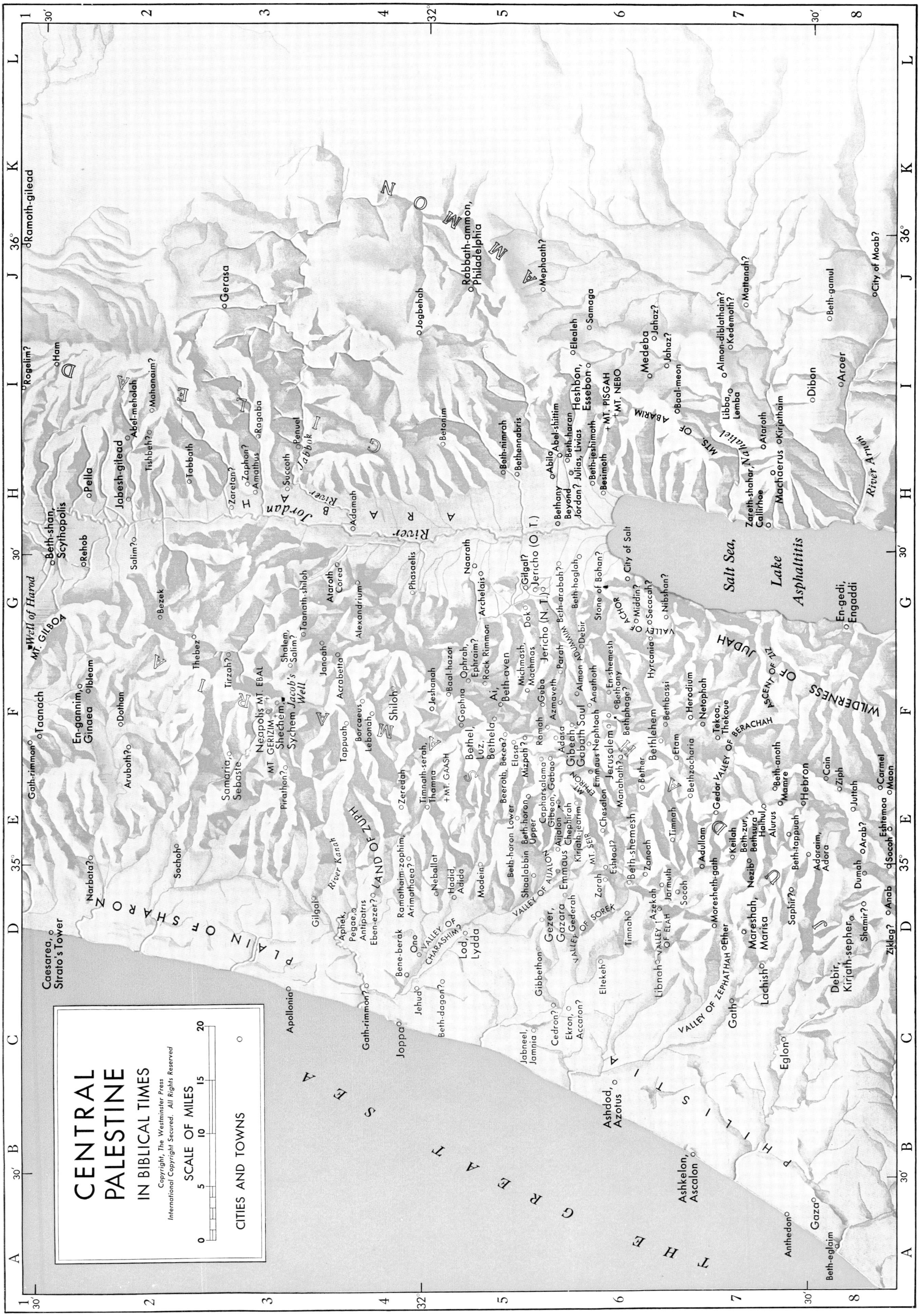

CENTRAL PALESTINE
IN BIBLICAL TIMES

SCALE OF MILES

CITIES AND TOWNS

THE GREAT SEA

Salt Sea,
Lake Asphaltitis

Jordan River

River Jabbok

River Arnon

PLAIN OF SHARON

LAND OF ZUPH

WILDERNESS OF ZIN

JUDAH

MTS. OF ABARIM

AMMON

MOAB

Caesarea, Strato's Tower
Apollonia
Joppa
Beth-dagon?
Jehud
Bene-berak
Ono
Lod, Lydda
Hadid, Adida
Neballat
Aphek, Antipatris
Pegae?
Eben-ezer?
Ramathaim-zophim, Arimathaea?
Modein
Gath-rimmon?
Gilgal?
River Kanah
Narbata?
Sochoh
Aruboth?
Dothan
En-gannim, Ginaea
Gath-rimmon
Taanach
Ibleam
Samaria, Sebaste
Piraton?
Neapolis, Shechem, Sychem, MT. GERIZIM
MT. EBAL
Sholem, Salim?
Taanath-shiloh
Tirzah?
Thebez
Bezek
Mt. GILBOA
Well of Harod
Beth-shan, Scythopolis
Rehob
Salim?
Zaretan?
Zaphon?
Amathus
Adamah
Tabbath
Tishbeh?
Jabesh-gilead
Abel-meholah
Mahanaim?
Pella
Ham
Rogelim?
Ramoth-gilead
Gerasa
Ragaba
Succoth
Penuel
Corea
Ataroth
Alexandrium
Acrabetta
Borcaeus,
Lebonah
Tappuah
Zeredah
Janoah?
Shiloh
Jeshanah
Baal-hazor
Gophna
Ophrah
Ephraim?
Rock Rimmon
Bethel
Luz
Bethel
Bethela
Ai,
Beth-aven
Berea?
Beeroth
Timnath-serah, Thamna
MT. GAASH
Jacob's Well
Phasaelis
Naarath
Archelais
Gilgal?
Jericho (O.T.)
Jericho (N.T.)
Beth-arabah?
Beth-hoglah
Stone of Bohan
City of Salt
Middin?
Secacah?
Nibshan?
VALLEY OF ACHOR
Hyrcania?
En-gedi, Engaddi
Dok
Parah
Debir
Almon
Anathoth
Geba
Azmaveth
Michmash,
Machmas
En-shemesh
Bethany
Bethphage?
Bethbassi
Herodium
Netophah
Tekoa, Thekoe
VALLEY OF BERACHAH
Beth-zacharia
Etam
Bethlehem
Bether
Jerusalem
Gibeah Saul
Gibeath
Nephtoah
Emmaus
Manahath?
Chesalon
MT. SEIR
Kiriath-jearim
Gederah
Emmaus Chephirah
Aijalon
Gibeon, Gabaon
Capharsalama?
Adasa
Ramah
Elasa?
Mizpah?
Beth-horon Upper
Beth-horon Lower
Shaalabbin
Beeroth
Gedor
Beth-anoth
Mamre
Hebron
Cain
Ziph
Juttah
Carmel
Maon
Eshtemoa
Socoh
Arab?
Adoraim, Adora
Dumah
Shamir?
Anab
Debir, Kiriath-sepher
Kiriath-sepher
Ziklag?
Lachish
Eglon
Gath
Mareshah, Marisa
Moresheth-gath
Nezib?
Keilah
Beth-zur
Bethsura
Halhul
Alurus
Beth-tappuah
Saphir?
Ether
VALLEY OF ZEPHATHAH
Socoh
Jarmuth
Azekah
VALLEY OF ELAH
Zanoah
Beth-shemesh
Zorah
Eshtaol
Timnah
Timnah
Adullam
VALLEY OF SOREK
Libnah
Timnah
Ekron, Accaron?
Cedron?
Jabneel, Jamnia
Ashdod, Azotus
Ashkelon, Ascalon
Gaza
Anthedon
Beth-eglaim
Gibbethon
Eltekeh
Gezer, Gazara
VALLEY OF AIJALON
VALLEY OF CHARASHIM?
Gaza
PHILISTIA
Beth-nimrah
Bethennabris
Betonim
Abila
Abel-shittim
Bethany Beyond Jordan?
Beth-haran Julias, Livias
Beth-jeshimoth
Besimoth
MT. PISGAH
MT. NEBO
Heshbon, Esebon
Elealeh
Jogbehah
Rabbath-ammon, Philadelphia
Samaga
Medeba
Jahaz?
Jahaz?
Baal-meon
Mephaath?
Libba?
Lemba
Almon-diblahaim?
Kedemoth?
Kirjathaim
Ataroth
Zareth-shahar, Nahaliel
Callihoe
Machaerus
Dibon
Aroer
Mattanah?
Beth-gamul
Beth-meon?
City of Moab?

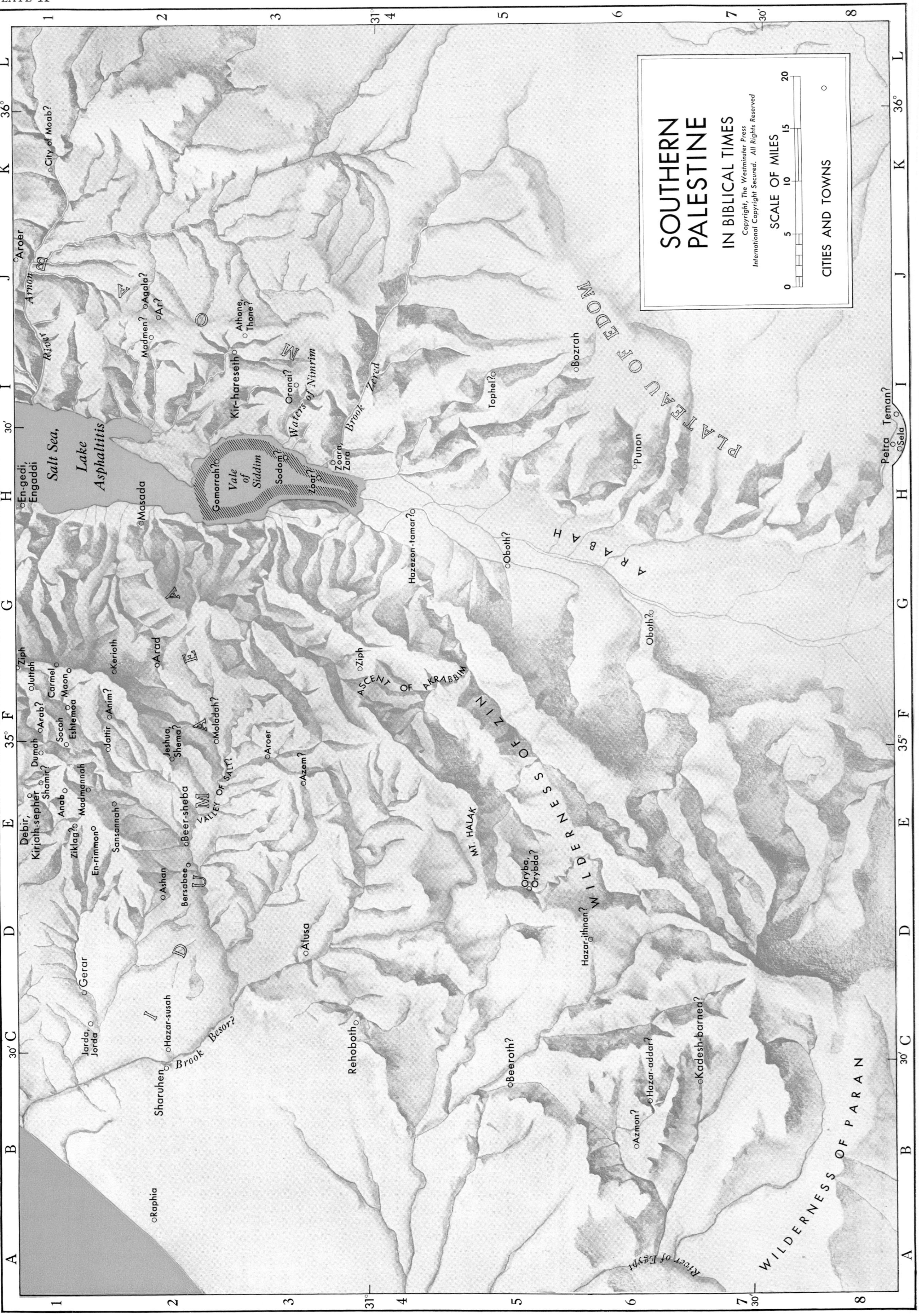
SOUTHERN PALESTINE
IN BIBLICAL TIMES
Copyright, The Westminster Press
International Copyright Secured. All Rights Reserved
SCALE OF MILES
0 5 10 15 20
CITIES AND TOWNS
PLATEAU OF EDOM
ARABAH
MOAB
JUDAEA
IDUMAEA
WILDERNESS OF ZIN
WILDERNESS OF PARAN
ASCENT OF AKRABBIM
VALLEY OF SALT?
MT. HALAK
Salt Sea, Lake Asphaltitis
Vale of Siddim
River Arnon
Brook Zered
Waters of Nimrim
Brook Besor?
River of Egypt
City of Moab?
Aroer
Agala?
Ar?
Madmen?
Athone, Thone?
Kir-hareseth
Oronai?
Tophel?
Bozrah
Punon
Petra
Sela
Teman?
En-gedi; Engaddi
Masada
Gomorrah?
Sodom?
Zoar?
Zoara, Zara
Hazezon-tamar?
Oboth?
Oboth?
Ziph
Juttah
Carmel
Maon
Kerioth
Arad
Ziph
Arab?
Socoh
Eshtemoa
Anim?
Dumah
Jattir
Jeshua, Shema?
Moladah?
Aroer
Shamir?
Anab
Madmannah
Azem?
Debir, Kirjath-sepher
Ziklag?
En-rimmon
Sansannah
Beer-sheba
Bersabee
Ashan
Oryba, Orybda?
Hazar-ithnan?
Alusa
Gerar
Jarda, Jorda
Hazar-susah
Sharuhen
Rehoboth
Beeroth?
Azmon?
Hazar-addar?
Kadesh-barnea?
Raphia
35°
36°
30′
31°
A B C D E F G H I J K L
1 2 3 4 5 6 7 8

FIG. 46. Jeshimon or the Wilderness of Judah, the barren wasteland to the east of the Judean watershed. The high plateau of Moab rises abruptly from the Dead Sea in the background. The bleakness of the area is forbidding, but the visitor to Palestine never tires of watching the ever-changing pastel shades of color in a view such as this.

SOUTHERN PALESTINE IN BIBLICAL TIMES

PLATE X

BELOW Hebron and Kirjath-sepher the hills of Judah drop down abruptly into relatively level plains, becoming drier as one goes south. This bleak, forbidding region, cut by countless dry valleys or wadis and dotted with sand dunes, was known in Biblical times as the *Negeb* (see p. 19), a word usually translated as "the south," though it originally meant "dry" or "parched." Through this sparsely populated desert wilderness ran Judah's traditional southern border, along the so-called "River of Egypt" (Plate X, A-6, and V, F-3) and the range of mountains lying between the Wilderness of Paran and the Wilderness of Zin, then into the Valley of the Arabah (X, G-H 4-8). Beyond the latter lay the ancient lands of Moab and Edom. The River of Egypt is not properly a river but one of the numerous dry valleys which carry off the excess water during the winter rains.

Leaving Hebron in Judah (IX, E-8), the traveler finds the hills descending rapidly to Beer-sheba, where evidence of intensive occupation in Biblical times immediately ceases. To the south the watershed lies in the region of Aroer (X, F-3). To the west of this watershed is an inhospitable desert of shifting sand dunes and soft, chalk-like limestone seamed with red flint. As the limestone crumbles, the flint is washed out so that it sometimes covers the surface of the ground for miles. Occasionally there is a small spring-watered valley or plain where the soil is sufficiently good to be cultivated. The Arab Bedouins who have lived here have depended on the brief winter rains for their crops. These rains, however, are so uncertain that frequently the grain is parched before it ripens to maturity, and rarely do the springs supply sufficient water for irrigation. In the summer the weather is extremely hot, and made the more unpleasant by the fine sand blown across the landscape by the wind. In the winter the cold is penetrating and made worse by winds which find nothing to check them in the rolling plains.

East of the watershed, the country is even more uninviting. This region is more arid and is filled with mountain ranges and deep valleys. The Ascent of Akrabbim (Num. 34:4; Josh. 15:3; Judg. 1:36), or "Pass of Scorpions," leading up from the Arabah to the plateau of Ziph and Aroer (X, F-4 and F-3) is an important landmark of this area.

In spite of the forbidding nature of the area, as has long been known, astonishing efforts were made between the fourth and the seventh centuries A.D. to occupy and cultivate it. Most remarkable are the ruins of numerous Christian churches and monasteries, especially those at Alusa (X, D-3), Oryba (*'Abda*, X, D-5), Subaita (XVIII, B-7), *'Aujā el-Ḥafīr* (XVIII, A-7), and *Kurnub* near Ziph (X, F-4). During the winter of 1935-1936 excavators at work on the churches of *'Aujā el-Ḥafīr* discovered a mass of papyrus documents, the first ever found in Palestine. They were written in Greek and Arabic, and dated

FIG. 47. An erosion dam at *Kurnub* (near Ziph; x, F-4), built by the Byzantine inhabitants as part of their energetic attempts at water and soil conservation.

in the sixth and seventh centuries A.D. Among them were deeds, contracts, receipts, letters, a list of Latin words and phrases from Virgil's *Aeneid* with their Greek equivalents (the work of some student who was laboriously trying to read Virgil), Christian legends, and fragments of the New Testament. While forts had been built in this region by the Romans to protect the trade route between Gaza and Arabia, the primary reason for the occupation here in the Byzantine period was undoubtedly religious. Christians who wished to withdraw from the active world found here a quiet place to practice the devotional life without interference from worldly interests. And here they stayed until the Mohammedan conquests.

Archaeological exploration has revealed, however, that the impressive Christian ruins of the Negeb are replicas of a civilization made possible by a remarkable people who preceded it. These were the Nabataeans (see below), who not only controlled the trade routes across the area, but settled it with numerous forts and villages. Previous occupation between c. 900 and 600 B.C. and especially between the twenty-first and nineteenth centuries B.C. was fairly intensive, though nowhere near what it was during New Testament times under the Nabataeans. It was once thought by some that there must have been more rainfall there in ancient times. Otherwise the people could not have existed in the region in such numbers. Now, however, we know that this was not the case. Habitation was made possible by the most spectacular efforts at water conservation. Dams, reservoirs, cisterns, and terrace walls still abound in the valleys of the region. Scarcely a drop of the scant winter rain was wasted. Today as Israel reoccupies the Negeb her people begin by repairing these ingenious waterworks of antiquity.

THE NEGEB DURING THE BIBLICAL PERIOD

The Negeb is first mentioned in the Biblical story during the journeys of Abraham and Isaac. Abraham lived here for a time (Gen. 13:1; 20:1), and passed through it on his way to and from Egypt. The main military and trade route lay along the coast, and was called in Ex. 13:17 "the way of the land of the Philistines" (Plate V). An inner route still used by nomads follows a series of springs from Beer-sheba to Rehoboth to Azmon, and then westward to Egypt (Plates IV and V). It was probably along this latter route that Abraham, and later the family of Jacob, journeyed to Egypt.

Both Abraham and Isaac are said to have had controversies with the king of Gerar (x, C-1), and Isaac, as we should expect, had trouble over wells he dug as far away as Rehoboth (x, C-3; Gen. 26:15 ff.). Archaeological deposits in the Negeb from about 2000 B.C. and shortly thereafter (Middle Bronze I) suggest the period to which the stories refer.

The most famous Biblical town in the area is Beer-sheba (x, E-2). "From Dan to Beer-sheba" was the common phrase describing the northern and southern limits respectively of Israelite territory. Like Dan, Beer-sheba was noted not merely as a geographical limit, and as an abode of the Patriarchs, but also as a holy place. Here Abraham planted a tamarisk tree and called on the name of his God (Gen. 21:33); here the sons of Samuel judged (I Sam. 8:2); here Elijah fled (I Kings 19:3); and here both Israel and Judah fell into pagan practices denounced by Amos (Amos 5:5 ff.; 8:14). The town is not mentioned in the New Testament, but later Christian writers say that it was a very large village, with a Roman garrison, and that it was the seat of a Christian bishopric. This Christian town was called Bersabee (x, E-2) and was located on the site of the modern Arab village. Nothing older than the Roman period has been found here, however, and it is probable that the Old Testament town was on the site of the mound of *Tell es-Seba'*, 2½ miles to the east.

After the Patriarchal period, the Negeb next played an important role during the period of the wandering in the wilderness. At this time the most important place in the narrative was Kadesh, or Kadesh-barnea (x, C-7). To this region the wanderers came from Sinai intending to obtain entrance to Canaan from the south (Plate V). They failed and stayed there a generation (Num., chs. 13 ff.), during which time Korah rebelled (Num., ch. 16) and Miriam died (ch. 20:1). Somewhere in this region north of Kadesh was Mount Hor, where Aaron died (vs. 22 ff.). The identity of this particular peak has been lost, however, among the many mountains in the area.

The ancient name of Kadesh is still preserved at a small spring called *'Ain Qedeis* (probably also the En-mishpat, "Spring of Judgment," of Gen. 14:7). The amount of water supplied by this spring is so limited, however, that few Israelites could have existed on its supply alone. About four miles northwest is the most copious spring of the whole area, *'Ain el-Qudeirât*, situated in a little valley made fertile by the spring's waters (Fig. 24). Between the tenth and eighth centuries B.C. a Judean fortress was built here; and some scholars have maintained that if any one site is to be identified with Kadesh, this must be the one. Yet in Josh. 15:3, 4 the southern border of Judah is described as running from the Salt Sea to the Maaleh-acrabbim (Ascent of Akrabbim, x, F-4), passing along the Wilderness of Zin to Kadesh-barnea, to Hazar-addar (to be read thus and not "Hezron" and "Adar"), turning to Karkaa, and thence to Azmon (x, B-6) and to the River of Egypt, following the latter to the Sea (cf. Plate VI). The three main springs in the area are *'Ain Qedeis*, *'Ain el-Qudeirât*, and *'Ain Qoseimeh*. It seems probable, therefore, that Kadesh was actually located at the first, Hazar-addar at the second, and Azmon at the third, with Karkaa perhaps lying at the junction of the valleys between Hazar-addar and Azmon. The simplest solution to the problem would be that the Israelites stayed, not merely at Kadesh, but in the general area, using all three of the springs.

Among the roving tribes who frequently appeared in the Negeb were the Amalekites, a people who occasioned repeated trouble for Israel (e.g., Num. 13:29; Judg. 6:3; I Sam. 15:1 ff.; 30:1ff.; Ps. 83:7). Tribes which were friendly to Judah were the Kenites and Jerahmeelites who lived near Arad (x, F-2) and Beer-sheba and were later absorbed into the tribe of Judah (VI, B-C 5; and I Sam. 27:10). Also absorbed by Judah were the tribes of Simeon and Caleb. Caleb was in possession of Hebron and the area south of it (Judg. 1:12 ff.; Josh., ch. 14), while Simeon occupied a group of villages in the area be-

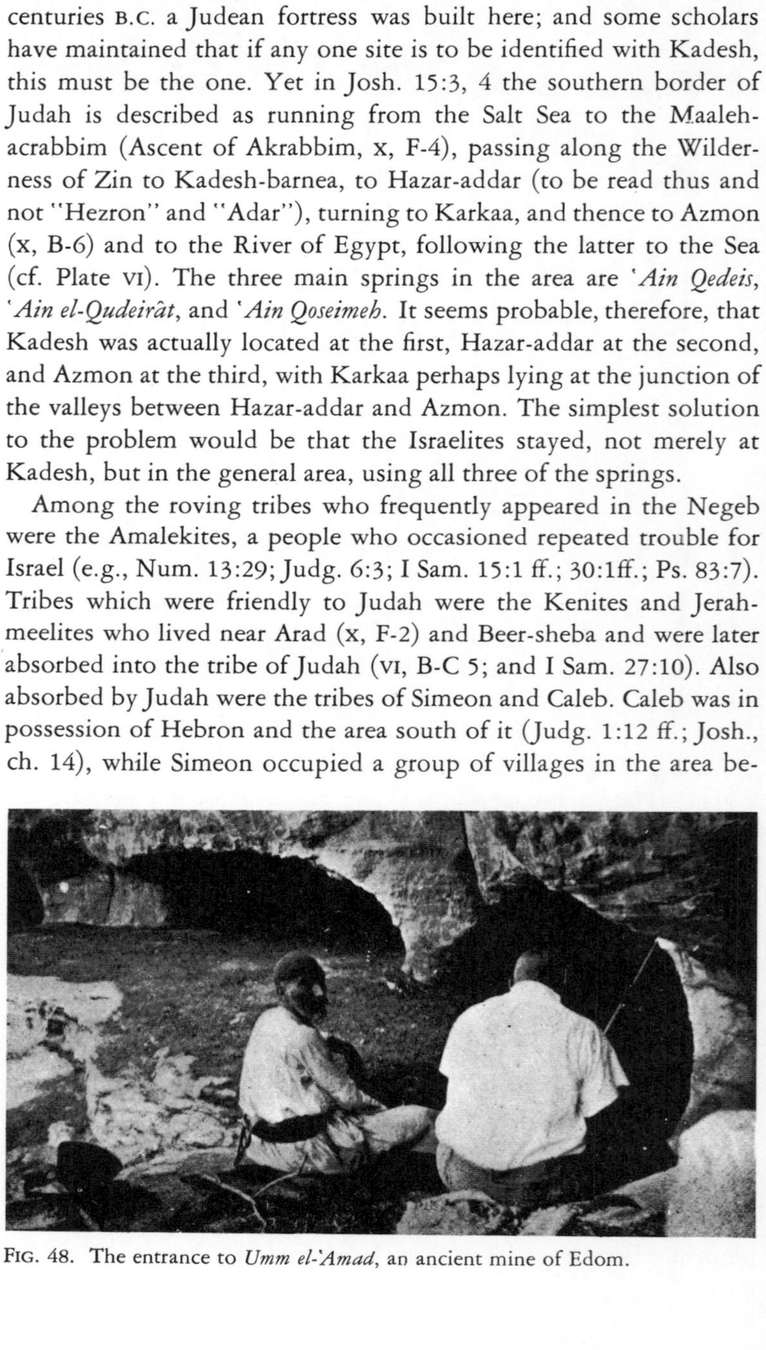

FIG. 48. The entrance to *Umm el-'Amad*, an ancient mine of Edom.

FIG. 49. *Qasr Abū el-Kharaq*, the best preserved of the ancient Moabite border fortresses. It is located just south of the probable site of the "City of Moab" (x, K-1).

tween Beer-sheba, Ziklag (x, E-1), and Sharuhen (x, C-2): see Josh. 19:1-9 and Plate VI.

During the course of David's life as an outlaw, fleeing from the jealous Saul, he spent most of his time in the northern portion of the Negeb. For a time he lived in the Judean wasteland southeast of Hebron. He spared Saul's life when he could have killed him at En-gedi (x, H-1) and again at Ziph (x, F-1; I Sam., chs. 24; 26). Nabal, of Maon, who had possessions at Carmel (x, F-1) refused to aid him and was saved from attack only by the intervention of Abigail (I Sam., ch. 25). Subsequently, David made Ziklag (x, E-1) his base for raiding the tribes of the Negeb (I Sam., chs. 27; 30).

The area east of the Judean watershed and extending northward the length of the Dead Sea was Jeshimon, the Wilderness of Judah (see also IX, F-G 7-8). It was an ideal place for a refuge, and has continued so to modern times. Few towns were situated in it because there was very little water. It was a barren, rugged wasteland, cut by numerous deep and jagged valleys leading down to the Dead Sea (Fig. 42). Masada (x, H-2) was the finest of the many natural fortresses in this region. It is an isolated, flat-topped hill along the cliffs of the Dead Sea, and inaccessible except by winding paths in two places. Here Herod the Great (see p. 83) erected a palace, and in A.D. 70 it was the last refuge of an army of Jewish patriots who fled there after Jerusalem had fallen to the Romans (see p. 84).

During the sixth century B.C. the Negeb was occupied by the Edomites, who were pushed out of their former territory by Arab tribes. Thus began Idumea, the Greek name for the new "Edom," which by the fifth century B.C. was ruled by Arabs (see p. 54).

SOUTHERN TRANSJORDAN DURING THE BIBLICAL PERIOD

While southern Transjordan is far more plentifully supplied with water and thus more fertile than the Negeb, it is more of a pastoral than an agricultural country. The writer of II Kings 3:4 calls Mesha, one of its kings in the ninth century B.C. (see Fig. 33), a "sheepmaster," whose yearly tribute to Israel was 100,000 lambs and the wool of 100,000 rams (see R.S.V.). The country is a plateau, deeply cut along the Dead Sea by east-west valleys which carry the winter rains down into the deep basin of the Sea. Chief of the valleys are the River Arnon and the Brook Zered. Below the Dead Sea the valleys run in a northwesterly direction into the Arabah, the continuation of the Jordan-Dead Sea cleft (see Plates V, X). The towns and villages appear in a narrow north-south belt, scarcely twenty-five miles wide. To the east the country gradually slips away into the vast expanse of Arabian desert without clearly marked boundary.

In Palestine generally, and in most of Transjordan, the rock underlying the thin topsoil and cropping out on every hillside is a soft, crumbling limestone. Along the eastern border of the Arabah, however, the valleys cut down through this limestone into an older, soft, colorful sandstone. This sandstone formation, one of the most important physical features of the country south of the Brook Zered, is the same as that of the region about Mount Sinai (V, E-F 5) and bears the same metallic ores. Recent exploration has shown that the Edomite ore contained both copper and iron in large amounts; and this explains the economic importance of the country. Small wonder, then, that its possession was so coveted by David, Solomon, and subsequent Judean kings that they were willing to risk large armies in an exceedingly difficult battlefield. Some of the ancient mines have been discovered (Fig. 48), and also a number of the mining camps and villages (for example Punon, X, H-6). The latter are usually surrounded with slag from which the metal has been extracted. Numerous small furnaces, once used for the preliminary smelting of the ore, are also found, though now in ruins.

Recent explorations reveal that Solomon was a most energetic exploiter of this ore, though the fact is not mentioned in the Bible. Great walled camps were built for the slave labor which was sent to work the mines; and a large smelter, employing some of the principles of the modern blast furnace, was constructed at Ezion-geber (V, G-4) to refine the metal. These discoveries at last explain the hitherto mysterious reference in Deuteronomy to the Promised Land as one "whose stones are iron, and out of whose hills thou mayest dig copper" (ch. 8:9).

The present sparse population of this region might give the impression that it was no more intensively occupied in Biblical times than was the Negeb. However, hundreds of ruined villages dot the country today, indicating that it was once thickly settled. The ancient names of these villages are not known; hence they do not appear on Biblical maps. The occupational history of the country as determined by recent exploration falls into three main periods: (1) c. 2300-1900 B.C.; (2) c. 1200-700 B.C.; and (3) c. 100 B.C. to A.D. 700.

During the first period an advanced civilization flourished for a time, and this may furnish the background for the invasion of the four kings described in Gen., ch. 14, though the matter is very uncertain. Centuries later the main highway through Transjordan (Plates IV and VI) was still called "The King's Highway" (see Fig. 25).

Several lines of evidence show that the cities of Sodom and Gomorrah were located somewhere in the southern part of the Jordan-Dead Sea basin. Study and exploration now indicate that they were at the southern end of the Dead Sea. The Vale of Siddim (Gen. 14:3) was located in all probability in what is now the basin of the sea below "the Tongue" which protrudes opposite Masada (X, H 2-3). This is the shallowest part of the sea today. In Roman times it was even shallower, for it was then possible to cross from the Tongue to the western shore. The level of the sea has been steadily rising, and is considerably higher today than it was a century ago. The clearest indications of this fact are the submerged forests still visible along the southern shore.

FIG. 50. *Umm el-Bayyârah*, site of Sela ("The Rock"), the virtually impregnable mountain-fortress of Edom.

FIG. 51. A Nabataean-Roman site, eight miles south of the Dead Sea, in the Edomite hills along the Arabah, illustrating Nabataean ability to wrest a living from bleak and marginal lands. Note the remains of the aqueduct which once led water to the enclosure.

Ruins of the Christian and medieval Zoar have been discovered in the area (x, H-3), and there is little doubt that the ruins of the Old Testament town, together with those of Sodom and Gomorrah, are now covered by the waters of the sea. That this region was once fertile and well-settled is indicated by the Biblical story of Abraham and Lot. When their herdsmen had quarreled the two families were separated. Lot chose the Plain of the Jordan which "was well watered every where, before the Lord destroyed Sodom and Gomorrah, even as the garden of the Lord [Eden], like the land of Egypt, as thou comest unto Zoar" (Gen. 13:10, A.V.). Lot then moved to Sodom, which with the other "cities of the Plain" (Gomorrah, Admah, Zeboiim, and Zoar) was located in the Vale of Siddim.

On some occasion in ancient times this vale with its cities was overwhelmed by a great conflagration, the memory of which is preserved not only in the Bible (Gen. 19:23-28), but also in later Greek and Latin writings. "The vale of Siddim was full of slime [asphalt] pits" according to a Biblical writer (Gen. 14:10), and petroleum deposits are still to be found in the region. Ancient writers also tell of the presence of gases which, though not observable today, were probably those commonly found in conjunction with petroleum deposits. The entire region is on the long fault line which formed the Jordan Valley, the Dead Sea, and the Arabah. Throughout history it has been the scene of frequent earthquakes. Geological activity, therefore, may well have been responsible for the settling of the valley's floor and for the disastrous petroleum, asphalt, and gaseous fires which accompanied the earthquakes. This would explain the "brimstone and fire" and the smoke which "went up as the smoke of a furnace" (Gen. 19:24, 28). The story of Lot's wife becoming a pillar of salt is certainly associated with the great salt mass in the valley, *Jebel Usdum* ("Mountain of Sodom"), a hill, some five miles long and three miles wide, stretching in a north-south direction at the southwestern end of the Dead Sea (the ridge west of the name Zoar, x, H-3).

The kingdoms of Moab and Edom (Plates IV-VI and p. 36) flourished during Transjordan's second period of intensive inhabitation and cultivation (1200-700 B.C.). During the six centuries prior to the founding of these kingdoms the inhabitants had reverted to a nomadic life. In the thirteenth century, however, people began to settle in villages once more. The kingdoms established were strongly fortified with walled cities and blockhouses along the borders and within the interior (Fig. 49). After the eighth century B.C. rapid disintegration set in once more and the power of the countries declined, probably because of prolonged warfare with Israel and Judah and aggression from Assyrian and Babylonian armies (see pp. 71 ff.).

The chief city of Moab was Kir-hareseth (x, I-3), located on a high and easily fortified hill. In the time of Elisha, Israelite and Judaean armies laid waste the country of Moab and besieged Kir, to which King Mesha had retired, but were unable to take it. When Mesha sacrificed his eldest son on the walls, the siege was broken (II Kings 3:25-27).

Teman (x, I-8) was one of the chief cities of Edom. Amos in his prophecy against Edom said: "Thus saith the Lord; For three transgressions of Edom, and for four, I will not turn away the punishment thereof . . .: but I will send a fire upon Teman, which shall devour the palaces of Bozrah" (ch. 1:11, 12, A.V.). Teman was the southernmost large city of Edom, and Bozrah the northernmost (x, I-6). The country was noted for its great wise men, many of whom lived in Teman (Jer. 49:7; Obad. 8, 9). One of them, Eliphaz, was the leader of the three friends of Job (ch. 2:11). While Teman was probably the actual capital of the country, the citadel to which the army fled in time of siege was Sela, "The Rock" (x, H-8). This was a virtually impregnable, flat-topped mountain (Fig. 50). The sense of security which it gave the Edomites is well described by Obad. 3: "The pride of thy heart hath deceived thee, O thou that dwellest in the clefts of Sela [R.S.V. marg.], whose habitation is high; that saith in his heart, Who shall bring me down to the ground?"

THE NABATAEANS

The civilization of southern Transjordan reached its peak during the third period of the country's history (100 B.C. to A.D. 100). This was the age of the Nabataeans, one of the most gifted and energetic peoples of ancient times. They were Arabs who invaded Edom between the sixth and fourth centuries, and gradually rose to a position of great wealth and power, controlling the rich trade routes between Arabia and Syria (see Plate XII:A-D). Their kingdom was highly organized and intensively populated. They took over the methods of defense which the Edomites and Moabites had worked out before them, but improved them and enlarged their scope. Villages and fortresses dotted the country. They pushed the border of arable land much farther into the desert than any people either before or since through remarkable efforts at water conservation. Cisterns and reservoirs were built wherever needed. Dry river beds were dammed in order to catch the heavy winter rains. Even aqueducts were constructed where needed (Fig. 51). Their pottery dishes represent a high point in ceramic art—highly decorated, of almost an eggshell thinness, delicately and beautifully worked.

The capital of Nabataea was Petra, a Greek translation of the Old Testament Sela (x, H-8). Part of it was literally carved out of rock, and is one of the most spectacular sights of modern Palestine. Houses, temples, and tombs were cut in the soft, multicolored sandstone cliffs. Flights of stairways, also hewn from the rock, lead up every hill. Free standing pillars before temples and tombs look as though they had been placed in position, and not hewn from the solid stone (Fig. 58). Beautiful murals still adorn some of the interiors. Petra was a resplendent and well-protected capital, on which heavily laden caravans converged from all directions. In the New Testament only one of its kings is mentioned, namely Aretas IV (9 B.C. to A.D. 40), who controlled Damascus at the time of Paul's conversion (II Cor. 11:32), and who also soundly defeated Herod Antipas of Galilee (called "that fox" by Jesus, Luke 13:32) when the latter divorced his first wife, Aretas' daughter.

The Nabataeans were conquered by the Roman emperor Trajan in A.D. 106, after which their civilization soon disappeared. During the next centuries Roman roads (Fig. 25) and fortresses were constructed in strategic places, so that the lucrative trade routes could now be under Roman control. Never again, however, did the country attain the prosperity which it had reached during the time of Jesus.

FIG. 52. One of the Cilician Gates (XI:D, B-2). These "gates" are a series of sharp defiles which cut through the Taurus Mountains in a space of some ten miles. Through them runs the main highway into Asia Minor from Cilicia, Syria, and Mesopotamia. For over four thousand years this highway has been a well-traveled trade and military route. Hittite, Assyrian, Greek, and Roman armies have passed through the mountain gap shown in this photograph. Such a picture as this is now rare because for some time the area has been prohibited to photographers.

THE GREAT EMPIRES OF ISRAELITE TIMES

PLATE XI

THE story of man's oft-repeated attempt to dominate his world by the use of totalitarian power is a fascinating account. It is the story of ambitious men who consolidate their power over a people, and turn the total resources of that people toward world conquest. Strangely enough, the conquest has not always been an unmixed evil. The organizing energy required often stirred creative powers to such an extent that great prosperity resulted and achievements in science and art were phenomenal.

Yet conquest was more often a dreadful thing, draining the resources of subject peoples and keeping them in a state of poverty, terror, and seething hatred. The mounds which dot the ancient Near East are filled with the evidence of this state of affairs. In Palestine and Syria especially the average city was frequently destroyed in war. Small wonder that Israel was so concerned with death and judgment and salvation! Small wonder that the psalms are filled with the pleading of tortured men that they may be delivered from the hands of their enemies!

The period of the Old and New Testaments was the first great epoch of empire-building, and in its maelstrom of tragedy and triumph the Hebrew people were inevitably caught. The Egyptian Empire of the fifteenth century B.C. was the greatest which the world had seen (Plate III). Yet it was dwarfed by the achievements which followed. During the eighth and seventh centuries the Assyrian Empire was formed, including in its scope the whole of Mesopotamia, Palestine-Syria, southern Asia Minor (Plate XI:A), and even for a time Egypt. By 600 B.C. Assyria had fallen and Babylonia had taken its place, ruling over substantially the same territory (Plate XI:B). Babylonia soon fell, however, to the Medes and the Persians, and by 500 B.C. the Persian Empire included in its scope the whole of Western Asia, Egypt, and Thrace in Europe; and its armies were threatening Greece (Plate XI:C). By 330 B.C. Alexander the Great had mastered Greece and the Persian Empire. After his death three great Hellenistic empires divided his domain (Plate XI:D). Then in the first century before Christ, the Romans, with a military power and organizing genius unparalleled in antiquity, conquered and unified the entire Mediterranean world (Plate XIII).

Such was the procession of empires in which the small country of Palestine was caught. Geographical situation decreed that political independence could be achieved in that country only during the brief periods when a dominant empire weakened and could no longer control its dependencies.

THE EMPIRE OF ASSYRIA

The country of Assyria lay along the upper Tigris River, and in the early period of its history Assur (or Asshur) was its chief city (XI:A, C-2). As early as 1900 B.C. the people of this small region were prosperous traders. One of their trading colonies was as far away as Kanish in Asia Minor, where an active interest in the silver mines of the area was one of the chief concerns (II, E-2; III, C-2).

In the thirteenth century Assyrian armies had crossed the Euphrates, and about 1100 B.C. an Assyrian monarch led his troops to the shores of the Mediterranean Sea. These conquests, however, were of a temporary nature. During the second half of the tenth century there began a series of rulers whose conquests during the subsequent century give evidence of a planned program of empire-building. This program was carried out with extraordinary vigor and determination. After securing the back door to Assyria in the highland regions to the north and east, and after subduing Babylon, the kings pushed westward.

The middle Euphrates region around Gozan (XI:A, C-2) and Haran (XI:A, B-2) and the area east of the watershed in Syria from Hamath to Damascus (XI:A, B 2-3), were in the hands of Aramean invaders, who were destined to flood the whole area with traders and settlers, and after 500 B.C. to make their language its official tongue. Around the turn of the ninth century the Assyrian monarchs, Adad-nirari II and Tukulti-Ninurta II, conquered Aramaean territory within the great northern bend of the Euphrates with the result that virtually the whole of Mesopotamia was firmly organized under Assyrian control. The major political story from Western Asia during the ninth century, however, concerns the exploits of the two Assyrian emperors whose reigns occupy the greater part of that century. The first of these, Asshurnasirpal II (883-859 B.C.), is the first of the emperors about whom detailed information is available. It was found in the excavation of his capital, Calah (XI: A, C-2), the modern *Nimrûd*. In a form of braggadocio which typifies the royal inscriptions for the next two and one half centuries Asshurnasirpal describes his conquest of northern Syria, the types and amounts of the booty he received, and the sadistic brutality which he visited upon all who refused to submit to him without battle. From this time forth the Assyrian kings describe their exploits in similar vein. Their armies were so powerful that none could withstand them. Their rapacious cruelty was so terrible that the hatred of them spilled over into the literature of a people as far away as Judah (cf. Nahum, chs. 2 to 3 and Jonah).

Northern Syria at that time was controlled by a number of Hittite dynasties, with their city-states, which were survivals from the fourteenth century B.C. when the region was first conquered by the Hittites of Asia Minor. Indeed both the Assyrians and the Israelites speak of Syria as "Land of the Hittites" (e.g., Josh. 1:4; cf. I Kings 10:29; Gen. 10:15). While the Aramaeans had pushed into the area by this period, they had rapidly assimilated the Syro-Hittite culture. Illustration of the latter has been revealed by the excavations at Carchemish and Samal (XI:A, B-2). After the Assyrian conquest, the culture of the area was rapidly brought under Assyrian influence. The Lebanon district along the coast of southern Syria was not conquered by Asshurnasirpal, but all its cities fearfully purchased their freedom from him by the payment of tribute.

His successor was Shalmaneser III (859-824 B.C.), by whose time the conquering armies were ready to turn southward toward Hadadezer (or Ben-hadad) of Damascus, the king who was probably the strongest ruler of the Syro-Palestinian region. In 853 B.C. the battle of Qarqar took place between Shalmaneser and a coalition headed by Hadadezer (Ben-hadad). Qarqar was south of Hamath and probably on the Orontes River. We have no mention of this battle in the Old Testament, but Shalmaneser lists among his opponents the following: 1,200 chariots, 1,200 cavalry and 20,000 infantry of Hadadezer of Damascus; 700 chariots, an equal number of cavalry and 10,000 infantry of Irhuleni of Hamath; and "2,000 chariots, 10,000 infantry of Ahab, the Israelite." Other smaller contingents of troops were present from places as far away as Que (the area of Tarsus; XI:A, B-2) and Ammon. In other words the strongest kings in Asia, between northern Syria and Egypt, were those of Damascus, Hamath, and Israel. The last-mentioned had not yet taken up the newly introduced cavalry as a weapon of war, but he was able to supply more chariots than the other two together. The Assyrian monarch claimed the victory, saying in contradictory fashion in different inscriptions that he killed 14,000, 20,500, and 25,000 of his enemy. Nevertheless, he retired from the scene and we may assume that the battle was drawn.*

FIG. 53. A cast of the Black Obelisk of the Assyrian monarch Shalmaneser III (859-824 B. C.). On this stone the king gave a brief account of his wars, and pictured various nations bringing tribute to him. In the second scene from the top the embassy of Israel is humbly offering to his majesty "the tribute of Jehu," consisting chiefly of silver, gold, and lead vessels and bars. Jehu himself is shown kissing the ground at Shalmaneser's feet.

As a result of the religious revolution in Israel, which under Elijah and Elisha not only swept the dynasty of Ahab from the throne but also deposed Ben-hadad of Damascus, the coalition was broken up (II Kings 8:7-15; chs. 9;10). Shalmaneser was quick to take advantage of this fact, and in 841 B.C. pictured the embassy of Jehu, the new king of Israel, bringing tribute to him (Fig. 53). The tribute was probably received after Shalmaneser's fifth attack on Damascus, following which he had taken his army into Phoenicia. While there he says that he received the tribute of Tyre, Sidon, and of Jehu, and that he placed his portrait on the cliff of *Ba'lira'si*. This portrait, along with that of Rameses II of Egypt (see pp. 29 f., 37), may still be seen on the cliff at the mouth of the Dog River, north of Beirut (Biruta; III, C-3; see Fig. 54). After 837 B.C. Damascus was not troubled again by Assyria until 805 B.C., when its kingdom was devastated and forced to pay heavy tribute by Shalmaneser's grandson, Adad-nirari II (810-783 B.C.). In the years before this, Hazael of Damascus had been able to bring Israel to her knees and even to extract tribute from Judah. The defeat of Damascus was a great boon to Israel and permitted her rapid recovery.

For the next sixty years (c. 805-745 B.C.) the west was given a breathing space because the rulers of Assyria were not strong men. The kingdom of Urartu (Biblical Ararat) to the north (XI:A-B, C-2) gathered its resources and pressed southward. Babylon and most of Syria freed themselves, while Israel and Judah reached the climax of their powers under Jeroboam II and Uzziah. Then another series of vigorous Assyrians began anew the relentless push of conquest. Tiglath-pileser III (745-727 B.C.), after consolidating his borders to the east and north, led his armies westward. His policy was to divide the west into subject provinces, each with its own governor, though leaving the native kings on the thrones of certain outlying areas, provided they paid a regular tribute (see Plate VII:C). He also instituted a policy of exchanging large sections of the populations of conquered territories, to break up nationalistic feeling and to make the population less united and more pliable.

After subduing Urartu, he struck at Syria, and within a comparatively short time he had conquered the whole of it as far south as Arvad and Hamath (XI:A, B-2). Then internal political problems in Palestine gave him his opportunity there. In 738 B.C. he received tribute from Menahem of Israel, who thus purchased Assyrian support for his hold upon his throne (II Kings 15:19). Tiglath-pileser confirms this Biblical statement by saying in his annals that Menahem "fled like a bird, alone" and bowed at his feet. He then returned Menahem to the throne and imposed a tribute upon him.

It was not until c. 734 B.C. that Damascus and Israel took the lead in attempting to form a coalition of all the southern powers against the Assyrians. Yet this time Ahaz of Judah refused to join, and his northern neighbors attacked him. He appealed for aid to Tiglath-pileser (II Kings 16:7), who was evidently delighted to have

*For the texts referred to here and subsequently in this chapter, see J. B. Pritchard, ed., *Ancient Near Eastern Texts Relating to the Old Testament* (Princeton, 1950), pp. 274 ff.

such a fine chance to intervene. Between 734 and 732 he conquered Philistia; Galilee and Transjordan were taken from Israel; and Damascus, finally, was destroyed. The whole of this territory was then incorporated into the Assyrian provincial system, ruled by Assyrian officials. Galilee, for example, was ruled from Megiddo where a large fort was erected, probably as the administrative center (VII:C, C-4). A fragment of the famous Babylonian Epic of Gilgamesh, recently found at Megiddo, may perhaps be evidence of the presence here of Mesopotamian officials, though it may date from an earlier period. The much-reduced Israel, as well as Judah, Ammon, Moab, and Edom, he left under their native rulers, whom he required to pay tribute (cf. II Kings 15:27 ff.; 16:5 ff.; Isa., ch. 7). Within a few years, however, Israel had revolted again and was this time utterly destroyed. The siege of Samaria, begun in 724 by Shalmaneser V (727-722), was completed early in 721 by his successor, Sargon II (722-705 B.C.; see Fig. 55). The latter tells us that he carried away captive from Samaria 27,290 people. Some of them were exiled in "the (Valley of the) Habor, the river of Gozan" (II Kings 17:6; III, D-2; XI:A, C-2). In the years that followed, people deported from Babylonia, Elam, and Syria were forced to live in Samaria.

During the reign of Sargon, Hezekiah of Judah reasserted the Davidic claims to rule all of Palestine, and to that end instituted a religious reform in both south and north (II Chron. 29-31). He probably attempted this, not as a rebellion against Assyria, but as a readjustment within the empire, whereby he claimed control over the provinces of Samaria and Megiddo (Galilee). Probably because he believed he could secure his end in this manner, he refused to aid the king of Ashdod, Assyrian sources inform us, when the latter was attacked by Sargon in 711 B.C. (cf. Isa., ch. 20) and had his territory reorganized into an Assyrian province. Yet subsequently he evidently concluded that the role of client-king was inadequate for his aims. After Sargon's death in 705 B.C., he allied himself with Babylon and Egypt and became the leader of all the smaller states of his area in a revolt against the new emperor, Sennacherib (705-681 B.C.). In 701 B.C. the latter retaliated (II Kings 18:13 ff.). He claims to have reduced forty-six fortified Judean cities and to have shut up Hezekiah "like a caged bird in Jerusalem." He did not wish to ruin the country; he simply broke down city fortifications, besieged Jerusalem but did not destroy it when the latter surrendered and paid a high tribute. The chief Judean fortress-city was Lachish, and its capture was pictured on a relief in the royal palace at Nineveh (Fig. 36). While our sources are obscure and difficult to harmonize in places, it is not improbable that still another rebellion took place a few years later. Whereas before the first revolt the prophecies of Isaiah appear to have envisaged the fall of Judah to Assyria and to have interpreted the event as the just judgment of God, another group of later prophecies, delivered during a second siege of Judah, predicted the defeat of Assyria and the salvation of Jerusalem. According to II Kings 19:35, 36, which is confirmed by the Greek historian Herodotus, Sennacherib actually did retire quickly from the west when a plague broke out among his troops.

The most notable event of the seventh century came in the seventies and sixties when the Assyrian kings Esarhaddon (681-669 B.C.) and Asshurbanapal (669-c.633 B.C.) conquered Egypt. The fall of Thebes, the capital of Upper Egypt (XI:A, B-4), in 663 B.C. was still remembered by the Judean prophet Nahum a half century later ("No" in Nahum 3:8). Between 652 and 648 B.C. a serious revolt against Assyria occurred which was again led by Babylon. This was the probable occasion when Manasseh of Judah also revolted (II Chron. 33:10-13). Other than that the latter's reign was chiefly notable for the introduction of Canaanite and Assyrian religious cults into Judah and for the attempt to convert the Judean faith into polytheism with Yahweh at the head of a pantheon (II Kings 21: 2-9).

When the revolt of Babylon was suppressed, the Assyrian power began rapidly to wane. Egypt was soon free, and the Assyrians found their energies completely absorbed in defensive warfare in various directions. The golden age of the empire was drawing to a close.

FIG. 54. Reliefs of the Egyptian Pharaoh, Rameses II (c. 1290-1224 B.C.), on the right and an Assyrian king, probably Shalmaneser III (859-824 B.C.), on the left. They were carved by the respective monarchs on the cliffs of the Dog River in Lebanon.

The remarkably detailed knowledge which we have about the Assyrians comes largely from vast palaces and imposing temple-towers built by the kings along the Tigris, especially from *Dur Sharrukin* ("Sargonburg"), Nineveh, and Calah (XI:A, C-2). The first was a magnificent royal residence erected by Sargon II on a grander scale than the ancient world had yet seen. It was abandoned, however, by his son Sennacherib, who made Nineveh his capital. This city then became renowned the world over as the symbol of Assyrian power and aggression. It extended some two and a half miles along the Tigris, and the circumference of the inner walls was about eight miles. The palace was a tremendous structure. In one place the excavators cleared seventy-one halls, lined with stone reliefs, nearly two miles in total length, depicting various activities of the king and his armies.

Asshurbanapal also made Nineveh his capital, and the reliefs in his palace represent the finest examples of Assyrian art. This king was much interested in intellectual matters, and took pride in his mastery of the art of writing. One of the greatest discoveries ever made by archaeologists occurred in the unearthing at Nineveh of his great library, composed of some 22,000 clay tablets. Here the king had systematically collected the religious, scientific, and literary works of the past. They represent our chief source of knowledge regarding life and thought in ancient Mesopotamia.

THE BABYLONIAN EMPIRE

On the death of Asshurbanapal c. 633 B.C. the great empire of Assyria fell rapidly to pieces. For centuries the Chaldeans, Semitic nomads, had been slowly moving into Babylonia. They now gained control of that country, and the first king of these Neo-Babylonians, Nabopolassar, declared his independence of Assyria c. 625 B.C. Meanwhile the Medes in the area of northern Iran (XI:A, C-D, 2-3) were becoming another threat to the security of Assyria. Under their king Cyaxares they captured Asshur in 614 B.C. The Babylonians then joined them, and together they attacked and conquered Nineveh in 612 B.C. As the Babylonian Chronicle put it, "the city they turned into mounds and heaps of ruins." This was a momentous date in ancient history. The greatest power that the world had yet known had fallen, and from the subject peoples there arose a chorus of gratitude, hatred, and new hope. To this sternly exultant mood the Hebrew prophet Nahum gave most vivid expression: "The Lord is slow to anger, and great in power, but the Lord will surely not acquit the guilty. . . . Woe to the bloody city, all of it filled with lies and robbery. . . . Everyone who hears the news of thee shall clap their hands over thee, for over whom hath not thy wickedness passed continually" (chs. 1:3; 3:1, 19).

The Assyrian army fell back on Haran (XI:B, B-2), and in 609 B.C. the Babylonians attacked. Meanwhile Pharaoh Necho of Egypt marched north through Palestine to aid the Assyrians. King Josiah attempted to halt him at Megiddo, but was killed in the attempt (II Kings 23:29 ff.). The Assyrians were defeated at Haran, and Necho took over their territory in Syria-Palestine. The new Egyptian empire in Asia was short-lived, however, for in 605 B.C. the vigorous Nebuchadnezzar arrived in Syria with a Babylonian army, administered a crushing defeat to the Egyptians at Carchemish (XI:B, B-2), and took over the whole of the west to the border of Egypt. The new hopes which the fall of Assyria had raised among the subject peoples were dashed. Babylon was substituted for Nineveh.

We do not possess the same detailed information about the exploits of Nebuchadnezzar as we do about those of the Assyrian kings. Babylonian tradition permitted him to write about his religious and architectural activity but not about his military exploits. Apart from the Bible our main source of information has been the Babylonian Chronicle, an official document which simply recorded the chief events in the empire year by year. One portion, published by C. J. Gadd in 1923, described the fall of Nineveh and for the first time fixed its date in 612 B.C. In 1956 D. J. Wiseman published four more tablets of the Chronicle. These are especially important in that they give itemized information about the chief events from 626 to 594 B.C., with a break of only six years. For the first time we learn the details of Babylonia's struggle against Assyria, and after 609 B.C. her war with Egypt. In 605 B.C. Nebuchadnezzar completely annihilated the army of Pharaoh Necho, but the death of his father caused him to hurry home to be crowned king so that he was unable to pursue his advantage. Hitherto unknown is the record of a major battle with the Egyptians in 601 B.C. in which Nebuchadnezzar was defeated. The new documents for the first time also describe and give the precise date of Nebuchadnezzar's capture of Jerusalem in his seventh year (see p. 55).

Apart from his wars, the chief work of Nebuchadnezzar was the enlargement and beautification of Babylon, which now surpassed Nineveh in architectural glory. He repaired the great Temple of Marduk, the Tower of Babel (see Fig. 11, and p. 24), and erected a vast imperial palace, on top of which, rising terrace upon terrace, was a garden. This place was called "The House at Which Men Marvel," and the "Hanging Gardens" were listed by the Greeks among the Seven Wonders of the World (Figs. 56 and 57).

FIG. 55. A remarkable portrait of Sargon II (722-705 B.C.), the conqueror of Samaria.

Nebuchadnezzar was the only great king of the newly erected Babylonian kingdom. If he had had strong successors, the extent of the empire would probably have equaled that of Assyria. His thirteen-year siege of Tyre did not result in the city's capture, though it did eventually acknowledge his sovereignty. In the latter part of his life he began the conquest of Egypt, but his death and weak successors prevented more than a purely temporary success (cf. Ezek. 29:17-20). Nabonidus (555-539 B.C.) was the last vigorous personality of the dynasty. Yet that vigor was not so observable in political and administrative matters as it was in those of religion and archaeology. He excavated and repaired ancient temples. He took a great interest in archaic religious matters. He apparently had definite opinions of his own about cultic practices and even dared interfere in priestly ceremonies and customs in Babylon. During the latter part of his life he retired to Tema in Arabia (XI: A, B-4) and stayed there year after year, probably insane. Administrative matters in Babylon were left to the crown prince Belshazzar, whom The Book of Daniel knows as "king" (Dan., ch. 5). Meanwhile the annual New Year's festival could not be celebrated in Babylon. In this festival the king acted the part of the god Marduk and ritually refought and rewon the battle that took place with chaos at the beginning of time. It was undoubtedly believed that when this ceremony was not repeated annually, world order was threatened. All in all Nabonidus succeeded in making himself so unpopular that the arrival of Cyrus, the Persian, at the gates of Babylon was welcomed, at least by the priests of Marduk, as heartily as it was by the Jewish exiles (cf. Isa. 45: 1-8).

Commerce, literature, art, and science flourished during this age. The Chaldeans were the founders of astronomy as a science. Careful astronomical observations were continuously kept for over 360 years, and these calculations form the longest series ever made. One great Chaldean astronomer, living shortly after the completion of this period of observation, was able to calculate the length of the year as 365 days, 6 hrs., 15 mins., and 41 secs.—a measurement which the modern telescope has shown to be only 26 mins., 26 secs. too long! His calculations on the diameter of the face of the moon were far more accurate than those of Copernicus. Certain measurements of celestial motions by another Chaldean astronomer actually surpass in accuracy the figures long in practical use among modern astronomers.

THE PERSIAN EMPIRE

During the days of Nebuchadnezzar two powerful empires, the Median and Lydian, existed to the east, north, and northwest of Babylon. By a treaty the boundary between them had been fixed at the Halys River in Asia Minor (Plate XI:B). The Medes, who had captured Asshur in 614 B.C. and assisted the Babylonians in destroying Nineveh in 612 B.C., had their capital at Achmetha (Ecbatana; XI:C, C-2). By 549 B.C. a Persian named Cyrus had united the people of his land and defeated the Median king. The attention of the west was now focused on the career of this extraordinary individual. A Judean prophet rightly interpreted the signs of the times, and saw in Cyrus one anointed of the Lord, who "giveth nations before him, and maketh him rule over kings" (Isa. 41:2; 44:28; 45:1). By 546 B.C. Sepharad or Sardis, the capital of Lydia (XI:C, A-2), had fallen to Cyrus, and Croesus, its king, was a prisoner. Cyrus was then ready to strike at Babylonia; in 539 B.C. he easily defeated the Chaldean army (led by the crown prince Belshazzar? Cf. Dan., ch. 5) and entered Babylon without opposition.

Thus just seventy years after the final Assyrian defeat at Haran in 609 B.C., the days of the Semitic empires were past. The Persian, Greek, and Roman empires were ruled by Indo-Europeans or Aryans. In 525 B.C. Egypt was added to the Persian Empire by Cyrus' son. In the space of twenty-five years the whole civilized east as far as India was brought under the firm control of Persia (Plate XI:C). Repeated attempts were made to add Greece (XI:C, A-2) to this empire. One was led by Darius the Great, who was defeated by the Greeks at Marathon in 490 B.C.; another, ten years later, was led by Xerxes, who was defeated in a naval battle off Salamis. Unable to subdue Greece, the Persians nevertheless held a firm hold over Asia for almost two centuries.

The organization of the great empire was a colossal task, brought to completion by Darius the Great (522-486 B.C.). While ruling Egypt and Babylonia directly as actual king, he divided the rest of the empire into twenty "satrapies" or provinces, each under a governor or "satrap"—a development of the earlier Assyrian provincial system. Aramaic, the language of Aramean ("Syrian") traders, which by this time had become the commercial tongue of the Fertile Crescent, was made the official language of government. Stamped coinage, an idea borrowed from Greece, was introduced throughout the empire as a convenience for business and government alike. A fleet was organized, and to provide a sea route from Egypt to Persia, a canal was dug between the Nile and the Red Sea.

Babylon and Susa (Shushan; XI:C, C-3) were used as royal residences. Cyrus had built a palace at Pasargadae, and there he was buried (XI:C, D-3). Darius, however, erected a magnificent palace with attendant buildings at Persepolis (XI:C, D-3), structures which surpassed in grandeur even the work of Nebuchadnezzar in Babylon. It is most unfortunate that Alexander the Great saw fit in 330 B.C. to burn them, leaving only the ruins for the modern excavator to uncover (Fig. 3).

The Assyrian and Babylonian policy of suppressing subject peoples by deportation and merciless taxation was reversed by the Persians, whose enlightened policies won a measure of gratitude from subject peoples. They were the only rulers of Palestine who did not incur the wrath of the Hebrew people. When Cyrus came to the throne of Babylon in 539 B.C., he evidently had himself proclaimed king and thus the legitimate successor to Nabonidus. In so doing he did not have to reconquer the Babylonian empire; instead, as he said in an inscription written for Babylonians, the god Marduk had searched through all countries and selected him as "righteous ruler" in place of the "weakling," Nabonidus, who babbled incorrect prayers and changed Marduk's worship into an abomination. Once within Babylon his troops were not permitted to loot the city; he returned exiles to their countries, rebuilt their sanctuaries, and restored the statues of their gods. In Ezra 1:2-4 and ch. 6: 3-5 there are preserved two accounts of the decree by which Judeans were permitted to return to Jerusalem and rebuild the Temple. Recent study of these two documents in the light of our present knowledge of royal decrees suggests that they are actually two different statements of the one decree. The second is in Aramaic, the official language of the Persian administration. It was entitled a *dikrona*, a term for a memorandum that recorded the decision of a king or official and was not for publication but for filing in government archives. The document in Ezra 1: 2-4, on the other hand, is in Hebrew and probably preserves the essence of the royal proclamation made to Judeans throughout the empire. The words, "The Lord, the God of heaven, has given me all the kingdoms of the earth, and has charged me to build him a house in Jerusalem," are precisely in keeping with the type of address Cyrus had previously used to the Babylonians; indeed the document was probably framed with the aid of a Judean adviser who knew what a contemporary Judean prophet was saying about Cyrus as the Lord's Anointed (Isa. 45:1). In any event, the exiles from Judah benefited from the new policies. During the years that followed, quite a number returned to the Jerusalem area, established a small province called *Yehud* (Judah), built a new Temple between 520 and 515 B.C. (Ezra, chs. 5; 6), and rebuilt the walls of Jerusalem under the leadership of a Jewish governor, Nehemiah, after 445 B.C. (Neh., chs. 2 to 6).

The best of the Persian monarchs felt obligated to rule justly and righteously. Their acts and words set them apart from Assyrian kings in this regard, and the reason is probably to be sought in their religion. Darius and his immediate successors, at least, were followers of

FIG. 56. Ruins of the Ishtar Gate of Babylon. The animals shown were made of highly colored glazed tile. For a reconstruction see Fig. 57.

Zoroaster, a Median religious reformer who lived about 600 B.C. Zoroaster saw life as a ceaseless struggle between the forces of good and evil. The good, the light, he believed, was a supreme being, named Ahura Mazda. Opposed to him and the helpers he created were the evil spirits; but the good Ahura Mazda would ultimately prevail over them. Zoroaster called men to take their stand on the side of the good, and worship "the righteous Master of Righteousness." The influence of this religion spread widely, and even Judaism by the second century B.C. had borrowed certain conceptions from it.

Evidence for Jews living in foreign countries during the fifth century B.C. has been found in both Mesopotamia and Egypt. Several hundred commercial tablets found at Nippur in Babylon (XI:C, C-3) are in the archives of the commercial firm of Murashu Sons. They reveal the great mixture of peoples who lived in the area; the large number of Hebrew names shows that one sizable element in the population was certainly Jewish. The Elephantine papyri from Upper Egypt indicate that on the island of Elephantine at the first cataract a group of Jews were living as mercenaries, guarding Egypt's southern frontier (XI:C, B-4). They were scarcely orthodox Jews, for they had a temple of their own on the island. The Persian satrap of Egypt during the latter part of the fifth century was a man named Arsham. This we know from recently published correspondence from him and his officials. Putting all the evidence together, we infer that while Arsham was absent in Mesopotamia between 410 and 408 B.C. there were disturbances in Egypt which resulted in the razing of the Jewish temple at Elephantine. The Jews at the fortress wrote to the high priest in Jerusalem and to the sons of Sanballat, former governor of Samaria, for aid in getting the temple rebuilt. The former, as we should expect, did not reply. The latter and Bagoas, governor of Judah, advised that they petition Arsham. This they did, and a copy of the petition is preserved. The letter carefully states that no animal offering will be burnt in the temple if it is rebuilt. Some years earlier, in 419 B.C., Arsham through his commissioner for Jewish affairs had ordered the community at Elephantine to celebrate the Passover according to certain precise regulations, which, we note, accord with

FIG. 57. A reconstruction of ancient Babylon in the time of Nebuchadnezzar, showing a royal procession passing through the Ishtar Gate on its way to the palace. The latter had on its roof the famous "Hanging Gardens," shown in the upper right. In the distant background is the Tower of Babel (see Fig. 11).

Pentateuchal law. These two bits of evidence suggest what we would infer from the Bible, namely, that the religious reforms in Jerusalem and the new priestly community there soon made their influence felt on Jewish affairs throughout the empire. The Elephantine temple was rebuilt, and from that fact we gather that the compromise regarding animal offerings was effective. The priesthood in Jerusalem, of course, held that such offerings were reserved for the Jerusalem altar, for that, they believed, was the altar meant in Deut. 12: 5-7. Reconciliation with the Samaritan sect at Mt. Gerizim, on the other hand, was impossible precisely because the latter believed that Shechem was the place which God had chosen for the central altar.

THE HELLENISTIC EMPIRES

In the fourth century B.C. the center of political power moved westward while Greek culture was making an energetic and partially effective attempt to penetrate the east. Culturally, Greece had long been important. Its brilliant cluster of city-states had generated a vitality and originality still unsurpassed. Particularly at Athens (XI:D, A-2) political vigor, expressed in civic interest, extensive sea power, and outreaching colonies, had joined with intellectual and artistic genius to create a permanently stimulating heritage.

An eastward movement of Greek influence may appear strange. Greek colonies and trade had previously been limited to the Mediterranean and the Black Sea (Plate XI:B). Two factors, however, directed attention eastward. The Greek cities in Asia Minor were inevitably bound up with trends farther east. Moreover, the competing city-states of Greece recognized that Persia, which at Marathon and Salamis had tried to conquer the Greeks, was still a threat.

These divided city-states found unity and protection, but only through unwilling subjection to Macedonia (XI:D, A 1-2). Philip of Macedon (359-336 B.C.), whose capital was at Pella (XI:D, A-1), extended his power southward until a decisive battle in 338 B.C. gave him control of all Greece except Sparta (XI:D, A-2).

It fell to Philip's son, Alexander the Great (336-323 B.C.), to carry out the war Philip had planned against Persia. This brilliant pupil of Aristotle, a provincial governor at sixteen, able general at eighteen, and king at twenty, swiftly won loyalty in Macedonia and Greece. In 334 B.C. he crossed the Hellespont into Asia Minor to challenge Persia. A victory at the River Granicus (XI:D, A-2) opened Asia Minor to conquest. The next spring, he passed through the Cilician Gates (XI:D, B-2; Fig. 52) and decisively defeated the Persian army of Darius at Issus (XI:D, B-2). Turning south, he subdued Syria, Palestine, and Egypt (XI:D, B 2-4). At the western mouth of the Nile he founded the famous city of Alexandria (XI:D, A-3). Returning northward, he crossed the Euphrates at Thapsacus (XI:D, B-2), moved east, and in 331 B.C., at Gaugamela, near Arbela (XI:D, C-2), he crushed the remaining forces of Darius and was master of the Persian Empire.

Alexander continued eastward. His route took him through Babylon (XI:D, C-3), Susa (XI:D, C-3), Persepolis (XI:D, D-3), Ecbatana (XI:D, C-2), and Zadracarta (XI:D, D-2). At Prophthasia, in Drangiana (XI:D, E-3), when it had become apparent that he wanted to unite East and West in one great brotherhood, revolt was brewing among his followers, but he crushed it, and moved on into Bactria (XI:D, E-1), Sogdiana (XI:D, E-1), and India. There his troops mutinied and refused to go farther. He returned westward, moving his troops partly by sea and partly by a land route through Gedrosia (XI:D, E-3) and Carmania (XI:D, D-3). At Babylon death ended his plan to create a world brotherhood with a culture prevailingly Greek (323 B.C.). He had proved a military genius; he had planted Greek cities and Greek influence in a wide area. But he made no deep and lasting imprint on the eastern regions he conquered. His work and the later Roman conquest did much, however, to determine the direction in which Judaism and Christianity were later to spread.

At his death there was no logical successor to hold the empire intact, and Alexander's generals fell to fighting among themselves. One of the many rivals, Ptolemy Lagi, emerged with secure possession of Egypt. Seleucus, another general, was able in 312 B.C. to establish the Seleucid dynasty in Syria and the east. The battle of Ipsus (XI:D, B-2) in 301 B.C. finally excluded from Asia the Antigonid dynasty, which henceforth contented itself with Macedonia. By 275 B.C. the situation shown on Plate XI:D had resulted. Three great empires existed, and they continued in essentially the same form until the eastern expansion of Rome absorbed them one by one. In Macedonia, Antigonus Gonatas ruled (283-239 B.C.). He was not able, however, to bring Greece under his control. In Egypt the Ptolemaic dynasty was firmly established, and Ptolemy II Philadelphus (285-246 B.C.) ruled also Cyrene, the southern part of the Aegean Sea, Lycia, Cyprus, and Palestine.

The dry climate of Egypt has permitted the survival of thousands of papyri, and from these records much of our knowledge of ancient life and history is derived. Tradition dates the translation of the Pentateuch from Hebrew into Greek in the reign of Ptolemy Philadelphus. The number of Greek-speaking Jews in Egypt, especially in Alexandria, was increasing, and they needed a Greek translation of their Scriptures.

The greater part of Alexander's empire, however, was in the hand of the Seleucid Antiochus I (280-262 B.C.), whose capital was at Antioch in Syria (XI:D, B-2). Northern Asia Minor, including Bithynia under Nicomedes (XI:D, B-1), Pontus under Mithridates (XI:D, B-1), and Galatia (XI:D, B-2), where the invading Gauls had just settled, was outside his control. But his empire extended from Thrace in Europe to the borders of India, although the effectiveness of his control over the eastern provinces is open to doubt. These eastern areas were soon to be lost, and Parthia (XI:D, D-2) was soon to begin its rise to power.

At this time Palestine was fulfilling its usual role of border region. Ptolemy Lagi had obtained control of it when Alexander's empire began to break up, and Ptolemaic control, though challenged more than once by the Seleucids, continued until 198 B.C., when Antiochus III added Palestine to the Seleucid empire. From that time until the coming of the Romans in 63 B.C. the history of Palestine was closely linked with that of Syria (see pp. 77 ff.).

MACCABEAN AND HERODIAN PALESTINE

Plate XII

The history of Maccabean and Herodian Palestine includes outstanding religious developments. At least one Old Testament writing, The Book of Daniel, was produced. Formation of the Hebrew canon of the Old Testament, a process already well advanced when the Maccabean period began, was practically completed. Noteworthy Jewish sects, the Pharisees, Sadducees, and Essenes, emerged into prominence. Among these sects, the Pharisees proved of the greatest ultimate importance; they developed the oral tradition which in its later written form gives orthodox Judaism its basic character. Above all, the Christian movement appeared and entered upon its missionary career. Obviously neither Judaism nor Christianity can be understood without careful study of this significant period.

PALESTINE UNDER SYRIA

During the decades preceding the Maccabean period, the struggle between Syria and Egypt for the control of Palestine came to a decisive issue (see p. 76). For over a century after Alexander the Great's empire had been divided among his generals, Egypt dominated Palestine. For several centuries Jews had lived in Egypt, and this gave Egypt a special tie with the Jewish homeland. Syria, however, was constantly seeking to extend its power southward, and under Antiochus III (223-187 B.C.) finally succeeded. His first effort, to be sure, was thwarted when in 217 B.C. he was beaten in battle at Raphia (Plate XII:A, A-6). In 198 B.C., however, he defeated the Egyptian forces at Paneas (XII:B, D-2) and became master of Palestine.

It would be wrong to ignore the continuing importance of Egyptian Judaism or its many ties with Palestine. Minor threats to these ties were not lacking. As early as the sixth century B.C. there were Jews in Egypt, and the Elephantine Papyri show that one group had a temple which was destroyed about 410 B.C. and apparently rebuilt. Later, about 160 B.C., Onias IV of the Jewish high-priestly circle fled to Egypt. Josephus reports that Onias appealed to Ptolemy VI Philometor (181-145 B.C.) for permission to build a Jewish temple at Leontopolis in the district of Heliopolis. He found Scriptural support for this surprising project in Isa. 19:19-21, which promised that an altar "with sacrifice and burnt offering" would be erected among the Egyptians. Such a project must have appealed to the Egyptian ruler after he had lost control of Palestine; it would give the Jews in Egypt an Egyptian center for their worship. In the long run, however, this temple did not divert the attention of Egyptian Jews from Jerusalem; its influence was probably local. The future of Judaism still centered in Palestine, which was now securely in the hands of the Seleucid ruler.

The policy of the Syrian rulers was to promote influences that would effect unity of culture in their territory. Hence they looked with disapproval upon the strangely different Jewish religion, and were ready to strengthen Hellenistic culture in Palestine. They were urged to this attitude by the Hellenistic wing of the Jewish people. Even some of the younger priests at Jerusalem took up the Greek language, athletic sports, and manner of dress. The Jews were deeply divided over the issue.

THE MACCABEAN REVOLT

This was the situation when Antiochus IV, called Epiphanes or "(God-) Manifest" (175-163 B.C.), became impatient with the stubborn opponents of his policy and determined to stamp out the Jewish religion. In 168 or 167 B.C. he desecrated the Jewish Temple at Jerusalem; he prohibited the Jewish sacrifices and built a pagan altar on the Jewish altar of burnt offering; he also prescribed the death penalty for Jews who possessed a copy of their Law, kept the Sabbath, or practiced circumcision. Representatives of the king erected pagan altars in various places and tested the loyalty of the Jews by requiring them to offer pagan sacrifice.

Obviously devout Jews now faced a life-and-death decision, and resistance soon appeared. The revolt began at the little town of Modein (XII:A, C-5), in the hill country northwest of Jerusalem. Here lived the aged Mattathias, a priest of the Hasmonean house. When summoned to sacrifice he refused, killed a Jew who was willing to abandon his ancestral faith, and also slew the Syrian officer. Then, with his five sons, he fled into the hills, where he was joined by many who were ready to die rather than give up their faith.

Such loyal Jews were in a difficult position. They faced civil war with other Jews, and they were in revolt against the king. Mattathias was too old to lead the movement; on his deathbed, shortly after the revolt began, he appointed his son Judas to captain the rebel forces. From the title given Judas comes the name Maccabean; Judas was called Maccabaeus, which is usually explained to mean "Hammerer" and to refer to his sudden, heavy blows against the enemy. But it would be quite wrong to think of Judas as the general of a large and disciplined army. The Syrian forces controlled most of Palestine, and Judas depended much upon sudden thrusts and brilliant surprise attacks. Yet the desperation of the Jews, who were fighting not only for their lives but also for their faith, made them the equal of an army many times their number.

The campaign of Judas took place mainly in the region of Judaea. Employing the methods of guerrilla warfare, he won victories at Beth-horon, Emmaus (XII:D, C-5), and Bethsura (XII:A, C-5). When the Syrian leaders withdrew to Antioch to prepare greater forces for

Fig. 58. The *Sîq* and *el-Khazneh* at Petra. The approach to this site of rugged grandeur and great defensive strength is through the *Wâdī Mûsā*, which for a mile and a quarter forms a narrow gorge, the *Sîq*, with side walls 100 to 160 feet high. At a final turn there comes into view the *Khazneh*, or "Treasury" of Pharaoh, as the Arabs call it. This famous temple, whose front is carved in the red sandstone side of the valley, is over ninety feet high. It is dated in the second century A. D. or earlier.

the war, Judas led his forces to Jerusalem, and although the Syrians still held the Citadel, he cleansed the Temple of pagan objects, rebuilt the altar, and resumed the sacrifices in December, 164 B.C. Since that time the Jews have observed the Feast of Dedication, or Hanukkah, in memory of this occasion. The profanation of the Temple and the struggle of the Maccabeans to rescue it from the control of the Gentiles is the background of The Book of Daniel (c. 166 B.C.); it describes the pagan altar built on the Jewish altar of burnt offering at Jerusalem as "the abomination that makes desolate" (ch. 11:31; 12:11).

Judas and his brothers next made expeditions to Gilead, Galilee, and Idumaea to rescue loyal Jews. In other words, for a brief time the band of loyal Jews was limited to the central part of Judaea, and did not constitute the whole of the population even in that small area. Judas, however, after bringing to safety Jews in other regions who were in danger from the Gentiles or more often from their own countrymen, had to meet the armies of the Syrian king, who was now determined to crush the growing rebellion. His general, Lysias, forced Judas to withdraw from battle at Bethzacharia (XII:A, C-5), where Eleazar, the brother of Judas, lost his life. Bethsura (Bethzur; Fig. 59), an important military center which changed hands several times in these decades, had to surrender to the Syrians. Then, however, rivalry between Lysias and Philip for control of the boy king, Antiochus V Eupator, gave Judas unexpected help. Lysias, eager to hurry back to Antioch to forestall his rival, was forced to make peace with Judas and grant religious freedom to the Jews.

THE FIGHT FOR POLITICAL FREEDOM

This concession by Lysias achieved the aim with which the revolt began. However, it did not satisfy the Maccabean leaders. They began to work for complete political independence, thinking, no doubt, that their religious freedom would never be entirely certain as long as they were politically subject to the Syrians. To strengthen their diplomatic position, they undertook to gain support from the Romans, with whom they formed a league of friendship about 161 B.C. This league, however, was of no immediate benefit to the Jews; the Romans, though glad to embarrass the Syrian ruler by showing friendship for the Jews, did not intervene in Palestine until they were ready to take it over and control it (63 B.C.). The immediate future held in store more conflict between the Maccabees and the Syrians, who were called in by the pro-Syrian party of the Jews to fight against Judas. After an indecisive fight at Capharsalama (XII:A, C-5), the Syrians were defeated and their general Nicanor killed at Adasa (XII:A, C-5). But the forces of Judas had suffered heavy losses. When Bacchides came down from Syria with another army and met Judas at Elasa (XII:A, C-5), few Jews rallied to the battle. Judas was killed and his army crushed (160 B.C.).

His brother Jonathan assumed the leadership, but had pitifully few soldiers to support him. He was, indeed, almost a fugitive, and at first could wage only furtive guerrilla warfare. For a time he dwelt at Machmas, i.e., Michmash (XII:A, C-5). His first successes were due not so much to Jewish military prowess as to Syria's internal troubles, which so occupied the Syrians that Jonathan was able to get control of all Jerusalem except the Citadel. Hard-pressed by their troubles at home, the Syrians also evacuated many of their strongholds in Judaea, although they did not give up the important fortress at Bethsura. Jonathan took Joppa (XII:A, B-4), won a victory near Azotus (XII:A, B-5), and was given Accaron, i.e., Ekron (XII:A, B-5). In an attempt to strengthen his political position, he renewed the alliance of the Jews with Rome.

Emboldened by success, Jonathan went to meet the Syrian general Trypho at Scythopolis (XII:A, D-4). Trypho, however, avoided battle; instead he enticed Jonathan to a parley at Ptolemais (XII:A, C-3), and treacherously took him prisoner. He then began to move against Jerusalem, using his captive as a hostage. Jonathan's brother Simon, however, assumed command of the Jews, and Trypho, finding himself balked, finally put Jonathan to death (142 B.C.).

Simon gained an apparent grant of political freedom in 142 B.C. from Demetrius II, who was trying to hold the Syrian throne against Trypho. The Jews dated a new era from this year. Nevertheless, as soon as Syria's internal affairs permitted, her leaders resumed attempts to subjugate the Jews. In the meantime, however, Simon won noteworthy successes. He finally forced the Syrian garrison out of the Citadel at Jerusalem. He took Gazara (XII:A, B-5), Joppa, and Bethsura, and is said to have made Joppa a usable Jewish port. At Joppa he defeated the Syrian general Cendebaeus, who was attempting to re-establish the Syrian rule of Palestine.

The Jews honored Simon as "their leader and high priest forever, until a trustworthy prophet should arise" (I Maccabees 14:41). His successful career was soon cut short, however, by the treachery of his son-in-law Ptolemy (134 B.C.). Ptolemy murdered Simon and two of his sons at Dok (XII:A, C-5), near Jericho, and sent agents to seize Jerusalem and to murder Simon's other son, John Hyrcanus, who was at Gazara. John, however, learned of the plot, and hastening to Jerusalem he gained control of it before Ptolemy's supporters could reach it. John was promptly recognized as the rightful successor of his father, and became both ruler and high priest.

THE PERIOD OF TERRITORIAL EXPANSION

John Hyrcanus had a long and successful reign (134-104 B.C.). In its early years he was forced to admit the control of the Syrian king for a time, but he later renounced this control and extended the range of Jewish power. For instance, he gained possession of Medeba (XII:A, D-5), east of the Jordan. He broke the resistance of the re-

FIG. 59. Beth-zur (Bethsura). Air view while the 1931 excavation was in progress. Particularly during the Maccabean period this isolated hill was an important military stronghold. Note the hilly character of the Judean upland, and the way the rocks are cleared from the field and used in soil conservation.

A

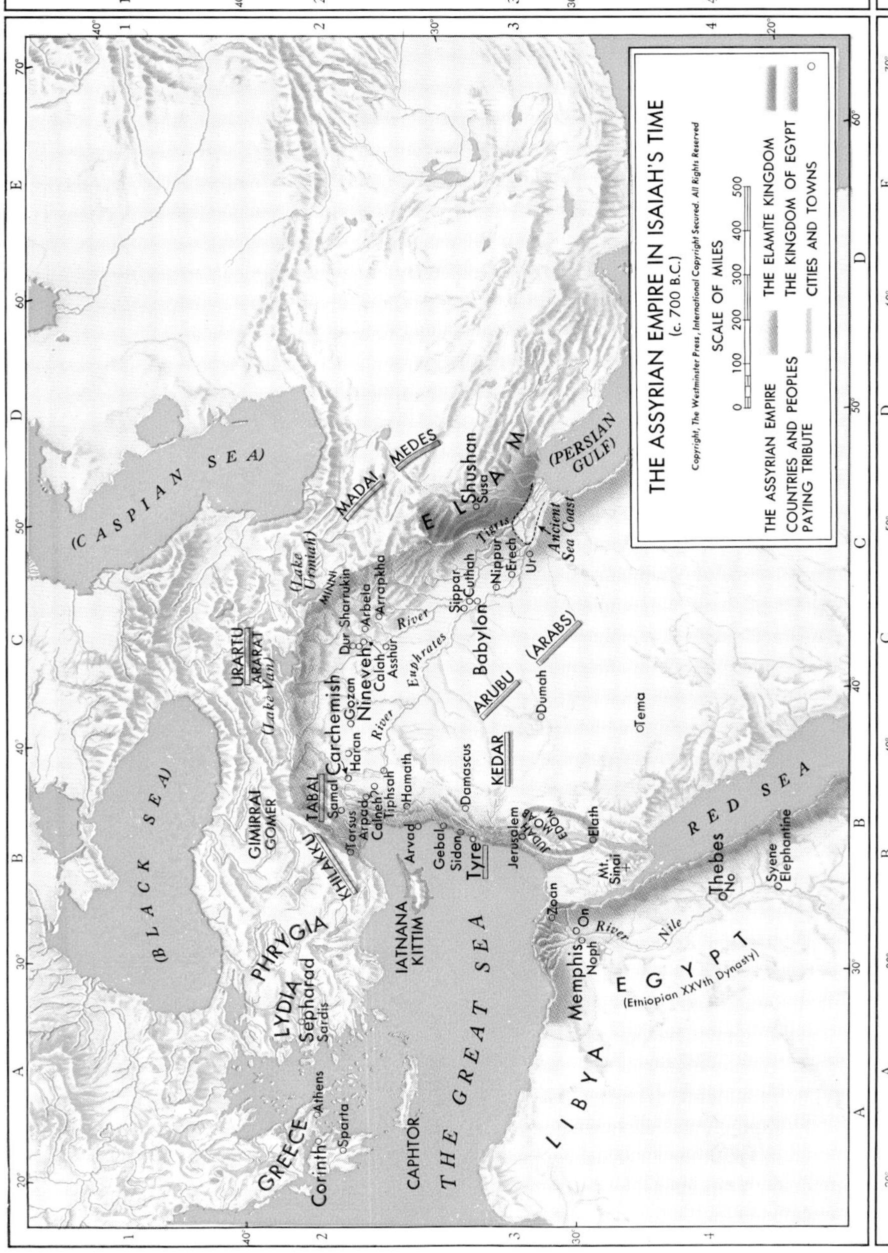
THE ASSYRIAN EMPIRE IN ISAIAH'S TIME
(c. 700 B.C.)
Copyright, The Westminster Press, International Copyright Secured. All Rights Reserved
SCALE OF MILES
0 100 200 300 400 500
THE ASSYRIAN EMPIRE
COUNTRIES AND PEOPLES PAYING TRIBUTE
THE ELAMITE KINGDOM
THE KINGDOM OF EGYPT
CITIES AND TOWNS
(CASPIAN SEA)
(BLACK SEA)
THE GREAT SEA
RED SEA
(PERSIAN GULF)
EGYPT
(Ethiopian XXVth Dynasty)
LIBYA
GREECE
LYDIA
PHRYGIA
URARTU
ARARAT
MADAI
MEDES
ELAM
ARUBU
(ARABS)
KEDAR
CAPHTOR
IATNANA
KITTIM
Nineveh
Babylon
Carchemish
Memphis
Thebes

B

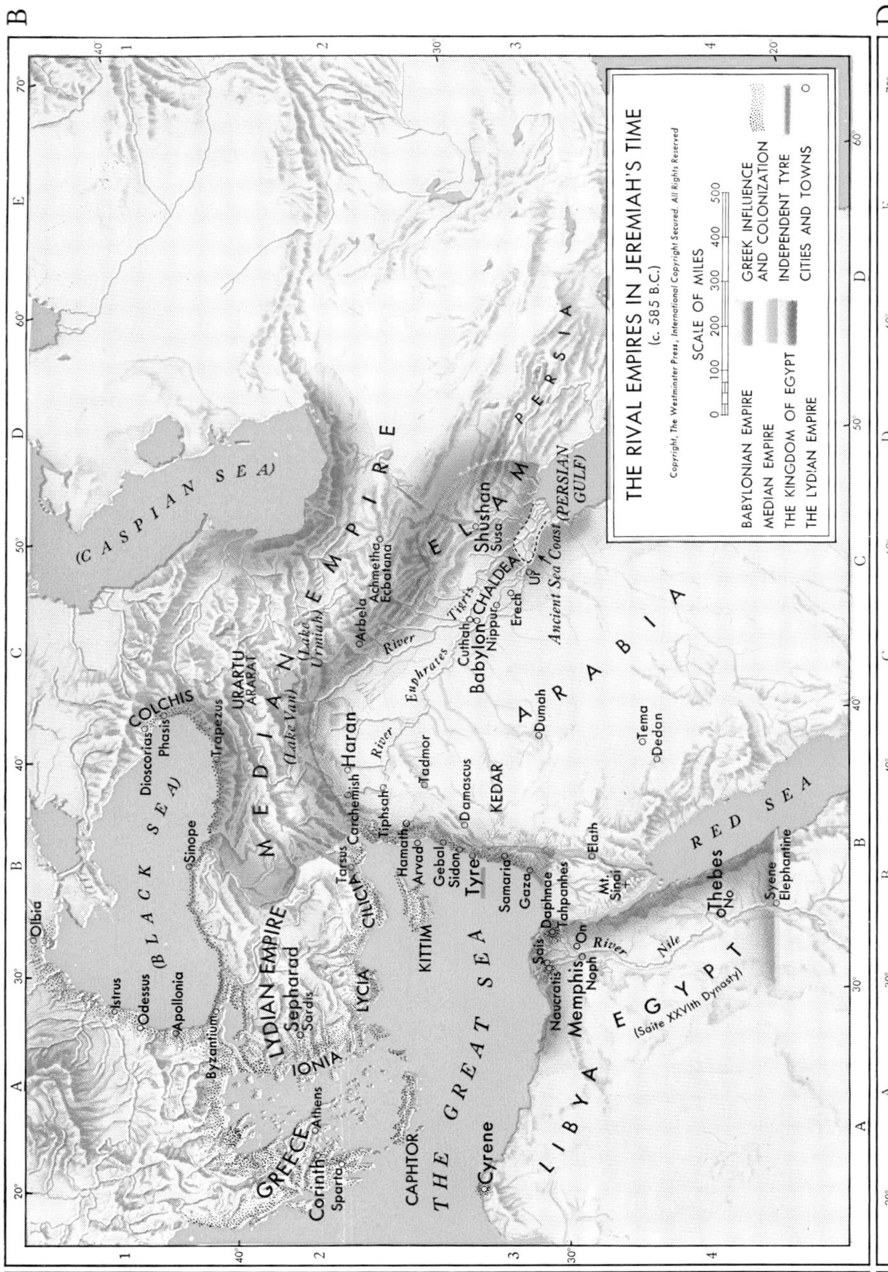
THE RIVAL EMPIRES IN JEREMIAH'S TIME
(c. 585 B.C.)
Copyright, The Westminster Press, International Copyright Secured. All Rights Reserved
SCALE OF MILES
0 100 200 300 400 500
BABYLONIAN EMPIRE
MEDIAN EMPIRE
THE KINGDOM OF EGYPT
THE LYDIAN EMPIRE
GREEK INFLUENCE AND COLONIZATION
INDEPENDENT TYRE
CITIES AND TOWNS
(CASPIAN SEA)
(BLACK SEA)
THE GREAT SEA
RED SEA
(PERSIAN GULF)
MEDIAN EMPIRE
LYDIAN EMPIRE
EGYPT
(Saite XXVIth Dynasty)
LIBYA
ARABIA
GREECE
ELAM
PERSIA
CHALDEA
COLCHIS
URARTU
ARARAT
IONIA
LYCIA
CILICIA
KEDAR
KITTIM
CAPHTOR
Babylon
Shushan
Haran
Tyre
Memphis
Thebes

C

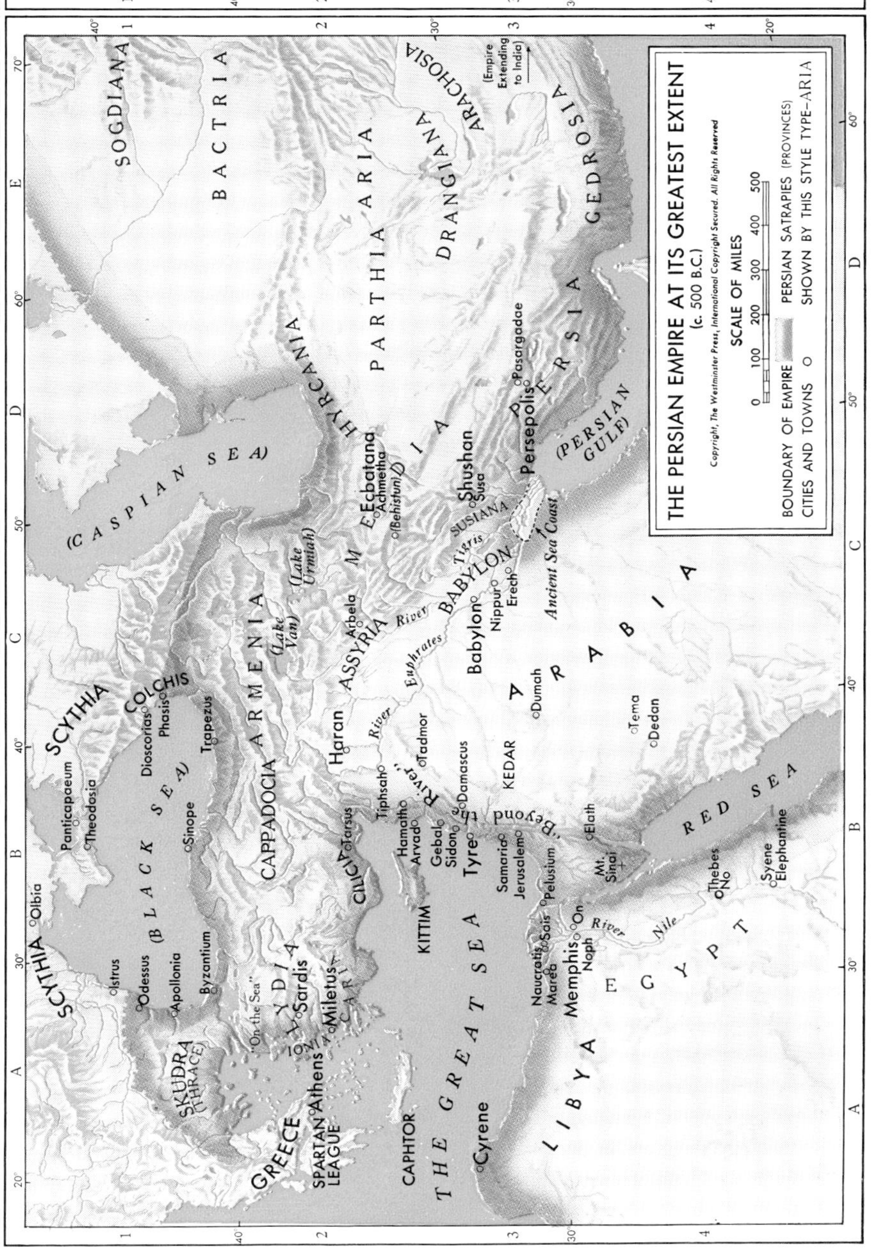
THE PERSIAN EMPIRE AT ITS GREATEST EXTENT
(c. 500 B.C.)
Copyright, The Westminster Press, International Copyright Secured. All Rights Reserved
SCALE OF MILES
0 100 200 300 400 500
BOUNDARY OF EMPIRE
CITIES AND TOWNS
PERSIAN SATRAPIES (PROVINCES) SHOWN BY THIS STYLE TYPE–ARIA
(CASPIAN SEA)
(BLACK SEA)
THE GREAT SEA
RED SEA
(PERSIAN GULF)
SCYTHIA
SOGDIANA
BACTRIA
HYRCANIA
PARTHIA
ARIA
DRANGIANA
ARACHOSIA
GEDROSIA
PERSIA
MEDIA
ARMENIA
CAPPADOCIA
ASSYRIA
BABYLON
ARABIA
EGYPT
LIBYA
GREECE
SKUDRA
(THRACE)
SPARTAN LEAGUE
(Empire Extending to India)
Persepolis
Pasargadae
Shushan
Ecbatana
Babylon
Memphis

D

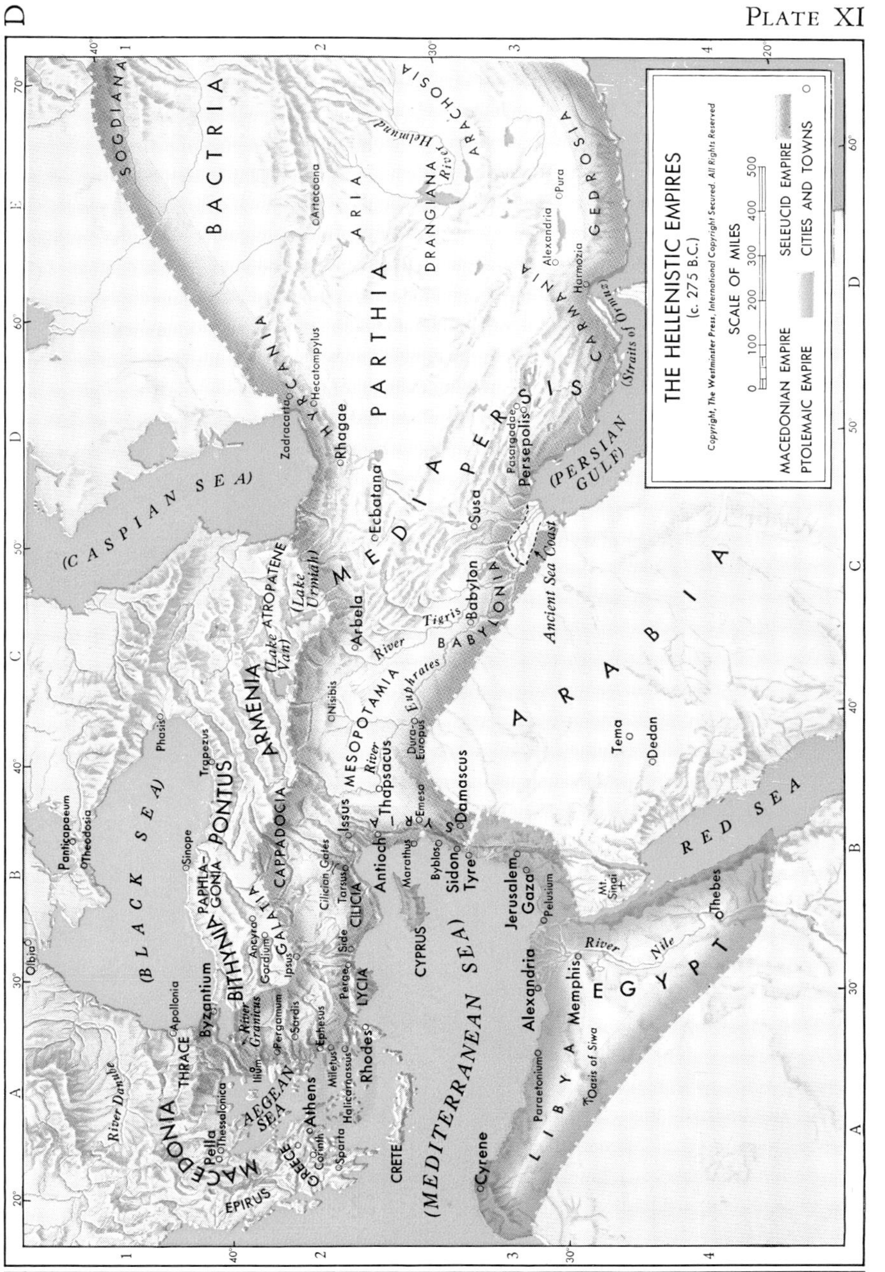
THE HELLENISTIC EMPIRES
(c. 275 B.C.)
Copyright, The Westminster Press, International Copyright Secured. All Rights Reserved
SCALE OF MILES
0 100 200 300 400 500
MACEDONIAN EMPIRE
PTOLEMAIC EMPIRE
SELEUCID EMPIRE
CITIES AND TOWNS
(CASPIAN SEA)
(BLACK SEA)
(MEDITERRANEAN SEA)
AEGEAN SEA
RED SEA
(PERSIAN GULF)
MACEDONIA
THRACE
BITHYNIA
PONTUS
CAPPADOCIA
ARMENIA
ATROPATENE
MEDIA
PARTHIA
HYRCANIA
BACTRIA
SOGDIANA
ARIA
DRANGIANA
ARACHOSIA
CARMANIA
GEDROSIA
PERSIA
MESOPOTAMIA
BABYLONIA
ARABIA
EGYPT
LIBYA
CILICIA
LYCIA
CYPRUS
CRETE
Alexandria
Antioch
Seleucia
Persepolis
Ecbatana
Babylon

A

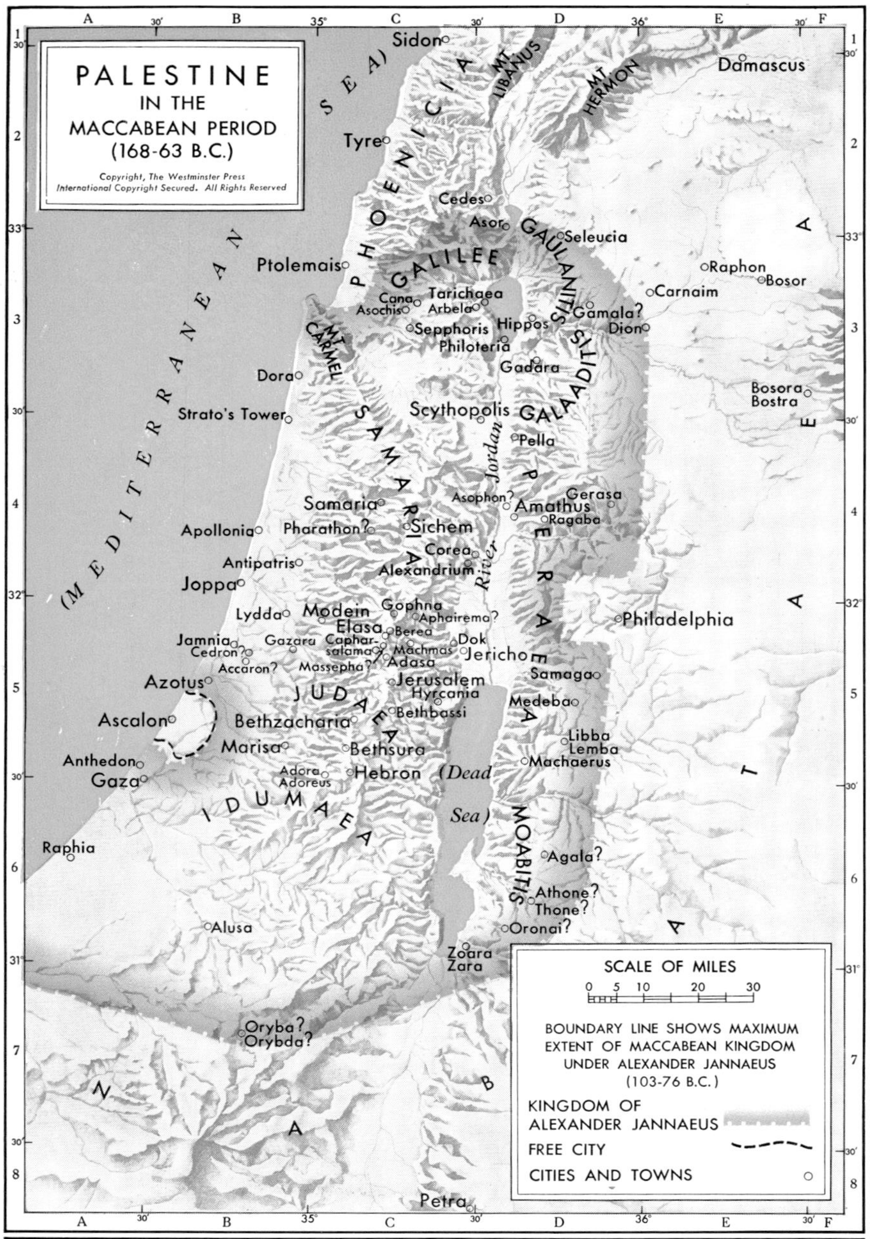
PALESTINE
IN THE
MACCABEAN PERIOD
(168-63 B.C.)
Copyright, The Westminster Press
International Copyright Secured. All Rights Reserved
Sidon
Tyre
Damascus
MT. LIBANUS
MT. HERMON
PHOENICIA
Cedes
Asor
Seleucia
GAULANITIS
GALILEE
Ptolemais
Raphon
Bosor
Carnaim
Cana
Tarichaea
Asochis
Arbela
Gamala?
Sepphoris
Hippos
Dion
Philoteria
MT. CARMEL
Gadara
Dora
GALAADITIS
Bosora
Bostra
Strato's Tower
Scythopolis
Pella
SAMARIA
Samaria
Asophon?
Gerasa
Amathus
Ragaba
Apollonia
Pharathon?
Sichem
Corea
Antipatris
Alexandrium
Joppa
Gophna
Lydda
Modein
Aphairema?
Philadelphia
Elasa
Berea
Jamnia
Gazara
Caphar-salama
Machmas
Dok
Cedron
Jericho
Accaron?
Massepha?
Adasa
Samaga
Azotus
Jerusalem
Hyrcania
JUDAEA
Bethbassi
Medeba
Ascalon
Bethzacharia
Marisa
Bethsura
Libba
Lemba
Anthedon
Adora
Adoreus
Hebron
Machaerus
Gaza
(Dead Sea)
IDUMAEA
MOABITIS
PERAEA
Raphia
Agala?
Athone?
Thone?
Alusa
Oronai?
Zoara
Zara
Oryba?
Orybda?
Petra
(MEDITERRANEAN SEA)
NABATAEA
River Jordan
SCALE OF MILES
0 5 10 20 30
BOUNDARY LINE SHOWS MAXIMUM EXTENT OF MACCABEAN KINGDOM UNDER ALEXANDER JANNAEUS (103-76 B.C.)
KINGDOM OF ALEXANDER JANNAEUS
FREE CITY
CITIES AND TOWNS

PALESTINE
UNDER
HEROD THE GREAT
(40-4 B.C.)
Copyright, The Westminster Press
International Copyright Secured. All Rights Reserved
Sidon
Tyre
Damascus
MT. LIBANUS
MT. HERMON
Paneas
PHOENICIA
TRACHONITIS
ULATHA
BATANAEA
Ecdippa
GAULANITIS
GALILEE
Ptolemais
Tarichaea
Magdala
AURANITIS
Arbela
Gamala?
Canatha
Sepphoris
Hippos
Gaba
Nazareth
MT. CARMEL
MT. TABOR
Gadara
Dora
Caesarea
Strato's Tower
Scythopolis
Pella
DECAPOLIS
SAMARIA
Sebaste
Samaria
MT. GERIZIM
Amathus
Apollonia
Antipatris
Alexandrium
Joppa
Phasaelis
Philadelphia
Jamnia
Gazara
Jericho
Essebon
Esbus
Jerusalem
Azotus
Bethlehem
Hyrcania
Herodium
Ascalon
JUDAEA
Marisa
Callirhoe
Machaerus
Anthedon
Adora
Hebron
Gaza
(Dead Sea)
Masada
IDUMAEA
PERAEA
Raphia
(MEDITERRANEAN SEA)
NABATAEA
River Jordan
Petra
SCALE OF MILES
0 5 10 20 30
KINGDOM OF HEROD THE GREAT
DECAPOLIS
FREE CITY
CITIES AND TOWNS

C

PALESTINE
UNDER
HEROD AGRIPPA I
(41-44 A.D.)
Copyright, The Westminster Press
International Copyright Secured. All Rights Reserved
Sidon
Tyre
ABILENE
Damascus
MT. LIBANUS
MT. HERMON
Caesarea Philippi
PHOENICIA
TRACHONITIS
ULATHA
GAULANITIS
BATANAEA
Ptolemais
GALILEE
Bethsaida
Julias
Tiberias
Gamala?
AURANITIS
Sepphoris
Hippos
Nazareth
MT. CARMEL
Gadara
Dora
Caesarea
Scythopolis
Pella
DECAPOLIS
SAMARIA
Sebaste
Samaria
MT. GERIZIM
Joppa
Phasaelis
Archelais
Philadelphia
Jamnia
Emmaus
Jericho
Julias
Livias
Essebon
Esbus
Betharamphtha
Azotus
Jerusalem
Bethlehem
Herodium
Ascalon
JUDAEA
Hebron
Gaza
(Dead Sea)
IDUMAEA
PERAEA
Raphia
(MEDITERRANEAN SEA)
NABATAEA
River Jordan
Petra
SCALE OF MILES
0 5 10 20 30
KINGDOM OF HEROD AGRIPPA I
DECAPOLIS
FREE CITY
CITIES AND TOWNS

PALESTINE
IN THE TIME OF
HEROD AGRIPPA II
AND THE
ROMAN PROCURATORS
(54-66 A.D.)
Copyright, The Westminster Press
International Copyright Secured. All Rights Reserved
Sidon
Tyre
ABILENE
Damascus
MT. LIBANUS
MT. HERMON
Caesarea Philippi
Daphne
PHOENICIA
TRACHONITIS
Cedasa
Gischala
GAULANITIS
Seleucia
BATANAEA
Ptolemais
GALILEE
Capernaum
Bethsaida
Julias
Gabara
Tarichaea
Jotapata
Tiberias
Gamala?
AURANITIS
Sepphoris
Garis?
Ammathus
Hippos
Japha
Sennabris
Dabaritta
Gadara
MT. CARMEL
Caesarea
Narbata?
Scythopolis
Pella
DECAPOLIS
SAMARIA
Sebaste
Samaria
Neapolis
Gerasa
Antipatris
Acrabetta
Corea
Joppa
Thamna
Lydda
Adida
Gophna
Ephraim?
Philadelphia
Bethela
Beth-horon Upper
Jericho
Bethennabris
Jamnia
Emmaus
Gabao
Abila
Gabath Saul
Julias
Essebon
Emmaus
Esbus
Azotus
Jerusalem
Besimoth
Herodium
Thekoue
Ascalon
JUDAEA
Alurus
Anthedon
Machaerus
Hebron
Gaza
(Dead Sea)
Engaddi
Masada
IDUMAEA
PERAEA
Raphia
Zoara
Zara
(MEDITERRANEAN SEA)
NABATAEA
River Jordan
Petra
SCALE OF MILES
0 5 10 20 30
RULED BY ROMAN PROCURATOR
DECAPOLIS
KINGDOM OF HEROD AGRIPPA II
FREE CITY
CITIES AND TOWNS

gion of Samaria, and captured Sichem (XII:A, C-4). After seizing the Samaritan temple on Mount Gerizim, he destroyed this ancient rival of the Temple in Jerusalem (cf. John 4:20). He took the city of Samaria (XII:A, C-4) and razed it. He also captured Scythopolis and successfully asserted control over the Plain of Jezreel.

His son and successor Aristobulus I ruled but a year (104-103 B.C.). He extended Jewish control northward to Galilee, which Judas had abandoned to the Gentiles. Josephus states that Aristobulus was the first Maccabean to assume the title of king.

In the reign of Alexander Jannaeus (103-76 B.C.) the territory under Maccabean control reached its maximum extent, approximately that shown on Plate XII:A. His reign was by no means without its conflicts. When he attacked Ptolemais, that city appealed to Ptolemy of Egypt for help. Ptolemy saw a chance to extend his power to the north, and undertook against Alexander Jannaeus a futile campaign which included battles at Asochis (XII:A, C-3) in Galilee and Asophon (XII:A, D-4) in the Jordan Valley. Alexander was able to take Gadara (XII:A, D-3) and Amathus (XII:A, D-4) on the east side of the Jordan. In the southwestern corner of Judaea he took Raphia, Anthedon, and Gaza (XII:A, A 5-6). By this time, however, the worldly character of Maccabean ambitions and methods had grown until Alexander was using foreign mercenary soldiers to aid him in his warfare. The movement which started out to protect religious freedom had become so secular and nationalistic that many of his devout countrymen supported the Syrian ruler against him. He almost lost his life and throne in a battle with the Syrian Demetrius at Sichem, but was saved by last-minute support from some Jews who at first fought against him.

Further difficulty for Alexander arose when the Syrian ruler came boldly into Palestine to meet Aretas, the Nabatean king, in battle. The latter defeated and killed the Syrian king, and later overcame Alexander in battle at Adida (XII:D, B-5), a town near Lydda in Judaea. By some concession Alexander induced Aretas to withdraw, and continued his attempt at further conquest until on a campaign against Ragaba (XII:A, D-4), east of the Jordan, he died.

His widow Alexandra succeeded him (76-67 B.C.). Upon her death her two sons fought for the rule; Hyrcanus II was defeated near Jericho (XII:A, C-5) and Aristobulus II gained the throne. At this point a decisive change occurred. The Idumaean Antipater took the side of Hyrcanus. He saw that he could gain power for himself by championing the cause of Hyrcanus, and enlisted Aretas III of the Nabatean Kingdom in an attempt to put Hyrcanus on the Jewish throne. Thus backed, Hyrcanus brought forces to Jerusalem and sought to gain control of that city. At this juncture both Aristobulus and Hyrcanus appealed to Pompey, the Roman general who at the time was in Syria. He came to Jerusalem and took control of it for the Romans. This was in 63 B.C. After that date the Jews never again enjoyed political independence in Palestine until the recent establishment of the State of Israel.

THE RISE OF JEWISH SECTS

The Maccabean period saw the emergence of the Jewish sects which furnished the background of Rabbinic Judaism and New Testament Christianity. We must pause, therefore, in our historical survey to note the forms which Jewish religious life was taking.

Several factors stimulated the rise of such sects. The Temple not only symbolized for all Israel the unity of their people; it was a special concern of the dominant priestly group and their leadership in its worship and sacrifices gave them special distinction. How rigidly the Law should be applied to all of the daily life of Israel was an issue. Differences arose as to how much and which tradition to adopt in order to apply the Law to new conditions of life. The pressure of Gentile practices and culture, not only on Jews living in Gentile lands, but also in Palestine itself, raised problems which received varying answers; some Jews, especially those whose public position or business forced them to deal with Gentiles, made concessions, while others, spurning compromise, insisted on strict legal observance or in some cases even withdrew into isolation to avoid ceremonial defilement from pagan or careless neighbors. The threat to political freedom led some to make liberty for God's chosen people their first concern.

While most of the Jews never allied themselves with any specific sect, three main parties clearly emerged as the second century B.C. passed. The Sadducees, apparently so named after Zadok (I Kings 2:35), were the priestly party; their life naturally centered in the Temple ministry. They had little interest in the prophetic movement and writings. When Palestine was under foreign rule, their official contacts with Gentiles led them to accept many Hellenistic ways. They were in general an aristocratic class, conservative in religious and political questions. When the Temple was destroyed in A.D. 70, they ceased to play any significant role in Judaism.

Out of the line of Pious Men devoted to the Law of Israel came the Pharisees, whose name seems to mean "the Separated Ones." They loyally supported the Temple, for the Law so directed, but their deep concern for separation from defilement and for strict observance of the Law led them to develop an extensive oral tradition which applied the Law to the changing conditions of life. Their interest in teaching the Law led them to emphasize the synagogue and its program of worship and education in the local community. While not a large group—Josephus says that in Herod's day they numbered a little over 6,000—their earnestness and dedication won them wide respect and influence. They were the most vital Jewish party of their time, and their group and tradition survived the fall of Jerusalem to live on in Talmudic and Orthodox Judaism.

FIG. 60. *Khirbet Qumrân*, the Essene center just before and during the time of Christ. The picture is taken from the cliff that rises high above the site and looks east toward the Dead Sea. *Wâdī Qumrân*, dry except during the rainy season, is to the right. Just above it in the fourth "pillar" (counting from the camera) of the corrugated cliffs, Bedouins found Cave 4, in which manuscript fragments were found in greatest number. Cave 1, from which the complete Isaiah Scroll came, is in the cliffs about three quarters of a mile to the north (left).

Least characteristic of Judaism and little known until recent times were the Essenes. For centuries they were known mainly from three literary sources. Pliny the Elder, a Roman writer who died A.D. 79, writes of them as a monastic group located on the northern stretch of the west side of the Dead Sea. Two first-century Jewish writers, Philo of Alexandria and Josephus, agree that the Essenes, while they kept aloof from normal society, were found in numerous cities, with a total number of about 4,000. They practiced community of property and lived a hard-working and frugal life under strict discipline; except for a few "marrying Essenes," they practiced celibacy.

Perhaps the most sensational archaeological discovery of recent years has been the finding of ruins of just such a monastic center on the northwest shore of the Dead Sea, at *Khirbet Qumrân* (XIV, C-5). The ruins at that site had long been known, but their antiquity and importance had not been realized. The finding of the Dead Sea Scrolls in a nearby cave was the first discovery (1947). It included a magnificent complete manuscript of Isaiah, another fragmentary manuscript of Isaiah, a commentary on Habakkuk, a Manual of Discipline for the sect, an idealistic and ritualistic set of directions for the War of the Sons of Light with the Sons of Darkness, and a collection of Thanksgiving Psalms. This and nearby caves have yielded fragments of ancient pottery and cloth as well as hundreds of other (fragmentary) manuscripts of Old Testament and noncanonical works.

Kinship of the sectarian writings with other ancient Jewish works was noted at once. In 1910 some "Fragments of a Zadokite Work," found in the Cairo Genizah, had been published. They came from an ancient Jewish sect which in protest against the current religious leadership had withdrawn under their own honored leader to "Damascus" (perhaps meant allegorically rather than literally). These fragments are related to the *Qumrân* writings; parts of several manuscripts of the "Zadokite Work" have been found in one of the caves near *Qumrân*.

Other ancient Jewish writings contain parallels to the Dead Sea Scrolls. The Book of Jubilees and the Testaments of the Twelve Patriarchs show the most striking kinship, but other books, such as the Psalms of Solomon, have important points of similarity.

FIG. 61. The clay table and portions of a bench found at *Khirbet Qumrân* as they are reconstructed in the Palestine Archaeological Museum in Jerusalem. On this table the scribes of the Essene community copied the manuscripts, so many fragments of which have been found. In the same room with the table were found two inkpots, one of clay and one of bronze, and a double basin which was evidently used for ritual washing when a scribe worked on the sacred texts.

Excavation of the ruins at *Khirbet Qumrân* was carried out, beginning in 1951, with striking results (Fig. 60). The site proved to be the residence of an ancient monastic sect which practiced frequent lustrations, for which there were a number of pools or cisterns. The group ate at a common table and practiced community of goods. They carried on active literary work. The long writing table found (Fig. 61) shows that the hundreds of manuscripts in the cave were not put there by temporary refugees from Jerusalem, but by members of the sect, who continuously copied the Scriptures and wrote and copied other religious works. The fact that their Scriptural writings usually have a better format, script, and writing material than do their other writings indicates that the sect had clear ideas concerning the canon of the Old Testament.

The numerous burials near the main building are almost all of men. The burials number about twelve hundred. This may imply that about 200 members of the order were resident at one time. The caves nearby may well have been used as living quarters by many.

The date of the manuscripts and ruins has been vigorously debated. It now seems clear, however, that the *Qumrân* site was occupied by the sect from about 100 B.C. to about A.D. 68. The manuscripts found are in some cases older than the first use of the site by the sect, but none is later than the middle of the first century A.D. These conclusions are supported by the converging evidence of style of writing, pottery, cloth (tested by the carbon-14 process), coins, and masonry. Some evidence suggests temporary withdrawal from the site during the time of Herod the Great. The sect abandoned it about A.D. 68, and Roman soldiers then occupied it for a time.

It is not yet possible to write a clear history of this sect. It appears that the group originated with Jewish priests who withdrew to the wilderness in violent protest against what they considered evil religious leadership at Jerusalem. About 100 B.C. or shortly thereafter a Teacher of Righteousness, evidently an able leader, gave definite form to the life of the sect. It lived under strict discipline, with severe penalties for infractions of rules. Each member was ranked annually on the basis of his record. New members had to undergo a time of probation and searching examinations. The sect shared property and common meals, and maintained a continuous study of the Law. It lived with a strong eschatological expectation, and looked forward to a Messianic age. In fact, two Messiahs may have been expected. At least, in rules for the common feast, probably described in anticipation of the eschatological banquet to come, we find a Messiah of Aaron, who is given first place; next to him appears the priestly group; and only then is mentioned the Messiah of Israel, who may be assumed to be of Davidic descent.

The importance of these discoveries at *Qumrân* is at least fivefold. First of all, this group appears to be Essene; at the least it was closely related to the Essene sect. In the second place, the discovery of over a hundred ancient Biblical manuscripts provides our earliest material for study of the text of the Old Testament books. In the third place, the presence in the sect's writings of Iranian and other Near Eastern influences throws light on the complex nature of ancient Palestinian Judaism, and shows the presence in Palestine of features which some scholars had felt compelled to seek in Gentile lands. In the fourth place, the relation of the sect's writings to other noncanonical documents calls for restudy of the Jewish literature of that period; and the parallels with several New Testament works, such as the Gospels of Matthew and John and the letters of Paul and Hebrews, show that the background of these writings was more Palestinian than has often been thought. Finally, the presence of such a sect in Jesus' day raises again the question of his relation to the Essenes. He was not an Essene, and there is no evidence that he knew the *Qumrân* monastery. But it is possible—though not certain—that John the Baptist in his wilderness stay did know the *Qumrân* sect and their monastery.

The importance of these new discoveries is great, but it must not be overestimated. The *Qumrân* sect left no lasting impress on Judaism. And for all its parallels with New Testament writings, the differences are even more striking. It does not explain the rise of Christianity, and Jesus is no mere duplicate of its great Teacher of Righteousness. The "friend of tax collectors and sinners" (Luke 7:34) lived in an entirely different atmosphere than did the priestly, hierarchical, ritualistic sect. So we resume the history of the Jews under the Romans, knowing that while the *Qumrân* sect illumines first-century Judaism and Christianity, it does not represent their central nature and content.

ROME TAKES CONTROL

Pompey removed from Jewish control the coastal cities, Samaria, and the non-Jewish cities on the east of the Jordan. However, he left Judaea, Idumaea, Galilee, and Peraea under Jewish rule. The entire region was put under the supervision of the Roman representative in Syria. Thus the link with Syria, which had continued to a greater or lesser extent since 198 B.C., continued under Rome in a new form.

Rome was entering upon the series of internal struggles which finally resulted in the establishment of the empire. Pompey was defeated by Julius Caesar, who made Hyrcanus II the ethnarch of the Jews. Caesar recognized, however, that the brains behind Hyrcanus were those of Antipater, and he therefore made Antipater procurator of Judaea. He also gave Joppa back to the Jews (47 B.C.). Antipater used his sons Phasael and Herod in the administration of his territory; Herod, though only twenty-five years old at the time, showed special skill and energy in suppressing brigands in Galilee.

Caesar was assassinated, however, in 44 B.C., and Palestine again suffered from uncertainty. Cassius demanded seven hundred talents from Judaea, which Antipater raised and paid. Shortly thereafter (43 B.C.) Antipater was murdered, and Antigonus, son of Aristobulus II, tried to gain control of Judaea. To further his purpose he called upon the Parthians, who at the time were trying to expand westward into Syria, and the Parthians helped him to gain control of Jerusalem (40 B.C.). This temporary success proved his undoing. The Parthians were not able to maintain their westward thrust, and the Romans naturally did not want a Parthian ally in control of Judaea. Herod sought the help of Rome, and in 40 B.C. was declared king of Judaea; the term Judaea was here used in its wider sense, practically equivalent to Palestine. It was three years, however, before he was able, with Roman help, to establish effective rule over all his realm. Thus he held his kingdom by the grant and power of Rome.

THE REIGN OF HEROD THE GREAT

The reign of Herod the Great lasted until his death in 4 B.C. It is notable in history as the reign under which Jesus was born (Matt. 2:1). The early years of his rule were not easy. The Roman Antony gave to Cleopatra, whose political ambitions reached far beyond her kingdom of Egypt, the coastal cities of Palestine and the commercially lucrative balsam groves near Jericho.

When Octavian, later known as Augustus, defeated Antony and became ruler of Rome (31 B.C.), he confirmed Herod's position as king of Judaea. After the death of Cleopatra in 30 B.C. Herod also received the cities which Antony had given her. He further received a number of other cities—Gadara, Hippos (XII:B, D-3), Samaria, Gaza, Anthedon, Joppa, and Strato's Tower (XII:B, B-4). These cities, which had been taken from the Jews in order to protect their Gentile population and culture, could be given to Herod because, while he sought to keep on good terms with the Jews, he also was eager to promote Hellenistic culture and loyalty to Rome. A short time later, for helping the Romans, Herod was given Trachonitis, Batanaea, and Auranitis (XII:B, D-F 2-3). In 20 B.C., it seems, he was given that part of the former lands of Zenodorus which lay between Galilee and northern Trachonitis. His kingdom thus took on the wide extent shown in Plate XII:B.

Indeed, Herod seemed on the verge of becoming even more widely influential. Augustus appointed him procurator of all Syria. However, his effective power was exercised in Palestine and the wider extension of it did not materialize. To add distinction to his rule and to promote Hellenistic influences, Herod undertook numerous am-

FIG. 62. One of "Solomon's Pools," so called under the influence of Eccl. 2: 6. Two aqueducts were built to carry the water from the three pools to Jerusalem, seven miles distant. The date of pools and aqueducts is uncertain, but the pools were probably built not later than the second century B. C. It appears that Pontius Pilate built or repaired one of the aqueducts.

bitious building projects. He rebuilt Samaria and named it Sebaste, a name which still survives in its modern Arabic name Sebasṭiyeh. He rebuilt Strato's Tower on a grand scale, and named it Caesarea in honor of the emperor. Antipatris (XII:B, B-4) in the Coastal Plain and Phasaelis (XII:B, C-4) in the Jordan Valley he laid out and named after his father and brother, respectively. He restored Anthedon (XII:B, A-5) and renamed it Agrippias or Agrippium in honor of Marcus Agrippa, the friend and son-in-law of Augustus; but this new name soon fell into disuse. It was probably Herod rather than his son Archelaus who originally built the winter palace, fortresses, and hippodrome at New Testament Jericho. Part of this Herodian Jericho has recently been excavated (see p. 117). Herod constructed many fortresses for the defense of his territory—Alexandrium (XII:B, C-4), Hyrcania (XII:B, C-5), Herodium (XII:B, C-5), Masada (XII:B, C-6), and Machaerus (XII:B, D-5); at the first two of these he built palaces.

One of his most ambitious projects, not finished in his lifetime, was the rebuilding of the Temple in Jerusalem. This was begun in 20-19 B.C. (which suggests A.D. 27-28 for the date of the debate in John 2:20). The main building was soon finished, but the outlying structures were not completed until A.D. 64, only a few years before the whole was destroyed (A.D. 70). Herod was not content, however, to build magnificent cities and buildings in Palestine. With the taxes from his burdened subjects he constructed buildings and made gifts not only in many cities near Palestine, such as Damascus (XII:B, E-2), Tyre (XII:B, C-2), and Sidon (XII:B, C-1), but also in places as far away as Rhodes and Athens. He thus sought to make his zeal for Hellenistic architecture and culture widely known and recognized.

THE KINGDOM OF HEROD AGRIPPA I

The terms of Herod's will are described in the discussion which accompanies Plate XIV (see p. 92). His son Archelaus ruled Judaea, Samaria, and Idumaea for ten years (4 B.C. to A.D. 6). The Romans then deposed him, and from A.D. 6 to 41 Roman procurators ruled this area. Herod Antipas governed Galilee and Peraea as tetrarch from 4 B.C. until the Romans, hearing that he planned revolt, exiled him in A.D. 39. A third son of Herod the Great, Philip, was tetrarch of the region east and northeast of the Sea of Galilee from 4 B.C.

until his death in A.D. 34. Plate XIV depicts the situation in the time of Jesus' ministry. We here resume the story with the rule of Herod Agrippa I (A.D. 41-44).

Agrippa, extravagant and impoverished grandson of Herod the Great, held ambitions which long seemed doomed to disappointment. Indeed, in Rome he was once imprisoned by the Emperor Tiberius for remarking that he wished Tiberius would die, so that Caligula could succeed him. When Caligula did become emperor in A.D. 37, he released Agrippa and made him king of both the former tetrarchy of Philip and the region Lysanias had ruled in Abilene (XII:C, E-1). This aroused the jealousy of Herodias (Mark 6:17), who urged her husband, Herod Antipas, to go to Rome and ask for the title of king instead of tetrarch. Upon arrival there, however, he was accused of plotting against the emperor, was deposed and banished to Gaul. Galilee and Peraea were added to Agrippa's realm.

Agrippa had little zeal to prove a good ruler, and spent much time in Rome. He was there in the last days of Caligula's life, and induced the emperor, who had decreed that his statue must be set up in the Temple at Jerusalem, to revoke the order. When Claudius succeeded Caligula (A.D. 41), Agrippa was again fortunate in having a friend as emperor. Claudius added to Agrippa's kingdom the territory of Judaea and Samaria. Thus in A.D. 41 Agrippa was king over all the territory which his grandfather, Herod the Great, had ruled; in addition, his kingdom included Abilene. He persecuted the Christians; he executed James the son of Zebedee and imprisoned Peter (Acts 12:2-4). But he soon died a painful death at Caesarea, according to both The Acts (ch. 12:20-23) and the Jewish historian Josephus.

HEROD AGRIPPA II AND THE ROMAN PROCURATORS

When Herod Agrippa I died in A.D. 44, his son Herod Agrippa II was but seventeen years old. Since it did not seem wise to entrust power to one so young, Palestine was put under a Roman procurator. The young man was not forgotten, however, and in c. A.D. 50 he was made king of Chalcis, a territory just to the north of Abilene. The procurators Cuspius Fadus and Tiberius Alexander seem to have had no great trouble, but under Cumanus (A.D. 48-52) friction led to outbreaks at Jerusalem and Samaria. Felix, under whom Paul was imprisoned at Jerusalem and sent to Caesarea (Acts 21:27 to 24:27), was proconsul from A.D. 52 to about A.D. 60 (when his term ended is uncertain; it was not earlier than A.D. 55 or later than A.D. 60).

By this time Agrippa II was coming into prominence (see XII:D). In A.D. 53, he had been transferred by Rome from the kingdom of Chalcis to a kingdom which included not only the former tetrarchy of Philip, east and northeast of the Sea of Galilee, but also Abilene. When Nero became emperor in A.D. 54, he added to Agrippa's kingdom Tarichaea and Tiberias (XII:D, D-3) in Galilee, and in Peraea, Abila and Julias (XII:D, D-5), with the villages round about. Agrippa appears to have retained his power until his death near the end of the first century A.D.

Felix was succeeded by Porcius Festus, who was procurator from about A.D. 60 to 62. It was before Festus that Paul made his defense and appealed to Caesar (Acts 25:1-12). The next procurator was Albinus (A.D. 62-64). Before the arrival of Albinus in Palestine the Jewish high priest had instigated the murder of James the brother of the Lord, the leader of the Church in Jerusalem. Friction between the Jews and the Romans grew under these final procurators, and under Gessius Florus (A.D. 64-66) it flamed into open rebellion.

Neither the power of Florus nor the influence of Herod Agrippa II, who had considerable weight with the Jews, could quiet the people. The Roman legate in Syria attempted to intervene. He took Sepphoris (XII:D, C-3) in Galilee, but was routed at Beth-horon (XII:D, C-5). The Jewish rebels seized Masada (XII:D, C-6) and organized resistance in other parts of the country. Josephus, a young Jerusalem priest, was sent to Galilee to lead activities against the Romans. He competed with John of Gischala (XII:D, C-2) for the Jewish leadership until captured by the Roman general Vespasian at Jotapata (XII:D, C-3). Josephus then became a champion of the Roman cause, and sought to induce his countrymen to submit. Later at Rome he wrote the history of his people, and so provided one of our most important sources for ancient Jewish history.

The Romans completed the subjugation of Galilee in A.D. 67. In A.D. 68 Vespasian took Gadara (XII:D, D-3), Antipatris (XII:D, B-4), and Emmaus (XII:D, B-5), overran Idumaea and Samaria, and took Jericho and Adida (XII:D, B-5). In other words, he overcame all organized resistance outside of Jerusalem which might harass him when he took up the siege of the capital city itself. The death of Nero, however, in A.D. 68, interrupted the campaign; Vespasian's troops proclaimed him emperor, and little more was done to quell the Jewish revolt until Vespasian was firmly established as emperor at Rome. The Jews meanwhile quarreled among themselves and became weaker. Titus, Vespasian's son, took up the siege of Jerusalem in A.D. 70, and succeeded in capturing the city after hard fighting. The Temple was destroyed and has never been rebuilt. Upon the occasion of his triumph in Rome the army of Titus carried vessels from the Temple, and the Triumphal Arch of Titus, which still stands in Rome (Fig. 66), pictures the procession and tokens of victory.

The capture of Jerusalem was the decisive victory of the war, which ended with the taking of certain fortresses, such as Herodium, Machaerus, and finally Masada. Roman troops were quartered at Jerusalem. Decades later, under the Emperor Hadrian (A.D. 117-138), another revolt took place about A.D. 132-135. It was led by Bar-Cochba. Recent discoveries in the *Wâdī Murabba'at*, ten miles south of *Qumrân*, give coins and documents from the time of this revolt, and include not only letters which mention Bar-Cochba as Simon Ben-Kosebah, but also two letters which seem to be written by him. When the revolt he led had been crushed, Hadrian carried out the plan which he had already conceived, and rebuilt Jerusalem as a Gentile city. He called it Aelia Capitolina, and no Jew was permitted to enter it. Although this severe exclusion was relaxed in later centuries, the Jews never again had political control of any of Palestine until the recent establishment of the State of Israel.

FIG. 63. An older view across Lake Huleh, 230 feet above sea level, to Mount Hermon, whose heights, c. 9,100 feet above sea level, are always snow-capped. Steps have been taken recently to drain this lake and use the reclaimed land.

THE ROMAN EMPIRE AT THE BIRTH OF JESUS

Plate XIII

THE rise of Rome to world power made Europe the center of political history. Prior to the emergence of Rome as a rival for empire, Asia had been the home of the most vigorous ruling powers. Alexander the Great transferred the focal point of history to southeastern Europe for a few brief years; but as a result of his attempt to extend his rule east to India the European portion of his empire was overshadowed, and when his territory was divided up after his death, Syria and Egypt became more important than Macedonia. It fell to Rome to effect the long lasting location of political dominance in Europe.

THE RISE OF THE ROMAN EMPIRE

In the early centuries of its history the city of Rome (Roma, Plate xiii, C-2) had little more than local importance. By 338 B.C., however, she had ended the Latin League by imposing her rule on its other members. She was then undisputed mistress of all Latium, the southern part of Etruria, and the northern section of Campania; in other words, she controlled about half of the western portion of the Italian peninsula. At the outbreak of the First Punic War in 264 B.C., when the serious challenge to Roman power by Carthage (Carthago, xiii, B-2) had to be met, almost all of the peninsula of Italy up to the valley of the Po River (Padus, xiii, Inset: F-3) was already firmly under Roman control.

The next two centuries were a time of spectacular expansion. Once Carthage had been defeated and destroyed, no powerful rival existed in the Mediterranean area, and Rome extended her rule in all directions. In 63 B.C. Pompey completed his work of taking over the eastern Mediterranean lands, including Palestine. The Roman power was then acknowledged in a series of provinces, protectorates, and client states which ringed the Mediterranean and made it indeed what the Romans liked to call it, *Mare Nostrum* ("Our Sea").

The empire did not reach its largest extent until A.D. 117, under the Emperor Trajan (A.D. 98-117). He added Dacia (xiii, D 1-2), Armenia (xiii, F-2), Assyria, Mesopotamia (xiii, E-F 2-3), and Arabia, the former Nabataea (xiii, E-3), to the list of Roman provinces. Nevertheless, the essential outlines of the empire were established by the beginning of the Christian era. All of northern Africa was under direct or indirect control. Europe west of the Rhine (Rhenus) and south of the Danube (Danuvius) was subject to the Roman will. Practically all of Asia Minor, as well as Syria and Palestine, was Roman territory. Plate xiii depicts the outreach of Rome at that time. Except for the Parthian Empire on the eastern frontier (xiii, E-H 2-3) and the turbulent tribes of northern Europe east of the Rhine (xiii, Inset, E-F 1-2), there was no serious threat to Roman domination.

THE EMPEROR AUGUSTUS

The development of Rome from city-state to world empire inevitably compelled alteration of her original political structure. In the earliest times the patricians had governed. Generations of determined struggle enabled the plebeians to gain a fair measure of participation in government, and by 366 B.C. their right to hold high office had been established. The machinery of government was that of a city-state. There were a popular assembly and various elective officers, most important of whom were two consuls who held office for a single year. In case of emergency one of the consuls could appoint a dictator. There was a senate, which, since it was composed of leading men and included those who had held high office, contained experienced leaders.

Nevertheless, the system devised for a city-state was not well adapted to efficient imperial administration. With the expansion of Roman control, the administrative problems which the Government faced grew increasingly complex and heavy. As a consequence, the republic fell into difficulties, and by the first century B.C. the situation was acute. Strong men began to emerge and exercise special powers. One of these was Pompey, who in 67 B.C. was entrusted with the task of stamping out piracy in the eastern Mediterranean. He successfully concluded this campaign and extended the power of Rome to the east.

Shortly thereafter Julius Caesar proved to be a leader of outstanding military and governmental talents. After his successful campaign in Gaul and his less fruitful campaigns in Britain, he gained the ascendancy over his chief rival, Pompey, became dictator of Rome, and no doubt would have developed the republic into an empire had

FIG. 64. The Appian Way. This, the oldest of the famous Roman roads, was begun in 312 B.C. It originally ran south from Rome to Capua, but was later extended until it reached Brundisium. In places the ancient road is still in use. In the background, one of the aqueducts by which water was carried into Rome on a line of arches.

not his life been cut short by assassination in 44 B.C. His death led, not to restoration of the republic, but to further intrigues for control of the empire. The republic, for all practical purposes, was already dead. After a time of confusion, in which rival alliances of competing candidates fought for power, Octavian finally crushed his most formidable opponents, Mark Antony and Cleopatra, and emerged as virtual emperor.

It is difficult to determine the date which marked the actual beginning of the empire. Octavian's strategy was to maintain the forms of the republic; for example, in 22 B.C., several years after he was in complete control, he refused to accept the position of dictator and consul for life. Nevertheless, the main dates which mark the establishment of his reign are clear. The battle of Actium (XIII, C-2) in 31 B.C. was a decisive defeat for Antony, who committed suicide the next year. Thus in 30 B.C. the last strong rival was removed, and in the same year tribunitian power was conferred on Octavian for life. However, the actual start of imperial rule may be dated in 27 B.C., when, in an Act of Settlement which ostensibly restored the republic and returned the power of rule to the senate, Octavian received control of all the difficult provinces and was given the title Augustus. From this time he carefully kept the control of the empire in his hands, while his cautious and outwardly conservative methods prevented any effective protest against his assumption of permanent supreme control.

Augustus was an able ruler. He organized a permanent standing army and placed its legions where danger was likely to arise. He traveled extensively throughout the empire, organizing the provinces and settling basic problems of administration. Something like eleven years of his reign were spent outside of Rome, a fact which witnesses to the care he devoted to provincial control. He was perhaps too cautious in failing to press a campaign for subjugation of the central European tribes, which were thus left to destroy the empire in a later century; he decided against further efforts to conquer Germania (XIII, Inset: E-F 1-2) after a rather unsuccessful beginning. His decision on this point may be criticized, but he gave peace to a war-weary empire and stability to the Roman government.

FIG. 65. The Roman Emperor Augustus. Photograph of a statue now in the Vatican in Rome.

THE ARMY

The power of Rome was never based upon its navy. Indeed, after the establishment of the empire there was little need for a strong naval force. Rome controlled the entire Mediterranean area and no naval power existed to challenge her rule of the sea. The army, therefore, was the basis of the Roman empire.

In the days of the republic the army was a citizen's militia, in which the Roman served only temporarily and as needed in emergency. The growth of the empire, however, called for a more permanent military force, and the Roman general Marius, in the war against Jugurtha in 107 B.C., developed what was practically a permanent professional army. During the period of the civil wars in the first century B.C., great numbers of men were brought under arms, but Augustus retired many, with proper provision for their livelihood, and organized his standing army on a much smaller scale.

The policy of Augustus was to station the Roman legions where revolt or invasion was to be feared. A quick survey of their stations shortly before his death in A.D. 14 will show this. In Spain (XIII, A 1-2), which had only recently been completely subjugated and organized, there were three legions. The Rhine front had four in the lower region and four in the upper Rhine district. Along the Danube three were located in Pannonia (XIII, C-1), two in Moesia (XIII, D-2), and two in Illyricum or Dalmatia (XIII, C 1-2). In the east, where Parthia was a constant threat, Syria (XIII, E 2-3) had four legions. Egypt (XIII, D-E 3-4), vital for grain and commerce, had two. The province of Africa (XIII, B-C 2-3) had one. The legions were thus used to guard the frontiers; the location of four in Syria indicates the military danger in that area and suggests the political tension in the region where the Christian movement had its origin.

The legion contained ten cohorts of infantry, each cohort having 480 men; it had also a cavalry company and an artillery unit. It was made up of Italians in the early empire; but auxiliaries enlisted from other regions were attached, so that the total personnel of a legion force amounted to about 10,000 men. Important among the officers of the legion were the centurions. As the name indicates, each commanded a company of a hundred men. It is not surprising that the New Testament always speaks of centurions with respect; they were the key men in the practical functioning of the legion. Rulers of client states, such as Herod Antipas, appear to have organized their forces on the Roman model (cf. Luke 7:2 ff.).

The empire had other police forces, noteworthy among which was the Praetorian Guard at Rome, probably referred to in Phil. 1:13.

ADMINISTRATION OF PROVINCES

Roman influence usually extended much further than the limits of formal organized control. Particularly in the early stages of domination in a border area, the Romans were content with indirect rule, and generally preferred to support a local ruler who was loyal to Rome and acceptable to the native population. The use of the Herods in Palestine is well known; Octavian and the senate designated Herod the Great as king (40 B.C.) and gave him such support as would further Roman interests, while he in return recognized that Rome was his master and must pass on the question of his successor or successors. At the time of the birth of Jesus, Augustus was continuing this policy, which had proved so successful in enabling the Romans to take over territory without resorting to armed conquest. In Africa, Mauretania (XIII, A-B 2) was under Roman influence. In southeastern Europe, Thracia (XIII, D-2) was in a similar situation. On the east side of Asia Minor, the Kingdom of Polemo, Armenia Minor, and Cappadocia (XIII, E-F 2) illustrate the same method.

This procedure was used in certain border states. The basic unit of imperial administration, however, was the province. By the Act of Settlement of 27 B.C. provinces were divided into two classes. Those of normal and stable life were under the Roman senate, which sent out a governor for a single year. Most desirable and remunerative

FIG. 66. Roman Forum and Arch of Titus. In earliest times, this Forum was the center of political and religious assemblies. It was later covered with columns, statues, arches, and other monuments. In the distance, the Arch of Titus, which commemorates Titus' victory over the Jews and destruction of Jerusalem in A. D. 70.

were the governorships of the provinces of Asia (XIII, D-2) and Africa, traditionally assigned to the consuls who had just retired from office. The governors of all provinces under the senate, however, were called proconsuls, so that the New Testament is correct in calling the governors of Cyprus (XIII, E-2; cf. Acts 13:7, R.S.V.) and Achaia (XIII, C-D 2; cf. Acts 18:12, R.S.V.) by this title.

The provinces of the other class, known as imperial, were under direct control of the emperor, who delegated his power, usually for several years, to legates (cf. Luke 2:2) and procurators (cf. Matt. 27:2). The original group of imperial provinces included Egypt, Syria, and those in Gaul and Spain; as new provinces were organized, they were added to the imperial class. Moreover, the emperor reserved the right to make changes in the division. When a senatorial province offered an urgent problem he could take it over and control its administration directly. On the other hand, when there was no further need of maintaining personal supervision of a province, he committed its management to the senate. Such changes occurred under later emperors.

One province, however, held a special position. Egypt was so productive in crops and trade, and its grain supply was so vital to the peace of Italy, that Augustus kept it as his personal domain. No Roman senator or other possible political rival visited there without special permission. Rome had a dangerously large proportion of its population (about 200,000) on a free grain allowance; it was dependent on Egypt for a large share of its food supply, and Augustus could not run any risk of having this supply cut off. The Apostle Paul, on his journey to Rome to be tried before the emperor, no doubt traveled on two of the many grain ships operating between Egypt and Rome (Acts 27:6; 28:11).

ROMAN COLONIES AND CITIZENSHIP

The fact that Augustus had to provide a grain allowance for 200,000 persons at Rome suggests the need of a population outlet from the capital city. From an early time the attempt was made to meet this problem by founding colonies, first in Italy, later in remoter parts of the empire. In them were settled Roman citizens, especially veteran soldiers who were ready to retire from active duty. These colonies were often already existing cities, which thus received an added population. Among those founded before or during the reign of Augustus were such widely separated cities as Corduba, Hispalis, and Emerita (XIII, A-2) in Spain; Narbo, Lugdunum, Vienna, and Arelate (XIII, B-1) in Gaul; Carthago in Africa; Corinthus (XIII, D-2) in Achaia; Philippi (XIII, D-2) in Macedonia; and Berytus (XIII, E-3) in Syria. The native residents of such colonies were granted Roman citizenship and thus enjoyed a favored position in the empire.

The removal of surplus population from Rome was by no means the only object in establishing colonies. Each such city became a center of loyalty to Rome, and promoted political stability in its region. Moreover, because so many of the settlers were veteran soldiers still able to serve in defensive warfare, the Roman colony often became an outpost of Roman military strength and was useful in cowing the inhabitants of a restless area. Furthermore, the network of colonies, stretching across the empire, served to foster trade and promote economic unity.

In addition to colonies marked by the presence of citizens sent out from Rome, other cities possessed citizenship by the grant of the Romans. Certain cities had entered into treaty relationship to Rome and enjoyed certain privileges, including exemption from ordinary taxes and the right to use their own laws; such were Athens (Athenae; XIII, D-2), Rhodes (Rhodus; XIII, D-2), and Tyre (Tyrus; XIII, E-3). In general, the Romans followed the policy of "divide and rule"; to prevent the cities of an area from uniting against Rome, they fostered various forms of direct and privileged relation to the empire. This tended to check any desire which a city might feel to revolt or plot against its benefactor.

The mention of colonies recalls the fact that Roman citizenship was widely held. It was gradually extended not only to the people of Italy but to increasing numbers throughout the empire. A rapid extension of the privilege took place in the first century B.C., when during the Civil Wars the number of citizens rose from 400,000 to 4,000,000. Augustus was cautious in this as in other matters, and during his reign the number increased less than a million. It was not until the time of the Emperor Caracalla that an edict granted full citizenship to practically all free residents of the provinces (A.D. 212).

A special class of citizens were the freedmen. Slaves set free by the emperor or a citizen became citizens of the empire. Many slaves had been acquired by war and purchase, and emancipation became common. This seemed a threat to the stability of Roman life and blood, and Augustus sharply limited the right of masters to free slaves and grant them citizenship.

It should be remembered, however, that the possession of citizenship did not involve such participation in government as we connect with the privilege today. The emperor, and to a minor degree other officials at Rome, guided the course of the empire. Roman citizenship, nevertheless, did give desirable advantages to favored residents of the provinces. They enjoyed not only a certain social prestige, but also added legal rights and definite economic benefits. The Apostle

Paul, who like his father before him was a Roman citizen, was able when unfairly treated by a provincial official to appeal to Caesar and thus transfer his case to the imperial court (Acts 22:28; 25:11).

TRAVEL IN THE EMPIRE

Efficiency of administration, military security, and trade interests demanded the development of easy communication throughout the empire. The Romans made great use of the sea in transporting grain to Rome from Egypt, Africa, and the Black Sea region. In a day of sailing vessels, however, the stormy winter season compelled a general intermission of sea traffic. To stop for the winter at such places as Crete (Creta; XIII, D-2; Acts 27:12) or Malta (Melita; XV, B-4; Acts 28:11) was the common practice of ships which were unable to make harbor in Italy before wintry storms rendered sea travel dangerous. A further disadvantage was that on certain sea lanes the prevailing winds permitted travel in only one direction. This explains why ships sailing from Alexandria to Rome first went north or northeast, to the southern coast of Asia Minor, and then worked their way westward (Acts 27:6).

Many rocky points were danger spots which sailors preferred to avoid. This explains in part the importance of Corinth. Because the southern coast of Achaia was rocky and dangerous, much traffic crossed the Isthmus of Corinth (XIII, D-2), using the two ports near Corinth, Lechaeum on the west side of the isthmus and Cenchreae (Acts 18:18) on the east side. To save the time and expense of unloading, land transport, and reloading, smaller ships were actually hauled over the narrow, low isthmus on a causeway. A few decades after Augustus' reign, Nero (A.D. 54-68) made a futile attempt to dig a canal through the isthmus; the attempt was renewed successfully in modern times, along the same line which Nero marked out (see Fig. 59). In Egypt a canal from the Nile (Nilus; XIII, E 3-4) to the extreme northwest arm of the Arabian Gulf (Sinus Arabicus; XIII, E-F 3-4) was dug long before Roman times and restored by Trajan (A.D. 98-117); it furthered trade with countries east of the empire.

The chief port of Rome was Puteoli (XIII, C-2), at least for grain trade, but Ostia (XIII, C-2) was much closer and continued to retain considerable importance.

The remarkable network of Roman roads, one of the outstanding achievements of Roman administrative and engineering skill, proved more important in many ways than the sea lanes. These justly famous roads provided facilities for land travel not surpassed until the coming of the railroad. Constant use of the highways was made possible by a well-built, well-drained, well-kept system of hard roads, marked by milestones.

In the reign of Augustus, the road network was by no means so large or well-built as it was in the later years of the empire. In newer provinces there had not been time to construct the highways needed for easiest communication and greatest military mobility. For example, in Palestine, which was still under a vassal king, the system of Roman roads, still partially marked out today by the many milestones which have been discovered, was not yet under construction. In older parts of the empire, however, excellent roads were already in existence. Noteworthy examples are the famous Appian Way, along which travelers from Puteoli proceeded on the last part of their land trip to Rome (Acts 28:13, 14; see Fig. 64), and the Egnatian Way which enabled travelers from Italy to cross over from Brundisium (XIII, C-2) to Dyrrhachium (XIII, C-2) or Apollonia (XIII, C-2) and thence go east by land to Thessalonica (XIII, D-2) and eastern points.

Such excellent roads greatly promoted trade and travel. Free and safe communication between all parts of the empire also did much to develop wider horizons, a more cosmopolitan spirit, and a continuous interchange of intellectual and spiritual treasures.

RELIGION AND CULTURE

The Roman policy concerning religion was to maintain the ancestral worship of the gods of Rome and at the same time show tolerance toward the deities of other peoples in the empire. This was possible because polytheism was basic in Roman religion, and the gods of the provincial peoples could either be identified with the ancestral deities at Rome or tolerated as additional objects of worship. Even the Jews, who insisted on a monotheistic faith and would join in no pagan rites, found tolerance, especially from the time of Julius Caesar on, and received special privileges which protected them in the exercise of their worship. New faiths were frowned upon, and cults with obviously degrading features were suppressed, but tolerance was the general practice.

FIG. 67. Corinth Canal. Finished in 1893. Nearly four miles long, 70 feet wide, 26 feet deep. It follows the line along which Nero attempted to dig a canal about A. D. 67.

One significant development, the practice of emperor worship, was hardly visible in the time of Augustus. The beginnings, however, were already present. Julius Caesar received suspiciously high honors while still alive and was declared a god after his death. Augustus had taken a name which suggested majesty and perhaps more than human rank. The eastern provinces were used to paying their rulers divine honors. The way was being prepared for the outrageous demand of the mad Caligula (A.D. 37-41) that his statue be set up in the Temple at Jerusalem and for the open claim of Domitian (A.D. 81-96) to be "lord and god" (contrast John 20:28).

In the day of Augustus, as in the later days of persecution, many refused to take such claims seriously. They regarded the paying of divine honors as merely the manifestation of patriotism. They doubtless considered religion, especially the state religion, a useful means of fostering and maintaining unity in the empire. Indeed, there was a widespread skepticism about all the old gods of pagan Rome.

The truth is that Rome had neither the spiritual nor the cultural vitality to infuse inner unity and strength into the empire. Not even Greece had the spiritual gift which the empire needed. It took Christianity to provide that. But Greece did have the cultural heritage which was the cohesive factor in the intellectual life of the time. Indeed, at the opening of the Christian era the prevailing culture was not Roman but Hellenistic. The Greek language was so widely spoken that it was the common medium of communication in such widely separated regions as Africa, Spain, Italy, and Asia Minor. It was a rival of Aramaic in Syria and Palestine. Athens, Tarsus, and Alexandria were among the centers of study and learning to which Romans went. Greek culture came to Rome not only from free traveling scholars and teachers but also from well-educated slaves, acquired in war or by purchase. Rome gave stable political unity under which the Christian faith could rise and spread, but it was the heritage of Greece which provided the language and intellectual background which made possible one far-flung Church.

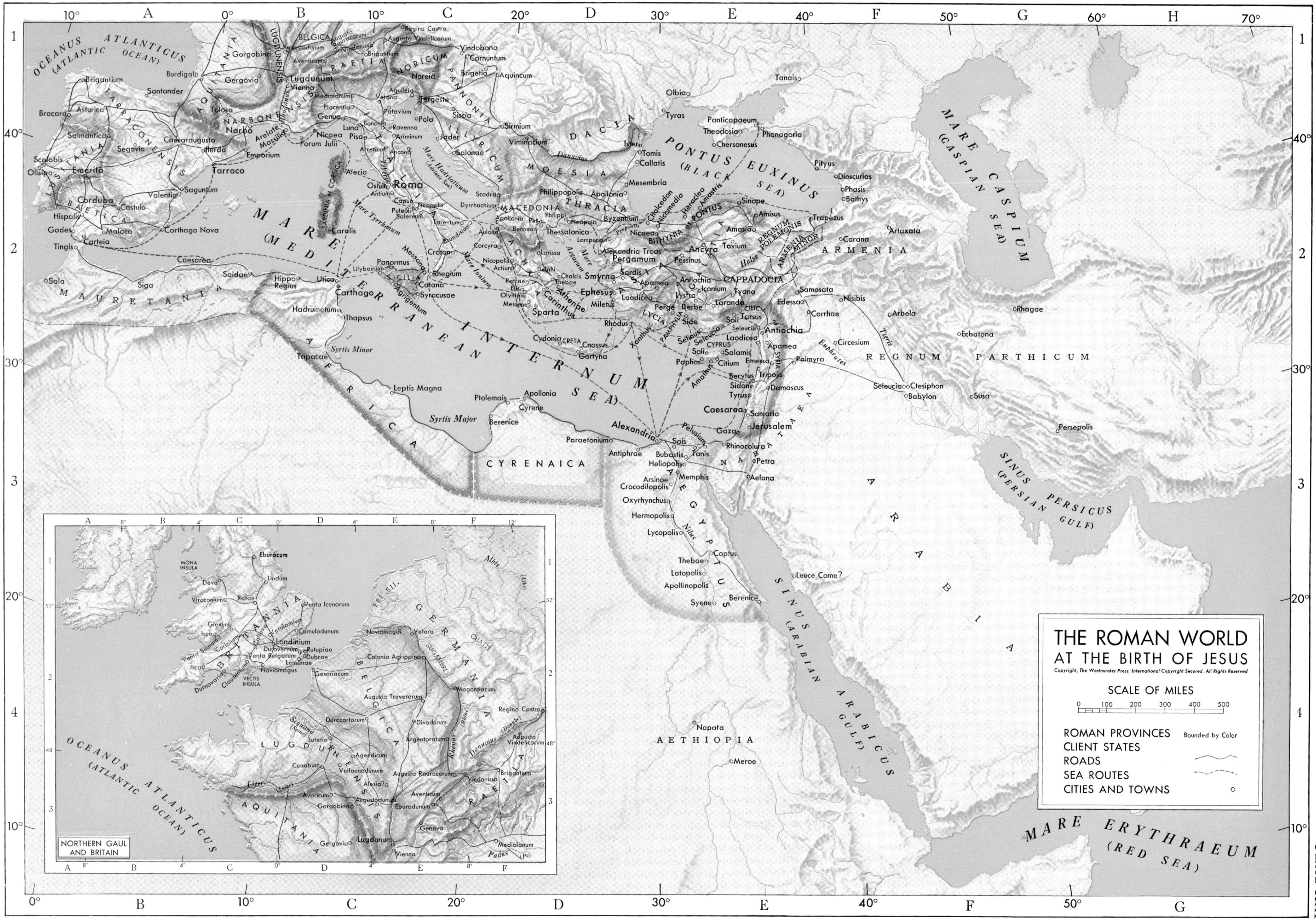
THE ROMAN WORLD
AT THE BIRTH OF JESUS
SCALE OF MILES
0 100 200 300 400 500
ROMAN PROVINCES
Bounded by Color
CLIENT STATES
ROADS
SEA ROUTES
CITIES AND TOWNS
MARE INTERNUM (MEDITERRANEAN SEA)
PONTUS EUXINUS (BLACK SEA)
MARE CASPIUM (CASPIAN SEA)
SINUS PERSICUS (PERSIAN GULF)
SINUS ARABICUS (ARABIAN GULF)
MARE ERYTHRAEUM (RED SEA)
OCEANUS ATLANTICUS (ATLANTIC OCEAN)
REGNUM PARTHICUM
ARABIA
AEGYPTUS
AETHIOPIA
CYRENAICA
AFRICA
MAURETANIA
ARMENIA
CAPPADOCIA
MACEDONIA
THRACIA
MOESIA
DACIA
ILLYRICUM
PANNONIA
NORICUM
RAETIA
ITALIA
TARRACONENSIS
LUSITANIA
BAETICA
NARBONENSIS
AQUITANIA
LUGDUNENSIS
BELGICA
Roma
Alexandria
Jerusalem
Antiochia
Carthago
Athenae
Corinthus
Ephesus
Babylon
Ctesiphon
Damascus
Caesarea
Tarsus
Byzantium
NORTHERN GAUL AND BRITAIN
OCEANUS ATLANTICUS (ATLANTIC OCEAN)
BRITANNIA
GERMANIA
Londinium
Eburacum
Lugdunum
Lutetia
Colonia Agrippina

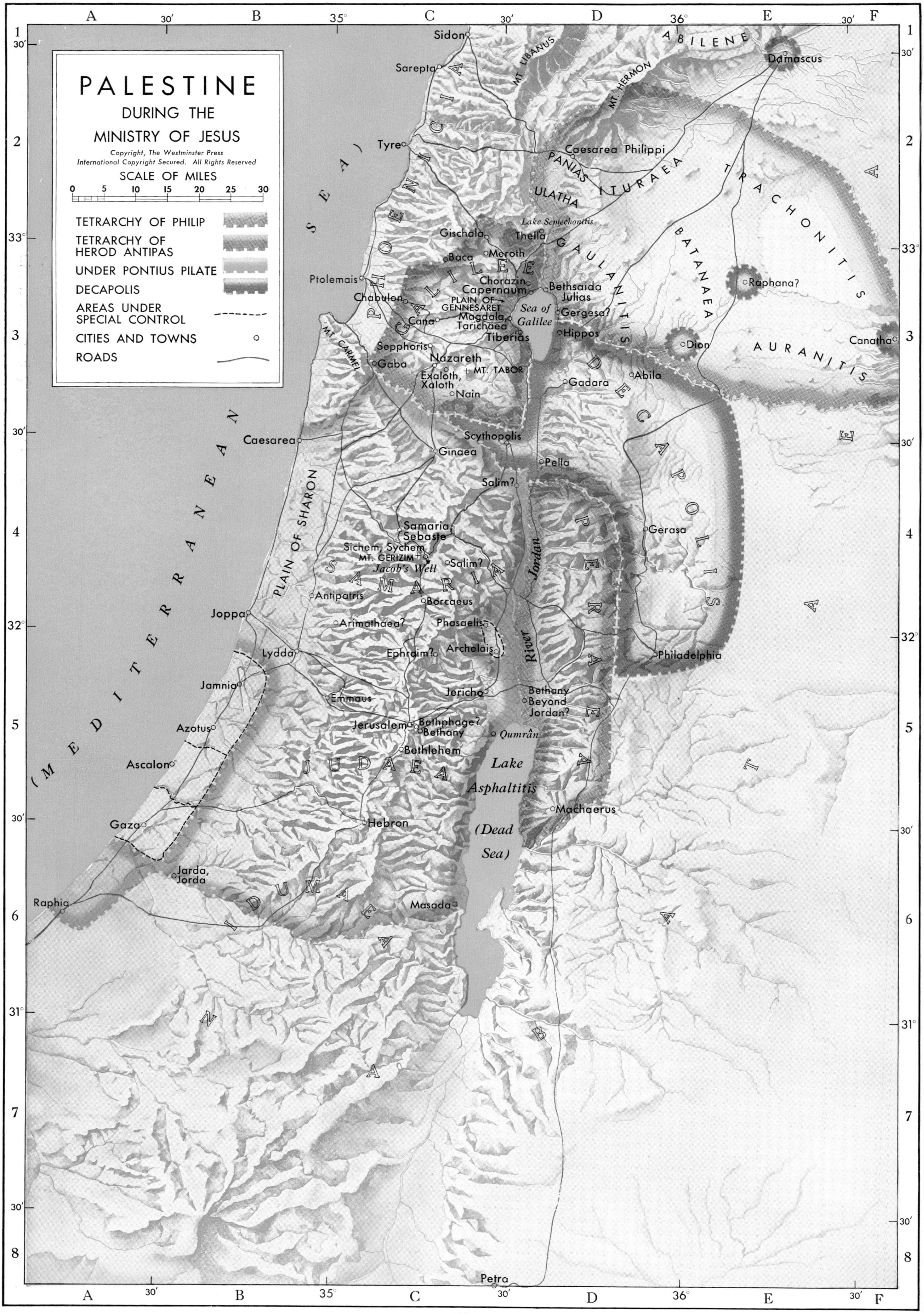
PALESTINE
DURING THE
MINISTRY OF JESUS
Copyright, The Westminster Press
International Copyright Secured. All Rights Reserved
SCALE OF MILES
0 5 10 15 20 25 30
TETRARCHY OF PHILIP
TETRARCHY OF HEROD ANTIPAS
UNDER PONTIUS PILATE
DECAPOLIS
AREAS UNDER SPECIAL CONTROL
CITIES AND TOWNS
ROADS
A B C D E F
1 2 3 4 5 6 7 8
30′ 35° 36° 33° 32° 31°
(MEDITERRANEAN SEA)
PHOENICIA
GALILEE
SAMARIA
JUDAEA
IDUMAEA
ABILENE
ITURAEA
PANIAS
ULATHA
GAULANITIS
TRACHONITIS
BATANAEA
AURANITIS
DECAPOLIS
PERAEA
NABATAEA
ARABIA
PLAIN OF SHARON
MT. CARMEL
MT. LIBANUS
MT. HERMON
MT. TABOR
MT. GERIZIM
PLAIN OF GENNESARET
Sidon
Sarepta
Tyre
Damascus
Caesarea Philippi
Lake Semechonitis
Gischala
Thella
Baca
Meroth
Ptolemais
Chorazin
Capernaum
Bethsaida Julias
Chabulon
Magdala, Tarichaea
Sea of Galilee
Gergesa?
Raphana?
Cana
Tiberias
Hippos
Dion
Canatha
Sepphoris
Gaba
Nazareth
Exaloth, Xaloth
Nain
Gadara
Abila
Caesarea
Scythopolis
Ginaea
Pella
Salim?
Samaria, Sebaste
Gerasa
Sichem, Sychem
Jacob's Well
Salim?
Jordan
Antipatris
Borcaeus
Joppa
Arimathaea?
Phasaelis
Lydda
Ephraim?
Archelais
River
Philadelphia
Jamnia
Emmaus
Jericho
Bethany Beyond Jordan?
Jerusalem
Bethphage?
Bethany
Qumrân
Azotus
Bethlehem
Ascalon
Lake Asphaltitis
(Dead Sea)
Machaerus
Gaza
Hebron
Jarda, Jorda
Raphia
Masada
Petra

FIG. 68. Sea of Galilee. View northward along the northwest shore of the lake. Just left of the foreground is the Plain of Gennesaret.

PALESTINE DURING THE MINISTRY OF JESUS

PLATE XIV

TO GAIN an understanding of the geographical background of the ministry of Jesus it is not enough to seek out individual sites. Students of the Gospels must grasp the larger setting of his life and work. This requires first of all an examination of the relation of Palestine to Rome.

During the public ministry of Jesus, Palestine was a border region on the eastern frontier of the Roman Empire. To the south and east stretched the desert area of the Nabatean kingdom, which centered in Petra (Plate XIV, C-8) but extended northwest to the Mediterranean and north to the vicinity of Damascus (XIV, E-1). To the northeast was the Parthian Empire, which in 40 B.C. had attempted to control Palestine and still constituted a threat to Rome's mastery. Since there were thus forces near Palestine which required watching, and rebellious spirits within the country were always plotting to throw off Roman control, Rome was constantly on the alert against invasion or uprising. Hence a charge that Jesus was trying to make himself king (Luke 23:2) was something to take seriously.

PALESTINE'S RELATION TO SYRIA

Only to the north was there direct contact with Roman territory and strength. To be sure, not far to the southwest lay Egypt (XIII, E-3), constantly in communication with Palestine and securely under Rome's control. But the Nabataeans, though generally friendly to Rome, broke the land link between Egypt and Palestine. The basic political connection of Palestine was with Syria on the north.

It was the task of the Roman governors in the more stable province of Syria to exercise supervisory control of Palestine in critical times. Palestine was definitely under their protection and watchful oversight. A vivid illustration of this occurred in A.D. 36; Pontius Pilate, the Roman procurator ruling Samaria, Judaea, and part of Idumaea, was under suspicion of acting unwisely in crushing a Samaritan disturbance, and Vitellius, the governor of Syria, deposed him and sent him to Rome for trial.

Further facts show the close interlocking of Palestine with Syria. The Roman province of Syria extended down the coast to include Phoenicia and Mount Carmel (XIV, B-C 1-3). Gaza (XIV, A-6), located in southwest Palestine, was detached from Palestine and made a part of the province of Syria. An even more striking evidence of the subordinate relation of Palestine to Syria is the fact that the governor of Syria protected and watched over the Decapolis (XIV, C-F 1-5).

THE DECAPOLIS

To those who think of first-century Palestine as a strictly Jewish country, the facts about the Decapolis will bring a startling correction. The word "Decapolis" is Greek; it combines the words *deka*, "ten," and *polis*, "city," and refers to a federation of cities marked by Hellenistic organization and culture. The original league of ten cities probably came into being under Roman protection after Pompey took over the region in 63 B.C.

The earliest mention of the Decapolis is in the Gospels (Mark 5:20; 7:31; Matt. 4:25), Josephus' *Wars of the Jews* (c. A.D. 75), and the *Natural History* of the elder Pliny (c. A.D. 77). Pliny lists the cities as follows (all on Plate XIV): Damascus (E-1), Philadelphia (D-5), Raphana (E-3), Scythopolis (C-4), Gadara (D-3), Hippos (D-3),

FIG. 69. The Jerusalem-Jericho Road. Between these two cities, fifteen miles apart in a direct line, the road descends 3,300 feet through wild country which has always offered hiding places for robbers (cf. Luke 10:30).

Dion (E-3), Pella (D-4), Gerasa (D-4), and Canatha (F-3). Ptolemy, a second-century writer, names eighteen cities; he omits Raphana and includes not only Abila (XIV, D-3) but also eight other cities. This fact, and a late reference to a fourteen-city federation, proves that the number varied from time to time. The map shows the ten cities named by Pliny and in addition Abila, which may have a better claim than Raphana to be one of the original ten.

Scythopolis, which Josephus calls the greatest city of the Decapolis, was the only member west of the Jordan. The other cities were all on the east side, spread out from Damascus on the north to Philadelphia on the south. It is impossible to represent this league clearly on the map. Each city evidently controlled the region immediately surrounding it, but how far such control extended cannot be determined. Plainly, however, the Decapolis was not a compact and definitely bounded political unit. Damascus was in Syria; Dion, Raphana, and Canatha were in the territory ruled by Philip; and Herod Antipas must have had some recognized and lawful way to move troops and messengers freely from Galilee (XIV, C-3) to Peraea (XIV, D 4-5). The Decapolis seems, therefore, to have been a league of independent cities under the protection of the governor of Syria, each controlling a greater or smaller area immediately about it. The region from Hippos to Philadelphia was so largely dominated by these cities that it may be regarded as in a particular sense the region of the Decapolis.

Why did these cities band together in this way? The answer may be in part that since they were on the frontier they needed to protect themselves from Nabataeans, Parthians, or other enemies who might attack them or cut their lines of trade. Probably, however, they banded together mainly to defend their interests and the cause of Hellenistic culture against the Jewish and other Semitic interests which were strong around them. For this was not merely a political frontier; it was also a cultural borderland.

Centuries before the days of Jesus the infiltration of Greek influence into the land of Palestine had begun. By the time of Jesus, this Hellenistic influence was operative in almost all parts of Palestine. Along the coast and in the Jordan Valley many cities were Greek in organization and cultural connection. No doubt Jewish and other Semitic influences were found in them, but the dominant features were Hellenistic. For example, outposts of Greek culture were present in Caesarea (XIV, B-4), Pilate's capital city during his rule in Palestine; Tiberias (XIV, D-3), built by Herod Antipas to be the capital of his tetrarchy; Samaria (XIV, C-4); and Jericho (XIV, C-5), near the Old Testament site but a little south of it.

Of all the expressions of this penetrating Greek influence, however, the Decapolis was the most powerful and impressive. Excavations at Gerasa have made clear the Greek plan of the city. The Greek theaters, temples, stadium, forum, colonnades, and inscriptions reflect the Greek manner of life (Fig. 45). Although these remains date almost entirely from a time later than the ministry of Jesus, their earliest portions reach back into his day. They show how different a city of the Decapolis was from a truly Jewish city.

Against the background of this cultural clash between Hellenistic and Jewish elements we must understand the situation of Jesus' day. The visible challenge to Jewish faith and customs probably does much to explain why the Pharisees were so strict in the observance of their ceremonial laws. It also added to the fiery spirit of revolt which the Zealots showed against the Romans. Many Jewish patriots felt that Roman power, which supported Hellenistic influences, was directed against both their liberty and their entire way of life. Palestine had become a battleground of cultural worlds. Jesus could not have been ignorant of Hellenistic forces, or of such complicated mingling of Iranian, Hellenistic, and Jewish forces as we see in the monastic sect of the Essenes (the *Qumrân* Sect; see pp. 81 ff.).

THE POLITICAL DIVISIONS OF PALESTINE

With the exception of the areas under the rule or protection of Syria, Palestine in Jesus' day fell into three main political divisions. This partition was based on the will of Herod the Great. When he died in 4 B.C., he bequeathed to his son Archelaus his title of king, and gave him control of Samaria, Judaea, and the northern part of Idumaea (cf. Matt. 2:22). To his son Herod Antipas he left Galilee and Peraea. To another son, Philip, he left the region east of the upper Jordan, from Mount Hermon (XIV, D-2; see Fig. 63) to the River Yarmuk (I, D-3). The Roman emperor Augustus, whose right it was to approve or reject this division of Herod's kingdom, approved it except that he granted Archelaus merely the rank of ethnarch. Ten years later, however, in A.D. 6, complaints against the rule of Archelaus became so serious that Augustus deposed him, and in his place appointed a Roman procurator, directly responsible to the emperor but dependent upon the Roman governor of Syria for military help and emergency supervision. This arrangement lasted until A.D. 41.

PONTIUS PILATE, "GOVERNOR OF JUDAEA"

The fifth in the line of succession of these procurators was Pontius Pilate (Luke 3:1). He was appointed by the Emperor Tiberius in A.D. 26, and remained in office until Vitellius, Roman governor of Syria, sent him to Rome in A.D. 36 to stand trial on the charge of unfair sternness toward turbulent Samaritans. While his control extended over Samaria, Judaea, and part of Idumaea, the city of Gaza, as noted, was detached from this district and joined to Syria. Other small areas also were under special control—always, of course, by the decision and under the final control of the emperor. Ascalon (XIV, B-5) continued to be an independent city of Hellenistic culture, as it had been for over a century. Nominally free, it actually depended upon the Roman Empire for its liberties and protection. Jamnia and Azotus (XIV, B-5), Phasaelis (XIV, C-4) and Archelais (XIV, C-5) were left by Herod the Great to his sister Salome. Upon her death, some time between A.D. 9 and 12, she left this possession by will to Livia, the wife of Augustus. Upon Livia's death these places passed into the hands of the Emperor Tiberius (A.D. 14-37), who controlled them by a specially appointed officer. Probably such areas depended upon the Roman procurator for military defense. The purpose in granting them to an individual was not so much to give political power as to provide a source of income and prestige for some favored person.

To the modern Christian, as to the first-century Jew, the outstanding city under Pilate's rule was Jerusalem (XIV, C-5). This was not the Roman view. Other cities, such as Samaria and Jericho, were more important as centers of Graeco-Roman life. Other religious centers, such as Mount Gerizim, where the Samaritans gathered, and Samaria, where a magnificent temple of Augustus crowned the western brow of the hill, probably seemed more important to a Roman than they do to a modern Jew or Christian. Moreover, for political purposes Caesarea (XIV, B-4) took first place. Here lived the governor. Built by Herod the king, provided with a man-made harbor, and equipped with a royal palace, it was an attractive location for the Roman procurator, and he lived regularly in the palace which Herod had built. However, at Passover time, when nationalistic feelings might cause the Jews to think of revolt, the procurator took up temporary residence in Jerusalem. It was this custom which explains Pilate's presence there when Jesus came up to keep the Passover (Mark 15:1).

HEROD ANTIPAS GOVERNS GALILEE AND PERAEA

From 4 B.C. to A.D. 39 Herod Antipas was tetrarch of Galilee and Peraea (cf. Luke 3:1). These districts appear separated on the map by territory under the influence of the Decapolis cities Gadara, Scythopolis, and Pella. It may be taken for granted, however, that Herod Antipas had free passageway from Galilee to Peraea.

The region of Peraea was less thickly populated than Galilee and figures little in the Gospel story. It began a little below Pella and ended just south of the border fortress Machaerus (XIV, D-5), where, according to Josephus, John the Baptist was imprisoned and executed.

The main attention of Herod Antipas must have been devoted to Galilee. His capital and residence were there. At first he governed from Sepphoris (XIV, C-3). This city had participated in the revolt against Rome in A.D. 6, and as a result the Romans ruthlessly destroyed it. Shortly thereafter it was rebuilt. All this occurred during the boyhood of Jesus, and he must have known the entire tragic story, since he lived not far to the south in Nazareth (XIV, C-3). At a later time, perhaps about A.D. 20, Herod Antipas built the city of Tiberias, on the western shore of the Sea of Galilee, and moved his capital and residence thither. Built on the site of a cemetery, and peopled by foreigners and lax Jews, it was at first shunned by most loyal Jewish people.

Galilee was bounded on the east by the Jordan River and the Sea of Galilee. In practice, however, the northern part of the sea's eastern shore was reckoned to Galilee. Gaulanitis (XIV, D-3) was a high plateau region over two thousand feet above the level of the Sea of Galilee. The steep, forbidding slope on the east side of the sea discouraged contacts between the lake region and the upland. It was easier for inhabitants on the eastern shore to communicate with residents on the other sides of the lake than to deal with people in Gaulanitis.

On the north, Galilee extended to Thella (XIV, D-2) and Gischala (XIV, C-2). The western border ran just west of Baca (XIV, C-3), Chabulon (XIV, C-3), and Gaba (XIV, C-3). On the south, Josephus places the border at Xaloth (XIV, C-3); but, since he speaks of Ginaea (XIV, C-4) as the northern limit of Samaria, it is probable that the border ran through the plain between these two towns.

FIG. 70. Gethsemane. In the center of the picture, just east of the Brook Kidron, is one traditional site of the Garden of Gethsemane (Mark 14:32; John 18:1). To the right is a church built to commemorate Jesus' struggle in the Garden. To the left, in a semicircular area, is the Grotto of the Agony, where another tradition places the event. Quite probably the original Garden into which Jesus entered was in the area pictured. The Mount of Olives rises to the east. Running across the Kidron and up the slope to the right is the road to Bethany and Jericho.

THE TETRARCHY OF PHILIP

From 4 B.C. until his death in A.D. 34 Philip was tetrarch of the region northeast of the Sea of Galilee (XIV, D-F 2-3). It is not possible to fix accurately the eastern borders of his territory. Moreover, his control of the area marked on the map cannot have been complete and rigid. Three cities of the Decapolis were in his tetrarchy; each had its local sphere of influence and its free lines of communication with other Decapolis cities.

Philip seems to have been a good ruler, conscientious, fair, and respected. In honor of the emperor he built a city at Paneas; to distinguish it from other cities of the same name he called it Caesarea Philippi, i.e., Philip's Caesarea (XIV, D-2; cf. Mark 8:27). Pagan shrines marked its non-Jewish character; indeed, the region ruled by Philip was prevailingly Gentile. For his capital Philip rebuilt Bethsaida, on the lake, and named it after Julia, the daughter of the Emperor Augustus. It is sometimes called Julias or Bethsaida Julias; in the Gospels the older name Bethsaida is still used (XIV, D-3; cf. Mark 6:45).

THE BASIC UNITY OF PALESTINE

The existence of so many separate units of political administration may give the impression that Palestine was a group of entirely distinct areas. In fact, however, Rome's control of the entire region gave it essential unity. All rulers held their power by grant from Rome and only so long as they furthered her interests. All were under the eye of the Roman governor in Syria.

Hence travel was free and constant between all sections of Palestine. Jesus could go freely, not only throughout Galilee, but also into Philip's territory (Mark 8:27), into the Decapolis (Mark 7:31), and into the region ruled by Pilate. He could even go without challenge into regions which were part of the province of Syria (Mark 7:24).

One caution, however, is in place. We often read of the excellent Roman roads. But these Roman roads of Palestine are later than the time of Jesus. What are shown on the map as roads are not the solidly constructed highways of Roman engineering genius but, rather, regularly used ancient lines of travel. Some of these were not capable of year-round use. The road down the west side of the Jordan Valley, for example, was probably not passable in the wet season of the year, at least in the district south of Scythopolis.

THE SCENES OF JESUS' MINISTRY

The modern tourist has no difficulty in finding the sites where Jesus lived and taught. Indeed, he is sometimes embarrassed to find two or more sites for the same event! There is in human nature a deeply rooted desire to know exactly where significant Biblical events occurred, and traditions confidently provide explicit answers to such desires.

As a matter of sober historical fact, however, the student of the Gospels must confess that he cannot locate some of the sites mentioned in the narrative. This becomes painfully clear when we begin to study the work of John the Baptist. He is said to have baptized at Aenon near to Salim (John 3:23). Aenon cannot be found. It is not even certain where this Salim was located. An ancient tradition favors a site six miles south of Scythopolis (XIV, C-4); strong arguments are also made for the Salim east of Mount Gerizim (XIV, C-4). Both are shown on Plate XIV; no decision is possible. Similarly, Bethany beyond Jordan (John 1:28) is a puzzle. It is even disputed whether this is the correct name of the place; Origen, a third-century Christian scholar residing in Palestine, insisted that the name was Bethabara. Early Gospel manuscripts do not appear to support him, however, and we may conclude that a place named Bethany was meant. In the very nature of the case, a place used for baptism would be hard to

FIG. 71. The Wailing Wall in Jerusalem. This is the outside western wall of the ancient Temple area. Note the size of the hewn stones. Jews here lament the loss of their Temple and national home.

locate in later times, and all we can do is to show on a map the place which from ancient times was regarded as the place where John baptized (XIV, D-5).

In like manner places referred to in the story of Jesus' ministry are often impossible to locate. He is said to have delivered a sermon on a "mount" (Matt. 5:1); none of the rival sites west and north of the Sea of Galilee appear to be more than early guesses.

Some have sought the scene of the transfiguration on Mount Hermon (Fig. 61). Others have upheld the claims of Mount Tabor (XIV, C-3; Fig. 39), where two churches have been built to commemorate the event. Both sites are mere conjecture.

Nor can a definite decision be made about Gergesa (XIV, D-3). The name itself is uncertain; in all three Gospels the manuscripts vary greatly, offering three alternatives, Gergesa, Gerasa, and Gadara (Matt. 8:28; Mark 5:1; Luke 8:26, 37). Even if, as seems probable, Gergesa is original, the location is doubtful. The modern *Kursî*, where Gergesa is placed on the map, shows the approximate location, but this Arabic name is not the exact equivalent of the Greek word "Gergesa." Even more baffling is Dalmanutha (Mark 8:10); no town of this name is known, and ancient manuscripts of Mark vary greatly in their spelling of the name; so the mystery seems incapable of solution.

Once such limitations of knowledge are honestly confessed, it is gratifying to find that we can identify the main sites of Jesus' life and ministry. The birthplace, Bethlehem (XIV, C-5), and the childhood residence, Nazareth (XIV, C-3), are certainly known. Concerning the Sea of Galilee, Cana (XIV, C-3), Nain (XIV, C-3), Capernaum (XIV, D-3), and Chorazin (XIV, D-3) there can be no reasonable doubt. There was long a dispute about the location of Capernaum, but it seems clear now that this center of Jesus' Galilean ministry was at *Tell Hûm*. It must be added, however, that the synagogue whose ruins are seen today at *Tell Hûm* is not that mentioned in the Gospels, but was built later, possibly in the third century (Fig. 41). Bethsaida (XIV, D-3) may be two miles north of the Sea of Galilee, at *et-Tell*, but is most probably at *el 'Araj*, on the shore of the sea.

On most of his trips to Jerusalem, Jesus probably followed the usual Galilean custom, journeying down the Jordan Valley on the east side of the river, crossing the river near Jericho (XIV, C-5; cf. Matt. 19:1; Mark 10:1; Luke 19:1), and going up the road from Jericho to Jerusalem (see Fig. 69). The Gospel of John tells of one journey through Samaria, and mentions a stop near Sychar (John 4:5). Modern tradition wrongly locates this town at the village *'Askar* (Fig. 6). Sychar must have been close to Jacob's Well (XIV, C-4); perhaps the correct name was Sichem, that is, Shechem.

The sites in Jerusalem appear on Plate XVII:B. It is important, however, to note the location of Bethany (XIV, C-5), southeast of Jerusalem; there Jesus found a welcome and refreshment in the home of friends (Mark 11:11; John 12:1). Bethphage was not far from Bethany, probably just northwest (XIV, C-5), but no certainty is attainable. The beautiful resurrection story in the Gospel of Luke (ch. 24:13 ff.) seems to refer not to the Emmaus close to Jerusalem (XII:D, C-5), but to *'Amwâs*, where Emmaus appears on this map (XIV, B-5).

GENERAL CONCLUSIONS

One gains from the study of the geography of the Gospels three strong impressions. First of all, we know the general framework of the life of Jesus. The political background is plain. The places of his birth, childhood, and death are known; the center of the Galilean ministry was at Capernaum; the major portion of his ministry was exercised north and west of the Sea of Galilee (see Fig. 68).

A second observation, however, is not so often made. In spite of the definite framework of the ministry, few places are definitely named as scenes of the activity of Jesus. Most of the sayings and actions which the Gospels report are not located in a particular place, and it is usually wrong to assign such incidents to the place mentioned in a neighboring paragraph of the Gospel story. Only fourteen or fifteen places in all Galilee are named as places where Jesus lived or worked. That he visited numerous other cities and towns may be regarded as certain; what those places were we do not know.

The third observation is that Jesus worked consistently in centers of Jewish life, and had very little to do with the many Hellenistic centers which dotted the landscape of Palestine. He avoided Sepphoris and Tiberias, outstanding Hellenistic cities of Galilee. There is no mention that he went to the coastal cities of Judaea, almost all of which were strongly Hellenistic in organization and culture. He never more than touched or passed through the region of the Decapolis, and no passage reports that he entered a Decapolis city (cf. Mark 5:1, 20; 7:31). He had nothing to do with the notably Hellenistic city of Samaria.

Apparent exceptions do not prove valid or significant when examined. It has been asserted that Jesus went to Tyre (XIV, C-2) and Sidon (XIV, C-1). The fact is that this journey into "the parts of Tyre and Sidon" (Matt. 15:21; Mark 7:24) was a retirement into rural seclusion; he went, not into those cities, but into the "parts" or regions connected with them. That is, he withdrew northwest from Galilee into a lonely region, and spent some time there with his disciples. Similarly, the romantic pictures which writers sometimes draw of Jesus at Caesarea Philippi, a city noted for Greek temples and other signs of Hellenistic culture, are without foundation. What the Gospels say is that he went into the "parts" (Matt. 16:13) or outlying "villages" (Mark 8:27) of Caesarea Philippi. There also he was alone with his disciples in a time of withdrawal from public ministry. He is said in Mark 8:22 to have touched at Bethsaida (XIV, D-3). This city, however, was not only Philip's capital; it included a Jewish settlement, composed partly of fishermen, which antedated Philip's time. Undoubtedly Jesus was interested in the Jewish section of the city. Jesus passed through the Hellenistic city of Jericho, it is true; but he had to do this to go to Jerusalem, and he lodged there in the home of a Jewish taxgatherer, Zacchaeus (Luke 19:5). The Gospels report but few contacts of Jesus with Gentiles, and such occasions are clearly represented as exceptional (e.g., Mark 7:27; cf. Matt. 15:24). When Jesus heals a Gentile, he does so without entering a Gentile home (Matt. 8:5-13; Mark 7:24-30).

Had the writers of the Gospels, who were providing writings intended in part at least to appeal to Gentiles, been able to tell that Jesus ministered freely to Gentiles in Galilee and elsewhere, they would certainly have done so. The conclusion is clear. The ministry of Jesus was deliberately limited to the Jews, and was confined almost entirely to centers free from strong Gentile influence. There is no trace of a planned effort to reach the Gentiles who were all about him. The mission to Gentiles had roots in the teaching and attitudes of Jesus, but its actual inauguration waited until the Apostolic Age.

THE JOURNEYS OF PAUL

Plate XV

THE Apostle Paul was providentially prepared to lead the early missionary expansion of Christianity. He was a Jew, thoroughly grounded in his ancestral faith. But he was a Jew of the Dispersion; hence he knew something of the larger world of his day. He not only knew the Hebrew in which the Old Testament was written and the Aramaic in which most residents of Palestine conversed, but he was most at home in the common Greek tongue which was then used almost everywhere in the Roman world. He was a Roman citizen (Acts 22:25, 28) as well as a citizen of Tarsus (Plate xv, F-3; cf. Acts 21:39). It was therefore no unprepared development when Saul—to use his Jewish name—became the leading missionary of the Apostolic Age.

EARLY PREPARATION

Although the famous Christian scholar Jerome wrote in the fourth century that Saul was born in Galilee at Gischala (viii, F-4), it is said in The Acts that he was born in Tarsus of Cilicia (ch. 22: 3). This city was noted for its vigorous intellectual and commercial life, and many have thought that Saul was greatly influenced by its Gentile thought. The apostle, however, states quite definitely in Phil. 3:5 that he was brought up in the strict Jewish tradition and became a Pharisee. He went to Jerusalem (xv, G-5) and with Gamaliel as teacher (Acts 22:3) took up the systematic study of the ancestral tradition (Gal. 1:13, 14). This faith he jealously championed against the newly arisen Christian movement. Not content with active efforts to suppress the new sect in Jerusalem (Acts 8:1, 3), he set out for Damascus (xv, G-4), where "the Way" was making inroads into the synagogues (Acts 9:1, 2). On the road, near Damascus, he had the vision of the living Christ which transformed his life and affected the course of history. Soon, while lodging in the street called Straight (Acts 9:11; Fig. 65), he made contact with Christian disciples and was baptized.

For a period of unknown length, Saul then withdrew into Arabia (Gal. 1:17). Writers of romantic temperament often picture him going far south to Mount Sinai (cf. Gal. 4:25). Arabia, however, was a vast desert area which reached almost to Damascus itself (xv, F-G 4-5). It is doubtful that Saul went on a long journey, since he next appeared in the same city of Damascus (Gal. 1:17). When Jewish hostility threatened his life there, he escaped with the help of friends, who during the night let him down to the ground through a window in the wall (Acts 9:25; II Cor. 11:33).

Thus three years after conversion (Gal. 1:18) Saul came to Jerusalem, met Peter and James, and according to Acts 9:29 preached to the Greek-speaking Jews (cf. Fig. 72). In fifteen days he aroused such hostility that the leaders of the Jerusalem Church urged him to leave. Christians conducted him to Caesarea (xv, G-5), where he took ship for Tarsus.

During the next few years Saul's vigorous personality impelled him to active Christian work. He himself writes in Gal. 1:22, 23 that his evangelistic work was reported even in Jerusalem. The Churches in Cilicia (xv, F-G 3; cf. Acts 15:23, 41) almost certainly owed their existence to his work.

When, therefore, Barnabas, in need of an able helper at Antioch in Syria (xv, G-4), journeyed to Tarsus to induce Saul to join him (Acts 11:25), he was seeking a man of proved energy and ability. Saul went to Antioch, the capital of Syria and third city of the Roman Empire, and for a year assisted Barnabas. When a famine brought the Christians of Judaea into severe straits, and the energetic Antioch Church sent relief, Barnabas and Saul were entrusted with the funds. They fulfilled the trust and brought back with them John Mark, son of a devout and well-to-do Christian lady of Jerusalem (Acts 12:12, 25). Saul then continued his work as a prophet and teacher in the Church at Antioch (Acts 13:1).

THE FIRST MISSIONARY JOURNEY

Through an unnamed leader, recognized as the spokesman of the Holy Spirit, the Church at Antioch was called upon to surrender Barnabas and Saul for wider activity (Acts 13:2). Barnabas was the Antioch Church's most trusted leader, Saul his most promising assistant. These men, with John Mark as helper, set out to spread the Christian faith.

From Antioch, located inland upon the Orontes River, the party went some sixteen miles west to Seleucia (xv, G-4). It was five miles north of the mouth of the Orontes, where the roadstead would not be silted up by deposits from the river. Thence the missionaries took ship for Cyprus (xv, F-4), important for copper mines and timber and governed by the Roman senate through a proconsul. They landed at Salamis (xv, F-4), chief business center of the island (Acts 13:5). Their method was to preach in synagogues as opportunity opened; nothing is yet said of a direct mission to Gentiles.

By what route the apostles crossed the island is not reported, nor are we told how much they preached as they went. In general, it appears to have been Paul's policy throughout his journeys to establish himself in cities of importance and let the Gospel spread from such central places. In any event, the next definite word of his work is connected with Paphos (xv, F-4), the capital of the province (Acts 13:6). There the apostles were called to preach before the proconsul, Sergius Paulus, and in connection with this occasion The Acts begins to call the apostle Paul. The change to this name suggests that Paul had become the real leader of the party.

From Paphos, Paul and his companions crossed to the small Roman province of Pamphylia (xv, F-3). They may have landed at Attalia (xv, F-3). Perga (xv, F-3), the first city they are said to have visited (Acts 13:13), was several miles inland. Without John Mark, who returned to Jerusalem for some reason which Paul thought distinctly inadequate (Acts 15:38), the party struck north into the higher country of central Asia Minor. Was it due to illness that they made this journey? So Ramsay thinks, supposing that Paul suffered from malaria along the coast land. Or did they stop in central Asia Minor on account of an illness which first seized Paul there? We cannot say (cf. Gal. 4:13).

The cities to which Paul came contained many Jews, and Paul found synagogues in which to begin his work. The cities in which missionary preaching now occurred were Antioch, Iconium, Lystra,

Fig. 72. Theodotus synagogue inscription. Theodotus built a synagogue and guest rooms for the convenience of Jewish pilgrims to Jerusalem. The inscription which told of his generous act was found in 1914 during excavations on the hill Ophel. It is in Greek, and reflects the presence of Greek-speaking Jews in Jerusalem. In such a synagogue Saul of Tarsus may have disputed with Christians (cf. Acts 6:9).

FIG. 73. "Straight Street," Damascus. A modern view of one of the most ancient streets in the world. Cf. Acts 9:11.

and Derbe (xv, F-3). All four were in the Roman Province of Galatia (xv, F-G 2-3), and probably it was to these Churches that Paul later wrote his letter to the Galatians. Further north, in the valley of the Halys River, lay the section settled by Gauls who came from Europe in the early third century B.C. Their chief cities were Ancyra (xv, F-2), the modern Ankara, capital of Turkey; Pessinus (xv, F-3); and Tavium (xv, F-2). It was long held that Galatians was written to these cities; more likely Paul wrote it to the Churches that he had founded on his First Journey and later revisited (Acts 13:14 to 14:23; 16:6; 18:23).

At Antioch—often called Pisidian Antioch (Acts 13:14) to distinguish it from Antioch in Syria—the great majority of the Jews refused to hear Paul. He turned directly to the Gentiles and invited them to accept the Christian Gospel without observing the distinctive rites of Judaism. In Iconium, the modern Konya, he again won both Jews and Gentiles to the faith. In Lystra there may have been fewer Jews; the lack of mention of any Jewish synagogue and the fact that Timothy had not been circumcised (Acts 16:3) suggest that the Jews were not so numerous or strict here. Yet they could hardly have been entirely lacking, since Jewish leaders from Antioch and Iconium were able to stir up a mob against Paul in Lystra (Acts 14:19). After preaching with success at Derbe, on the southeastern border of the Province of Galatia, the apostles retraced their route, came down to Attalia, and sailed to Seleucia (Acts 14:20-26). At Antioch they were able to report the conversion of a modest number of Jews and large numbers of Gentiles.

THE COUNCIL AT JERUSALEM

Strict Jewish Christians soon challenged Paul's practice of accepting Gentiles into the Church without requiring them to observe the Jewish law (Acts 15:1). Since the Church at Antioch was itself a mixed group, in which both Jews and Gentiles joined in worship and fellowship, its existence, as well as the results of Paul's wider mission, was thus threatened. The issue was taken to Jerusalem. Paul, Barnabas, and others apparently journeyed by land, since they "passed through both Phoenicia and Samaria" (Acts 15:3); but it is possible that they went on a ship stopping at the Phoenician ports and disembarked at Ptolemais (xv, G-4) or Caesarea (xv, G-5). When Paul's mission to the Gentiles had been essentially approved by the conference in Jerusalem, the Antioch representatives returned home and reported the result (Acts 15:30).

THE SECOND MISSIONARY JOURNEY

On the Second Journey, in which Paul had Silas to help him, the route led north by land through Cilicia to the Cilician Gates (xv, G-3; Fig. 48), a pass leading through the Taurus Mountains into the high country of inland Asia Minor (Acts 15:40, 41). The travelers visited the Churches of South Galatia, and from Lystra took with them Timothy, who probably had been converted on the First Journey (Acts 16:1-6). Then followed a period of uncertainty. Paul was seeking a new field, but felt led to avoid for the time both the Province of Asia (xv, E-F 2-3) and Bithynia (xv, E-F 2). Finally, after moving north through Phrygia (xv, F-3) and west through Mysia (xv, E-3), he came to Troas (xv, E-3), an important port on the Aegean Sea, not far south of the Hellespont (Acts 16:6-8). Here Paul saw in a dream a man in Macedonian garb, who urged him to preach in Macedonia (xv, C-D 2). This he took to be the divine guidance he needed. Since The Acts begins at this point to use "we" and "us" (Acts 16:10), it seems that at Troas Paul enlisted the help of Luke, the writer of The Acts.

The party sailed for Macedonia. One day's journey took them to the island of Samothrace (xv, E-2); the next day they reached Neapolis (xv, D-2) in Macedonia. They went immediately ten miles northwest to Philippi (xv, D-2), a leading city in that part of Macedonia, and a Roman colony with special privileges. No synagogue is mentioned at Philippi, and at the Jewish place of prayer, located outside the city at a place convenient for the washings which Jewish ceremonies prescribed, Paul found only a group of women. Among those won to the faith by Paul's preaching was Lydia, a Gentile of Thyatira (xv, E-3) in Asia Minor. She was a seller of purple cloth (Acts 16:14). Paul restored to sanity a slave girl whose mysterious psychic powers were being exploited by her masters, and they made frantic complaint. The Philippian authorities stripped Paul and Silas, and ordered them beaten and imprisoned. The apostles were soon released, however, and the magistrates forced to apologize for having dealt illegally with Roman citizens (Acts 16:16-40).

Following the Egnatian Way westward, the evangelists passed through Amphipolis and Apollonia (xv, D-2) and came to Thessalonica (Acts 17:1). This city (xv, D-2), on the main road, with a good harbor and sustained by a rich valley behind it, was inevitably a commercial center, and has remained so into modern times. The unusual title "*politarchai*," which The Acts uses to designate the rulers there (ch. 17:6), has been proved correct by inscriptions. Jews were numerous there as well as at the next stop, Beroea (xv, D-2), which was some forty miles southwest of Thessalonica, and not on the Egnatian Way. When Jewish opposition forced Paul to leave Beroea, friends conducted him to Athens (Acts 17:14 f.). Whether they took him by the land road or by ship is disputed, but a man who had been shipwrecked three times before writing II Cor. 11:25 must have used the sea route whenever possible.

In its golden age Athens (xv, D-3) had been the center of the classical culture of ancient times. On its Acropolis stood famous masterpieces of art and architecture. In Paul's day Athens was less brilliant, but it was still a city to thrill any lover of culture. Objects of art abounded; interest in poetry, mythology, and philosophy continued; tradition was rich. All this made little impression on Paul, who knew but one God and one Lord (I Cor. 8:6). According to The Acts, he tried to catch and mold the mood of this polytheistic and philosophical city, but with little success (Acts 17:16-34; Fig. 74). No letter to Athens survives; he mentions no Church there; his work had little fruit. He moved on to Corinth (xv, D-3).

Corinth was the political and commercial center of the Province of Achaia. It lay at the foot of a rocky citadel at the southwest end of the isthmus which connected the Peloponnesus with the Grecian mainland. Much traffic crossed the isthmus to avoid rounding the storm-haunted capes at the southern tip of Achaia (see p. 80). There were ports on the west and east sides of the isthmus; on the west was Lechaeum, on the east Cenchreae (xv, D-3). Paul passed through the latter port (Acts 18:18); the later existence of a Christian group there is attested by Paul's reference to Phoebe as active in its work (Rom. 16:1). Corinth itself, after a century of eclipse due to its destruction in 146 B.C., was rebuilt by Caesar in 46 B.C. and soon became a populous and thriving center of trade. The contents of I Corinthians make it clear that there were Jews in the Church Paul founded there, and their presence in Corinth is also indicated by a Greek inscription, which, though fragmentary, seems to read, "Synagogue of the Hebrews."

In Corinth Paul was brought before the Roman proconsul, Gallio, and excavations have uncovered the rostrum on which Gallio may have appeared before the mob. Gallio is mentioned as proconsul of Achaia in an inscription found at Delphi (XIII, D-2). This inscription gives one of the few dependable clues to the chronology of the life of Paul. It indicates that Gallio came to Corinth for his year as proconsul in either A.D. 51 or 52. Paul then, according to Acts 18:11, 12, must have arrived there about A.D. 50.

When Paul left Corinth, he sailed from Cenchreae to Ephesus (xv, E-3) and visited the synagogue there (Acts 18:19), but apparently only to determine the desirability of a future visit, for he refused an invitation to stay longer and sailed to Caesarea. The Church which he then "went up and saluted" was probably that in Jerusalem. Very soon, however, he went north to Syrian Antioch; this rather than Jerusalem was his home base.

THE THIRD MISSIONARY JOURNEY

After a stay in Antioch, Paul again went north by land through the Cilician Gates and visited the Churches in Southern Galatia (Acts 18:23). From Pisidian Antioch he went westward to Ephesus (Acts 19:1), his chief center of work on this Third Journey. Beginning in the synagogue, as was his custom, he moved after three months into a lecture hall which he rented. Thus he opened a successful two-year mission to Gentiles. He also sent out workers into other cities of the Province of Asia; in this way Churches were established in Colossae, Hierapolis, and Laodicea (xv, E-3; Col. 1:2; 4:13).

As at Philippi, so at Ephesus commercial greed ended Paul's work. Demetrius, a silversmith who made shrines of the goddess Artemis for sale to pilgrims to the great temple in Ephesus, saw that his business was suffering by reason of Paul's work. He aroused the silversmiths, by a blended appeal to religious fanaticism and business profits, and drew a great mob into the large theater (Acts 19:29; Fig. 67). Some of the Asiarchs, officials who had responsibility in the religious festivals of the city, urged Paul not to brave the mob, and the town clerk quieted and dismissed the crowd without bloodshed (Acts 19:31-41).

The situation, however, made impossible effective preaching in the immediate future. Paul, therefore, soon left for Macedonia (Acts 20:1), either by land to Troas and thence by sea to Neapolis, or by ship from Ephesus to Neapolis. He then followed the Egnatian Way west to Thessalonica, and proceeded south to Greece. He may have followed the route of his Second Journey, encouraging the Christians in Beroea, and thence going south to Athens and Corinth. Since, however, he later says that he had preached as far as Illyricum (xv, C 1-2; Rom. 15:19), and since we find embedded in the Pastoral Epistles a reference (which may date from this time) to his purpose to winter at Nicopolis (xv, D-3; Titus 3:12), the possibility remains that from Thessalonica he went west by the Egnatian Way to Dyrrhachium or Apollonia (xv, C-2), south to Nicopolis for the winter, and later to Athens or Corinth. We do not know the exact route of Paul's journeys; in most cases the map can show only a possible or probable route. The certain thing is that Paul spent three months in Greece (Acts 20:3), most of it perhaps at Corinth, and made his plans for his last visit to Jerusalem. His purpose was to take thither a collection for the poor Christians of Palestine.

His plan had been to go by ship to Syria and thence—from Ptolemais, perhaps, or Caesarea—to Jerusalem. A plot against his life by some Jews led him to change his plan and double back through Macedonia. He then crossed from Neapolis to Troas (Acts 20:3-5). Here he joined representatives of the Churches who were to go with him to take the collection to Jerusalem. When the ship left Troas, going south, Paul for some reason went by land as far as Assos (xv, E-3), where he boarded the ship (Acts 20:13, 14). Then began Paul's last voyage to Jerusalem. The first day the ship came to Mitylene (xv, E-3), chief city of the island of Lesbos (Acts 20:14). The next day they reached a point by Chios (xv, E-3); the third day they touched at Samos (xv, E-3); on the following day they came to Miletus. Here the ship stopped long enough for Paul to send to Ephesus, thirty miles away, and summon the elders of that Church to Miletus for final instructions (Acts 20:17). From Miletus the voyage led straight to the island or city of Cos (xv, E-3), then to Rhodes (xv, E-4), and next to Patara (xv, E-4), a port in Lycia (Acts 21:1). There they boarded another ship, sailed southeast, passing within sight of the west end of Cyprus, and came down to Phoenicia at Tyre (xv, G-4), where Paul visited Christian disciples before the ship went on to Ptolemais (Acts 21:3-7). From Ptolemais the party went on to Caesarea, the capital city of Palestine, either by sea or on the land route rounding Mount Carmel and following the coastal road south. After a few days in Caesarea they went up to Jerusalem (Acts 21:8-10, 15), to present the collection and to observe Pentecost.

FIG. 74. Areopagus, Athens. The smaller hill in the center of the picture is the Areopagus, "Mars' Hill," where Paul may have spoken to the Athenians (cf. Acts 17:22). Behind it is the Acropolis, on which stand the remains of the Parthenon.

FIG. 75. Ruins of the theater at Ephesus. Scene of the riot described in Acts 19:29–41. In the lower left center is the orchestra, around which the spectators' seats rise in semicircular tiers. The theater is said to have had a capacity of nearly 25,000. Note the street running toward the sea.

PAUL THE PRISONER

After the Roman guard seized Paul during the riot scene in the Temple court, they took him to the "castle" or Tower of Antonia at the northwest corner of the Temple area (Acts 22:24). When a plot against his life became known, the centurion sent him by way of Antipatris (xv, G-5) to the governor, Felix, in Caesarea (Acts 23:31-33). He was kept a prisoner in the palace which Herod the Great had built. After two years Festus replaced Felix (c. A.D. 60). Festus desired to take Paul to Jerusalem for examination; but Paul, a Roman citizen, appealed to Caesar (Acts 25:11). He then had to be taken to Rome for a hearing before the emperor or his representative.

THE VOYAGE TO ROME

Luke's account of Paul's voyage to Rome is a marvel of graphic description. The centurion Julius and his soldiers embarked with Paul and other prisoners on a boat that touched at Caesarea. The vessel was going to Asia Minor and, as it seems (Acts 27:2), intended to go up the western coast to its home port, Adramyttium (xv, E-3). Since the winds did not permit a direct northwest course, the ship went north to Sidon (xv, G-4), where Paul was permitted to visit Christian friends. Thence the ship continued north, keeping east of Cyprus, and sailed west along the southern shore of Asia Minor to Myra in Lycia (xv, F-4). There the centurion transferred his charges to an Alexandrian ship headed for Italy (Acts 27:5 f.).

By slow sailing the ship worked westward until it was just south of the island of Cnidus (xv, E-4). It then struck south to come under the lee of Crete, passing by the promontory of Salmone (xv, E-4; cf. Acts 27:7). Under the protection of Crete the ship worked west to Fair Havens (xv, E-4), an anchorage near Lasaea. Winter, when sea travel was too dangerous for sailing vessels, was at hand, and the problem was to find the best place to stay during the stormy winter months. Fair Havens was too open to storms, and the sailors, with full knowledge of the risk, tried to sail west to Phoenix (xv, D-4), a safe harbor (Acts 27:12, 13). But a violent wind caught the ship and drove it away from the land. It came under the shelter of the small island of Cauda (xv, D-4), and the crew sought to strengthen the ship for the strain of the storm (Acts 27:16, 17). Then, for fear that they might be driven into Syrtis Major (xv, C-5), the treacherous shallows off the northern coast of Africa, they permitted the ship to be driven west in the sea called Adria, a name which then applied not only to the Adriatic Sea between Italy and Illyricum but also to the open sea west of Crete (xv, C-D 3-4).

After fourteen days of wild buffeting the ship drew near to land during the night (Acts 27:27). Anchors warded off disaster until dawn. Then a bay with a beach appeared (Acts 27:39), and the one chance of safety seemed to be to beach the ship. When this was attempted, however, clashing currents "where two seas met" drove the ship aground, and it broke up under the beating of the waves. The soldiers wanted to kill the prisoners lest they escape; but the centurion, friendly to Paul, vetoed this plan and permitted all to try to reach land. Some could swim; the others clung to wreckage and were washed ashore by the waves (Acts 27:43, 44).

They found (Acts 28:1) that the island was Melita or Melitene (xv, B-4), the modern Malta. There they were forced to winter. Fortunately for them, another ship of Alexandria was wintering there. When spring permitted, this ship, carrying the centurion and his party, sailed for Italy (Acts 28:11). The first stop was at Syracuse in Sicily (xv, B-3), an excellent harbor where they stayed three days. Then they made a circuit to Rhegium (xv, C-3), on the Italian side of the Straits of Messina (where were located the mythical Scylla and Charybdis). The final stage of the voyage was from Rhegium to Puteoli (Acts 28:13), a favored harbor for large ships coming from Egypt. From Puteoli (xv, B-2) the apostle was taken by road to Rome (xv, B-2). At Appii Forum and Tres Tabernae he was met by Christian friends. During the latter part of the land journey to Rome, Paul traveled the famous Appian Way (Fig. 64). Upon arrival, he was permitted to live in his own lodging under guard (Acts 28:15, 16, 30, 31).

Thus ends the book of The Acts. Paul had wanted to go to Spain (Rom. 15:24, 28). There is an ancient tradition that after two years he was released from prison, traveled in East and West, was again imprisoned, and finally was executed in Rome. Indeed, if the Pastoral Epistles in their present length come from Paul, they seem to require us to accept this tradition. But the authorship of the Pastoral Epistles is disputed. Perhaps only in a shorter form did they come from Paul. Yet, even if Paul took such journeys, we can say nothing definite about his itinerary.

Certain facts, however, are clear. Paul found the Christian movement a small fellowship, little known outside of Palestine and Syria, and left it a growing movement planted in almost all of the important provinces of the empire. He found it a movement just beginning to take root among Gentiles and left it a greatly enlarged Church open to Jew and Gentile alike. The Apostle Paul did more than any other man to plant the Church in the centers where it was destined to shape the future of Europe and America.

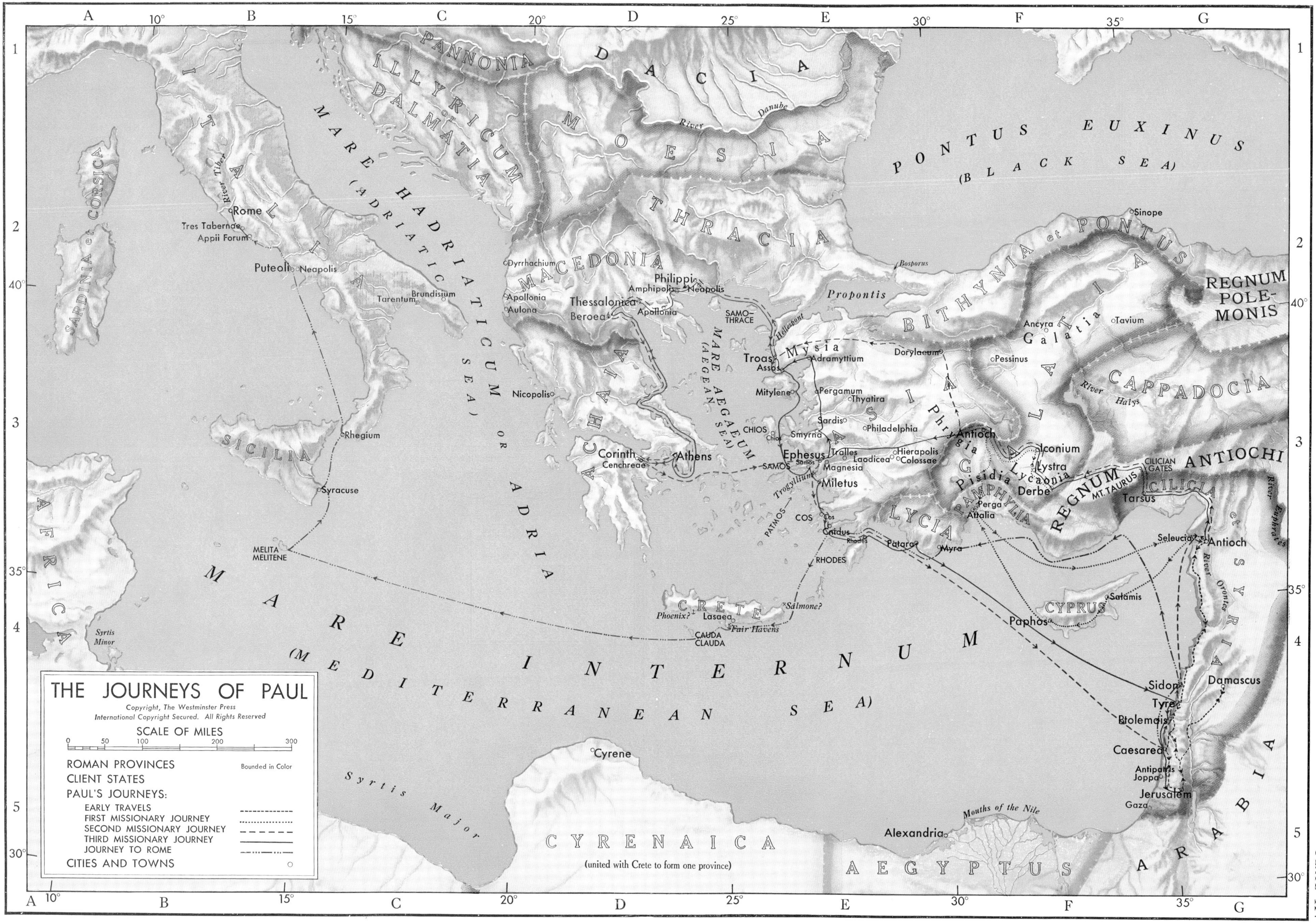
THE JOURNEYS OF PAUL
Copyright, The Westminster Press
International Copyright Secured. All Rights Reserved
SCALE OF MILES
0 50 100 200 300
ROMAN PROVINCES
CLIENT STATES
Bounded in Color
PAUL'S JOURNEYS:
EARLY TRAVELS
FIRST MISSIONARY JOURNEY
SECOND MISSIONARY JOURNEY
THIRD MISSIONARY JOURNEY
JOURNEY TO ROME
CITIES AND TOWNS
PANNONIA
DACIA
ILLYRICUM or DALMATIA
MOESIA
THRACIA
MACEDONIA
ACHAIA
ITALIA
SARDINIA et CORSICA
SICILIA
AFRICA
CYRENAICA
(united with Crete to form one province)
AEGYPTUS
ARABIA
SYRIA
CILICIA
REGNUM ANTIOCHI
REGNUM POLEMONIS
BITHYNIA et PONTUS
GALATIA
CAPPADOCIA
ASIA
LYCIA
PAMPHYLIA
Pisidia
Lycaonia
Phrygia
Galatia
Mysia
CRETE
CYPRUS
PONTUS EUXINUS
(BLACK SEA)
MARE HADRIATICUM OR ADRIA
(ADRIATIC SEA)
MARE AEGAEUM
(AEGEAN SEA)
MARE INTERNUM
(MEDITERRANEAN SEA)
Propontis
Hellespont
Bosporus
Syrtis Major
Syrtis Minor
Mouths of the Nile
River Tiber
River Danube
River Halys
River Euphrates
River Orontes
MT. TAURUS
CILICIAN GATES
Rome
Tres Tabernae
Appii Forum
Puteoli
Neapolis
Tarentum
Brundisium
Rhegium
Syracuse
MELITA MELITENE
Dyrrhachium
Apollonia
Aulona
Nicopolis
Thessalonica
Beroea
Amphipolis
Philippi
Neapolis
Apollonia
SAMOTHRACE
Corinth
Cenchreae
Athens
Troas
Assos
Adramyttium
Mitylene
Pergamum
Thyatira
Sardis
Philadelphia
CHIOS
Chios
Smyrna
Ephesus
SAMOS
Samos
Trogyllium
Tralles
Magnesia
Miletus
Laodicea
Hierapolis
Colossae
PATMOS
COS
Cos
Cnidus
RHODES
Rhodes
Patara
Myra
Perga
Attalia
Antioch
Iconium
Lystra
Derbe
Dorylaeum
Pessinus
Ancyra
Tavium
Sinope
Tarsus
Seleucia
Antioch
Salamis
Paphos
Salmone?
Phoenix?
Lasaea
Fair Havens
CAUDA CLAUDA
Cyrene
Alexandria
Sidon
Tyre
Ptolemais
Caesarea
Antipatris
Joppa
Jerusalem
Gaza
Damascus
A B C D E F G
1 2 3 4 5
10° 15° 20° 25° 30° 35° 40°

A

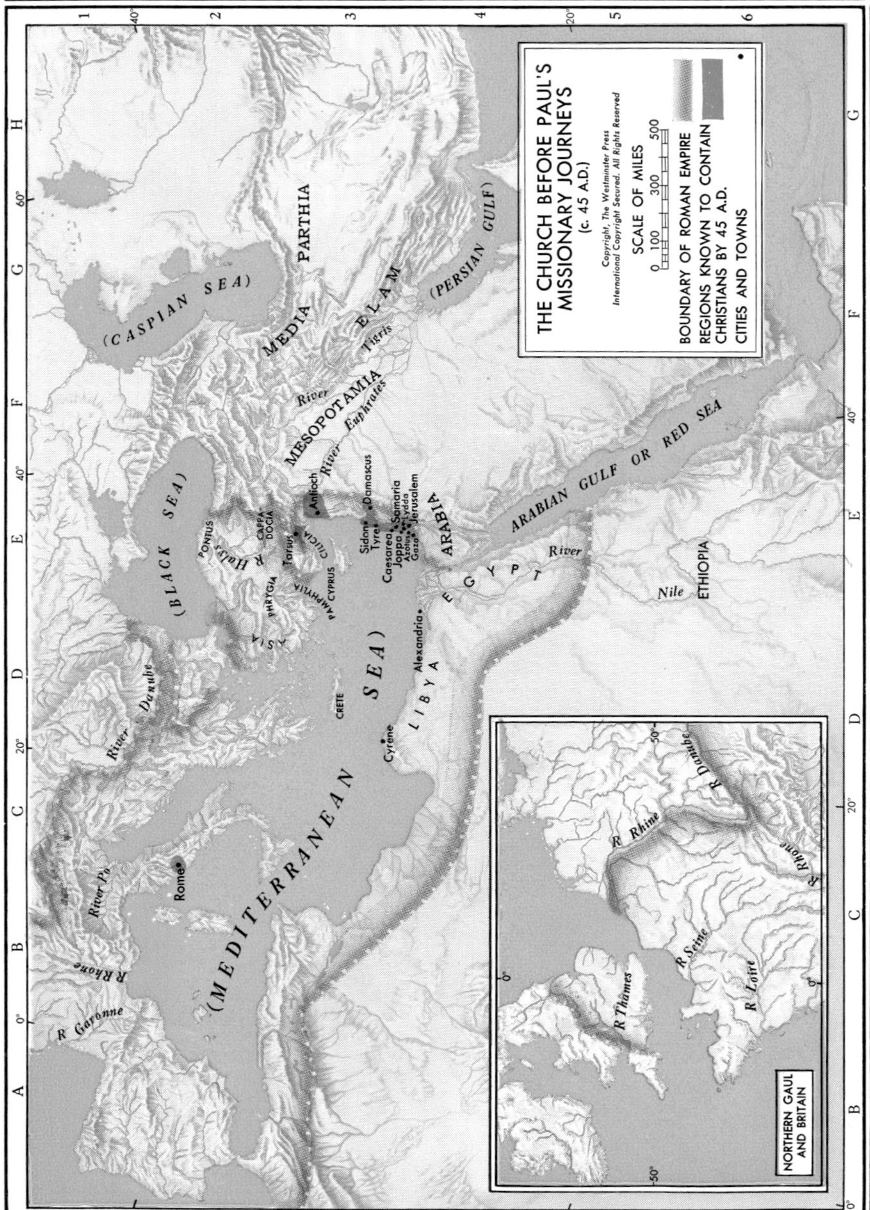

THE CHURCH BEFORE PAUL'S MISSIONARY JOURNEYS
(c. 45 A.D.)
Copyright, The Westminster Press
International Copyright Secured. All Rights Reserved
SCALE OF MILES
0 100 300 500
BOUNDARY OF ROMAN EMPIRE
REGIONS KNOWN TO CONTAIN CHRISTIANS BY 45 A.D.
CITIES AND TOWNS
NORTHERN GAUL AND BRITAIN

B

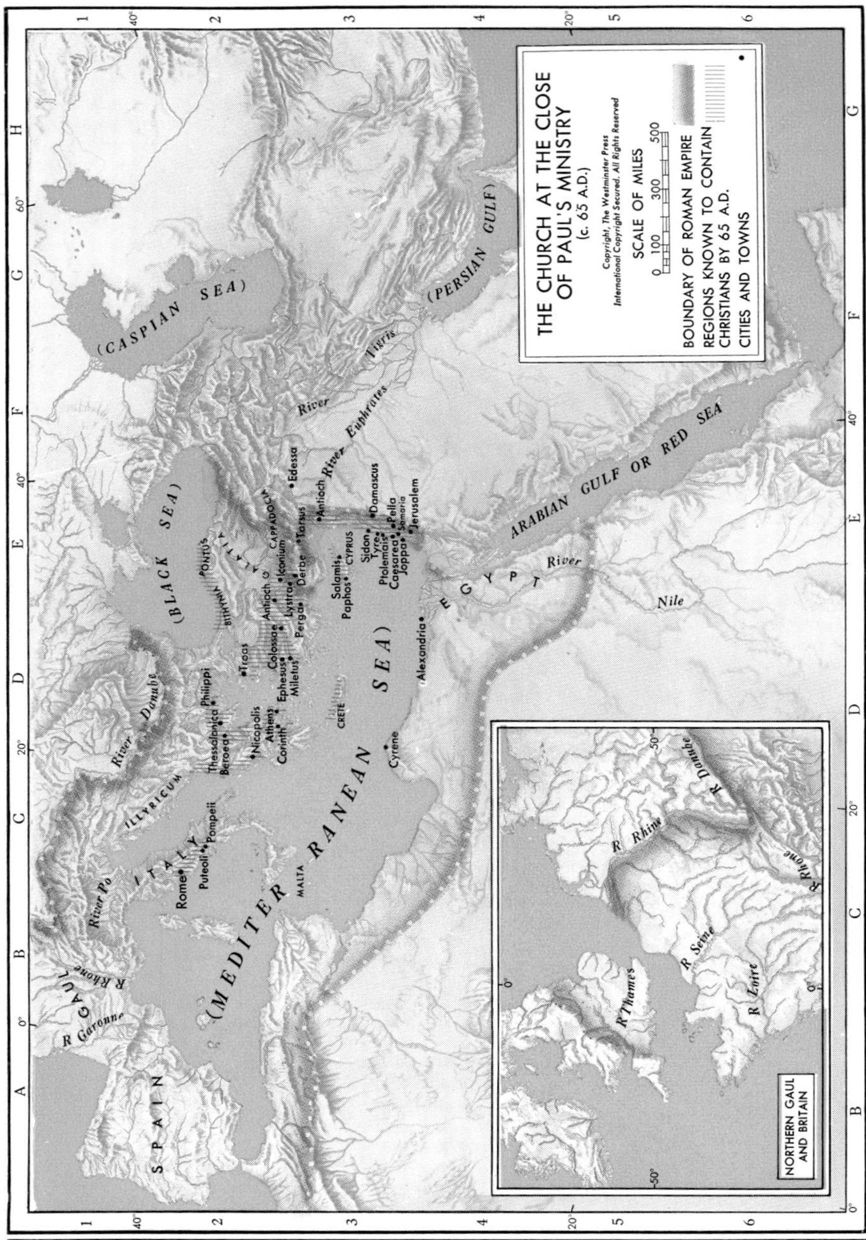

THE CHURCH AT THE CLOSE OF PAUL'S MINISTRY
(c. 65 A.D.)
Copyright, The Westminster Press
International Copyright Secured. All Rights Reserved
SCALE OF MILES
0 100 300 500
BOUNDARY OF ROMAN EMPIRE
REGIONS KNOWN TO CONTAIN CHRISTIANS BY 65 A.D.
CITIES AND TOWNS
NORTHERN GAUL AND BRITAIN

C

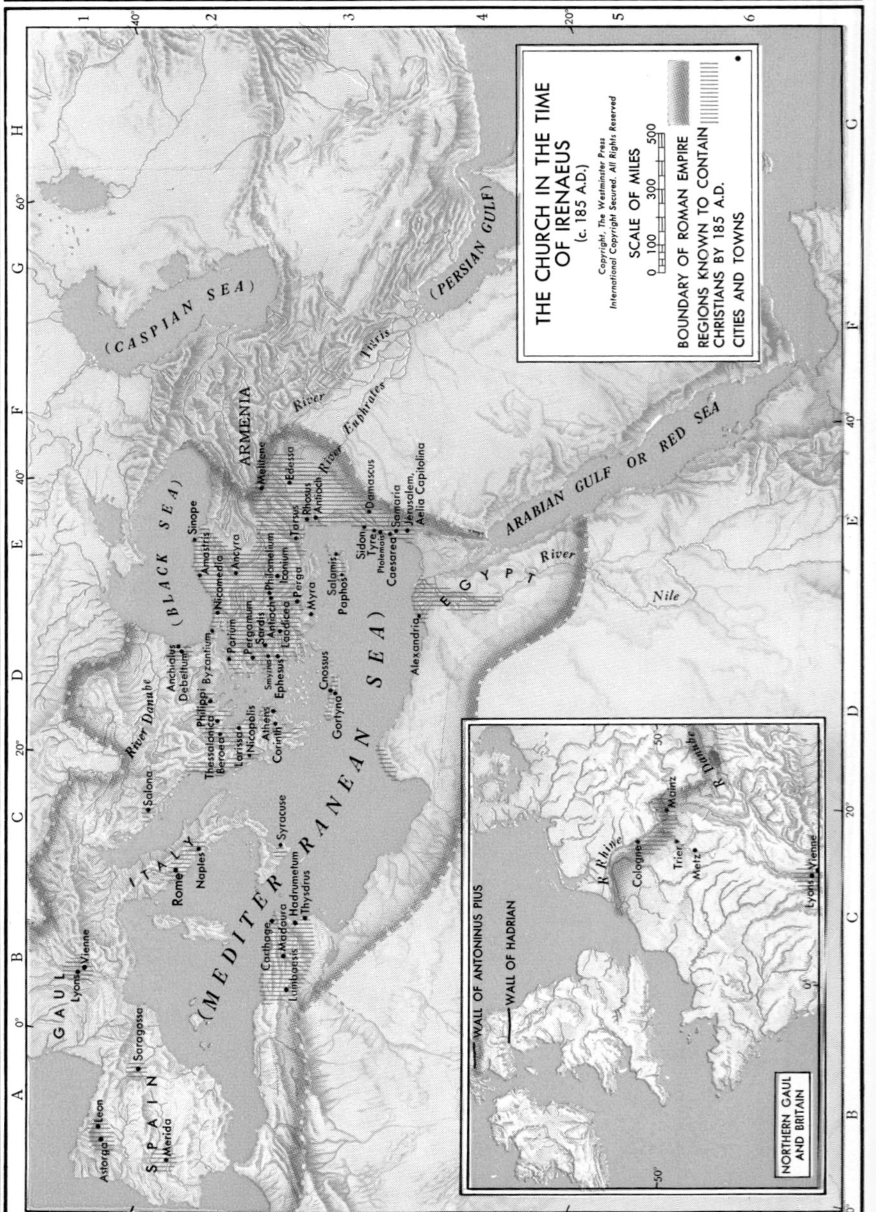

THE CHURCH IN THE TIME OF IRENAEUS
(c. 185 A.D.)
Copyright, The Westminster Press
International Copyright Secured. All Rights Reserved
SCALE OF MILES
0 100 300 500
BOUNDARY OF ROMAN EMPIRE
REGIONS KNOWN TO CONTAIN CHRISTIANS BY 185 A.D.
CITIES AND TOWNS
WALL OF ANTONINUS PIUS
WALL OF HADRIAN
NORTHERN GAUL AND BRITAIN

D

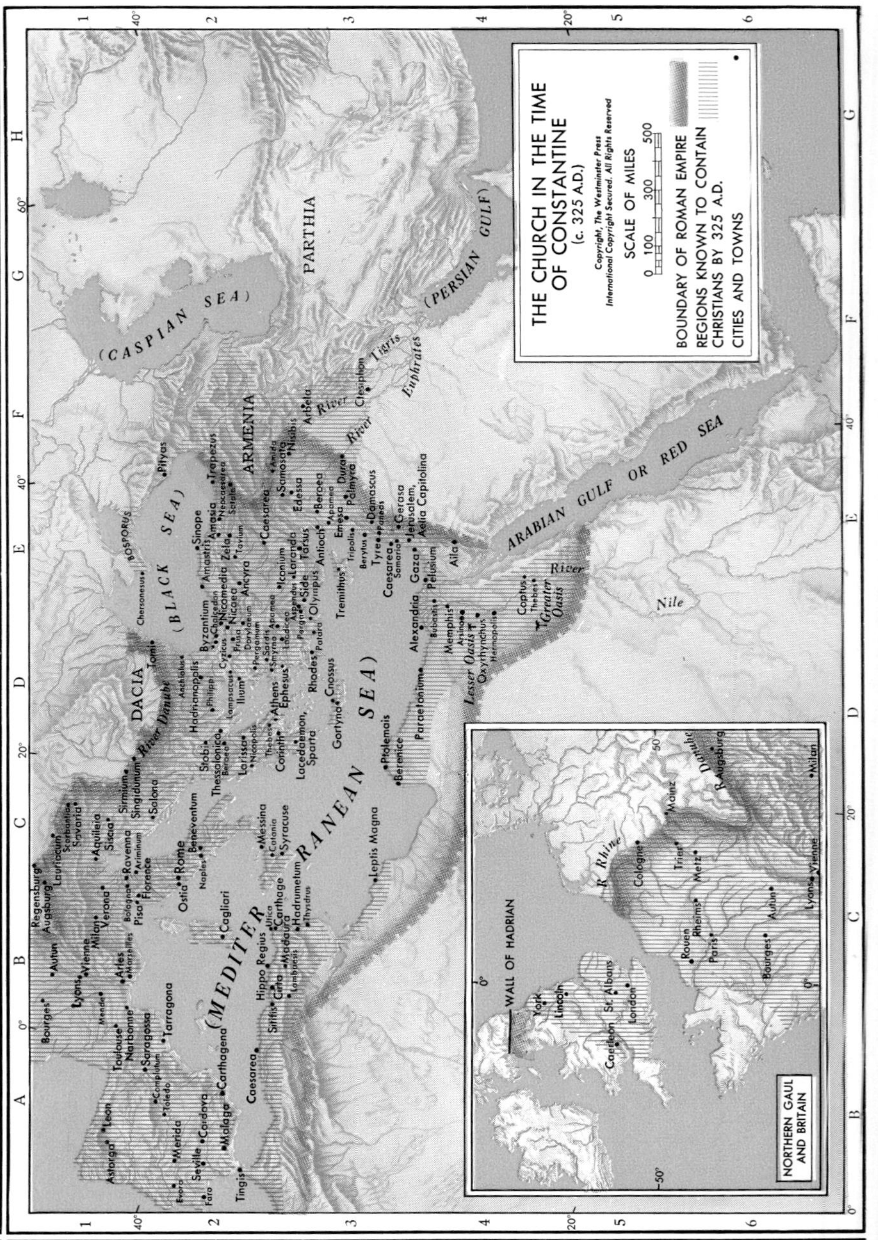

THE CHURCH IN THE TIME OF CONSTANTINE
(c. 325 A.D.)
Copyright, The Westminster Press
International Copyright Secured. All Rights Reserved
SCALE OF MILES
0 100 300 500
BOUNDARY OF ROMAN EMPIRE
REGIONS KNOWN TO CONTAIN CHRISTIANS BY 325 A.D.
CITIES AND TOWNS
WALL OF HADRIAN
NORTHERN GAUL AND BRITAIN

Fig. 76. Pompeii and Vesuvius. In A. D. 79 a violent eruption of volcanic Vesuvius covered with cinders and ashes the famous Italian resort city of Pompeii. Excavations during the last two centuries have thrown much light on the architecture, art, amusements, and daily life of the ancient Romans. This view looks across the forum.

THE EXPANSION OF CHRISTIANITY

Plate XVI

IT IS often futile to ask why history happened as it did, but the student of Christian missions will understand the expansion of Christianity better if he inquires why the new faith so promptly spread west to find its center and greatest future in Europe. Certainly such a result could not have been clearly foreseen. Although the Apostle Paul is reported to have said that "this thing was not done in a corner" (Acts 26:26), a sophisticated Roman citizen residing in the capital of the empire might have asserted the very opposite, for Christianity arose on the far eastern border where the empire met and clashed with Oriental powers and influences. It originated in an obscure and apparently backward region of the empire, in a very small subdivision under the rule of a minor official. It emerged among a people who were constantly drawing criticism but from whom no empire-molding was expected.

Moreover, these Jews among whom Jesus appeared were by no means confined to the Roman Empire. They were also found in regions to the east, which were under Parthian control (Plate xiii, E-H 2-3). This fact is forcefully emphasized by the Pentecost story in Acts, ch. 2. When one carefully examines the list of places from which the Jews present at Pentecost had come, it is found that almost half of the regions mentioned are located outside of the eastern borders of the Roman Empire, and, with the exception of the city of Rome, those parts of the empire that are included in the enumeration are in the eastern half.

Palestine seemed poised between West and East, and there was no outward sign to guarantee that the rising Christian Church would move mainly to the west. Jesus in his ministry had seemed to shun cities of Hellenistic connection. Basically untouched by influences from the west, he had confined himself almost entirely to a ministry among Palestinian Aramaic-speaking Jews. These facts give added interest to the question, Why did the Church almost immediately turn westward?

WHY CHRISTIANITY SPREAD WESTWARD

Five factors go far to explain this somewhat unexpected development. In the first place, the possibility of such a growth was implicit in the purpose and program of Christ. For all his faithful loyalty to his people, he presented a message concerned with basic human needs and traits, and exhibited freedom from external, divisive elements of current religious life. He thus laid the foundation for a Church which made a universal appeal and increasingly transcended racial barriers.

A second factor was the wide westward dispersion of the Jews. In the first century, many more Jews lived outside of Palestine than in their homeland. While they were found in regions farther east, particularly in Babylonia, they were notably numerous in Egypt, Syria, Asia Minor, Cyprus, Cyrenaica, and Italy. Indeed, in almost every important center of the empire were Jews to whom Jewish Christians could take their gospel message.

Still a third factor was the presence in Palestine, even among many of the Jews, of a strong strain of Hellenistic culture or influence. Here is probably the greatest significance of the Hellenistic expansion into Asia which Alexander the Great so greatly furthered and promoted. That eastward expansion of Hellenistic life established in the Semitic world a bridgehead which, although not permanent, furnished a transition point from which a religious movement arising among Aramaic-speaking Jews could find its way into the entire Roman Empire.

Basic to this transfer was a fourth factor, the widespread use of the Greek language, not only by most Gentile residents of the Roman Empire, but also by great numbers of its Jews. Most of these members of the Dispersion spoke Greek. Indeed, so did many Jews who lived in Palestine, and from this group came some of the members of the very early Church. This tie of common language, present in

FIG. 77. Coliseum and Arch of Constantine, Rome. The Coliseum, begun in A. D. 75 by Vespasian and completed in A. D. 80 by Titus, seated 80,000 spectators around an arena 282 x 148 feet. In this arena gladiatorial combats took place and during times of persecution Christians were forced to fight with wild beasts. The Arch of Constantine was erected by the Senate and People of Rome in A. D. 315 to commemorate Constantine's victory over Maxentius three years earlier. Constantine was the first Christian emperor; his victory over Maxentius, in which he is said to have seen a vision of the cross, gave him mastery of the western part of the Roman Empire.

Palestine, led out into all parts of the empire and even beyond, and enabled missionaries to go everywhere without the necessity of acquiring a new tongue before presenting the Gospel message.

The fifth important factor which promoted the westward trend of Christianity was the Roman Empire itself. Even though the new faith appeared on the very frontier, it was still within the sphere of Roman control and contacts and could move into other parts of the empire without international complications.

Plate XVI shows four stages in the expansion which Christianity made in the first three centuries. It must be confessed that the information one needs to make such maps is often far from adequate. The student of the ancient Church frequently has the feeling that there must have been Christian groups in a certain place at a given time, yet he lacks the evidence to support the surmise. He is often attracted by general references which early Christian writers make to the spread of the faith, but such statements are too vague to give real help. At other times there are full and confident traditions; but they are late and open to grave suspicion, which prevents their use in serious study. Yet, with all the drawbacks which the character and incompleteness of our sources create, evidence suffices to enable us to trace the general lines of the development in a dependable way.

THE CHURCH BEFORE PAUL'S JOURNEYS

Because the Apostle Paul brought about so great an enlargement in the territory touched by Christianity, it is well to begin by seeing what the Church had done before he entered upon his systematic mission. In this earliest period, the center of the Christian movement was in Jerusalem. Galilee, which had been so prominent in the ministry of Jesus, is mentioned but once in this connection in The Acts (ch. 9:31) and played no controlling role in the Apostolic Church. From Jerusalem the Christian Church spread out into Judaea, Samaria, and the coastal plain, where Lydda, Joppa, and especially Caesarea (XVI:A, E-3) became centers remembered in Christian tradition (Acts, ch. 8). Churches arose in Phoenicia, evidently at first among Jews (Acts 11:19; 15:3). Tyre and Sidon (XVI:A, E-3) were apparently early Christian centers there (Acts 21:4; 27:3). Greek-speaking Jews driven from Jerusalem after the martyrdom of Stephen founded a most important Church in Syria at Antioch (XVI:A, E-3), where there were large numbers of Jews. Here a Church containing both Jews and Gentiles marked a new stage in the growth of the Church (Acts 11:20). At some very early date a group of believers was formed in Damascus (XVI:A, E-3). When Saul, i.e., Paul, went to his home city Tarsus (XVI:A, E-3) after his conversion, he preached and founded Churches there and elsewhere in Cilicia (Gal. 1:21, 23; Acts 15:41).

Although men of Cyprus (XVI:A, E-3) and Cyrene (XVI:A, D-3) are mentioned in this period of the Church (Acts 11:20), there is no reason to suppose that Churches already existed in these two areas. Neither does the mention of the conversion of the Ethiopian eunuch (Acts 8:38) warrant the conclusion that there was already a Christian movement in his country by A.D. 45. Moreover, there is no trustworthy witness that Christianity had reached Egypt (XVI:A, E-4) in this early period.

We may regard it as a well-supported conclusion, however, that a Christian group existed in Rome by A.D. 45. To be sure, the tradition, so widely circulated in later times, that the Apostle Peter founded the Roman Church must certainly be rejected. Yet other evidence more substantial must be heard. About A.D. 49 the Emperor Claudius expelled the Jews from Rome for rioting over "one Chrestus," and this is quite likely a reference to disputes in the synagogues over Christian claims that Jesus was the Christ. In the middle fifties, when Paul wrote a letter to the Church at Rome, he implied that it had been founded a considerable number of years before. These facts, combined with the fact that messages from all parts of the empire naturally traveled to Rome, warrant the view that by A.D. 45 there were Christians in the capital. Whether the Christian Gospel was brought there by Jews who had been present at Pentecost (Acts 2:10), or by immigrants who had been converted in the eastern parts of the empire, or by travelers or traders temporarily in the capital, cannot be determined.

The overwhelming proportion of the Christians in this earliest period were Jews, although a large proportion of the Jewish Christians were Greek-speaking. Groups of believers were found in Palestine, Phoenicia, Syria, Cilicia, and no doubt in Rome. As yet, however, they constituted an apparently negligible fraction of the empire's population.

AT THE CLOSE OF PAUL'S MINISTRY

The wide extension of the Church in the next fifteen years was due largely to the energetic and statesmanlike work of the Apostle Paul. He developed a strategy of following main trade routes and stopping in important cities, from which the Gospel could spread out into adjacent territory. His journeys may be traced on Plate XV. Here we need only survey the extent of his achievements.

Paul and Barnabas brought Cyprus into the Christian circle. In this island, as in other regions which Paul touched, there was no thorough approach to the entire population. What the apostles did was to establish centers in Salamis and Paphos (XVI:B, E-3), and probably in other points (Acts 13:5 f.). In Asia Minor Paul's work took place in southern and western regions. He probably founded Churches in the province of Pamphylia (XV, F-3; Acts 13:13 f.; 14:25). The Churches of Galatia (Gal. 1:2) were probably those in Antioch, Iconium, Lystra, and Derbe (XVI:B, E 2–3; see Acts, chs. 13;14); the alternative theory that they were farther north in Ancyra, Pessinus, and Tavium (XV, F 2-3) is less likely. But the greatest work of Paul in Asia Minor was in the Roman province of Asia. The chief center was Ephesus (XVI:B, D-3), from which the Gospel was carried out to other cities of the province, such as Colossae (XVI:B, D-2), Laodicea, and Hierapolis (XV, E-3; Col. 4:13). The existence of a Christian group at Troas (XVI:B, D-2) is also clearly attested, and one at Assos is implied (XV, E-3; Acts 20:6-13).

In Macedonia and Achaia Paul founded Churches in Philippi (XVI:B, D-2), Thessalonica (XVI:B, D-2), Beroea (XVI:B, D-2), Corinth (XVI:B, D-2), and likewise at Athens (XVI:B, D-2), although the extent of his success there was limited (cf. Acts 17:32-34). In minor places also, such as Amphipolis and Apollonia in Macedonia (XV, D-2), and Cenchreae in Achaia (XV, D-3), it is likely that groups of believers were formed. Paul's reference to saints in "all Achaia" (II Cor. 1:1) suggests a rather vigorous outreach of influence from his center at Corinth; indeed, such outreach may be assumed to have occurred from every center where the apostle made a stay of any length.

Since Paul says that he preached the Gospel "round about unto

Illyricum" (XVI:B, C 1-2; Rom. 15:19), it is clear that there were then Christians on the western border of Macedonia. Whether Paul himself went there or whether he sent assistants to preach in that region is not easy to decide, but the existence of Churches on the west coast of Macedonia and probably also of Achaia must be accepted. If, as seems probable, the personal references in the Pastoral Epistles are from Paul, he evidently extended his work to the island of Crete (XVI:B, D-3; Titus 1:5) and took thought for a further ministry there.

The fact that The Acts centers its attention so largely upon Paul may give us a somewhat misleading picture. That Paul's work was the outstanding and permanently significant missionary achievement of the period is indisputable, but he certainly was not the only Christian actively engaged in such pioneer mission preaching. Yet the names and accomplishments of these contemporaries of Paul are unknown, and we cannot be sure how far their labors extended. No clear evidence survives of early work east of Syria. Egypt still receives no mention; the reference to Apollos as an Alexandrian does not prove the presence of a Church in Alexandria (XVI:B, D-4), since it does not appear that he had a clear understanding of Christianity when he came to Ephesus (Acts 18:25).

In two regions, however, we find an extension of the Church beyond the area covered by Paul. One is in northern Asia Minor. Indeed, if The First Epistle of Peter dated from the lifetime of Paul it would be sufficient to prove that practically all of Asia Minor was sprinkled with Churches at that time; for it mentions Pontus (XVI:B, E-2), Galatia (XVI:B, E-2), Cappadocia (XVI:B, E-2), Asia (XVI:A, D-2), and Bithynia (XVI:B, D-E 2; cf. I Peter 1:1). But even if this epistle is to be dated somewhat later, as is assumed to be the case for the purposes of this map, it still suggests the possibility that there were Christian Churches in northern Asia Minor as early as Paul's time. Hints from other sources support this view. Early in the second century A.D., Pliny wrote to the Emperor Trajan (A.D. 98-117) about conditions in Bithynia, and his letter reflects a long-established and numerically prominent Church whose origin may well extend back into Paul's day. More important is the fact that Paul felt definitely led to avoid Mysia (XV, E-3) and Bithynia (Acts 16:7 f.). In view of his policy of not working where others had laid the foundation of the Church (Rom. 15:20), the most likely explanation of his action is that there were already Churches in these regions.

The other region where further expansion of Christianity can be documented in this time was in and near Puteoli in Italy (XVI:B, C-2). When Paul landed there as a prisoner he found "brethren" (Acts 28:14). It is probable that by this time there were Christians also in the neighboring city of Pompeii (XVI:B, C-2; cf. Fig. 76).

In this second period of the expansion of Christianity the almost exclusively Jewish character of the Church gave way to a mixed membership, a development which was largely effected and successfully defended by Paul. The Church spread through most of Asia Minor, established itself in Macedonia, Achaia, and Crete, and further extended its bounds in Italy. Outstanding centers were Jerusalem, Antioch in Syria, Ephesus, Corinth, and Rome. Numerically the Church still constituted a very small proportion of the inhabitants of the Roman Empire.

THE TIME OF IRENAEUS

For the period which follows Paul's journeys we lack the data to trace even in broad outline the continuous development of the Church. The next three decades are almost a complete blank. From about A.D. 95 on we get glimpses and episodes. A little help comes from First Clement, a letter of the Roman Church to Corinth about A.D. 96. Some time about A.D. 115 Ignatius journeyed from Antioch in Syria (XVI:C, E-3) through Asia Minor, where he met with Christian leaders and wrote letters, still extant, to Churches in the area. He was being taken in chains to Rome, where he anticipated martyrdom. Between one and two generations later Marcion came from Pontus, where he had already become a Christian, to Rome. Other Roman leaders are known; rivalry between Ephesus and Rome is attested; the Montanist movement arose in Phrygia (XVI:A, D-E 2); Polycarp was martyred in Smyrna (XVI:C, D-2); and clues to the life of the Church throughout the empire begin to appear. But a connected, comprehensive story cannot be written.

The situation changes, however, about A.D. 185, when we may date the chief writing of the influential Christian leader Irenaeus. He gives much information about the situation in the Church, and thereafter the evidence of a succession of writers and sources makes it possible to present a more detailed picture of the successive stages in the life of the Church.

When in the time of Irenaeus the information becomes more abundant, it is clear that the Church has made tremendous strides. Extension to the east has begun. There are Churches in Edessa (XVI:C, E-3), the first place where Christianity became the official religion, and in Melitene (XVI:C, E-2), where the faith found adherents among soldiers. Egypt now appears as an important center of Christian life and scholarship. The discovery in recent years of

FIG. 78. Air view of Dura-Europos, on the Euphrates River (XVI:D, F-3). This city, a Roman military outpost on the eastern frontier, was destroyed in or shortly after A. D. 258. Recent excavations have uncovered not only pagan temples, but also a Jewish synagogue, adorned with striking wall paintings of Biblical scenes; a Christian church, built by remodeling a private home and containing not only a room for worship but also a baptistry marked by distinctive wall paintings; and a parchment sheet of Tatian's *Diatessaron* in Greek, clear proof of the presence of Greek-speaking Christians in Dura in the first half of the third century.

FIG. 79. Church of the Holy Sepulcher, Jerusalem. Built on the traditional site of the crucifixion and burial of Jesus. Constantine erected the first Christian church here in the early fourth century. After repeated destructions and rebuildings, essentially the present form appeared after the destructive fire of 1808. The present church is architecturally unsatisfying and structurally weak. Its parts are partitioned among various Christian groups, chiefly the Armenian, Greek Orthodox, and Roman Catholic groups.

Christian papyri dating from the early second century A.D. proves that Egyptian Christianity was not then confined to Alexandria (XVI:C, D-4) and the section near the sea, but extended up the Nile into the dry regions where papyri have been preserved in the sand through the centuries. In Cyrenaica, also, there were Christians in the region about Cyrene (XVI:B, D-3), although the sources mention other cities without including Cyrene itself. Farther west in Africa, the area about Carthage (XVI:C, B-2) was proving to be a fruitful field for Christian evangelism. Asia Minor was dotted with Christian centers. Macedonia and Achaia were likewise largely included in the sphere of Christian influence. A few cities of Thrace are known to have had Churches. North of Macedonia, in Dalmatia on the Adriatic Sea, the faith was beginning to take root. Beginnings at Syracuse (XVI:C, C-3), and further extension throughout Italy, are to be noted.

It is difficult to show on the map the evidence of Early Church writers concerning Christian advances in some portions of the empire. They mention the existence of Churches in a province, but fail to tell in what cities Christian missionaries have successfully preached. This is in part true of their references to the region of Gaul (modern France: XVI:C, A-B 1). It is definitely known that there were Christian Churches in Lyons and Vienne (XVI:C, B-1); for the story of persecutions there, about A.D. 177, makes the fact clear, and suggests that farther south in Gaul there were probably Churches. The mention of Churches in the Rhine River valley, however, is not explicit as to location; the most likely centers in that region may well be Cologne and Mainz (XVI:C, C-5). Christians are mentioned in Spain only a few years after the time of Irenaeus, and it may be taken as certain that Christian centers were found there by A.D. 185. The exact location of such centers is uncertain, but the cities of Astorga (XVI:C, A-1), Leon (XVI:C, A-1), Merida (XVI:C, A-2), and Saragossa (XVI:C, A-1) appear to be the most likely choices.

The early history of Christianity in Britain is obscure. It is entirely possible that there were Churches in the southeast portion of Britain in the latter part of the second century, but it is not possible to be certain of this.

Thus by the close of the third period which our survey covers the Church was established in many centers over the Roman Empire and had also crossed the eastern border. The predominantly Gentile character of the Church had long been a fact, and the center of leadership had moved westward. Jerusalem, rebuilt by the Romans as a Gentile city and renamed Aelia Capitolina, had dropped from its commanding role shortly after Paul's ministry. Antioch in Syria was not so dominant as in Paul's day. Alexandria, Ephesus, and Rome were outstanding centers. The remarkable geographical extension of the Church, however, must not obscure the fact that as yet the Christian group constituted but a small portion of the total population. It was a vigorous minority movement.

THE AGE OF CONSTANTINE

The fourth period witnessed both intensive and extensive advance of Christianity. For this period the evidence is gratifyingly full and explicit. Such documents as the lists of bishops who attended the Council of Arles (XVI:D, B-1) in A.D. 314 and the Council of Nicaea (XVI:D, D-2) in A.D. 325 provide clear proof that the Christian movement was not confined to key cities of provinces, but had taken root in most of the important centers of population in every portion of the empire. The cities shown on Plate XVI:D are only part of those in which it is known that Christian bishops then had their residence, but they are sufficient to give an impression of the intensive spread of Christianity in the Roman Empire. Practically every province is seen to be well covered with Churches. In Mauretania (XIII, A-B 2), in the provinces along the River Danube (XVI:D, C-D 1-2), in western Gaul and in England (see XVI:D, Inset) there is now clear evidence of a firmly established Christian Church.

In addition to the intensive growth of the Church in regions previously reached by Christian missionaries, there was also in this period a considerable geographical expansion into new areas, particularly in the east. Evidence appears of Christians in Arabia, for example at Aila (XVI:D, E-4). There were Churches in Mesopotamia, Babylonia, and even farther east, beyond the Tigris (XVI:D, F-3), on the borders of Persia. Indeed, suggestions of Christian centers as far east as Bactria and India are not lacking, although it is extremely difficult to know what to make of the traditions concerning these regions. Part at least of the eastward outreach was connected with the Greek-speaking Church, as has been shown by the discovery at Dura-Europos (XVI:D, F-3; Fig. 78), on the Euphrates River, of a Christian chapel and a sheet of Tatian's *Diatessaron* in Greek. Farther north, Armenia (XVI:D, F-2) had become the first country of any size to become officially Christian. On the north side of Armenia, between the southern part of the Black and Caspian Seas, the region of Georgia may have been the scene of missionary work by the time of Constantine. In the region north and west of the Black Sea the Goths had had contact with Christianity, but the exact location and number of Christian groups in that area is unknown.

By the time of Constantine (A.D. 306-337), therefore, the Christian Church had established itself throughout most of the Roman Empire and was reaching out far beyond its eastern borders. The greater number of Christians undoubtedly lived within the empire, where Greek and to a lesser degree Latin were the languages used by Christians. In the eastern extension of the Church the use of Syriac and other tongues was involved, although, as stated, Greek was used even in regions where other tongues were widely employed. The Church was of course by then overwhelmingly Gentile in composition. It was particularly strong in Italy, North Africa, Asia Minor, and Egypt.

It is worthy of note that up to this time the Church had been largely an urban movement. In spite of the fact that the ministry of Jesus was centered in villages and open country, the Church from its early days at Jerusalem took to the cities and preserved its urban emphasis throughout the period of our study.

It should also be held in mind that Christianity was still a minority movement at the close of our survey. Though Churches had been established throughout a wide area, a numerical majority had been attained in few places. With the conversion of Constantine, however, there arose a new situation, in which the former governmental attitude of tolerance or persecution gave way to active support. Thus encouraged, the Church was able in the next two centuries to bring a majority of the residents of the empire into the Christian fellowship.

THE HISTORY OF JERUSALEM

Plate XVII

JERUSALEM is by far the most important city in the Bible. In it was the Temple, the focal point of Israelite and Jewish religious life and aspiration. Here David and Solomon, Isaiah and Jeremiah, Ezra and Nehemiah, lived and labored. Here too a portion of the ministry of Jesus took place; here he was crucified and raised up, and here the Christian Church was founded. During the seventh century A.D. Jerusalem was conquered by the Mohammedans and became, next to Mecca and Medina in Arabia, the most important holy place of the Moslem world. To Jews, Christians, and Mohammedans, therefore, it is in a special way the "holy city" (cf. Rev. 21:2, 24).

THE TOPOGRAPHY OF JERUSALEM

The site of Jerusalem has never been forgotten. In different periods its limits have varied, but one spot has remained constant. Unbroken tradition fixes the sacred area of the First or Solomonic Temple, the Second Temple, and the Herodian Temple of Jesus' day on the site now called the *Haram esh-Sherîf* (Plate XVII:D, D-E 4-5). In Old Testament times the city proper lay chiefly south of this area. In the New Testament period it lay largely west and north.

Jerusalem is located on the central ridge of the hill country, 33 miles east of the Mediterranean and 14 miles west of the northern tip of the Dead Sea. Its highest part is 2,550 feet above sea level. To the east is the Mount of Olives, separated from the city by the Kidron Valley (or "The Brook," II Chron. 32:4). The Valley of Hinnom (this is the original meaning of the New Testament word Gehenna) lies south and west; during the period of the Judges this valley formed the boundary between the tribes of Judah and Benjamin (Josh. 15:8; 18:16; see Plate VI). Between these two main valleys stood a plateau connected with the central ridge on the north. A smaller north-south valley, which Josephus calls the Tyropoeon (i.e., valley of "cheese-makers") divides the plateau into two parts. Of these the Western Hill is larger than the Eastern, and also higher. Hence it was later called the Upper City (XVII: B-C, C 5-6).

Two springs were the main sources of the early city's water supply. The chief one, in the Kidron Valley, was called the Gihon (XVII:A, E-5). Another, just below the juncture of the Kidron and Hinnom Valleys, was called En-rogel (XVII:A, E-7). It may also be the Dragon's (or Jackal's, R.V. and R.S.V.) Well of Neh. 2:13.

The location of the water supply determined that the earliest settlements should be located on the Eastern Hill, south of the Temple area and above the Gihon spring. In ancient times this hill was called, in its northern part at least, Ophel (XVII:A, D-E 5; Micah 4:8, R.V. marg.; II Chron. 27:3; 33:14; Neh. 3:26 f.; 11:21). This was also the site of the City of David, or Zion, and of the Jebusite city before it. This part of the Eastern Hill is not formidable in appearance, and since the fourth century A.D. tradition has associated Zion with the southern part of the Western Hill, where guides still show tourists the traditional Tomb of David (XVII:D, C-6). Archaeological investigation, however, has proved that Zion was south of the Temple area, as indeed it had to be in order to be near its water supply. In Old Testament times it was higher than at present; the Hasmonaeans in the second century B.C. removed the top of the Eastern Hill in order that it might not rival the Temple in height. By the time of Jesus the city had spread north and west; because of the use of aqueducts and cisterns, the Gihon spring was no longer the chief source of water (see Fig. 62). It is known that Pontius Pilate, Roman governor of Judaea from A.D. 26 to 36, built or repaired an aqueduct into the city and paid for the work with funds from the Temple treasury. This aqueduct may have run along the general line of the later Lower Aqueduct shown on Plate XVII: D, B-D 4-7.

JERUSALEM DURING THE OLD TESTAMENT PERIOD

Little is known of the history of Jerusalem before the fourteenth century B.C. The earliest archaeological remains on Ophel date from c. 3000 B.C. The name "Jerusalem" first occurs in Egyptian texts dating about 1900 B.C. In the fourteenth and thirteenth centuries B.C., before and during the conquest, the city was one of the main Canaanite city-states (see pp. 34, 44) of southern Palestine, with a mixed population (cf. Ezek. 16:3).

Shortly after 1000 B.C., the city was captured by David, who made it his capital (II Sam. 5:6 ff.; I Chron. 11:4, 5). As his personal property, it was now named the City of David. Plate XVII:A shows its approximate size. It was a small but powerfully fortified "stronghold" (II Sam. 5:7, 9). At its northern end was the Millo, apparently a raised platform on which the palace-citadel of David was erected. This palace, like that of Solomon, was built for David by Phoenician artisans of Hiram of Tyre (II Sam. 5:11).

No certain trace of Davidic building has been recovered. A portion of the Jebusite city wall and one of the gates have been excavated. The wall was exceedingly strong, being twenty-seven feet in width, and so well built that it was repaired and used as the main fortification of the City of David. A tower and revetment added to this wall above the Gihon spring have been excavated; they were probably built by David or Solomon.

Solomon found the City of David too small. He enlarged the city to the north and erected the Temple, his palace, and administrative buildings in the area of the present *Ḥaram*. Near the center of this area today the beautiful "Dome of the Rock" (Fig. 81) covers an old sacred rock on which the altar of burnt offering once stood. The Temple itself was directly west of this point, and the court surrounding it (the Inner Court of I Kings 6:36 and the Upper Court of Jer. 36:10) probably had the approximate extent of the large platform on which the "Dome of the Rock" now stands. Directly south of the Temple, probably on a lower terraced level, were the palace of the king and that of his queen, Pharaoh's daughter. South of the palace were other administrative structures. Solomon thus built a separate governmental quarter in a special walled-in court (the Outer or Great Court; cf. I Kings 7:12).

While the Canaanites still controlled Jerusalem, they dug a rock

FIG. 80. Citadel and city wall, Jerusalem. On the left, the western exterior of the Citadel. On the right is seen the city wall running to the southwest corner of Jerusalem. The Citadel is on the site of Herod's Palace.

tunnel from near the top of the hill down to the Gihon, to give protection to those who drew water. Perhaps David's men gained access to the city by going up this watercourse, though it is doubtful that the Hebrew of II Sam. 5:8 contains any mention of it. In any event, at some later date, an aqueduct (cf. Isa. 7:3) was constructed along the edge of the hill from the Gihon to the Old or Lower Pool (XVII:A, D-E 5-6). Hezekiah abandoned these older waterworks and built the Siloam Tunnel, to carry the water of the Gihon to the new Upper Pool or Pool of Siloam or Shiloah (Neh. 3:15 has Shelah; XVII:A, D-6). He probably then built an outer wall at the south, enclosing the new pool so that water would be available in case of siege (XVII:A, D-6; II Chron. 32:4, 5, 30; Isa. 22:9 ff.; II Kings 20:20).

Various Old Testament passages seem to distinguish between the city of Jerusalem as a whole and the City of David. Even in Solomon's day, the city was probably spreading to the Western Hill. In fact, the First North Wall mentioned by Josephus (first century A.D.; see below) was perhaps built in part by Solomon. In the time of Manasseh and Josiah (seventh century B.C.), we first hear of the *Mishneh* or Second Quarter, in which were located the Fish Gate and the house of Huldah the prophetess (Zeph. 1:10; II Kings 22:14, R.V.); it was probably west or northwest of the Temple area. We are unable, however, to sketch the westward limits of Jerusalem at that time.

After North Israel fell, in 721 B.C., Jerusalem became increasingly important as the religious center and the symbol of the people's unity. Its capture and devastation by Nebuchadnezzar in 587 B.C. was a severe blow. Under Zerubbabel's leadership a new but smaller Temple was completed in 516 B.C., and under Nehemiah's direction the city fortifications were rebuilt (Ezra, chs. 5; 6; Neh., chs. 2 ff.).

For the next century Jerusalem was small and politically unimportant, although involved in trouble with the Persians which led to stern reprisals or possibly to actual capture and destruction. Two important developments, however, were in process. One was the increase in the proportion of Jewish population located outside of Palestine. Yet Judaism still centered in Jerusalem, and to this focal point its life flowed back in pilgrimages and gifts.

The other development was the increase of Greek influence in Palestine. Contacts and trade between Palestine and lands of Greek culture existed over a century before Alexander the Great appeared in 332 B.C. Under his successors, however, the program of achieving political unity by promoting cultural unity on a Hellenistic basis was purposefully developed. By the first half of the second century B.C. Greek dress, games, and customs were finding favor in Jerusalem. Most Jews, then as always, rejected such practices, yet athletic exercises were carried on in the Tyropoeon Valley, and some priests adopted Hellenistic ways.

When, therefore, in 168 B.C., Antiochus Epiphanes, determined to stamp out the Jewish religion, profaned the Temple and stopped the sacrifices, he must have counted on considerable support among the Jews. Nor did the Maccabean revolt at first appear a serious threat to his plans. He held not only the Temple area, but also the Acra or Citadel, a fortress probably located just south of the Temple precincts (XVII:C, D-5). After three years the Maccabeans regained control of the Temple and rededicated it, an occasion still recalled by Jews in December at the Feast of Dedication (see John 10:22 f.). The Maccabeans also built a fortress called Baris on a strategic rock elevation at the northwest corner of the Temple area. Not until some time after 142 B.C., however, did they expel the Syrians from the Acra. They then destroyed that citadel and cut down the top of the hill so that it no longer threatened the Temple.

The existence of a separate, distinct Judaism was thus assured, and the importance of Jerusalem preserved. But the later Maccabees, also called Hasmonaeans, became as devoted to Hellenistic ways as had been the Syrians. One building of this period which was still in use in Jesus' day was the Palace of the Hasmonaeans, located on the northeast brow of the Western Hill (XVII:B, D-5). The coming of Roman rule in 63 B.C., therefore, marked no decisive cultural break, although in the decades just before and after this date the city was subjected to several damaging sieges which resulted from the unsettled political conditions. When Rome made Herod the Great king in 40 B.C., he followed the Roman pattern of promoting Hellenistic influence.

JERUSALEM IN HEROD'S DAY

Herod carried out extensive building projects in numerous places, but particularly in Jerusalem. He must have repaired the city walls, which Pompey had breached a few years before. The characteristic masonry of this period can still be seen in many places, as, for example, at the Wailing Wall (XVII:D, D 4-5; see Fig. 71).

At the northwest corner of the Western Hill, Herod built a fortified palace, with gardens, pools, and porticoes (XVII:B, B-C 5). On the north, where gates gave entrance and attacks were most to be feared, Herod built three great towers: Hippicus, Phasael, and Mariamme, named in honor of a friend, a brother, and Herod's favorite wife. Recent excavations show that the tower Phasael was located where the Tower of David now stands (XVII:D, C-5). Hippicus must have stood slightly southwest, Mariamme a little east of Phasael. All three were built into the old city wall.

Herod rebuilt the Baris and renamed it Antonia (XVII:B, D 3-4). At each of its corners was a tower. Two stairways or bridges connected it with the Temple porticoes, to enable its garrison to watch and control the Temple courts. There must have been some space between the porticoes and Antonia, for in the Jewish revolt the Jews isolated the Temple by cutting away the stairs, and Josephus describes fighting between the Temple and Antonia.

Herod erected many other buildings in Jerusalem—a theater, amphitheater, hippodrome, et cetera—but his most ambitious project was the rebuilding of the Temple. He used specially trained priests in the building work and so executed the plan that the worship of the Temple was not interrupted. The rebuilding of the sanctuary proper, begun in 20-19 B.C., was completed in eighteen months, but the complete reconstruction of the entire plan Herod did not live to achieve. Indeed, it was not completed until A.D. 64. For this larger plan Herod prepared a larger Temple area. By the use of massive retaining walls on the slopes of the Temple Hill he extended the area of the outer court, although probably not so far northward as it now reaches.

The main parts of the Temple area are indicated on Plate XVII:B. It had at least eight gates: four on the west, two on the south, and one each on east and north. Around the outer court ran porticoes. The Royal Porch, on the south, was wider than the others. On the east was Solomon's Porch. Inside these porticoes was the Court of the Gentiles, the only court which Gentiles could enter. Signs in Greek at the gates leading to the inner courts warned Gentiles not to go farther. Two such notices have been discovered; they read:

> No foreigner is allowed within the balustrade and embankment about the sanctuary. Whoever is caught [violating this rule] will be personally responsible for his ensuing death.

On the east side of the inner structure steps led up to the main gate of entrance; probably this was the Beautiful Gate (cf. Acts 3:2, 10). Within was the Court of the Women, the last court which Jewish women could enter. Here were collection boxes into which gifts were put (Mark 12:41). The men of Israel could go up the steps into the Court of Israel, where they could watch the sacrifices being offered on the altar of burnt offering in the center of the Court of the Priests. West of the altar, steps led up into an ornamental porch, through which ministering priests entered the Holy Place, a room 30 x 60 feet. West of this room, behind a veil, was the Most Holy Place, 30 x 30 feet, into which the high priest entered on the Day of Atonement. Around the sides of the sanctuary were storerooms and treasuries. Special chambers for the priests were located at appropriate places in the Temple area, especially in the northern part. Meetings of religious leaders were held on occasion in the Council Chamber just west of the Temple area (XVII:B, D-4), and a viaduct across the Tyropoeon Valley gave easy access to the Upper City (XVII:B, D-5).

JESUS IN JERUSALEM

Jerusalem was the scene of comparatively little of Jesus' ministry, but his dramatic and momentous experiences there merit careful attention. His visit to Jerusalem when twelve years of age (Luke 2:42) recalls the fact that great throngs went there for the three great festivals of the Jewish year. It also reminds us that pilgrimages and religious devotion gave Jerusalem much of its economic support.

Of places mentioned in the Gospels, the Pool of Siloam is certainly known (XVII:B, D-6). The Pool of Bethesda is probably not the Pool of Israel (XVII:D, D-E 3) or the Virgin's Spring (Gihon) or the Pool of Siloam, but the pool, now many feet below the surface, near the present Church of St. Anne (XVII:B, D-3). Solomon's Porch, where Jesus walked in December for protection from wintry winds (John 10:23), was the east portico.

In the triumphal entry Jesus used a gate located approximately where the walled-up Golden Gate now stands (XVII:D, E-4). When he cleansed the Temple he drove traders and money-changers from the Court of the Gentiles; only this part of the Temple area was a "house of prayer for all the nations" (Mark 11:17). The place of the Last Supper is not certainly known; strong ancient tradition fixes the site at the modern Coenaculum (XVII:D, C-6). The modern Grotto of the Agony and the Gethsemane Church (XVII:D, E 3-4) show approximately where Jesus withdrew for prayer on his last night (Mark 14: 26, 32). Dubious tradition locates the house of Caiaphas just north of the Coenaculum (XVII:D, C-6).

The Praetorium where Jesus stood before Pilate was probably in the Palace of Herod rather than in the barracks at Antonia. If this is so, the traditional Via Dolorosa (XVII:D, C-D 3-4) cannot have been the path from Pilate's residence to the crucifixion. To take Jesus to Herod Antipas (Luke 23:7), then, the guard would have taken Jesus from the Palace of Herod to the Palace of the Hasmonaeans.

The traditional site of the crucifixion, continuously identified as such since the time of Constantine (C.A.D. 325), is where the Church of the Holy Sepulcher now stands (XVII:D, C-4). A recent rival claim for a hillock called Gordon's Calvary (XVII:D, C-3) has little strength, and the "Garden Tomb" near by, in which some hold that Jesus was buried, probably dates several centuries later than the first.

THE FIRST-CENTURY WALLS

Discussion of the site of the crucifixion requires a study of the walls of first-century Jerusalem. On the south, the wall ran approximately as seen on Plate XVII:C. Later, however, the south wall, as excavations show, ran northeast to the Temple area along the line JKLMN, leaving the southern Tyropoeon and the ancient City of David outside the wall. Another later course followed much the line of the modern wall.

On the north were at least four ancient walls. The earliest ran eastward from the Palace of Herod to the Temple area. The second north wall is discussed below. Herod Agrippa I began a third wall about A.D. 42; it enclosed the hill Bezetha and other sections north of the second wall. This third wall was long thought identical in course with the present north wall A century ago, however, traces of it were found much farther north, and recently nearly 800 yards of it have been discovered. The rest of its course can be conjectured by noting the elevation of the land. The tower of Psephinus, at its northwest corner, probably lay on the slight ridge running to the northwest.

Ancient remains along the course of the present north wall are proved by recent soundings to be from a wall built by Hadrian about A.D. 135. Before that date there was no wall along this line.

The second north wall began at the Gate Gennath, which was probably between the towers Hippicus and Phasael, encircled a section north of the first wall, and ended at Antonia. Four courses for it have been suggested. The circular course indicated by the letters ABCDP is unlikely; some evidence indicates this wall ran west, not north, from Antonia. The course AEFH encloses too small an area, and places the Gate Gennath too far east. Prevailing tradition favors the course AEFGP. Archaeological remains of walls, pavements, and cisterns give considerable support to this view. No other course proposed has such strong archaeological support. This, however, is a queer course for a city wall. Walls were built for defense; yet the middle section of the course AEFGP runs on comparatively low ground. Moreover, the traditional view assumes that the wall left a hillock, Golgotha, just outside. Military judgment would have dictated the inclusion of such a hillock within the wall. No certain conclusion seems possible. The wall may have followed the course AEFGP, or it may have run west from E and then south to G, in which case the traditional site of Golgotha is not authentic and the place of the crucifixion and burial of Jesus is unknown.

EARLY CHRISTIAN JERUSALEM

Apostolic Christianity was closely linked with Jerusalem and the Temple. The disciples met in Solomon's Porch; Peter and John went up to the Temple at the hour of prayer; they healed the lame man at the Beautiful Gate; even Paul the Apostle to the Gentiles was fulfilling a vow in the Temple when his enemies started a riot, dragged him out of the inner court, and caused the Roman guards to rush down from the Tower of Antonia and arrest him. From the stairs leading to the tower he addressed the crowd. Later he was confined in Antonia until sent to Caesarea. It was not until the Jewish revolt began in A.D. 66 that the Christian group, prompted by an oracle, left the city and moved to Pella, east of the Jordan. In A.D. 70 Jerusalem with its Temple was destroyed by the Romans. It was later rebuilt as a pagan city by the Romans, who renamed it Aelia Capitolina.

The Christian emperor Constantine gave the city new prestige as a Christian center and began the building of great churches to commemorate events in the life of Christ. From the seventh century to the First World War, with a few interludes, such as the Crusades, when Palestine was held by Christian armies, Jerusalem was under Mohammedan rulers; a mosque stood, as one still does, on the Temple site (Fig. 81). The Kingdom of Jordan now controls the walled city; the State of Israel controls the west and northwest suburbs.

FIG. 81. Dome of the Rock, Jerusalem. The sacred rock under the dome is probably the site of the ancient Jewish altar of burnt offering. The beautiful octagonal structure, built late in the seventh century, stands on a raised platform some ten feet above the surrounding area.

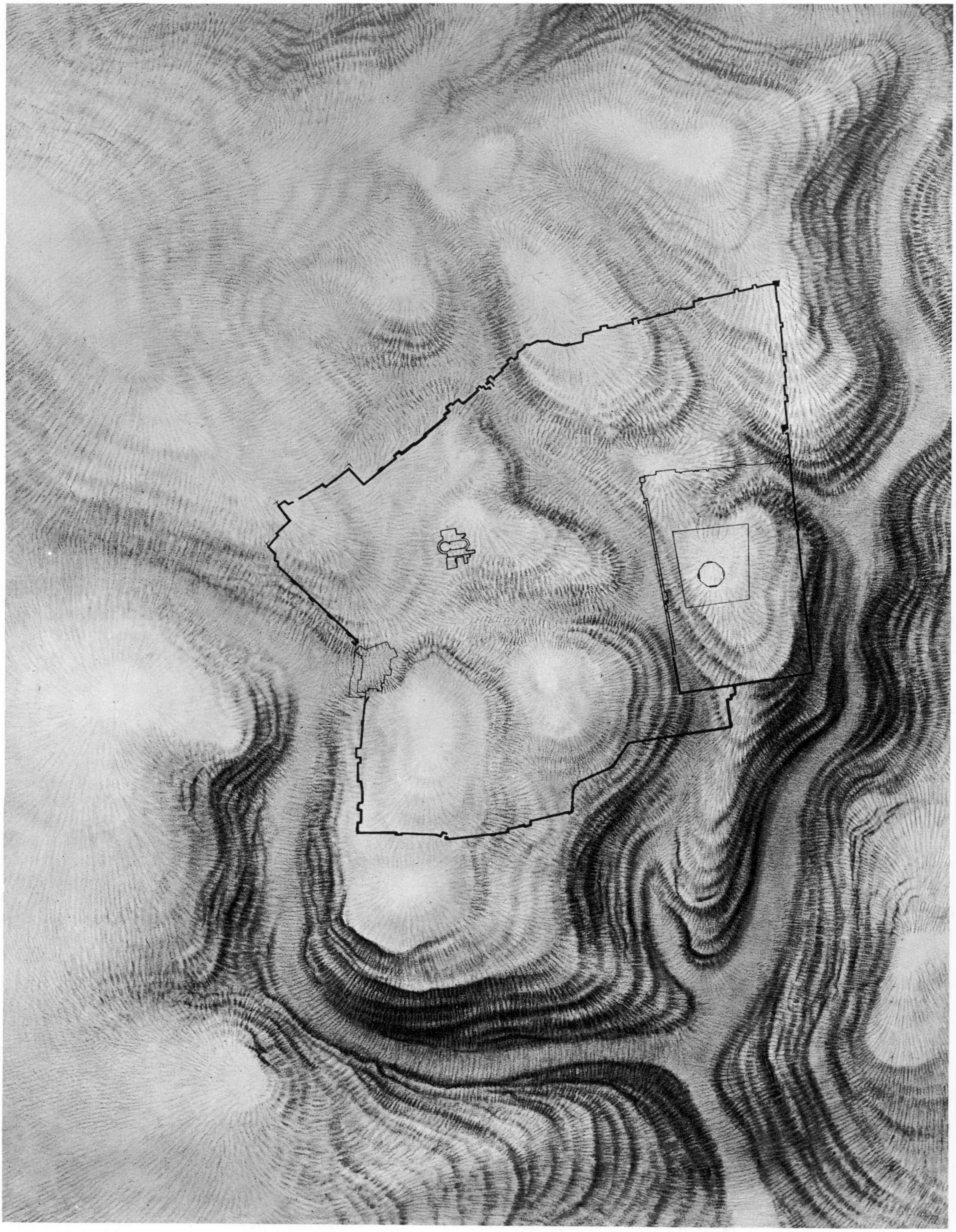

FIG. 82. The relief of ancient Jerusalem as reconstructed for this volume. By comparing it with the maps on Plate XVII, the main features can be quickly identified. Note especially the Hinnom and Kidron valleys which surround the site except on its northern side, and the Tyropoeon Valley which cut the city in two in Jesus' day, but which through the centuries has gradually filled. The ancient city of Old Testament times was largely confined to the spur on the right of the Tyropoeon; the existence of the Gihon spring at its foot and the necessity of fortifying a relatively confined area dictated the choice of this hill. In New Testament times, however, few people inhabited the old city. Most of the population lived on the western (left) hill and to the west of the Temple area. The whole was strongly fortified, especially at the weakest point topographically, where the first and second walls joined and where Herod the Great erected three remarkable towers.

A

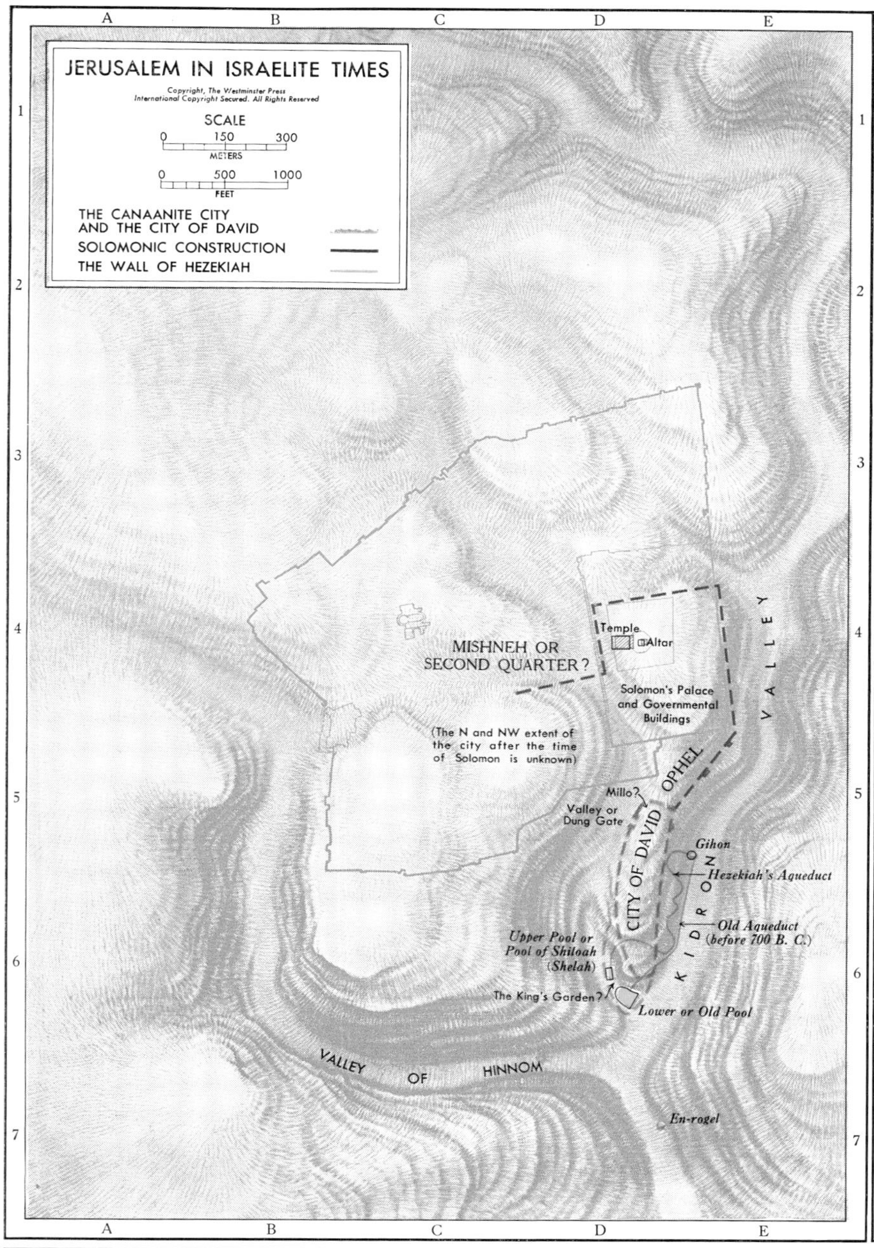
JERUSALEM IN ISRAELITE TIMES
Copyright, The Westminster Press
International Copyright Secured. All Rights Reserved
SCALE
0 150 300
METERS
0 500 1000
FEET
THE CANAANITE CITY AND THE CITY OF DAVID
SOLOMONIC CONSTRUCTION
THE WALL OF HEZEKIAH
MISHNEH OR SECOND QUARTER?
Temple
Altar
Solomon's Palace and Governmental Buildings
(The N and NW extent of the city after the time of Solomon is unknown)
OPHEL
Millo?
Valley or Dung Gate
CITY OF DAVID
Gihon
Hezekiah's Aqueduct
KIDRON
VALLEY
Old Aqueduct (before 700 B. C.)
Upper Pool or Pool of Shiloah (Shelah)
The King's Garden?
Lower or Old Pool
VALLEY OF HINNOM
En-rogel

B

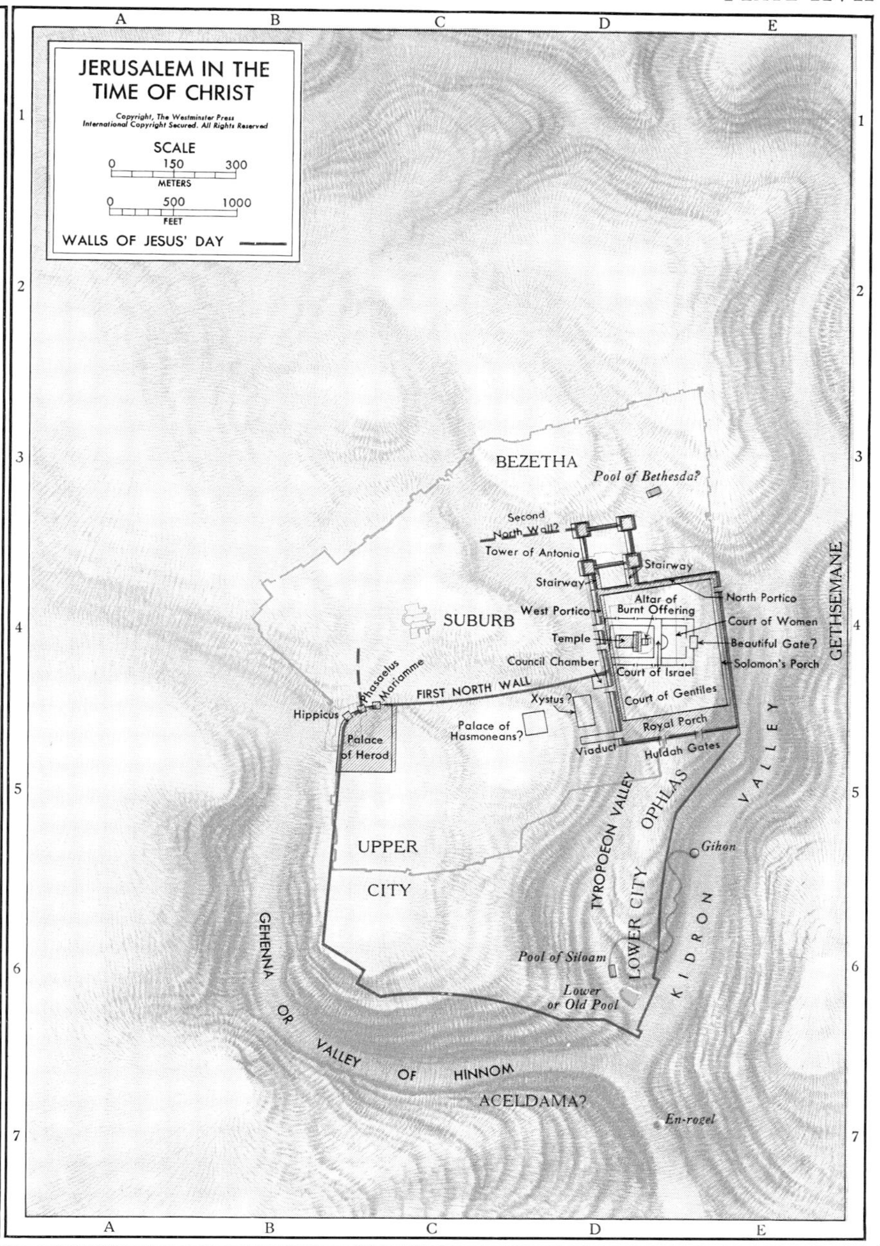
JERUSALEM IN THE TIME OF CHRIST
Copyright, The Westminster Press
International Copyright Secured. All Rights Reserved
SCALE
0 150 300
METERS
0 500 1000
FEET
WALLS OF JESUS' DAY
BEZETHA
Pool of Bethesda?
Second North Wall?
Tower of Antonia
Stairway
Stairway
North Portico
Altar of Burnt Offering
Court of Women
West Portico
SUBURB
Temple
Beautiful Gate?
Council Chamber
Solomon's Porch
Court of Israel
GETHSEMANE
Phasaelus
Mariamme
FIRST NORTH WALL
Court of Gentiles
Hippicus
Xystus?
Palace of Hasmoneans?
Royal Porch
Palace of Herod
Viaduct
Huldah Gates
UPPER CITY
TYROPOEON VALLEY
OPHLAS
LOWER CITY
Gihon
KIDRON
VALLEY
GEHENNA OR VALLEY OF HINNOM
Pool of Siloam
Lower or Old Pool
ACELDAMA?
En-rogel

C

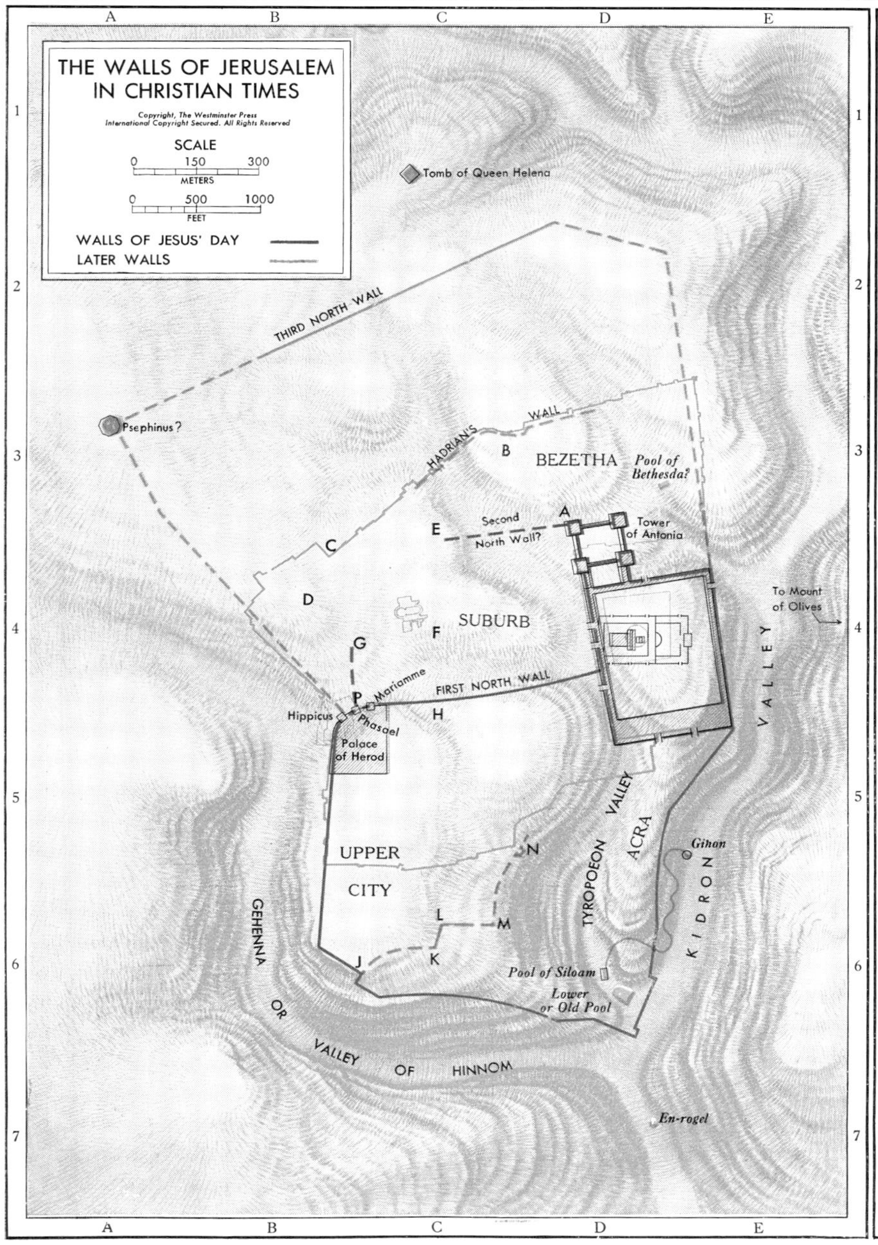
THE WALLS OF JERUSALEM IN CHRISTIAN TIMES
Copyright, The Westminster Press
International Copyright Secured. All Rights Reserved
SCALE
0 150 300
METERS
0 500 1000
FEET
WALLS OF JESUS' DAY
LATER WALLS
Tomb of Queen Helena
THIRD NORTH WALL
Psephinus?
HADRIAN'S WALL
B
BEZETHA
Pool of Bethesda?
C
E
Second North Wall?
A
Tower of Antonia
D
To Mount of Olives
G
F
SUBURB
P
Mariamme
FIRST NORTH WALL
Hippicus
Phasael
H
Palace of Herod
VALLEY
UPPER CITY
N
TYROPOEON VALLEY
ACRA
Gihon
KIDRON
L
M
J
K
Pool of Siloam
Lower or Old Pool
GEHENNA OR VALLEY OF HINNOM
En-rogel

D

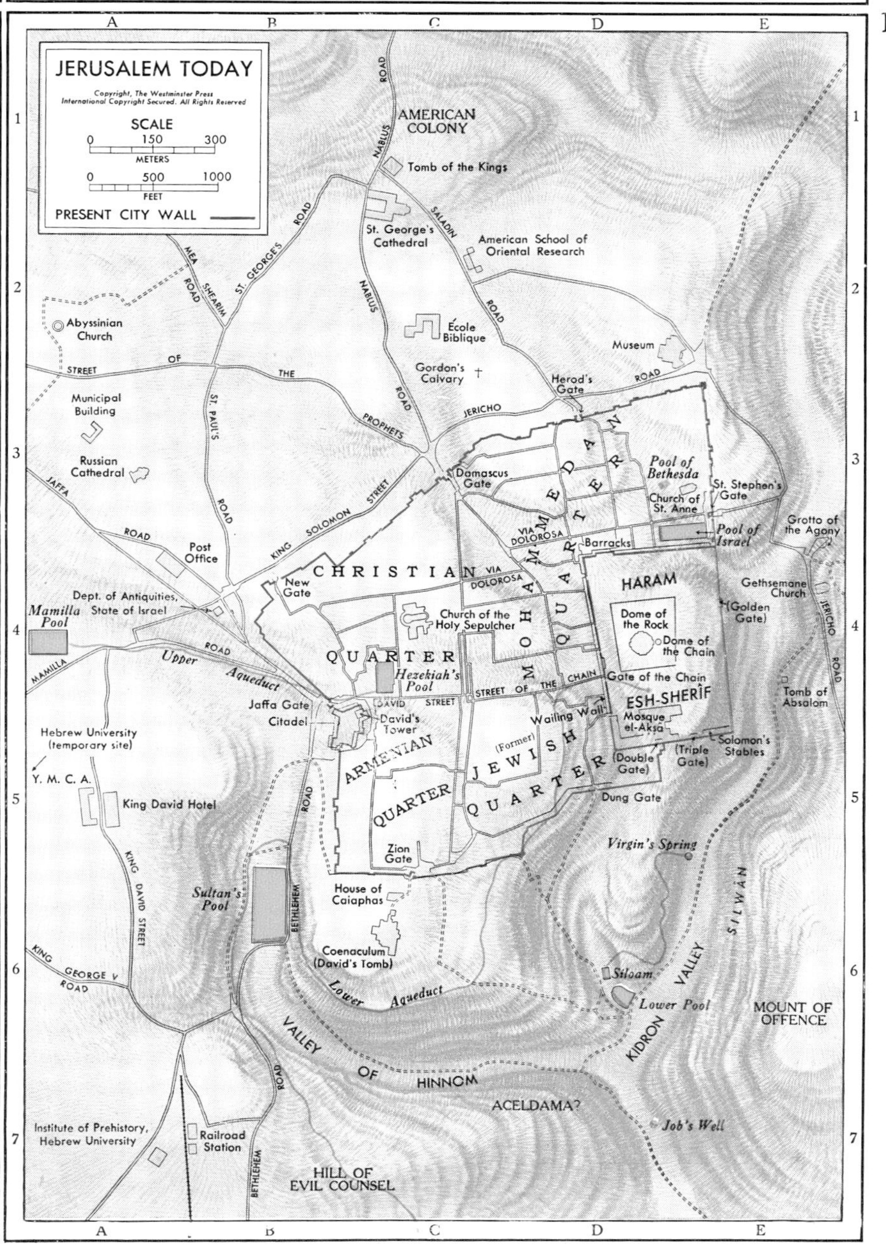
JERUSALEM TODAY
Copyright, The Westminster Press
International Copyright Secured. All Rights Reserved
SCALE
0 150 300
METERS
0 500 1000
FEET
PRESENT CITY WALL
AMERICAN COLONY
Tomb of the Kings
NABLUS ROAD
St. George's Cathedral
SALADIN
American School of Oriental Research
MEA SHEARIM ROAD
ST. GEORGE'S ROAD
Abyssinian Church
École Biblique
STREET OF THE PROPHETS
Gordon's Calvary
Museum
Herod's Gate
JERICHO ROAD
Municipal Building
ST. PAUL'S ROAD
Russian Cathedral
Damascus Gate
Pool of Bethesda
St. Stephen's Gate
JAFFA ROAD
KING SOLOMON STREET
Church of St. Anne
Pool of Israel
Grotto of the Agony
Post Office
VIA DOLOROSA
Barracks
CHRISTIAN QUARTER
MOHAMMEDAN QUARTER
HARAM
New Gate
Gethsemane Church
Dept. of Antiquities, State of Israel
Church of the Holy Sepulcher
Dome of the Rock
(Golden Gate)
Mamilla Pool
Dome of the Chain
Upper Aqueduct
Hezekiah's Pool
Gate of the Chain
MAMILLA ROAD
Jaffa Gate
Citadel
David's Tower
DAVID STREET
STREET OF THE CHAIN
Wailing Wall
ESH-SHERIF
Tomb of Absalom
Hebrew University (temporary site)
ARMENIAN QUARTER
(Former) JEWISH QUARTER
Mosque el-Aksa
Solomon's Stables
(Double Gate)
(Triple Gate)
Y. M. C. A.
King David Hotel
Dung Gate
Zion Gate
Virgin's Spring
KING DAVID STREET
Sultan's Pool
House of Caiaphas
BETHLEHEM ROAD
Coenaculum (David's Tomb)
SILWAN
KING GEORGE V ROAD
Lower Aqueduct
Siloam
KIDRON VALLEY
Lower Pool
MOUNT OF OFFENCE
VALLEY OF HINNOM
ACELDAMA?
Job's Well
Institute of Prehistory, Hebrew University
Railroad Station
HILL OF EVIL COUNSEL

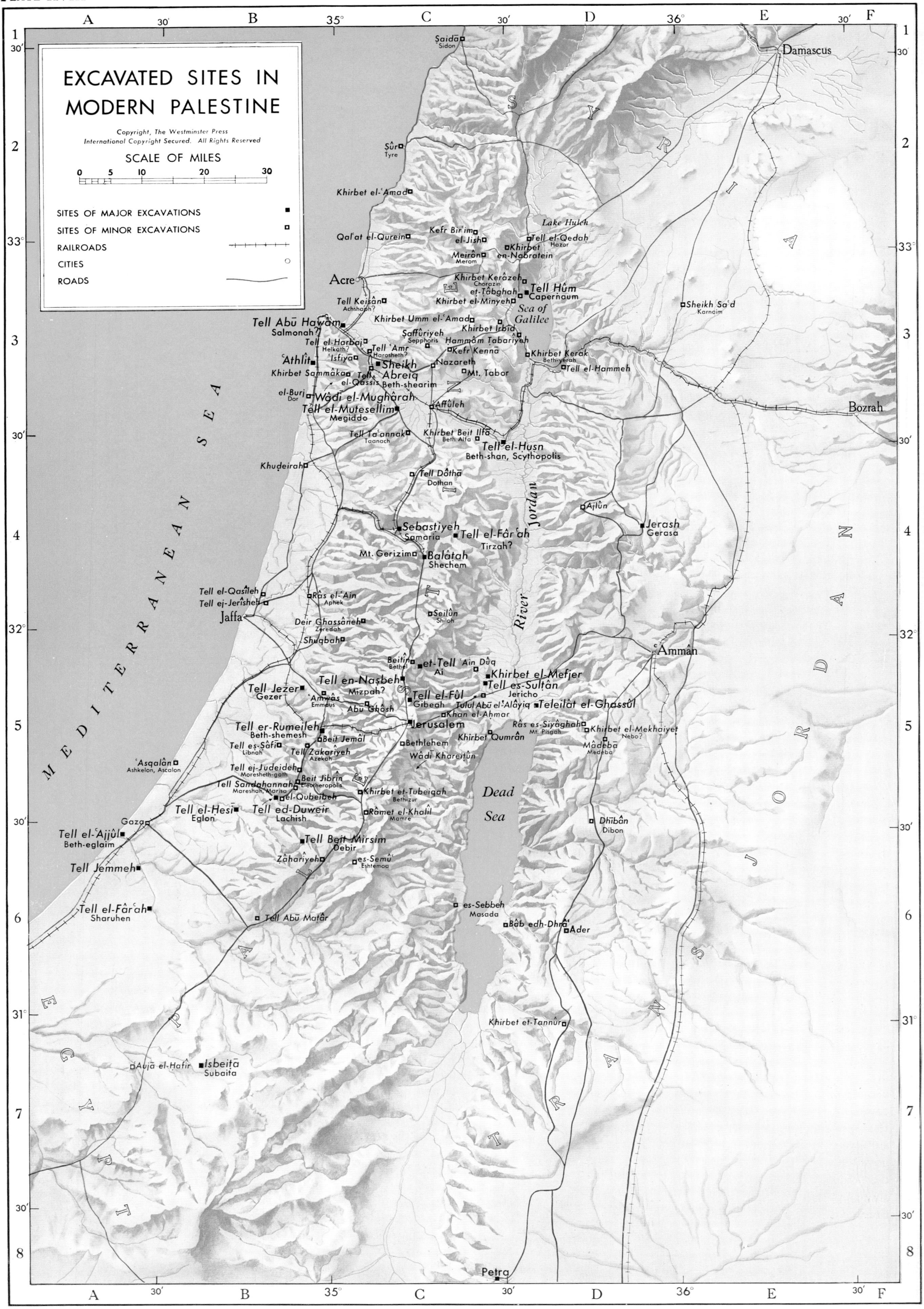

EXCAVATED SITES IN MODERN PALESTINE
Copyright, The Westminster Press
International Copyright Secured. All Rights Reserved
SCALE OF MILES
0 5 10 20 30
SITES OF MAJOR EXCAVATIONS
SITES OF MINOR EXCAVATIONS
RAILROADS
CITIES
ROADS
A
30′
B
35°
C
D
36°
E
F
1
2
3
4
5
6
7
8
33°
32°
31°
Saidā
Sidon
Damascus
S Y R I A
Sûr
Tyre
Khirbet el-ʿAmad
Lake Huleh
Kefr Birʿim
el-Jish
Qalʿat el-Qurein
Tell el-Qedah
Hazor
Khirbet en-Nabratein
Meirôn
Merom
Acre
Khirbet Kerâzeh
Chorazin
Tell Hûm
Capernaum
et-Tabghah
Khirbet el-Minyeh
Sea of Galilee
Tell Keisân
Achshaph?
Sheikh Saʿd
Karnaim
Tell Abū Hawâm
Salmonah?
Khirbet Umm el-ʿAmad
Saffûriyeh
Sepphoris
Khirbet Irbid
Hammâm Tabarîyeh
Tell el-Harbaj
Helkath?
Tell ʿAmr
Harosheth?
ʿIsfiya
Kefr Kennâ
Khirbet Kerak
Beth-yerah
ʿAthlit
Sheikh Abreiq
Beth-shearim
Nazareth
Tell el-Hammeh
Khirbet Sammâka
Tell el-Qassis
Mt. Tabor
el-Burj
Dor
Wâdi el-Mughârah
Tell el-Mutesellim
Megiddo
ʿAffûleh
Bozrah
Tell Taʿannak
Taanach
Khirbet Beit Ilfâ
Beth Alfa
Tell el-Husn
Beth-shan, Scythopolis
Khudeirah
Tell Dôthâ
Dothan
MEDITERRANEAN SEA
Jordan
ʿAjlûn
Sebastiyeh
Samaria
Tell el-Fârʿah
Tirzah?
Jerash
Gerasa
Mt. Gerizim
Balâtah
Shechem
River
Tell el-Qasileh
Tell ej-Jerisheh
Râs el-ʿAin
Aphek
Seilûn
Shiloh
Jaffa
Deir Ghassâneh
Zeredah
Shuqbah
ʿAmmân
Beitin
Bethel
et-Tell
Ai
ʿAin Dûq
Tell en-Nasbeh
Mizpah?
Khirbet el-Mefjer
Tell es-Sultân
Jericho
Tell Jezer
Gezer
ʿAmwâs
Emmaus
Tell el-Fûl
Gibeah
Abū Ghôsh
Tulul Abū el-ʿAlâyiq
Teleilât el-Ghassûl
Khan el-Ahmar
Tell er-Rumeileh
Beth-shemesh
Jerusalem
Râs es-Siyâghah
Mt. Pisgah
Khirbet el-Mekhaiyet
Nebo?
Beit Jemâl
Bethlehem
Khirbet Qumrân
Mâdebâ
Medeba
Tell es-Sâfi
Libnah
Tell Zakarîyeh
Azekah
Wâdi Khareitûn
ʿAsqalân
Ashkelon, Ascalon
Tell ej-Judeideh
Moresheth-gath
Beit Jibrîn
Eleutheropolis
Tell Sandahannah
Mareshah, Marisa
el-Qubeibeh
Khirbet et-Tubeiqah
Beth-zur
Dead Sea
Tell el-Hesi
Eglon
Tell ed-Duweir
Lachish
Râmet el-Khalîl
Mamre
Gaza
Dhībân
Dibon
Tell el-ʿAjjûl
Beth-eglaim
Tell Beit Mirsim
Debir
Zâhariyeh
es-Semûʿ
Eshtemoa
Tell Jemmeh
es-Sebbeh
Masada
Tell el-Fârʿah
Sharuhen
Tell Abū Matâr
Bâb edh-Dhrâʿ
Ader
TRANSJORDAN
Khirbet et-Tannûr
EGYPT
PALESTINE
ʿAujā el-Hafîr
Isbeitā
Subaita
Petra

FIG. 83. *Tell el-Ḥuṣn*, the mound containing the ruins of ancient Beth-shan. In the Roman-Byzantine period the town, then called Scythopolis, was situated on level ground mainly to the south (right) of the *tell*, but the cathedral was constructed on top of the mound over the ruins of a long series of earlier pagan temples.

EXCAVATIONS IN MODERN PALESTINE

PLATE XVIII

A LARGE part of what has been written in the pages of this *Atlas* could not have been written, nor could the maps themselves have been prepared, had it not been for the many years of intensive exploration in the Holy Land by scores of devoted students of the Bible. On Plate XVIII may be found the places where excavations have been conducted to determine the nature and history of the ancient towns, though the mere listing of the sites does not tell the complete story, nor does it give any inkling of the problems that have been solved or of the reasons for solving them. Chief among these problems are: how to locate and identify the ancient sites, how to dig the ruins properly, and how to date what is found. These matters have been discussed by Professor Albright on pp. 9-14. Here we need only mention that the journeys of Edward Robinson in 1838 and 1852 and the Survey of Western Palestine by the Palestine Exploration Fund between 1872 and 1878 were the first great achievements in Palestinian archaeology, achievements which formed the basis of all later topographical work.

Between 1920 and 1940 a number of well-trained scholars have studied and traveled extensively through the country and have arrived at a point far beyond that reached by their predecessors. Modern explorers like Albright and Glueck have been able to advance beyond their forerunners, in large part because they have developed new and refined methods for checking conclusions and for dating the ruins explored. For example, Num. 33:49 tells us that the Israelites after the conquest of Transjordan "encamped by the Jordan, from Beth-jeshimoth even unto Abel-shittim in the plains of Moab." Study of the places where these towns had been located by former explorers now reveals that the ruins could not be those of the Israelite period because they date from Roman times. The earlier sites have been discovered a little farther back in the hills along the same valleys (IX, H 5-6; the names Besimoth and Abila of the New Testament period are given to the later ruins). When peace prevailed under a stable government, the people moved their towns out into the plain near their crops; but before that they had to live in the hills near good springs at sites which possessed natural features to aid in fortification and defense even though they were some distance from the fields.

EARLY EXCAVATIONS

The ability to date the ancient ruins is the result of years of excavation. It is comparatively easy to recognize the typical site where an ancient city once stood in western Asia. It is in the shape of a truncated cone, possessing a flat top and steep, sloping sides (Fig. 83). This shape is preserved because the stumps of old city walls remain in the slopes and prevent erosion. The name which the Arabs use for such a mound is *tell*, a word which is very old, occurring not only in the Old Testament but in Babylonian literature as well. The Authorized Version of Josh. 11:13 reads as follows: "But as for the cities that stood still in their strength, Israel burned none of them, save Hazor only." The word here translated "strength" is really *tell*, and the words should be translated, "the cities that stood on their *tells*" (cf. R.V. and R.S.V.).

When one digs into an ancient *tell*, he usually finds the ruins arranged in layers or strata, one above another. The reason for this is that the typical city was repeatedly destroyed and rebuilt through the centuries of its history. *Tell el-Ḥuṣn* ("Mound of the Fortress"), on which ancient Beth-shan was located, contains eighteen different strata of debris and ruined houses, accumulated during the four thousand years of its intermittent occupation (XVIII, C-4). The depth of the debris from the topmost layer to virgin soil was about seventy-nine feet. The smaller Judean mound of *Tell Beit Mirsim* (XVIII, B-6), occupied for some two thousand years, has about twenty feet of debris and ten strata.

It is not surprising that the translators of the Authorized Version did not understand the significance of a *tell*. Neither Edward Robinson nor the Survey of Western Palestine understood its full significance. The first demonstration of its true nature came in 1872-1874 with the excavations conducted by Schliemann at Troy (II, D-2). Even so, many years passed before the archaeological world as a whole was convinced. Lacking, therefore, a knowledge of the nature of a mound, and, more important, lacking an ability to date the ruins uncovered, early excavations were little more than treasure hunts. The "Tomb of the Kings" in Jerusalem, for instance, was so com-

FIG. 84. The American School of Oriental Research in Jerusalem. For its location in the city, see XVII: D, C-2.

pletely misinterpreted that, while actually dating from the first century A.D., it was thought to be the mausoleum of the kings of Judah (XVII:D, C-1)! Excavations around the walls of Jerusalem by Warren (1867-1870) were carried out with great vigor, but the information gained was scarcely commensurate with the effort required.

The year 1890 was a turning point in archaeological work, for in that year W. M. Flinders Petrie made a small excavation at *Tell el-Hesī* (XVIII, B-5). Here he showed that the pottery varied greatly in the different levels and that it was possible to set up a chronological scheme by means of it. This was the key needed to determine the date of excavated ruins. In a poor country like Palestine where monumental inscriptions are few, and the moist climate destroys papyrus documents, some other means of dating must be found. In the fifty years since Petrie's work the study of Palestinian pottery has been greatly advanced; and today, given a representative collection of broken fragments, it is usually possible for the expert to date them within a century, though the pottery styles of some periods are better known than others.

Between 1890 and 1914 there were a number of important excavations. In 1891-1893 an American named Frederick Jones Bliss continued Petrie's work at *Tell el-Hesī* for the Palestine Exploration Fund, clearing one third of the mound to bedrock. So little money was available for the publication of the discoveries, however, that neither they nor their stratification were adequately described. Between 1894 and 1897, Bliss conducted excavations in the southern part of Jerusalem to determine the line of the ancient walls and the extent of the city. Ruined fortifications along the southern edge of both the western and the eastern hills were unearthed (XVII:C, B-D 6), but their date was not precisely determined. Those which he found on the western hill probably do not go back to the time of Christ, as many have thought. They date chiefly from the Byzantine and Crusader periods, though they may follow the lines of earlier walls.

In 1898, Bliss was joined by R. A. S. Macalister, a young English archaeologist, and together they examined four *tells* in the Judean Shephelah: *Tell eṣ-Ṣâfī*, *Tell Zakarîyeh*, *Tell ej-Judeideh*, and *Tell Sandaḥannah* (XVIII, B-5). Judean ruins were found in the first three; the most important was a strongly walled citadel at *Tell Zakarîyeh* (Azekah) which may have been built by Rehoboam (II Chron. 11:9), though the exact date was not determined. At *Tell Sandahannah* the best preserved Hellenistic town yet found in Palestine was unearthed. None of the discoveries were adequately published, however, and little can be said about them.

Macalister then undertook the first major excavation of a mound at *Tell Jezer* (XVIII, B-5). Most of the site was cleared in five campaigns between 1902 and 1909. This was a great achievement, the more so because Macalister directed the work alone, with no assistance except that of an able Arab foreman. He divided the mound into north-south strips, each forty feet wide, and dug the strips one at a time. At first he was able to keep check on the strata and the objects found in each. As time went on, however, he found it increasingly difficult to correlate the strata of one strip with those of other strips near by and to observe and record accurately the precise level from which the objects came. Hence, the value of his energetic work is largely dissipated. In general terms we can now recount the history of the site and its fortifications, but we cannot be precise. The most interesting discovery was that of a Canaanite sacred area in which there were a number of large, upright stones (Hebrew *maṣṣēbôth*). Similar installations have been found elsewhere, particularly at *Tell el-Qedaḥ* (XVIII, D-2) and Ader (XVIII, D-6) in Palestine, at Ugarit in Syria and Asshur in Iraq. The evidence suggests that they were memorial shrines for important people who were deceased.

The accomplishments of German archaeologists between 1901 and 1905 at Taanach and Megiddo (XVIII, C-3) were far less even than that of Macalister. They destroyed far more evidence than they recovered. At Taanach the most important discovery was a Canaanite structure which contained a few cuneiform tablets dating about a century earlier than the Amarna period. The meaning of the seemingly chaotic results of the Megiddo expedition has been clarified only in part by recent excavations (see below). Interesting objects were discovered, among which was the official seal of "Shema, servant of Jeroboam." This individual is not mentioned in the Old Testament, but the Jeroboam of the seal was undoubtedly the king who reigned in Israel during the early part of the eighth century. The expression "servant" on this and other similar seals means "royal official."

German work at Jericho (1907-1909) was a great improvement over previous excavations, because for the first time the importance of an adequate trained staff was realized. This was the second major excavation before the First World War, and considerable information was gained about the houses and fortifications of Jericho, though some of the strata were misdated by several centuries (see further below).

The third major excavation of this period, and by far the most important, was the work of Harvard University at Samaria (XVIII, C-4), directed by the Americans George A. Reisner and Clarence S. Fisher between 1908 and 1910. Important discoveries were made, including a magnificent temple built by Herod the Great, under which were the ruins of the palace of the Israelite kings (see further below). Equally important was the development by these excavators of the method of excavation now in use throughout the Near East (see p. 10).

EXCAVATIONS BETWEEN 1920 AND 1955

In the story of Palestinian excavations the period before 1920 must be considered largely as one of preparation for what was to come. There were significant discoveries, but none were so important as the knowledge of how to dig and how to date what was found. Consequently, when excavations began again after the war, far more valuable results were obtained. In addition, a number of organizations now entered the field whose co-operative endeavor and sharing of information made advance more rapid. One of the most significant events occurred in 1920, when the Department of Antiquities in Palestine was established by the British Government. Digging by unauthorized and untrained persons was now forbidden, but the work of trained and well-equipped expeditions was greatly encouraged. Before the war the latter were hampered by a corrupt Turkish Government and oppressive laws. Since the division of Palestine in 1948, both Jordan and Israel have continued the policies of the British mandate with regard to the care of antiquities and the careful oversight of excavations.

Another significant organization was the American School of Oriental Research in Jerusalem, which has done much to encourage co-operation between national and religious groups and institutions, serving as a clearing house for information, and providing a place where students can study (Fig. 84). Likewise important was the interest taken by the Rockefeller Foundation, which gave to the Government of Palestine $2,000,000 for the establishment of the Palestine Archaeological Museum. In addition, numerous educational institutions have taken a direct interest in the work on a scale far greater than before 1914.

The largest and most elaborate excavation ever planned in Palestine was that at Megiddo (XVIII, C-3; and Fig. 5) by the Oriental Institute of the University of Chicago. The entire site was purchased so that it could be completely dug as a model excavation for the whole of the Near East. The work began in 1925, and during the following decade the first four strata were entirely removed. These dated from the fourth back to the tenth century B.C. After some ten years of work the comprehensiveness of the excavation's plan had to be abandoned. Between 1935 and 1939 sections were dug deep into the debris, as shown in Figure 85. Area AA on the north was found to be the place where great Canaanite palaces were built next to the successive city gates. A portion of the ancient roadway leading up to the gateway was exposed and is shown in the lower right corner of the photograph. Area BB on the east is the only one dug to bedrock. Below the Solomonic horse stables discovered here (as well as in Area CC), there was found the Canaanite sacred area with a series of temples going back to 3000 B.C. On the western side of the mound may be seen a depression which is a great water shaft dug down into bedrock and then tunneled horizontally to the mound's edge where the main spring exits. The water of the spring was made to flow into the city through this tunnel by the Canaanites sometime before 1200 B.C., and this continued as the main water system for centuries thereafter.

The history of the site may now be reconstructed somewhat as follows: Stratum XX is the designation for some scattered remains found on the rock at the bottom of the mound in Area BB. They indicate that people lived there as early as 4000 B.C. (Early Chalcolithic). There is no indication of intensive occupation until Stratum XIX where the first architecture, including a small, rectangular temple, appears. This cannot be dated before c. 3100-3000 B.C. (Early Bronze I B). Strata XVIII-XVI, dating between c. 3000 and 2600 B.C. (Early Bronze II and III A) exhibit the period of Palestine's first great flowering of civilization. One of the most spectacular products of a highly developed community organization at this time is the massive stone city wall of XVIII, originally between thirteen and sixteen feet wide, and later widened to nearly twenty-six feet. Fortifications of the preceding period (Early Bronze I), though evidently not as massive, have been found in the south at Jericho and Ai. As in all major sites of early Palestine, the Early Bronze civilization was violently destroyed during the course of Early Bronze III (c. 2700-2400 B.C.) and the site lay unoccupied until the twentieth century B.C. Stratum XV marks the beginning of a new and great era c. 1900 B.C. At that time three adjoining temples were erected, with a large altar of unhewn stone, twenty-six feet in diameter and four and one-half feet high, standing in a courtyard at their rear. This is the first great altar of burnt offering found intact in Palestine.

Strata XV-XIII, c. 1900-1700 B.C., provide the best collection of material from Middle Bronze II A that we now have. Among the finds was a portion of a statue of an Egyptian official, probably the Egyptian ambassador or high commissioner at Megiddo. Strata XII-XI, c. 1700 to 1550 B.C., belong to the most prosperous period of Palestine's pre-Roman history (Middle Bronze II B), when it was controlled by the Asiatic rulers whom the Egyptians called Hyksos (pp. 27-28). After these foreigners were expelled by the Egyptians and the latter took control of Palestine again, Stratum X was erected with a new fortification system. This remained in use until the destruction of the Bronze Age Canaanite city c. 1140-1130 B.C. Stratum IX was destroyed in 1468 B.C. by the great Egyptian conqueror, Thutmose III, during a Syro-Palestinian rebellion. In Strata VIII and VII, dating from the fifteenth to the third quarter of the twelfth century, the main features were the royal palace and temple. Both were partially destroyed and repaired repeatedly. In the palace two hoards of treasure, or what remained of them, were found, one dating from the early thirteenth century and the other from the early twelfth. The latter was a large collection of Canaanite ivories, carved and decorated for use in numerous ways (games, inlays, boudoir objects, etc., Figs. 28-29). The temple is a special type of Canaanite structure which we may call a *migdal* or fortress-temple, rectangular in shape, with walls eleven and one-half feet wide. An even larger example of the type has been found at Shechem with walls c. sixteen and one-half feet wide. Both the Solomonic and Herodian temples in Jerusalem had similar thick walls and probably represented later modifications of the same type of structure (cf. Fig. 31).

For a half century or more after the destruction of City VII the mound lay in ruins. Stratum VI probably represents the period of Philistine control in the eleventh century (c. 1075-1000 B.C.), whereas V (or V B, c. 1000-970 B.C.) was a prosperous town of Davidic times. Reconstructing the situation from the excavator's reports, we find that the most important age in Megiddo's history was the age of Solomon, represented in the southern areas by Stratum IV B and in the northern by Stratum V A. In spite of the different designations IV B and V A represent one and the same period when the city was made into an important administrative center of the Solomonic State, with palace for the district officer, stables for several groups of chariot horses (c. 500 in all), a new city fortification and an elaborate gateway. This complex was captured by Shishak of Egypt c. 918 B.C., partially destroyed, and then rebuilt as City IV (IV A) which lasted until presumably destroyed by Hazael of Damascus just before 800 B.C. City III was no longer a headquarters of government in the old sense. The elaborate administrative center was not needed by the government of Samaria, not many miles away. It was destroyed by Tiglath-pileser III in 733 B.C., rebuilt with a very large fort (Stratum II) to serve as the Assyrian headquarters for the province of Galilee. This was in turn destroyed by Necho of Egypt who fought and killed Josiah there in 609 B.C. The surface remains of Stratum I indicate that a village continued to occupy the mound until the fourth century, when it was abandoned and not reoccupied.

Megiddo is here described in detail, not only because of its intrinsic importance, but also to indicate how the story of one city as reconstructed by archaeological evidence vividly reflects a major segment of the history of the country. Equally important for archaeologists has been the excavation of *Tell Beit Mirsim* (XVIII, B-6) by the American School of Oriental Research in Jerusalem and the Xenia (now Pittsburgh-Xenia) Theological Seminary, under the direction of W. F. Albright between 1926 and 1932. This is a small Judean mound only half the size of Megiddo, the southernmost of the Canaanite royal cities in the Shephelah (Lowland) conquered by Joshua. Ten periods of occupation were discovered dating from a period just after Megiddo XVI in Early Bronze III B (c. 2500 B.C.) to 587 B.C. when it was destroyed by Nebuchadnezzar and never reoccupied. It is a minor and rather poor site when compared with

FIG. 85. Air view of the mound of Megiddo after excavation. The whole top has been removed to Stratum IV (c. 918-815 B.C.). Area AA is the location of the successive fortified gateways and of the Canaanite palaces of local kings. In Areas BB and CC were found the Solomonic stables. Below the stables in BB were a series of Canaanite temples, the earliest of which was erected about 3100 B.C.

FIG. 86. Air view of the mound of ancient Jericho, taken after many years of excavation, all too often by trenching. The view is toward the south. On the left the main road passes between the mound and the concrete reservoir which collects the water of the spring. Except for a time after the eighteenth century the spring lay outside the city's fortifications. On the mound just above it is the only place there where architecture of the seventeenth–sixteenth centuries has been found, and possibly some heavy walls of a fort of the following centuries. Elsewhere most remains belong to the third and fifth millenniums B.C. About 4500 B.C. it was already a large city with a heavy fortification wall, the oldest city thus far known to archaeologists. Only in northern Iraq have village remains of comparable date been found.

Megiddo. Its importance lies in the excellence of excavation, observation, and publication on the part of the director, W. F. Albright. His reports on his findings constitute the greatest single monument to archaeological scholarship in Palestine. Not only do they describe the history of the site, but everything found is set in the perspective of other discoveries in Palestine and the Near East, with the result that the volumes constitute a comparative and critically reconstructive study of Palestinian archaeology as a whole. Of particular importance is the thorough and comparative study of the pottery sequence; it marks a major transition in ceramic chronology in the Near East, when dating by a disciplined "intuition" finally gave way to a careful typological and stratigraphical treatment that others may study and evaluate.

Next in importance must be placed the excavation of Beth-shan (XVIII, C-4; Fig. 83) between 1921 and 1933 by the University Museum of Philadelphia. The major discoveries were a Byzantine Church and monastery, a Hellenistic temple of the third century B.C., and a series of Canaanite temples dating between the fourteenth and tenth centuries B.C. The Hellenistic structure is a good illustration of the general type of Phoenician temple plan and is similar in its main features to the Solomonic Temple (Fig. 31). The Canaanite temples and their contents are our most important source of information regarding the material equipment of Canaanite religion. Two of them, the "houses" of Ashtoreth and Dagon, are mentioned in the Old Testament (I Sam. 31:10; I Chron. 10:10), and were probably destroyed by David. In any event, the city was laid waste shortly after 1000 B.C. and remained virtually unoccupied for centuries. Between the fifteenth and early twelfth centuries an Egyptian garrison was stationed there, and at least three Pharaohs left their stelae (monumental inscriptions) in the temple area.

The important discoveries at Beth-shan have not been as usable as they should have been because of long delays and inadequate provision for publication on the part of the University Museum. Another complicating factor was the tendency on the part of the chief archaeologist, Alan Rowe, to date his strata by means of Egyptian objects while excluding the scholarly consideration of other typological and stratigraphical factors. The Canaanite temples, as a result, were dated too early, and their strata were labeled by the names of Egyptian Pharaohs. A redating of the material has been necessary with the result that the nomenclature is confusing. Those who use the publications must substitute numbers for the Pharaohs and reorganize the material into a new framework. The history of the site may now be described somewhat as follows: The town was founded c. 3400-3300 B.C. and was occupied more or less continuously until its destruction c. 2400 B.C. (Levels XVIII-XI). In the small excavated portion of the mound at this depth there is a gap of over eight hundred years, so that Level X is to be dated in the sixteenth and fifteenth centuries. In Level IX (Rowe's "Thothmes III" stratum) the series of Canaanite temples begins; it dates in the fourteenth century. Levels VIII and VII ("Pre-Amenophis III" and "Amenophis III") cover the end of the fourteenth and the thirteenth century; Level VI ("Seti I") is from the twelfth and early eleventh centuries; and Level V ("Rameses III" or "II") dates from the time when the Philistines controlled the city and hanged Saul's body on its walls before it was captured and destroyed by David (end of eleventh and early tenth century). After considerable time had elapsed people began to drift back to the mound, and Levels IV and III date for the most part from the Persian, Hellenistic, and Roman periods, while Levels II and I are Byzantine and Arabic.

Of particular interest to students of the Old Testament have been the British excavations at Jericho (XVIII, C-5). German work before the First World War (see above) had already revealed something of the city's history. It was known that the site was occupied in the Early and Middle Bronze Ages (c. 2500-1500 B.C.), though the Germans labeled the three strata of those periods "Canaanite," "Late Canaanite," and "Israelite." Actually their "Canaanite" is Early Bronze, their "Late Canaanite" is Middle Bronze I (c. 2100-1900 B.C.) and their "Israelite" is Middle Bronze II B–C (c. 1700-1500 B.C.). After a long period during which the site lay waste, it was reoccupied during the tenth and ninth centuries and people continued to live on the mound during the eighth and perhaps seventh centuries, but probably not thereafter (this is the material called "Jewish" by the Germans).

Between 1930 and 1936 Professor John Garstang of the University of Liverpool returned to the mound to investigate it anew. His main work was concerned (1) with the investigation of the city walls, (2) with the area just above the spring on the east side where a Middle Bronze Age palace had evidently existed, (3) with some marvelous Bronze Age tombs, and (4) with a deep cut which revealed an earlier history at the site than was known to exist in any other Palestinian or Syrian mound. In this deep probing, his levels IX through XVII (the lowest) are to be dated in the Neolithic or Late Stone Age c. 4500 B.C. Levels X-XVII are a series of successive floor levels of one building which is probably the earliest temple known. In it were found the earliest known statues, probably of gods; they are in threes, father, mother, and child. Level IX marks the first introduction of pottery vessels. After this there is a gap in the occupation of the mound for a thousand years, except for a brief time about 4000 B.C. (Level VIII). Levels VII-V contained a city wall and a small temple of Early Bronze I (c. 3300-3000 B.C.). Very little was found in the Garstang Level IV of Early Bronze II (c. 3000-2700 B.C.), but Level III was associated with another city wall. Hence the excavator called the city of the first wall City A, and that associated with Level III, City B. City C was the name reserved for the Middle Bronze Age city, with its great sloping-stone revetment against the mound's side topped by a brick parapet (c. seventeenth and sixteenth centuries). To the fifteenth century two more walls on the summit, one outside the other, were attributed, together with some remains inside of them, and the whole was called City D. There was considerable evidence of destruction, and this was credited to Joshua, who in the excavator's opinion was responsible for laying City D waste between c. 1400 and 1385 B.C. Other archaeologists believed the evidence as presented called for a date somewhat later, probably sometime after 1350 B.C.

Beginning in 1952 a third excavation began at the old mound of Jericho under the direction of Kathleen Kenyon. Her main discoveries have been threefold. 1. The city walls which Professor Garstang dated to City D of Joshua's time were discovered in one place to be overlaid with the series of Middle Bronze Age revetments. This means that they cannot be Late Bronze Age, but earlier than the seventeenth century fortifications. Indeed, they are only two of some fourteen different walls or wall reconstructions of the Early Bronze Age between c. 3300 and 2400 B.C. Wherever one digs into the mound he encounters Early Bronze Age or earlier material almost at the surface. The only later remains from the Middle Bronze and perhaps Late Bronze Ages are found in the area above the spring. Yet the only evidence of a possible city of the Late Bronze time are a few pieces of pottery from three tombs, a handful of sherds (broken fragments) from the spring area, and some heavy walls, possibly a fort, in the same region—all of these found by Professor Garstang. Miss Kenyon, on her part, can find nothing further (see p. 39). 2. The most remarkable discoveries of the Kenyon expedition have been in the Neolithic period. The town of that time was surprisingly large and supplied with at least two successive stone city walls, the earliest known, testifying to a larger degree of social organization than was thought possible for such an early time. Several skulls with mud-plaster on them are remarkably lifelike and are the earliest examples of attempted portraiture ever found. 3. A series of Middle Bronze Age tombs proved to be so perfectly sealed that remains of food and furniture still existed in them when they were opened.

Between 1931 and 1935 excavation was resumed at the old capital of North Israel, Samaria (XVIII, C-4), under the direction of the English archaeologist, J. W. Crowfoot. We can now summarize the city's history somewhat as follows: Period I, as the Crowfoot expedition calls it, dates from the time of the Omri Dynasty, c. 876-842 B.C., when the site was purchased and made the capital. A large palace with its courtyard was erected on the top of the mound and surrounded by a beautifully built wall (the "inner wall"), about five feet wide, which in turn was enclosed by two more walls around the slopes and base of the hill. Period II is marked by a new and spectacular fortification (the "casemate wall") around the summit on the north, west, and part of the south sides. Two parallel walls, connected with cross walls, were erected and the intervening spaces filled in with rubble. On the north the resulting fortification was about thirty-one feet wide. These city defenses were so well made that they were kept in repair and not replaced until c. 150 B.C. The excavator believes the casemate wall may have been built by Ahab, but it is far more probable that it was the work of the Jehu Dynasty, perhaps by Jehu himself (c. 842-815 B.C.). The buildings of Period II suffered a partial destruction, and the most probable time for this would have been between c. 815 B.C. and 805 B.C., at which time Hazael of Damascus caused Israel much trouble, destroying also the Solomonic buildings remaining in Stratum IV at Megiddo. Period III, when the Samaria palace was evidently rebuilt, would then belong to the first part of the eighth century. The Samaria ivories (comparable to those found at Megiddo, see above) date within these first three periods, while the Samaria ostraca, sixty-three potsherds with inscriptions on them, date from c. 778, 777, 772 and 770 B.C. in the reign of Jeroboam II. They record shipments of wine and oil to the palace in Samaria. Periods IV, V, and VI evidently represent minor repair and rebuilding in the last decades before the city's destruction by the Assyrians in 721 B.C. Period VII contains evidence of Assyrian or at least foreign occupation during the seventh century. Period VIII represents a time when most of the mound's summit was an enclosed garden or orchard, perhaps belonging to the Babylonian administrators of the area in the sixth century. Period IX represents the scanty remains discovered between the sixth and first centuries B.C. During the fourth or third centuries the old Israelite walls were strengthened by the addition of large round towers. This whole system was finally replaced c. 150 B.C. when the pagan inhabitants erected a new "Fort Wall" for protection against the Maccabees.

The greatest time in the city's history, next to its days as a capital in the ninth-eighth centuries, began with Herod the Great (37-4 B.C.). In honor of Augustus Caesar he built a magnificent and famous temple over the site of the palace of the Israelite kings. A stadium for games, a forum and a new wall were also erected. The last great architectural age at Samaria was between c. A.D. 180 and 230 when a new stadium was erected to replace the old; new columns were installed to enclose the forum and to flank the street leading up to the summit; and a large theater and a basilica were built, the last being turned into a church during the fourth century.

From 1932 to 1938 exceedingly important work was done at Lachish (XVIII, B-5) by the Wellcome-Marston Archaeological Research Expedition, directed by J. L. Starkey before his tragic murder by Arab brigands early in 1938. By that time only a beginning had been made on top of the mound in digging it stratigraphically, so that very little below Level III was laid bare in normal sequence. On the other hand, numerous important discoveries had come to light while clearances were made for debris, tombs excavated, and the city fortifications explored. In general, nine occupational levels were discovered, of which VI through IX were of the Bronze Age, beginning about 2500 B.C. Belonging to the period of VI was a Canaanite temple; both it and the whole city of VI were violently destroyed, evidently by Israel at the end of the thirteenth century. After some two centuries went by, building began anew in the early tenth century when David erected a provincial administrative center there, with palace and storehouse for taxes paid in kind (Level V). A double city wall was subsequently built around the mound, presumably by King Rehoboam of Judah (cf. II Chron. 11:5-12); it probably belongs to the beginning of Level IV, though the contents of this stratum have not been sufficiently excavated to enable us to be sure. At any rate, the city of Level III was evidently destroyed in the first invasion of Nebuchadnezzar in 598-7 B.C., at which time the palace, gateway, and part of the main wall were destroyed. The fortifications were quickly rebuilt (Level II) with stone taken from a deep quarry dug in an unoccupied part of the mound, but the site was completely laid waste by Nebuchadnezzar in 587 B.C. Between the two final destructions in a layer of burned debris within the city gate eighteen letters were found, written with ink on broken pottery vessels. Two others were found elsewhere, one in the old roadway and another near the palace. Most of them were correspondence from the officer in charge of a neighboring outpost between Lachish and Azekah to the commandant at Lachish. They date shortly before the final siege, and reflect the same tension in the country which is to be observed in the Book of Jeremiah. As was the case after the end of Level VI, some time elapsed before the mound was reoccupied. During the fifth century B.C., however, the Judean fortifications were repaired and a new palace erected on the ruins of the old (Level I). In other words, the site was made a new administrative center, probably by Geshem the Arab (see p. 56). After the fourth century, the mound ceased to

FIG. 87. A reconstruction of the fortifications of *Tell en-Nasbeh* (XVIII, C-5). The high wall, some 26 feet wide, was built c. 900 B.C. during the civil war between Israel and Judah. It is a good example of ancient fortifications: see also Figs. 18 and 37.

FIG. 88. Prehistoric caves in the *Wâdī el-Mughârah* (Plate XVIII, C-3) where a stratified sequence of human occupation some seventy feet deep has been excavated. The cave in the center is *Mughâret el-Wâd* in which two levels of the Mesolithic or Middle Stone Age were found and below them five levels of Paleolithic. At least sixty-four individuals were found to have been buried in the cave or on the terrace in front of it.

be of any importance because the district center shifted to the nearby Mareshah.

In 1923-1925 and again in 1927-1928 the Palestine Exploration Fund sent new expeditions to explore the City of David. The first, under the direction of R. A. S. Macalister and J. G. Duncan, excavated a portion of the old city wall above the Gihon spring (XVII:A, E-6). A tower and revetment, both probably built by David, were found. The second expedition, directed by J. W. Crowfoot, worked on the western side of the hill and found the massive towers of a Jebusite city gate (XVII:A, E-6). Whether it was the Valley or Dung Gate of ancient Jerusalem is a matter of debate.

The only German excavations in Palestine since the First War have been at Shechem (XVIII, C-4). From 1925 to 1928 a series of yearly campaigns were directed by Ernst Sellin, who was succeeded by his chief archaeologist, G. Welter, from 1928 to 1932. The latter had to be recalled because of poor work, and Sellin with the help of Hans Steckeweh returned for one month in 1934. The only serious attention to pottery and stratigraphy during the whole excavation was confined to that final month. The result is that the history of the site is only sketchily known. It is clear that the city was occupied from the seventeenth to the first century B.C. How long before that the city flourished is not certain. Its mention in Egyptian texts of the nineteenth century B.C. as one of the important places of Palestine suggests a much earlier history; and the "Sychar" of John 4:5 is probably a mistake for Sychem (Shechem), which suggests that the city existed during the first century A.D., probably to the time of the First Jewish Revolt (A.D. 66-70). The most important features of the site are: 1. The citadel near the well-preserved gateway in the northwest area of the mound. The main identifiable building is a huge *migdal* or fortress-temple, larger even than the one found at Megiddo (see above; cf. Judg. 9:4). 2. The main fortification system which presumably protected the city during the Late Bronze Age (c. 1500-1200 B.C.). The wall is one of the greatest ever found in Palestine, built of stone like the one at Jericho against the sloping side of the mound. Some of the stones in the base of this fortification are great blocks six to seven feet long. 3. From a later period a second fortification (a casemate wall) with a new gate on the northeast reused the old Bronze Age gate on the northwest. It is similar to work at Beth-shemesh and Debir in Judah and may belong to the tenth century B.C.

During 1933-34 there was an interesting French excavation at Ai (XVIII, C-5), directed by Mme. Marquet-Krause. This was found to have been an important Early Bronze Age city, founded c. 3300 B.C. and destroyed c. 2400 B.C. A fine building was unearthed at the mound's crest; judging from its plan it was a large temple, one of the best preserved from ancient Palestine. A small Israelite settlement of the eleventh or tenth century is the only later occupation on the mound. An excavation by W. F. Albright in 1934 and continued by J. L. Kelso in 1954-1956 at Bethel, one and one-half miles away, showed that this town was probably established to take Ai's place. The ruins of Bethel bare vivid marks of violent destruction during the course of the thirteenth century (cf. Judg. 1:22 ff.). The simplest explanation of the story of Ai's capture by Joshua (Josh., chs. 7; 8) is that the narrative of the destruction of Bethel by Joshua was subsequently transferred to Ai, the great ruin nearby.

Among other smaller undertakings, mainly on the part of institutions connected with the American Schools of Oriental Research, we may mention the following: (1) The uncovering of Saul's fortress at Gibeah (XVIII, C-5), first capital of united Israel, by the American School under the direction of W. F. Albright in 1922-23 and 1933. (2) The excavation of Beth-shemesh (XVIII, B-5) by Haverford College, directed by Elihu Grant between 1928 and 1933, a continuation of earlier British work in 1911-12. The town was founded about the same time as Bethel, but its most prosperous period was c. 1500-918 B.C. Its destruction in 587 B.C. marked its end except for a Byzantine monastery. (3) The excavation of *Tell en-Naṣbeh* (XVIII, C-5) by the Pacific School of Religion, directed by W. F. Badè between 1926 and 1935. This was a small Israelite mound dating between the twelfth and fourth centuries B.C. mainly, but chiefly notable for its role in the wars between Israel and Judah (Fig. 87 and p. 50) and in the Post-Exilic period. (4) The excavation of the Maccabean fortress and earlier remains at Beth-zur (XVIII, C-5; Fig. 59) by the Presbyterian (now McCormick) Theological Seminary in Chicago, directed by O. R. Sellers in 1931. (5) Beginning in 1950 the various staffs of the American School in Jerusalem have been carrying on work for short periods at a time in Dibon (XVIII, D-5), the capital of ancient Moab. (6) Wheaton College began work in 1953 at Dothan (XVIII, C-4), an important mound on which occupation began c. 3100 B.C. and continued into the eighth century at least, with a small Hellenistic settlement on the *tell*'s summit.

Also of interest is the work of a small Danish expedition at Shiloh (XVIII, C-4) between 1926 and 1932, which discovered that the town was destroyed in the days of Eli and Samuel (cf. Jer. 7:12-14). Sir Flinders Petrie returned to Palestine between 1927 and 1937 with important discoveries at *Tell el-ʿAjjûl*, *Tell Jemmeh* and *Tell el-Fârʿah* (XVIII, A-6). The material is poorly published and the chronology so individualistic, however, that the results must be used with caution. Of great importance is the work of the Dominican School in Jerusalem at *Tell el-Fârʿah* in north central Palestine (XVIII, C-4). The expedition began work in 1946 under the direction of Père R. de Vaux. It was discovered that the site was first settled during the fourth millennium and was occupied more or less continuously down to the ninth century B.C. when it was destroyed—a history that lends support to W. F. Albright's contention that this great mound was ancient Tirzah (cf. I Kings 16:8 ff.). One of the great cities of early Palestine was at Khirbet Kerak (XVIII, C-D 3) at the southern end of the Sea of Galilee. Four strata from the end of the fourth and from the early third millenniums were found by the Jewish Palestine Exploration Society, beginning in 1944. The city was destroyed c. 2400 B.C. and not reoccupied until a Hellenistic town was established on the old site. The small mound of *Tell Qasîleh*, excavated by Benjamin Mazar (Maisler) between 1948 and 1950, is of great importance, particularly for the ceramic chronology of the period between the twelfth century, when it was first established, and the ninth century. The neighboring *Tell ej-Jerîsheh*, excavated by E. L. Sukenik between 1934 and 1951, contains the remains of a town dating from the Early Bronze Age to the end of the tenth century, and the suggestion that it is the Biblical Gath-rimmon seems quite probable.

A major excavation at *Tell el-Qedaḥ* in Galilee (XVIII, D-2) was begun in 1955 by an Israeli expedition headed by Yigael Yadin. This was Hazor, the ancient capital of Galilee and the only city of that region which Joshua destroyed (Josh. 11:10). It was found to contain some seventeen strata of occupation beginning in the fourth millennium and evidently ending in 733 B.C. when the Assyrian king,

Tiglath-pileser III, destroyed it. After that time there was only a small village from the late eighth and early seventh centuries and a Hellenistic fort. The site consists of a great mound, comprising more than twenty-five acres in area, to the north of which lies a huge rectangular plateau, surrounded where necessary by a great earthen wall which in turn was protected on the outside by a dry moat. This enclosure is approximately 3,000 feet long by 2,000 feet wide, and was built by the Hyksos about 1700 B.C. as a camp for their horses and chariots (see pp. 27-28). When destroyed in the thirteenth century B.C., the whole camp area was filled with houses. Its estimated population was some 40,000 people; it was probably the largest city of Palestine at that time.

Very little has been done in Palestinian towns of the time of Jesus, apart from Jerusalem (see pp. 105-107) and Samaria (where a great temple and numerous houses built during the time of Herod the Great have been found). A number of Herodian forts and palaces have been identified. In 1950 and 1951 expeditions directed by J. L. Kelso and J. B. Pritchard unearthed a portion of the constructions of Herod at *Tulûl Abū el-'Alâyiq*, near Jericho. In 1955 an Israeli expedition began work on the Herodian palace at Masada (XVIII, C-6). A very different type of construction has been unearthed at *Khirbet Qumrân* by Pere R. de Vaux, beginning in 1951 (see p. 82). Larger excavations have been made in later Roman and Byzantine ruins. The largest has been at *Jerash* (XVIII, D-4) by the British and American schools and Yale University. Here was laid bare the best-preserved Roman city in Palestine, with its wall and gates, colonnaded streets, temples, theaters, baths, and stadium (see Fig. 45). During the Byzantine Age between the fourth and seventh centuries, the city was filled with a dozen churches, witnessing to a large Christian population. Numerous other churches of the age have also been excavated, among the most interesting of which may be mentioned the Church of the Multiplying of the Loaves at *eṭ-Ṭâbghah* (XVIII, D-3), the Cathedral of Scythopolis (Beth-shan), and the church at *Mâdebā* (XVIII, D-5) which contained a mosaic floor with a large map of Palestine worked in it. The Colt Archaeological Expedition to the Negeb, working on the churches at *'Auja el-Ḥafîr* in 1935-1936, found a large group of papyri, the most significant documents of the age yet found in Palestine (see pp. 67 f.). Judging from the exceedingly large number of churches, chapels, and monasteries built in the country during Byzantine times, there can be no doubt that the country was predominantly Christian.

Similarly, a wealth of information is now at hand about Jewish synagogues and burial customs. The synagogues of Galilee had attracted the attention of Edward Robinson who described several of them, namely at Capernaum (XVIII, D-3), *Meirôn* (XVIII, C-3), *Kefr Bir'im* (XVIII, C-2), and *Khirbet Irbid* (XVIII, C-3). Two German archaeologists examined these and others by means of soundings in 1905. After the First World War the one at Capernaum, the finest yet discovered in Palestine, was completely cleared and partially restored by the Franciscans (see Fig. 41). Unfortunately, however, it is not the same one which existed there in the time of Jesus, since it dates from about the third century A.D. In fact, there appear to be no synagogues thus far found which belong to the period of the New Testament, probably because most of them were destroyed during the first and second revolts against Rome in A.D. 66-70 and A.D. 131-135. Two of the most interesting and important synagogues excavated since the First World War are those at *Khirbet Beit Ilfā* (XVIII, C-3) and *'Ain Dûq* (XVIII, C-5). Both contained well-preserved mosaic floors with elaborate designs, pictures, and inscriptions. After the Byzantine period, a reaction against such things set in and they were no longer tolerated in the synagogues. One of the most significant excavations into Jewish antiquity is that at *Sheikh Abreiq* (begun 1936; XVIII, C-3) in burial catacombs filled with pictorial representations and inscriptions. From the latter we learn that between the second and fifth centuries A.D. this was one of the most famous burial grounds of Judaism, and Jews from many parts of the Roman world came there to die and to be buried on sacred soil.

One of the most astonishing results of Palestinian excavations in the period since the First World War has been in the field of prehistoric archaeology. Indeed, the country has become one of the centers of the search for early civilization. The lowest levels of such sites as Megiddo, Beth-shan, and Gezer show that a number of Palestine's leading cities in the Biblical period had been founded as early as the fourth millennium B.C. The period between c. 3300 and 2400 B.C. was one of great prosperity for the country. Among the cities then in existence were Ai (XVIII, C-5), Jerusalem, Jericho, Gezer, Beth-shan, Megiddo, and Khirbet Kerak (XVIII, D-3). The last mentioned is a good illustration of the prosperity of the period, for it is a huge site, covering nearly sixty acres. In Roman times a number of Palestinian cities were this large or larger, but during the days of the Old Testament the average city was much smaller, sometimes comprising twelve to twenty-five acres (Megiddo covered thirteen), but usually much less. Excavations at *Teleilât el-Ghassûl* (XVIII, D-5) and *Tell Abū Maṭar* (XVIII, B-6) have uncovered small villages from the middle of the fourth millennium or a bit earlier, while the lowest levels at Jericho go back to the Late Stone or Neolithic Age (see above) when villages were first being established during the fifth millennium B.C. Palestine's sequence of early village cultures can thus be outlined somewhat as follows: (1) Neolithic, of which the only town excavated in Palestine is Jericho, though Jarmo in Iraq belongs to the same horizon; (2) Ghassulian (c. 4000-3300 B.C.), found in a number of places, but its development from beginning to end has yet to be discovered stratigraphically; and (3) Early Bronze (c. 3300-2100 B.C.), the period when the city-states were first extensively developed.

In the Early and Middle Stone Ages, covering the long dark ages of prehistory, most of the people of Palestine apparently lived in caves. In the *Wâdī el-Mughârah* (XVIII, B-C 3), the *Wâdī Khareitûn* (XVIII, C-5), *Shuqbah* (XVIII, C-5), and Galilee such caves have yielded a great store of information about early man, including the first complete Stone Age skeletons ever found. At *Shuqbah* some forty-five skeletons belonging to the Middle Stone Age probably represent the earliest appearance of the native race which lived in the country during historical times. In the *Wâdī el-Mughârah* seventy feet of deposit, representing mainly the life of Early Stone Age man, were excavated, and from them ten skeletons and fragments of others were recovered. They are approximately contemporary with Neanderthal man in Europe, and some of them look like Neanderthalers. Others, however, show characteristics of modern man (*homo sapiens*), which means that already at this early period there was racial mixture.

This by no means completes the story of modern excavations in Palestine; yet enough has been written to indicate that the recovery of the ancient life of the country is still in its initial stages. Many years of intensive effort have had to be spent in solving problems of method. Most of the earlier excavators and many of the more modern, without proper knowledge of how to dig, record, or publish, have unwittingly destroyed or lost much of the evidence needed to discover the meaning of their findings. Today the most pressing of these problems have been solved, and we stand at the threshold of a new era in Biblical study. Neither in Palestine nor in any of the Biblical lands has the point of diminishing returns in exploration and discovery yet been reached or even seen upon the distant horizon. When one considers what is yet to be learned, he can only conclude that the districts of Galilee, Samaria, Philistia, Transjordan, Bashan, Damascus, and Phoenicia have barely been touched. In addition, a vast body of material already discovered needs intensive study and assimilation. After the First World War progress was unprecedentedly rapid, and there is reason to believe that the results will be no less astonishing during the years to come. No one would have dared predict the discovery of the Dead Sea Scrolls (see p. 82), but there is no reason to doubt that even greater things may yet be in store for those who seek.

INDEX TO THE TEXT

LETTERS are used with the page numbers to help the reader to find the reference. Note the following examples: 9, the subject is treated in both columns on p.9; 9a, the reference is to the first column of p. 9; 9b, the reference is to the second column of p.9; *p*9, the subject is illustrated in the picture on p.9; *c*9, the subject is discussed in caption to picture on p.9.

Abana River, 58a
Abel, geographer, 14a
Abilene, 84a
Abraham, 23, 25a, 26a, 30b, 68
Absha, *c*23, 29a
Accadian, 30b
Accho, 18a, 35a, 57a
Accho (Acre), Plain of, 18b, 19a
Achaia, 87a, 96b, 97a, 102b, 103a
Achmetha (Ecbatana), 74b
Achor, Valley of, 62b
Acropolis, Athens, 96b, *p*97
Act of Settlement (27 B.C.), 86
Actium, battle of, 86a
Adria, Adriatic Sea, 98a
Aelia Capitolina, 84b, 104a, 107b; *see also* Jerusalem
Aenon, 63a, 93b
Agriculture, Egypt, 28b, 87a; Palestine, 20, 61a; Coastal Plain, 19a; Damascus, 58a; Galilee, 19a, 20a, 59b; Haurân, 20b, 59a; Hill Country, 20b, 62b, 63a; Jezreel, 34b; Negeb, 19b, 67b; Shephelah, 19b, 62b; Phoenicia, 57a
Agrippa, *see* Herod Agrippa
Ahab, 53a, 72b, 115a
Ahaz, 54b, 72b
Ai, 33a, 39b, 40a, 116
Aijalon, Valley of, 34a, 40a, 62b
'Ain Dûq, 117a
'Ain el-Qudeirât, *c*39, 68b
Akhnaton, see Amenophis IV
Albright, 6, *c*48, *c*49, 111a, 114a, 116b
Alexander the Great, career and purpose, 76; destroyed Persepolis, *c*12, 75a; significance, 85a, 101b
Alexander Jannaeus, 81a
Alexandra, Queen, 81a
Alexandria, in Egypt, 76b, 88b, 103a
Alphabet, origin and transmission, 30b, 33b, 57b
Alt, A., 14a
Altar of Burnt Offering, 105b, *c*107
Amalekites, 68b
Amarna, *see* Tell el-Amarna
Amenophis IV (Akhnaton), 13a, 29b, *p*34, 35a
American Schools of Oriental Research, *p*112; Bulletin, 10b; value, 9a, 14a; excavation leadership, 112b, 113a, 116a
Ammon, Kingdom of, location, 20b, 64a; date established, 36a, 40b; oppressed Israel, 43, 44b; David conquered, 47b, 48a; later history, 54b, 55b
Ammon, Persian province, 56b
Amorites, *c*23, 24b, 25a, 35b, 36a
Amos, prophet, 54a, 63a
Anthedon, 83a
Antigonid dynasty, 76b
Antioch, Pisidian, 96a
Antioch, Syrian, 58b, 95, 96, 97a; 102a, 104
Antiochus Epiphanes, 77a, 106a
Antipater, 83a
Antonia, Tower of, 98a, 106b, 107
Antony, Mark, 83a, 86a
'Apiru, 35a
Appian Way, *p*85, 88a, 98b
Aqabah, Gulf of, 17a, 38b
Aqueducts, Jerusalem, *c*83, 105a, 106a; Nabataean, *p*70, 70; Roman, *p*85
Arabah, 17b, 20, 39a, 43a, 67, 69a, *p*70; mines, 50a
Arabia, situation and importance for Israel, 5, 23; Semitic invasion of Fertile Crescent from, 24a; Arameans from, 46b; Nabataeans in, 64a; Paul visited, 95a; Roman province, 85a
Aram, 25a
Aram ("Syria"), **Kingdom of**, in Damascus region, 33b, 58a; history, 33b, 34b, 43b, 46b, 48a, 50b, 53, 54a, 58a, 72a; *see also* Zobah, Kingdom of
Aramaic, 71b, 75a, 88b, 95a, 101
Arameans, in Damascus region, *see* Aram, Kingdom of; in Euphrates Valley, 46b, 71b, 75a; their language official in Persian Empire, 75a
Ararat, 25b
Arch of Constantine, *p*102
Arch of Titus, 84b, *p*87
Archaeology, recent advance in, 6a, 9; methodology, 9-14, 111-117; survey of modern excavations, 111-117; importance of pottery, 10, 112a; of accurate recording, 10; contribution to linguistic study, 11b; to chronology, 12b, 13; use in identifying sites, 13b, 14; prehistoric, 117b; light on patriarchal narratives, 25, 26, 30; on conquest of Canaan and time of Judges, 39b, 40, 45, 46; on Solomon's business ventures, 48b, 57b; on empires of O.T. times, 72-76; on Judaism, synagogues, 60b, 117a; on Negeb, 67b, 68a; *see also* Inscriptions
Archelais, 63b, 92b
Archelaus, 83b, 92b
Areopagus, Athens, *p*97
Aretas IV, Nabataean king, 70b
Aristobulus I, 81a
Aristobulus II, 81a
Ark, in Flood story, 25b; of Covenant, 44b, 46a, 49b, 62b
Arles, Council of, 104b
Armenia, 29a; Christian, 104b
Army, of David, 47b; Roman, 86
Arnon, 20b, 39a, 69a
Arsham, satrap, 75b
Art, in Solomon's Temple, 34a, 49; in synagogues, 60b, 117a
Artaxerxes I, 56b
Artaxerxes II, 56b
Artemis, temple of, *p*64
Aryans, *see* Indo-Europeans
Asa, king of Judah, 50b
Ascalon, 62b, 92b
Ascent of Akrabbim, 67b, 68b
Asher, tribe of, 46b
Asherah, goddess, 36b
Ashtoreth, 6a, 36b
Asia, Province of, 87a, 96b, 97a, 102b
Asia Minor, 76a, 102b, 103, 104a
Asiarchs, 97a
Asiatic Captives Making Bricks in Egypt, *p*37
Asiatics Entering Egypt, *p*23, 25a, 29a
Asochis, Plain of, 59b
Asphalt ("slime") **pits**, 70a
Asphaltitis, Lake (Dead Sea), 20b
Asshur (Assur), 71b
Asshurbanapal, 55a, 73
Asshurnasirpal II, 72a
Assyria, Assyrians, colony in Kanish, 23b; subjugate Mitanni, 30a, 36a; history of empire, 44b, 46b, 47a, 48a, 53-55, 71-74; power in Palestine, 53-55; legal code, 30b
Assyrian language, 12a; codes, 30b
Astronomy, Chaldean, 74b
Athens, 76a, 83b, 87b, 88b, 96b, *p*97
Augustus, 83, 85-88, *p*86, 92b
'Aujā el-Ḥafîr, 117a; papyri, 67b
Avaris, 26a, 28a, 37b; *see* Raamses; Tanis
Azekah, 19b, *p*47, 50b, 62b, 112a
Azotus, 62b, 92b

Baal, Baalism, 6a, *p*35, 36b, 44b, 57a
Baal-Hazor, 19a, 61b
Baal-zephon, 38b
Baasha, king of Israel, 50b
Babel, Tower of, 24b, *p*25, 25b, 26a, 74a, *p*76
Babylon, *p*25, *p*75, *p*76; enlarged by Hammurabi, 24b; by Nebuchadnezzar, 74a; fall, 74b
Babylonia, *c*28; under First Dynasty, 24b, 29a; under Kassites, 29; empire of, 55b, 56a, 73, 74; architecture and science of, 74; fall, 74b
Babylonian, deciphered, *c*9
Babylonian Chronicle, 13a, 55b, 73b, 74a
Badè, 116b
Balaam, diviner, 24b
Balah, Lake, 38b
Bar-Cochba, 84b
Baris, 106b
Barnabas, 95, 96a
Basalt, black, 20b, 59a
Bashan, situation, 20b, 58b; geology, 59a; Israelite settlement, 43b; Aramean invasion, 46b, 50b; later history, 59a, 83a, 93b
Bauer, 11b
Beer-sheba, 19b, 26a, 67a, 68
Behistun "Rock," *p*9
Belshazzar, 74b
Ben-hadad, 72
Bersabee, 68b
Bethabara, 93b
Bethany, beyond Jordan, 64b, 93b
Bethel, patriarchal, 26a; border city, 61b; capture by Israel, 40; excavation, 116b
Bethesda, Pool of, 107a
Bethlehem, *c*63
Bethphage, 94b
Bethsaida Julias, 59a, 93b, 94
Beth-shan, *c*18, 33a, *p*111; Egyptian control, 35a, 60a; Canaanites in, 44a, 45a, 60a; Canaanite temples, 45a; Philistine control, 46a; excavation 111b, 114; *see also* Scythopolis
Beth-shemesh, 19b, 48b, 116b
Beth-yerah, 33a
Beth-zur, Bethsura, 77b, 78, *p*78, 116b
Bezetha, 107a
Bible, origin of word, 33b; roots in history and geography, 5a; textual criticism, 14
Bithynia, Christian, 103a
Blackman, 12a
Black Sea, 76a, 88a
Bliss, 112a
Boghazköy, Hittite center, 9b
Borchardt, 13
Bossert, H., 12b
Bozrah, 59a, 70b
Breasted, 12a, 13b
Brickmaking, *p*37
Bridges, over Jordan, 20a
Britain, Christians in, 104
British in Palestine, 18a, 112b
Bronze Age chronology, 13b
Burrows, M., 6b
Byblos, 24b, 33

Caesarea, 57a, 63a, 92a, 93a, 96b
Caesarea Philippi, 59a, 93b, 94b
Calah, 72a, 73b
Calendar, Egyptian, 13a
Caligula, 84a, 88b
Camel, early use, *c*23, 45a
Cameron, G., 6b, *c*9
Canaan, meaning of name, 33a; geographical extent, 33a; people of, 35b, 36; *see also* Canaanites
Canaanite Captives in Egypt, *p*24
Canaanite Fortress, *p*33
Canaanites, appearance, *p*24, *p*29, *p*33, *p*45, *p*46; original inhabitants of Palestine-Syria, 23b, 35b; Semitic (Gen., ch. 10) 26b, 28a; identified with Phoenicians, 33a; relation to *'Apiru*, 35; importance for civilization, 33, 34a; developed alphabet, 33b; commercial activity, 45a, 46b; social and political organization, 34-36; chief cities, location, 35, 36a; mainly in plains, 34; used chariots, 46a; religious literature, 9b, 11b, 30b; religion, 34a, *p*35, 36b, 44b; temples, 45a, 113a, 114a; reason for weakness, 36; poetry and music, 33b; influence on Israel, 30b, 33b; Patriarchal Age, 24b, 26; Hyksos period, 28; Late Bronze Age, 29a, 33-36; Egyptian rule of, 25a, 26b, 29b, 30a, 34b, 35a; conquest by Israel, 33b, 39, 40; time of Judges, 43-46; in Galilee and Esdraelon, 60a; in Megiddo, 113a; in Jerusalem, 105b; *see also* City-states; Phoenicia; Râs Shamrah
Canals, from Euphrates, *c*28; Nile to Red Sea, 75a, 88a; through Isthmus of Corinth, *p*88, 88a
Canon, Old Testament, 82b
Capernaum, 94; synagogue, *p*60, 60b, 117a
Caracalla, 87b
Carchemish, battle, 55b, 72a, 74a
Carmel, Mount, 18, 19a, *p*47, 57a, 59b
Carthage, 57a, 85a, 104a
Cartography, Palestinian, 9b, 10a, 13b, 14
Catacombs, Jewish, 60b, 117a
Caves, prehistoric *p*116, 117b
Cedar of Lebanon, *p*13
Cenchreae, 97a, 102b
Census records of Israel, 38a
Centurions, 86b
Chalcolithic Age, defined, 24a
Chaldean astronomers, 74b
Chariots, *c*28, 28a, 34b, 44a, 46a, 53a, 72b
Cherethites, 46a
Cherubim, *c*45
Childe, V. G., 24a
Chinnereth, Sea of, *see* Galilee, Sea of
Chorazin, 59a, 60b
Christianity, in Jerusalem, 107; in Galilee, 60b; Transjordan, 59a, 64b, 117a; Samaria, 63b; Philistia, 62b; Negeb, 67b, 68a; sketch of expansion in ancient times, 101-104; why westward spread, 101, 102a; expansion before Paul's mission, 102; Paul's mission work, 95-98, 102b, 103; time of Irenaeus, 103b, 104; of Constantine, 104b
Chronology, archaeological data for, 9b; methods of fixing ancient dates, 12b, 13; absolute and comparative, 11a; most important ancient dates, 15, 16
Church of Holy Sepulcher, *p*104, 107a
Churches, Dura, *c*103, 104b; Jerash, 117a; Jerusalem, 107a; Gethsemane, *p*93, 107a; Holy Sepulcher, *p*104, 107a; St. Anne, 107a; *Mâdebâ*, 117a; Negeb, 67b, 117a; Samaria, 63b; Scythopolis, *c*111, 114a; *eṭ-Ṭâbghah*, 117a
Cilician Gates, *p*71, 76b, 96b, 97a
Citadel, Jerusalem, ancient, 78b; modern, *p*105
Citizenship, Roman, 87, 88a, 95a, 96b, 98a; Tarsus, 95a
Citrus fruits, 19a, 61a
City of David, Jerusalem, 61b, 105, 106a, 107a, 116a
City-states, Canaanite, 24b, 28a, 34a, 35a, 36a, 39b, 40b, 44b, 46b, 57a, 105b; Greek, 76a; Philistine, 46a; Rome, 85; under Rome, 87b; *see also* Ascalon; Gaza
Clark, J. G. D., 24a
Claudius, 84a, 102b
Cleopatra, 83a, 86a
Climate of Palestine, 17, 36b
Coast line, Palestine, 6a, 57a
Coastal Plain near Ramleh; *p*62; *see also* Plain, Coastal
Coinage, Jewish, 56b; Persian, 75a
Coliseum, Rome, *p*102
Colonies, Greek, 30a, 76a; Phoenician, 26b, 33b, 57a; Roman, 87, 96b; Zionist, 20a
Colt Expedition, 14b, 117a
Conder, 14a
Conquest of Canaan, 35a, 39, 40, 43, 44a
Constantine, *c*102, *c*104, 104b, 107b
Corinth, 96b, 97a, 102b
Corinth, Isthmus of, 88a, 96b
Corinth Canal, *p*88
Council at Jerusalem, 96
Covenant relation, 26b
Creation story, 25b
Crete, 24a, 25a, 30a, 45b, 88a, 103b
Crowfoot, J. W., 115a, 116a
Cuneiform writing, 9a, 11b, 12b, *p*30, 30b, 101b
Cyprus, 30a, 45a, 87a, 95b, 102b
Cyrenaica, Cyrene, 101b, 102b, 104a
Cyrus, 74b, 75a

Dalman, G., 14a
Dalmanutha, 94a
Dam at *Kurnub*, *p*68
Damascus, 43b, 48a, 53, 54, 58, 59a, 70b, 72, 83b, 92a, 96a
Dan, tribe of, moved, 46a
Darius I, *c*9, *c*12, 56a, 75a
David, and Goliath, 62b; in Negeb and Jeshimon, 69a; reign, 47, 48; conquests, 48, 61b, 64a, 105b; Jerusalem his city, 61b, 105b; census, 38a
Dead Sea, 17, 19b, *p*20, 20, 26a, *p*61, 69, 70a, *p*81
Dead Sea Scrolls, *c*61, *c*81, 82, 117b; *see* Qumrân
Debir, 19b, 40b, 48b
Decapolis, meaning of word, 91b; cities included, 91b, 92a; purpose and history of the league, 58b, 64a, 91b-94
Delphi inscription, 97a
Department of Antiquities, 10b, 112b
Desert, Arabian, 5, 17b, 20b, 23b, 24, 35b, 45a, 61a, 64a, 95a
Desert of Sinai, *p*38
De Vaux, 117a
Dhorme, 11b
Diatessaron, *c*103, 104b
Dibon, *c*50, 53b, 116b
Dispersion of Jews, 6a, 75b
Divination, Mesopotamian, 24b
Documents, decipherment, 9b, 11b; interpretation, 11b, 12; use in chronology, 12b, 13; in topography, 14; Patriarchal Age, 24b, 25; Sojourn period, 30; *Qumrân*, 82; *see also* Inscriptions; Papyri
Dog River, 72b, *c*73
Dome of the Rock, 105b, *p*107
Dominican School, 116b
Domitian, 88b
Dophkah, 39a
Dor, 18b, 45b
Dothan, 26a, 116b
Duncan, 116a
Dur-Sharrukin, 73b
Dura-Europos, *p*103

Early Bronze Age, defined, 24a
Ebal, Mount, *c*18, 19a, 63a
Economic condition of Palestine, under David and Solomon, 48b-50a; under later kings, 47a
Edgerton, 13b
Edom, Kingdom of, territory, 20b; date founded, 35b, 36a; history, 39a, 40b, 43a, 44b, 53b, 54b, 55b, 56, 64a, 69a, 70; area under Persians, 56b; succeeded by Nabataeans, 69a, 70b; copper and iron mines, 20b, *p*68, 69b
Edomites, origin, 36a; territory, 20b; occupied Negeb, 69a
Eglon, 40b, 49a
Egnatian Way, 88a, 96b, 97b
Egypt, cultural influence on Palestine, 5a; early excavation in, 10a; chronology of, 12b, 13; Nile basis of life in, 23a; trade with Edom and desert, 20b; Patriarchal Age, 24b; refuge of nomads in famine, 25a, 29a; Sojourn and Exodus period (Hyksos and New Kingdom), 27-30a, *p*33, 34b, 35a, 36a, *p*37, 37, 38, 40, 71a, 113; weak in David's day, 48b; raid of Shishak, 50b; time of Jeremiah, 74; Persia rules, 74b; Alexander in, 76b; Ptolemaic dynasty, 76b, 77a; Roman province, 87a, 91a; Christianity in, 102b-104; grain, 28b, 87a; *see also* Papyri
Egypt, River of, 67a
Egyptian language, literature, 12a
El, Canaanite god, 36b
El Shaddai, meaning, 26b
Elah, Valley of, 40b, *p*47, 62b
Elam, Indo-European, 26b; Kingdom of, about 1600 B.C., 29
Elamite inscription, *c*9
Elephantine, 9b, 56b, 75b, 76a, 77a
Eleutheropolis, 62b
Elijah, 57b
Elim, 39a

Emmaus, 94b
Emperor worship, 88b
En-rogel, 105a
Ephesus, 97, p98, 102b
Erman, 12a
Esarhaddon, 55a, 73a
Esdraelon, p47, c58, 59b, 60a; *see also* Jezreel, Valley of
Essenes, 63a, c81, 82, 92b
Ethical quality of Israelite religion, 36b
Ethiopia, 102b
Etymologies, popular, 14b
Euphrates River, 23a, p25, p28, p103
Europe, in age of Abraham, 24a; later political center, 85a
Excavation, methods, 6a, 10, 11a; in Palestine, 111-117
Exile, northern tribes, 54b, 73a; Judah, 55b, 56a, 75a
Exodus from Egypt, 37-41; date, 28a; route, 38, 39a
Ezion-geber, 39a, 50a, 57b, 69b
Ezra, 56b

Fair Havens, 98a
Famine, in Egypt, 28b; in Palestine, 25a, 29a, 95a
Feast of Dedication, 78a, 106a
Felix, 84a, 98a
Fertile Crescent, 5, 23, 24, 27a
Festus, 84, 98a
First Peter, 103a
Fisher, 112b
Flood story, 25b, 26a
Foreign Captives before Pharaoh, p29
Forests, ancient, Palestine, Sharon, 18b, 63a; Philistia lacked, 19a; Hill Country, 34a; Transjordan, 20b; palm and balsam groves at Jericho, 63b, 83a; Lebanon, 34b; Cyprus, 95b
Fortifications, city, Hyksos, 28a, p28; Egyptian, in Palestine, 35a; Canaanite, p33, 36, 113a; period of Judges, 45b; Davidic, 48b; Samaria, 53, p54, 54a, 115a; *Tell en-Naṣbeh*, 50b, p115; Jericho, 114b; *Tell Zakarîyeh*, 112a; Jerusalem 105-107; Lachish, c56, 115b
Forum, Gerasa, p64; Rome, p87
Freedmen, 87b

Gad, tribe, settled, 36a, 43, 63b
Gadd, C. J., 74a
Galatia, 76b, 96, 97, 102b
Galatians, Epistle to, 96a
Galilee, geographical situation, p17, 19a, 57a, 59; Canaanites in, 60a; mixed population, 60; history, 54b, 59b, 60, 93; Jesus' ministry in, 94; Christianity in, 102a; Judaism in, 60b
Galilee, Sea of, 17, 19a, 20a, p59, 59a, 60b, p91; connection with Jesus' ministry, 93, 94
Gallio, 97a
Garden Tomb, 107a
Gardiner, 12a
Garstang, 14b, 40a, 114b, 115a
Gaul, Christians in, 104
Gaulanitis, 93a
Gaza, location, 18b; trade center, 20b, 62; Egyptian administration center, 34b; attached to Syria, 91b, 92b
Gehenna, 103a
Gelb, I. J., 6b
Genesis patriarchal stories, 26b
Gennath, Gate, 107b
Gennesaret, Plain of, 20a, 59b, p91; Lake, *see* Galilee, Sea of
Gentile Christianity, 102, 103b, 104
Gentile mission, 94b, 95b, 96, 98b
Gentiles in Galilee, 60b, 78a, 94b
Geography, importance for Biblical study, 5, 6a; of Palestine, 17-20; of Northern Palestine, 57-60; of Central Palestine, 61-64; of Southern Palestine, 67-71
Geology, of Palestine, rocky hill country, 19a, p78; Jordan Valley, 20; Transjordan, 20b; limestone, 19a, 20b, 59a, 67a, 69a; basalt, 59a; flint, 67a; lava, 58b; sandstone, 69a; *see also* Mines
Georgia, 104b
Gerasa, p64, 64b, 92
Gergesa, 94a
Gerizim, Mount, c18, 19, 62a, 63a, 76a, 81a, 92b
Germania, 86a
Geshem the Arab, 56b, 115b
Gethsemane, Garden of, p93
Gezer, early, 24b, 33a; in time of Judges and monarchy, 40a, 44a; date destroyed, 44a; Solomonic building at, 49a; excavation of, 112
Gibeah, 47b, 50b, 61b, 116b
Gibeon, 36a, 39b, 61b
Gibeonite tetrapolis, *see* Hivites
Gihon, 105, 106a, c108
Gilboa, Mount, 19a, 45a, 59b
Gilead, 20b, 39b, 54b, 63b
Gilgamesh epic, 24b, 73a
Ginsberg, H. L., 11b
Girgashites, 36a
Glueck, N., 5b, 11a, 14a, 111a
Golgotha, 107b
Gomorrah, 20b, 26a, 69b, 70a
Gordon, C., 11b
Gordon's Calvary, 107a
Goshen, 28, 29a, 37, 38a
Goths, 104b
Granicus River, 76b
Grant, E., 116b
Grazing, in Palestine, 20b, 25a, 26a, 34b, 61a, 62b, 69a
Greece, basis of chronology of, 13b; prehistoric, 24a; in period of Sojourn and Conquest of Canaan, 30a; development of culture, 33b, 76; Exilic and post-Exilic periods, 75a, 76; coinage, 75a; *see also* Achaia; Hellenistic culture
Greek, 67b, 70a, 77a, 88b, 95a, 101b, 104b, 106; among Jews, 76b, c95, 97a, 101b, 102; at Dura, c103, 104b
Greek culture, *see* Hellenistic culture
Greek O.T., 76b; use in topography, 14
Guthe, H., 14a

Hadad, or Baal, 36b
Hadrian, 84b
Ham, father of African peoples, 26b
Hamath, 33a, 48, 53
Hammath synagogue, 60b
Hammurabi, 13a, 27b, 29a; Code of, 24b, p26, 30b; date, 24b
Hanging Gardens, 74b, p76
Hanukkah, 78a
Ḥaram esh-Sherîf, 105
Haran, 25, 71b, 74a
Harbors, Palestine, 18, 57a; Phoenicia, 18a, 57; Seleucia, for Syrian Antioch, 95b; Cenchreae and Lechaeum, for Corinth, 97a; Phoenix, 98a; Syracuse, 98b; Puteoli and Ostia, for Rome, 88a, 98b
Har-magedon, 19a
Haurân, 20b, 58b, 59a; never strongly Israelite, 59a; *see also* Bashan
Hays, A. A., 6b
Hazael, King, 53b, 72b
Hazor, 14b, 39b, 40b, 60a, 116b
Hebrews, meaning of word, 35b; relation to *Khabiru*, 35; in Goshen, 37a
Hebron, 19b, 26a, 40b, 61b, 67a
Hellenistic culture, under Alexander the Great, 76; under Seleucids, 77a; promoted by Herod the Great, 63b, 83, 106b; in Roman Empire, 88b, 101; in Palestine, especially Decapolis, 6a, 58b, 59a, 62b, 63b, 64a, 77a, 81b, 83, 92, 101, 106a
Hellenistic empires, 76
Hermon, Mount, 6a, 17, 20a, c57, 57b, p84, 94a
Herod Agrippa I, 84a, 107a
Herod Agrippa II, 84
Herod Antipas, ruled Galilee and Peraea, 64b, 83b, 92b, 93; built Tiberias, 20a, 60b, 92a; army 86b; defeated by Aretas, 70b; seized John the Baptist, 64b
Herod the Great, given kingdom by Rome, 86b; reign, 83; fortresses, 62b, 83b; building work at Caesarea, 63a, 83b, 93a, 98a; at Jericho, 63b; at Jerusalem, including Temple, 83b, 106b, c108; at Samaria, 63b, 83b; fled to Masada, 69a; sons and will, 83b, 92b
Herodium, 62b, 83b, 84b
Herodotus, 73a
Hezekiah, 54b, 73a
Hill Country, of Palestine, geography, 17, 18a, 19, 20b, 59b, 62b, 63a; military approach by way of Shephelah, 40; in Patriarchal Age, 26a, 34b, 36b; not center of Canaanites, 34a; Hebrews settled first in, 20b, 34b; time of Judges, 44a, 45b; later history, 55a
Hinnom, Valley of, 61b, 105a, c108
Hippicus, tower, 106b, 107b
Hiram of Tyre, 33b, 49b
History, geographical conditions, 5, 6a
Hittite language, 12b, 29a
Hittites, appearance, c24, p29; Kingdom of, 23b, 26a, 29b, 30a, 36a; in Palestine, 35b; in Syria, 72a; legal code, 30b; kept secret method of smelting iron, 46a
Hivites, i.e., Horites, 35b, 36a
Hor, Mount, unidentified, 39a, 68b
Horeb, 38b
Horites, 35b; *see also* Hurrians
Hormah, 39a
Horses, c28, 28a, 50a, 53a, 72b, 113, 117a
Hosea, 54a, 63a
Huffmon, H. B., 6b
Huleh, Lake, 17b, 20a, 58a, p84
Hurrian language, 12b, 29b
Hurrians, 29; *see also* Mitanni
Hyksos, 26a, 27b-29a, 37b, 113a
Hyksos enclosure, p28, 28a
Hyrcania, 62b, 83b
Hyrcanus, John, 62a, 78b, 81a
Hyrcanus II, 81a, 83a

Idumaea, 69a
Ignatius, 103b
Illyricum, 97b, 103a
Indo-European empires, 69a; peoples, 23b, 26b, 27b
Indo-Iranians in Mitanni, 29a
Inscriptions, discovery and decipherment, 9b, 11b; interpretation, 11b, 12; Behistun "Rock," p9; *Râs Shamrah*, 11b, 30; Khorsabad list Assyrian kings, 12b, 13a; Mari texts, 13a, 24b; Kanish, 23b; Code of Hammurabi, 24b, p26; Sinai, 25a; Nuzi tablets, p30, 30b; *Tell el-Amarna* letters, 30b, 35a; Black Obelisk of Shalmaneser III, p72; Mesha Stone, p50, 53b; Lachish letters, 56a; Nineveh, library Ashurbanapal, 73b; Theodotus synagogue, p95; Corinth synagogue, 97a; Delphi (Gallio), 97a; Temple, Jerusalem, 106b; *see also* Documents; Papyri
Irenaeus, 103b, 104a
Iron, 46a, 48b; Iron Age, 46a
Irrigation, 23a; in Negeb, 19b; Jordan Valley, 20a, 63b
Isaiah, 54, 73a
Ishtar Gate, Babylon, p75, p76
Israel, Kingdom of, in period of united monarchy, 47-50; in ninth-eighth centuries, 50b, 53, 54; civil war with Judah, 50b, 61b, 62a; fall of, 54b, 62a
Israel, State of, 10b, 107b, 112b
Israelites, appearance, p23, p24, p29, p72; Law influenced by ancient codes, 24b, 30b; Sojourn in Egypt, 27a, 28, 29a; oppression, p37, 37; Exodus, 38, 39a; number involved, 37b, 38a; conquest of Palestine, 33b, 35a, 39, 40; settlement, 43, 44, 60a; period of Judges, 44b-46; under monarchy, 47-50, 53-56a, 57b
Ivory work, Megiddo, p45, p46, 113a; Samaria, 115a

Jabbok, 20b, 43b, 63b
Jacob's Well, c18, 94a
Jamnia, 62b, 92b
Japheth, children of, 23b, 26b
Jebusite Gate, Jerusalem, 116a
Jebusites, 35b
Jehu, 53, 72b
Jehud, to be read Iazor, 14
Jerahmeelites, 68b
Jerash, ancient Gerasa, p64, 117a
Jeremiah, 55, 56a
Jericho, altitude and climate, 17; in Canaanite period, 28a, 33a; fall of, 39b, 40a; in N.T. period, 63b, 92, 94b; excavation of, 112b, p114, 114b, 115a
Jeroboam I, 50b
Jeroboam II, 53b, 54a, 72b, 112b
Jerome, 95a
Jerusalem, altitude and climate, 17a, 19b; topography, 105a; early, 24b, 33a, 34a; Jebusite city, 105; David captures, 48a, 61b, 105b; Solomonic building, 49a; O.T. period, 39b, 40, 54b, 55a, 105b, 106a; destroyed, rebuilt, 55b, 56, 75a; Maccabean period, 77, 78, 81a; under Herod the Great, 83b, 106b; Jesus in, 107a; first century walls, 107; Christian center, 102a, 103b, 104, 107b; destroyed, 107b; modern, p104, p105; excavations, p95, 112a, 115b
Jerusalem-Jericho Road, p92
Jeshimon, *see* Judah, Wilderness of
Jesus, not an Essene, 82b; knew Hellenistic forces, 92b; centered ministry in Galilee, 60b; scenes of ministry, 93b, 94; in Jerusalem, 107a; accused of political aims, 91a; purpose and message, 101b
Jewish Palestine Exploration Society, 116b
Jews, fight for religious freedom, 77, 78a; for political freedom, 78; under Rome, 83, 84, 88b; dispersion, 75b, 101a
Jezebel, 53a, 63a
Jezreel, Valley of, p17, 19a, 20b, 34; *see also* Esdraelon
John the Baptist, 20a, 64b, 82b, 93a; Church of, Samaria, 63b
Jonah, prophet, 54a
Jonathan, Maccabean, 78b
Joppa, 18b, 34b, 78b, 83a, 102a
Jordan, Kingdom of, 10a, 107b, 112b
Jordan River and Valley, sources, 20a, p57; views, p19, p20; bridges, 20a; divides Palestine, 6a, 64; geographical data, 17, 18a, 20, 59a, c61; history, 26a, 34a, 59a, 63, 64a, 93b, 94a; *see also* Galilee, Sea of
Joseph story, 28
Josephus, 20, 64b, 81, 82a, 84, 91b, 92a, 93, 106a
Joshua, 35b, 36, 39b, 40
Joshua, ch. 1, 39b; **ch. 10**, 40; **chs. 15 to 19**, 43b, 44a
Josiah, 55a, 74a
Judaea, wider meaning, 83a
Judah, geography, 19, 62, p63; wilderness of, 19b, 62b, 63a, p67, 69a; Philistia and, 62, 63a; conquest by Joshua, 39b, 40; Kingdom of, 47-50, 53-56; civil war with Israel, 50b, 61b, 62a, p115; captivity of, 55b, 56a; post-Exilic period, 56a
Judaism, 6a, 60b, 77a, 101b, 117
Judas Maccabaeus, 77b, 78a
Judges, ch. 1, 39b, 40a; **ch. 5**, by eyewitness, 45a
Judges, Period of, 43-46, 63b
Julius Caesar, 83a, 85b, 88b, 97a

Kadesh, 29b; battle at, 30a
Kadesh-barnea, 19b, 39a, c39, 68b
Kampffmeyer, 14b
Kanish, 23b, 71b
Karnak, ruins of, p27, 50b
Kassites, 29
Kelso, J. L., 116b, 117a
Kenites, metal smiths, 38b, 68b
Kenyon, Kathleen, 114b, 115a
Khabiru, 35b
Khazneh, at Petra, p77
Khirbet Beit Ilfa, 117a
Khirbet Kerak, 14b, 116b
Khirbet Qumrân, 63a, p81, 82, c82, 117a
Khorsabad List, 12b, 13a
Kidron, Valley of, p93, 105a, c108
King's Highway, 39a, p40, 69b
Kir-hareseth, 20b, 44b, 70b
Kirjath-sepher, 40b
Kishon, "river," 19a, 44a
Kitchener, 14a
Kramer, S. N., 9b, 12a
Kugler, F.X., 13a
Kurnub, dam, p68

Lab'aya, 35
Lachish, at *Tell ed-Duweir*, 14b; palace, 48b; reconstruction of, p56; Israelite capture of, 19b, 40b; Assyrian destruction of, 54b, p55, 73a; Babylonian destruction of, 56a; letters, 50b, 115b; excavation of, 40b, 115b
Laish, 46a
Landsberger, 12a
Late Bronze Age, 27a
Latin, 78a, 104b
Lebanon, Mount, geographical facts, 19a, 20a, 59b; northern barrier of Galilee, 6a, 57b, 58a; forests, 34b; cedar of, p13
Lebonah, Plain of, p44
Legal codes, 30b
Legions, Roman, 86b
Leontopolis, 77a
Libnah, 19b, 40b, c47, 62b
Libyan, p29
Limestone throughout Palestine, 19a, 20b, 58b, 67a, 69a
Luckenbill, 12a
Luke, 96b
Lydian Empire, fall, 74b

Macalister, 112a, 116a
Maccabaeus, meaning, 77a
Maccabean period, 60a, 77-81, 106a
Macedonian Empire, 76
Machaerus, 64, 83b, 84b, 93a
Magdala, 60b
Malta, 88a, 98b
Mamre, 26a
Manasseh, east of Jordan, 43, 59a
Manasseh, king of Judah, 55a, 73a
Manetho, on Hyksos, 27b, 28a
Manna, 37b
Manuscripts, *see* Documents
Marah, 39a
Marcion, 103b
Marduk, 74, 75a
Mari, 24b, 25a; tablets, 13a
Mariamme, tower, 106b
Mariette, 10a
Marquet-Krause, Mme., 116a
Mars' Hill, *see* Areopagus
Masada, 69a, 83b, 84b, 117a
Masterman, 14b
Mattathias, 77b
Mazar (Maisler), 116b
Medeba, 64b, 78b, 117a
Medes, Media, 29a, 73b, 74b
Mediterranean, under Roman control, 85a; travel on, 88a; no good harbors in Palestine, 6a, 18, 57a; *see also* Harbors
Megalithic tombs, 24a
Megiddo, guarded pass from Esdraelon to coastal plain, p17, 19a, 44a; early, 24b, 33a, 35a; period of Judges, 39b, 44a, 45; Solomonic, 49, 60a; battle of, 55b; ivories, 45, p45, p46; excavation, 112b, 113, p113
Megiddo, Pass of, 19a, p43, 59b
Melitene, Christian, 103b
Menahem, 54b, 72b
Mercenary troops, 35a, 81a
Merenptah, Pharaoh, 40b
Mesha, king of Moab, 49a, c50, 53b, 69a, 70b
Mesopotamia, 23a; chronology, 12b, 13a; literature, 12, 25b, 26a
Meyer, 13b
Midianites, in Sinai region, 38b; oppressors of Israel in period of Judges, 44b, 45a
Millo, 105b
Mines, in Edom, iron and copper, 20b, 50a, p68, 69b; in Nubia, gold, 25a; in Sinai, copper and turquoise, 25a, 38b; in Taurus Mountains, silver, 23b
Minos, Minoan culture, 30a
Mishneh, Second Quarter, 106a
Mitanni, 29, 30, 36a
Mizpah, 50b
Mizpah, benediction, 26b
Moab, Kingdom of, location, 20b, 43, p67, 69a; origin and date established, 36a, 40b, 70; avoided by Israel on way to Canaan, 39a; oppressed Israel in time of Judges, 44b; David conquered, 48a; displaced Reuben, 43b; independent, p50, 53b; tribute to Assyria, 54b; chief city, 70b; border fortress, p69
Modein, 77b
Mohammed, 5b
Monarchy, Hebrew, set up, 47b
Monasteries, in Negeb, 67b
Monotheism, of Akhnaton, c34
Moreh, Hill of, 19a, 45a, 60a
Mosaics, Medeba map, 60b, 117a; synagogues, 60b, 117a
Moses, 28a, 37b
Mot, Canaanite god, 36b
Museum, at Jerusalem, 112b
Mycenaean culture, 30a
Mythology, Canaanite, 25b, 30b, 36b

Nabataeans, origin and history, 70b; capital Petra, 70b; Kingdom of, 70b, 81a, 91a; in Transjordan, 59a, 64a, 68
Nabataean-Roman site, p70
Nabonidus, 74b, 75a
Nabopolassar, 73b
Nahum, 73a
Navy, Roman, 86b

INDEX TO THE TEXT

Nazareth, 60b, 93a
Neanderthal man, 117b
Nebuchadnezzar, *c*25, 55b, 57b, 74, 75a
Necho, 55b, 74a
Negeb, "Southland," 19b; history of, 67, 68; views, *p*39, *p*68; Christianity in, 67b, 68a; papyri found in, 67b, 68a
Nehemiah, 56b, 75a
Nero, 84, *c*88, 88a
Nicaea, Council of, 104b
Nile, 23a, 25a, *c*27, 29a
Nineveh, 55b, 73b
Nippur, 12a, 75b
Nofretete, Queen, *p*34
Nuzi tablets, 25b, *p*30, 30b

Obelisk, Shalmaneser III, *p*72
Octavian, *see* Augustus
Og, Kingdom of, 36a, 39a, 43
Olives, Mount of, *p*93, 105a
Olive trees, *p*62, *p*63
Omri, 53, 57b, 63a
Onias IV, 77a
Ophel, *c*95, 105
Oriental Institute, 12a, 113a
Origen, 93b

Paddan-aram, 25a
Palace of Hasmonaeans, 106a, 107a
Palace of Herod, *c*105, 106b, 107a
Palestine, origin of word, 19a, 45b; size, 17a; climatic contrasts in, 17; geography of, 5, 6a, 17-20; Northern, 18a, 19a, 20, 57-60; Central, 18-20, 61-64; Southern, 19b, 20, 67-71; lack of geographical unity, 6a; limited detachment, 5, 6a; no good harbors, 6a, 57a; not wealthy, 5b; not mainly urban, 5b, 61a; focal point of Biblical history, 5a; cultural ties, 5a; bridge between civilizations and border region of empires, 23a, 33a, 76b, 101a; population, 61; prehistoric period, 117; Patriarchal Age, 24b, 25a, 26; Late Bronze Age, 33-36; Israelite conquest, 39b, 40; period of Judges, 43-46; period of monarchy, 47-50, 53-56; post-Exilic period, 56, 76b; Maccabean, 77-81; Rome takes over, 81a, 83a; Herodian, 83, 84; in time of Jesus, 91-94; rise of Church in, 101, 102; excavations in, 111-117; economic life, 48b, 57, 61, 63a, 67, 69; Roman roads, 88a, 93b
Palestine Exploration Fund, 103a, 112a, 116a
Pamphylia, 95b
Papyri, *c*30; found mainly in Egypt, 76b; Elephantine, 9b, *c*23, 75b; Christian Egypt, 104a; *'Aujā el-Ḥafīr* in Negeb, 19b, 67b, 68a, 117a
Parthian Empire, 59a, 76b, 85b, 86b, 91a, 92a; Jews in, 101a
Pasargadae, 75a
Pastoral Epistles, 97b, 98b, 103a
Patriarchs, probable appearance, *p*23; origin, 25a; customs and life, 25b, 26, 30b; Patriarchal Age, 24-26, 35; settled in Hill Country, 34b; in Negeb, 68; patriarchal structure of Israelite society, 5b, 43a; religion, 26b
Paul, Apostle, 87a, 88a; journeys, 95-98; mission strategy, 95b, 102, 103
Pella, 36a, 60a, 64b, 107b
Pentateuch, sources, 9b; date, 56b
Pentecost, 101a, 102b
Peraea, 64b, 93a
Perizzites, 36a
Persepolis, *p*12, 75a
Persian Empire, 56, 74-76
Petra, 17b, 20b, 70b, *p*77
Petrie, F., 9b, 10a, 112a, 116b
Petroleum deposits, 70a
Pharisees, 81b, 92b
Pharpar River, 58
Phasael, tower, 106b, 107b
Phasaelis, 63b, 83b, 92b
Philip, tetrarch, 83b, 92b, 93b
Philip of Macedon, 76
Philippi, 96b
Philistia, Philistine Plain, geographical features, 18b, 19a, 62, *p*62; rarely controlled by Israelites or Jews, 62a; political and economic importance, 62; Hellenistic influence in, 62b; *see also* Philistines
Philistines, 18b; appearance, *p*29; origin, 45b; settlement in Palestine, 26b, 39b, 45b; control of iron in days of Judges, 46a; oppressed Israel, 44b, 46a; Saul and David defeated, 46a, 47, 48; chief cities, 46a, 62a; Uzziah subdued, 62a
Philo of Alexandria, 82a
Phoenicia, meaning of word, 33a; situation, 18a, 20b, 57; *see also* Phoenicians
Phoenicians, identified with Canaanites, 33a; seafaring people, 53; organized state, 46b; colonies, 26b, 57a; commercial activity, 30a, 33, 46b, 57; aid to Solomon, 48b, 57b; Israel's debt to, 33b, 57b
Pithom, 37a, 38a, 40b
Plain, of Accho, 18b, 19a; of Asochis, 59b; Coastal, 17a, 18, 19a, 20b, 44a, 62a, 102a; Esdraelon, 19a, 34b; in Galilee, 19a; Gennesaret, 20a, 59b, *p*91; Lebonah, *p*44; "Plains of Moab," 63b; Philistine, 18b, 19a; Sharon, 18b, 44a; Shechem, *p*18; "Cities of the Plain," 26a, 70a
Plateau, Transjordan, 17b, 18a, 20b, 63b, 64a, 69a; Ḥaurân, 58b, 59a; Judean, 19b; Moab, *p*67
Pliny the elder, 82a, 91b
Pliny the younger, 103a
Poebel, 12
Politarchs, 96b
Polycarp, 103b
Polytheism, 5b, 26b, 88
Pompeii, *p*101; Christians in, 103b
Pompey, 81a, 83a, 85, 91b
Pontius Pilate, *c*83, 91b, 92b, 93, 105a
Population, of Canaan before conquest, 34a, 35b; of Palestine, 61, 63a; of Galilee, mixed, 60b; of Transjordan, 69b; of Rome, 87
Pottery, Canaanite, 33b; Nabatean, 70b; Philistine, 45b; use in dating, 10, 11a, 112a
Praetorian Guard, 86b
Praetorium, 107a
Pritchard, J. B., 12a, 72b, 117a
Proconsuls, 87a, 95b
Procurators, 83, 84, 87a, 92b, 93a
Prophets, nomadic heritage, 5b; fought pagan culture, 5b; international outlook, 5b
Provinces, Roman, 86, 87
Psephinus, tower, 107b
Ptolemaic canon, 13a
Ptolemaic Empire, 76b
Ptolemais, 18a, 57a, 96b
Ptolemy, geographer, 92a
Punon, mining center, 39a, 69b
Punt, 25a
Purple dyes, 33a, 57b
Puteoli, 88a, 98b, 103a
Pyramids, *p*11, 24b

Qarqar, battle at, 72
Qumrân, *c*61, 63a, *p*81, *c*82, 82, 83a, 84b, 92b, 117a

Raamses, Rameses, 37, 38a, 40b, *p*73
Rabbath-ammon, 20b, 36a, 43b, 44b, 64a
Racial types, *c*29
Rainfall, Palestine, 17b, 19b, 61a, 67b, 68a
Rameses, *see* Raamses
Rameses II, 29b, 37, 45a
Ramsay, 95b
Râs Shamrah (Ugarit), 24b, *c*35, 46b; texts: discovery, interpretation, 11b, 26a; contents, 30b, 36b
Rawlinson, H., *c*9
Red Sea, 20a, 38a, 39a, 50a
Reed Sea, 38
Rehoboam, 50b, *c*56
Reisner, G. A., 10a, 112b
Reland, A., 13b
Religion under Romans, 88
Rephidim, 39a
Reuben, tribe, 36a, 43, 63b
Rhodes, 83b, 87b
River of Egypt, 67a, 68b
Roads, in Esdraelon, 19a; in Galilee, 57a; to Gaza, 18b, 62b, 68a; Jerusalem-Jericho, 64a, *p*92, *p*93; Jordan Valley, 20a, 59b, 94a; King's Highway, 39a, *p*40, 69b; past Megiddo, 19a, *p*43, 59b; Samaria, *p*18, 19b, *p*44, 59b; Way of Land of Philistines, 38a, 68a; Way of Sea, 58; through Cilician Gates, *c*71, 76b; Roman, *c*40, 70b, 88a, 93b
Robinson, E., 9b, 13b, 111, 117a
Roman Empire, rise of, 85; Augustus ruler of, 85-88; army, 86; provinces, 86b, 87a; colonies, 87; citizenship, 87, 95a, 98a; travel in, 88a; religion and culture, 88; in Palestine, 6a, 59a, 61a, 81a, 83, 84; Christianity in, 101-104; roads, *p*40, 70b, 88a, 93b
Roman Forum, *p*87
Rome, rise, 85; population, 87; Christianity in, 102b, 103b, 104b; *see also* Roman Empire
Rowe, A., 114a

Sadducees, 81b
Salim, 63a, 93b
Salt hill s.w. of Dead Sea, 70a
Salt Sea, *see* Dead Sea
Samaria, city, built by Omri, 53a, *p*53, *p*54; refortified, 53b, 54a; Damascene quarter, 58b; fall of, 54b, 73a; Hyrcanus destroyed, 81a; Herod rebuilt, 63b, 83; Jesus avoided, 94b; excavation of, 112b, 115
Samaria, country, geographical situation, 19, 63; separation from Galilee, 59b; rivalry with Judah, 61b, 62a; fertile, 63a; boundary, 61b, 93b; historical data, 56, 61b, 62a, 63, 92b
Samaritans, 19b, 56, 62a, 76a
Samson, 62b
Sanballat, 56b
Sandstone, 69a, 70b
Sargon II, 54b, 73, *p*74
Satrapies, 75a
Saul, King, 47b
Schaeffer, C. F. A., 11b
Schliemann, 111b
Scylla and Charybdis, 98b
Scythopolis, *c*18, 81a, 92a, *c*111
Sea peoples, 45b, 46
Sea travel under Rome, 86b, 88a, 96-98
"Seat of Moses," 60b
Sela, 44b, *p*69, 70b
Seleucia, port of Antioch, 95b
Seleucid Empire, 76b
Sellers, O. R., 6b, 116b
Sellin, E., 116a
Semechonitis, Lake, *see* Huleh, Lake
Semites, physical appearance, *p*23, *p*24, *p*29, *p*37; origin, 5b; peoples included, 23, 26b
Senate, Roman, 85b-87a
Sennacherib, 14b, 54b, *p*55, 73
Sepharad (Sardis), 74b
Sepphoris, 60b, 93a, 94b
Sethe, 12a
Sethos I (Seti), 13a, 29b, 37b, 38a, 45a
Shalmaneser III, 53, 54b, *c*72, 72, *p*73
Sharon, Plain of, 18b, 19a, 44a, 63a
Sharuhen, 29a, 43b, 50b, 68b
Shechem, *c*18, 24b, 26a, 28a, 35, 39b, 40a, *c*44, 49b, 50b, 63a, 94a, 113b, 116a
Shechem, Plain of, *p*18
Shefar'am, location, name, 14b
Sheikh Abreiq, 60b, 117a
Shem, father of Semites, 23a, 26b
Shephelah, 19b, 34a, 40, 50b, 62b
Shepherds, Egyptians despise, 28b, *c*34
Shepherds' Field, Bethlehem, *p*63
Sheshbazzar, 56a
Shiloh, 43a, 46a, 116b
Ships, grain, 87a, 98; Persian fleet, 75a; Sea of Galilee, 60b; Solomon's, 50a, 57b
Shishak, raids Palestine, 50b
Shuqbah, 117b
Siddim, Vale of, 20b, 26a, 69b, 70a
Sidon, 18a, 57, 83b, 94b
Sihon, Kingdom of, 36a, 39a, 43
Siloam, Tunnel, 54b, 106a; Pool, 107a
Silversmiths, Ephesus, 97a
Simon the Maccabee, 78b
Sinai, Mount, 26b, *p*38, 38b, 39a
Sinai, peninsula, 38b; mines, 25a, 38b
Sinuhe, Tale of, 25a
Sîq, at Petra, *p*77
Sirocco, east wind, 17b, 61a
Sites, how identified, 13b, 14
Slaves, laborers, 44a, 69b; educated, 88b
Smelter, Ezion-geber, 50a, 57b, 69b
Smith, G. A., 14a
Sodom, 20b, 26a, 69b, 70a
Sojourn in Egypt, 27-29a, 37a
Solomon, reign of, 49, 50a; administrative districts, 50a, 60a, 113b; Temple of, *p*48, *p*49, 49, 105b; mining and smelting, 50a, 57b, 69b; other trade, 50a; buildings in Megiddo, 113b; dealings with Hiram of Tyre, 33b, 49b
Solomon's Pools, *p*83
Sorek, Valley of, 62b
Sothic cycle, 13a
Source of Jordan, *p*57
South, Southland, *see* Negeb
Spain, Christians in, 98b, 104a
Speiser, E. A., 12b
Sphinx and Pyramids, *p*11
Starkey, J. L., 115b
Stone Age, 23a, 24a, 117b
Straight Street, Damascus, 95a, *p*96
Stratigraphy, 10, 11a, 111b
Succoth, location, 38
Sumerian language, literature, 9b, 12
Survey, Northern Transjordan, Schumacher, 10a; Transjordan, Glueck, 11a, 14a; Western Palestine, 10a, 14a, 111
Susa, *c*26
Sychar, location, *c*18, 63a, 94a
Synagogues, 60b, 95-97a, 117a; Capernaum, *p*60, 94a; Dura, *c*103
Syria, for meaning "Aram," *see* Aram
Syria, geology, 19a, 20a; cultural contribution to Palestine, 5; mountain barrier on south, 6a, 57b; Hyksos rule, 28a; Egyptian rule, 24b, 25a, 29a; sea peoples invade, 46b; Seleucid empire, 76b; Antioch capital, 58b; rule of Palestine, 77-81; Roman rule, 83a, 86b, 87a, 91; Christianity in, 102
Syriac, 104b
Syrians, *see* Arameans
Syrtis Major, 98a

Taanach, *p*43, 112b
Table of Nations, 26b
Tabor, Mount, *p*17, 19a, 45a, *p*58, 60a, 94a
Tahpanhes, 38b
Tanis, is Raamses, 37b
Tarichaea, location, 14b, 60b
Tarshish, "smelter," 26b
Tarsus, 88b, 95a, 102a
Tatian, *c*103, 104b
Taurus Mountains, 23b, *c*71, 96b
Taxes, to Egypt, 34b; Solomon, 50a; Herod, 83b
Taylor Prism, Sennacherib, 14b
Teacher of Righteousness, 82b, 83a
Teleilât el-Ghassûl, 117b
Tell, *p*17, *p*111; described, 111b
Tell el-Amarna tablets, 9b, 30b, *c*34, 35, 36a, 40, 60a
Tell Aviv, 62b
Tell Beit Mirsim, 111b, 113b
Tell ed-Duweir, 14b
Tell el-Fâr'ah, 116b
Tell el-Ḥesī, 10a, 112a
Tell Hûm, 94a
Tell el-Ḥuṣn, *p*111, 111b
Tell Jezer, 112
Tell en-Naṣbeh, 50b, *p*115, 116b
Tell Qasîleh, 116b
Tell el-Qedaḥ, 116b
Tell Sandaḥannah, 112a
Tell el-Yehûdîyeh, *p*28
Tell Zakarîyeh, *p*47, 112a
Teman, 44b, 70b
Temple, Jerusalem, Solomon's, 34a, *c*45, *p*48, *p*49, 49, 55b, 105b; Zerubbabel's, 56a, 75a, 77a, 78a, 81b, 106a; Herodian, 83b, 84b, *c*94, 105a, 106b, 107; Babylon (Marduk), 74a; Beth-shan, 45a, *c*111, 114; Gerizim, 62a, 81a; Karnak, *p*27; Lachish, 115b; Megiddo, 113a; Shechem, 113b; Elephantine, 75b, 76a, 77a; Samaria (Augustus), 63b, 92b, 115a
Textile dyes, 33a, 57b
Textual criticism, place names, 14a
Theater, Ephesus, 97a, *p*98
Thebes (Egypt), *p*27, 28a, 29a, 30a, 37b, 73a
Theodotus inscription, *p*95
Thessalonica, 88a, 96b
Tiberias, 20a, *p*59, 60b, 92a, 93a, 94b
Tiberias, Sea of, 20a
Tiberius, emperor, 84a, 92b
Tiglath-pileser III, 54, 72b, 73a
Tigris River, 23a, 71b
Timsâh, Lake, 29a, 37a, 38a
Tirzah, 50b, 63a
Titus, emperor, 84b, *c*87, *c*102
Tobiah, 56b
Tomb of the Kings, 111b
Topography, method of identifying ancient sites, 13b, 14; survey of topographical features of Palestine, 17-20, 57-64, 67-70; Exodus route, 38, 39a
Toponymy, 14
Trachonitis, lava, 58b
Trajan, 85a, 88a, 103a
Transfiguration, 94a
Transjordan, survey, 14a; geographical features, 17b, 20b, 63b, 64, 69, 70; King's Highway, 39a, *p*40, 65b; early history, 24b, 34b, 36a, 39a, 40b; Israelite, 43, 44b, 59b; Hellenistic (Decapolis), 58b, 59a, 64a, 84; Christianity in, 59a, 64b
Travel, under Romans, 88a, 93b
Tribal boundaries, 43, 44a
Troas, 96b, 97b
Trypho, 78b
Tulul Abu el-ʿAlayik, 117a
Tunip, *p*33
Tutankhamun, tomb, *c*27
Typology, 10, 11a
Tyre, 18a, 57, 74b, 83b, 87b, 94b
Tyropoeon Valley, 105a, 106, *c*108

Ugarit, *see* Râs Shamrah
Ugaritic, 11b; texts, 30b
University Museum, Philadelphia, 114a
Ur of the Chaldees, 25a
Urartu (Ararat), 72b
Urban nature of Early Church, 104b
Uzziah (Azariah), 54, 62a, 72b

Vespasian, 84b, *c*102
Vesuvius, Mount, *p*101
Via Dolorosa, 107a
Virgin's Spring, Gihon, 107a
Virolleaud, 11b
Vitellius, 91b, 92b
Volcanoes, Ḥaurân, 20b, 58b; Midian, 38b, 39a

Wâdī, defined, 29a
Wâdī el-Mughârah, *p*116, 117b
Wâdī Muraba'at, 84b
Wâdī Mûsā, *p*77
Wâdī Qudeirât, *p*39
Wâdī Qumrân, *p*81
Wâdī Ṭumilât, 29a, 38a
Wailing Wall, Jerusalem, *p*94, 106b
Walls, Jerusalem, Jebusite, 105b; Solomon, 106a; Hezekiah, 106a; Nehemiah, 56a; first century, 106b, 107; modern, *p*105; other ancient walls: Canaanite, *p*33, 36a; Jericho, 36, 114b; Lachish, *p*56; Samaria, 53a, *p*54, 54a, 115a; Shechem, 116a; *Tell-en-Naṣbeh*, 116b
Warren, 112a
Water supply, Ḥaurân, 59a; Judah, 67; Nabataea, *p*66, 66b; Negeb, 19b, 68a; Jerusalem, *p*83, 105a, 106a
Watershed, Judean, 62b, *c*67, 67, 69a
Way of Land of Philistines, 38a, 68a
Way of the Sea, 58a
Weapons of Patriarchs, 34b
Wenamon, 45b
Wheaton College, 116b
Wilderness of Judah, 19b, 62b, 63a, *p*67, 69a
Wilderness of Paran, 39a, 67a
Wilderness of Sin, 39a
Wilderness of Zin, 39a, 67a
Winds, Palestine, 17b, 18a, 61a; Mediterranean, 88a
Wiseman, D. J., 74a

Yadin, Y., 116b
Yarmuk, 20b, 59a

Zadokite work, 82a
Zealots, 92b
Zedekiah, king, 55b
Zephath, location, 14b
Zephathah, Valley of, 62b
Zered, Brook, 20b, 39a, *p*40, 43a, 69a
Zerubbabel, 56a
Ziggurat, *p*25, *c*49, 49b
Zilu (Thel), 38b
Zimri-Lim, 24b
Zion, location, 105a
Zoar, 20b, 70a
Zobah, Kingdom of, 46b, 48a
Zoroaster, date and religion of, 75a

INDEX TO THE MAPS

INCLUDING A TOPOGRAPHICAL CONCORDANCE TO THE BIBLE

This index has three purposes: (1) to give the location of the sites and geographical features on the maps; (2) to provide a topographical concordance of all places mentioned in the Bible and indicate their location; and (3) to present accurately (with the aid of Professor W. F. Albright) the modern names of the places where ancient sites are located. (The system of transliteration of Semitic place names is one in use among scholars; the markings on the vowels do not represent the same sounds as in English.)

Where two or more places had the same name, the different sites are indicated by numbers; e g., Abel 1 and 2. If two or more sites of the same name are mentioned in the Bible, the Biblical references are given for all but one; all other references to that name refer to the site for which no references are given.

Note the use of certain words and phrases:

see—used after the name of a site which does not occur on any map; it introduces another name or spelling for the same site which is found on one or more of the maps.

see also—indicates that the place just named occurs on the maps or in the Bible under the following name or names.

?—The question mark after the identification of a site means that the location is possible or probable but not certain.

uncertain—all proposed locations for the site seem to the Editors quite unconvincing.

unknown—the location of the site cannot be determined.

near—used when only approximate location of site can be given.

Abana, River, *Nahr Baradā:* IV, E-1; VI, E-1; VIII, J-1
Abarim, Mountains of: IX, I-6
Abdon, *Khirbet 'Abdeh:* IV, C-2; VI, C-2; VIII, D-4
Abel
1—I Sam. 6:18, near Beth-shemesh 1; unknown
2—*see also* Abel-beth-maachah, *Tell Abil (âbil):* IV, D-2; VII: A-D, C-3
Abel-beth-maachah, *Tell Abil (âbil):* VI, D-2; VIII, F-3
Abelcheramim (R.V.), near Rabbath-ammon; uncertain
Abel-maim, *see* Abel-beth-maachah
Abel-meholah, *Tell el-Maqlûb:* VI, D-4; IX, H-2
Abel-mizraim, in Transjordan; uncertain
Abel-shittim (in N.T. times Abila), *Tell el-Ḥammâm:* V, G-2; VI, D-5; IX, H-5
Abez, in Issachar; uncertain
Ab-i-Diz, River; III, E-3
Abila
1—(in O.T. times Abel-shittim), *Khirbet el-Kefrein:* IX, H-5; XII: D, D-5
2—*Tell Abil (âbil):* VIII, H-7; XIV, D-3
Abilene, district N.E. of Mt. Hermon: XII: C-D, E-1; XIV, E-1
Abū Ghôsh: XVIII, C-5
Abydos, *'Arabet el-Madfûneh:* II, E-3
Accad, capital of Babylonia, *c.* 2400 B.C.; unknown
Accaron (in O.T. times Ekron), *Qaṭrā?:* IX, C-6; XII: A, B-5
Accho (in N.T. times Ptolemais), *Tell el-Fukhkhâr:* I, C-3; III, B-3; IV, C-3; VI, C-3; VII: A-D, C-4; VIII, C-5
Aceldama, "field of blood," southern side of lower Valley of Hinnom?: XVII: B, D, D-7
Achaia, *cf.* Greece; Roman province: XIII, D-2; XV, D-3
Achmetha, *see also* Ecbatana, *Hamadân:* XI: B-C, C-2
Achor, Valley of, *el-Buqei'ah:* IX, G-6
Achshaph, *Tell Kisân?:* IV, C-3; VI, C-3; VIII, D-5; XVIII, C-3
Achzib
1—Josh. 15:44; Mic. 1:14; *Tell el-Beiḍā*, S.W. of Adullam?
2—(in N.T. times Ecdippa), *ez-Zîb:* IV, C-2; VI, C-2; VIII, D-4
Acra, hill (citadel) S. of temple area in Jerusalem: XVII: C, D-5
Acrabetta, *'Aqrabeh:* IX, F-4; XII: D, C-4
Acre, *see also* Accho and Ptolemais: XVIII, C-3
Actium, *La Punta:* XIII, C-2
Adab, *Bismâya:* III, E-3
Adadah, probably the same as Aroer 3
Adam, *see* Adamah 1
Adamah
1—*Tell ed-Dâmiyeh:* IV, D-4; VI, D-4; VII: A, C-4; IX, H-4
2—Josh. 19:36; in Naphtali; uncertain
Adami, *Khirbet Dâmiyeh:* IV, C-3; VI, C-3; VIII, F-6
Adar, *see* Hazar-addar
Adasa, *Khirbet 'Addâseh:* IX, F-6; XII: A, C-5
Addan, Addon, unknown
Ader: XVIII, D-6
Adida, *see also* Hadid, *el-Ḥadîtheh:* IX, D-5; XII: D, B-5
Adithaim, near Beth-shemesh 1; uncertain
Admah, near Sodom; unknown
Adora, *see also* Adoraim, Adoreus, *Dûrā:* IX, E-8; XII: A-B, C-5
Adoraim, *see also* Adora, Adoreus, *Dûrā:* IX, E-8
Adoreus, *see also* Adora, Adoraim, *Dûrā:* XII: A, C-5
Adramyttium, harbor, near *Edremit:* XV, E-3
Adria, *see also* Adriatic Sea *and* Hadriaticum, Mare, XV, C-2
Adriatic Sea, *see also* Adria *and* Hadriaticum, Mare, XIII, C-2; XV, C-2
Adullam, *Tell esh-Sheikh Madhkûr:* VI, C-5; IX, E-7
Adummim, Ascent of, *Tal'at ed-Damm:* IX, G-6
Aduru, *Dûrā:* IV, D-3
Aegaeum, Mare, *see also* Aegean Sea: XIII, D-2; XV, D-2
Aegean Sea, *see also* Aegaeum, Mare: XIII, D-2; XV, D-3
Aegyptus, *see also* Egypt: XIII, E-3; XV, E-5
Aelana, *see also* Aila, c. 1 mi. WNW of *'Aqabah:* XIII, E-3
Aelia Capitolina, *see also* Jebus *and* Jerusalem, *el-Quds:* XVI: C-D, E-4
Aenon, John 3:23, "near to Salim" (*q.v.*); unknown
Aethiopia, *see also* Ethiopia *and* Cush: XIII, E-4
'Affûleh: XVIII, C-3
Afghanistan: II, H-2
Africa, Roman Province in N. Africa: XIII, B-3; XV, A-4
Afyonkarahisar: III, B-2
Agala, *Rujm el-Jilimeh?:* X, J-2; XII: A, D-6
Agendicum, Agedincum, *Sens:* XIII Inset, D-3
Agrigentum, *Girgenti:* XIII, C-2
Agrippias, *see* Anthedon
Ahava, River or Canal, in Mesopotamia; unknown
Ahlab, Meheleb, *Khirbet el-Maḥâlib:* IV, C-2; VI, C-2; VIII, D-2
Ahnâs el-Medîneh, *see also* Heracleopolis: V, B-4
Ai, original name probably Beth-aven, *et-Tell:* IV, C-5; V, G-2; VI, C-5; IX, F-5; XVIII, C-5
Aiath, *Khirbet Haiyân*, near Ai?
Aija, *see* Aiath
Aijalon or **Ajalon**
1—*Yâlô:* IV, C-5; V, G-2; VI, C-5; IX, E-6
2—Judg. 12:12; near Rimmon 2; *Khirbet el-Lôn* or *Tell el-Buṭmeh?*
Aijalon or **Ajalon, Valley of**, *Wâdī Selmân:* IX, D-5
Aila, *see also* Aelana, c. 1 mi. WNW of *'Aqabah:* XVI: D, E-4
Ain
1—Num. 34:11, near Riblah; uncertain
2—*see* En-rimmon
'Ain Dûq, *see also* Noarah: XVIII, C-5
Ajalon, *see* Aijalon 1
'Ajlûn: XVIII, D-4
Akhetaton, *Tell el-Amarna ('Amârneh):* V, B-6
Akrabbim, Ascent of, *Naqb eṣ-Ṣafâ:* VI, C-7; X, F-4
Alaca Hüyük: III, B-1
Alalakh, *Tell 'Aṭshânah:* II, E-2; III, C-3
Alammelech, near Helkath, unknown
Alashiya, *see also* Elishah, Kittim, Iatnana, *and* Cyprus: II, E-2; III, B-3
Albis, *see also* Elbe, a river: XIII Inset, F-1
Alemeth, *see* Almon
Aleppo, *see also* Khalab, *Ḥaleb:* II, E-2; III, C-2
Aleria, city in Corsica, near S. side of mouth of R. Rhotanus (modern *Tavignano*): XIII, B-2
Alesia, near *Alise Saint-Reine?:* XIII Inset, E-3
Alexandria
1—*Iskanderiyeh:* XI: D, A-3; XIII, D-3; XV, F-5; XVI: A-D, D-4
2—*Gulashkird:* XI: D, E-3
Alexandria Troas, *see also* Troas, *Eskistanbul:* XIII, D-2
Alexandrium, *Qarn Sarṭabeh:* IX, G-4; XII: A-B, C-4
Allon, to be read with Zaanannim as Elon-bezaanannim; near Adami; uncertain
Allon-bachuth, near Bethel 1, unknown
Almon, *Khirbet 'Almît:* IX, F-6
Almon-diblathaim, *Khirbet Deleilât esh-Sherqîyeh?:* IX, I-7
Aloth, I Kings 4:16; text uncertain
Alps, The: II, C-1
Alurus, *see also* Halhul, *Ḥalḥûl:* IX, E-7; XII: D, C-5
Alusa, *also called* Elusa, *Khalaṣa:* X, D-3; XII: A, B-6
Alush, near Dophkah; uncertain
Amad, near Helkath; unknown
Amalekites: III, B-4
Amam, near Beer-sheba; unknown
Amana, Mt., *Jebel Zebedâni:* VII: B-D, D-3
Amasia, *Amasya:* XIII, E-2; XVI: D, E-2
Amastris, *Amasra:* XIII, E-2; XVI: C-D, E-2
Amathus
1—*Tell 'Ammatā:* IX, H-3; XII: A-B, D-4
2—on S. coast of Cyprus; near *Limassol:* XIII, E-2
Amida, *Diyarbekir:* XVI: D, F-2
Amisus, *Samsun:* XIII, E-2
Amki, *el-Biqâ':* III, C-3
Ammah, Hill of, near Gibeon; unknown
'Ammân, *see also* Rabbath-ammon, Philadelphia, XVIII, D-5
Ammathus (in O.T. times Hammath), *Ḥammâm Tabarîyeh:* VIII, F-6; XII: D, D-3
Ammon, Kingdom of, I, E-5; IV, E-5; V, H-2; VI, E-5; VII: A-D, D-5; IX, J-5
Amorites, Land of the: II, F-2
Amphipolis, *Neochori:* XV, D-2
'Amwâs, *see also* Emmaus 1: XVIII, B-5
Anab, *Khirbet 'Anâb:* IX, D-8; X, E-1
Anaharath, *en-Na'ûrah:* IV, C-3; VIII, E-7
Ananiah, O.T. name for Bethany
Anathoth, *Râs el-Kharrûbeh:* IX, F-6
Anchialus, *Ankhialo:* XVI: C-D, D-2
Ancona: XIII, C-2
Ancyra, *Ankara (q.v.):* XI: D, B-2; XIII, E-2; XV, F-3; XVI: C-D, E-2
Anem, *'Olam ('ôlam)?:* VI, D-3; VIII, F-7
Aner, *see* Taanach
Anim, *Khirbet Ghuwein et-Taḥtā?:* X, F-1
Ankara, *see also* Ancyra: III, B-1
Ankuwa, *Alişar Hüyük?:* II, E-2
Anthedon, *also called* Agrippias, *el-Blâḥiyeh:* IX, A-7; XII: A-B, D, A-5
Antioch
1—*see also* Antiochia 1; *Anṭâkiyeh:* XI: D, B-2; XV, G-4; XVI: A-D, E-3
2—*see also* Antiochia 2; Acts 13:14; 14:19, 21; II Tim. 3:11, *Yalvaç:* XV, F-3; XVI: B-C, E-2
Antiochia
1—*see also* Antioch 1, *Anṭâkiyeh:* XIII, E-2
2—*see also* Antioch 2, *Yalvaç:* XIII, E-2
Antipatris, *see also* Aphek *and* Pegae, *Râs el-'Ain:* IX, D-4; XII: A-B, D, B-4; XIV, B-4; XV, G-5
Antiphrae, close to the coast in W. Egypt: XIII, D-3
Antium, *Anzio:* XIII, C-2
Apamea
1—*Qal'at el-Muḍîq:* XIII, E-2; XVI: D, E-3
2—*Diner:* XIII, D-2; XVI: D, D-2
Aphairema *or* **Apherema**; *see also* Ephraim; *same as* Ophrah 1?, *eṭ-Ṭaiyibeh?:* XII: A, C-5
Aphek
1—*see also* Pegae *and* Antipatris, *Râs el-'Ain:* IV, B-4; VI, B-4; IX, D-4; XVIII, B-4
2—Josh. 13:4; *Afqā* E of Byblos
3—Josh. 19:30, *Tell Kurdâneh?:* VIII, D-6
4—I Kings 20:26, 30; II Kings 13:17; *Fîq:* VI, D-3; VIII, G-6
Aphekah, near Hebron; uncertain
Aphik, *see* Aphek 3
Aphrah, *see* Beth-le-aphrah (R.V. and R.S.V.)
Apollinopolis, *Edfu:* XIII, E-3
Apollonia
1—*Arsûf:* IX, C-3; XII: A-B, B-4
2—*Sizeboli:* XI: B-D, A-1; XIII, D-2
3—several miles N. of *Valona:* XIII, C-2; XV, C-2
4—in Cirenaica, *Marsa Susa:* XIII, D-3
5—S. of *Lake Bolbe;* uncertain: XV, D-2
Appii Forum, i.e., Market of Appius, near *Foro Appio:* XV, B-2
Aqabah, Gulf of: V, F-5
Aquileia: XIII, C-1; XVI: D, C-1
Aquincum, *Buda (Budapest):* XIII, C-1
Aquitania, Roman province in southwest Gaul: XIII, A-1; XIII, Inset, C-3
Ar, *el-Miṣna'?:* VI, D-6; VII: A-C, C-5; X, J-2
Arab, *er-Râbiyeh?:* IX, E-8; X, F-1
Arabah, *el-Ghôr* (Jordan Valley) N of Dead Sea and *Wâdī el-'Arabah* S of it: I, C-8; III, B-4; V, G-3; IX, H-4; X, G-6
Arabah, Sea of, *see* Salt Sea
Arabia, Arabian Desert: II, F-3; III, C-3; V, H-4; VII: A-B, D, E-4; XI: B-D, C-3; XIII, F-3; XV, G-5; XVI: A, E-4
Arabian Gulf, *see also* Sinus Arabicus, Red Sea: XIII, F-4; XVI: A-D, E-4
Arabs, *see* Arubu *and* Arabia
Arabs, Arabians, mentioned in Neh. 4:7; 6:1: VII: D, B-6
Arachosia, district on W. side of R. Indus: XI: C-D, E-3
Arad, *Tell 'Arâd:* IV, C-6; V, G-2; VI, C-6; X, F-2
Aral Sea: II, H-1
Aram, *see also* Syria, Zobah, Ube: II, Inset; VII: B, D-3; VIII, J-2
Aram-maacah, *see* Maachah
Aram-naharaim, *same as* Padan (Paddan)-aram
Aram-rehob, district around Beth-rehob
Aram-zobah, *see* Zobah
Ararat, *see also* Armenia, Urartu: XI: A-B, C-2
Arbah, City of, *see* Kirjath-arba
Arbela
1—*Khirbet Irbid (q.v.):* VIII, F-6; XII: A-B, C-3
2—in Assyria, *Erbil:* III, D-2; XI: A-D, C-2; XIII, F-2; XVI: D, F-3
Archelais, *Khirbet 'Aujā et-Taḥtânī:* IX, G-5; XII: C, C-5; XIV, C-5
Archi, not a place, but a clan which owned Ataroth 3
Ardata, *Ardat:* III, C-3
Arelate, *Arles (q.v.):* XIII, B-1
Argentoratum, *Strassburg:* XIII Inset, F-2
Argob: VI, E-3
Aria: XI: C-D, E-2
Ariel, *see* Jerusalem
Arimathaea, *see also* Ramathaim-zophim, *Rentis?:* IX, E-4; XIV, C-4
Ariminum, *Rimini:* XIII, C-2; XVI: D, C-1
Arles, *see also* Arelate: XVI: D, B-1
Armenia, *see also* Ararat, Urartu: III, D-2; XI: C-D, C-2; XIII, F-2; XVI: C-D, F-2
Armenia Minor: XIII, E-2
Arnon, River, *Wâdī el-Môjib:* I, D-6; IV, D-6; V, G-2; VI, D-6; IX, H-8; X, J-1
Aroer
1—Josh. 13:25; Judg. 11:26, 33; near Rabbath-ammon; uncertain
2—*'Arâ'ir:* VI, D-6; IX, I-8; X, J-1

3—I Sam. 20 : 28 ; *'Ar'arah:* IV, B-6 ; VI, B-6 ; X, F-3
Aron, *Tell 'Arā ('ârā):* IV, C-4
Arpad, Arphad, *Tell Erfâd:* III, C-2 ; XI : A, B-2
Arrapkha, *Kirkûk:* II, F-2 ; III, D-2 ; XI : A, C-2
Arretium, *Arezzo:* XIII, C-2
Arsinoe, *see also* Crocodilopolis, *Medinet el-Faiyûm:* XIII, E-3 ; XVI : D, D-4
Artacoana, at or near *Herat:* XI : D, D-2
Artaxata, *Ardashir:* XIII, F-2
Aruboth, or **Arruboth**, *'Arrâbeh?:* IV, C-4 ; VI, C-4 ; IX, F-2
Arubu, *see also* Arabs, Arabia : VII : C, E-5 ; XI : A, C-3
Arumah, near Shechem ; uncertain
Arvad, *Erwâd:* II, E-2 ; III, C-3 ; VII : A-D, C-2 ; XI : A-C, B-2
Arzawa: III, B-2
Ascalon (in O.T. times Ashkelon), *'Asqalân (q.v.):* IX, B-7 ; XII : A-D, B-5 ; XIV, B-5 ; XVIII, B-5
Asdudu, Assyrian Province: VII : C, B-5
Ashan, *Khirbet 'Asan:* VI, B-6 ; X, D-2
Ashdod
1—Persian Province, VII : D, B-5
2—(in N.T. times Azotus), *Esdûd:* IV, B-5 ; V, F-2 ; VI, B-5 ; VII : A-D, B-5 ; IX, C-6
Ashdoth-pisgah, *see* Pisgah
Asher
1—Tribal District: VI, C-3
2—Josh. 17 : 7 ; near Shechem ; unknown
Ashkelon (in N.T. times Ascalon), *'Asqalân:* II, E-3 ; IV, B-5 ; V, F-2 ; VI, B-5 ; VII : A-D, B-5 ; IX, B-7 ; XVIII, B-5
Ashkenaz: II, Inset
el-Ashmûnein, *see also* Hermopolis : V, B-6
Ashnah
1—Josh. 15 : 33 ; near Zorah ; uncertain
2—Josh. 15 : 43 ; *Idhnā,* near Mareshah?
Ashtaroth, *Tell 'Ashtarah:* III, C-3 ; IV, E-3 ; VI, E-3 ; VII : A-D, D-4 ; VIII, I-6
Asia, Roman province in western Asia Minor : XIII, D-2 ; XV, E-3 ; XVI : A, D-2
Askelon, *see* Ashkelon
Asochis, *Khirbet el-Lôn:* VIII, D-6 ; XII : A, C-3
Asophon, *or* Asaphon ; *cf.* Zaphon ; at or near *Tell es-Sa'idiyeh?:* XII : A, D-4
Asor (in O.T. times Hazor), *Tell el-Qedaḥ* (or *Waqqâṣ*) : VIII, F-4 ; XII : A, D-2
Aspendus, c. 7 mi. from mouth of Eurymedon R. : XVI : D, E-3
Asphaltitis, Lake, *see also* Dead Sea *and* Salt Sea, *Baḥr Lûṭ:* IX, G-7 ; X, H-1 ; XIV, C-5
'Asqalân, *see also* Ashkelon *and* Ascalon : XVIII, B-5
Asshur
1—*see also* Assyria : II, Inset
2—*Qal'ât Sherqât:* II, F-2 ; III, D-2 ; XI : A, C-2
Assos, *Behramköy:* XV, E-3
Assyria, *see also* Asshur 1 : II, F-2 ; III, D-2 ; XI : C, C-2
Astorga, *see also* Asturica : XVI : C-D, A-1
Asturica, *Astorga (q.v.):* XIII, A-1
Atad, in Transjordan ; unknown
Atania, *Adana:* III, C-2
Ataroth
1—Num. 32 : 3, 34, *Khirbet 'Aṭṭārûs:* VI, D-5 ; IX, H-7
2—Josh. 16 : 7. *See also* Corea ; *Tell el-Mazâr:* VI, C-4 ; IX, G-4
3—of the Archite clan, near Mizpah 2 ; unknown
4—I Chron. 2 : 54, near Bethlehem ; unknown
Ataroth-addar (or **-adar**), *see* Ataroth 3
Athach, *see* Ether 2
Athenae, *see also* Athens, *Athēnai:* XIII, D-2
Athens, *see also* Athenae, *Athēnai:* XI : A-D, A-2 ; XV, D-3 ; XVI : B-D, D-2
'Athlît: XVIII, B-3
Athone, *see also* Thone, *Khirbet eṭ-Ṭeniyeh?:* X, I-3 ; XII : A, D-6
Athribis, *Tell Atrîb:* V, C-3
Atlantic Ocean, *see also* Oceanus Atlanticus : XIII, A-1 ; XIII Inset, B-3
Atropatene, a district : XI : D, C-2
Atroth, read Atroth-shophan ; near Jogbehah ; unknown
Attalia, *Adalia:* XV, F-3
Augsburg, *see also* Augusta Vindelicorum : XVI : D, B-1 ; XVI : D, C-6
Augusta Rauracorum, *Augst:* XIII, B-1 ; XIII Inset, F-3
Augusta Treverorum, *Trier (q.v.)* : XIII Inset, E-2
Augusta Vindelicorum, *Augsburg (q.v.)* : XIII, C-1 ; XIII Inset, F-2
Augustodunum, *Autun (q.v.)* : XIII, B-1 ; XIII Inset E-3
'Aujā el-Ḥafîr: XVIII, A-7
Aulona, *Valona:* XIII, C-2 ; XV, C-2
Auranitis, *see also* Hauran ; southeastern *Ḥaurân:* XII : B-D, E-3 ; XIV, E-3
Autun, *see also* Augustodunum : XVI : D, B-1 ; XVI : D, B-6
Ava, *see* Ivah
Avaricum, *Bourges:* XIII Inset, D-3
Avaris, *see also* Rameses, Tanis, *and* Zoan, *Ṣân el-Ḥagar:* II, E-3 ; III, B-4 ; V, C-3
Aven
1—Ezek. 30 : 17, *see* On
2—Hos. 10 : 8, *see* Beth-aven
Aven, Plain (Valley) of, *el-Biqa'* near *Ba'albek? (see* Chun)
Aventicum, *Avenches:* XIII, B-1 ; XIII Inset, F-3
Avim, same as Ai?
Avith, in Edom ; uncertain
Ayyanu, *'Ayyûn:* IV, D-3
Azal, unknown
Azekah, *Tell ez-Zakarîyah:* IV, B-5 ; V, F-2 ; VI, B-5 ; IX, D-6 ; XVIII, B-5
Azem, *Umm el-'Aẓam?:* VI, B-6 ; X, E-3
Azmaveth, *Ḥizmeh:* IX, F-6
Azmon, *Qeṣeimeh?:* VI, A-7 ; X, B-6
Aznoth-tabor, *Umm Jebeil* near Mt. Tabor?
Azotus (in O.T. times Ashdod), *Esdûd:* IX, C-6 ; XII : A-D, B-5 ; XIV, B-5 ; XVI : A, E-4
Azzah, *see* Gaza

Baal, *see* Baalath-beer
Baalah
1—*See* Kirjath-baal
2—Josh. 15 : 29 ; 19 : 3 ; in Simeon ; uncertain
Baalah, Mount, Josh. 15 : 11, near Jabneel ; uncertain
Baalath, near Mt. Baalah ; uncertain
Baalath-beer, near Rehoboth 1 ; unknown
Baale, *see* Kirjath-baal
Baal-gad, in the valley west of Mt. Hermon ; uncertain
Baal-hamon, unknown
Baal-hazor, *Jebel 'Aṣûr:* I, C-5 ; V, C-5 ; VI, C-5 ; IX, F-5
Baal-hermon, near or on Mt. Hermon ; uncertain
Baal-meon, *Ma'în:* VI, D-5 ; IX, I-7
Baal-peor, *see* Beth-peor
Baal-perazim, *Sheikh Bedr* near Jerusalem?
Baal-shalisha, in central Palestine ; uncertain
Baal-tamar, near Gibeah ; uncertain
Baal-zephon, *Tell Defneh:* V, D-3
Bâb edh-Dhrâ': XVIII, D-6
Babel, *see* Babylon
Babylon, Babel: II, F-3 ; III, E-3 ; XI : A-D, C-3 ; XIII, F-3
Babylonia: II, F-3 ; II, Inset ; III, E-3 ; XI : D, C-3
Baca, *el-Buqei'ah:* VIII, E-5 ; XIV, C-3
Baca, Valley of, unknown
Bactria, region between Hindu Kush Mts. and Oxus R. : XI : C-D, E-1
Baetica, Roman province : XIII, A-2
Bahurim, *Râs eṭ-Ṭmim,* just east of Mt. Scopus near Jerusalem
Bajith, not a place name ; corrupt text
Balah, *see* Baalah 2
Balaḥ, Lake: V, D-3
Balâṭah, *see also* Shechem *and* Sichem : XVIII, C-4
Balearic Islands: II, A-2
Balîkh River: III, C-2
Baluchistan: II, H-3
Bamoth, *see* Bamoth-baal
Bamoth-baal, near Mt. Nebo ; uncertain
Bashan, *see also* Batanaea, southern *Ḥaurân:* I, D-3 ; VI, D-3 ; VIII, H-5
Bashan-havoth-jair, *see* Havoth-jair
Batanaea, *see also* Bashan, southern *Ḥaurân:* XII : B-D, E-3 ; XIV, E-3
Bathys, port on E. shore of Black Sea : XIII, F-2
Bealoth, *see* Baalath-beer
Beer
1—Num. 21 : 16, a spring or well in the valley east of Mattanah
2—Judg. 9 : 21, *el-Bîreh* near Hapharaim
Beer-elim, in Moab ; same as Beer 1?
Beer-lahai-roi, a spring near Kadesh-barnea ; uncertain
Beeroth
1—Deut. 10 : 6, *Birein?:* X, C-5
2—(in N.T. times Berea), *Râs eṭ-Ṭaḥûneh?:* IV, C-5 ; VI, C-5 ; IX, F-5
Beer-sheba (in N.T. times Bersabee), *Tell es-Seba':* I, B-6 ; II, E-3 ; III, B-4 ; IV, B-6 ; V, F-2 ; VI, B-6 ; VII : A-D, B-5 ; X, E-2
Beeshterah, *see* Ashtaroth
Behistun, *see also* Bisitun, III, E-3 ; XI : C, D-2
Beitîn, *see also* Bethel 1, Bethela, *and* Luz 1 : XVIII, C-5
Beit Jemâl: XVIII, B-5
Beit Jibrîn, *see also* Eleutheropolis : XVIII, B-5
Bela, *see* Zoar
Belgica, Roman province in NE Gaul : XIII, B-1 ; XIII Inset, E-2
Bene-berak, *Ibn-ibrâq:* IV, B-4 ; VI, B-4 ; IX, D-4
Bene-jaakan, *see* Beeroth 1
Beneventum, *Benevento:* XVI : D, C-2
Beni-hasan, *see also* Speos Artemidos : II, E-3 ; V, B-6
Benjamin, tribal district : VI, C-5
Beon, *see* Baal-meon
Berachah, Valley of, *Wâdî el-'Arrûb:* IX, F-7
Berea (in O.T. times Beeroth), *el-Bîreh?:* IX, F-5 ; XII : A, C-5
Bered, in the district of Kadesh-barnea ; uncertain
Berenice
1—Egyptian port on Red Sea : XIII, E-4
2—*Bengasi:* XIII, C-3 ; XVI : D, C-3
Beroea
1—*Verria:* XIII, D-2 ; XV, D-2 ; XVI : B-D, D-2
2—*Aleppo:* XVI : D, E-3
Berothah, *see* Berothai
Berothai, *Bereitân:* III, C-3 ; VII : A-D, D-3
Bersabee (in O.T. times Beer-sheba), *Khirbet Bîr es-Seba':* X, E-2
Berytus, *see also* Biruta, *Beirût:* XIII, E-3 ; XVI : D, E-3
Besimoth (in O.T. times Beth-jeshimoth), *Khirbet es-Sweimeh:* IX, H-6 ; XII : D, D-5
Besor, Brook, *Wâdī Ghazzeh?:* VI, B-6 ; X, C-2
Betah, *see* Tibhath
Beten, *Abṭûn?:* VIII, D-6
Beth Alfa, *Khirbet Beit Ilfā:* XVIII, C-4
Beth-anath, *el-Ba'neh?:* IV, C-3 ; VI, C-3 ; VIII, D-5
Beth-anoth, *Beit 'Ainûn:* IX, E-7
Bethany, *el-'Azarîyeh:* IX, F-6 ; XIV, C-5
Bethany Beyond Jordan, in *Wâdī el-Kharrâr?:* IX, H-6 ; XIV, D-5
Beth-arabah, *el-Gharabeh?:* IX, G-6
Beth-aram, *see* Beth-haran
Betharamphtha, *see also* Julias, Livias ; *cf.* O.T. Beth-haran, *Tell er-Râmeh:* XII : C, D-5
Beth-arbel, *Irbid:* IV, D-3 ; VIII, H-7
Beth-aven, probably the original name of Ai
Beth-azmaveth, *see* Azmaveth
Beth-baal-meon, *see* Baal-meon
Beth-barah, in Jordan Valley ; uncertain
Bethbassi, *Khirbet Beit Baṣṣa:* IX, F-6 ; XII : A, C-5
Beth-birei, in the tribal district of Simeon ; unknown
Beth-car, both text and location uncertain ; near Ebenezer ; perhaps Beth-horon Lower
Beth-dagon
1—*Khirbet Dajûn?:* IX, C-4
2—Josh. 19 : 27, on or near Mt. Carmel ; uncertain
Beth-diblathaim, *see* Almon-diblathaim
Beth-eglaim, *Tell el-'Ajjûl:* IV, A-6 ; IX, A-8 ; XVIII, A-6
Bethel
1—*See also* Luz 1 (in N.T. times Bethela), *Beitîn:* III, B-3 ; IV, C-5 ; V, G-2 ; VI, C-5 ; VII : A-D, C-5 ; IX, F-5 ; XVIII, C-5
2—I Sam. 30 : 27, *see* Bethul
Bethel, Mount, hill country around Bethel 1
Bethela, *see also* Bethel 1, Luz 1, *Beitîn:* IX, F-5 ; XII : D, C-5
Beth-emek, *Tell Mîmâs:* VI, C-3 ; VIII, D-5
Bethennabris (in O.T. times Beth-nimrah), *Tell Nimrîn:* IX, H-5 ; XII : D, D-5
Bether, *Bittîr:* IX, E-6
Beth-ezel, *Deir el-'Aṣal* near Debir 1?
Beth-gader, *same as* Gedor 1?
Beth-gamul, *Khirbet ej-Jumeil:* IX, J-8
Beth-gilgal, *see* Gilgal 1
Beth-haccerem, *'Ain Kârim,* west of Jerusalem
Beth-hanan, I Kings 4 : 9, *Beit 'Anân* east of Aijalon 1
Beth-haran (in N.T. times Julias, Livias, Betharamphtha), *Tell Iktanû:* IX, H-6
Beth-hoglah, at or near *'Ain Ḥajlah:* VI, C-5 ; IX, G-6
Beth-horon Lower, *Beit 'Ur ('ûr) et-Taḥtā:* IV, C-5 ; V, G-2 ; VI, C-5 ; IX, E-5
Beth-horon Upper, *Beit 'Ur ('ûr) el-Fôqā:* IX, E-5 ; XII : D, C-5
Beth-jeshimoth (in N.T. times Besimoth), *Tell el-'Azeimeh:* IX, H-6
Beth-le-aphrah, *eṭ-Ṭaiyibeh* near Hebron?
Beth-lebaoth, *see* Lebaoth
Bethlehem
1—*Beit Laḥm:* IV, C-5 ; VI, C-5 ; IX, F-6 ; XII : B-C, C-5 ; XIV, C-5 ; XVIII, C-5
2—Josh. 19 : 15 ; Judg. 12 : 8, *Beit Laḥm:* VI, C-3 ; VIII, D-6
Beth-maachah, *see* Abel-beth-maachah
Beth-marcaboth, near Ziklag ; uncertain
Beth-meon, *see* Baal-meon
Beth-nimrah (in N.T. times Bethennabris), *Tell el-Bleibil:* VI, D-5 ; IX, H-5
Beth-palet(-pelet), near Beersheba ; uncertain
Beth-pazzez, near En-haddah ; uncertain
Beth-peor, near Mt. Pisgah ; uncertain
Bethphage, *Kefr eṭ-Ṭûr?:* IX, F-6 ; XIV, C-5
Beth-phelet, *see* Beth-palet
Beth-rehob, near Dan ; unknown
Bethsaida Julias, east end of *el-'Araj:* VIII, F-5 ; XII : C-D, D-3 ; XIV, D-3
Beth-shan (in N.T. times Scythopolis), *Tell el-Ḥuṣn (q.v.):* III, C-3 ; IV, C-4 ; VI, C-4 ; VIII, F-8 ; IX, G-1 ; XVIII, C-4
Beth-shean, *see* Beth-shan
Beth-shearim, *Sheikh Abreiq:* XVIII, C-3
Beth-shemesh
1—*Tell er-Rumeileh:* IV, B-5 ; VI, B-5 ; IX, D-6 ; XVIII, B-5
2—Josh. 19 : 22 : near Anem ; at *el-'Abeidiyeh?*
3—Josh. 19 : 38 ; Judg. 1 : 33 ; in northern Naphtali ; unknown
4—Jer. 43 : 13 ; *see* Heliopolis *and* On
Beth-shittah, near Zaretan ; uncertain
Bethsura, *see also* Beth-zur, *Khirbet eṭ-Ṭubeiqah (q.v.):* IX, E-7 ; XII : A, C-5
Beth-tappuah, *Taffûḥ:* IX, E-7
Bethul, near Hormah ; uncertain
Bethuel, *see* Bethul
Beth-yerah, *see also* Philoteria, *Khirbet Kerak:* XVIII, D-3
Bethzacharia, *Khirbet Beit Skâriā:* IX, E-7 ; XII : A, C-5
Beth-zur, *see also* Bethsura ; *Khirbet eṭ-Ṭubeiqah (q.v.):* VI, C-5 ; VII : D, C-5 ; IX, E-7 ; XVIII, C-5
Betonim, *Khirbet Baṭneh:* VI, D-5 ; IX, H-5
Bezek
1—Judg. 1 : 4, 5, uncertain ; *Khirbet Bezqa* near Gezer?
2—*Khirbet Ibzîq:* IV, C-4 ; VI, C-4 ; IX, G-2
Bezer, in the tribe of Reuben ; uncertain
Bezetha, hill N. of Temple Area at Jerusalem : XVII : B-C, D-3
Bileam, *see* Ibleam
Bilhah, *see* Baalah 2
Biruta, *see also* Berytus, *Beirût:* III, C-3
Bisitun, *see also* Behistun : III, E-3
Bithron, district or valley leading from the Jordan to Mahanaim ; uncertain
Bithynia, district in N. Asia Minor : XI : D, B-2 ; XIII, E-2 ; XV, F-2 ; XVI : B, D-2
Bitter Lakes: V, D-3
Bizjothjah, near Beer-sheba if text is not corrupt ; unknown
Black Sea, *see also* Pontus Euxinus : II, E-2 ; III, B-1 ; XI : A-D, B-1 ; XIII, E-2 ; XV, F-2 ; XVI : A-D, E-2
Bochim, *same as* Allon-bachuth?
Bohan, Stone of, *Ḥajar el-Aṣbaḥ?:* VI, C-5 ; IX, G-6
Bologna, *see also* Bononia : XVI : D, B-1
Bononia, *Bologna:* XIII, C-1
Borcaeus, *Khirbet Berqît:* IX, F-4 ; XIV, C-4
Borsippa, *Birs Nimrûd:* III, D-3
Boscath, *see* Bozkath
Bosor, *Buṣr el-Ḥarîrî:* VIII, K-5 ; XII : A, E-3
Bosora, *see also* Bostra *and* Bozrah 1, *Buṣra-Eski Shâm:* VIII, L-7 ; XII : A, F-3
Bosporus
1—strait connecting Black Sea and Propontis : XV, E-2
2—kingdom on both sides of Cimmerian Bosporus, on N. side of Black Sea : XVI : D, E-1
Bostra, *see also* Bosora *and* Bozrah 1, *Buṣra-Eski Shâm:* XII : A, F-3
Bourges, *see also* Avaricum : XVI : D, B-1 ; XVI : D, B-6
Bozez, rocky escarpment, near Michmash along the *Wâdī eṣ-Ṣuweinîṭ*
Bozkath, near Lachish ; unknown
Bozrah
1—(not mentioned in O.T. ; in N.T. times Bosora, Bostra), *Buṣra-Eski Shâm:* IV, F-3 ; VIII, L-7 ; XVIII, F-3
2—*Buṣeirah:* V, G-3 ; VI, D-7 ; VII : A-C, C-6 ; X, I-6
3—Jer. 48 : 24 : *same as* Bezer?
Bracara, *Braga:* XIII, A-1
Brigantium
1—*La Coruña?:* XIII, A-1
2—*Bregenz:* XIII, B-1 ; XIII Inset, F-3
Brigetio, *Bratislava?:* XIII, C-1
Britain, *see also* Brittania : XVI : A-D, A-6
Britannia, *Britain:* XIII Inset, C-2
Brundisium, *Brindisi:* XIII, C-2 ; XV, C-2
Bubastis, *see also* Pi-beseth, *Tell Basṭa:* III, B-4 ; XIII, E-3 ; XVI : D, E-4
Burdigala, *Bordeaux:* XIII, A-1
el-Burj, *see also* Dor, Dora : XVIII, B-3
Busiris, *Abû Ṣîr:* III, B-4 ; V, C-3
Buto, *Tell el-Ferâ'în:* III, A-4
Buz, in Arabia ; uncertain
Byblos, Byblus, *see also* Gebal 1, *Jebeil:* II, E-3 ; III, C-3 ; VII : A-D, C-2 ; XI : D, B-3
Byblos, Persian Province : VII : D, C-3
Byzantium, *Constantinople:* XI : B-D, A-1 ; XIII, D-2 ; XVI : C-D, D-2

Cabbon, near Lachish ; uncertain
Cabul (in N.T. times Chabulon), *Kâbûl:* IV, C-3 ; VI, C-3 ; VII : A-B, C-4 ; VIII, D-5
Caerleon, *see also* Isca 1 : XVI : D, A-5
Caesaraugusta, *Saragossa (q.v.):* XIII, A-2
Caesarea
1—*see also* Strato's Tower, *Qeiṣâriyeh:* I, B-4 ; VIII, B-8 ; IX, D-1 ; XII : B-D, B-4 ; XIII, E-3 ; XIV, B-4 ; XV, G-5 ; XVI : A-D, E-3
2—*also* called Iol, *Cherchel:* XIII, A-2 ; XVI : D, A-2
3—*Kayseri:* XVI : D, E-2
Caesarea Philippi, *see also* Paneas, *Bâniyâs:* VIII, G-3 ; XII : C-D, D-2 ; XIV, D-2
Cagliari, *see also* Caralis : XVI : D, B-2
Cain, *Khirbet Yaqîn:* IX, E-8

Calah, *Nimrûd:* XI: A, C-2
Caleb, tribe affiliated with Judah: VI, C-6
Caleb-ephratah, text corrupt, but *see* Ephratah
Callatis, *Mangalia:* XIII, D-2
Calleva, *Silchester:* XIII Inset, C-2
Callirhoe (in O.T. times Zareth-shahar), *Zārât:* IX, H-7; XII: B, D-5
Calneh
1—Gen. 10: 10; probably not a place name, but a word to be translated "all of them"
2—*Kullanköy?:* XI: A, B-2
Calno, *see* Calneh 2
Camon, *Qammm?:* VI, D-3; VIII, G-7
Camulodunum, *Colchester:* XIII Inset, D-2
Cana, *Khirbet Qânâ:* VIII, E-6; XII: A, C-3; XIV, C-3
Canaan: II, Inset; III, B-3; IV, G-2; V, G-2
Canatha, *see also* Kenath, Nobah 1, Qanu, *Qanawât:* VIII, L-6; XII: B, F-3; XIV, F-3
Canneh, near Haran; unknown
Capernaum, *Tell Ḥûm (q.v.):* VIII, F-5; XII: D, D-3; XIV, D-3; XVIII, D-3
Capharsalama, *Khirbet Selmah ('Id):* IX, E-5; XII: A, C-5
Caphtor, *Crete (q.v.):* II, D-2; II, Inset; III, A-2; XI: A-C, A-2
Cappadocia: XI: C-D, B-2; XIII, E-2; XV, G-3; XVI: A-B, E-2
Capua, *Santa Maria di Capua:* XIII, C-2
Caralis, *Cagliari:* XIII, B-2
Carana, *Erzerum (q.v.):* XIII, F-2
Carchemish, *Jerablus:* II, E-2; III, C-2; XI: A-B, B-2
Caria: XI: C, A-2
Carmania: XI: D, D-3
Carmel, *Kermel:* VI, C-6; IX, E-8; X, F-1
Carmel, Mt., *see also* "Holy Cape," *Jebel Mâr Elyâs:* I, B-3; VI, B-3; VIII, C-6; XII: A-D, B-3; XIV, B-3
Carnaim (in O.T. times Karnaim), *Sheikh Sa'd:* VIII, I-5; XII: A, E-3
Carnuntum, *Petronel:* XIII, C-1
Carpathians, Mts.: II, D-1
Carrhae (in O.T. times Haran), *Ḥarrân:* XIII, F-2
Carteia, on *Bay of Algeciras:* XIII, A-2
Carthage, *see also* Carthago, on *Gulf of Tunis:* XVI: C-D, B-2
Carthagena, *or* **Cartagena;** *see also* Carthago Nova: XVI: D, A-2
Carthago, *see also* Carthage on *Gulf of Tunis:* XIII, B-2
Carthago Nova, *Carthagena (q.v.):* XIII, A-2
Casiphia, unknown
Caspian Sea, *see also* Mare Caspium: II, G-2; III, E-2; XI: A-D, D-1; XIII, G-2; XVI: A-D, G-2
Caspium, Mare, *see also* Caspian Sea: XIII, G-2
Castulo, *Cazlona:* XIII, A-2
Catana, *Catania (q.v.):* XIII, C-2
Catania, *see also* Catana: XVI: D, C-2
Caucasus: II, F-2
Cauda, *see also* Clauda, *Gozzo:* XV, D-4
Cedasa, *see also* Cedes, Kedesh 3, *Tell Qades:* XII: D, D-2
Cedes, *see also* Cedasa *and* Kedesh 3, *Tell Qades:* VIII, F-4; XII: A, D-2
Cedron, *Mughâr?:* IX, C-5; XII: A, B-5
Cenabum, *Orléans:* XIII, Inset D-3
Cenchreae, *Kechries:* XV, D-3
Chabulon, in O.T. times Cabul, *Kābûl:* VIII, D-5; XIV, C-3
Chalcedon, *Kadiköy:* XIII, D-2; XVI: D, D-2
Chalcis: XIII, D-2
Chaldea: XI: B, C-3
Charashim, Valley of, near Lod and Ono; *Wâdī esh-Shellâl?:* IX, D-4
Chatti, a tribe in ancient Germania: XIII Inset, F-2
Chebar, River, canal near Babylon
Chephar-haammonai, in Benjamin; unknown
Chephirah, *Tell Kefîreh:* IV, C-5; IX, E-6
Cherith, Brook, a stream flowing into the Jordan opposite Samaria; *Wâdī Yâbis?*
Cherethites, Cretans: VI, A-6
Chersonesus, near *Sevastopol:* XIII, E-2; XVI: D, E-1
Cherub, unknown
Chesalon: *Keslā:* VI, C-5; IX, E-6
Chesil, *same as* Bethul?
Chesulloth (in N.T. times Exaloth or Xaloth), *Iksâl:* VI, C-3; VIII, E-7
Chezib, *see* Achzib 1
Chidon, Threshing Floor of, near Jerusalem; unknown
Chilmad, unknown
Chinnereth, *Tell el-'Oreimeh:* IV, D-3; VI, D-3; VIII, F-5
Chinnereth, Sea of, *see also* Galilee, Sea of, *and* Tiberias, Sea of; *Baḥr Ṭabarîyeh:* IV, D-3; VI, D-3; VIII, F-6
Chinneroth, *see* Chinnereth
Chios
1—island in Aegean Sea, III, A-2; XV, E-3
2—city on island Chios, XV, E-3
Chisloth-tabor, *see* Chesulloth
Chittim, *see* Kittim
Chorashan, *see* Ashan
Chorazin, *Khirbet Kerâzeh (q.v.):* VIII, F-5; XIV, D-3; XVIII, D-3
Chozeba, *see* Achzib 1
Chub, *see* Lud
Chun, *Râs Ba'albek:* VII: A-D, D-2
Cilicia: XI: B-D, B-2; XIII, E-2; XV, G-3; XVI: A, E-3
Cilician Gates, a pass through the Taurus Mts.: III, C-2; XI: D, B-2; XV, G-3
Cinneroth, district around Chinnereth
Circesium, at junction of *R. Khābûr* with Euphrates: XIII, F-2
Cirta, *Constantine:* XVI: D, B-2
Citium, *Larnaka:* III, B-3; XIII, E-2
City of Salt, *Khirbet Qumrân:* IX, G-6; XIV, C-5; XVIII, C-5
Clauda, *see also* Cauda, *Gozzo:* XV, D-4
Clausentum, at or near *Southampton:* XIII Inset, C-2
Cnidus, on *Cape Krio* in Caria: XV, E-4
Cnossus, near *Candia*, on Crete: II, D-2; XIII, D-2; XVI: C-D, D-3
Colchis: XI: B-C, C-1
Cologne, *or* Köln; *see also* Colonia Agrippina: XVI: C-D, C-5
Colonia Agrippina, *Cologne (q.v.):* XIII Inset, E-2
Colossae, 3 mi. N.W. of *Khonai:* XV, E-3; XVI: B, D-2
Complutum, *Alcala de Henares:* XVI: D, A-2
Coptus, *Kuft:* XIII, E-3; XVI: D, E-4
Corcyra, *Corfu:* XIII, C-2
Cordova, *see also* Corduba: XVI: D, A-2
Corduba, *Cordova (q.v.):* XIII, A-2
Corea, *see also* Ataroth 2, *Tell el-Mazâr:* IX, G-4; XII: A, D, C-4
Corinium, *Cirencester:* XIII Inset, C-2
Corinth, *see also* Corinthus; 3 mi. S.W. of *Korinthus:* XI: A-B, C, A-2; XV, D-3; XVI: B-D, D-3
Corinthus, *see also* Corinth; 3 mi. SW of *Korinthus:* XIII, D-2
Corsica, *Corse:* XIII, B-2; XV, A-2
Cos
1—island: XV, E-3
2—city: XV, E-3
Craftsmen, Valley of, *see* Charashim, Valley of
Creta, *see also* Crete *and* Caphtor: XIII, D-2
Cretans, *see* Cherethites
Crete, *see also* Creta *and* Caphtor: II, D-2; XI: D, A-2; XV, D-4; XVI: A-B, D-3
Crocodilopolis, *see also* Arsinoe, *Medinet el-Faiyûm:* XIII, E-3
Croton, *Cotrone:* XIII, C-2
Ctesiphon, on Tigris R., below Baghdad, opposite Seleucia: XIII, F-3; XVI: D, F-3
Cush, *see also* Aethiopia *and* Ethiopia: II, E-4; II, Inset
Cuthah, *Tell Ibrâhîm:* XI: A-B, C-3
Cyclades: II, D-2
Cydonia, *Khania:* XIII, D-2
Cyprus, *see also* Alashiya, Elishah, Kittim: II, E-2; VII: A-D, B-1; XI: D, B-2; XIII, E-2; XV, F-4; XVI: A-B, E-3
Cyrenaica, *Cirenaica:* XIII, D-3; XV, D-5
Cyrene, *Cirene:* XI: B-D, A-3; XIII, D-3; XV, D-5; XVI: A-B, C-3
Cyzicus, on the Propontis, i.e., the modern Sea of Marmara: XVI: D, D-2

Dabareh (in N.T. times Dabarittha), *Debûriyeh:* VIII, E-7
Dabarittha (in O.T. times Dabareh), *Khirbet Debûriyeh:* VIII, E-7; XIII: D, C-3
Dabbasheth, near Jokneam; uncertain
Daberath, *see* Dabareh
Dacia, region of Transylvania and Rumania: XIII, D-1; XV, D-1; XVI: D, D-1
Dalmanutha, Mark 8: 10; uncertain
Dalmatia, *see also* Illyricum: XV, C-1
Damascus, *esh-Shâm:* I, E-2; II, E-3; III, C-3; IV, E-2; VI, E-2; VII: A-D, D-3; VIII, J-1; XI: A-D, B-3; XII: A-D, E-2; XIII, E-3; XIV, E-2; XV, G-4; XVI: A-D, E-3; XVIII, E-2
Damietta Mouth of the Nile River: V, C-2
Dan
1—tribal district before the 11th cent.: VI, B-5
2—tribal district after the 11th cent.: VI, D-2
3—*see also* Laish, *Tell el-Qâḍî:* I, D-2; IV, D-2; VI, D-2; VII: A-D, C-3; VIII, G-3
Dan-jaan, uncertain text, but reference is to the city of Dan
Dannah, near Debir 1; uncertain
Danube, River, *see also* Danuvius: XI: D, A-1; XIII Inset; XV, E-2; XVI: A-D, D-2; XVI: A-D, D-6
Danuvius, *see also* River Danube: XIII, D-2; XIII Inset, F-3
Daphnae, *see also* Tahpanhes, *Tell Defneh:* XI: B, B-3
Daphne, *Khirbet Dafneh:* VIII, G-3; XII: D, D-2
David, City of, *see also* Jerusalem, Jebus: XVII: A, D-5
Dead Sea, *see also* Salt Sea *and* Lake Asphaltitis, *Baḥr Lûṭ:* I, C-6; XII: A-D, C-6; XIV, C-6; XVIII, C-6
Debeltum, in eastern Thrace: XVI: C, D-2
Debir
1—*see also* Kirjath-sepher, *Tell Beit Mirsim:* IV, B-6; V, F-2; VI, B-6; IX, D-8; X, E-1; XVIII, B-6
2—Josh. 15: 7, *Thoghret ed-Debr:* VI, C-5; IX, G-6
3—Josh. 13: 26, *see* Lo-debar
Decapolis, "ten cities," sphere of influence of federation of Greek cities in E. Palestine: XII: B-D, D-3; XIV, D-3
Dedan, *el-'Ulā;* II, Inset; XI: B-D, B-4
Deir Ghassâneh, *see also* Zeredah: XVIII, C-4
Delphi, on lower south slope of Mt. Parnassus: XIII, D-2
Der, *Bedrai:* II, F-3; III, E-3
Derbe, near *Zosta:* XIII, E-2; XV, F-3; XVI: B, E-3
Deva, *Chester:* XIII Inset, C-1
Dhîbân, *see also* Dibon: XVIII, D-5
Diblath, *see* Riblah
Dibon
1—*Dhībân:* V, G-2; VI, D-5; VII: A-C, C-5; IX, I-8; XVIII, D-5
2—Neh. 11: 25, *see* Dimonah
Dibon-gad, *see* Dibon 1
Diklah, in southern Arabia; uncertain
Dilean, near Lachish; uncertain
Dimasqu, Assyrian Province: VII: C, D-3
Dimnah, *see* Rimmon 2
Dimon, Waters of, stream near Madmen?
Dimonah, near Aroer 3; uncertain
Dinhabah, in Edom; unknown
Dion, *Tell el-Ash 'arī:* VIII, I-6; XII: A, E-3; XIV, E-3
Dioscurias, Dioscurias, *Sukhum:* XI: B-C, C-1; XIII, F-2
Divodurum, *Metz (q.v.):* XIII Inset, E-2
Diyâlā River: III, E-3
Dizahab, unknown
Dok, *Jebel Qaranṭal:* IX, G-5; XII: A, C-5
Dophkah, *Serābîṭ el-Khâdim?:* V, E-5
Dor
1—in N.T. times Dora, *el-Burj* north of *eṭ-Ṭanṭûrah:* IV, B-3; VI, B-3; VII: A-D, B-4; VIII, C-7; XVIII, B-3
2—Persian Province: VII: D, B-4
Dora, *see also* Dor, *el-Burj* north of *eṭ-Ṭanṭûrah:* VIII, C-7; XII: A-C, B-3
Dorylaeum, just N. of *Eskişehir:* XV, E-3; XVI: D, D-2
Dothan, *Tell Dôthā:* IV, C-4; VI, C-4; IX, F-2; XVIII, C-4
Dragon's Well, *same as* En-rogel?
Drangiana, region in E. Iran and W. Afghanistan: XI: C-D, E-3
Dubrae, *Dover:* XIII Inset, D-2
Dumah
1—Josh. 15: 52, *ed-Dômeh:* IX, D-8; X, F-1
2—*Dûmet ej-Jendel:* III, D-4; XI: A-C, C-3
Dura, Plain of, near Babylon; uncertain
Dura, Dura-Europus, *Ṣâliḥîyeh:* XI: D, C-2; XVI: D, F-3
Dur-belḫarran-shadua, Assyrian Province: VII: C, C-4
Durnovaria, *Dorchester:* XIII Inset, C-2
Durocortorum, *Rheims (q.v.):* XIII Inset, E-2
Durovernum, *Canterbury:* XIII Inset, D-2
Dur Sharrukin, *Khorsabad:* XI: A, C-2
Du'ru, Assyrian Province of Dor: VII: C, B-4
Dyrrhachium, *Durazzo:* XIII, C-2; XV, C-2

East Sea, *see* Salt Sea
Ebal, Mt., *Jebel Eslāmīyeh:* I, C-4; IV, C-4; VI, C-4; IX, F-3
Eben-ezer, *Mejdel Yâbâ?:* VI, B-4; IX, D-4
Ebronah, in Sinai; uncertain
Eburacum, *York:* XIII Inset, C-1
Eburodunum, *Yverdon:* XIII Inset, E-3
Ecbatana, *see also* Achmetha, *Hamadân:* III, E-3; XI: B-D, D-2; XIII, G-2
Ecdippa (in O.T. times Achzib), *ez-Zîb:* VIII, D-4; XII: B, C-2
Edar, Tower of, unknown
Eden, House of (Beth-eden), a district near Haran
Eder, same as Arad?
Edessa, *Urfa:* XIII, E-2; XVI: B-D, E-3
Edom: I, D-7; IV, C-7; V, G-3; VI, C-8; VII: A-C, C-6; X, I-6; XI: A, B-3
Edrei
1—*Der'ā:* III, C-3; IV, E-3; VI, E-3; VII: A-D, D-4; VIII, I-7
2—Josh. 19: 37; near Kedesh 3; uncertain
Eglaim, in Moab; unknown
Eglon, *Tell el-Ḥesī:* IV, B-5; V, F-2; VI, B-5; IX, C-7; XVIII, B-5
Egypt, *see also* Aegyptus: II, D-3; II Inset; III, B-4; V, B-4; XI: A-D, A-4; XVI: A-C, E-4; XVIII, A-7
Egypt, River of, *Wâdī el-'Arîsh:* III, B-4; V, F-3; VI, A-7; VII: A-D, B-6; X, A-6
Ekron (in N.T. times Accaron), *Qaṭrā?:* IV, B-5; VI, B-5; IX, C-6
Elah, Valley of, *Wâdī es-Sanṭ:* IX, D-6
Elam: II, G-3; II Inset; III, E-3; XI: A-B, D-3; XVI: A, G-3
Elasa, *Khirbet el-'Ashshī:* IX, F-5; XII: A, C-5
Elath, either the same as or near Ezion-geber; *Tell el-Kheleifeh?:* VII: C-D, B-7; XI: A-C, B-3
Elbe, *see also* Albis, a river: XIII Inset, F-1
Elealeh, *el-'Al ('âl):* VI, D-5; IX, I-6
Eleph, to be read with preceding word as Zelah-eleph; *see* Zelah
Elephantine, *see also* Syene *and* Seveneh, *Aswân:* II, E-4; XI: A-C, B-4
Eleutheropolis, *Beit Jibrîn:* XVIII, B-5
Elim, *Wâdī Gharandel?:* V, D-4
Elis, *Kalaskopi:* XIII, D-2
Elishah, *see also* Cyprus, Kittim, Alashiya: II, Inset; III, B-3
Elkosh, unknown
Ellasar, *see* Larsa
Elon
1—Josh. 19: 43, near Timnah 2; uncertain
2—I Kings 4: 9, same as Aijalon 1
Eloth, *see* Elath
El-paran, in the Wilderness of Paran; unknown
Eltekeh, *Khirbet el-Muqenna':* VI, B-5; IX, D-6
Eltekon, in Judah; uncertain
Eltolad, in Simeon; uncertain
Elusa, *see* Alusa
Emerita, *Merida (q.v.):* XIII, A-2
Emesa, Emessa, *Homs:* XI: D, B-2; XIII, E-2; XVI: D, E-3
Emmaus
1—*'Amwâs:* IX, D-6; XII: C-D, B-5; XIV, B-5; XVIII, B-5
2—*Qalôniyeh:* IX, E-6; XII: D, C-5
Emporium, in N.E. Spain, near mouth of Muga River: XIII, B-2
Enam, near Jarmuth 1; uncertain
En-dor, *Endôr:* VI, C-3; VIII, E-7
En-eglaim, *'Ain Feshkah* near *Qumrân (q.v.)*
Engaddi (in O.T. times En-gedi), *'Ain Jidi:* IX, G-8; X, H-1, XII: D, C-6
En-gannim
1—Josh. 15: 34, near Beth-shemesh 1; *Beit Jemâl?*
2—(in N.T. times Ginaea), *Jenîn:* VI, C-4; VIII, E-8; IX, F-1
En-gedi (in N.T. times Engaddi), at *'Ain Jidi:* VI, C-6; IX, G-8; X, H-1
En-haddah, *el-Hadetheh:* VIII, F-7
En-hakkore, spring in Lehi
En-hazor, *Ḥazzûr?:* VI, C-2; VIII, E-4
Enkomi: III, B-3
En-mishpat, *see* Kadesh-barnea
Enoch, unknown
En-rimmon, *Khirbet Umm er-Ramâmîn:* VI, B-6; X, E-1
En-rogel, spring in Jerusalem; *see also* Job's Well, *Bîr Ayyûb:* XVII: A-C, E-7
En-shemesh, *'Ain el-Hôd:* VI, C-5; IX, F-6
En-tappuah, *see* Tappuah 2
Enu-anabi, *Nâb:* IV, D-3
Ephes-dammim, between Socoh 1 and Azekah; uncertain
Ephesus, c. 3 mi. from mouth of Cayster R., on S. side: III, A-2; XI: D, A-2; XIII, D-2; XV, E-3; XVI: B-D, D-3
Ephraim
1—*see also* Aphairema; *same as* Ophrah 1?; *eṭ-Ṭaiyibeh?:* IX, F-5; XII: D, C-5; XIV, C-5
2—tribal district: VI, C-4
Ephraim, Mt. or hill country of, region north of Bethel
Ephrain, *see* Ephraim 1
Ephratah, *see* Bethlehem 1
Ephrath, *see* Ephratah
Ephron, II Chron. 13: 19 (R.S.V.); *see* Ephraim 1
Ephron, Mt.: IX, E-6
Epirus, region in N.W. ancient Greece: XI: D, A-2
Erech, Uruk, *Warka:* II, F-3; III, E-3; XI: A-C, C-3
Eridu, *Abū Shahrein:* II, F-3; III, E-4
Erythraeum, Mare, lit., Red Sea, usually of the gulf so named in II, E-4; *also* used as here of Indian Ocean: XIII, H-4
Erzerum, *see also* Carana: III, D-1
Esbus, *see also* Essebon, Heshbon, *Ḥesbân:* XII: B-D, D-5
Esdraelon, *see also* Jezreel, Valley of, *Merj Ibn 'Amir ('âmir):* VIII, D-7
Eshcol, Brook or Valley of, one of the valleys of Hebron area
Eshean, near Dumah 1; uncertain
Eshnunna, *Tell el-Asmar:* II, F-3; III, E-3
Eshtaol, *Eshwa'* (or *Ishwa'*)?: IX, E-6
Eshtemoa, *es-Semû':* VI, C-6; IX, E-8; X, F-1; XVIII, C-6
Eshtemoh, *see* Eshtemoa
Eskişehir: III, B-1
Essebon, *see also* Esbus, Heshbon, *Ḥesbân:* IX, I-6; XII: B-D, D-5
Etam
1—*Khirbet el-Khôkh:* IX, F-7
2—near En-rimmon; uncertain
Etam, Rock, in northern Judah; uncertain
Etham, in Sinai; uncertain
Ether
1—Josh. 15: 42, *Khirbet el-'Ater:* IX, D-7
2—*Khirbet 'Attîr;* near En-rimmon
Ethiopia, *see also* Aethiopia, Cush: II, Inset; XVI: A, E-6
Euphrates River, *Shaṭṭ el-Furât:* II, F-2; III, D-3; XI: A-D, C-2; XIII, F-2; XV, G-3; XVI: A-D, F-3
Evora, ancient Ebora: XVI: D, A-2
Exaloth, *see also* Xaloth (in O.T. times Chesulloth), *Iksâl:* VIII, E-7; XIV, C-3
Ezek, Well of, near Gerar in the *Wâdī Ghazzeh;* unknown
Ezel, Stone of, unknown
Ezem, *see* Azem

Location of plates: I, p. 21; II, p. 22; III, p. 31; IV, p. 32; V, p. 41; VI, p. 42; VII, p. 51; VIII, p. 52; IX, p. 65; X, p. 66; XI, p. 79; XII, p. 80; XIII, p. 89; XIV, p. 90; XV, p. 99; XVI, p. 100; XVII, p. 109; XVIII, p. 110.

Ezion-geber, *see also* Elath, *Tell el-Kheleifeh:* III, B-4; V, G-4; VII: A-B, B-7

Fair Havens, *Limenes Kali:* XV, E-4
Faiyûm: V, B-4
Faro, city in S. Portugal: XVI: D, A-2
Florence, ancient Florentia, *Firenze:* XVI: D, B-1
Forum Julii, *Fréjus:* XIII, B-2
Frisii, ancient tribe in N. Germania: XIII Inset, E-1
Fuller's Field, in Jerusalem; uncertain

Gaash, Mt., by Timnath-serah: IX, E-5
Gaba
1—*see* Geba
2—*el-Ḥârithîyeh:* VIII, D-6; XII: B, C-3; XIV, C-3
Gabao, *see also* Gibeon, *ej-Jîb:* IX, E-5; XII: D, C-5
Gabara, *'Arrâbet el-Baṭṭôf:* VIII, E-5; XII: D, C-3
Gabath Saul (in O.T. times Gibeah 3), *Tell el-Fûl:* IX, F-6; XII: D, C-5
Gad, tribal district: VI, D-5
Gad, River or Valley of, *see* Arnon, River
Gadara, *Muqeis:* VIII, G-7; XII: A-D, D-3; XIV, D-3
Gades *Cádiz:* XIII, A-2
Galaaditis, *see also* Gilead: XII: A, D-3
Galatia
1—district settled by Gauls in north central Asia Minor: XI: D, B-2; XV, F-3
2—Roman province in central Asia Minor: XIII, E-2; XVI: B, E-2; XV, F-3
Gal'aza, Assyrian Province of Gilead: VII: C, C-4
Galeed, *see* Mizpah 1
Galilee: I, C-3; VIII, D-6; XII: A-D, C-3; XIV, C-3
Galilee, Sea of, *see also* Chinnereth, Sea of, *Baḥr Ṭabarîyeh:* I, D-3; VIII, F-6; XIV, D-3; XVIII, D-3
Gallim, *Khirbet Ka'kûl,* near Anathoth
Gamala, *Râs el-Ḥâl* at *Jamleh?:* VIII, H-6; XII: A-D, D-3
Gareb, hill near Jerusalem; unknown
Garis, *Khirbet Kennā?:* VIII, E-6; XII: D, C-3
Garonne, River, ancient Garumna: XVI: A-B, B-1
Garu: IV, D-3
Gath, *'Arâq el-Menshîyeh:* IV, B-5; VI, B-5; VII: A-C, B-5; IX, C-7
Gath-carmel, *Jett:* IV, C-4
Gath-hepher, *Khirbet ez-Zurrâ':* IV, C-3; VI, C-3; VIII, E-6
Gath-rimmon
1—Josh. 21:25, *Rummâneh:* VIII, D-8; IX, F-1
2—*Tell ej-Jerîsheh:* IX, D-4; XVIII, B-4
Gaul: XVI: B-C, B-1
Gaul, Northern: XVI: A-D, Inset
Gaulanitis, region E. and N.E. of Sea of Galilee: XII: A-D, D-3; XIV, D-3
Gaza, *Ghazzeh:* I, A-6; III, B-3; IV, A-6; V, F-2; VI, A-6; VII: A-D, B-5; IX, A-8; XI: B, D, B-3; XII: A-D, A-6; XIII, E-3; XIV, A-6; XV, G-5; XVI: A, D, E-4; XVIII, A-6
Gazara (in O.T. times Gezer), *Tell Jezer:* IX, D-5; XII: A-B, B-5
Geba, *Jeba':* IX, F-5
Gebal
1—*see also* Byblos, *Jebeil:* III, C-3; VII: A-D, C-2; XI: A-C, B-3
2—Ps. 83:7, northern Edom?
Gebim, in Benjamin; uncertain
Geder, near Debir 1; unknown
Gederah
1—Josh. 15:36, *Jedîreh:* IX, D-6
2—I Chron. 12:4, *Jedîreh* near Gibeon
Gederoth, near Beth-dagon 1; uncertain
Gederothaim, textual corruption?
Gedor
1—Josh. 15:58, *Khirbet Jedûr:* IX, E-7
2—I Chron. 4:18, 39, in Judah; uncertain
3—I Chron. 12:7, uncertain
Gedrosia, region in S.E. Iran: XI: C-D, E-3
Gehenna, *see also* Valley of Hinnom, *Wâdî er-Rabâbi:* XVII: B-C, B-6
Gelil ha-Goim, Persian Province of Galilee: VII: D, C-4
Geliloth, *see* Gilgal 3
Genava, *Geneva:* XIII Inset, E-3
Gennesaret, Plain of, *el-Ghuweir:* XIV, C-3
Genua, *Genoa:* XIII, B-1
Gerar, *Tell Abū Hureirah:* I, B-6; II, E-3; IV, B-6; V, E-3; VI, B-6; VII: A-D, B-5; X, C-1
Gerasa, *Jerash (q.v.):* IX, J-3; XII: A, D, D-4; XIV, D-4; XVI: D, E-3; XVIII, D-4
Gergesa, *Kursī?:* VIII, G-6; XIV, D-3
Gergovia, *Gergovie:* XIII, B-1; XIII Inset, D-3
Gerizim, Mt., *Jebel eṭ-Ṭôr:* I, C-4; IV, C-4; VI, C-4; IX, F-3; XII: B-C, C-4; XIV, C-4; XVIII, C-4
Germania: XIII Inset, F-2
Geshur
1—Aramean district in Bashan: VII: A, C-4
2—Josh. 13:2, I Sam. 27:8, district in northern Sinai or on southern border of Palestine
Gesoriacum, *Boulogne:* XIII Inset, D-2
Gethsemane, garden on E. side of Kidron Valley: XVII: B, E-4
Gezer (in N.T. times Gazara), *Tell Jezer:* IV, B-5; III, B-3; V, F-2; VI, B-5; IX, D-5; XVIII, B-5
Giah, near Gibeon; unknown
Gibbar, corruption of Gibeon?
Gibbethon, *Tell el-Melât:* IX, D-5
Gibeah
1—Josh. 15:57, in Judah; uncertain
2—I Sam. 7:1 ("hill"), II Sam. 6:3, near Kirjath-jearim; unknown
3—(in N.T. times Gabath Saul), *Tell el-Fûl:* VI, C-5; IX, F-6; XVIII, C-5
Gibeath, *same as* Gibeah 3?
Gibeon (in N.T. times Gabao), *ej-Jîb:* IV, C-5; V, G-2; IX, E-5
Gibeonite Tetrapolis, composed of the Hivite cities, Gibeon, Beeroth, Chephirah, Kirjath-baal: IV, C-5
Gidom, near Rock Rimmon; unknown
Gihon, spring in Jerusalem; *see also* Virgin's Spring; *'Ain Sittī Maryam:* XVII: A-C, E-5
Gilboa, Mt., *Jebel Fuqû'ah:* I, C-4; VI, C-4; VIII, E-8; IX, G-1
Gilead
1—*see also* Galaaditis: I, D-4; IX, H-4
2—Persian Province: VII: D, C-4
Gilgal
1—*Khirbet el-Mefjer?:* V, G-2; VI, C-5; VII: C, C-5; IX, G-5; XVIII, C-5
2—Josh. 12:23, *Jiljûlieh:* IV, B-4; IX, D-3
3—Josh. 15:7; near Debir 2; uncertain
Giloh, in Judah; uncertain
Gimirrai, *see also* Gomer: XI: A, B-2
Gimzo, *Jimzū,* near Lod
Ginaea (in O.T. times En-gannim), *Jenin:* VIII, E-8; IX, F-1; XIV, C-4
Gischala, *el-Jish (q.v.):* VIII, F-4; XII: D, C-2; XIV, C-2
Gittah-hepher, *see* Gath-hepher
Gittaim, near Lod; uncertain
Gîzeh: V, C-4
Glevum, *Gloucester:* XIII Inset, C-2
Goath, near Jerusalem; unknown
Gob, unknown
Golan, *Saḥem el-Jōlân?:* VI, D-3; VIII, H-6
Gomer, *see also* Gimirrai: II, Inset; XI: A, B-2
Gomorrah, under waters of the Dead Sea at the S.E. end, exact spot unknown: X, H-2
Gophna, *Jifnah:* IX, F-5; XII: A, D, C-5
Gordium, near *Pebi:* XI: D, B-2
Gorgobina, in upper Loire valley: XIII, B-1 and Inset, D-3
Gortyna, *Gortyn:* XIII, D-2; XVI: C-D, D-3
Goshen
1—Land of: III, B-4; V, C-3
2—Josh. 10:41, 11:16, district in southern Palestine; exact area uncertain
3—Josh. 15:51, town near Anim; unknown
Gozan, *Tell Ḥalâf:* XI: A, C-2
Granicus, River, small river in N.W. Asia Minor: XI: D, A-2
Great Sea, *see also* Mare Internum *and* Mediterranean Sea
Greater Oasis, W of Nile, c. 25° N lat., 30° E long.: XVI: D, D-5
Greece, *see also* Achaia: XI: A-D, A-2
Gudgodah, in Sinai; uncertain
Gur, the going up of, near Ibleam; unknown
Gur-baal, unknown
Gurgum, *Maraṣ:* III, C-2

Habor River, *Nahr el-Khābûr:* III, D-3
Hachilah, Hill of, near Ziph 2; uncertain
Hadashah, near Gath; uncertain
Hadattah, read with preceding word as Hazor-hadattah; in Negeb of Judah; uncertain
Hadid, *see also* Adida, *el-Ḥadîtheh:* IV, B-5; IX, D-5
Hadrach, Land of, district of Syria north of Hamath
Hadrianopolis, *Adrianople:* XVI: D, D-2
Hadriaticum, Mare, *see also* Adriatic Sea *and* Adria, XIII, C-2; XV, C-2
Hadrumetum, *Sousse:* XIII, B-2; XVI: C-D, B-3
Hai, *see* Ai
Halah, in N. Mesopotamia; unknown
Halak, Mt., *Jebel Halâq:* VI, B-7; X, E-5
Halhul (in N.T. times Alurus), *Ḥalḥûl:* IX, E-7
Hali, near Helkath; uncertain
Halicarnassus, *Bodrum:* XI: D, A-2
Halys River, *Kizil Irmak:* II, E-2; III, B-2; XIII, E-2; XV, G-3; XVI: A, E-2
Ham, *Hâm:* IV, D-4; VIII, H-8; IX, I-1
Hamadân, *see also* Achmetha, Ecbatana: III, E-3
Hamat *(ḫamat),* Assyrian Province: VII: C, D-1
Hamath
1—*Ḥamā:* II, E-2; III, C-3; VII: A-D, D-1; XI: A-C, B-2
2—Persian Province: VII: D, D-2
Hamath-zobah, *see* Zobah
Hammâm Tabarîyeh *(Ḥammâm Ṭabarîyeh), see also* Hammath *and* Ammathus: XVIII, D-3
Hammat, *Tell el-Ḥammeh:* IV, C-4
Hammath (in N.T. times Ammathus), *Ḥammâm Ṭabarîyeh:* IV, D-3; VI, D-3; VIII, F-6
Hammon
1—Josh. 19:28, *Umm el 'Awāmîd?:* IV, C-2; VI, C-2; VIII, D-4
2—I Chron. 6:76, *same as* Hammath?
Hammoth-dor, *same as* Hammath?
Hamonah, unknown
Hamon-gog, Valley of, unknown
Hanes, *see* Tahpanhes
Hannathon, *Tell el-Bedeiwîyeh?:* IV, C-3; VI, C-3; VIII, E-6
Hapharaim, *eṭ-Ṭaiyibeh:* IV, C-3; VI, C-3; VIII, E-7
Hara, unknown
Haradah, in Sinai, uncertain
Haran, *see also* Carrhae, *Ḥarrân:* II, F-2; III, C-2; XI: A-C, B-2
Hareth, Forest of, at *Kharâs* near Keilah?
Hariph, *see* Haruph
Harmozia, port N. of Straits of Ormuz: XI: D, E-3
Harod, Well of, *'Ain Jâlûd:* VI, C-3; VIII, E-8; IX, G-1
Harosheth, *Tell 'Amr?:* IV, C-3; VIII, D-6; XVIII, C-3
Harput: III, C-2
Haruph, in southern Judah; uncertain
Hashmonah, near Kadesh-barnea; uncertain
Hauran, *see also* Auranitis, *Haurân:* VII: D, D-4; VIII, J-6
Haurina, (ḫaurina), Assyrian Province: VII: C, D-4
Havilah: II, Inset
Havoth-jair: VI, D-3
Hazar-addar, *Khirbet el-Qudeirât?:* V, F-3; VI, A-7; X, B-6
Hazar-enan, *Qaryatein?:* VII: A-D, E-2
Hazar-gaddah, near Beer-sheba; uncertain
Hazar-hatticon, in Hauran; uncertain
Hazar-ithnan, Josh. 15:23, *el-Jebarîyeh* on the *Wâdī Umm Ethnân?:* X, D-6
Hazarmaveth, *Wâdī Hadramaut:* II, Inset
Hazar-shual, near Beer-sheba; uncertain
Hazar-susah, *Sbalat Abū Sûsein:* X, C-2
Hazerim, to be rendered "villages"
Hazeroth, *'Ain Khaḍrā?:* V, F-5
Hazezon-tamar, at or near *'Ain el-'Arûs?:* VI, C-7; X, H-4
Hazor
1—in N.T. times Asor, *Tell el-Qedaḥ* (or *Waqqâṣ*): II, E-3; III, C-3; IV, D-2; VI, D-2; VIII, F-4; XVIII, D-2
2—Josh. 15:25, *see* Hezron 2
3—Neh. 11:33, *Khirbet Hazzûr* near Gibeon?
4—Josh. 15:23, *see* Hazar-ithnan
Hazor-hadattah, *see* Hadattah
Hebron
1—*see also* Kirjath-arba, *el-Khalîl:* I, C-6; III, B-3; IV, C-6; V, G-2; VI, C-5; VII: A-D, C-5; IX, E-8; XII: A-D, C-5; XIV, C-6
2—Josh. 19:28, *see* Abdon
Hecatompylus, *Damghan* (or *Shahrud*): XI: D, D-2
Helam, uncertain
Helbah, *same as* Ahlab?
Helbon, *Halbûn:* VII: A-D, D-3
Heleph, near Mt. Tabor; uncertain
Heliopolis, *see also* On *and* Beth-shemesh 4, *Tell Ḥuṣn:* II, E-3; III, B-4; V, C-3; XIII, E-3
Helkath, *Tell el-Harbaj?:* IV, C-3; VI, C-3; VIII, D-6; XVIII, C-3
Helkath-hazzurim, *see* Gibeon
Hellespont, *Dardanelles:* XV, E-3
Helmund, River, in Afghanistan: XI: D, E-2
Hemath, *see* Hamath
Hena, in Syria; unknown
Hepher, in Manasseh; uncertain
Heraclea, *Eregli:* XIII, E-2
Heracleopolis, *Ahnâs el-Medîneh:* II, E-3; V, B-4
Heres, Mt., *see* Beth-shemesh 1
Hermon, Mt., *Jebel esh-Sheikh:* I, D-2; IV, D-2; VI, D-2; VII: A-D, C-3; VIII, H-2; XII: A-D, D-2; XIV, D-2
Hermopolis, *el-Ashmûnein:* V, B-6; XIII, E-3; XVI: D, D-4
Herodium, *Jebel Fureidîs:* IX, F-7; XII: B-D, C-5
Heshbon (in N.T. times Esbus, Essebon), *Ḥesbân:* V, G-2; VI, D-5; VII: A-D, C-5; IX, I-6
Heshmon, near Beer-sheba; uncertain
Hethlon, in Syria; uncertain
Hezron
1—*see* Hazar-addar
2—Josh. 15:25, unknown; text corrupt?
Hiddekel, River, *see* Tigris River
Hierapolis, *Pambuk Kalesi:* XV, E-3
Hilen, *see* Holon 1
Hinnom, Valley of, *see also* Gehenna, *Wâdī er-Rabâbeh:* XVII: A-D, C-7
Hippo Regius, near *Bône:* XIII, B-2; XVI: D, B-2
Hippos, *Qal'at el-Ḥuṣn:* VIII, G-6; XII: A-D, D-3; XIV, D-3
Hispalis, *Seville (q.v.):* XIII, A-2
Hittite Empire: III, B-2
Hivite Tetrapolis, *see* Gibeonite Tetrapolis
Hobah, near Damascus; uncertain
Holon
1—*Khirbet 'Alîn,* near Beth-zur
2—Jer. 48:21, near Medeba; unknown
"Holy Cape," an Egyptian name for Mt. Carmel: VI, B-3
Hor, Mt.
1—Num. 34:7, 8; uncertain
2—in the area north of Kadesh-barnea; uncertain
Horeb, *see also* Sinai, Mt., *Jebel Mûsā?:* V, E-5
Horem, near Iron; uncertain
Hor-hagidgad, *see* Gudgodah
Horites, Land of the, *see also* Mitanni: III, D-2
Hormah, *see also* Zephath, near Ziklag; unknown
Horonaim, in Moab; uncertain
Hosah, near Tyre; uncertain
Hukkok, *Yâqûq:* VI, C-3; VIII, F-5
Hukok, *see* Helkath
Huleh, Lake, *see also* Lake Semechonitis, *Baḥret el-Ḥûleh* (or *Baḥret el-Kheiṭ*): I, D-2; XVIII, D-2
Humtah, near Hebron; unknown
Hyrcania
1—*Khirbet Mird:* IX, G-6; XII: A-B, C-5
2—Persian Satrapy: XI: C-D, D-2

Iatnana, *see also* Cyprus, Alashiya, Kittim: XI: A, B-2
Ibleam, *Tell Bel'ameh:* IV, C-4; VI, C-4; VIII, E-8; IX, F-2
Iconium, *Konya:* III, B-2; XIII, E-2; XV, F-3; XVI: B-D, E-3
Idalah, *Khirbet el-Ḥawârah* near Bethlehem 2?
Idiglat River, *see also* Hiddekel, River, *and* Tigris River: *Shaṭṭ ed-Dijleh:* III, D-3
Idumaea: VII: D, B-5; X, C-2; XII: A-D, B-6; XIV, B-6
Iim
1—*see* Ije-abarim
2—Josh. 15:29, near Azem; uncertain
Ije-abarim, near Brook Zered: uncertain
Ijon, *Tell ed-Dibbîn?:* IV, D-2; VII: A-D, C-3; VIII, G-2
Ilerda, *Lerida:* XIII, A-2
Ilium *see also* Troy, *Hissarlik:* XI: D, A-2; XVI: D, D-2
Illyricum *see also* Dalmatia: XIII, C-2; XVI: B, C-2; XV, C-1
Immer, unknown
Indian Ocean *see also* Mare Erythraeum: II, H-4
Ionia: XI: B-C, A-2
Ionium, Mare, *Ionian Sea:* XIII, C-2
Ipsus, *near Saklî?:* XI: D, B-2
Ir-nahash, in Judah; uncertain
Iron, *Yārûn:* VI, C-2; VIII, E-4
Irpeel, in Benjamin; uncertain
Irqata, *Tell 'Arqah:* III, C-3
Ir-shemesh, *see* Beth-shemesh 1
Isbeitā, *see also* Subaita: XVIII, B-7
Isca
1—*Caerleon (q.v.):* XIII Inset, C-2
2—*Exeter:* XIII Inset, C-2
'Isfīyā: XVIII, C-3
Ishtob, *see* Tob
Israel, the ten northern tribes: VII: A-B, C-4
Issachar, tribal district: VI, C-3
Issus, on N.E. shore of Gulf of Alexandretta: XI: D, B-2
Ister, *see also* Istrus: *Karanasib:* XIII, D-2
Istrus, *see also* Ister: *Karanasib:* XI: B-C, A-1
Italia, *see also* Italy: XIII, C-2; XV, B-1
Italy, *see also* Italia: XVI: B-C, C-2
Ithnan, *see* Hazar-ithnan
Ittah-kazin, near Gath-hepher; uncertain
Ituraea, district S. of Mt. Hermon: XIV, D-2
Ivah, Ava, *Tell Kefr 'Ayā* near Riblah?

Jaazer, *see* Jazer
Jabbok, River, *Nahr ez-Zerqā:* I, D-4; IV, D-4; VI, D-4; IX, H-3
Jabesh-gilead, *Tell Abū Kharaz:* IV, D-4; VI, D-4; IX, H-2
Jabez, near Arad; unknown
Jabneel, *see also* Jamnia, Jabneh
1—*Yebnā:* VI, B-5; IX, C-5
2—Josh. 19:33, *Yemmā?:* VI, D-3; VIII, F-6
Jabneh, *see also* Jabneel 1, Jamnia, *Yebnā:* IX, C-5
Jacob's Well, *Bir Ya'qûb:* IX, F-3; XIV, C-4
Jader, *Zara:* XIII, C-2
Jaffa, *see also* Joppa, *Yâfā:* XVIII, B-4
Jagur, in S. Judah; uncertain
Jahaz, either *Jâlûl* or *Khirbet et-Teim?:* IX, I-6
Jahaza, Jahazah, *see* Jahaz
Jahzah, *see* Jahaz
Jamnia, *see also* Jabneel 1, Jabneh, *Yebnā:* IX, C-5; XII: A-D, B-5; XIV, B-5
Janoah
1—*Khirbet Yânûn:* VI, C-4; IX, G-3
2—II Kings 15:29, near Kedesh 3; unknown
Janohah, *see* Janoah 1
Janum, near Hebron; unknown
Japha, *see also* Japhia, *Yâfā* in Galilee: VIII, E-7; XII: D, C-3
Japhia, *see also* Japha, *Yâfā* in Galilee: IV, C-3; VI, C-3; VIII, E-7

Japhleti, a clan, not a town
Japho, *see* Joppa
Jarda, *or* **Jardan**; *see also* Jorda, *Khirbet 'Irq:* X, C-1; XIV, B-6
Jarmuth
1—*Khirbet Yarmûk:* IV, B-5; VI, B-5; IX, D-6
2—Josh. 21:29; *see* Remeth
Jashubi-lehem, to be translated "the dwellers in Bethlehem [1]"
Jattir, *Khirbet 'Attîr:* X, F-1
Javan: II, Inset
Jazer, west or northwest of Rabbath-ammon; uncertain
Jearim, Mt., same as or near Mt. Seir 2
Jebus, *see also* Jerusalem *and* Aelia Capitolina, *el-Quds:* IV, C-5; VI, C-5
Jebusi, *see* Jebus
Jegar-sahadutha, *see* Mizpah 1
Jehoshaphat, Valley of, uncertain
Jehud, the proper rendering should be Jazur, *Yazûr:* VI, B-4; IX, C-4
Jekabzeel, *see* Kabzeel
Jerahmeel (tribe affiliated with Judah): VI, B-6
Jerash, *see also* Gerasa: XVIII, D-4
Jericho
1—O.T. site, *Tell es-Sulṭân:* I, C-5; III, C-3; IV, C-5; V, G-2; VI, C-5; VII: B, C-5; IX, G-5; XVIII, C-5
2—N.T. site, S. of *Tell es-Sulṭân* and N.W. of *Erîkhâ:* IX, G-5; XII: A-D, C-5; XIV, C-5
Jeruel, Wilderness of, S.E. of Tekoa
Jerusalem, *see also* Jebus *and* Aelia Capitolina, *el-Quds:* I, C-5; II, E-3; III, B-3; IV, C-5; V, G-2; VI, C-5; VII: A-D, C-5; IX, F-6; XI: A, C-D, B-3; XII: A-D, C-5; XIII, E-3; XIV, C-5; XV, G-5; XVI: A-D, E-4; XVII: A-D; XVIII, C-5
Jeshanah, *Burj el-Isâneh:* IX, F-4
Jeshimon, *see* Judah, Wilderness of
Jeshua, *see also* Shema, *Tell es-Sa'wî?:* X, F-2
Jethlah, near Aijalon 1; uncertain
Jezreel
1—*Zer'în:* VI, C-3; VIII, E-7
2—Josh. 15:56, I Sam. 25:43; near Ziph 2; uncertain
Jezreel, Valley of, *see also* Esdraelon, *Merj Ibn 'Amir ('âmir):* I, C-3; VI, C-3; VIII, D-7
Jiphtah, near Ashan; uncertain
Jiphtah-el, Valley of, *Wâdî el-Melek:* VI, C-3; VIII, D-6
el-Jish, *see also* Gischala: XVIII, C-2
Job's Well, *see also* En-rogel, *Bîr Ayyûb:* XVII: D, E-7
Jogbehah, *Jubeihât* (or *Ajbeihât*): VI, D-4; IX, J-4
Jokdeam, *Khirbet Raqa'* near Ziph 2?
Jokmeam, I Chron. 6:68, *see* Kibzaim
Jokneam, *Tell Qeimûn:* IV, C-3; VI, C-3; VIII, D-7
Joktan: II, Inset
Joktheel
1—near Lachish; unknown
2—II Kings 14:7, *see* Sela
Joppa, *see also* Jaffa, *Yâfâ:* I, B-4; IV, B-4; V, F-1; VI, B-4; VII: A-D, B-4; XII: A-D, B-4; XIV, B-4; IX, C-4; XV, G-5; XVI: A-B, E-3
Jorda, or **Jordan**; *see also* Jarda, *Khirbet 'Irq:* X, C-1; XIV, B-6
Jordan, River, *esh-Sherî'ah el-Kebîreh:* I, D-4; IV, D-4; VI, D-4; VIII, F-7; IX, H-3; XII: A-D, D-4; XIV, D-4; XVIII, D-4
Joseph, Tomb of, near Shechem; traditional site is *Kabr Yûsef* near Jacob's Well
Jotapata, *see also* Jotbah, *Khirbet Jefât:* VIII, E-6; XII: D, C-3
Jotbah, *see also* Jotapata, *Khirbet Jefât:* VIII, E-6
Jotbath, Jotbathah, in Arabah N of Ezion-geber; uncertain
Judaea, *cf.* Judah: XII: A-D, C-5; XIV, C-5
Judah
1—tribal district and state; *cf.* N.T. Judaea: I, C-5; VI, B-5; VII: A-D, C-5; IX, D-8; XI: A, B-3
2—Josh. 19:34, not a place name; corrupt text
Judah, City of, *see* Jerusalem
Judah, Wilderness of, *see also* Jeshimon: IX, G-7
Julias, *see also* Livias *and* Beth-aramphtha, *Tell er-Râmeh:* IX, H-6; XII: C-D, D-5
Juttah, *Yaṭṭâ:* IX, E-8; X, F-1

Kabzeel, near Arad; uncertain
Kadesh
1—*see* Kadesh-barnea
2—(not mentioned in the Bible), *Tell Nebî Mend:* III, C-3; VII: A-C, D-2
Kadesh-barnea, *'Ain Qedeis?:* I, A-7; III, B-4; IV, A-7; V, F-3; VI, A-7; VII: A-D, B-6; X, C-7
Kanah, *Qânah:* IV, C-2; VI, C-2; VIII, E-3
Kanah, River, *Wâdî Qânah:* VI, C-4; IX, E-4
Kanish, *Kültepe:* II, E-2; III, C-2
Kar-ashshur-akha-iddin, Assyrian Province: VII: C, C-3
Karem, LXX of Josh. 15:59b, *'Ain Kârim*, c. 3 miles W of Jerusalem
Karkaa, near Hazar-addar; uncertain
Karkor, *Qarqar* in the *Wâdî Sirḥân*
Karnaim (in N.T. times Carnaim), *Sheikh Sa'd:* IV, E-3; VI, E-3; VIII, I-5; XVIII, E-3
Kartah, near Jokneam; uncertain
Kartan, *Khirbet el-Qureiyeh:* VIII. E-4
Kashshuwa: III, C-2
Kattath, *Khirbet Qoṭeina*, S.W. of Jokneam?
Kedar: XI: A-C, B-3
Kedemoth, *ez-Za'ferân?:* IX, I-7
Kedesh
1—Josh. 15:23, *see* Kadesh-barnea
2—I Chron. 6:72, in Issachar; unknown
3—(in N.T. times Cedes, Cedasa), *Tell Qades:* IV, D-2; VI, D-2; VIII, F-4
Kefr Bir'im: XVIII, C-2
Kefr Kennâ: XVIII, C-3
Kehelathah, in Sinai; uncertain
Keilah, *Khirbet Qîlâ:* IV, C-5; VI, C-5; IX, E-7
Kenath, *see also* Nobah 1, Qanu; in N.T. times Canatha, *Qanawât:* III, C-3; IV, F-3; VIII, L-6
Kenites (tribe affiliated with Judah): VI, C-6
Kerioth
1—*Khirbet el-Qaryatein:* X, F-2
2—Jer. 48:24, 41, in Moab: uncertain
Keziz, Valley of, near Beth-hoglah; uncertain
Khâbûr River, *see also* Habor River: III, D-2
Khalab, *see also* Aleppo, *Ḥaleb:* II, E-2; III, C-2
Khan el-Aḥmar: XVIII, C-5
Kharṭûm: II, E-4
Khattushash, *Boğazköy:* II, E-2; III, B-1
Khilakku, *see also* Cilicia: XI: A, B-2
Khirbet el-'Amad: XVIII, C-2
Khirbet Beit Ilfâ: XVIII, C-3
Khirbet Irbid, *see also* Arbela 1: XVIII, C-3
Khirbet Kerak, *see also* Beth-yerah, Philoteria: XVIII, D-3
Khirbet Kerâzeh, *see also* Chorazin: XVIII, D-3
Khirbet el-Mefjer: XVIII, C-5
Khirbet el-Mekhaiyeṭ, *see also* Nebo 1: XVIII, D-5
Khirbet el-Minyeh: XVIII, D-3
Khirbet en-Nabratein: XVIII, D-3
Khirbet Qumrân, *see also* City of Salt: IX, G-6; XIV, C-5; XVIII, C-5
Khirbet Sammâka: XVIII, C-3
Khirbet et-Tannûr: XVIII, D-7
Khirbet eṭ-Ṭubeiqah, *see also* Bethzur, Bethsura: XVIII, C-5
Khirbet Umm el-'Amad: XVIII, C-3
Khubishna, Kybistra, *Eregli:* III, B-2
Khuḍeirah: XVIII, B-4
Khuru IV, C 2-6
Kibroth-hattaavah, in Sinai; uncertain
Kibzaim, in Ephraim; uncertain
Kidron Valley, *Wâdî en-Nâr:* XVII: A-D, E-6
Kinah, near Arad on the *Wâdî el-Qeini;* uncertain
King's Highway, The: V, G-3; VI, D-7
Kir, unknown
Kir-haraseth, *see* Kir-hareseth
Kir-hareseth, *el-Kerak:* I, D-6; V, G-2; VI, D-6; VII: A-C, C-5; X, I-3
Kir-haresh, Kir-heres, Kir of Moab, *see* Kir-hareseth
Kiriathaim, *see* Kirjathaim 1
Kirioth, *see* Kerioth 2
Kirjath, Josh. 18:28, *see* Kirjath-jearim
Kirjathaim
1—*el-Qereiyât:* VI, D-5; IX, I-7
2—I Chron. 6:76, *see* Kartan
Kirjath-arba, *see also* Hebron, *el-Khalîl:* IV, C-5
Kirjatharim, *see* Kirjath-jearim
Kirjath-baal, *see also* Kirjath-jearim, *Tell el-Azhar:* IV, C-5
Kirjath-huzoth, in Moab; uncertain
Kirjath-jearim, *Tell el-Azhar:* IV, C-5; VI, C-5; IX, E-6
Kirjath-sannah, to be corrected to Kirjath-sepher
Kirjath-sepher, *see also* Debir 1, *Tell Beit Mirsim:* IV, B-6; IX, D-8; X, E-1
Kish, *Tell el-Oḥeimer:* II, F-3; III, E-3
Kishion, *see* Kishon
Kishon, in Issachar; uncertain
Kishon, River, *Nahr el-Muqaṭṭa':* I, C-3; VI, C-3; VIII, D-6
Kithlish, near Eglon; uncertain
Kitron, near Nahalal; uncertain
Kittim, *see also* Cyprus, Alashiya, Elishah, Iatnana: II, Inset; XI: A-C, B-3
Kizzuwatna: III, C-2
Konya, *see also* Iconium: III, B-2
Kue, *see* Cilicia
Kusura: III, A-2

Laban, Deut. 1:1; uncertain
Lacedaemon, *see also* Sparta, *Spartē:* XVI: D, D-3
Lachish, *Tell ed-Duweir:* I, B-5; III, B-3; IV, B-5; V, F-2; VI, B-5; VII: A-D, B-5; IX, D-7, XVIII, B-5
Lagash, *Tell Lô (Telloh):* III, E-3
Lahman, *Khirbet el-Laḥm* near Lachish?
Laish, *see also* Dan, *Tell el-Qâḍî:* IV, D-2; VIII, G-3
Laishah, *el-'Isâwiyeh ('isâwiyeh)* N.E. of Jerusalem
Lakum, *Khirbet el-Manṣûrah* near Anem?
Lambaesis, *Lambessa:* XVI: C-D, B-3
Lampsacus, *Lapsaki:* XIII, D-2; XVI: D, D-2
Laodicea
1—*Eskihisar* near *Denizli:* XIII, D-2; XV, E-3; XVI: C-D, D-3
2—*Lâdhiqiyeh:* XIII, E-2
Lapithos: III, B-3
Laranda, *Karaman:* XIII, E-2; XVI: D, E-3
Larissa, *Larisa:* XIII, D-2; XVI: C-D, D-2
Larnaka, *see also* Citium: III, B-3
Larsa, *Senkereh:* II, F-3; III, E-3
Lasaea, c. 5 mi. E. of Fair Havens and 1 mi. E. of Cape Leona: XV, D-4
Lasha, uncertain
Lasharon, uncertain text
Latopolis, *Esneh:* XIII, E-3
Lauriacum, near *Enns:* XVI: D, C-1
Lebanon, Mt., *see also* Mt. Libanus, *Jebel Libnân:* I, D-1; IV, D-1; VI, D-1; VII: A-C, C-3; VIII, G-1
Lebaoth, near Sharuhen; unknown
Lebonah, *Lubban:* VI, C-4; IX, F-4
Lehabim, *see also* Lubim *and* Libya: II, Inset
Lehi, probably in the area of Beth-shemesh 1; unknown
Lemanae, *Lympne:* XIII Inset, D-2
Lemba, *see also* Libba, *Khirbet Libb:* IX, I-7; XII: A, D-5
Lemnos: III, A-1
Leon, ancient *Legio Septima Gemina:* XVI: C-D, A-1
Leptis Magna, on coast a few miles E. of Homs in Tripolitania: XIII, C-3; XVI: D, C-3
Lesbos: III, A-2
Leshem, *see* Laish
Lesser Oasis, in desert W. of Nile, 28° 30′ N. lat. and 29° 30′ E. long.: XVI: D, D-4
Leuce Come, at mouth of *Wâdî el-Hamd?:* XIII, E-3
Libanus, Mt., *see also* Mt. Lebanon, *Jebel Libnân:* XII: A-D, D-2; XIV, D-2
Libba, *see also* Lemba, *Khirbet Libb:* IX, I-7; XII: A, D-5
Libnah
1—*Tell eṣ-Ṣâfî:* IV, B-5; V, F-2; VI, B-5; IX, D-6; XVIII, B-5
2—Num. 33:20–21, in Sinai; uncertain
Libya, *see also* Lehabim *and* Lubim: II, D-3; II Inset; III, A-4; V, A-3; XI: A-D, A-3; XVI: A, D-4
Liger, *River Loire (q.v.):* XIII Inset, C-3
Lilybaeum, *Marsala:* XIII, C-2
Lincoln, *see also* Lindum; XVI: D, B-5
Lindum, *Lincoln (q.v.):* XIII Inset, C-1
Litani, River, *Nahr el-Lîṭânî:* I, D-2
Livias, *see also* Julias *and* Beth-aramphtha, *Tell er-Râmeh:* IX, H-6; XII: C, D-5
Lod (in N.T. times Lydda), *Ludd:* IV, B-5; VI, B-5; IX, D-5
Lo-debar, *see also* Debir 3, *Umm ed-Dabar (or Dubar):* VIII, G-7
Loire River, *see also* Liger, XIII Inset, D-3; XVI: A-B, B-6
Londinium, *London (q.v.):* XIII Inset, C-2
London, *see also* Londinium: XVI: D, B-5
Lubim, *see also* Lehabim *and* Libya: II, Inset
Lud, *see also* Lydia: II, Inset
Lugdunensis, Roman province in ancient Gaul: XIII, B-1; XIII, Inset, D-3
Lugdunum, *Lyons (q.v.):* XIII, B-1; XIII, Inset, E-3
Luhith, Ascent of, in Moab; uncertain
Luna, *Luni* on the Gulf of Spezia: XIII, B-1
Luristan: III, E-3
Lusitania, Roman province: XIII, A-2
Lutetia, *Paris (q.v.):* XIII Inset, D-2
Luz
1—*See also* Bethel 1 *and* Bethela, *Beitîn:* IV, C-5; IX, F-5
2—Judg. 1:26; uncertain
Lycaonia, district in Asia Minor: XV, F-3
Lycia, country and district in Asia Minor: XI: B, D, A-2; XIII, D-2; XV, E-3
Lycopolis, near *Assiûṭ:* XIII, E-3
Lydda (in O.T. times Lod): *Ludd:* IX, D-5; XII: A, D, B-5; XIV, B-5; XVI: A, E-3
Lydia, *see also* Lud: XI: A-C, A-2
Lyons, *see also* Lugdunum: XVI: C-D, B-1; XVI: C-D, B-6
Lystra, *Zoldera* near *Khatyn Serai:* XIII, E-2; XV, F-3; XVI: B, E-3

Maacah, Maachah, district around Abel-beth-maachah: VII: A, C-3
Maaleh-acrabbim, *see* Akrabbim, Ascent of
Maarath, near Hebron; uncertain
Macedonia: II, D-2; XI: D, A-1; XIII, D-2; XV, D-2
Machaerus, *Mukâwer:* IX, H-7; XII: A-B, D, D-5; XIV, D-5
Machir, a clan: VI, D-4
Machmas (in O.T. times Michmash), *Mukhmâs:* IX, F-5; XII: A, C-5
Machpelah, Cave of, in or near Hebron; traditional site in the *Ḥarâm* in Hebron
Madai, *see also* Medes: II, Inset; XI: A, D-2
Madaura, town in ancient Numidia: XVI: C-D, B-3
Mâdebâ, *see also* Medeba: XVIII, D-5
Madmannah, *Umm Deimneh:* X, E-1
Madmen, *Khirbet Dimneh?:* X, I-2
Madmenah, in Benjamin; uncertain
Madon, *Qarn Ḥaṭṭîn:* IV, C-3; VI, C-3; VIII, F-6
Magadan, Matt. 15:39, uncertain
Magbish, in central Palestine; uncertain
Magdala, *see also* Tarichaea, *Mejdel:* VIII, F-6; XII: B, D-3; XIV, D-3
Magidu, Assyrian Province of Megiddo: VII: C, C-4
Magnesia, *Inek-bazar?:* XV, E-3
Mahanaim, *Khirbet Maḥneh?:* VI, D-4; VII: A-B, C-4; IX, I-2
Mahaneh-dan, near Kirjath-jearim; unknown
Mainz, *see also* Mogontiacum: XVI: C-D, C-5
Makaz, near Beth-shemesh 1; uncertain
Makheloth, in Sinai; unknown
Makkedah, near Azekah; uncertain
Maktesh, unknown
Malaca, *Malaga:* XIII, A-2
Malaga, *see also* Malaca: XVI: D, A-2
Malatya: III, C-2
Malta, island, *see also* Melita, Melitene: XVI: B, C-3
Mamre, *Râmet el-Khalîl:* II, E-3; IX, E-7; XVIII, C-5
Manahath, *Mâlḥâ?:* IX, E-6
Manasseh, tribal districts: VI, C-4, D-4
Manṣuate, Assyrian Province: VII: C, D-2
Maon, *Tell Ma'în:* VI, C-6; IX, E-8; X, F-1
Maon, Wilderness of, country east of Maon
Marah, *'Ain Ḥawârah?:* V, D-4
Maralah, in Zebulun; uncertain
Marathus, *Amrît:* XI: D, B-2
Marea, *Amriyeh:* XI: C, A-3
Mare Internum, *see also* Great Sea *and* Mediterranean Sea: XIII, B-2
Mareshah (in N.T. times Marisa), *Tell Sandaḥannah:* IV, B-5; VI, B-5; IX, D-7; XVIII, B-5
Mari, *Tell el-Ḥarîrî:* II, F-2; III, D-3
Marisa, *see also* Mareshah, *Tell Sandaḥannah (q.v.):* IX, D-7; XII: A-B, B-5; XVIII, B-5
Maroth, same as Maarath?
Marseilles, *see also* Massilia: XVI: D, B-1
Masada, *es-Sebbeh:* X, H-2; XII: B, D, C-6; XIV, C-6; XVIII, C-6
Mashal, *see* Mishal
Masrekah, in Edom; uncertain
Massah, *see also* Meribah, near Mt. Sinai; unknown
Massepha (in O.T. times Mizpah 2), *Tell en-Naṣbeh?:* XII: A, C-5
Massilia, *Marseilles (q.v.):* XIII, B-1
Massyas, Persian Province: VII: D, C-3
Mattanah, *Khirbet el-Medeiyineh?:* VI, D-5; IX, J-7
Mauretania, ancient kingdom in N.W. Africa: XIII, A-2
Mearah, *Mogheiriyeh* near Sidon?
Medeba, *Mâdebâ:* V, G-2; VI, D-5; VII: A-D, C-5; IX, I-6; XII: A, D-5; XVIII, D-5
Medes, *see also* Madai: II, Inset; XI: A, D-3
Media: III, E-2; XI: C-D, D-2; XVI: A, G-3
Median Empire: XI: B, B-2
Mediolanum, *Milan (q.v.):* XIII, B-1; XIII Inset, F-3
Mediterranean Sea, *see also* Great Sea *and* Mare Internum, I, A-5; II, B-2; III, A-3; XI: D, A-3; XII: A-D, A-4; XIII, B-2; XIV, A-5; XV, C-4; XVI: A-D, B-2; XVIII, A-5
Megiddo, *Tell el-Mutesellim:* III, B-3; IV, C-3; VI, C-3; VII: A-C, C-4; VIII, D-7; XVIII, C-3
Megiddo, Valley of, *see* Jezreel, Valley of
Megiddo, Waters of, sources of River Kishon at Megiddo
Meheleb, probably correct reading of Ahlab; *Khirbet el-Maḥâlib:* IV, C-2; VI, C-2; VIII, D-2
Meirôn, *see also* Merom, Meroth: XVIII, C-3
Me-jarkon, *Nahr el-'Aujâ:* XVIII, B-4
Mekonah, near Ziklag; unknown
Melita, *see also* Melitene 1, *Malta (q.v.):* XV, B-4
Melitene
1—*See also* Melita, *Malta (q.v.):* XV, B-4
2—*Malatia:* XVI: C, E-2
Memphis, *see also* Noph, *Mît Rahneh:* II, E-3; III, B-4; V, C-4; XI: A-D, B-3; XIII, E-3; XVI: D, D-4
Mende: XVI: D, B-1
Menzaleh, Lake: V, D-2
Meonenim, near Shechem; unknown
Mephaath, *Tell ej-Jâwah?:* IX, J-5
Meribah
1—Ex. 17:7, *see* Massah
2—*see* Kadesh-barnea
Merida, *see also* Emerita: XVI: C-D, A-2
Meroe: II, E-4; XIII, E-4
Merom, *see also* Meroth, *Meirôn:* IV, C-3; VIII, E-5; XVIII, C-3
Merom, Waters of, *Wâdî Meirôn:* VI, C-3; VIII, F-5
Meronoth, near Gibeah; unknown
Meroth, *see also* Merom, *Meirôn:* VIII, E-5; XIV, C-3
Meroz, in or near the Valley of Jezreel; uncertain
Mersin: II, E-2
Mesembria, *Mesivri:* XIII, D-2
Mesha, in Arabia; uncertain

Meshech: II, Inset
Mesopotamia: XI: D, C-2; XVI: A, F-3
Messana, *Messina:* XIII, C-2
Messene, *Mavromati:* XIII, D-2
Messina, see also Messana: XVI: D, C-2
Metz, see also Divodurum: XVI: C-D, C-6
Michmash (in N.T. times Machmas), *Mukhmâs:* VI, C-5; IX, F-5
Michmethah, *Khirbet Makhneh el-Fôqā* near Shechem?
Middin, *Khirbet Abū Ṭabaq?:* IX, G-6
Midian, Land of: V, G-4
Midianites: III, B-4
Migdal-el, near Iron; uncertain
Migdal-gad, near Lachish; uncertain
Migdol
1—on the border of Egypt; uncertain
2—Jer. 44:1, 46:14, *Tell el-Ḥeir* near Pelusium
Migron, *Tell Miriam* S.W. of Michmash?
Milan, see also Mediolanum: XVI: D, B-1, D-6
Miletus, near *Palatia:* XI: C-D, A-2; XIII, D-2; XV, E-3; XVI: B, D-3
Millo
1—David's citadel in Jerusalem: XVII: A, D-5
2—Judg. 9:6, 20; citadel in Shechem
Minni: XI: A, C-2
Minnith, near Rabbath-ammon; unknown
Misgab, in Moab; unknown
Mishal, Misheal, in the plain of Accho; unknown
Mishneh, or Second Quarter in Jerusalem: XVII: A, C-4
Misrephoth-maim, *Khirbet el-Musheirefeh:* VI, C-2; VIII, D-4
Mitanni: III, D-2
Mithcah, in Sinai, unknown
Mitylene, city on island called Lesbos or Mytilene: XV, E-3
Mizar, Hill, near Mt. Hermon; unknown
Mizpah
1—Gen. 31:49, in northern Transjordan; unknown
2—(in N.T. times Massepha), *Tell en-Naṣbeh?:* IX, F-5; XVIII, C-5
Mizpeh
1—I Sam. 22:3, in Moab; uncertain
2—Josh. 15:38, near Lachish; unknown
Mizpeh, Land or Valley of, uncertain
Mizraim, see also Egypt: II, Inset
Moab, see also Moabitis, *Belqā:* I, D-6; IV, D-6; V, G-2; VI, D-6; VII: A-D, C-5; X, I-3; XI: A, B-3
Moab, City of, Num. 22:36; Deut. 2:36; Josh. 13:9, 16; II Sam. 24:5; *Khirbet el-Medeiyineh?:* IX, J-8; X, K-1
Moabitis, see also Moab, *Belqā:* XII: A, D-6
Modein, *el-Arba'in:* IX, E-5; XII: A, C-5
Moeris, Lake, see also Faiyûm: V, B-4
Moesia, Roman province: XIII, D-2; XV, D-2
Mogontiacum, *Mainz (q.v.):* XIII Inset, F-2
Moladah, *Tell el-Milḥ?:* X, F-2
Mona Insula, *Anglesey:* XIII Inset, B-1
Moph, see Noph
Moreh, Gen. 12:6, Deut. 11:30; name of an oak tree or trees near Shechem
Moreh, Hill of, *Nebī Daḥī:* I, C-3; VI, C-3; VIII, E-7
Moresheth-gath, *Tell ej-Judeideh:* IX, D-7; XVIII, B-5
Moriah, Land of, Jerusalem?
Mosera, near Mt. Hor and Beeroth 1; unknown
Moseroth, see Mosera
Mount of Corruption, II Kings 23:13, see Olives, Mt. of
Mozah, see also Emmaus 2, *Qalôniyeh* (or *Qâlunyah*) near Nephtoah
Myra, name used for both Myra and its port Andriaca, *Dembre:* XV, F-4; XVI: C, D-3
Mysia, district in N.W. Asia Minor: XV, E-3

Naamah, *Khirbet Fered* near Timnah 1?
Naaran, see Naarath
Naarath (in N.T. times Noarah), *Khirbet el-'Ayâsh:* VI, D-5; IX, G-5
Nabataea: XII: A-D, A-7; XIII, E-3; XIV, B-7
Nahalal, Nahallal, *Tell en-Naḥl?:* VIII, C-6
Nahaliel, stream, *Wâdī Zerqā Mâ'în:* IX, H-7
Nahalol, see Nahalal
Nahr 'Aujā see also Me-jarkon (Josh. 19:46): I, B-4
Nahr Bereighith: I, D-2
Nahr Ḥasbānī: I, D-2
Nahr Iskanderûneh: I, B-4
Nahr Jâlûd: I, C-3
Nahr Līṭânī: I, D-2
Nahr Muqaṭṭa': I, C-3
Nahr Yarmûk: I, D-3
Nahr Zerqā, near Mt. Carmel: I, B-3
Nahr Zerqā, in Transjordan: I, D-4
Nain, *Nein:* VIII, E-7; XIV, C-3
Naioth, in or near Ramah 1; unknown
Nakhita, *Niğde:* III, B-2
Napata, in Ethiopia, by the Nile, just below the fourth cataract, near *Jebel Barkal:* XIII, E-4
Naphtali, tribal district: VI, C-3
Naples, see also Neapolis 2: XVI: C-D, C-2
Narbata, *Khirbet Beidûs?:* VIII, C-8; IX, E-2; XII: D, C-4
Narbo, *Narbonne (q.v.):* XIII, B-1
Narbonensis, Roman province: XIII, B-1
Narbonne, see also Narbo: XVI: D, B-1
Naucratis, *Kûm Ga'if:* XI: B-C, B-3
Nazareth, *en-Nâṣirah:* I, C-3; VIII, E-6; XII: B-C, C-3; XIV, C-3; XVIII, C-3
Neah, near Rimmon 2; uncertain
Neapolis
1—*Nâblus:* IX, F-3; XII: D, C-4
2—*Naples:* XIII, C-2; XV, B-2
3—*Kavalla:* XIII, D-2; XV, D-2
Neballat, *Beit Nabala:* IX, D-4
Nebo
1—*Khirbet el-Mekhaiyeṭ?:* XVIII, D-5
2—Ezra 2:29, Neh. 7:33; *Nûbâ* near Aijalon 1
Nebo, Mt., *Jebel Nebā:* I, D-5; V, G-2; VI, D-5; IX, I-6
Negeb, or "South": I, A-7
Neiel, *Khirbet Ya'nîn:* IV, C-3; VI, C-3; VIII, D-5
Nekeb, *el-Baṣṣah* near Adami?
Nekheb, *el-Kâb:* II, E-3
Nekhen, *Kôm el-Aḥmar:* II, E-3
Neocaesarea, *Niksar:* XVI: D, E-2
Nephtoah, *Liftā:* IX, F-6
Netophah, *Khirbet Bedd Fālûḥ:* IX, F-7
Nezib, *Khirbet Beit Neṣîb:* IX, E-7
Nibshan, *Khirbet el-Maqârī?:* IX, G-6
Nicaea
1—*Nice:* XIII, B-1
2—*Iznik:* XIII, D-2; XVI: D, D-2
Nicomedia, *Izmit:* XIII, D-2; XVI: C-D, E-2
Nicopolis, on Ambracian Gulf, c. 4 mi. N. of *Preveza:* XIII, C-2; XV, D-3; XVI: B-D, C-2
Nile, Blue: II, E-4
Nile, Mouths of the: XV, F-5
Nile River, see also Nilus: II, E-3; III, B-4; V, C-4; XI: A-D, B-4; XVI: A-D, E-5
Nile, White: II, E-4
Nilus, see also Nile R.: XIII, E-3
Nimrah, see Beth-nimrah
Nimrim, Waters of, *Wâdī en-Numeirah:* X, I-3
Nineveh, *Tell Quyunjiq* and *Tell Nebi Yûnus:* II, F-2; III, D-2; XI: A, C-2
Nippur, *Nuffar:* II, F-3; III, E-3; XI: A-C, C-3
Nisibis, near *Niṣibîn:* XI: D, C-2; XIII, F-2; XVI: D, F-3
No, see also Thebes 1, *Karnak, Luxor,* and neighboring ruins: XI: A-C, B-4
Noarah (in O.T. times Naaran, Naarath), *Khirbet el-'Ayâsh*
Nob, *eṭ-Ṭôr* on Mount of Olives?
Nobah
1—see also Kenath, Qanu; in N.T. times Canatha, *Qanawât:* IV, F-3; VI, F-3; VII: A-D, D-4; VIII, L-6
2—Judg. 8:11, near Jogbehah; unknown
Noph, see also Memphis, *Mît Rahneh:* III, B-4; V, C-4; XI: A-C, B-4
Nophah, text uncertain; probably not a place name
Noreia, *Neumarkt:* XIII, C-1
Noricum, Roman province, XIII, C-1
Noviomagus
1—*Chichester:* XIII Inset, C-2
2—*Nijmegen:* XIII Inset, E-2
Nukhashshe: III, C-2
Nuzi, *Yorghan Tepe:* III, D-2

Oboth at *'Ain el-Weiba* or *'Ain Ḥoṣob?:* V, G-3; X, G-5 for the latter; X, G-6 for the former
Oceanus Atlanticus, see also Atlantic Ocean: XIII, A-1; XIII Inset, B-3
Odessus, near *Varna:* XI: B-C, A-1
Og, Kingdom of: IV, E-3
Olbia, near *Nikolaev?:* XI: B-D, B-1; XIII, E-1
Olisipo, *Lisbon:* XIII, A-2
Olivet, Olives, Mt. of, *Jebel eṭ-Ṭûr,* rising E. from the Kidron Valley, Jerusalem: XVII: C, E-4
Olympia, plain in S.E. Ellis, N.E. of junction of Cladus and Alpheus rivers: XIII, D-2
Olympus, city in E. Lycia: XVI: D, D-3
On, see also Heliopolis and Beth-shemesh 4, *Tell Ḥuṣn:* II, E-3; III, B-4; V, C-3; XI: A-C, B-3
Ono *Kefr 'Anā:* IV, B-4; VI, B-4; IX, D-4
Ophel, see also Ophlas: XVII: A, D-5
Ophir, S.W. Arabia and perhaps also some portion of the neighboring African coast: II, Inset
Ophlas, see also Ophel, XVII: B, D-5
Ophni, Josh. 18:24, see Gophna
Ophrah
1—(in N.T. times Aphairema or Ephraim?), *eṭ-Ṭaiyibeh:* VI, C-5; IX, F-5
2—Judg. 6:11, 24; 8:27, 32; 9:5; in Manasseh; uncertain
Oreb, Rock in the Jordan Valley; unknown
Ormuz, Straits of: XI: D, E-3
Oronai, *el-'Araq?:* X, I-3; XII: A, D-6
Orontes River, *Nahr el-'Aṣi ('âṣi):* III, C-2; XV, G-4
Oryba, Orybda, *'Abdeh?:* X, D-5; XII: A, B-7
Ostia, c. ½ mi. below modern Ostia, at mouth of Tiber: XIII, C-2; XVI: D, C-2
Oxyrhynchus, *Behneseh:* XIII, E-3; XVI: D, D-4

Padan-aram, Paddan-aram, see also Aram-naharaim: II, F-2
Padus, *Po River (q.v.):* XIII Inset, F-3
Pai, see Pau
Palm Trees, City of, uncertain
Palmyra, see also Tadmor, *Tudmur:* XIII, E-2; XVI: D, E-3
Pamphylia, district and Roman province in S. Asia Minor: XIII, E-2; XV, F-3; XVI: A, E-3
Paneas, see also Caesarea Philippi, *Bâniyâs:* VIII, G-3; XII: B, D-2; XVI: D, E-3
Panias, or **Paneas,** district southwest of Mt. Hermon: XIV, D-2
Pannonia, Roman province: XIII, C-1; XV, C-1
Panormus, *Palermo:* XIII, C-2
Panticapaeum, *Kerch:* XI: C-D, B-1; XIII, E-1
Paphlagonia, district in N. Asia Minor: XI: D, B-1
Paphos, *Baffo,* 1 mi. S. of *Ktima:* XIII, E-2; XV, F-4; XVI: B-C, E-3
Paraetonium, near *Maṭrûh:* XI: D, A-3; XIII, D-3; XVI: D, D-4
Parah, *Khirbet el-Fârah:* IX, F-6
Paran, Wilderness of: V, F-4; VI, B-8; X, A-7
Paris, see also Lutetia XVI: D, B-6
Parium, seaport in ancient Mysia, near eastern end of the Hellespont: XVI: C, D-2
Parthia: XI: C-D, D-2; XVI: A, D, G-3
Parvaim, in Arabia?; uncertain
Pasargadae, in the *Murghab Plain:* XI: C-D, D-3
Pas-dammim, see Ephes-dammim
Patara, port in ancient Lycia; at *Gelemish:* XV, E-4; XVI: D, D-3
Patavium, *Padua:* XIII, C-1
Pathros, upper Egypt: II, Inset
Patmos, island west of Asia Minor: XV, E-3
Patrae, *Patras:* XIII, D-2
Pau, in Edom; unknown
Pegae, see also Antipatris and Aphek, *Râs el-'Ain:* IX, D-4
Pella
1—*Khirbet Faḥil:* III, C-3; IV, D-4; VIII, F-8; IX, H-2; XII: A-D, D-4; XIV, D-4; XVI: B, E-3
2—in Macedonia, at *Neochori:* XI: D, A-1; XIII, D-2
Pelusium, *Tell Faramâ:* V, D-3; XI: C-D, B-3; XIII, E-3; XVI: D, E-4
Peniel, see Penuel
Penuel, *Tulûl edh-Dhahab:* IV, D-4; VI, D-4; IX, H-3
Peor, Top of, mountain peak near Beth-peor; uncertain
Peraea: XII: A-D, D-4; XIV, D-4
Perazim, Mt., see Baal-perazim
Perez-uzzah, threshing floor of, near Jerusalem; unknown
Perga, see also Perge, *Murtana:* XV, F-3; XVI: B-D, D-3
Pergamum, *Bergama:* XI: D, A-2; XIII, D-2; XV, E-3; XVI: C-D, D-2
Perge, see also Perga, *Murtana:* XI: D, A-2; XIII, E-2
Persepolis, *Takht-i-Jamshîd:* XI: C-D, D-3; XIII, G-3
Persia, see also Persis: XI: B-C, D-3
Persian Gulf, see also Sinus Persicus: II, G-3; III, E-4; XI: A-D, D-3; XIII, G-3; XVI: A-D, G-4
Persis, see also Persia: XI: D, D-3
Pessinus, *Balahisar:* XIII, E-2; XV, F-3
Pethor, in northern Mesopotamia; unknown
Petra, cf. Sela, in *Wâdī Mûsâ:* I, C-8; X, H-8; XII: A-D, C-8; XIII, E-3; XIV, C-8; XVIII, C-8
Phanagoria, *Taman:* XIII, E-1
Pharathon (in O.T. times Pirathon), *Far'âtâ:* XII: A, C-4
Pharpar, River, *Nahr el-A'waj:* VI, E-2; XVII, J-2
Phasaelis, *Khirbet Faṣâ'il:* IX, G-4; XII: B-C, C-4; XIV, C-4
Phasis, *Poti:* XI: B-D, C-1; XIII, F-2
Phiale, Pool of, *Birket er-Râm* or *er-Rân:* VIII, G-3
Philadelphia
1—see also Rabbath-ammon, *'Ammân:* IX, J-5; XII: A-D, D-5; XIV, D-5
2—*Alashehir:* XV, E-3
Philippi, *Filibedjik:* XIII, D-2; XV, D-2; XVI: B-D, D-2
Philippopolis, *Plovdiv:* XIII, D-2
Philistia, Philistine Plain: I, B-5; VII: A-B, B-5; IX, B-7
Philistines: VI, B-5
Philomelium, *Akshehir:* XVI: C, E-2
Philoteria, see also Beth-yerah, *Khirbet Kerak (q.v.):* VIII, F-6; XII: A, D-3
Phoenicia: VII: A-B, C-3; VIII, D-4; XII: A-D, C-2; XIV, C-2
Phoenix, a harbor, *Lutro?:* XV, D-4
Phrygia: XI: A, B-2; XV, F-3; XVI: A, E-2
Phut: II, Inset
Pi-beseth, see also Bubastis, *Tell Basṭa:* III, B-3
Pi-hahiroth, on the N.E. border of Egypt; unknown
Pirathon (in N.T. times Pharathon), *Far'âtâ?:* VI, C-4; IX, E-3
Pisa: XIII, B-2; XVI: D, B-1
Pisgah, Mt., *Râs es-Siâghah:* IX, I-6; XVIII, D-5
Pisidia: XV, F-3
Pison, River, uncertain
Pithom, *Tell er-Reṭâbeh:* V, C-3
Pityus, *Pitsunda:* XIII, F-2; XVI: D, F-2
Placentia, *Piacenza:* XIII, B-1
Po River, see also Padus: XIII Inset, F-3; XVI: A-B, B-1
Pola: XIII, C-1
Pompeii: XVI: B, C-2
Pontus, district in N. Asia Minor: XI: D, B-1; XIII, E-2; XV, F-2; XVI: A-B, E-2
Pontus Euxinus, see also Black Sea: XIII, E-2; XV, F-2
Propontis, *Sea of Marmara:* XIII, D-2; XV, E-2
Prusa, *Bursa:* XVI: D, D-2
Psephinus, a tower at N.W. corner of third north wall of Jerusalem: XVII: C, A-3
Ptolemais
1—(in O.T. times Accho), *'Akkā:* VIII, C-5; XII: A-D, C-3; XIV, C-3; XV, G-4; XVI: B-C, E-3
2—*Tolmeta:* XIII, C-3; XVI: D, C-3
Punon, *Feinân:* II, E-3; V, G-3; VI, C-7; VII: A-C, C-6, X, H-6
Punt: II, F-4
Pura, *Fahraj:* XI: D, D-3
Purattu River, see also Euphrates River, *Shaṭṭ el-Furât:* III, D-3
Puteoli, near *Pozzuoli:* XIII, C-2; XV, B-2; XVI: B, C-2
Pyramids: V, C-4
Pyrenees: II, A-1

Qal'at el-Qurein: XVIII, C-2
Qanṭîr: V, C-3
Qanu, see also Kenath, Nobah 1 (in N.T. times Canatha), *Qanawât:* IV, F-3
Qara Su, River: III, E-3
Qarnaim, Persian Province: VII: D, C-4
Qarnini, Assyrian Province: VII: C, C-4
Qatna, *el-Mishrifeh:* II, E-2; III, C-3
el-Qubeibeh: XVIII, B-5
Qumrân, see *Khirbet Qumrân*

Raamah: II, Inset
Raamses, see Rameses
Rabbah
1—Josh. 15:60, near Kirjath-jearim; uncertain
2—see also Rabbath-ammon, *'Ammân:* VII: A, C-5
Rabbath-ammon, Rabbath of the Ammonites; see also Rabbah (in N.T. times Philadelphia); *'Ammân:* I, D-5; IV, D-5; V, G-2; VI, D-5; VII: A-D, C-5; IX, J-5
Rabbith, to be read Dabareh
Rachal, original text probably read Carmel (town in Judah)
Rachel, Tomb of, *Qubbet Râḥil* near Bethlehem is the traditional site
Raetia, Roman province, XIII, B-1; XIII Inset, F-3
Ragaba, *Râjib:* IX, I-3; XII: A, D-4
Rakkath, *Tell Eqlâṭiyeh?:* IV, D-3; VIII, F-6
Rakkon, *Tell er-Reqqeit:* VI, B-4
Ramah
1—*er-Râm:* VI, C-5; IX, F-5
2—Josh. 19:36, *er-Râmeh:* VI, C-3; VIII, E-5
3—Josh. 19:29, in Asher; either same as Ramah 2 of Naphtali, or else a site near Tyre
4—see also Ramathaim-zophim; the home of Samuel, probably to be distinguished from Ramah 1 in I Sam. 1:19; 2:11; 7:17; 8:4; 15:34; 16:13; 19:18-23; 25:1; 28:3
5—II Chron. 22:6, see Ramoth-gilead
Ramath of the South (Negeb), prob. same as Baalath-beer
Ramathaim-zophim, see also Arimathaea, *Rentis?:* VI, B-4; IX, E-4
Ramath-lehi, see Lehi
Ramath-mizpeh, see Mizpah 1
Rameses, see also Tanis, Avaris, Zoan, *Ṣân el-Ḥagar:* V, C-3
Râmet el-Khalîl, see also Mamre: XVIII, C-5
Ramoth
1—see Ramoth-gilead
2—I Sam. 30:27, see Ramath of the South
3—I Chron. 6:73, *Kôkab el-Hawâ?:* VIII, F-7
Ramoth-gilead, *Tell Râmîth:* I, E-3; IV, E-3; VI, E-3; VII: A-D, D-4; VIII, I-8; IX, J-1
Raphana, see also Raphon, *er-Râfeh:* VIII, J-5; XIV, E-3
Raphia, *Rafah:* IV, A-6; V, F-2; X, A-2; XII: A-D, A-6; XIV, A-6
Raphon, see also Raphana, *er-Râfeh:* IV, E-3; VIII, J-5; XII: A, E-3
Râs el-'Ain, see also Aphek 1, Antipatris, Pegae: XVIII, B-4
Râs es-Siyâghah, see also Pisgah, Mt.: XVIII, D-5
Ratae, *Leicester:* XIII Inset, C-1
Ravenna: XIII, C-1; XVI: D, C-1
Rechah, I Chron. 4:12; unknown
Red Sea
1—see also Arabian Gulf; cf. Mare Erythraeum: II, E-4; V, F-6; XI: A-D, B-4; XVI: A-D, E-4
2—see also Mare Erythraeum: XIII, H-4

Regensburg, *see also* Regina Castra: XVI: D, C-1
Regina Castra, *Regensburg:* XIII, C-1; XIII Inset, F-2
Regnum Antiochi, *i.e.,* Kingdom of Antiochus, client king under Roman control: XV, F-3
Regnum Parthicum, *i.e.,* Parthian Empire: XIII, F-2
Regnum Polemonis, *i.e.,* Kingdom of Polemon; client state under Rome: XIII, E-2; XV, G-2
Rehob
1—Num. 13: 21; II Sam. 10: 8; *see* Beth-rehob
2—Josh. 19: 28, *same as* Rehob 3?
3—*Tell el-Gharbī* (or *Berweh*)?: IV, C-3; VI, C-3; VIII, D-5
4—not in Bible, *Tell eṣ-Ṣârem:* IV, C-4; VIII, F-8; IX, G-1
Rehoboth
1—near Nineveh; uncertain
2—Gen. 26: 22, *Ruḥeibeh:* VI, B-6; X, C-4
3—Gen. 36: 37; I Chron. 1: 48; in Edom near the Brook Zered; unknown
Rekem, in Benjamin; uncertain
Remeth, *see* Ramoth 3
Remmon, *see* En-rimmon
Remmon-methoar, *see* Rimmon 2
Rephaim, Valley of, *Baqa'* S.W. of Jerusalem
Rephidim, in the *Wâdī Refâyid?:* V, E-5
Resen, near Nineveh; unknown
Retenu, Egyptian name for Syria-Palestine: II, E-3
Reuben, tribal district: VI, D-5
Rezeph, Assyrian *Raṣappa;* unknown
Rhagae, a little S. of *Teheran:* XI: D, D-2; XIII, G-2
Rhegium, *Reggio:* XIII, C-2; XV, C-3
Rheims, *see also* Durocortorum: XVI: D, B-6
Rhenus, *i.e.,* Rhine River *(q.v.):* XIII Inset, F-3
Rhine River, *see also* Rhenus: XVI: A-D, C-5
Rhinocolura, *el-'Arîsh:* XIII, E-3
Rhodanus, *i.e.,* Rhone River *(q.v.):* XIII, B-1
Rhodes
1—city, *see also* Rhodus, *Rodi:* XI: D, A-2; XV, E-4; XVI: D, D-2
2—island, *Rodi:* III, A-2; XV, E-4
Rhodus, city, *see also* Rhodes, *Rodi:* XIII, D-2
Rhone River, *see also* Rhodanus: XVI: A-B, B-1; XVI: A-B, C-6
Rhosus, city on S. shore of Gulf of Alexandretta: XVI: C, E-3
Riblah, *Ribleh:* III, C-3; VII: A-D, D-2
Rimmon
1—*see* En-rimmon
2—I Chron. 6: 77, *Rummâneh:* VI, C-3; VIII, E-6
Rimmon-parez, in Sinai, uncertain
Rimmon, Rock, *Rammûn:* IX, F-5
Riphath: II, Inset
Rissah, in Sinai; uncertain
Rithmah, in Sinai; uncertain
Rogelim, *Bersinyâ?:* VI, D-3; VIII, G-8; IX, I-1
Roma, *see also* Rome: *Roma:* XIII, C-2
Rome, *see also* Roma: *Roma:* XV, B-2; XVI: A-D, C-2
Rosetta Mouth of the Nile: V, B-2
Rouen: XVI: D, B-6
Royal Park, special Persian district in Mt. Lebanon: VII: D, C-3
Rumah, *Khirbet Rûmeh,* near Rimmon 2?
Rutupiae, *Richborough:* XIII Inset, D-2

Saffûriyeh, *see also* Sepphoris: XVIII, C-3
Saguntum, *Sagunto:* XIII, A-2
Ṣaidâ, *see also* Sidon: XVIII, C-1
St. Albans, *see also* Verulamium: XVI: D, B-5
Sais, *Ṣân el-Ḥagar:* XI: B-C, B-3; XIII, E-3
Sala, *Salé:* XIII, A-2
Salamis, c. 3 mi. N.W. of *Famagusta:* XIII, E-2; XV, F-4; XVI: B-C, E-3
Salcah, *Salkhad:* VII: A-D, D-4
Salchah, *see* Salcah
Saldae, *Bougie:* XIII, B-2
Salem
1—Gen. 14: 18; uncertain
2—Psa. 76: 2; *see* Jerusalem
Salernum, *Salerno:* XIII, C-2
Salim
1—*see also* Shalem, *Sâlim?:* IX, F-3; XIV, C-4
2—*Umm el-'Amdân?:* IX, H-2; XIV, D-4
Salmantica, *Salamanca:* XIII, A-2
Salmon, Ps. 68: 14, site or mt. in Syria or same as Mt. Zalmon
Salmonah, *Tell Abû Hawâm?:* IV, C-3; XVIII, C-3
Salmone, *Cape Sidero?:* XV, E-4
Salona, *Split:* XVI: C-D, C-2
Salt, City of, in the Wilderness of Judah; uncertain
Salt Desert: II, G-2
Salt Sea, *see also* Dead Sea *and* Lake Asphaltitis, *Baḥr Lûṭ:* IV, C-6, V, G-2; VI, C-5; VII: A-D, C-5; IX, G-7; X, H-1
Salt, Valley of, *Wâdī el-Milḥ?:* VI, B-6; X, E-2
Samaga, *es-Sâmik:* IX, J-6; XII: A, D-5
Samal, *Zenjirli:* XI: A, B-2
Samaria
1—district of: I, C-4; IX, F-4; XII: A-D, C-4; XIV, C-4
2—Persian Province: VII: D, C-4
3—city of (in N.T. times Sebaste), *Sebasṭyeh (q.v.):* VII: B-D, C-4; IX, F-3; XI: B-C, B-3; XII: A-D, C-4; XIII, E-3; XIV, C-4; XVI: A-D, E-3; XVIII, C-4
Samerena, Assyrian Province of Samaria: VII: C, C-4
Samos
1—chief city of island of Samos; near *Tigani:* XV, E-3
2—island in Aegean Sea: III, A-2; XV, E-3
Samosata, *Samsat:* XIII, E-2; XVI: D, E-3
Samothrace, island in N.E. part of Aegean Sea: XV, E-2
Sansannah, *Khirbet esh-Shamsanîyât:* X, E-2
Santander: XIII, A-1
Saphir, *Khirbet el-Kôm?:* IX, D-7
Saqqârah: V, C-4
Saragossa, *see also* Caesaraugusta: XVI: C-D, A-1
Sardinia, island, *Sardegna:* XIII, B-2; XV, A-3
Sardis, *see also* Sepharad, *Sart:* III, A-2; XI: A-D, A-2; XIII, D-2; XV, E-3; XVI: C-D, D-2
Sarepta (in O.T. times Zarephath), *Ṣarafand:* VIII, E-2; XIV, C-2
Sarid, *Tell Shadûd:* IV, C-3; VI, C-3; VIII, D-7
Satala, city in Lesser Armenia: XVI: D, E-2
Savaria, *Stein?:* XVI: D, C-1
Scalabis, *Santarem:* XIII, A-2
Scarbantia, *Sopron:* XVI: D, C-1
Scodra, *Scutari:* XIII, C-2
Scopus, Mt.: I, C-5
Scythia: XI: C, A-1, C-1
Scythopolis (in O.T. times Beth-shan), *Tell el-Ḥuṣn (q.v.):* VIII, F-8; IX, G-1; XII: A-D, D-4; XIV, D-4; XVIII, C-4
Sebaste, *see also* Samaria, *Sebasṭiyeh:* IX, F-3; XII: B-D, C-4; XIV, C-4
Sebasṭiyeh, *see also* Samaria, City of, Sebaste: XVIII, C-4
es-Sebbeh, *see also* Masada: XVIII, C-6
Secacah, *Khirbet es-Samrah?:* IX, G-6
Sechu, near Ramathaim-zophim; unknown
Segovia: XIII, A-2
Seilûn, *see also* Shiloh: XVIII, C-4
Seine River, *see also* Sequana: XIII Inset, D-2; XVI: A-B, B-6
Seir
1—or Mt. Seir; *see also* Edom: VI, C-7
2—Mt., Josh. 15: 10, *Sârîs* near Chesalon may preserve the name: IX, E-6
Seirath, in Ephraim; uncertain
Sela, Selah, *cf.* Petra, *Umm el-Bayyârah:* I, C-8; V, G-3; VI, C-8; VII: A-C, C-6; X, H-8
Sela-hammahlekoth, *Wâdī el-Malâqi* east of Judean Carmel?
Seleucia
1—*Selûqiyeh:* VIII, G-5; XII: A, D, D-3
2—port of Syrian Antioch; 5 mi. N. of mouth of Orontes: *Selûqiyeh:* XIII, E-2; XV, G-4
3—*Silifke:* XIII, E-2
4—on Tigris R., opposite Ctesiphon; c. 20 mi. below modern Baghdad: XIII, F-3
Selinus, at *Gazipaşa:* XIII, E-2
Semechonitis, Lake, *see also* Lake Huleh, *Baḥret el-Ḥûleh* (or *Baḥret el-Kheiṭ*): VIII, F-4; XIV, D-2
Semneh: II, E-4
es-Semû', *see also* Eshtemoa: XVIII, C-6
Senaah, near Jericho; uncertain
Seneh, Rock of, escarpment near Michmash along the *Wâdī eṣ-Ṣuweiniṭ*
Senir, the same as Mt. Hermon in Deut. 3: 9; elsewhere probably a wider designation for the range of Antilebanon: VI, D-2; VIII, H-2
Sennabris, *Sinn en-Nabreh:* VIII, F-6; XII: D, D-3
Sephar, in southern Arabia
Sepharad, *see also* Sardis, *Sart:* XI: A-B, A-2
Sepharvaim, near Riblah; unknown
Sepphoris, *Ṣaffûriyeh (q.v.):* VIII, E-6; XII: A-D, C-3; XIV, C-3; XVIII, C-3
Sequana, *Seine R. (q.v.):* XIII Inset, D-2
Seveneh, *see* Syene
Seville, *see also* Hispalis: XVI: D, A-2
Shaalabbin, Shaalbim, *Selbît:* IX, D-5
Shaaraim
1—near Azekah; uncertain
2—I Chron. 4: 31, *see* Sharuhen
Shahazimah, in Issachar; uncertain
Shalem (in N.T. times Salim 1), *Sheikh Naṣrallah:* VI, C-4; IX, F-3
Shalim, Land of, *same as* Shual, Land of?
Shalisha, Land of, area around Baal-shalisha
Shamir
1—*el-Bîreh?:* IX, D-8; X, E-1
2—Judg. 10: 1-2, *same as* Samaria?
Shapher, Mt., in Sinai; uncertain
Sharaim, *see* Shaaraim 1
Sharon, I Chron. 5: 16, site or district in Gilead; uncertain
Sharon, Plain of: I, B-4; IX, D-2; XIV, B-4
Sharuhen, *Tell el-Fâr'ah:* III, B-4; IV, A-6; V, F-2; VI, A-6; X, C-2; XVIII, A-6
Shaveh, Valley of, uncertain, location depending on that of Salem 2
Shaveh Kiriathaim, plain by Kirjathaim 1
Sheba
1—Josh. 19: 2, *see* Shema
2—II, Inset
Shebah, Gen. 26: 33, *see* Beer-sheba
Shebam, *see* Sibmah
Shebarim, near Ai; unknown
Shechem (in N.T. times Sichem or Sychem), *Tell Balâṭah:* II, E-3; III, B-3; IV, C-4; VI, C-4; VII: A, C-4; IX, F-3; XVIII, C-4
Sheikh Abreiq, *see also* Beth-shearim: XVIII, C-3
Sheikh Sa'd, *see also* Karnaim: XVIII, E-3
Shema, *see also* Jeshua, *Tell es-Sa'wī?:* X, F-2
Shen, in region of Eben-ezer; uncertain
Shenir, *see* Senir
Shepham, in Syria; unknown
Shephelah, "lowlands": I, B-5
Sheshach, *see* Babylon
Shibaniba, *Tell Billah:* III, D-2
Shibmah, *see* Sibmah
Shicron, near Ekron; uncertain
Shihor
1—probably a branch of the Nile River near Rameses
2—Josh. 13: 3; I Chron. 13: 5, probably the same as Egypt, River of, *Wâdī el-'Arîsh*
Shihor-libnath, on or near Mt. Carmel; uncertain; probably two different sites
Shilhim, *see* Sharuhen
Shiloah, Waters of, Isa. 8: 6; an early water conduit in Jerusalem
Shiloh, *Seilûn:* V, G-1; VI, C-4; IX, F-4; XVIII, C-4
Shimron, in Zebulun; uncertain
Shinar: II, Inset
Shion, in Issachar; uncertain
Shittim, *see* Abel-shittim
Shittim, Valley of, near Abel-shittim
Shoco, Shocho, Shochoh, *see* Socoh 1
Shophan, *see* Atroth
Shual, Land of, area by Ophrah 1
Shunem, *Sôlem:* IV, C-3; VI, C-3; VIII, E-7
Shuqbah: XVIII, C-5
Shur, Wilderness of: III, B-4; V, E-3
Shushan, *see also* Susa, *Shush:* II, G-3; X: A-C, D-3
Sibmah, near Heshbon; uncertain
Sibraim, *see* Sepharvaim
Sichem, *see also* Sychem (in O.T. times Shechem), *Tell Balâṭah:* XII: A, C-4; XIV, C-4
Sicilia, *see also* Sicily: XIII, C-2; XV, B-3
Sicily, *see also* Sicilia, II, C-2
Siddim, Vale of, now below the S. end of Dead Sea: X, H-3
Side, *Eski Adalia:* XI: D, B-2; XIII, E-2; XVI: D, E-3
Sidon
1—*Ṣaidâ:* I, C-1; II, E-3; III, C-3; IV, C-1; VI, C-1; VII: A-D, C-3; VIII, E-1; XI: A-D, B-3; XII: A-D, C-1; XIII, E-3; XIV, C-1; XV, G-4; XVI: A-C, E-3; XVIII, C-1
2—Persian Province: VII: D, C-3
Siga, city on coast of ancient Mauretania: XIII, A-2
Sihon, Kingdom of: IV, D-5; V, G-2
Sihor, *see* Shihor
Siloah, Pool of, *see also* Siloam, Pool of: XVII: A, D-6
Siloam, Pool of, *see also* Siloah, Pool of: XVII: B-D, D-6
Silver Mts., Taurus Mts. *(q.v.):* III, C-2
Simeon, tribe affiliated with Judah: VI, B-6
Ṣimirra, Assyrian Province: VII: C, D-2
Sin, Ezek. 30: 15-16, *same as* Pelusium?
Sin, Wilderness of, *Debbet er-Ramleh?:* V, E-5
Sinai Mining District: II, E-3
Sinai, Mt., *see also* Horeb, Mt., *Jebel Mûsâ?:* V, F-5; XI: A-D, B-4
Sinai, Peninsula of: III, B-4; V, E-4
Sinai, Wilderness of, Ex. 19: 1, Num. 33: 16; plain of *er-Râḥa* at the foot of Mt. Sinai?
Singidunum, *Belgrade:* XVI: D, C-1
Sinim, unknown
Sinope, *Sinop:* XI: B-D, B-1; XIII, E-2; XV, G-2; XVI: C-D, E-2
Sinus Arabicus, *see also* Arabian Gulf, Red Sea: XIII, F-4
Sinus Persicus, *Persian Gulf (q.v.):* XIII, G-3
Sion, *see* Zion
Sion, Mt.
1—*see* Zion, Mt.
2—Deut. 4: 48; *see* Hermon, Mt.
Siphmoth, near Aroer 3; unknown
Sippar, *Abû Ḥabbah:* III, D-3; XI: A, C-3
Sirah, Well of, near *Ṣîret el-Bella'* north of Hebron
Sirbonis, Lake: V, E-2
Sirion, *see also* Hermon, Mt.; *Jebel esh-Sheikh:* VI, D-2; VIII, H-2
Sirmium, *near Mitrovica:* XIII, C-1; XVI: D, C-1
Siscia, *Sisak:* XIII, C-1; XVI: D, C-1
Sitifis, *Setif:* XVI: D, B-2
Sitnah, Well of, between Gerar and Rehoboth 2, unknown
Sivas: III, C-1
Siwa, Oasis of, in the Libyan Desert: XI: D, A-3
Skudra, *see also* Thrace: XI: C, A-1
Smyrna, *Izmir:* III, A-2; XIII, D-2; XV, E-3; XVI: C-D, D-2
Socoh, I Kings, 4: 10, *Tell er-Râs:* IV, C-4; VI, C-4; IX, E-2
Socoh
1—Josh. 15: 35, *Khirbet 'Abbâd:* IX, D-7
2—Josh. 15: 48, *Khirbet Shuweikeh:* IX, E-8; X, F-1
Sodom, in Vale of Siddim below southern end of Dead Sea; ruins undiscovered: X, H-3
Sogdiana: XI: C-D, E-1
Soli
1—in Cilicia; also called Pompeiopolis, *Mezetlü:* XIII, E-2
2—on Cyprus, *Aligora?:* XIII, E-2
Sorek, Valley of, *Wâdī eṣ-Ṣarâr:* IX, D-6
Spain: XVI: B-C, A-2
Sparta, *see also* Lacedaemon, *Spartē:* XI: A-B, D, A-2; XIII, D-2; XVI: D, D-3
Spartan League: XI: C, A-2
Speos Artemidos, *Beni-ḥasan:* V, B-6
Stobi, *Sirkovo:* XVI: D, D-2
Strato's Tower, *see also* Caesarea 1, *Qeiṣârîyeh:* VIII, B-8; IX, D-1, XII: A-B, B-4
Subaita, *Isbeiṭâ:* XVIII, B-7
Ṣubat, *see* Ṣubutu
Ṣubutu, Assyrian Province, *see also* Zobah: VII: C, D-2
Succoth
1—Ex. 12: 37, 13: 20, Num. 33: 5, 6; *Tell el-Maskhûṭah:* V, D-3
2—*Tell Deir'allâ:* IV, D-4; VI, D-4; IX, H-3
Suez Canal: III, B-4; V, D-3
Suez, Gulf of: V, E-5
Sugambri, a tribe in ancient Germania: XIII Inset, F-2
Ṣûr, *see also* Tyre: XVIII, C-2
Susa, *see also* Shushan, *Shush:* II, G-3; III, E-3; XI: A-D, D-3; XIII, G-3
Susiana, Persian Satrapy: XI: C, D-3
Sychar, corruption of Sychem?
Sychem, *see also* Sichem *and* Shechem, *Tell Balâṭah:* IX, F-3; XIV, C-4
Syene, *see also* Elephantine, Seveneh: *Aswân:* XI: A-C, B-4; XIII, E-4
Syracusae, *see also* Syracuse, *Siracusa:* XIII, C-2
Syracuse, *see also* Syracusae, *Siracusa:* XV, B-3; XVI: C-D, C-3
Syria
1—*See also* Aram; the Aramean region north of Bashan with center at Damascus: VII: B, D-3; VIII, I-2
2—territory or province extending from Cilician border S. to Palestine: XI: D, B-2; XIII, E-2; XV, G-4
Syrtis Major, *Gulf of Sidra:* XIII, C-3; XV, C-5
Syrtis Minor, *Gulf of Gabes:* XIII, B-2; XV, B-4

Taanach, *Tell Ta'annak:* IV, C-4; VI, C-4; VIII, D-8; IX, F-1; XVIII, C-4
Taanath-shiloh, *Khirbet Ta'nah el-Fôqâ:* VI, C-4; IX, G-3
Tabal, *see also* Tubal: XI: A, B-2
Tabbath, *Râs Abû Tâbât:* VI, D-4; IX, H-2
Taberah, in Sinai; unknown
eṭ-Ṭâbghah: XVIII, D-3
Tabor, I Chron. 6: 77; refers either to Mt. Tabor or to the village of Dabareh
Tabor, Mt., *Jebel eṭ-Ṭôr:* I, C-3; IV, C-3; VI, C-3; VIII, E-7; XII: B, C-3; XIV, C-3; XVIII, C-3
Tabor, Plain of, I Sam, 10: 3, to be translated "Oak of Tabor"; *see* Allon-bacuth
Tabriz: III, E-2
Tadmor, *see also* Palmyra, *Tudmur:* II, E-2; III, C-3; VII: A-D, F-2; XI: B-C, B-3
Tahapanes, *see* Tahpanhes
Tahath, in Sinai; uncertain
Tahpanhes, *see also* Daphnae, *Tell Defneh:* XI: B, B-3
Tahtim-hodshi, The Land of, to be read "to the land of the Hittites, to Kadesh"; *see* Kadesh 2
Tamar, *see* Hazezon-tamar
Tanach, *see* Taanach
Tanais, near *Nedrigofka:* XIII, E-1
Tanis, *see also* Avaris, Rameses, Zoan, *Ṣân el-Ḥagar:* II, E-3; V, C-3; XIII, E-3
Tapacae, *Gabes:* XIII, B-2
Tappuah
1—Josh. 15: 34, in Judah; uncertain
2—*Sheikh Abû Zarad:* IV, C-4; VI, C-4; IX, F-4
Tappuah, Land of, district around Tappuah 2
Tarah, in Sinai; unknown
Taralah, in Benjamin; uncertain
Tarantum, *Taranto:* XIII, C-2; XV, C-2
Tarichaea, *see also* Magdala, *Mejdel:* VIII, F-6; XII: A-B, D, D-3; XIV, D-3
Tarraco, *Tarragona (q.v.):* XIII, A-2
Tarraconensis, Roman Province: XIII, A-1
Tarragona, *see also* Tarraco: XVI: D, A-2
Tarshish, Phoenician smelting center in Spain or Sardinia: II, Inset
Tarsus: II, E-2; III, B-2; XI: A-D, B-2; XIII, E-2; XV, G-3; XVI: A-D, E-3

Taurus, Mt., *see also* Silver Mts.: XV, G-3

Tavium, *Nefezköy:* XIII, E-2; XV, G-2; XVI: D, E-2

Tegarama, *Gürün?:* III, C-2

Tehaphnehes, *see* Tahpanhes

Tekoa, Tekoah, *see also* Thekoue, *Teqû':* IX, F-7

Tekoa, Wilderness of, district around Tekoa

Telaim, near Ziph 1; uncertain

Telassar, in northern Mesopotamia; unknown

Teleilât el-Ghassûl: XVIII, D-5

Telem, *see* Telaim

Tel-harsa, Tel-haresha, in Mesopotamia; unknown

et-Tell, *see also* Ai: XVIII, C-5

Tell-abib, near Babylon; unknown

Tell Abû Hawâm, *see also* Salmonah: XVIII, C-3

Tell Abû Maṭar: XVIII, B-6

Tell el-'Ajjûl, *see also* Beth-eglaim: XVIII, A-6

Tell el-Amarna, *see also* Akhetaton: V, B-6

Tell 'Amr, *see also* Harosheth: XVIII, C-3

Tell Beit Mirsim, *see also* Debir *and* Kirjath-sepher: XVIII, B-6

Tell Brâk: III, D-2

Tell Chagar Bazar: III, D-2

Tell Dôthâ, *see also* Dothan: XVIII, C-4

Tell ed-Duweir, *see also* Lachish: XVIII, B-5

Tell el-Fâr'ah, *see also* Tirzah: XVIII, C-4

Tell el-Fâr'ah, *see also* Sharuhen: XVIII, A-6

Tell el-Fûl, *see also* Gibeah 3: XVIII, C-5

Tell Halâf, *see also* Gozan: III, D-2

Tell el-Ḥammeh: XVIII, D-3

Tell el-Harbaj, *see also* Helkath: XVIII, C-3

Tell el-Ḥesî, *see also* Eglon: XVIII, B-5

Tell Hûm, *see also* Capernaum: XVIII, D-3

Tell el-Ḥuṣn, *see also* Beth-shan *and* Scythopolis: XVIII, C-4

Tell Jemmeh: XVIII, A-6

Tell ej-Jerîsheh, *see also* Gath-rimmon 2: XVIII, B-4

Tell Jezer, *see also* Gezer: XVIII, B-5

Tell ej-Judeideh
1—*see also* Moresheth-gath: XVIII, B-5
2—in N. Syria: III, C-2

Tell Keisân, *see also* Achshaph: XVIII, C-3

Tell el-Mutesellim, *see also* Megiddo: XVIII, C-3

Tell en-Naṣbeh, *see also* Mizpah 2: XVIII, C-5

Tell el-Qasîleh: XVIII, B-4

Tell el-Qassîs: XVIII, C-3

Tell el-Qedaḥ, *see also* Hazor: XVIII, D-2

Tell er-Rumeileh, *see also* Beth-Shemesh 1: XVIII, B-5

Tell eṣ-Ṣâfî, *see also* Libnah: XVIII, B-5

Tell Sandaḥannah, *see also* Mareshah *and* Marisa: XVIII, B-5

Tell es-Sulṭân, *see also* Jericho: XVIII, C-5

Tell Ta'annak, *see also* Taanach: XVIII, C-3

Tell el-Yehûdîyeh: V, C-3

Tell Zakarîyeh, *see also* Azekah: XVIII, B-5

Tel-melah, in Mesopotamia, unknown

Tema, *Teimā:* XI: A-D, C-4

Teman, *Tawîlân?:* V, G-3; VI, D-8; VII: A-C, C-6; X, I-8

Tepe Gawra: II, F-2

Tepe Giyan: II, G-2; III, E-3

Tepe Sialk: II, G-2

Tergeste, *Trieste:* XIII, C-1

Thames, River: XVI: A-B, B-5

Thamna, *see also* Timnath-serah, *Khirbet Tibneh:* IX, E-4; XII: D, C-4

Thapsacus, *see also* Tiphsah 1, *Dibseh:* XI: D, B-2

Thapsus, on coast E. of *Teboulba:* XIII, B-2

Thebae
1—*see also* Thebes 1 *and* No; comprises *Karnak, Luxor, Deir el-Baḥrî, Medinet Habu,* etc.: XIII, E-3
2—*See also* Thebes 2; in Boeotia: XIII, D-2

Thebes
1—*see also* Thebae 1 *and* No; comprises *Karnak, Luxor, Deir el-Baḥrî, Medinet Habu,* etc.: II E-3; XI: A-D, B-4: XVI: D, E-4
2—*see also* Thebae 2; *in* Boeotia: XVI: D, D-2

Thebez, *Ṭûbâṣ:* VI, C-4; IX, G-2

Thekoue, *see also* Tekoa, *Teqû':* IX, F-7; XII: D, C-5

Thelasar, *see* Telassar

Thella, *et-Tuleil:* VIII, F-4; XIV, D-2

Theodosia: *Feodosiya:* XI: C-D, B-1; XIII, E-1

Thessalonica, *Salonika:* XI: D, A-1; XIII, D-2; XV, D-2; XVI: B-D, D-2

Thessaly: II, D-2

Thimnathah, *see* Timmah 1

Thone, *see also* Athone, *Khirbet eṭ-Ṭeniyeh?:* X, I-3; XII: A, D-6

Thrace, *see also* Skudra: XI: C-D, A-1

Thracia, kingdom, later Roman province, in S.E. Europe: XIII, D-2; XV, D-2

Three Taverns, *see* Tres Tabernae

Thyatira, *Akhisar:* XV, E-3

Thysdrus, *el-Djem:* XVI: C-D, B-3

Tiber, River, *see also* Tiberis: XV, B-2

Tiberias, *Ṭabarîyeh:* VIII, F-6; XII: C-D, D-3; XIV, D-3

Tiberias, Sea of, *see* Chinnereth, Sea of, *and* Galilee, Sea of: *Baḥr Ṭabarîyeh:* VIII, F-6

Tiberis, *see also* Tiber, River: XIII, C-2

Tibhath, in Syria; unknown

Tigris River, *also called* Hiddekel *or* Idiglat, *Shaṭṭ ed-Dijleh:* II, F-2; III, D-3; XI: A-D, C-3; XIII, F-2; XVI: A-D, F-3

Til-Barsip, *Tell el-Aḥmar:* II, E-2; III, C-2

Timnah
1—*Khirbet Tibnah:* VI, B-5; IX, D-6
2—Josh. 15:57, *Tibnah:* IX, E-6

Timnath
1—Gen. 38:12-14, *see* Timnah 2
2—Judg. 14:1-5, see Timnah 1

Timnath-heres, *see* Timnath-serah

Timnath-serah, *see also* Thamna, *Khirbet Tibneh:* VI, C-5; IX, E-4

Timsâḥ, Lake: V, D-3

Tingis, *Tangier:* XIII, A-2; XVI: D, A-2

Tiphsah
1—*see also* Thapsacus, *Dibseh:* XI: A-C, B-2
2—II Kings 15:16, in the area of Shechem; uncertain

Tirqa, *Tell 'Ashârah:* II, F-2; III, D-3

Tirzah, *Tell el-Fâr'ah?:* IV, C-4; VI, C-4; IX, F-3; XVIII, C-4

Tishbeh, I Kings 17:1, *Lisdib?:* VII: B, C-4; IX, H-2

Tob, *eṭ-Ṭaiyibeh?:* IV, E-3; VI, E-3; VIII, J-7

Tochen, near En-rimmon; uncertain

Togarmah: II, Inset

Tolad, *see* Eltolad

Toledo: XVI: D, A-2

Tolosa, *Toulouse:* XIII, B-1

Tomi, Tomis, *Constanta:* XIII, D-2; XVI: D, D-2

Tophel, *eṭ-Ṭafîleh?:* X, I-5

Topheth, Tophet, in the Valley of Hinnom

Toulouse, *see also* Tolosa: XVI: D, A-1

Trachonitis, region of lava deposits east of Hauran: VIII, K-4; XII: B-D, E-2; XIV, E-2

Tralles, *Aydin:* XV, E-3

Transjordan: I, D-E 4-7; XVIII, D-E 4-7

Trapezus, *Trabzon (Trebizond):* XI: B-D, C-1; XIII, F-2; XVI: D, F-2

Tremithus, in Cyprus: XVI: D, E-3

Tres Tabernae, *i.e.,* Three Taverns; on Appian Way, c. 33 mi. from Rome: XV, B-2

Trier, *see also* Augusta Treverorum: XVI: C-D, C-5

Tripolis
1—*Ṭarâbulus:* VII: D, C-2; XIII, E-3; XVI: D, E-3
2—Persian Province: VII: D, D-2

Troas, *see also* Alexandria Troas, *Eskistanbul:* XV, E-3; XVI: B, D-2

Trogyllium, promontory on W. Asia Minor, just S. of island of Samos: XV, E-3

Troy, *see also* Ilium, *Hisarlik:* II, D-2; III, A-1

Tubal, *see also* Tabal: II, Inset

Tulûl Abû el-'Alâyiq: XVIII, C-D 5

Turkestan: II, H-1

Tuttul, *Hît:* II, F-3; III, D-3

Tuwana, Tyana, *Kilisehisar:* III, B-2; XIII, E-2

Tyras, at mouth of Dniester R.: XIII, E-1

Tyre
1—*see also* Tyrus, *Ṣûr:* I, C-2; II, E-3; III, B-3; IV, C-2; VI, C-2; VII: A-D, C-3; VIII, D-3; XI: A-D, B-3; XII: A-D, C-2; XIV, C-2; XV, G-4; XVI: A-D, E-3; XVIII, C-2
2—Persian Province: VII: D, C-3

Tyropoeon Valley, "Valley of Cheesemakers," *el-Wâd:* XVII: B-C, D-5

Tyrrhenum, Mare, *Tyrrhenian Sea:* XIII, B-2

Tyrus, *see also* Tyre 1, *Ṣûr:* XIII, E-3

Ube, *see also* Aram: IV, E-2; III, C-3

Ugarit, *Râs esh-Shamrah:* II, E-2; III, C-2

Ulai, River, near Susa; uncertain

Ulatha, district just N.E. of Lake Huleh: XII: B-C, D-2; XIV, D-2

Umma, *Jôkha:* III, E-3

Ummah, *see* Accho

Uphaz, *same as* Ophir?

Ur, *el-Muqaiyar:* II, F-3; III, E-4; XI: A-B, C-3

Urartu, *see also* Ararat, Armenia: XI: A-B, C-2

Urmiah, Lake: II, F-2; III, D-2; XI: A-D, C-2

Ursu: III, C-2

Utica, in ancient times at mouth of Bagradas (now *Medjerda*) R.: XIII, B-2; XVI: D, B-2

Uz, in Arabia; uncertain

Uzzen-sherah, near the two Beth-horons; uncertain

Valentia, *Valencia:* XIII, A-2

Van, Lake: II, F-2; III, D-2; XI: A-D, C-2

Vectis Insula, *Isle of Wight:* XIII Inset, C-2

Vellaunodunum, *Montargis:* XIII Inset, D-3

Venta Belgarum, *Winchester:* XIII Inset, C-2

Venta Icenorum, *Caistor:* XIII Inset, D-1

Venta Silurum, *Caerwent:* XIII Inset, C-2

Verona: XIII, C-1; XVI: D, B-1

Verulamium, *St. Albans (q.v.):* XIII Inset, C-2

Vetera, near *Xanten:* XIII Inset, E-2

Vienna, *Vienne (q.v.):* XIII, B-1; XIII Inset, E-3

Vienne, *see also* Vienna: XVI: C-D, B-1; XVI: C-D, C-6

Viminacium, *Kostolatz?:* XIII, D-2

Vindobona, *Vienna:* XIII, C-1

Vindonissa, *Windisch:* XIII, B-1; XIII Inset, F-3

Virgin's Spring, *see also* Gihon, *'Ain Sittî Maryam:* XVII: D, E-5

Viroconium, *Wroxeter:* XIII Inset, C-1

Vounous: III, B-3

Wâdî 'Arab: I, D-3

Wâdî 'Arîsh: I, A-7

Wâdî Bîreh: I, D-3

Wâdî Fâr'ah: I, C-4

Wâdî Ghazzeh: I, A-6

Wâdî Ḥesā: I, D-7

Wâdî Ḥesî: I, B-5

Wâdî Jurm: I, D-4

Wâdî Kefrein: I, D-5

Wâdî Khareiṭûn: XVIII, C-5

Wâdî Khuḍeirah: I, B-4

Wâdî Kufrinjeh: I, D-4

Wâdî Mâliḥ: I, C-4

Wâdî Meirôn: I, C-3

Wâdî Môjib: I, D-6

Wâdî Mughârah: XVIII, C-3

Wâdî Murabba'ât: I, C-5

Wâdî Nâr: I, C-5

Wâdî Nimrîn: I, D-5

Wâdî Qelt: I, C-5

Wâdî Qubeibeh: I, B-5

Wâdî Qumrân: I, C-5

Wâdî Râjeb: I, D-4

Wâdî Râmeh: I, D-5

Wâdî Sanṭ: I, B-5

Wâdî Ṣarâr: I, B-5

Wâdî Sayyâl: I, C-6

Wâdî Sherî'ah: I, B-6

Wâdî Selmân: I, B-5

Wâdî Sirḥân: III, C-4

Wâdî Wâlā: I, D-6

Wâdî Yâbis: I, D-4

Wâdî Ziqlâb: I, D-4

Washshukanni, *Tell Fekherîyeh?:* III, D-2

Xaloth, *see also* Exaloth; in O.T. times Chesulloth, *Iksâl:* XIV, C-3

Xanthus, near *Günük:* XIII, D-2

Yaham, *Tell el-Asâwir:* IV, C-4

Yano'am, *Tell en-Nâ'meh:* IV, D-2

Yarmuk, River, *Sherî'at el-Menâdireh:* I, D-3

York, *see also* Eburacum: XVI: D, B-5

Zaanaim, Plain of, to be read Elon-bezaanim; near Kedesh 3; unknown

Zaanan, *see* Zenan

Zaanannim, *see* Allon

Zab, Great, *Zâb el-A'lā:* III, D-2

Zab, Little, *Zâb eṣ-Saghîr:* III, D-2

Zadracarta, city in N. Parthia: XI: D, D-2

Zagros Mts.: III, E-3

Zair, *see* Zior

Ẓaharîyeh: XVIII, B-6

Zalmon, Mount, the southern part of Mt. Gerizim?

Zalmonah, in the Arabah near Punon; uncertain

Zanoah
1—*Khirbet Zānû'* (or *Zānûḥ*): IX, D-6
2—Josh. 15:56, *Zanûtâ* near Jattir?

Zaphon (in N.T. times Asophon?), *Tell el-Qôs?:* IV, D-4; IX, H-3

Zara, *see also* Zoara; *cf.* Zoar; *Khirbet Sheikh 'Isā:* X, H-3; XII: A, D, C-6

Zareah, *see* Zorah

Zared, Valley of, *see* Zered, Brook

Zarephath (in N.T. times Sarepta), *Ṣarafand:* IV, C-2; VI, C-2; VIII, E-2

Zaretan, Zarethan, *Tell es-Sa'idîyeh?:* IV, D-4; IX, H-3

Zareth-shahar (in N.T. times Callirhoe), *Zārât:* IX, H-7

Zartanah, Zarthan, *see* Zaretan

Zeboim, Zeboiim
1—Near Sodom under Dead Sea; precise location unknown
2—Neh. 11:34, near Hadid; uncertain

Zeboim, Valley of, *Wâdî Abû Dabā'* near Debir 2?

Zebulun, tribal district: VI, C-3

Zedad, *Ṣadâd:* VII: A-D, D-2

Zela, *Zile:* XVI: D, E-2

Zelah, to be read Zelah-eleph; in Benjamin; uncertain

Zelzah, in Benjamin; uncertain

Zemaraim, at or near *Râs ez-Zeimara* near Ophrah 1?

Zemaraim, Mt., near Zemaraim; uncertain

Zenan, near Lachish; uncertain

Zephath, *see also* Hormah; uncertain

Zephathah, Valley of, *Wâdî Zeitā?:* IX, C-7

Zer, in Naphtali; uncertain

Zered, Brook, *Wâdî el-Ḥesā:* I, D-7; IV, D-7; V, G-3; VI, D-7; X, I-4

Zeredah, Zereda, *Deir Ghassâneh:* VI, C-4; IX, E-4; XVIII, C-4

Zeredathah, *see* Zaretan

Zererath, *see* Zaretan

Ziddim, near Madon; uncertain

Zidon, *see* Sidon

Ziklag, *Tell el-Khuweilfeh?:* VI, B-6; IX, D-8; X, E-1

Zilu, *Tell Abû Seifah:* III, B-4; V, D-3

Zin, Wilderness of: V, F-3; VI, B-7; X, E-6

Zion, *see* Jerusalem

Zion, Mt., *see* Jerusalem

Zior, in Judah; uncertain

Ziph
1—Josh. 15:24, I Sam. 15:4, *ez-Zeifeh:* X, F-4
2—*Tell Zîf:* VI, C-6; IX, E-8; X, F-1

Ziph, Wilderness of, area around Ziph 2

Ziphron, in Syria; uncertain

Ziz, Ascent of, or "Cliff of," *Wâdî Ḥaṣâṣah:* IX, F-7

Zoan, *see also* Rameses, Tanis, Avaris, *Ṣân el-Ḥagar:* V, C-2; XI: A, B-3

Zoar (in N.T. times Zoara or Zara), the O.T. site is probably beneath the S.E. end of the Dead Sea: X, H-3

Zoara, *see also* Zara: *cf.* Zoar; *Khirbet Sheikh 'Isā:* X, H-3; XII: A, D, C-6

Zobah, *see also* Ṣubat, Ṣubutu: VII: A, D-3

Zoheleth, Stone of, near En-rogel, Jerusalem

Zophim, Field of, portion of Moabite plateau near Mt. Pisgah

Zorah, *Ṣar'ah:* IV, B-5; VI, B-5; IX, D-6

Zuph, Land of, near Ramathaim-zophim: IX, E-4

Location of plates: I, p. 21; II, p. 22; III, p. 31; IV, p. 32; V, p. 41; VI, p. 42; VII, p. 51; VIII, p. 52; IX, p. 65; X, p. 66; XI, p. 79; XII, p. 80; XIII, p. 89; XIV, p. 90; XV, p. 99; XVI, p. 100; XVII, p. 109; XVIII, p. 110.

INDEX OF ARABIC NAMES

IDENTIFIED WITH BIBLICAL PLACES IN SYRIA AND PALESTINE

(The Biblical name following the Arabic may be consulted in the Index to the Maps for its occurrence on the maps.)

'Abdeh, Oryba?
Abṭûn, Beten?
Afqā, Aphek 2
'Ain el-'Arûs, Hazezon-tamar (at or near)?
-Hôd, En-shemesh
-Weiba, Oboth (at)?
Feshkha (near Khirbet Qumrân), En-eglaim
Ḥajlah, Beth-hoglah (at or near)
Ḥoṣob, Oboth (at)?
Jālûd, Well of Harod
Jidi, Engaddi
Kârim, Beth-haccerem
Qedeis, Kadesh-barnea?
Sittī Maryam, Virgin's Spring (Gihon)
Ajbeihât, Jogbehah
'Akkā, Ptolemais 1
Aleppo, Beroea
'Ammân, Rabbah 2 (Rabbath-ammon)
Amrît, Marathus
'Amwâs, Emmaus 1
Anṭâkiyeh, Antioch 1
'Aqrabeh, Acrabetta
'Arâ'ir, Aroer 2
'Arâq el-Menshîyeh, Gath
'Ar'arah, Aroer 3
Ardat, Ardata
'Arrâbeh, Aruboth?
'Arrâbet el-Baṭṭôf, Gabara
Arsûf, Apollonia 1
'Asqalân, Ascalon (Ashkelon)
'Ayyûn, Ayyanu

Baḥr Lûṭ, Dead Sea
Ṭabarîyeh, Sea of Galilee
'Baḥret el-Ḥûleh, Lake Huleh
-Kheit, Lake Huleh
Bâniyâs, Paneas (Caesarea Philippi)
Baqa', Valley of Rephaim (S.W. of Jerusalem)
Bei Laḥm, Bethlehem 1
Beirût, Berytus
Beit 'Ainûn, Beth-anoth
'Anân, Beth-hanan
Jemâl, En-gannim 1?
Jibrîn, Eleutheropolis
Laḥm, Bethlehem 2
Nabala, Neballat
'Ur ('ûr) el-Fôqā, Beth-horon Upper
et-Taḥtā, Beth-horon Lower
Beitîn, Bethel 1 (Luz 1; Bethela)
Belqā, Moab
Bereitân, Berothai
Bersînyā, Rogelim?
Bîr Ayyûb, En-rogel (Job's Well)
Ya'qûb, Jacob's Well
Birein, Beeroth 1?
Birket er-Râm, Pool of Phiale
-Rân, Pool of Phiale
Bittîr, Bether
Burj el-Isâneh, Jeshanah
Buṣeirah, Bozrah 2
Buṣr el-Ḥarîrī, Bosor
Buṣra-Eski Shâm, Bosora

Debbet er-Ramleh, Wilderness of Sin?
Debûriyeh, Dabareh
Deir el-'Aṣal, Beth-ezel?
Ghassâneh, Zeredah
Der'ā, Edrei 1
Dhîbân, Dibon
Dibseh, Thapsacus (Tiphsah 1)
Dûrā, Adora
Dûrā, Aduru

ed-Dômeh, Dumah 1
ej-Jîb, Gibeon (Gabao)
el-'Abeidiyeh, Beth-shemesh 2?
-'Al ('âl), Elealeh
-'Araj (east end), Bethsaida Julius
-'Araq, Oronai?
-Arba'în, Modein
-'Arîsh, Rhinocolura
-'Azarîyeh, Bethany
-Ba'neh, Beth-anath?
-Baṣṣah (near Adami), Nekeb?
-Biqâ', Amki
-Bîreh, Berea?
-Bîreh (near Hapharaim), Beer 2
-Bîreh, Shamir?
-Blâḥiyeh, Anthedon
-Buqei'ah, Baca
-Buqei'ah, Valley of Achor
-Burj (north of eṭ-Ṭanṭûrah), Dor 1 (Dora)
-Gharabeh, Beth-arabah?
-Ghôr, Arabah
-Ghuweir, Plain of Gennesaret
-Hadetheh, En-haddah
-Ḥadîtheh, Adida (Hadid)
-Ḥârithîyeh, Gaba 2
-'Isâwîyeh ('Isâwîyeh) (N.E. of Jerusalem), Laishah

el-Jebarîyeh (on the Wâdī Umm Ethnân), Hazar-ithnan?
-Jish, Gischala
-Kerak, Kir-hareseth
-Khalîl, Hebron 1 (Kirjath-arba)
-Mishrifeh, Qatna
-Miṣna', Ar?
-Qereiyât, Kirjathaim 1
-Quds, Jerusalem
-Wâd, Tyropoeon Valley
Endôr, En-dor
en-Nâṣirah, Nazareth
-Na'ûrah, Anaharath
er-Râfeh, Raphana
-Râm, Ramah 1
-Râmeh, Ramah 2
Erwâd, Arvad
Esdûd, Ashdod 2 (Azotus)
es-Sâmik, Samaga
-Sebbeh, Masada
-Semû', Eshtemoa
Eshwa', Eshtaol?
esh-Shâm, Damascus
-Sherî'ah el-Kebîreh, River Jordan
eṭ-Ṭafîleh, Tophel?
-Taiyibeh (near Hebron), Aphrah?
-Taiyibeh, Ophrah 1 (Ephraim 1?; Aphairema?)
-Taiyibeh, Hapharaim
-Ṭaiyibeh (E. of Jordan), Tob?
-Tell, Ai
-Tôr (on Mt. of Olives), Nob?
-Tuleil, Thella
ez-Za'ferân, Kedemoth?
-Zeifeh, Ziph 1
-Zîb, Achzib 2 (Ecdippa)

Far'âtā, Pirathon (Parathon)?
Feinân, Punon
Fîq, Aphek 4

Ghazzeh, Gaza

Ḥajar el-Aṣbaḥ, Stone of Bohan?
Halbûn, Helbon
Ḥaleb, Khalab (Aleppo)
Ḥalḥûl, Alurus (Halhul)
Ḥâm, Ham
Ḥamā, Hamath 1
Ḥammân Ṭabarîyeh, Hammath (Ammathus)
Ḥazzûr, En-hazor?
Ḥesbân, Heshbon (Esbus; Essebon)
Ḥizmeh, Azmaveth
Homs, Emesa

Ibn-ibrâq, Bene-berak
Idhna, Ashnah 2?
Iksâl, Chesulloth (Exaloth)
Irbid, Beth-arbel
Isbeiṭa, Subaita
Ishwa', Eshtaol?

Jâlûl, Jahaz?
Jebeil, Byblos
Jebel 'Aṣûr, Baal-hazor
esh-Sheikh, Mt. Hermon (Sirion)
Eslâmîyeh, Mt. Ebal
eṭ-Ṭôr, Mt. Tabor
-Ṭôr, Mt. Gerizim
-Ṭûr, Mt. of Olives (Olivet)
Fuqû'ah, Mt. Gilboa
Fureidîs, Herodium
Halâq, Mt. Halak
Libnân, Mt. Lebanon
Mâr Elyâs, Mt. Carmel
Nebā, Mt. Nebo
Qaranṭal, Dok
Zebedânî, Mt. Amana
Jedîreh (near Gibeon), Gederah 2
Jedîreh, Gederah 1
Jenîn, En-gannim 2 (Ginaea)
Jerablus, Carchemish
Jerash, Gerasa
Jett, Gath-carmel
Jifnah, Gophna
Jiljûlieh, Gilgal 2
Jimzū (near Lod), Gimzo
Jubeihât, Jogbehah

Kâbûl, Cabul (Chabulon)
Kefr 'Anā, Ono
eṭ-Ṭûr, Bethphage?
Kermel, Carmel
Keslā, Chesalon
Khalaṣa, Alusa
Khirbet 'Abbâd, Socoh 1
'Abdeh, Abdon
Abū Ṭabaq, Middin?
'Addâseh, Adasa
'Alîn, Holon
'Almît, Almon
'Anâb, Anab
'Asan, Ashan
Khirbet 'Aṭṭârûs, Ataroth 1
'Attîr, Jattir
'Attîr (near En-rimmon), Ether 2
'Aujā et-Taḥtânī, Archelais
Baṭneh, Betonin
Bedd Fâlûḥ, Netophah
Beidûs, Narbata?
Beit Baṣṣa, Bethbassi
Ilfā, Beth Alfa
Neṣîb, Nezib
Skâriā, Bethzacharia
Berqît, Borcaeus
Bezqa, Bezek 1?
Bîr es-Seba', Bersabee
Dafneh, Daphne
Dajûn, Beth-dagon 1?
Dâmiyeh, Adami
Debûriyeh, Dabarittha
Deleilât esh-Sherqîyeh, Almon-diblathaim?
Dimneh, Madmen?
ej-Jumeil, Beth-gamul
el-'Ashshī, Elasa
-'Ater, Ether 1
-'Ayâsh, Naarath (Noarah)
-Fârah, Parah
-Ḥawârah, Idalah?
-Kefrein, Abila 1
-Khôkh, Etam 1
-Kôm, Saphir?
-Laḥm (near Lachish), Lahman?
-Lôn, Asochis
-Lôn (near Rimmon 2), Aijalon 2?
-Maḥâlib, Ahlab (Meheleb)
-Manṣûrah (near Anem), Lakum?
-Maqarī, Nibshan?
-Medeiyineh, City of Moab?
-Medeiyineh, Mattanah?
-Mefjer, Gilgal 1
-Mekhaiyeṭ, Nebo 1?
-Muqenna', Eltekeh
-Musheirefeh, Misrephoth-maim
-Qaryatein, Kerioth 1
-Qudeirât, Hazar-addar?
-Qureiyeh, Kartan
es-Samrah, Secacah?
-Sweimeh, Besimoth
esh-Shamsanîyât, Sansannah
et-Teim, Jahaz?
-Ṭeniyeh, Athone (Thone)?
-Ṭubeiqah, Beth-zur (Bethsura)
ez-Zurrâ', Gath-hepher
Faḥil, Pella 1
Faṣâ'il, Phasaelis
Fered (near Timnah 1), Naamah?
Ghuwein et-Taḥtā, Anim?
Haiyân, Aiath?
Hazzûr (near Gibeon), Hazor 3
Ibzîq, Bezek 2
Irbid, Arbela 1
'Irq, Jarda (Jorda)
Jedûr, Gedor 1
Jefât, Jotapata
Ka'kûl, Gallim
Kennā, Garis?
Kerak, Beth-yerah (Philoteria)
Kerâzeh, Chorazin
Libb, Lemba (Libba)
Maḥneh, Mahanaim?
Makhneh el-Fôqā (near Shechem), Michmethah?
Mird, Hyrcania 1
Qânā, Cana
Qîlā, Keilah
Qoṭeina (S.W. of Jokneam), Kattath?
Qumrân, City of Salt
Raqa' (near Ziph 2), Jokdeam?
Rûmeh (near Rimmon 2), Rumah
Selmah ('Id), Capharsalama
Sheikh 'Isā, Zoara (Zara)
Shuweikeh, Socoh 2
Ta'nah el-Fôqā, Taanath-shiloh
Tibnah, Timnah 1
Tibneh, Timnath-serah (Thamna)
Umm er-Ramâmîn, En-rimmon
Ya'nîn, Neiel
Yānûn, Janoah 1
Yaqîn, Cain
Yarmûk, Jarmuth 1
Zānû', Zanoah 1
Zānûḥ, Zanoah 1
Kôkab el-Hawā, Ramoth 3?
Kullanköy, Calneh 2?
Kursī, Gergesa?

Lâdhiqîyeh, Laodicea 2
Liftā, Nephtoah
Lisdib, Tishbeh?
Lubban, Lebonah
Ludd, Lod (Lydda)

Mâdebā, Medeba
Ma'în, Baal-meon
Mâlḥā, Manahath?
Meirôn, Merom (Meroth)
Mejdel, Magdala (Tarichaea)
Yâbā, Eben-ezer?
Merj Ibn 'Amir ('âmir), Esdraelon (Valley of Jezreel)
Mogheiriyeh (near Sidon), Mearah?
Mughâr, Cedron?
Mukâwer, Machaerus
Mukhmâs, Michmash (Machmas)
Muqeis, Gadara

Nâb, Enu-anabi
Nâblus, Neapolis 1
Nahr Baradā, River Abana
el-'Aṣī ('âṣī), Orontes River
-'Aujā (north of Joppa), Me-jarkon
-A'waj, River Pharpar
-Liṭânī, River Litani
-Muqaṭṭa', River Kishon
ez-Zerqā, River Jabbok
Naqb eṣ-Ṣafā, Ascent of Akrabbim
Nebī Daḥī, Hill of Moreh
Nein, Nain
Nûbā (near Aijalon 1), Nebo 2

'Olam ('ôlam), Anem?

Qal'at el-Ḥuṣn, Hippos
-Muḍîq, Apamea 1
Qalônîyeh (near Nephtoah), Emmaus 2 (Mozah)
Qâlunyah (near Nephtoah), Mozah
Qamm, Camon?
Qânah, Kanah
Qanawât, Kenath (Nobah 1; Qanu; Canatha)
Qarn Ḥaṭṭîn, Madon
Sarṭabeh, Alexandrium
Qaryatein, Hazar-enan?
Qaṭrā, Ekron (Accaron)?
Qeisârîyeh, Caesarea 1 (Strato's Tower)
Qeṣeimeh, Azmon?

Rafah, Raphia
Râjib, Ragaba
Râmet el-Khalîl, Mamre
Rammûn, Rock Rimmon
Râs Abū Ṭâbât, Tabbath
Râs Abū Ṭâbât, Tabbath
Ba'albek, Chun
el-'Ain, Aphek 1 (Pegae; Antipatris)
-Hâl (at Jamleh), Gamala?
-Kharrûbeh, Anathoth
es-Siâghah, Mt. Pisgah
esh-Shamrah, Ugarit
eṭ-Ṭaḥûneh, Beeroth 2?
-Ṭmîm, Bahurim
ez-Zeimara (near Ophrah 1), Zemaraim (at or near)?
Rentîs, Ramathaim-zophim (Arimathaea)?
Ribleh, Riblah
Ruḥeibeh, Rehoboth 2
Rujm el-Jilîmeh, Agala?
Rummâneh, Gath-rimmon 1
Rummâneh, Rimmon 2

Ṣadâd, Zedad
Ṣaffûriyeh, Sepphoris
Ṣaḥem el-Jōlân, Golan?
Ṣaidā, Sidon
Ṣâlim, Salim 1?
Ṣarafand, Zarephath (Sarepta)
Ṣar'ah, Zorah
Ṣârîs (near Chesalon), Seir 2?
Sbalat Abū Sûsein, Hazar-susah
Sebasṭiyeh, Samaria 3 (Sebaste)
Seilûn, Shiloh
Selbît, Shaalabbin
Selûqiyeh, Seleucia 1
Selûqîyeh (Med. port), Seleucia 2
Sheikh Abreiq, Beth-shearim
Abū Zarad, Tappuah 2
Bedr, Baal-perazim?
Nasrallah, Shalem
Sa'd, Karnaim
Sherî'at el-Menâdireh, River Yarmuk
Sinn en-Nabreh, Sennabris
Ṣîret el-Bella' (north of Hebron), Well of Sirah (near)
Sôlem, Shunem
Ṣûr, Tyre

Ṭabarîyeh, Tiberias
Taffûḥ, Beth-tappuah
Ṭal'at ed-Damm, Ascent of Adummim
Ṭarâbulus, Tripolis 1
Tawîlân, Teman?
Tell Abil (âbil), Abel-beth-maachah (Abel 2)